The Glory of Washington

The People and Events that Shaped the Husky Athletic Tradition

Jim Daves
and
W. Thomas Porter

Sports Publishing Inc.
Champaign Illinois

Director of Production: Susan M. Moyer
Interior design: Michelle R. Dressen
Cover and insert design: Christina Cary

ISBN: 1-58261-221-8

SPORTS PUBLISHING INC.
www.SportsPublishingInc.com

Printed in the United States

Contents

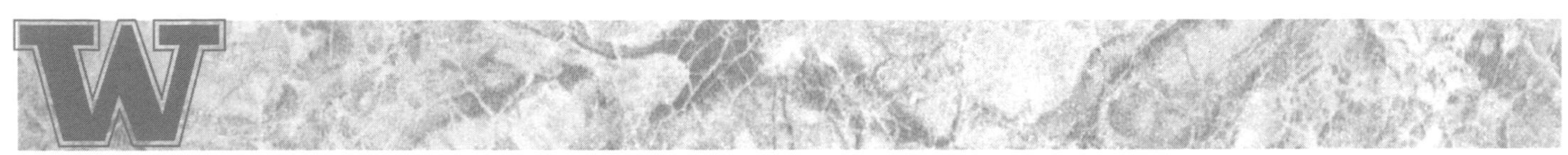

Acknowledgments

Primarily, we want to acknowledge the thousands of former athletes, coaches, students, faculty members, and Husky fans who have given their time, talents, resources, and loyalty to the Husky athletic program. We were motivated to write this book to chronicle the people and events that have shaped the University of Washington athletic program. We hope that the book will help you to learn about athletes and coaches who built some of the Washington tradition and to relive many Husky moments.

Many helped us in the research and development of this book. The University of Washington's Athletic Department has championed this project from the start, and we want to thank Athletic Director Barbara Hedges, Senior Associate Athletic Directors Gary Barta and Marie Tuite, Assistant Director Chip Lydum, and Director of Special Events Patti Daves. The Media Relations Department has provided extraordinary support and we thank Lisa Center, Bruce Terami, Joanie Komura, Jessica Dyer and previous sports information staffs who helped chronicle the history of Washington's athletic program.

We also thank the staff of the University's Manuscript, Special Collections, and University Archives Division of the University of Washington Libraries, particularly Jennifer Evans, Kris Kinsey, Sandra Kroupa, Janet Ness, and Carla Rickerson. Ruth Larson and Linda Nevarez at the U.S. Olympic Committee, Pamela Rene' at the Canadian Olympic Committee, and Wally Renfro at the NCAA have provided much assistance.

We are grateful to former athletes, coaches, and administrators who reviewed drafts of various sections of the book. They are John Buller, Chuck Carroll, Bud Ericksen, Dick Erickson, Bob Ernst, Ted Garhart, Gus Giovanelli, Eric Hughes, Jerry Johnson, Chip Lydum, Jim McCurdy, Don McKeta, Bob Moch, John Reid, Al Rossi, and Dick Sprague.

Michelle Dressen has done a simply wonderful job of designing the layout of the book and formatting all of the text. Thanks so much. We really appreciated the overall management of the project by B.J. Sohn and Susan Moyer's production direction at Sports Publishing Inc.

Special thanks to Rosie Leutzinger, Erin Shea, Micah Dunham, and Lyndee Regimbal for their work compiling the index.

Finally, we want to thank our wives, Patti Daves and Dixie Jo Porter who read drafts, provided wise counsel and helped in a number of other important ways. Thanks to Doug Porter, head track and field coach at Lakeside School in Seattle, for his overall research in the initial stages of the project and for his expertise on track and field resources and information. And special thanks to Beverly Franko and Jaimee Porter for transcribing almost 100 tape recordings of interviews.

The research for this book has been done through March of 2001 from information available up until that time. The list of letter winners is through June of 2000.

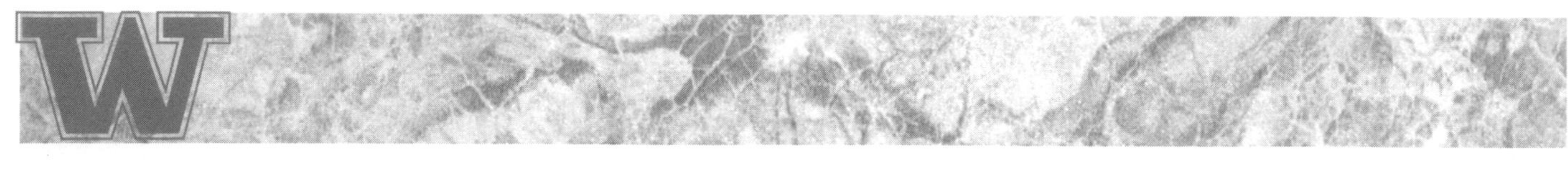

Foreword

In my 18 years as head football coach at the University of Washington, I was associated with some of the greatest teams and players in college football history. In addition, I had the opportunity to witness athletes and coaches in other Husky programs reach the highest levels of athletic performance. Washington is truly one of the finest academic institutions in the world and provides an outstanding environment to learn, grow, and mature as an individual.

For the student-athlete, Washington's broad base of athletic programs is led by a creative and focused administrative group and skilled and motivated coaches. The great athletic successes at Washington weave through every sport. Husky athletes excite and inspire and rally students, faculty, alumni, and the community around the program. They are proud of the Husky tradition and the support from our fans and alumni only encourages athletes to better performances.

The Glory of Washington chronicles the many men and women who have created the rich Husky history. This book helps all of us to relive the events and moments and rekindle our memories of Husky legends. It is great of Tom Porter and Jim Daves to gather this information and record it to be enjoyed for generations to come.

—Don James

If the Weather Gods didn't box their ears occasionally, the people who live in the Pacific Northwest would surely be the most complacent humans on the face of the earth. It is THAT good or WAS until the rest of the country discovered the quality of life that is available.

A major player in this evolution has been the University of Washington and especially its athletics and the marketing that has become an inseparable element in the whole image.

I lived and worked at KOMO-TV for 10 years in Seattle as the plucky people of the Pacific Northwest and the University of Washington opened new horizons. There was the football slush fund that brought sanctions from the NCAA that angered the Rowing Stewards who sent a good Husky crew off to the Henley Royal Regatta in England and then to the Soviet Union and an historic moment for them and for me.

And then came the dramatic back-to-back Rose Bowl wins with Coach Jim Owens and life in the Pacific Northwest hasn't been the same since. Those two games lifted the whole westside, and Seattle World's Fair then kicked open the future.

Enthusiasm can be catching, and certainly the Huskies have been a prime provider across the first century. *The Glory of Washington* does a masterful job of capturing the spirit of those young men and women who have helped Washington to achieve great heights in intercollegiate athletics. They are, after all, what makes college sports a wonderful spectacle.

—Keith Jackson

1889-99

1889 W 1890

Husky Moment

A Lively Contest Over The Yellow Egg—The First Football Game

The Seattle Fire, in June of 1889, launched what may have been the first football game ever played in the west. After the fire, which leveled 60 acres of the city, many stories were circulated throughout the country heralding the rebuilding of Seattle and its "boom town" nature. The city attracted young graduates of leading eastern colleges. These schools had been playing football since Nov. 6, 1869, when Rutgers beat Princeton 6-4 in the first collegiate game. The eastern adventurers formed a team—the Eastern Colleges Alumni—and on Thanksgiving day, Nov. 28, 1889, played against a University of Washington team. Only four of the 11 Washington players had ever played the game. It was not an official game; in fact, the University cast a severe institutional frown on the whole affair. The game was probably played at Jackson Street Park, at 27th and Jackson, littered with rocks and with only one crooked goal post. The Washington players, who didn't have any official uniforms—they could not afford them—wore woolen undershirts and baggy pants made of tent canvas. No players wore helmets because they had not been invented. Frank Griffith was the Washington captain. The team had no coach. About 400 spectators watched the alumni score three touchdowns (four points each), two extra points (two points each), and two safeties (two points each) to win 20-0.

UWMssSCUA

Territorial University on Denny's Knoll

Husky Spotlight

1904 Tyee

REVEREND DANIEL BAGLEY, often called the "founder of the university," was born in Pennsylvania and admitted to the Methodist ministry in Illinois. Sent as a missionary to Oregon in 1852, he moved to Seattle in 1860. Working with Arthur Denny and other territorial legislators, he persuaded them to locate the new territory's university in Seattle. Appointed president of the University Land Commission, he set about making the university a reality with a driving, irrepressible zeal. Bagley worked with Denny to obtain land for the university, directed land sales to fund construction of the university buildings, and oversaw all activities to open the University of the Territory of Washington in 1861.

Husky Highlight

Football in the 1890s was very different from today's game. The field was 110 yards long with two 50-yard lines, 10 yards apart, and with no end zones. The field was not reduced to 100 yards until 1912. A team received four points for a touchdown from 1883 to 1897 and five points from 1898 to 1911. Starting in 1912, a touchdown earned six points. A team secured five points for field goals from 1883 to 1903, four points from 1904 to 1908 and three points beginning in 1909. A conversion after a touchdown garnered two points from 1888 to 1897 and one point until the 1958 season. Then the two-point option came into effect. A safety has been worth two points since 1884.

Husky Legend

Starting Lineups for the First Football Game

University	Position	Eastern Alumni
H. Fredenberg	Left End	C.H. Rathbun
Otto Collings	Left Tackle	F.S. Bronson
Ed Nichols	Left Guard	B.H.Lee
John Weedin	Center	George R. Carter
Ralph Andrews	Right Guard	Francis Dana
Frank Griffith	Right Tackle	W.A. Deckey
John Carter	Right End	G.F. Folsom
Ellis Doughty	Quaterback	William Goodwin
Frank Atkins	Left Halfback	W.A. Peters
Delbert Ford	Right Halfback	F.B. Weistling
Edward Drew	Fullback	D.H. Baxter

HUSKY LIST

The following have been presidents of the University of Washington:

Asa Mercer, 1861-63
William Barnard, 1863-66
George Whitworth, 1866-68
University closed, 1868-69
John Hall, 1869-72
Eugene Hill, 1872-74
Mary (May) Thayer, 1874 (six months)
George Whitworth, 1875-76
Closed, 1876-77
Alexander Anderson, 1877-82
Leonard Powell, 1882-87
Thomas Gatch, 1887-95
Mark Harrington, 1895-97
William Edwards, 1897 (six months)
Charles Reeves, 1897-98
Frank Graves, 1898-1902
Thomas Kane, 1902-14
Henry Landes, 1914-15
Henry Suzzallo, 1915-26
David Thompson, 1926-27
Matthew Spencer, 1927-33
Hugo Winkenwerder, 1933-34
Lee Sieg, 1934-46
Raymond Allen, 1946-51
H.P. (Dick) Everest, 1952 (six months)
Henry Schmitz, 1952-58
Charles Odegaard, 1958-73
Philip Cartwright, 1973-74 (six months)
John Hogness, 1974-79
William Gerberding, 1979- 95
Richard McCormick, 1995-

FROM its beginning, the University of Washington was inspired by the vision and boldness of Washington Territory's pioneers. In 1855, the Territorial legislature established two universities, one in the two-year-old village of Seattle and the other in the more populous Lewis County. Both were to be "on the same footing with respect to funds and all other matters." In January 1858, the legislature repealed the 1855 action, and in late 1860 passed a bill relocating the University at Seattle on the condition that ten acres be donated for a suitable campus. In early 1861, the legislature established a University Land Commission and chose Reverend Daniel Bagley president. Arthur Denny, an original Seattle settler and King County legislative representative offered Capitol Hill—a spot originally offered to get the territorial capitol in Seattle. The commissioners found the Denny site "too far out in the woods." So Denny agreed to donate more than eight acres of his choicest forested land closer to the town on a knoll overlooking Elliott Bay. The remainder was donated by Charles and Mary Terry and Edward Lander. With the evangelism and zeal of a preacher man and the skill of a wild west trader, Bagley directed the clearing of the tract and the construction of the campus buildings. On Sept. 16, 1861, the Territorial University opened, the first public university on the west coast. Classes began on Nov. 4, 1861, with Asa Mercer as the temporary president and the school's only instructor. The institution became the University of Washington in November 1889 when Washington became a state.

1890 W 1891

Husky Moment

Scoreless Tie in Second Game

The second football game was played in Tacoma, on Nov. 27, 1890, against Washington College of Tacoma—a 0-0 tie. Scoreless in two games, the Washington lads were not quite mastering this game new to the Northwest. In the eastern part of the country, the Ivy schools had been at it for over a decade. Yale, Harvard, and Princeton systematized the game in the 1880s. Yale's Walter Camp developed many of the playing rules and promoted the sport through such inventions as the All-America team. Large crowds attended contests between major eastern school rivals generating sizable profits. From the beginning, winning was important. Recruiting and the use of "tramp athletes" were among the standard ways to win. The lack of standard college admission procedures and playing eligibility rules resulted in transfers of athletes from school to school and playing careers that extended well beyond school years. Schedules were erratic, many games were played against club teams, and a few against high school teams. Only a few colleges played football in the 1890s—particularly on the west coast where travel was difficult between those schools that did play. Students and alumni ran the teams; the faculty had no interest in the operation and governance of the sport. Head coaches were typically unpaid part-timers who showed up for the season and sometimes returned for the next year, but often did not. Washington had five coaches in its first ten seasons—none of them received pay. Player captains often trained the team and student managers took care of the scheduling. Athletic directors did not exist.

Husky Spotlight

The First Century at the University of Washington

Asa Mercer, first president of the Territorial University

SEATTLE PIONEER John Pike designed the first building on the downtown campus, a stately two-storied structure that featured an elegantly sculptured Ionic-columned portico, a balustrade roof, and a belfry. Construction was truly a regional effort—foundation stone came from a quarry near Port Orchard; fir lumber came from Port Madison and Port Gamble; white pine finishing wood from mills at Seabeck; brick and lime from Bellingham Bay; cement, paint, oils, glass and hardware from Victoria. Two other structures were built—a two-story president's house with ten rooms and a "plain box" boarding house for boys. Asa Mercer was the acting president and the school's only instructor. Girls lived in the president's house, under the supervision of Mercer's wife.

Husky Highlight

The University's early years were marked by economic and academic uncertainties—limited support from the territorial legislature, temporary closures, deteriorating facilities, an inadequate supply of students prepared for university work, and frequent turnover of presidents (six in the first 15 years). But by the end of the 1880s, enrollment approached 300 and facilities were crowded. Seattle—a city of 40,000 by the late 1880s—was growing around Denny's Knoll. University supporters wanted a new campus.

Husky Legend

Frank Griffith

Washington's first football captain and first two-time captain, 1889 and 1890, Frank Griffith (sometimes listed as Griffiths) organized Washington's first football team. He read about Yale's athletic exploits in Seattle newspapers. He sent away to Philadelphia for a rule book and an "oval pigskin." He recounts that it was "some time before we received our purchase. But the joyous day finally arrived and with it the rules and the ball...It was in 1889 before we got a team together with which we dared play a match game. We had no coach. We had to coach each other with only the rules for our guide...The difficulties encountered in creating interest, finding material for a team and getting any kind of equipment were most discouraging." Several days before the game the *Seattle Post-Intelligencer* reported, "In Mr. Griffith(s)...they have a fast runner and a good tackler..." After the game, the *P-I* failed to report that Washington might have won if Frank Griffith had played the entire match. Unfortunately, he departed with 15 minutes left, a sartorial wreck with nothing to wear. An Eastern Alumni brute had torn Mr. Griffith's clothes clean off.

HUSKY LIST

Football Captains in the 19th Century

1889	**Frank Griffith**
1890	**Frank Griffith**
1891	**No team**
1892	**Otto Collings**
1893	**Delbert Ford**
1894	**Ralph Nichols**
1895	**Martin Harrais**
1896	**Jack Lindsay**
1897	**Jack Lindsay**
1898	**Clarence Larson**
1899	**Stirling Hill**

THE existing structures of the University of Washington were 30 years old. They were becoming eyesores to the community and were cramped and unsuitable for the students and faculty. They were not able to meet the anticipated needs of a rapidly growing state. To deal with the situation, the legislature, under the leadership of Edmond S. Meany, member of the lower house, passed a law authorizing the governor to purchase 160 acres for a new university campus and to dispose of the old site. Several sites were considered—Jefferson Park, Fort Lawton, and Interlocken, an area near both Lake Union and Lake Washington. The Interlocken site was chosen without difficulty.

1891 W 1892

Husky Moment

New Campus At Interlocken

With no victories in two years, football was curtailed when only eight men turned out for practice. However, momentum was building for a much greater venue for all university activities—a new campus. The legislature granted the authority for developing a new university site and disposing of the old one to the Board of the University Land and Building Commission. Among its members were Elisha Ferry (first governor of the State); James Hayden, a Seattle businessman and University regent; and John Arthur, a Seattle attorney with considerable knowledge of University properties. To develop a comprehensive plan of the new campus, the commissioners hired a local architect, William Boone. Boone presented an ambitious plan that included a cluster of five major academic buildings romantically positioned along undulating paths and roads. This plan was accepted on Aug. 20, 1891. When construction bids were opened, the amounts far exceeded available funds, resulting in much public opposition. University advocate and legislative leader, Edmond Meany, never lost his vision and zeal to build a great university and he continued to work to obtain support. He sponsored Home Bill #470 which was passed on the last day of the 1893 legislature and signed by Governor McGraw on March 3, 1894. The bill authorized the purchase of the entire 580 acres of the Interlocken site for $28,313.75 backed by a $150,000 construction appropriation.The legislature abolished the Land and Building Commission and established a University regents subcommittee to develop the new campus.

The First Century at the University of Washington

New campus—Administration Building renamed Denny Hall

Husky Spotlight

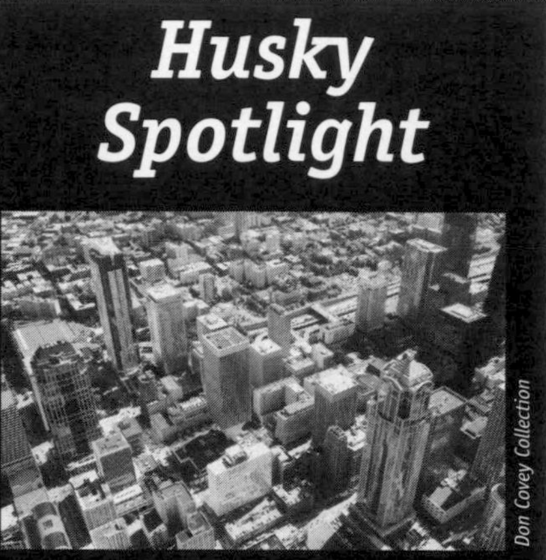

Don Covey Collection

The Metropolitan tract

THE LAND AND BUILDING Commission had to dispose of the original ten acre campus and to use the proceeds for the construction of facilities on the new campus. They were permitted to lease unsold portions of the property. The downtown campus was appraised at $250,000, and during the depression of the 1890s, attempts to sell the land failed. The legislature advanced money to acquire the new university site and construct the first buildings with the understanding that the advances were a loan to be repaid with receipts from the sale of the downtown tract. The Board of Regents resolved not to jeopardize the return from the tract through small transactions. Other than one small piece at Third and Union, the tract was kept intact and is known as the Metropolitan Tract—managed by UNICO Properties. It is bounded on the north by Union Street; on the south by Seneca; on the alley east behind the Skinner Building, east of the IBM Building; and the alley behind the Washington and Cobb buildings and the Financial Center. Other buildings in the tract are the Four Seasons Olympic Hotel and the Rainier Tower and Rainier Square Plaza.

Husky Highlight

University enrollment in the 1890s nearly doubled. In 1890, total enrollment was 273 students—about a half of them in the preparatory or pre-collegiate program. The preparatory program was established in the late 1860s. Very few high schools in the territory had programs to prepare students for college. The university set up the program to also increase enrollment when the university experienced difficulties. The preparatory program also provided boys for some of the early football teams. By 1900, enrollment was over 500 with about 25 percent in the prep program. Washington was becoming a true collegiate institution.

The First Century at the University of Washington

Husky Legend

Arthur A. Denny

Arthur Denny, together with Reverend Bagley, founded the University of Washington. He was born in 1822 near Salem, Indiana, and attended school in Illinois where his father was a member of the Illinois legislature in 1840-41 and a friend of Abraham Lincoln. Denny married Mary Ann Boren in 1843 and with their two daughters journeyed west to Portland in April 1851. In November, they set sail on a small vessel, the Exact, for Seattle and landed on the south rim of Elliott Bay (now Alki Point). Denny was one of the original Seattle settlers whose land claims covered all of the lower lands from the Seattle village to the south tip of what would later be called Lake Union and extending east into the forested lands. Denny soon became a Territorial legislator and together with two other legislators, Paul Tubbs of Port Townsend and Lewis Van Fleet of Vancouver, secured approval for the location of several prized territorial institutions. The choice one was the capitol—temporarily located in Olympia. Denny wanted it in Seattle; he even was ready to donate a site from land holdings he had named Capitol Hill. The Denny, Tubbs, Van Fleet coalition introduced three bills in the 1860-61 legislative session providing for the location of the capitol, the penitentiary and the university. The bills passed with the capitol transferred to Vancouver and the university placed in Seattle. Denny offered his Capitol Hill land for the university but the University Land Commission felt it was "too far out in the woods." Denny then agreed to donate his choice forested land closer to town on a knoll overlooking Elliott Bay. He wanted the land dedicated forever to educational purposes. Arthur Denny—a visionary, a pioneer, a statesman—died on Jan. 9, 1899.

HUSKY LIST

On Jan. 24, 1862, the legislature passed "An Act to Incorporate the University of the Territory of Washington." Nine regents were named in the law. They were to serve in a staggered cycle of three-year terms. On Jan. 29, 1862, the Regents held their first meeting with Reverend Daniel Bagley as the first chairman. Other members included: Edmund Carr, Frank Clark, Calvin Hale, J.P.Keller, Columbia Lancaster, Henry McGill, G. A. Meigs, and John Webster.

THE new campus on the shores of Lake Washington was unequaled in natural beauty. To the east, you could see the rugged peaks of the Cascades; to the west the snow-covered Olympics following the sound to the sea. Away to the south rose the great white watch-tower, Rainier.

1892 W 1893

Husky Moment

Washington Wins First Football Game

Football was revived in 1892, and for the first time, Washington had a coaching staff and they won a game. Washington opened its season by losing to the Seattle Athletic Club, 28-0. Two months later, on Dec. 17, 1892, Washington won the rematch 14-0. Frank Atkins, who played in Washington's first game in 1889, as a preparatory (pre-collegiate) student, scored the school's first touchdown on a fullback five-yard run up the center in the first half. Atkins' drop-kick for the points after touchdown failed when the ball skidded off the side of his foot and hit the ground 20 feet away. After Washington scored again, Atkins' kick again failed. So when Washington's Delbert Ford scored his second TD, Washington's third, captain Otto Collings commanded J. Howard Darlington, the team's quarterback, to kick the ball. With Collings holding, Darlington kicked it over the goal post and over the fence at Madison Park—recording the first points after touchdown for Washington. The final score was 14-0 in a very physical match. Washington players who competed in the historic win—other than Atkins, Collings, Darlington and Ford—were Tom Alderson, A.S. Burrows, M.E. Durham, Roger Green, H.L. Reese, C.H. Steffen, and Calvin Welbon. After the game, students paraded the streets. At the *Post-Intelligencer* office, where the score was chalked upon the bulletin board, the university lads gave three cheers. The parade was followed by a banquet at the Rainier Hotel where every member of the team responded to a toast. It ended with cheers for hotel manager Lee Willard and then for captain Collings.

1892 football team gets first win in Husky history (UWMssSCUA)

Husky Spotlight

FRANK ATKINS, Washington' fullback, scored the first touchdown in the school's history on Dec. 17, 1892 He was the starting left halfback in Washington's first football game in 1889 when he was a preparatory, not a collegiate student. In October 1891, as the youngest athlete, he won the all-around championship in a YMCA track meet. He won five events and scored 272 points out of a possible 500, coming within 20 points of the world's record. He established a number of Washington initial track and field records, including the hop-step-jump, the broad jump, the pole vault, the high jump, and 50 and 100 yard dashes.

Husky Highlight

Gymnasium and Denny Field on the new campus (1901 Tyee)

Early football games were played on several fields. The school's first game, on Nov. 28, 1889, was probably played at Jackson Street Park at 27th and Jackson, although various sources list the location as 18th and Jackson, 14th and Jefferson, and the YMCA Park at 12th and Jefferson. Before the university moved to the new campus site in 1895, they played at the old downtown campus; at a playground in West Seattle; and at Madison Park, near the end of the Madison Street cable line. After relocating, they practiced and had scrimmages on a field on campus—Denny Field—but continued to use other fields. When grandstands and bleachers were built around Denny Field, Washington began to play all games there—beginning on Oct. 23, 1906.

Husky Legend

W. B. Goodwin

William "Billy" Goodwin played a key role in establishing Washington football. He was the captain of the Eastern Alumni team that played Washington in its first football game on Nov. 28, 1889. He was Washington's first football coach. He coached for two seasons (1892 and 1893) and his teams recorded two wins, four losses, and one tie. He earned a varsity letter in rugby-football at Yale in 1884 when the Eli had an unbeaten season 8-0-1. He graduated in 1887 and came to Seattle, attracted by the prospect of rebuilding the city after the great fire of 1889. Shortly after his arrival, he befriended Washington students. He gave kicking demonstrations, instructions in rugby-football, and ran the students through scrimmages. His tutelage was a big factor in preparing Washington players for their first match in 1889. In 1893, he guided Washington in its first real schedule—five games—its first out of state game against the Multnomah Athletic Club in Portland, and its first collegiate opponent, Stanford. Goodwin also rowed for the Seattle Athletic Club in the first regatta in Seattle in August 1894. Four teams representing the Pacific Northwest Rowing Association competed. Seattle finished second to the Portland Rowing Club.

HUSKY LIST

Top 10 Winning Percentage of Washington Football Coaches (Minimum Three Seasons)

Coach	Record	Winning Percentage
Gil Dobie (1908-16)	58-0-3	.975
James Knight (1902-04)	15-4-1	.775
Don James (1975-92)	153-57-2	.726
Enoch Bagshaw (1921-29)	63-22-6	.725
Jim Lambright (1993-98)	44-25-1	.636
James Phelan (1930-41)	65-37-8	.627
Ralph Nichols (1895-96, 98)	7-4-1	.625
Claude Hunt (1917-19)	7-4-1	.625
Ralph Welch (1942-47)	27-20-3	.570
Jim Owens (1957-74)	99-82-6	.545

HUSKY LORE

IN 1892, Washington students agitated for organizations and symbols to promote "college spirit." An Athletic Association was formed. Then, an assembly was called to adopt school colors. A group called "the dormitory gang" made a determined bid to adopt the nation's colors. They reasoned that since the school was named after the "father of our country," it was obvious that red, white, and blue was the logical choice. Another group, "the townies," protested that it was improper to adopt the national colors for another purpose. After a spirited debate, Miss Louise Frazyer, a faculty member of English, Rhetoric and Elocution, asked for quiet. She opened a book and recited from Lord Byron's "The Destruction of Sennacherib." The first stanza of his six stanza poem is:

> The Assyrians came down like the wolf on the fold,
> And his cohorts were gleaming in purple and gold;
> And the sheen of their spears was like stars in the sea,
> When the blue wave rolls nightly on deep Galilee.

Miss Frazyer did it. She silenced the dormitory gang and rallied the assembly around "Purple and Gold."

1893 W 1894

Husky Moment

A Real Football Schedule

In 1893, Washington played an extensive schedule, including its first collegiate opponent. The first four games were against athletic club teams. Washington competed against such teams because there were few college teams in the west and because the school could not afford to send the team great distances to play. On three successive Saturdays, Washington beat the Viciendas team in Tacoma 8-4, lost to the Tacoma Athletic Club 6-4, and tied the Port Townsend Athletic Club, 6-6. On Thanksgiving, Nov. 30, 1893, Washington traveled to Portland, Oregon to play its first out-of-state opponent, the Multnomah Athletic Club. Multnomah easily won, 30-0. The landmark game occurred almost a month later. Stanford began football in 1891 and in 1893 its team was 4-0-1 when it headed north to play four games in the Northwest. Stanford lined up as Washington's first collegiate foe on Dec. 29, 1893, and won, 40-0, before 600 spectators in West Seattle. Stanford's road trip, the longest ever taken by a football team in the country, was very successful. They won all four games by an aggregate score of 154-0. With an unbeaten season, Stanford made its claim to Pacific Coast champions.

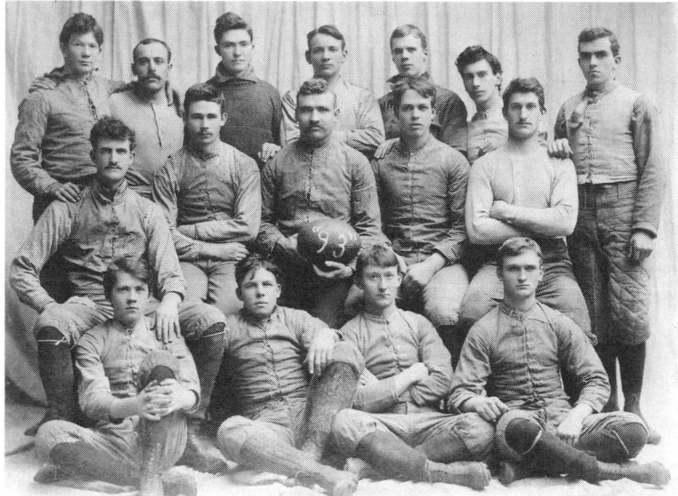

The 1893 football team played Stanford, Washington's first collegiate opponent.

UWMssSCUA

Husky Spotlight

NO SPORT EQUALED football for glamour, sensationalism, and gladiatorial qualities near the turn of the 20th century. Yet, other sports had their following. Of these, baseball was perhaps the most important. Although played informally as early as 1878, baseball became a Washington sport in 1894. It was not very popular—students did not show much interest, the Puget Sound climate created difficult playing conditions, and the team lacked financial support and coaching. So baseball was played as part of interclass activities until 1901 when Fred Schock was appointed Washington's first baseball coach.

1904 Tyee

Fred Schock

Husky Highlight

The Western Washington Intercollegiate Athletic Association (W.W.I.A.A.) admitted Washington in 1893. Members included the College of Puget Sound, Whitworth College (in Tacoma), Washington Agricultural College, and Vashon College, a small military school on Vashon Island. In 1902, the Northwest Intercollegiate Athletic Association was formed.

Husky Legend

Ralph Nichols

Celebrating 100 Years of Husky Football

Ralph Nichols, first football star, coach for six years

Ralph Nichols was probably the first gridiron star at Washington. He was the starting guard for three seasons starting in 1892. In 1893, he led the "Purple and Gold" in its first intercollegiate game against Stanford. Although the Indians won handily 40-0, Nichols so impressed Stanford's student manger that he offered Nichols a "free ride" if he would transfer to the Palo Alto school. The Stanford student manager was Herbert Hoover, a member of Stanford's first graduating class in 1895 and the 31st President of the United States. Nichols was Washington's football captain in 1894 and served as head coach in 1895, 1896, and 1898. His 1895 team recorded the first unbeaten football season in Washington history—four wins and one tie—scoring 98 points to its opponents' eight.

HUSKY LIST

Football Season Records in the 19th Century

Year	Wins	Losses	Ties	Points For	Points Against
1889	0	1	0	0	20
1890	0	0	1	0	0
1891		No games played			
1892	1	1	0	14	28
1893	1	3	1	18	86
1894	1	1	1	60	38
1895	4	0	1	98	8
1896	2	3	0	20	40
1897	1	2	0	16	26
1898	1	1	0	24	18
1899	4	1	1	71	21
TOTALS	15	13	5	321	285

ON March 14, 1894, the regents awarded the design of the first building on the new campus to Charles Saunders. After the acceptance of a low bid of $112,000, construction began. Saunders' design was French Renaissance style. The main rectangle of the building was capped by a belfry, marked by round towers flanking the entrance, and extended into rounded bays at the end. About 1,000 people, a mix of professors, students, and community leaders attended the cornerstone ceremonies on July 4, 1894. James Taylor, master mason, officiated. When finished, it was known as the Administration Building, renamed Denny Hall on Feb. 23, 1910.

1894 W 1895

Husky Moment

A State Championship

Washington played only three football games in 1894—the first, an away game in Port Townsend ending in a 14-14 tie; next, a loss to the Seattle Athletic Club, 24-0. Finally, the University's played its first collegiate road game, on November 22, in Walla Walla against Whitman College. Concerned that the game's attendance would be insufficient to cover expenses, Washington's student manager and starting end, Tom Alderson took a box lunch with lots of biscuits. Alderson may have taken home some uneaten biscuits since the trip was a great success. Once the team reached Walla Walla, they were warmly entertained and toured the penitentiary. Team members posed for a picture in the rogue's gallery. Over 5,000 spectators watched in awe as Alderson repeatedly brought Whitman runners down with flying tackles. Made on the run, the tackler would fly through the air and hit the opponent with crushing force. Washington romped, 46-0, and claimed the first collegiate state championship. 1894 marked the first football game played by Washington freshmen. On Dec. 1, the frosh beat Seattle High School, 16-0, on the Madison Park field.

The 1894 football team wins the state championship.

UWMssSCUA

Husky Spotlight

MARTIN HARRAIS is seated in the captain's position, holding a football, in team pictures of 1893, 1894, and 1895. Most accounts of his football exploits list him as the captain for 1895 only, but some credit him being captain for parts of the 1893 and 1894 seasons as well. He was one of the two first four-year starters in Washington history and, during his career, he wore a long flowing mustache. Harrais was chosen as the center on the all-time Washington football team selected in 1930.

Husky Highlight

Charles Cobb was hired to replace Billy Goodwin as football coach in 1894. Cobb, a former Harvard player, was the University's first salaried coach. By 1892, University officials had been pressured into financially supporting a football team—the school's first official endorsement of organized athletics. Because the treasury was in a deficit position at the end of the season, university officials could not pay Cobb and so they fired him.

Husky Legend

The First Century at the University of Washington

Edmond S. Meany

Meany was the principal leader in establishing the University's new campus. His contributions rank along with those of Reverend Bagley and Arthur Denny. A six-foot six-inch hustling journalist and promoter, he was elected to the state legislature in 1891. He became chairman of the university committee in the lower house and, later, chairman of a legislative joint committee to find, acquire, and guide a new campus. He graduated from the university in 1885. (Only 10 people had graduated before Meany's class of five, the first being Clara McCarty in 1876. McCarty Hall is named in her memory). Meany exhibited a consuming zeal to advance the interests of the university. His House Bill #470, signed by Governor McGraw on March 3, 1894, authorized purchase of the Interlocken site for the new campus for $28,313.75. Meany would later join the faculty and become involved in many important university events. He devoted his teaching and research to the history of the state and the Northwest. To generations of students, he represented excitement in learning because he never lost his own sense of excitement. He was one of the university's most indefatigable authors whose bibliography comprised more than 50 published items. He was one of the founders of the Mountaineers, and was one of the first to receive their honor badge for scaling Washington's six major peaks. He died in his University office on April 22, 1935, while preparing to meet a history class. Meany was a scholar, historian, mountaineer, and beloved citizen.

Husky List

Top Winning Percentage of Washington's Basketball Coaches (Minimum three seasons)

Coach	Record	Winning Percentage
Clarence "Hec" Edmundson (1921-1947)	488-195	.715
Tippy Dye (1951-1959)	156-91	.632
Marv Harshman (1972-1988)	246-146	.628
Art McLarney (1948-1950)	53-36	.596
Tex Winter (1969-1971)	45-35	.563
John Grayson (1960-1963)	57-49	.538

THE flying wedge was a formation used by many teams in the early years of football. A very formidable weapon, the wedge was taught to Washington players in 1892 by the legendary Walter Camp. Camp was hired as a consultant because of his knowledge of the game. He coached Stanford to a 12-3-3 record in three seasons (1892, 1894-95). He played and coached at Yale and is credited with creating the line of scrimmage, the 11 man team, signal calling, and the quarterback position. The wedge was in the shape of a V, with the ball carrier tucked neatly inside. The defense had limited options in grappling with the formation, none very pleasant to the point man in the V. One defensive tactic was for the defender to punch the point man in the face; another to render a quick knee to the point man's nose. A third option was for the defender to dive under the wedge and pile it up. With this option, the defender risked getting trampled as the force of the wedge moved on by. The wedge was abolished with a extensive revision of the rules in 1905, a season of record roughness and injuries throughout the nation.

Husky Moment

First Unbeaten Season

The Purple and Gold recorded its first unbeaten season in 1895. It opened the season with a 12-0 win over the Seattle Athletic Club on Oct. 19 with Ralph Nichols, a former Washington captain, coaching the team. A week later, Washington tied the Seattle Athletic Club in a fierce contest marred by rough and unsportmanslike play by one of the club players—an eastern college man who had also won laurels in the boxing ring. He evidently considered football a modified boxing match and was involved in slugging, choking, hair pulling and jumping with his knees upon downed opponents. Two victories were lopsided home wins (44-4 and 34-0) over Vashon College, a small military college. Due to injuries, Washington did not have enough players in the first game against Vashon, so Vashon loaned Washington a player. Apparently they loaned the wrong guy. K.C. Nieman ran for seven touchdowns, an all-time school record. He scored on runs of 97, 62, 48, 31, 17, 11 and eight yards. The Thanksgiving game was played in Tacoma. Washington triumphed 8-4, with Clarence Larson scoring on a 40-yard run. Will Turnbull, the team mascot, carrying the purple and gold, was lifted on the shoulders of two of the victors and carried triumphantly across the gridiron. Martin Harrais captained this team that outscored its opponents 98-8. He was one of two players who first represented Washington for four football seasons—Tom Alderson was the other.

UWMssSCUA

The 1895 football team records the first unbeaten season.

Husky Spotlight

BASKETBALL began on the new campus with class teams vying for the all-university title. The first men's contest against outside competition was in the winter of 1896 when the Seattle Athletic Club edged Washington, 3-2, in overtime. There was no coach. The women played three games in 1896. One game was against the Ellensburg Normal School before 600 spectators with Washington winning, two goals to one. The women played two more games—shutout wins over the Seattle Athletic Club (14-0) and the YMCA (16-0).

The first women's basketball team has a perfect season. *(1900 Tyee)*

Husky Highlight

The University's first gymnasium and drill hall was built in 1896, north of Denny Field. It was used for athletic training, military cadets' drill training, and men and women's basketball games. It was replaced in 1927 by the women's physical education building on a nearby site to the south. This building was later named Hutchinson Hall. The men moved into a new pavilion in 1927, later named the Clarence S. "Hec" Edmundson Pavilion.

Husky Legend

Charles Vander Veer

1916 Tyee

Washington appointed Charles Vander Veer as Professor of Physical Culture and Hygiene, Director of the gymnasium, and Manager of the track and field team. A graduate of Union College in New York, he was a Professor of Physical Culture at Union and then the Case School of Applied Sciences before moving to Seattle in 1893. He directed the athletic program for the Seattle Athletic Club until coming to Washington. He quickly went to work. He called for volunteer student help in constructing a track and cultivated students' interests in a broad array of sports and physical education. In track and field, he initiated indoor meets and offered prizes for the winners. Such innovations resulted in large turnouts for track and excellent performances. Vander Veer's 1902 team was undefeated, with a 103-13 win over Oregon, the largest Washington score until 1933. The 1903 team won the Pacific Northwest Conference championship, sharing the title with Idaho. With the scored tied, the final event—the mile relay—ended in dead heat. Coach Vander Veer resigned in the autumn of 1903 to become Athletic Director at the University of Idaho where Clarence Sinclair Edmundson was beginning to compete. Vander Veer returned to Washington in 1916 as head track and field coach. World War I limited university athletic activities but Vander Veer kept the track program operating on an intramural basis. Following the 1918 season, the "Father of Track and Field" retired.

HUSKY LIST

The Women's Athletic Association was organized in November 1895 with the following officers:

- **Jessie Hanford, president—Jessie was the left center on the basketball team**
- **Ina Pratt, vice-president**
- **Mabel Ward, secretary—Mabel was the captain and center on the basketball team**
- **Miss Ames, treasurer**

The association prepared a constitution, chose a yell, organized women's basketball games with other institutions, and conducted handball tournaments. A poem, *The Gym Girl,* mused on the benefits of women's athletics.

The pensive girl with the dreamy eyes may sit in the corner and pose,
But give me the girl that plays basketball with her cheeks the hue of the rose.
Her step is light, and her eyes are bright. She studies and works with a vim.
And it all is due to the exercise she takes at the dear old gym.
Then here's to the girl in the navy blue with her steps so light and free;
With the golden wealth of her matchless health—Oh! she is the girl for me.

SCHOOL colors, athletic associations, and school yells contributed to the development of school spirit. The men adopted one heavily endowed with Chinook Indian jargon:

U of W—Hiah, Hiah
U of W—Siah, Siah
Skookum, Skookum, Washington

The coeds countered with a more feminine cheer.

He-Ho-Hi
He-Ho-Hi
Konamox—Klatawa
Skookum—Squaw

1896 W 1897

Husky Moment

Washington Wins City Championship

Ralph Nichols was again the coach for the season. Jack Lindsay was the captain. The team opened with a loss to the Seattle Athletic Club (4-6), followed by two more losses to Port Townsend Athletic Club (18-0), and the Multnomah Athletic Club (10-0). Three days later, on Dec. 15, they beat the Seattle YMCA, 4-0. On Dec. 19, their third game in a week, Washington again played the Seattle Athletic Club. The game was characterized as the greatest university athletic event ever, up to that point. With only ten seconds remaining, the score was tied at 6-6. Washington was three yards from victory. A newspaper account describes the action: "...in the lurking gloom of the YMCA grounds at the close of the game which those that witnessed it will never forget...On the one hand, desperate determination to check the awful onslaught of bone and muscle and seek consolation in a tie rather than suffer the sting of defeat; on the other hand an overwhelming irresistible force of impending victory which sweeps all before it. The ball was passed to Captain Lindsay. The heavy U backs thundered against the exhausted line of the athletic club, staggered a few feet, then with one Herculean effort plunged over the line and the game was ... won and the university boys became the local champions."

UWMssCUA

The 1896 football team wins the city championship.

Husky Spotlight

Denny Field was the first stadium site on the new campus. Located on the north sector of the campus near 45th Street, the field was initially used for practices and scrimmages. Eventually, the field was fenced and flanked by wood-frame covered bleachers on both the north and south. In front of 9,000 fans, the final collegiate football game was played on this historic field on Nov. 5, 1920—Stanford scoring the only points on a Dink Templeton field goal. Dink Templeton won a gold medal on the U.S. rugby team in the 1920 Olympics. He finished fourth in the long jump. He was Stanford's track coach from 1921-1939. Denny Field today remains a grass student playfield bordered by tennis, volleyball and basketball courts.

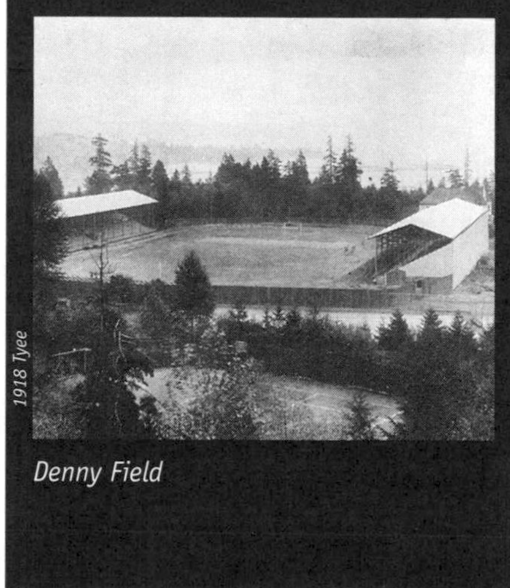

1918 Tyee

Denny Field

Husky Highlight

There have been eight two-time football captains.

Frank Griffith	1889, 1890
Jack Lindsay	1896, 1897
Fred McElmon	1902, 1904
Ray Eckman	1921, 1922
Sonny Sixkiller (co-captain)	1971, 1972
John Whitacre (co-captain)	1973, 1975
Ray Pinney (co-captain)	1974, 1975
Marques Tuiasosopo (co-captain)	1999, 2000

1900 Tyee

Husky Legend

Jack Lindsay

In describing early football greats, writers reserved the phrase "above all the great and only one" for Jack Lindsay. He scored every Washington touchdown during the 1896 and 1897 seasons and was a two-time captain. He was Washington's track captain in 1897. He set the Western Washington Intercollegiate Athletic Association record in the 50-yard dash in 1896 (5.75 seconds). A poem paid tribute to this outstanding young man.

Hurrah for Lindsay! the pride of our college.
The terror of foes, the wonder of all,
Cheer for his deeds in the wildest of carnage,
Crown him with laurel, the king of football.
Hurrah for Lindsay, the hero, the splendor,
The boast, the delight of our Washington,
Oh write his name on the bright scroll of glory
And honor, Oh College, thy peerless son.
Hurrah for Lindsay! hurrah for Lindsay!
He covers our college with endless fame,
We'll deck him with honors, we'll drown him with praises,
Hurrah for Lindsay—once more—and again!

Lindsay was selected to the All-Time Washington football team covering the years 1892-1930. In the spring of 1898, Lindsay and two teammates, Victor and Conrad Schmidt, drowned on an Alaskan expedition outfitted by Prince Luigi of Italy. On an old wooden schooner, 15 men headed for the rich Kotzebue Sound country. The boat's seams opened; and it sank with 11 of the 15 going down with her.

Husky List

Construction on the new campus quickly changed its landscape. Below is a list of the major buildings completed before the Alaska-Yukon-Pacific Exposition in 1909.

Building	Year Constructed
Denny Hall (originally named the Administration Building)	1895
Observatory	1895
Gymnasium	1896
Canoe House	1897
Lewis Hall (originally called the men's dormitory)	1899
Clark Hall (originally called the women's dormitory)	1899
Parrington Hall	1902

All of these buildings were located below the University's northern border along Northeast Forty-fifth Street. They were clustered around open spaces including Denny Field, the site of the first athletic field on the new campus.

Husky Lore

ON March 20, 1897, University president Mark W. Harrington resigned and a period of internal turbulence and weakened conditions followed until Frank Graves became president in May, 1898. Graves and his successor, Thomas Kane, both classical scholars, presided during a major transformation period (1898-1914) in the University's history. The small, once territorial college, changed into a true university with a complex of professional schools and centers of advanced study and research.

First Century at the University of Washington

University faculty with President Graves (bearded gentleman, hand in left pocket, in middle of first row)

Husky Moment

First Game In Corvallis, Oregon

In 1897, Carl Clemans replaced Ralph Nichols as head football coach. Considered to be one of the great fullbacks in Stanford history, Clemans was a star player on Stanford's first teams in 1891 and 1892. He became Stanford's sixth football coach in 1902. Washington played three games in 1897, winning only one against the YMCA, 10-0. On Thanksgiving day, they lost to their old rival, the Seattle Athletic Club, 10-6. On Dec. 4, they traveled to Corvallis to play their first out-of-state collegiate game. Oregon Agricultural College beat Washington, 16-0, in the rain before 1,500 spectators. It was a stubbornly contested affair with Washington twice forcing the ball within the 10-yard line. Each time, they lost their touchdown opportunities on downs, despite the efforts and exhortations of Captain Lindsay.

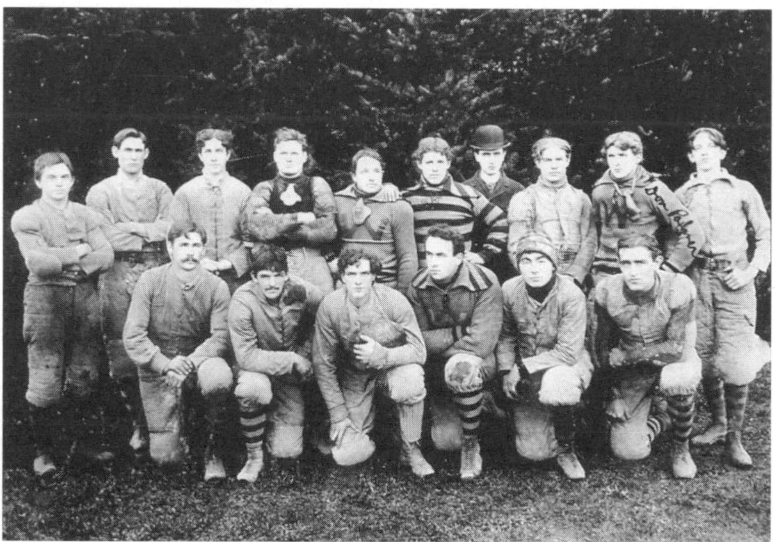

UWMsSCUA

The 1897 football team played the first out-of-state game against a collegiate opponent.

Husky Spotlight

John Condon

The head linesman for the Thanksgiving day game in 1897 against the Seattle Athletic Club was John Condon. In 1899, Washington established the School of Law. Condon, then a university professor, was appointed its first dean. He attended Washington from 1875-1879 and he received his L.L.B. from Michigan in 1891 and his L.L.M. from Northwestern in 1892. He served as a Washington faculty member until 1926. The School of Law was initially housed in the administrative building on the original campus near the business center of Seattle. A new law school building was constructed in 1932 as part of the Liberal Arts Quadrangle. It was named Condon Hall as was the new one built in 1973.

Husky Highlight

In the Oregon State (formerly Oregon Agricultural College) series, Washington leads 55-26-4. There have been 24 shutouts—Washington has 15, Oregon State six, and three games ending in a scoreless tie. Gil Dobie-coached teams recorded the longest shutout streak—four—from 1908 through 1911. In those four years, Washington scored a total of 109 points. After a 9-3 win in 1912, Washington recorded five more shutouts from 1913-1918. The biggest shutout victory in the series was in 1913 when Washington won 47-0.

UWMssSCUA

Husky Legend

Don Palmer

Don Palmer was one of the nation's top track and field performers, the best pole vaulter on the west coast. He participated from 1895-1899, graduating in 1899. Primarily a track athlete, he played football in 1897 and 1898. He was elected manager of the Athletic Association for the academic year, 1898-1899. He made his marks on the cinder lanes and runways in many events. In the Western Washington Intercollegiate Athletic Association (WWIAA) Field Day in May 1897, he scored in five events—first in the pole vault, second in the 120-yard high hurdles and broad jump, and third in the high jump. He also ran the final leg on the mile relay, helping his team set a new meet record. In August, he broke the Northwest record by vaulting 10-6. He was featured in the 1897 Spaulding Athletic Calendar as one of the nation's outstanding athletes. He established school and WWIAA records in 1898, in the 120-yard high hurdles. In March 1899, he set a Pacific Coast indoor pole vault record of 10-7¾. In that meet, he attempted a world record of 11-¼ with the vaulting standards elevated on wooden planks to get the crossbar to the record height. The winning vault in the 1896 and 1900 Olympics was 10-10. Palmer was Washington's unpaid athletic team physician from 1904 to 1947, a founder of the Big "W" Alumni Club, the Homecoming half-time blanket parade, and the 101 Club.

HUSKY LIST

The first game against Oregon Agricultural College (now Oregon State University) initiated a series that has been unbroken since 1902. The 10 games (six at home, four away) with the largest Washington margins of victory are:

Year	Score
1991 (away)	58-6
1913 (home)	47-0
1979 (home)	41-0
1981 (home)	56-17
1996 (home)	42-3
1989 (away)	51-14
1980 (away)	41-6
1916 (home)	35-0
1911 (home)	34-0
1978 (away)	34-0

HUSKY LORE

IT was not uncommon in the early years of Washington football for the starting 11 to play the whole game, both offensively and defensively. The substitutes, called scrums, usually played when the starters were injured. Few scrums earned the Big W emblem. In 1907, a football player had to play in four full halves of a game to earn a letter. In the early 1900s, the substitutes began to play on a "second" team against local high school teams.

Husky Moment

Ninety-four Yard Touchdown Run

All athletic programs were severely restricted during the academic year, 1898-1899, because of the Spanish-American War and inadequate financial support. Ralph Nichols organized a football team of Washington seniors late in the fall of 1898. After limited practice sessions, the team played two games against the Puyallup Indian Reservation squad. Indian schools, in the early days of football, produced some outstanding teams. The most notable was Carlisle College in Pennsylvania. Its most outstanding player was Jim Thorpe, a decathlon world-record holder and gold medalist in the 1912 Olympics and one of the greatest football players in history. The game against Puyallup was played in Tacoma on Dec. 17, and the Indians won 18-11. This game featured an 85-yard run by Craig, a former Carlisle player. A week later, Washington shut out the Indians in Seattle 13-0. At the close of the first half, neither team had scored. In the second half, Washington drove to the Indians' 10-yard line. On third down, Clarence Larson, team captain, shook off one tackler, brushed a teammate out of the way, and carried the ball to the five. On the next play, Stirling Hill raced around left end for Washington's first score. Tom Murphine's kick was good to make it 6-0. With only two minutes left and the fans filing out of the grandstand, Hill broke through an opening between left tackle and guard, created by Bert Durham and Henry Richardson. Larson blocked two Indians behind the scrimmage line and Edgar Wright escorted Hill all the way to the goal line. Wright kept the Indians from Hill on the final phase of this brilliant piece of teamwork. Hill's 94-yard touchdown run stands as the second longest one from scrimmage in Washington's history.

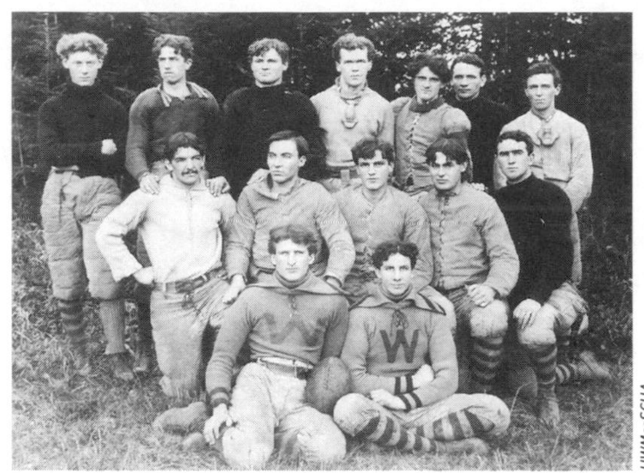
UWMsSCUA

The 1898 football team.

Husky Spotlight

Four Hill brothers played football at Washington. Three of them—Arthur, Climie, and Stirling played together on the 1896 team. Climie and Stirling played on the 1899 team and William Hill was on the 1902 and 1903 teams. In 1897, Climie set an early Washington record for the mile run: 4:53.4. William was a star basketball player. Their father, Eugene Hill, served as the fifth President of the University of Washington, from 1872-74.

1902 Tyee

Climie Hill

Husky Highlight

Stirling Hill's 94-yard touchdown run, on Dec. 24, 1898, was the second longest run from scrimmage in Washington's history. There have been four other ninety-yard plus rushing touchdowns. Royal Shaw recorded the longest run in Washington history—105 yards when the field was 110 yards long—in igniting a comeback win over Idaho (12-10) in 1904. Dean Derby went 92 yards for a score in Washington's win over Illinois (28-13) in 1956. Hugh McElhenney scored a 91-yarder to help beat Kansas State, 33-7, in 1950. Napoleon Kaufman also went 91 yards in Washington's win over San Jose State (34-20) in 1994.

Husky Legend

Clarence Larson

1900 Tyee

Clarence Larson was the football captain in 1898. Considered among the leading players in the state, his career apparently extended six seasons—from the fall of 1894 to the fall of 1899. During that period, he played in all 24 games. In the 1894 season, he was a left tackle. Showing great running ability, he started at right halfback in 1895 and, for three seasons, paired with Jack Lindsay to form one of the most powerful running combinations on the Pacific Coast. He played on the first unbeaten Washington team in 1895. He handled the kicking off and point-after kicks. He also participated on the track team and interclass baseball games as a pitcher.

Husky List

Whitman College was Washington's first Northwest rival. Others soon followed. Here are the all-time records with each Northwest school against which Washington has played at least 10 games.

School	First Game	Last Game	Series Summary
Col. of Puget Sound	1910	1934	13-0
Idaho	1900	Still active	30-2-2
Montana	1920	1951	16-1-1
Oregon	1900	Still active	56-33-5
Oregon State	1897	Still active	55-26-4
Washington State	1900	Still active	60-27-6
Whitman College	1894	1944	28-2-3
Willamette	1906	1944	9-0-1

Husky Lore

PUBLICATIONS became a part of early Washington students' enterprises. University newspapers dated back to territorial days, although the first student venture, the *Washington Venture*, had a very short publication life. In 1891, students made another attempt to publish a university newspaper. This venture also failed. In 1893, two football captains, Otto Collings and Delbert Ford, founded the *Pacific Wave*, a student weekly that carried reports of university events together with student comments and opinions. In 1895, a rival sheet, the *College Idea*, was started. Eventually, the two were consolidated under the banner of the *Wave*. In 1909, the *Wave* was renamed the *University of Washington Daily*. An annual, named the *Tyee*, began in 1900. Launched by the junior class, it continued to be a class book until 1911 when the Associated Students of the University of Washington took it over. These annuals preserved a wealth of detail about campus life at the turn of the century and beyond.

1899 W 1900

Husky Moment

Football Champions of Idaho and Washington

In 1899, Washington closed out the century with a very solid football season. With a 4-1-1 record, they outscored their opponents 71-27. A.S. Jeffs coached the team and was assisted by a former coach, Ralph Nichols. On Thanksgiving, Nov. 25, Washington hosted Whitman College for the championship of Idaho and Washington. In a heavy wind and rain storm, Washington won 6-5 behind the leadership of captain Stirling Hill and the outstanding play of Clarence Larson. It was Larson's 24th game over six seasons. He plunged through the line repeatedly for big gains. When the game ended, pandemonium reigned in the grandstand. Young women tore their bonnets from their heads and embraced one another. They shook hands with their male escorts and appeared flushed with joy.

1900 Tyee

The 1899 football team wins championship of Idaho and Washington.

Husky Spotlight

The track team competed in three meets in the spring of 1900. They beat Whitman, lost to Oregon by two points, and won a a triangular meet with Washington Agricultural College and the University of Idaho. In the Whitman contest, Glen Caulkins, a junior, competed in six events. He won four—the 100-yard dash, the 220-yard dash, the 120-yard high hurdles, and the broad jump. He took second in the high jump and the pole vault. The following athletes set school records:

- **Fred Chestnut—50-yard dash (5.4 seconds) and the 100-yard dash (10 seconds)**
- **Glen Caulkins—220-yard dash (22.8 seconds) and the 120-yard high hurdles (16.4)**
- **Richard Huntoon—440-yard dash (52.4 seconds)**
- **Carl Morford—880-yard run (2 minutes, 6.2 seconds)**
- **Fred Fields—Discus throw (101 feet, 1 and 1/4 inches)**

Husky Highlight

Carl "Peggy" Morford was the track and field team captain in 1900. He, together with Glen Caulkins, Fred Chestnut, and Lance Thayer, established a Pacific Coast record in the mile relay —3 minutes and 34 seconds. Morford is at the bottom of the picture, Thayer is at the top, Caulkins is left center, and Chestnut is right center.

1901 Tyee

Husky Legend

Stirling Bryant Hill

1900 Tyee

Stirling (sometimes listed as Sterling) Hill, was a very versatile football player who played four seasons for Washington. He played left halfback in 1896, backing up the great Jack Lindsay; right end in 1897; left halfback again in 1898 and 1899. He captained the team in 1899. He also was the punter. His three brothers played for Washington—Arthur, Climie, and William and his father, Eugene Hill, was the University's president from 1872-1874. Stirling was the president of the University's Athletic Association for the academic year 1899-1900. He also played baseball in interclass competition and also participated in track. He set a school record in the broad jump in 1904, competing as a graduate engineering scholar. His most famous feat was a 94-yard touchdown run, on Dec. 24, 1898, in the closing minutes of the game against the strong Puyallup Indian Reservation team. The run stands as the second longest touchdown, from the line of scrimmage, in Washington's football history.

HUSKY LIST

Below are the Washington athletes who won more than one individual Pacific Coast Conference championship in track and field.

Event	Name	Year	Performance
100 yard dash	Vic Hurley	1921	9.8
100 yard dash	Vic Hurley	1922	10.6
100 yard dash	Vic Hurley	1923	9.9
220 yard dash	Vic Hurley	1921	22.4
220 yard dash	Vic Hurley	1922	22.6
220 yard dash	Vic Hurley	1923	22.5
440 yard dash	Terry Tobacco	1957	46.9
440 yard dash	Terry Tobacco	1958	47.1
880 yard run	Jim Charteris	1925	1:56.5
880 yard run	Jim Charteris	1927	2:00.2
120 yard high hurdles	Chuck Frankland	1921	16.0
	Chuck Frankland	1922	16.0
120 yard high hurdles	Steve Anderson	1928	14.4
220 yard low hurdles	Vic Hurley	1921	25.0
220 yard low hurdles	Vic Hurley	1922	24.
220 yard low hurdles	Vic Hurley	1923	23.6
220 yard low hurdles	Steve Anderson	1928	23.6
High jump	Chuck Frankland	1922	6'1" (tie)
Shot put	Gus Pope	1921	45'8"
Discus throw	Gus Pope	1921	148'6"

ON Jan. 10, 1900, the University Book Store was opened next to the president's office in the Administration Building (now Denny Hall). In 1908, Percy Dearle was hired as the first full-time manager, a position he held until 1922. Total sales reached almost $50,000 in 1914. The book store prospered at several locations, including a billiard parlor on University Avenue, its home since 1925. The enterprise now has nine locations and annual sales in excess of $51.5 million. The University Book Store sells more books than any college book store in the U.S.

(University Bookstore)

The Original University Bookstore

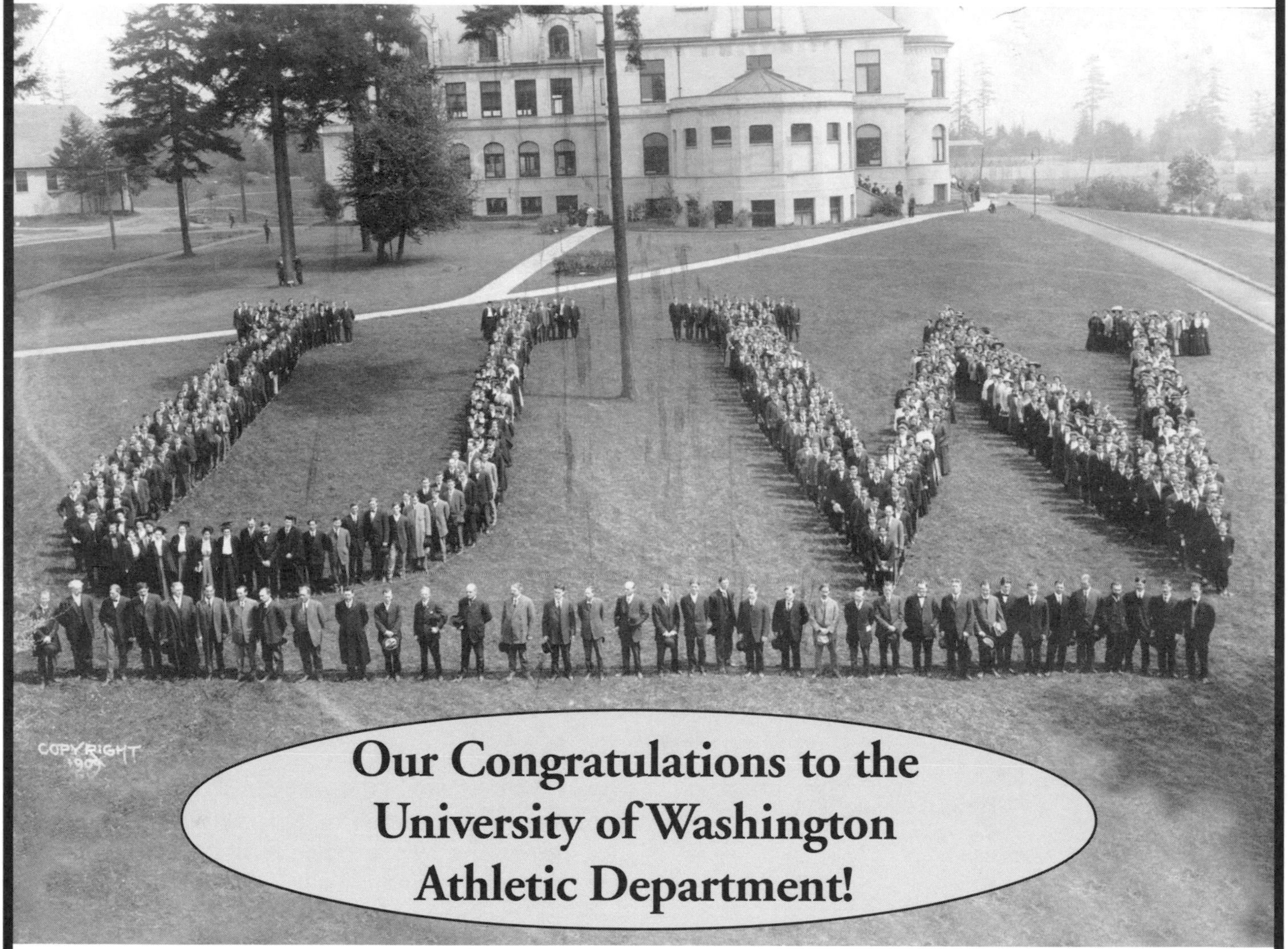

1900-09

1900 W 1901

Husky Moment

Washington Ties Unbeaten Washington Agricultural College

At the turn of the twentieth century, Washington hired J. Sayre Dodge, former end and captain of the University of Indiana, as football coach. He was the first paid coach, receiving $500 for the season. Also for the first time, the schedule included Idaho, Oregon and Washington Agricultural College. The team traveled to Walla Walla and tied Whitman on Oct. 27 (11-11). Three days later, Washington lost to Idaho, 12-6. Back in Seattle on Thanksgiving day, Washington tied an unbeaten Washington Agricultural College team, 5-5. Washington was motivated by the prophecy of Aggie coach, W.T. Allen that his boys would beat Washington 30-0. His confidence was not misplaced since the Aggies had not allowed an opponent to reach their 25-yard line all season. Twice, the Aggies had the ball on Washington's four-yard line, each time turning the ball over on downs. That evening, both teams sat in boxes as guests of the Grand Opera House to witness Hoyt's play—A Day and a Night. Several actresses carried the colors of the two teams and one wore a purple and gold gown. Early the next day, Washington entrained for Eugene, managing to arrive just before game time on Saturday. Washington fell easily to Oregon, 43-0. A trip to Oregon was a major undertaking in 1900.

The first game against Washington Agricultural College—now Washington State University.

1902 Tyee

Husky Spotlight

A Boat House for the Crew

In 1899, effort was made to establish a crew program at Washington. E.F. Blaine, a Seattle attorney, offered to help form a student rowing committee. The committee consisted of Frank Brightman (Chair), Stanley Hall, and J.A. Millett. In early 1900, Blaine and his law partner, Charles Denny, solicited funds from the business community and organized a student work party to build a boat house. A cutting bee was held at Madison Park Point and 10 cedars were cut to make a float. Blaine furnished the lumber for the construction and the students built a boat house on Lake Washington. In 1900, Blaine also helped the students to raise funds for two rowing barges that were built at the Moran Brothers Shipyards in Seattle. Class races were held in the spring of 1901.

Husky Highlight

1901 Tyee

Baseball began in the spring of 1901. Fred Shock was the first Washington coach and the team's best pitcher. Ken McPherson was the first captain. They played 10 games, winning four and losing six. They won their first game in Spokane against Gonzaaga 15-14. Washington played Washington Agricultural College six times, losing four and winning two, 9-8 and 12-1.

Husky Legend

Fred Chestnut

1904 Tyee

Glen Caulkins

1902 Tyee

Glen Caulkins and Fred Chestnut

Glen Caulkins and Fred Chestnut were outstanding track athletes at the turn of the century. Caulkins participated in 1900 and 1901, when he was team captain. He was named "Star Athlete of the Pacific Coast" for his sprinting and hurdling ability. He set school records in the 220-yard dash (22.8 seconds), 120-yard high hurdles (16 seconds), and the broad jump (21 feet, 5 inches). He also was a member of the mile relay team that established a Pacific Coast record (3 minutes and 34 seconds). His teammate in the mile relay was Fred Chestnut. Chestnut established Washington records in the 50-yard dash (5.4 seconds), 100-yard dash (10 seconds), and was on the mile relay team that set a new school record (3 minutes 33 seconds) in 1902. He was the captain of the 1902 team that beat Oregon 103 to 13, the largest score amassed by a Washington team until 1933. The team was undefeated in 1902. They also beat Whitman and Washington Agricultural College.

Husky List

The Oregon football series started in 1900. Through 2000, Washington leads the series 56-33-5 with Washington recording 13 shutouts. The 10 games with the largest margins of victory for Washington are:

Year	Score
1974 (home)	66-0
1951 (away)	63-6
1977 (away)	54-0
1952 (home)	49-0
1961 (away)	36-0
1986 (home)	38-3
1983 (away)	32-3
1911 (away)	29-3
1991 (home)	29-7
1990 (home)	38-17

Husky Lore

THE Athletic Association was responsible for the management of athletic activities in the 1890s. As athletics were gradually embraced by the student body, a Student Assembly was formed to sponsor activities not within the sphere of official university responsibilities. At first, funds were raised by individual solicitation and money-raising activities. In 1900 students were assessed a fee of fifty cents to stabilize support of student enterprises. In 1901, the Assembly and the Athletic Association were replaced by the Associated Students of the University of Washington (ASUW). The ASUW assumed the management of all matters of general student concern, including athletics, with a general manager in charge. The first general manager, William T. Laube, was selected in February 1903.

1901 W 1902

Husky Moment

A Six Game Season

Washington faced its largest schedule in 1901 with six opponents. Jack Wright, a former Columbia University player, was coach. A large number of football candidates turned out for what appeared to be a promising season. However, Washington lost its first two games—by identical 10-0 scores—to Whitman and Washington Agricultural College. They won two of the next three games played before dwindling crowds. On Thanksgiving day, the largest crowd for a football game in Seattle—about 2,000—came to watch Washington hold Idaho scoreless. Captain Dick Huntoon scored the first touchdown. The 1903 Tyee review of the game ended with a poem:

And in the nights of winter, when cold the north winds blow,
And the dripping of the eaves is heard amidst the snow.
With cheering and with laughter will the story then be told,
How well Washington won the game in the college days of old.

1902 Tyee

The 1901 football team played Washington's first six-game schedule.

Husky Spotlight

Climie Hill led the 1902 track team. As both an undergraduate and graduate student, Hill earned eight letters—five in track in 1896, 1897, 1900, 1901 and 1902 and three in football in 1895, 1896, and 1899. He set a school record (4:53.4)in the mile run in 1897. Climie and his brothers, Stirling and William, were three of many students who played in two or more sports. Some played while in college preparatory, undergraduate and graduate programs. In those days, little was done to enforce eligibility rules. The 1902 track team won all three meets by large margins and were undisputed champions of the Northwest. Outstanding performers included Joe and Robert Pearson in the sprints, Dave Grant in the pole vault, and Dick Huntoon in the 880- yard run. Washington crushed Oregon 103 to 13, the largest score by Washington until 1933.

Husky Highlight

Football players need to be students. That was the message of athletic manager Carl Eshelman, reflecting on the overall 1901-02 athletic year in the *Tyee.* Eshelman wrote of the Associated Students of the University of Washington's initial struggles to manage student affairs, including intercollegiate athletics. He also commented on the need for football players to be students with a real academic purpose, not players who only attend school during the football season. He believed that the best football men came from the rank and file students who have a loyalty to the institution and make an academic effort throughout the year.

Husky Legend

1995 Tyee

James Knight

James Knight was hired in June 1902 to become the football coach and Washington's first crew coach. He coached football for three seasons—1902 to 1904—compiling the second best winning percentage (.775) in Washington history. In 1902 and 1903, his record of 11-0 against collegiate competition was the best in the nation. He led Washington to its first Pacific Coast championship in 1903. He was an end on Princeton's 1895 football team and was a member of a champion gymnastics team in 1896, After graduating in 1896, he played football for the Chicago Athletic Club. From 1898 to 1900, he was a member of the Detroit Rowing Club and rowed in regattas in Canada and in the United States. In the fall of 1901, he entered Michigan Law School and played end on the football team and was the assistant coach. While at Washington, he initiated Washington's first intercollegiate rowing competition in 1903. He ignited so much interest in rowing that the ASUW officially recognized the sport in 1904. He was the crew coach from 1903 to 1905 and the track coach in 1904. He started a series of athletic social events to raise money for the crew program.

Husky List

Washington Football Success (Decade by Decade)

Years	Wins	Losses	Ties	Winning Percentage
1889	0	1	0	.000
1890-1899	15	12	5	.547
1900-1909	44	16	12	.694
1910-1919	52	4	3	.907
1920-1929	64	27	6	.691
1930-1939	53	31	8	.620
1940-1949	44	40	4	.523
1950-1959	49	48	4	.545
1960-1969	54	43	5	.554
1970-1979	67	44	0	.604
1980-1989	84	33	2	.714
1990-1999	82	35	1	.699
2000	11	1	0	.917

ONE of the true sporting spectacles in the early years of Washington baseball was the annual Seniors-Faculty game. In 1901, the faculty had won 27-12. On June 18, 1902, the confident and colorful faculty arrived—Paddy (English Professor Frederick Padelford) with his massive legs; Doc Byers (Horace Byers of Chemistry) in football attire; Roberts (Milnor Roberts, Dean of the School of Mines) in bloomers; and Haggett (Arthur Haggett, Professor of Greek and Latin) in last summer's bathing suit. President Kane was the faculty team's captain and catcher. It was a dangerous game; Roberts planted the first pitch square in Ed Duffy's ribs. "Priggy" Prigmore smashed a grounder to Byers playing second base, and the ball became entangled in the numerous hairs on Byers' face. Time was called until the ball was found. The final score was Seniors 27 - Faculty 4. The faculty, with heads bowed, retreated to an office where they freely partook of witch hazel and liniment, so the labels read.

1902 W 1903

Husky Moment

Washington's First Crew Race

Under the tutelage of James Knight, Washington's first paid crew coach, seven oarsmen regularly practiced in the spring of 1903. On May 14, Washington rowed against the James Bay Boat Club's junior crew in Victoria, British Columbia. Because of a series of mishaps, the race carried over to the next day when Washington won by a quarter of a boat length. On June 3, 1903, Washington competed in its first intercollegiate race. The University of California crew came to Seattle to race Washington in a four-oared event. Rowed in barges, the crews raced over a mile and a half course on Lake Washington. About 5,000 people lined the course to watch the Washington boat win by about three lengths in the time of nine minutes and thirty three seconds. The oarsmen in this first race with Cal were Fred McElmon, stroke; Clinton Lantz, number three seat; Dan Pullen, number two; and Captain Karl Van Kuran, bow. When the men crossed the finish line, thousands sent up a cheer and people on the spectator boats unfurled pennants—the nicest ovation ever paid the University, up to that point. The sport of rowing was introduced to Seattle.

1905 Tyee

Washington's first crew beats California in Washington's first collegiate race. Left to right: Van Kuran, Pullen, Lantz, McElmon.

Husky Spotlight

Washington recorded its first shutout of Washington Agricultural College on Nov. 27, 1902, 16-0. New football coach, James Knight developed his small squad into a strong combination. They beat all four collegiate foes, losing only to the Multnomah Athletic Club. In the game against the Aggies, Clinton Lantz was a battering ram on fullback plunges and Maxey Wells, left halfback, scored two touchdowns. The second one was a 90-yard run, with three minutes left, assisted by superb blocking around left end by Charles Sigrist, Bob Ewing and Lantz. Speidel escorted Wells into the secondary and knocked the last Aggie defensive back out cold with his block. Many writers and fans claimed Washington won the Northwest title over Oregon on the basis of comparative scores since Washington did not meet Oregon in 1902. Coach Knight was selected Northwest Coach of the Year by the Portland Oregonian.

Husky Highlight

The Northwest Intercollegiate Athletic Association (NWIAA) was organized in Spokane on Oct. 11, 1902. The NWIAA promoted intercollegiate athletics in its founding schools—Idaho, Montana, Montana Agricultural College, Oregon, Oregon Agricultural College, Pacific University, Washington, Washington Agricultural College, and Whitman. Included in the association's bylaws was a requirement that athletes be registered for at least 12 hours of credit while participating on a college team in a season.

Husky Legend

1902 Tyee

Fred McElmon

Fred McElmon was a two-time football captain (1902 and 1904) and the stroke of the first Washington crew in 1903. He was an outstanding football player for four years (1901-1904) making substantial yardage as a fullback and keying the defense. His play in the 1903 Nevada game contributed mightily to Washington's 2-0 win and its claim to the Pacific Coast championship. He blocked a field goal attempt in the closing moments in the shadow of Washington's goal line.

Husky List

Washington State (known as Washington Agricultural College until March 1905 when it became Washington State College) began its football series with Washington in 1900, with a 5-5 tie. Washington leads the series 60-27-6, recording 19 shutout wins. The 10 games with the largest Washington margins of victory are:

Year	Score
2000 (away)	51-3
1914 (home)	45-0
1990 (away)	55-10
1936 (home)	40-0
1991 (home)	56-21
1950 (away)	52-21
1978 (away)	38-8
1938 (home)	26-0
1911 (home)	30-6
1940 (home)	33-9

Husky Lore

WALTER CAMP wrote a series of articles about the 1902 college football season in *Collier's Weekly*. Apparently, neither he or other sportswriters of that day covered or cared about football played in schools 200 miles west of the Atlantic Ocean. Camp ranked the nation's top 15 teams in four groups.

Group One—Yale, Princeton, Harvard, West Point
Group Two—Dartmouth, Pennsylvania, Cornell
Group Three—Brown, Carlisle, Amherst, Bucknell
Group Four—Lehigh, Lafayette, Syracuse, Columbia

Walter Camp

Husky Moment

Pacific Coast Champions

The 1903 Washington football team beat its six collegiate opponents and lost only to the Multnomah Athletic Club. They won the West Coast championship by defeating Nevada 2-0. The game was billed as the championship because Washington had defeated all the Northwest schools and Nevada had beaten California and Stanford. The newspapers and the community's celebration heralded the memorable win. The game was a defensive struggle—the only score of the game was a safety early in the game. Friesell, Nevada's outstanding right halfback and punter, was unable to get a punt out of his end zone. The center snap was high and gave Washington players time to rush and force Friesell to drop in the end zone. Washington came close to scoring again. Bill Speidel's 35-yard field goal attempt fell short by six inches Two European immigrants played key roles in the victory. One was Alfred Strauss, a senior halfback from Hardheim, Germany. Strauss later would become a leading surgeon and cancer researcher and a significant Chicago-Midwest Washington recruiter. The other was Enoch Bagshaw from Flint, Wales. He was credited with a game-saving tackle near the end of the game. A Nevada halfback broke clear for a 30-yard run and Bagshaw was the only man left to beat in the secondary. The Welshman went on to earn an engineering degree and to become the first Washington coach to lead a team to the Rose Bowl.

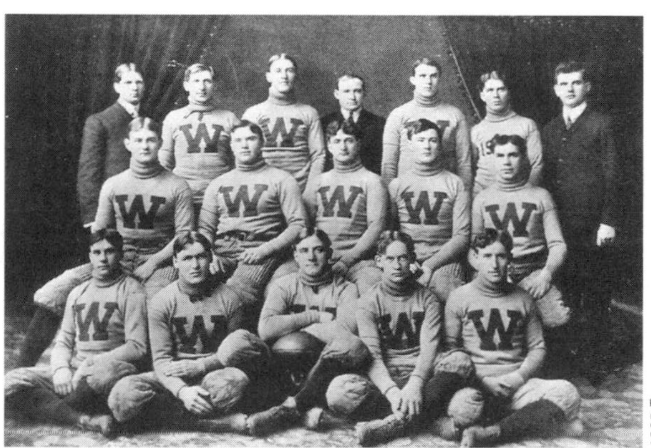

The 1903 football team claims the championship of the Pacific Coast.

1905 Tyee

Husky Spotlight

Joe Pearson

Joe Pearson sped on to the track scene in 1901 as a 16-year-old "Boy Wonder." He was an outstanding sprinter and established Pacific Coast records in 100-yard dash, 220 yard dash and school records in five events—100-yard dash (10 seconds), 220-yard dash (22.2). 440-yard dash (50.6), 220-yard hurdles (27.0), and the mile relay (3 minutes and 33 seconds). He was a star performer on the undefeated track and field teams of 1902 and 1903. In the 1903 Idaho meet, he placed in seven events. He won the 100, the 220, and anchored the mile relay; he was second in the 440-yard dash, the 220-yard low hurdles, and the high jump; he took third in the shot put. In the California meet in 1904 at Berkeley, he brought the crowd to its feet by taking the relay baton 25 yards behind the Cal anchor man and overtaking him in the final yards of the last leg of the mile relay event.

Husky Highlight

The men's and women's basketball teams continued to develop. Without a coach, the men's team went 2-4 in its first collegiate season (1902-03). The 1903-04 team was 6-3-1. The starting forward was William Hill, the last of the four Hill brothers to earn a varsity letter at Washington. The women's team won four games in the 1902-03 season, losing two away games in Ellensburg and Pullman. Next season, they beat Seattle High School 7-0, and split games with Vancouver College (2-5, 12-4).

Husky Legend

Bill Speidel

1905 Tyee

Bill Speidel was Washington's quarterback in 1902 and 1903 and team captain in 1903. He was selected by the *Portland Oregonian* to the first ever All-Northwest team. He was an outstanding field captain, calling both offensive and defensive plays. A punishing blocker, he cleared many opponents in the secondary on the long runs recorded by the Washington backs. He was probably best known for his punting and kicking. He boomed many long punts to pin the opposition deep on the field and get the ball out of danger for Washington. In 1903, he kicked five field goals out of eight attempts netting 25 of Washington's 65 points. The 1904 Tyee included a poem, Speidel's Famous Right Leg:

Among the college traditions of college men of fame,
Of many a winning touchdown and many a hard-fought game.
Of Lindsay's plunging line-bucks, when he held the leather egg.
You'll hear of "Spi," the quarter, and Speidel's famous leg.

Light up your pipe, old fellow, and let the smoke drift slow,
While visions of many a scrimmage across the smoke wreaths go;
Of Oregon defeated, and still the college tells
How we won the game with place-kicks from that leg of old Speidel's.

The smoke-wreaths drift and circle into another dream.
Old "Spi" is kicking spirals around the Pullman team;
Oh, hear the bleachers cheering, and shouting college yells,
For Washington victorious, and that leg of Bill Speidel's.

Husky List

The Washington-California men's crew dual series dates back to 1903, with 90 meetings between the two schools. At stake is the Schoch Cup, named after Washington oarsman Delos Schoch who lettered three years, 1934-1936. Through the 2000 season, Washington leads the series 64-25-1.

In the last 50 years, Washington has won the Schoch Cup 34 times. Here are the results for the last 10 years:

Year	Winner	Course	Time
1991	Washington	Montlake Cut, Seattle	5:42.0
1992	California	Oakland Estuary, Oakland	5:36.22
1993	Washington	Montlake Cut	6:26.3
1994	Washington	Oakland Estuary	5:50.8
1995	Washington	Montlake Cut	6:28.9
1996	Washington	Oakland Estuary	5:45.4
1997	Washington	Montlake Cut	5:30.0
1998	Washington	Redwood Shores, Ca.	6:13.06
1999	California	Montlake Cut	5:33
2000	California	Redwood Shores, Ca.	5:37.6

Husky Lore

ON Nov. 20, 1903, Chief Joseph, the famous Nez Perce leader, made his first visit to Seattle and attended the Washington-Nevada football game. Chief Joseph spent most of the game on the sidelines smoking a cigar. Asked his impression of the game, he said, "I saw a lot of white men almost fight today. I do not think this is good. This may be all right, but I believe it is not. I feel pleased that Washington won the game. Those men I should think would break their legs and arms, but they did not get mad. I had a good time at the game with my white friends."

UWMsSCUA

Chief Joseph

1904 W 1905

Husky Moment

The Longest Touchdown Run in Washington History

In 1904, Washington won four games, lost two, and tied a heavily favored California team. The most exciting win was over Idaho on Nov. 3. Outplayed in every phase of the game, Washington mounted one of the biggest comebacks in its history. With only 10 minutes to go, Idaho led 10-0 and Washington had just held Idaho on its five-yard line—105 yards away for a Washington touchdown (the field was 110 yards long until 1912). On first down, Royal Shaw got the call from Washington's quarterback, Dode Brinker. Big Tom McDonald and Herb Ziebarth opened the hole and Shaw darted through the line behind the secondary blocking of Brinker. He headed straight toward the Idaho safety. The safety's flying tackle staggered Shaw but buoyed by the wild cheers of the Washington rooters, he fought to stay up with an open field in front of him and the Idaho team in pursuit. Shaw flung his headgear to the ground and raced toward the goal line. He fell between the goal posts dragging two Idaho players with him—a 105-yard touchdown run, the longest in Husky history. It seemed the Washington crowd's demonstration would never end. Then a hush and another roar as Brinker's kick went right between the uprights. Idaho 10, Washington 6. When Washington got the ball back, Shaw broke another long gainer—40 yards—to Idaho's 30-yard line. With 30 seconds left, Washington had reached the 15-yard mark. Brinker sent the right halfback Dean wide to the right. As Idaho's defense shifted left on the snap of the ball, Dean countered back to the left, Idaho's defensive right side, broke several tackles and scored to put Washington ahead. Brinker's kick was again good, giving Washington the victory, 12-10. The season ended with a dramatic upset—a 6-6 tie with heavily favored Cal. Again, Shaw was a hero with a 25-yard score to tie the game. It was Coach Knight's last game as Washington's football coach. His record of 15-4-1 is the second best winning percentage (.775) in Washington football history—trailing only the legendary Gil Dobie (.975).

1906 Tyee

The 1904 football team

Husky Spotlight

First Regatta on Lake Washington

The first intercollegiate rowing regatta on Lake Washington was held on May 30, 1905. Probably the largest turnout—about 5,000—for a Seattle sporting event lined the course. In the first mile, Washington opened up a five-boat length lead over California with Stanford trailing. A launch, with its passengers wanting to see more closely Washington's long swinging stroke, threw waves of water in the racing boat. Other launches followed, The boat's rudder string broke and the Washington shell was half full of water. The fellows kept on rowing and finished second to California. At the finish, the Washington boat swamped, throwing the crew into the water.

Husky Highlight

The Washington men and women's basketball teams had very successful seasons in 1905. The men won four games and lost one, to Ellensburg Normal. William Hill, the youngest of the Hill brothers who played for Washington, was the top point scorer. Tom McDonald, an outstanding football player and track and field weight events' thrower, was considered one of the best big men on the coast. The women were victorious in all eight games, played mostly against high school teams. The 1905 baseball team had the best season ever—8-3-1—including two home games with Waseda University, in an initial series with Japanese universities.

Husky Legend

Tom McDonald

1905 Tyee

"Big Tom" McDonald was a multi-sport star. He was an outstanding offensive and defensive lineman for three years (1903 to 1905) and frequently lined up as rushing fullback. He was the football team's captain in 1905. In that year, he was also selected as the right guard on the All-Pacific football team. He set the school and Northwest record in 1904 in the shot put (42-3½) and hammer throw (143-10). For four years prior to coming to Washington, he played on a championship YMCA basketball team. He was acclaimed as one of the Pacific coast's best basketball big men during his two seasons on the Washington basketball team. Somehow he managed time to coach the women's basketball team in 1905. He was involved in many other student activities. He was on the debate team, hosted high school participants in the annual spring interscholastic sports meet, and gave rousing speeches to the student body on the value of athletics and school spirit.

HUSKY LIST

The California football series began in 1904. Through the 2000 season, Washington leads the series 44-32-4, with Washington recording eight shutout victories. The 10 games with the largest winning margins for Washington are:

Year	Score
1915 (away)	72-0
1982 (home)	50-7
1990 (home)	46-7
1986 (home)	50-18 (Washington's 500th win)
1984 (home)	44-14
1962 (home)	27-0
1997 (away)	30-3
1944 (away)	33-7
1971 (away)	30-7
1977 (away)	50-31

HUSKY LORE

UNIVERSITY of Washington students launched many enterprises, promoted special events, established traditions, and founded a diverse number of clubs and social organizations. They included fraternities and sororities, honorary societies, and professional, debate and dramatic clubs. Fraternities and sororities were formed in the early 1900s. By 1904, 10 had been founded with 160 members out of a university enrollment of about 700 students. At first, the fraternity and sorority houses were located in residences on Brooklyn Avenue and 14th Avenue. The organizations soon relocated in a section north of the campus and built large mansions to accommodate members who wanted to live in them. Their members were very active in student activities. Between 1905 and 1917, every football captain, all but two ASUW presidents, and every *Tyee* editor was a member of a Greek letter society.

1905 W 1906

Husky Moment

Last Football Game Against Indians

The 1905 football team was coached by a former Harvard All-America, Oliver Cutts. The season started well. Washington won three and tied one against mediocre competition. In the last four games, they reversed course, beating only the Sherman Indian Institute and losing to Idaho and Oregon Agricultural College and tying Oregon 12-12. The highlights of the season were two games against Indian schools—Chemawa Indian School from Oregon and Sherman from California. Washington beat Chemawa 11-6 in 1905 and shut them out, 40-0, in 1907. It was the last game scheduled with an Indian school in Washington football history. The 1905 Sherman Institute game was heralded as a big test for Washington. Sherman had made a remarkable showing against a good Stanford team, losing 6-4, and against California without some of their best players. They had three former players from the strong Carlisle College program and had a very big line. Washington played a superb first half, scoring all of their points in a 29-0 shutout win. The last touchdown was made when Billy Winsor smothered a Sherman punt, wrapped his arms around the ball, and rumbled 45 yards for the score.

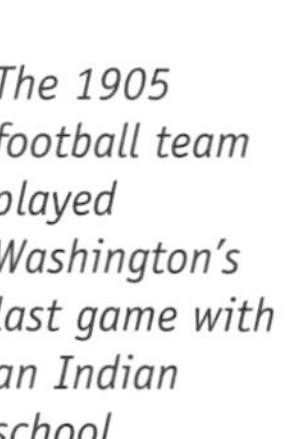

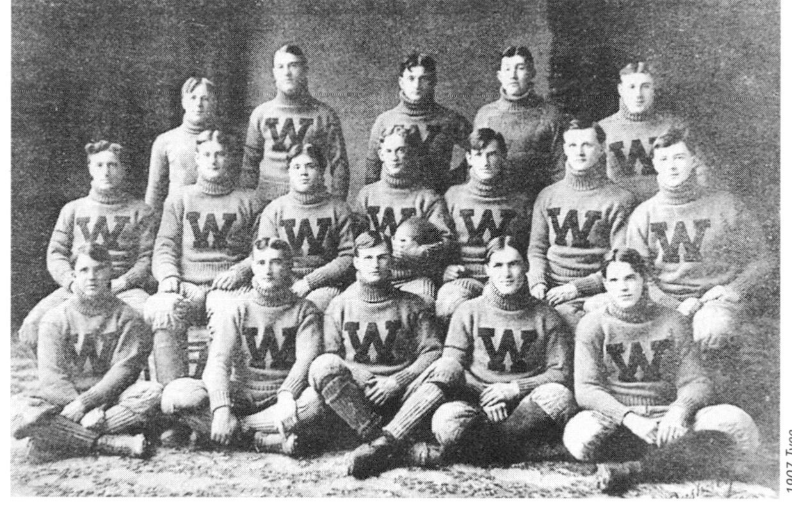

The 1905 football team played Washington's last game with an Indian school.

1907 Tyee

Husky Spotlight

William "Dode" Brinker was an outstanding pitcher on three baseball teams (1903-1905) and followed Bill Speidel as the quarterback on the 1904 football team. He occasionally played tackle on the 1905 team, the year he entered law school. He was editor of Washington's literary magazine, *The Goat*. He was the university's baseball coach in 1906, 1909, 1910, 1916, 1918, and 1919. His 1918 team was the first unbeaten team (6-0) in Washington history. His 1919 team was 10-0 and captured Washington's first Pacific Coast Conference championship. His overall record was 55 wins and 23 losses, a remarkable winning percentage of .705.

1905 Tyee

Dode Brinker

Husky Highlight

Washington did not have a crew coach at the start of the 1906 rowing season. George Strange, a former University of Toronto oarsman, and Mark O'Dell, who rowed at Cornell, volunteered to coach. The scheduled regatta in the San Francisco area was canceled because of the 1906 earthquake and fire in the city by the bay. No other races were held. The women's crew program began in 1906, with four women rowing in the only available barge in the morning practice session and the second four in the afternoon. Owen Crim was the coach. On Junior Day in 1907, the first women's class races were held. In the spring of 1908, 45 women turned out for crew, 64 in 1909.

1907 Tyee

Husky Legend

Dan Pullen

Dan Pullen, from Skagway, Alaska, may have been one of Washington's finest student athletes in the early years of the 20th century. The 1907 Tyee devoted a whole page to him, entitled "An Appreciation." Pullen was one of the best students in the Mechanical Engineering Department and actively participated in athletics during his entire college career. He made his initial appearance as a right halfback in the fall of 1902 and played in every game for the next three seasons, as guard, tackle and end. Teammates said they would rather play alongside Pullen than anyone. He was selected as right tackle on the 1905 All-Pacific football team. He was a member of the first three crews representing Washington in intercollegiate contests. He was the crew captain and stroke in 1905. After the regatta, on May 30, 1905, on Lake Washington, Coach Knight, a former oarsman, said: "Dan Pullen pulled the best oar of anyone in any crew, and he could step into any college boat in the world today and pull any oar." After finishing his junior year in mechanical engineering at Washington, he entered West Point, earned All-America football honors, and finished fourth in his class at Army. He became a Colonel in the Army Corps of Engineers and received the Distinguished Service Cross for his valor in France in World War I. The athletic field at Fort Belvoir, Virginia, is named after him.

Husky List

There have been many Washington athletes who have become Washington head coaches. Below are the athletes who coached for more than three seasons.

Baseball	**Dode Brinker (1906, 1909, 1910, 1916, 1918, 1919)**
	Ken Knutson (1993 to present)
Basketball	**Lynn Nance (1990-1993)**
Crew	**Ed Leader (1919-1922)**
	Rusty Callow (1923-1927)
	Al Ulbrickson (1928-1942, 1946-1958)
	Fil Leanderson (1959-1966)
	Dick Erickson (1967-1987)
	Jan Harville (1988-present)
Football	**Enoch Bagshaw (1921-1929)**
	John Cherberg (1953-1955)
	Jim Lambright (1993-1998)
Golf (Men)	**O.D. Vincent (1996 to present)**
Golf (Women)	**Edean Ihlanfeldt (1975-1981)**
	Mary Lou Mulflur (1983 to present)
Swimming	**Jack Torney (1933-1942, 1945-1962)**
	John Tallman (1962-1969)
Tennis	**Ed Brown (1916-1918, 1920)**
	Windy Langlie (1931-1933, 1947-1960)
	Jack Torney (1933-1941, 1946)
	Bill Quillian (1966-1973)
	Chip Zimmer (1975-1981)
	Doug Ruffin (1982-1984, 1986-1994)
Water Polo	**Arthur Kauffman (1968-1970)**
Wrestling	**Leonard Stevens (1931-1942)**

Husky Lore

IN 1906, football almost went out of existence in the East. President Theodore Roosevelt warned: "Clean up the game or I'll outlaw it." The 1905 season ended with a record number of injuries and fatalities. Roosevelt's criticism led to the elimination of mass plays such as the flying wedge. Also, the yardage required for a first down was lengthened to 10 yards from five. Seven men were required on the line of scrimmage. The forward pass was introduced to open up the game.

1906 W 1907

HUSKY MOMENT

First Pacific Coast Crew Championship

On June 1, 1907, Washington won its first Pacific Coast championship in rowing by beating Stanford. Stanford had beaten California in a race on April 29. On Saturday, April 27, Washington rowed in a triangular regatta against Cal and Stanford in Richardson Bay near Sausilito, California. Heavy winds and rough water caused all three boats to swamp. The race was rescheduled for Monday, April 29, but Washington could not stay. They had traveled to San Francisco by steamer—cheaper than by train—a trip taking about eight days. Because of Saturday's race conditions, the steamer ship had already waited past its scheduled departure time. The Washington crew was lifted out of the water and headed home. Stanford easily defeated Cal on April 29, and earned a trip north to row for the championship on Saturday, June 1. A light westerly breeze slightly rippled the water on the four-mile course and fanned Stanford and Washington pennants displayed by thousands of people lining the course and nestled in boats. Washington got off to a quick start, opened up a boat length and then settled into a steady stroke. Covering the four miles from Leschi Park to Laurelhurst Point in 23:38. Washington won by four-and-a-half boat lengths. The men in the course patrol boat, guiding the victorious shell to its moorage, congratulated Coach Conibear and exclaimed: "We will have to send you to Poughkeepsie if you keep this up."

Washington wins first Pacific Coast crew championship.

1909 Tyee

Husky Spotlight

With the arrival of its first two eight-oared shells on April 5, 1907, the Washington rowing program really got going. Once again, through the generosity of Seattle businessmen, Washington purchased two eights from Cornell. One was the sleek Henley shell in which Cornell established a new world record in 1902 on the Intercollegiate Rowing Association's Poughkeepsie course—18:53.2 for the four mile race. The boats were launched with much excitement. When the Washington oarsmen gently pushed the boats into Lake Washington, cheers echoed and reechoed as Washington took its place as the college Navy of the West.

HUSKY HIGHLIGHT

The trip to Eugene, Oregon, for a scheduled Saturday football game on Nov. 17, 1906, was indeed a journey. The team boarded a train on Thursday but was unable to get beyond Tacoma. Floods had washed out portions of track between Tacoma and Portland. The team spent Thursday and Friday evenings in Tacoma waiting for the railbed to be repaired. With repairs not completed, the team spent another night in Tacoma and, early Sunday morning, embarked on a boat for Portland. However, the boat detoured up the Cowlitz River to Castle Rock where the team once again boarded a train for Portland. They arrived in Portland about 11 p.m. on Sunday—tired and hungry. On Monday morning, they took a train to Eugene arriving in the afternoon. After a practice, they witnessed a march through the town headed by the Oregon band and many students. Singing and cheering, they ended the rally with a great big bonfire. The next day, Nov. 20, Oregon beat the weary Washington men, 16-6.

Husky Legend

Hiram Conibear

1913-14 Tyee

Hiram Conibear became the Washington crew coach in the spring of 1907. His innovations impacted rowing throughout the world. During his 10-year Washington coaching career, he implemented a rowing stroke—the Washington Stroke—that would lift Washington into the national limelight and eventually into international fame. Conibear became crew coach almost by default, taking the position because no one else was available. At that time, the long "layback" rowing stroke was the accepted standard. But Conibear felt the layback stroke was unnecessarily long and put undue strain on the rower's back, neck, and stomach muscles. He set out to find a more comfortable, rhythmic stroke that would also provide more power. He was originally hired to be Washington's football trainer and track coach in the fall of 1906. Lorin Grinstead, the ASUW's general manager, encouraged him to take the crew coaching job. Conibear remarked that he did not know the bow from the stern but that he would study up on the sport. And study and coach he did. He founded the Varsity Boat Club and the Board of Rowing Stewards and initiated fund raising activities for the rowing program. On Sept. 10, 1917, Conibear fell from a tree while harvesting fruit at his home and died instantly. He was a 1979 charter member of the Husky Hall of Fame and was regarded as one of the great sportsmen in Washington history. Conibear started a tradition of national and international excellence for the Washington crew program and dedcated his life to teaching young men and women not only the physical skills to be winners but the skills of dedication and commitment to make them champions in life.

HUSKY LIST

Washington Crew Coaches (for more than three seasons)

Men

James Knight	**1903-1905**
Hiram Conibear	**1907-1917**
Ed Leader	**1919-1922**
Rusty Callow	**1923-1927**
Al Ulbrickson	**1928-1942, 1946-1958**
Fil Leanderson	**1959-1966**
Dick Erickson	**1967-1987**
Bob Ernst	**1988 to present**

Women

John Lind	**1975-1979**
Bob Ernst	**1980-1987**
Jan Harville	**1988 to present**

HUSKY LORE

THE Department of Physical Culture expanded significantly under the direction of Professor Benjamin F. Roller, MD, and Instructor Lavina Rudberg. Men participated in calisenthics, gymnastics, cross country, rowing, boxing, wrestling and class day competitions in a variety of sports. In the women's program, there was class competition in baseball, basketball, cross country, field hockey, rowing and tennis. After 1906, women's intercollegiate athletic competition was discontinued and did not resume until 1974.

Benjamin Roller
1907 Tyee

Lavina Rudberg

1907 W 1908

Husky Moment

The Longest Unbeaten Streak in Football History

On Thanksgiving day, Nov. 28, 1907, Washington played a scoreless tie with Idaho to start a 63-game unbeaten streak, a record that has not been broken in college football. From the last game of the 1907 season until the second game of the 1917 season, Washington never lost a game—winning 59 and recording four ties. During the stretch of unbeaten games, Washington pieced together a 39-game win streak. During the perfect period (1908-1914), Washington outscored its opponents 1331 to 73, an average margin of 34-2 and recorded 26 shutouts. The 63-game unbeaten period ended with a 14-6 win over Whitman on Oct. 20, 1917.

1909 Tyee

A scoreless tie with Idaho starts the longest unbeaten streak in college football history.

Husky Spotlight

The Washington baseball team left for Japan on Aug. 18, 1908, for a two-month trip to play 10 games with Japanese universities' teams and club teams. They traveled to Japan on the steamer, Tosa Maru, landing on Sept. 3. They played their first game on Sept. 19 against Waseda University, winning 4 to 2. They lost the second game 6-3 to Waseda. In the remaining games, they lost three to Keio University and won five more including a 15-inning affair with Waseda late in the trip. The team had plenty of time for sightseeing and entertainment by the gracious Japanese officials.

Husky Highlight

The first intercollegiate tennis tournament in which Washington participated was held on May 29 and 30, 1908. Three schools participated—Oregon, Washington, and Washington State College. Each college entered a doubles and singles team. Mayberry Davis and E.C. Galbraith of Washington State won the doubles championship and Oregon's Charles McCnow won the singles championship.

UW Media Relations

Husky Legend

Enoch Bagshaw

Enoch Bagshaw was an outstanding football player from 1903 to 1907. He played end, halfback and quarterback. He was the team's captain in 1907 and was credited with throwing the first completed forward pass in Washington history on Oct. 10, 1906. He graduated in 1908 with a degree in engineering. He became Washington's head football coach in 1921. His teams compiled a 63-22-6 record over nine seasons, a .725 winning percentage, the fourth best in Washington history. His 1923 team played in Washington's first Rose Bowl on Jan. 1, 1924—a 14-14 tie with the Naval Academy. In 1925, the team won the Pacific Coast championship and again went to the Rose Bowl—losing 20-19, in a memorable game against Alabama on Jan. 1, 1926. He coached Washington's first and second consensus All-America football players—running backs George Wilson and Chuck Carroll. Bagshaw was inducted into the Husky Hall of Fame in 1980.

HUSKY LIST

Head Coaches in the Husky Hall of Fame (started in 1979)

Coach	Sport	Coaching Years	Year Inducted
Enoch Bagshaw	Football	1921-1929	1980
Rusty Callow	Crew	1923-1927	1982
John Cherberg	Football	1953-1955	1981
Hiram Conibear	Crew	1907-1917	1979
Gil Dobie	Football	1908-1916	1979
Tippy Dye	Basketball	1951-1959	1996
Hec Edmundson	Basketball and Track and Field	1919-1954	1979
Dick Erickson	Crew	1967-1987	1994
Tubby Graves	Baseball	1923-1946	1980
Marv Harshman	Basketball	1975-1993	1994
Eric Hughes	Gymnastics	1950-1978	1985
Edean Ihlanfeldt	Women's Golf	1974-1981	1989
Don James	Football	1975-1992	1994
Jim Owens	Football	1957-1974	1979
Jim Phelan	Football	1930-1941	1986
Bill Quillian	Tennis	1966-1973	1985
Jack Torney	Tennis and Swimming	1934-1941, 1946 1933-1942, 1946-1962	1981
Al Ulbrickson	Crew	1928-1942, 1946-1958	1979

SIX schools joined to form the Northwest Conference on Feb. 8, 1908. The schools were Idaho, Oregon, Oregon Agricultural College, Washington, Washington State and Whitman. They agreed on a set of rules to determine the eligibility of student athletes and to prohibit professionalism. Each student-athlete had to carry three-quarters of the required course work. Athletes could not be given scholarships or reduction in fees except on the basis of competitive examination or other methods open to non-athletes on the same terms. No student-athlete could play for an athletic club or organization other than his academic institution from the opening of the fall semester to the close of the spring term. Student-athletes, carrying the required amount of course work, could work part-time during the academic year, assuming they received no more than reasonable compensation for their services.

1908 W 1909

Husky Moment

Gil Dobie Coaches Washington

The 1908 football season was an historic one. Gil Dobie began his Washington coaching career and led Washington to its second unbeaten season. The team went 6-0-1; the only blemish on a perfect season being a tie with Washington State College. WSC came into the contest favored to win. Without a questionable official's call in the second half, giving WSC a safety, Washington might have won. In the first half, Washington drove twice inside the WSC seven- yard line but did not score. Three field-goal attempts failed. WSC scored on a field goal and Washington was able to garner a safety when the WSC punter could not handle a bad center snap and was dropped behind the goal line for a safety. The half ended with WSC up, 4-2. In its first drive of the second half, Washington drove to the WSC four-yard line where Max Eakins kicked a field goal to put Washington ahead, 6-4. Two more Washington drives ended in missed field goals. Late in the game, WSC punted deep in Washington territory. Arthur Clark, the Washington punt returner, fielded the punt on his two-yard line and was pushed back over the goal line for the questionable WSC safety. The final score was 6-6.

1910 Tyee

Action in 1908 Washington State College game.

Husky Spotlight

Guy Flaherty entered Washington having never played football. He was slender and weighed about 165 pounds. He played in every minute of every game during the 1906 and 1907 seasons. A severe case of boils on his arm prevented him from playing all but the first and last games of the 1908 season. When he was unable to play, Flaherty came to every practice and performed manager and assistant manager duties. His willing service to Washington football was recognized by every member of the team and a medal was named in his honor. The Guy Flaherty medal is awarded annually to the player voted "most inspirational" by his teammates. The award is considered the top award given at the end of each football season. The Guy Flaherty Award is believed to be the first inspirational award started in intercollegiate athletics in this country. In 1908, Guy Flaherty was the first recipient of the award.

UW Media Relations

Guy Flaherty

Husky Highlight

The women's rowing program began in 1906. By 1908, 45 turned out for practice. The women participated in interclass competition and had rowing form contests with points awarded for loading the boat, stroking, posture when ready to stroke, and unloading the boat. In 1908, the women's program was regarded as the largest in the country, if not in the world.

UW Media Relations

Husky Legend

Gil Dobie

Gil Dobie became Washington's football coach in 1908. Over the nine seasons—1908 through 1916—Dobie compiled an incredible record of 58 wins, no losses, and three ties. Washington won 39 consecutive games from late in the 1908 season to the middle of the 1914 season. This record stood for more than 40 years before Coach Bud Wilkinson's Oklahoma teams surpassed it. Dobie's nine teams—all undefeated—formed the base for Washington's phenomenal unbeaten streak of 63 games, still an NCAA record. Dobie attended the University of Minnesota. As a sophomore in 1900, he led the Golden Gophers to their first Big Ten Conference championship. After graduating in 1904, Dobie entered coaching. In his first head college coaching position at North Dakota State, he led his teams to unbeaten seasons in 1907 and 1908. His Washington teams were so well coached that they ran up a total of 1,930 points over his nine seasons compared to only 118 for his opponents. Dobie resigned after the 1916 season. He coached at Navy (1917-1919), Cornell (1920-1935), and Boston College (1936-1938) before retiring. His career record of 180 wins, 45 losses, and 15 ties ranks him among the winningest coaches of all time. He is a charter member of the Husky Hall of Fame, inducted in 1979. He was also enshrined into each of the Halls of Fame of the four other schools at which he coached. He is a member of the College Football Hall of Fame.

HUSKY LIST

Gil Dobie's Year-by-Year Record

Year	Record	Shutouts	Total Points (For and Against)
1908	6-0-1	4	128-15
1909	7-0-0	6	214-6
1910	6-0-0	5	150-8
1911	7-0-0	5	277-9
1912	6-0-0	4	190-17
1913	7-0-0	4	266-20
1914	6-0-1	5	242-13
1915	7-0-0	5	274-14
1916	6-0-1	4	189-16
TOTAL	58-0-3	42	1930-118

HUSKY LORE

THE Alaska-Yukon-Pacific Exposition (AYPE) opened on June 1, 1909, for four and a half months. It was a complete success. On the slope of the campus below Denny Hall, exhibition buildings were placed around a beautiful mall, with a pond and a fountain at its center. This spectacular corridor of buildings was oriented around the Mt. Rainier axis. This arrangement created an expansive outlook for the campus and an environmental partnership with the mountain. Eventually the fountain and the mountain would become the primary features of the Rainier Vista.

The First Century at Washington

1909 W 1910

Husky Moment

First Perfect Season

The 1909 football season was the first perfect season in Washington history. Gil Dobie's squad won all seven games and outscored its opponents 214 points to six. Oregon was the only team to score on Washington. When Oregon came to Denny Field for the last game of the seasaon on Thanksgiving day, Nov. 20, 7,000 people were waiting to watch a battle of two teams victorious over all collegiate foes. It was the largest football crowd ever in Seattle. Oregon was determined to crown itself champion of the Northwest. The game was a battle of two well-drilled teams. The rushing yards were pretty evenly matched. Washington's superb defense and passing game won the game. Washington scored at the 15-minute mark on a drive featuring a 20-yard run by Warren Grimm. Mel Mucklestone bucked over for the score and Wee Coyle made the conversion. A few minutes later, Oregon tied the score. Near the end of the first half, Washington scored again, with Warren Grimm grabbing a touchdown pass. Coyle's kick failed but just before the half ended, Coyle kicked a field goal, putting Washington up at the half 14-6. Neither team scored in the second half until near the end of the game, Grimm scored his second touchdown on a 75-yard pass play. Coyle's kick brought the final score to 20-6. Dobie's boys were becoming special.

Washington beats Oregon to notch its first perfect season.

1911 Tyee

Husky Spotlight

First Basketball Coach

After a two-year respite, the ASUW's Board of Control reinstated basketball as an intercollegiate sport. The team was coached by David Hall, Washington's first basketball coach. The team won five games and lost one. Hall graduated from Brown University where he was an outstanding track athlete. He was selected for the first modern day Olympics, in 1896, in Greece but could not finance the trip. Four years later, he represented the United States in the Paris Olympics. In 1908, he came to Washington as Director of the Department of Physical Training. He coached basketball for two seasons (1909 and 1910) and was the track coach for five seasons (1909, 1910, 1912-1914). Hall was a devoted medical practitioner and organized the US Medical Corps during World War I. In 1918, he returned to Washington to establish the university's health service. Hall's commitment led to the construction of a health center in 1936. It was named the David C. Hall Student Health Center in October, 1947. Hall retired in 1948 and maintained his active lifestyle into his 90s.

Husky Highlight

Washington won the Pacific Coast track meet on May 14, 1910, in Berkeley, California. Freshman Brailey Gish was the meet's outstanding performer. He scored 17 points by winning the 400-yard dash; taking second in the 100, the broad jump and the discus throw; placing third in the javelin throw; and anchoring the winning mile relay team. Washington athletes swept the next-to-last event—the javelin throw—to earn nine points and tie California at 51 points. In the last event—the mile relay—Gish ran the last quarter mile and beat the Cal anchor by one yard. Washington 56, Cal 51, Oregon 13, Stanford 10, Nevada 1.

Husky Legend

William "Wee" Coyle

UW Media Relations

Wee earned letters in three sports—football, baseball and track—over four years; 1908-1911. He was the football captain in 1911. Coyle is best remembered as the quarterback on four undefeated teams from 1908 to 1911. His teams won 26 games and tied one. He played right field on the baseball team and ran hurdles in track. He was the first-team quarterback on the all-time Washington team selected by fans in 1950. One of the voters said: "(Coyle) was the man who never made a mistake. Four straight years quarterbacking a major college team, 60 minutes of every game, and never in all that time calling a wrong number. Had Coyle's light not been hidden under the bushel of limited competition, much too far out in the Indian country to jolt Walter Camp from the Big Three (Harvard, Yale and Princeton) and Michigan, there is no doubt he would have been acclaimed one of the great quarterbacks of all time." He was inducted in the Husky Hall of Fame in 1980.

HUSKY LIST

Washington Head Coaches in More Than One Sport

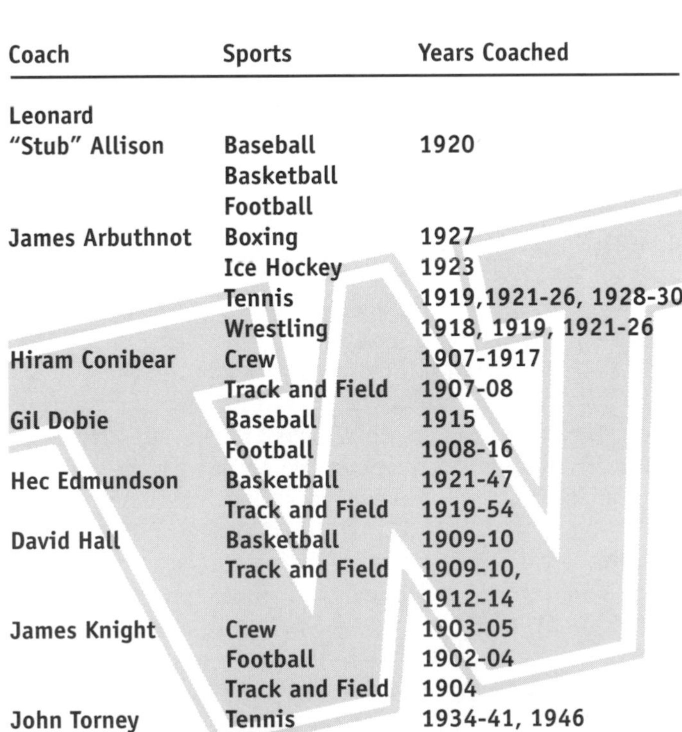

Coach	Sports	Years Coached
Leonard "Stub" Allison	Baseball	1920
	Basketball	
	Football	
James Arbuthnot	Boxing	1927
	Ice Hockey	1923
	Tennis	1919,1921-26, 1928-30
	Wrestling	1918, 1919, 1921-26
Hiram Conibear	Crew	1907-1917
	Track and Field	1907-08
Gil Dobie	Baseball	1915
	Football	1908-16
Hec Edmundson	Basketball	1921-47
	Track and Field	1919-54
David Hall	Basketball	1909-10
	Track and Field	1909-10, 1912-14
James Knight	Crew	1903-05
	Football	1902-04
	Track and Field	1904
John Torney	Tennis	1934-41, 1946
	Swimming	1933-42, 1946-62

HUSKY LORE

ON Lake Washington on May 26, 1910, Washington's crew beat Stanford for the Pacific Coast championship. Because of terrible course conditions the day before, the three-mile race was rerun. Again the waters were rough. Stanford stopped midway down the course because its boat was full of water. Washington's boat, nearly full of water, finished in a predictably slow time of 18:22.6. A few hours later, the victorious crew left for its first race in Madison, Wisconsin on June 4. Over a three-mile course on Lake Mendota, Wisconsin beat Washington in 16:06. Washington finished 15 seconds later in the best time ever recorded by a Washington crew up to that date. Washington realized it could row with the best Eastern crews.

Super Legend

Hiram Conibear

Perhaps the most famous rowing coach in Washington history never rowed a stroke in a racing shell in his life but his innovations revolutionized the sport. Born in 1871 in Mineral, Illinois, Hiram Conibear's love of sports led him first to coaching, training and conditioning bicycle racers and then to training college athletes. In 1895, Conibear became the trainer of track and football at the University of Chicago. After brief stints elsewhere, he returned to Chicago in 1906. As the Chicago White Sox trainer that summer, he met Bill Speidel, a young Chicago medical student. Speidel was a former Washington quarterback and 1903 team captain. Through Speidel's contacts with the Athletic Manager at Washington, Lorin Grinstead, Conibear was offered the position as Washington's athletic trainer.

Shortly after Conibear moved to Seattle, he and Grinstead were watching football practice. Grinstead said that Washington was in desperate need of a crew coach. Conibear jokingly replied: "I'd make a good one...(but) to tell you the truth, I don't know one end of a boat from another." Grinstead pressed on and told Conibear to study up on the subject of rowing by reading books in the library. In the spring of 1907, he became Washington's crew coach. Then the experiments began. Conibear borrowed a skeleton from a laboratory and dragged it up the boardwalk of Brooklyn Avenue and set it on a rowing seat in his basement. Into the skeleton's hands, he slid an old broom handle to serve as an oar. Then, with painstaking patience, he moved the skeleton through a stroke noting the position of the bones at each stage. Next, he turned an old bicycle upside down and began turning the wheel with the palm of his hand. In his mind, the wheel was the water, his palm the oar blade. He began to realize that unless the oar blade struck the water at a speed equal to or greater than the water's speed, there would be a moment of unwanted "drag." The Conibear stroke was taking shape. The results of his experiments led to a stroke with a shorter layback, a snap to the oar blade the instant it was inserted in the water, and a "shot" of the blade out of the water at the completion of the rower's drive.

Although, his innovations were successful, academic forces were working against him. Many wanted rowing to be taken over by the Physical Education Department under the supervision of a faculty member. Standing in the center of "his men" and surrounded by his detractors, Connie gave one of the most powerful orations in Washington athletic history. "I may be hard-boiled," he confessed. "I may cuss. I may do considerable more talking on the campus than I should. But, honestly I've put my heart and very soul into this work and, no matter what, I want to keep on." Pausing, he gazed about and with tears coursing down his leathery cheeks, he implored: "Don't fire me. Let me keep on. We are on the road to something really worthwhile!"

Conibear stayed on. With his enthusiasm and vision for the Washington rowing program, he persuaded George Pocock and his brother, Dick, to leave their boat-building business in Vancouver, British Columbia, and set up shop on the campus. In 1913, Conibear received an invitation to have Washington compete in Poughkeepsie at the Intercollegiate Rowing Association regatta.

Washington was the first western crew to appear in the elite event. The Purple and Gold challenged the eastern crews and threatened to win until Elmer Leader snapped his foot strap and was forced to pull himself back in the stroke with the strength of his stomach muscles. Despite Leader's difficulties, Washington finished third and the crew members returned to Seattle as heroes.

Four years later, Conibear's coaching career ended when, in September 1917, he died in a fall from a tree in his yard. "His men" continued on. Ed Leader, Elmer's twin brother, followed Conibear as Washington coach and then went to Yale. His varsity eight won the 1924 Olympic gold medal. Conibear's 1916 coxswain, Ky Ebright, would coach at California and gather Olympic golds in 1928, 1932, and 1948. Rusty Callow succeeded Leader as the Husky crew coach and his 1923 crew won Washington's first IRA championship. Callow's 1924 and 1926 crews, stroked by Al Ulbrickson, won again. After Callow moved on to Pennsylvania, Ulbrickson started his 31-year head-coaching career at Washington in 1928. Other Conibear disciples took over programs all over the country. Conibear had indeed started "... something really worthwhile."

Gil Dobie

1911 Tyee

Gilmour "Gil" Dobie hardly looked like a football coach. He was tall and thin, wore a black overcoat and smoked cigars or chewed on straw as he paced the sidelines. In terms of what he accomplished, Dobie certainly established himself as one of the best coaches in collegiate history.

In 1908, Washington appointed Dobie, a tall austere Scot, as head football coach. Dobie had starred at quarterback for the University of Minnesota, helping it win its first Conference championship in 1900. He obtained a law degree but decided to coach first at South Minneapolis High School. He led the "little Swedes" to an undefeated season and the state championship in 1903. He then became an assistant coach at Minnesota before going to North Dakota State as head coach. There, he was unbeaten over two seasons.

Dobie's impact at Washington was sudden. A group of entering freshmen was among the first to meet him. As one of them recalled: "No smile, no handshakes, no slap on the back—nothing but a pair of eyes peering coldly out of a dark face that was hidden partially by a slouch hat drawn loosely over a head of mussed black hair...He began to unfold himself from his lounging position. He seemed to mount into sections until his six feet and more of black overcoat had assumed an upright position. Those eyes were still working on us..." After a brief introduction, in his rasping voice, he said: "Remember, all you fellows, practice Monday starts at 2 P.M.. One thing I demand is promptness."

His concern for promptness and his preparation for games and his psychological skills paid off. During his nine years at Washington, Dobie's teams never lost a game—Washington won 58 games, tied three, and lost none. The Purple and Gold totaled 1,930 points and held opponents to 118. Washington's teams of that era ran had a streak of 63 games without a defeat (including the last game of 1907 and the first game of 1917). It still stands in the NCAA records as the all-time unbeaten streak.

Dobie's coaching was a combination of technical perfection and psychological warfare, the product of endless hours of practice. Wee Coyle, the star quarterback during the four seasons 1908-1911, recognized Dobie's genius: "He is one of the few coaches I ever heard of who could point his team for every game of the season."

Dobie knew his men, brought them to peak condition mentally, emotionally, and physically for each game, and remained in control at all times.

Coyle's talents were sharpened by Dobie's semi-weekly meetings in the coach's residence near campus. Intense meetings, they were conducted the night before a game and the night after each contest. The rooms of Dobie's small house were strewn with the sports pages of hundreds of newspapers and scraps on which football formations were scrawled. Amid the piles were always two sheets: one minutely describing Washington plays; the other detailing the defenses to be used against the opponent. These private conferences were always conducted with Dobie smoking a black cigar. As the smoke and smell filled the small rooms, Dobie would go over each play—when, where, and why they should be used.

"After about one cigar," Coyle relates, "I would begin getting uneasy, restless, and fed up on football...If I were lucky, I might be excused upon completion of his smoke, with probably this parting word: 'Coyle, you're a rotten quarterback and if I didn't have so many cripples, you'd be sitting on the bench. You've played your last two games like a man devoid of brains.'"

Dobie called the Washington-Oregon games of 1909 and 1914 as "the two best football games any man ever watched. (The 1909 and 1914) Washington teams could stand up with any outfit ever produced in the country," Dobie proclaimed in 1940 after his retirement from coaching, "providing you were limited to about 15 men. In each of those games, we played 11 men right through from start to finish."

Thanks to Coach Dobie, the University of Washington gained national prominence in intercollegiate football. After leaving Washington, Dobie coached at Navy, Cornell, and Boston College. He finished his coaching career in 1938 with a cumulative record of 180-45-15 (a winning percentage of .784). He was:

- Selected to the College Football Hall of Fame
- Selected as a charter member of the Football Coaches' Association when it was formed in 1921
- Selected as a charter member of the Husky Hall of Fame (1979) and the Halls of Fame of each of the four other schools where he coached.

1910-19

1910 W 1911

Husky Moment

First Basketball Northwest Conference Championship

In 1911, Washington won its first Northwest Conference championship with a season mark of 11 wins and one loss. Playing five games in six nights in January, they defeated Washington State twice, Idaho twice, and Whitman. They then played three games in Oregon in mid-February, losing to Oregon in one of the games, 27-13. They finished the season at home with four games in late February and early March. They took the first two from Washington State. The last two games were with Oregon with whom they were tied for the conference lead. Both schools had one loss. Washington won both games. In the second one, Oregon was ahead 17-10, with five minutes remaining in the game. Then Washington scored eight unanswered points to take the lead, with 30 seconds to go, and hung on to win 18-17. Center John St. John played the entire game with an injured knee and a sprained ankle. He and Captain C.C. Clementson, Rex Hosley, and Elmer Sugg played crucial roles in the final minutes. Clementson scored the tying and winning points by hitting two foul shots. Clementson was considered the best player in the Northwest based on outstanding quickness, leadership and coolness in crucial moments of the game. He and forward Oscar Olson made the all-Northwest first team.

1912 Tyee

The 1911 basketball team wins Northwest Conference championship.

Husky Spotlight

The football team completed its second perfect season, winning all six games with a scoring margin of 150-8. All eight points were scored by Whitman in a close game, with Washington winning 12-8. Two Washington fumbles early in the game gave Whitman its touchdowns. Washington recorded shutout victories over Lincoln High School, the College of Puget Sound, Idaho, Washington State, and Oregon Agricultural College.

1910 Tyee

Husky Highlight

Wrestling was established as an intercollegiate sport in 1909. The team held one match, losing to Oregon Agricultural College in Corvallis. In 1911, letters were first awarded to wrestling team members after they won the Northwest title by beating Washington State and the Aggies. The first eight-oared freshmen's race on the Pacific Coast was held in the spring of 1911 between Cal and Washington. Washington won. The baseball team played its first series with Cal. In the three games, Cal won the first two—3-2 and 7-2; Washington winning the third game, 6-4.

1911 Tyee

Husky Legend

Polly Grimm

Huber "Polly" Grimm was an amazing athlete. He starred on the 1905, 1907, 1909, and 1910 football teams as a tackle, place-kicker, punter, and runner in a tackle-around-play. On occasion, he was a passer and pass receiver. He was a weight man in track and field events and was a pitcher on the 1908 baseball team that made the first trip to Japan. Grimm was the national Amateur Athletic Union (AAU) heavyweight wrestling champion in 1911. Only the lack of expense funds kept him from representing the United States in wrestling in the 1912 Olympics. He wrestled professionally after being shunned by the U.S. Olympic Committee. He was the 1910 football captain and was picked as a third team All-America by Walter Camp, the first Washington player to receive national honors. Grimm was the only Washington and western college player picked by Gil Dobie, in 1925, on his all-time national football team. Polly had two brothers who played for Washington. Warren was an outstanding end and a terrific pass receiver from 1908 to 1911 and Bill was a star tackle in 1915, 1916, 1919,and 1922. Warren was killed by gunfire from members of the Industrial Workers of the World while marching in an Armistice Day parade in 1919 in his hometown of Centralia. He was a prominent attorney, as was Polly, and led anti-Communist activities as a commander of the local American Legion.

HUSKY LIST

Top 10 Men's Basketball Seasons (Minimum of 20 Wins)

Year	Record	Pct.	Coach	Conference Finish
1953	**28-3**	**.903**	**Tippy Dye**	**First N.D, won playoff (NCAA, Third)**
1931	**25-3**	**.893**	**Hec Edmundson**	**First N.D., won playoff**
1976	**23-5**	**.821**	**Marv Harshman**	**Third in Pac-8**
1944	**26-6**	**.813**	**Hec Edmundson**	**First N.D., playoff not held because of WW II**
1952	**25-6**	**.807**	**Tippy Dye**	**First N.D., lost playoff**
1938	**29-7**	**.806**	**Hec Edmundson**	**Second N.D.**
1934	**20-5**	**.800**	**Hec Edmundson**	**First N.D., won playoff**
1939	**20-5**	**.800**	**Hec Edmundson**	**Second N.D.**
1951	**24-6**	**.800**	**Tippy Dye**	**First N.D., won playoff**
1928	**22-6**	**.786**	**Hec Edmundson**	**First N.D., lost playoff**
1933	**22-6**	**.786**	**Hec Edmundson**	**Second N.D.**

N.D. is the Northern Division of the Pacific Coast Conference
Playoff was between the Northern Division and Southern Division champion for the Pacific Coast Conference championship

HUSKY LORE

IN the early 1900s, the University established the Puget Sound Marine Station at Friday Harbor on San Juan Island for instruction and research in marine biology. Other institutions were invited to share in the sponsorship of the program. A council was appointed with representatives from the Universities of Idaho, Kansas, Oregon, Puget Sound, Whitman College, and the normal schools at Ellensburg and Bellingham. Students in these institutions could earn credits in courses such as zoology, botany, and animal ecology. This program would eventually become as well known on the Pacific Coast as Wood's Hole, in Massachusetts, would be on the Atlantic.

1911 W 1912

Husky Moment

Baseball's Championship Series in California

Washington's baseball team did not have a great season, winning four and dropping five, but the series in California was memorable. It was the first trip to California for a Washington baseball team. First, Washington played three games at Stanford. Jack Johnson, the pitcher, homered in the second inning. John Patten laced the field with a triple, two doubles and a single in four times at bat. Robin Welts tripled and singled to help Washington win 6-2. Stanford rebounded to win 5-4 in the second game. Washington won the series by taking the loosely played third game, 13-9. Two days later, a great Santa Clara team beat Washington, 3-1. Washington traveled on to Berkeley for another three games. Cal won the first game, 1-0. Thirteen innings were required to decide the second game. Washington scored two runs in the top of the 13th to win, 3-1. Captain Fred Hickingbottom's double drove in the winning run and he scored on a wild throw. Will Boatman mowed down the Cal hitters, striking out 26. Cal won the third game 3-1. The Blue and Gold scored in the second inning on an error, a stolen base, a single, and another error. The score remained 1-0 until the eighth inning. Helped by two Washington errors, Cal collected five hits to score two more runs for the victory.

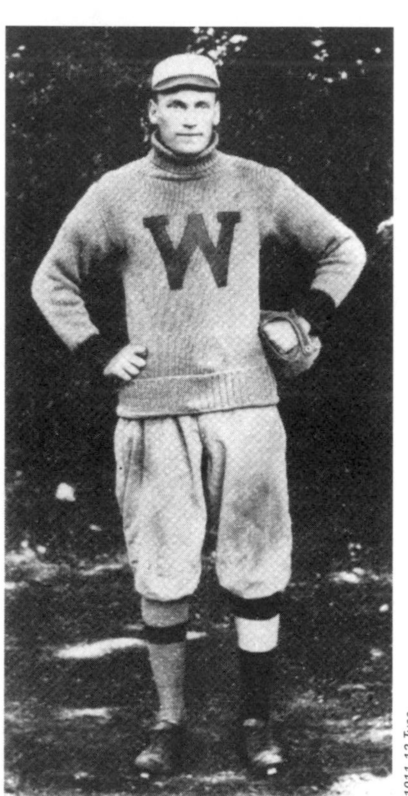
1911-12 Tyee

Fred Hickingbottom, 1912 baseball captain.

Husky Spotlight

For the fourth consecutive year, Washington completed an unbeaten football season in 1911, winning seven games. The Thanksgiving game on Nov. 30, a 30-6 win over Washington State College, was the last one for the "Old Guard—" Wee Coyle, quarterback; Warren Grimm, left end; Mel Mucklestone, right halfback; Royal Pullen, right guard; and Walter Wand, left halfback. When these players were replaced by substitutes near the end of a contest, Washington fans considered it time to start homeward. Many loyal supporters did not think that the Dobie football machine ran smoothly with one of these players out of the game. Coyle, Grimm, and Mucklestone were captains; Grimm received the Flaherty award. All were selected to Northwest all-star teams.

1911-12 Tyee

Mel Muckleston

Husky Highlight

The crew season commenced with the opening of school in September 1911 and ended on Junior Day on May 11, 1912. The Seattle City Park Board made available to the University single, double, and four-oared boats, used by the public in the summer. This gave the program ample shells for fall training. Coach Conibear held two fall regattas on Lake Union. Intra-college races were held in March and the inter-class regatta was held in late April. Over 70 turned out for the varsity program. In the California triangular regatta, Stanford beat Washington by a boat length and Cal by two.

1911-12 Tyee

Husky Legend

J. Ira Courtney

J. Ira Courtney was an outstanding sprinter for Washington in 1911 and 1912. He grew up in Minneapolis and first discovered his speed when policemen tried to catch him and his older brother after routing them from a neighbor's orchard. Short and stocky, he set interscholastic dash records at Seattle's Broadway High School. In a Pacific Northwest Association meet in the summer of 1911, he won the 100-yard dash in 9.8 seconds. In May 1912 meet in Pullman, he set a Washington record for the 100 meters (10.8). This time equaled the world record. In the same meet, he established a Washington record for the 200-meter dash (21.8), two-tenths of a second slower than the world record. In the 1912 Olympic Trials in San Francisco, he won the 100-meter dash (10.8) and the 200-meter dash (21.8), becoming the first Washington athlete to make a U.S. Olympic team. In the 1912 Stockholm Olympics, he won his heats in the 100- and 200-meter races, but lost in the semifinals. The 400-meter relay team, of which he was a member, was disqualified on a violation, after winning the semifinals.

Husky List

Washington Track and Field Athletes Who Participated in the Olympic Games

Year	Athlete	Event(s)
1912	Ira Courtney	100, 200 meters, 4 X 100 meter relay
1920	Gus Pope	Discus Throw
1924	Gus Pope	Discus Throw
1928	Steve Anderson	110 meter High Hurdles
	Herman Brix	Shot Put
1932	Ed Genung	800 meters, 4 x 400 meter relay
	Paul Jessup	Discus Throw
1936	Bruce Humbar (Canada)	100, 200 meters, 4 X 100 meter relay
1952	Bob Hutchinson (Canada)	100, 200 meters, 4 X 100 meter relay
	George Widenfeldt (Sweden)	Decathlon
1956	Terry Tobacco (Canada)	400 meter, 4 x 400 meter relay
1960	Terry Tobacco (Canada)	400 meters
1964	Phil Shinnick	Long Jump
	Wariboko West (Nigeria)	Long Jump
1972	Jim Seymour	400 meter, Intermediate Hurdles
	Fred Luke	Javelin Throw
1976	Borys Chambul (Canada)	Discus Throw
1980*	Duncan Atwood	Javelin Throw
	Rod Ewaliko	Javelin Throw
	Scott Neilson	Hammer Throw
1984	Duncan Atwood	Javelin Throw
	Sterling Hinds (Canada)	4 X 400 meter relay
	Regina Joyce (Ireland)	Marathon
1996	Adam Setliff	Discus Throw
	Aretha Hill	Discus Throw
2000	Christian Belz (Switzerland)	Steeplechase
	Ja'Warren Hooker	4 x 400 meter relay
	Adam Setliff	Discus throw

*Atwood, Ewaliko, and Neilson did not compete due to boycott

Husky Lore

WASHINGTON Yell Leader, Bill Horseley, became a legend in 1911. Wearing a cap with a long peak and clad in peg-top trousers, Bill taught the student body at Washington how to cheer as a unit. The Washington Rooting Club was established to organize cheering at all intercollegiate athletic contests. For the Thanksgiving day football game in 1911, he led the fans in a serpentine on the field. The 1911-12 *Tyee* devoted two pages to laud Horseley's abilities to lead the fans. It observed that he seemed to know the exact moment a yell was needed, how to spur on the Washington teams, and when yelling was out of place. In addition to his yell-leading activities, Horseley, who received his Bachelor of Arts degree in 1913, was the Managing Editor of the *Daily*. He was the president of the Senior Class and a member of the Oval Club, the senior-junior men's honor society.

1912 W 1913

Husky Moment

First Crew Race at Poughkeepsie

On June 21, 1913, Washington's varsity eight was the first crew west of the Rocky Mountains to race at the historic annual Intercollegiate Rowing Association (IRA) regatta on the Hudson River. The eight earned an invitation to row at Poughkeepsie by winning the Pacific Coast regatta on the Oakland Estuary on April 19. Washington beat Stanford by 12 boat lengths and Cal by 20 over a three-mile course. The crew raced in a new boat designed and built by George Pocock. The ASUW's Board of Control accepted the IRA bid and public-spirited citizens backed the drive for funds to make the trip. Regatta day dawned bright and hot as the seasoned crews of Columbia, Cornell, Pennsylvania, Syracuse, and Wisconsin lined up with Washington. Columbia jumped into an early lead with Cornell and Syracuse close behind. In last place was Washington—but not for long. Increasing the strokes per minute, the Westerners closed fast, soon challenging the leaders. Then came disaster. Elmer Leader, one of the Leader twins in the boat, snapped his foot strap. He had to row the last three miles of the four-mile race, pulling himself back and forth with the strength of his stomach muscles. Washington finished third, five seconds behind the winner, Syracuse, and two seconds behind Cornell. Coach Conibear was initially very disappointed but when he found out about Leader's broken foot strap, he was proud. When those at home learned about the unfortunate mishap, they welcomed the returning crew as conquering heroes.

Washington's first Intercollegiate Rowing Association regatta appearance.

1913-14 Tyee

Husky Spotlight

Max Walske was Washington's first oarsman to be selected as an All-American. He was the only sophomore on the 1913 crew - rowing in the number five position. The big (6′ 2½″, 190 pounds), bronze fellow from Auburn was the finest physical specimen Coach Conibear had ever seen. One day, Max refused to row with both arms moving inside his knees as the convention suggested. Max persisted on rowing with one arm outside his knee. It worked so well and proved so natural that the method became part of Conibear's comfortable rowing stroke.

1914 Tyee

Husky Highlight

Tom Wand, a reserve quarterback in 1911 and 1912, was the first athlete in Washington history to receive the Flaherty Award twice. The award was given annually, starting in 1908, to the football player voted "most inspirational" by his teammates. Wand was also a member of 1911-1913 basketball teams. Don McKeta is the only other football player to receive the Flaherty Award twice—in 1959 and 1960. McKeta is the only player in Husky history to captain two Rose Bowl teams (1960-61).

Husky Legend

George Pocock

Ready All!

George Pocock was the most famous boatbuilder of his day. Leading rowing programs boated their crews in the handiwork of the Seattle Master. In 1911, George and his older brother Dick, came to Vancouver, B.C. after completing an apprenticeship in their father's shop at Eton College in England. They started their shell building in "The Float" on Coal Harbor in Vancouver Bay in 1912. The Float was the original headquarters of the Vancouver Rowing Club, and it was there that the Pocock brothers lived and worked. Soon their reputation spread and they began to receive orders for shells. Hearing of their skills, Hiram Conibear, the Washington crew coach, rowed out to their shop in the bay. He discussed his ambitious plans for the Washington program and ordered 12 eight-oared shells for a starter and asked the Pococks to move to Seattle to set up shop on the campus. Although the order was reduced to one shell because Conibear could not raise sufficient funds for 12, orders from other programs increased and the Pococks moved to Seattle near the end of 1913. They continued their boat building until 1917 when they accepted Bill Boeing's offer to build wooden pontoons for float planes during World War I and stayed at Boeing until 1922. Dick Pocock accepted Ed Leader's invitation to be the shell builder at Yale when Leader left Washington to accept the coaching job at Yale. Rusty Callow, who had succeeded Leader as Washington's coach, persuaded George to come back to campus to renew his old love, boatbuilding. That love lasted for another 54 years, until his death in 1976. During that period, he became a revered international figure in the crew world not only because of his boatbuilding craft but because of his inspiration to so many rowers. In 1969, he was inducted into the Helms Rowing Hall of Fame. He was selected to the Husky Hall of Fame in 1989.

Husky Lists

The 1912 football season was another unbeaten one—the fourth consecutive perfect season. The top seasons (with a minimum of seven games) in Washington football history are:

Year	Record	Coach
1991	12-0-0	Don James
1909	7-0-0	Gil Dobie
1911	7-0-0	Gil Dobie
1913	7-0-0	Gil Dobie
1915	7-0-0	Gil Dobie
1984	11-1-0	Don James
2000	11-1-0	Rick Neuheisel
1959	10-1-0	Jim Owens
1960	10-1-0	Jim Owens
1923	10-1-1	Enoch Bagshaw
1925	10-1-1	Enoch Bagshaw

WASHINGTON'S fight song was written by Lester Wilson in 1913. Following are the lyrics:

Bow down to Washington, Bow down to Washington,
Mighty are the men who wear the Purple and the Gold,
Joyfully we welcome them within the victors fold.
We will carve their names in the Hall of Fame
To preserve the memory of our devotion.
Heaven help the foes of Washington;
They're trembling at the feet of mighty Washington,
The boys are there with bells, Their Fighting blood excels,
It's harder to push them over the line
Than pass the Dardenelles.
Victory the cry of Washington...
Leather lungs together with a Rah! Rah! Rah!
And o'er the land our loyal band
Will sing the Glory of Washington forever.

Fans first sang the song at the California football game on Nov. 6, 1915.

1913 W 1914

Husky Moment

Five Consecutive Perfect Seasons

The 1913 football season was the last of five consecutive perfect ones under Gil Dobie. The team shut out four of its seven opponents including lopsided wins over Whitworth (100-0) and Oregon Agricultural College (47-0). The closest game was on Nov. 15, against Oregon, in Portland. There were 8,000 spectators including 500 Washington rooters. Washington scored in the first quarter on a drive which featured two pass plays and a seven-yard line plunge by "Hap" Miller. Wayne Sutton kicked the point. In the second quarter, Oregon's fine running back, Parsons, scored on a 37-yard run. Fenton's conversion was good to tie the game, 7-7. In the fourth quarter, Washington's quarterback, Charlie Smith called a drop-kick from a running formation. He backed up from his backfield position and calmly booted the ball through the uprights to win the game, 10-7. Oregon threatened to tie the score. Oregon's Fenton tried a place kick but Walt Shiel blocked the kick and Shiel and Sutton recovered the ball. Washington closed out the season with a 20-0 win over Washington State.

The 1913 football team records Washington's fifth straight perfect season.

1913-14 Tyee

Husky Spotlight

Washington won another Northwest Conference basketball title in 1914. Led by Captain and player-coach Tony Savage, the team went 12-2. It played only three teams. Washington beat Oregon Agricultural College in five out of six games, Oregon in five of six, and Idaho twice. Savage and guard, Jack Fancher, made the all-Northwest team.

1914 Tyee

Jack Fancher

Husky Highlight

Tennis became a major sport in 1914 and claimed the Northwest Conference championship. At the conference tournament held in Eugene, Ore., Washington beat Washington State College and Oregon beat Oregon Agricultural College in the first rounds. In the finals, Oregon won two of the three singles matches with Washington. Washington won the first doubles match and then Oregon forfeited the other doubles match giving Washington the double's title and the conference championship. Given its victories in the singles matches, Oregon disputed the crowning of Washington as the conference championship.

1912-13 Tyee

Husky Legend

Ed and Elmer Leader

The Leader twins, Ed and Elmer, starred in three sports—baseball, crew, and football. As high school students, they had manned oars in heavy fishing boats on the Columbia River, earning sufficient resources to enter Washington in the fall of 1912. They were both members of the crew that first raced in the Intercollegiate Rowing Association (IRA) regatta in Poughkeepsie in 1913. Ed also rowed on the 1916 crew. Elmer was a hard-hitting catcher on the 1914, 1915, and 1916 baseball teams. Ed was a pitcher on the 1913, 1914, and 1915 teams. Ed played on Gil Dobie's 1912 and 1913 football teams and Elmer was the left tackle on the 1913, 1914, and 1915 teams. Ed loved rowing and provided valuable information to Coach Conibear on "body angle" and "stealing" the slide for the catch. After Washington's crew coach, Hiram Conibear died in 1917, and after the war-time cessation of rowing in 1918, Ed Leader became Washington's third rowing coach. George Pocock compared Ed with Gil Dobie. Leader was a perfectionist and insisted that the oarsmen execute his instructions exactly. He coached Washington to a second-place finish in the 1922 IRA regatta. In the three-mile race, Washington lost by less than a boat length to Navy in a record time of 13:33.6 seconds. After the 1922 season, Ed went to Yale University where his crews were among the best in the nation. His 1924 crew won the Olympics in Paris. He became one of the most respected and beloved crew coaches in Yale history.

HUSKY LIST

Washington has achieved notable success in the Pacific Coast Conference and its successor conferences. Washington has won 166 team championships in 18 sports (through March 2001). USC with 190, Stanford with 181, and UCLA with 172 lead the Huskies. (Note: Championships include ties. They also include titles won where sports are split into Northern and Southern divisions.)

Sport	Number of Conference Championships Men	Women
Baseball	12	
Basketball	9	3
Cross Country	1	1
Football	15	
Golf	3	
Gymnastics	3	
Rowing	26	10
Soccer	1	1
Softball		2
Swimming	20	
Tennis	38	9
Track and Field	9	
Wrestling	3	
TOTAL	140	26

GEORGE POCOCK'S legacy was not only his craftsmanship as a shell builder but his rowing creed.

It's a great art, is rowing.
It's the finest art there is.
It's a symphony of motion.
And when you're rowing well
Why it's nearing perfection ——
And when you reach perfection
You're touching the Divine.
It touches the you of you's
Which is your soul.

1914 W 1915

Husky Moment

39-Game Winning Streak Ends

The 1914 season brought an end to the 39-game winning streak starting with the Nov. 14, 1908, win over Oregon and ending with a victory over Whitman, on Oct. 24, 1914. The next week, the streak ended when Washington journeyed to Albany, Ore., to play Oregon Agricultural College on a muddy, sloppy field. The game ended in a scoreless tie. OAC had a weight advantage and tore into the fray with a ferocity that seriously threatened Washington's unbeaten streak. Washington had several bad breaks. First, referee George Varnell, also a Seattle newspaper sports columnist, ruled Mike Hunt, Washington's left end, out of the game for running into the punter. The punter was not knocked off his feet. Washington's left halfback, "Hap" Miller, was knocked cold twice and saw limited action. Five men who had never won their "W" were put into battle. In the first quarter, Washington missed scoring by six inches when the two chalk marks on the goal line confused Miller. He did not know he had to get beyond the second line and fell short of the end zone. Washington closed the season with shutout wins over Oregon (10-0) and Washington State (45-0).

Oregon Agricultural College ends Washington's winning streak.

1914-15 Tyee

Husky Spotlight

Washington again won the Northwest Conference basketball title with a 11-1 conference record (17-2 overall), losing only to Washington State (29-28) in Pullman. Tony Savage, in his fourth year on the team, outplayed every center in the conference. He led the team in scoring while developing the team as a coach. It was his second year as player-coach. In both years, his teams won Northwest championships. Savage also played end on the 1914 football team and lettered as a first baseman on the 1914 team. He was elected to Phi Beta Kappa and was vice-president of the student body. He was Washington's football coach in 1918.

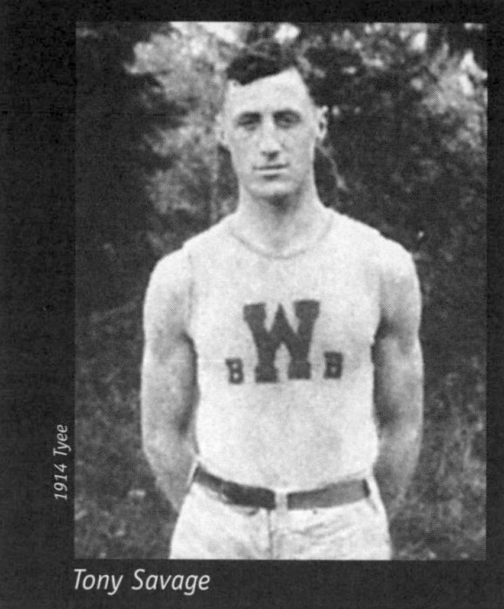

1914 Tyee

Tony Savage

Husky Highlight

Rupert Edmonds broke the American collegiate record for the discus throw on May 24, 1915, in a dual meet on Denny Field with Washington State. His mark of 140-11 was three inches better than a record throw by Marks of Wisconsin a week earlier. Edmonds finished second in the Northwest conference meet held at Corvallis. The events were conducted indoors because of wet conditions.

UW Media Relations

Husky Legend

Russell "Rusty" Callow

Called Rusty because of his flaming red hair, Callow entered Washington in the fall of 1911 having graduated as valedictorian of the 1909 class of Olympia High School. He taught in a one room schoolhouse for two years before coming to Washington. He played freshmen football in 1911 and competed in crew in the spring of 1912. He was a member of the first Washington crew team to go to the Intercollegiate Rowing Association (IRA) regatta in Poughkeepsie in 1913, rowing in a four-oared shell as an alternate on the varsity eight. He rowed in the number seven position on the 1914 and 1915 teams and was the crew captain in 1915. He also earned a varsity letter in track and served as president of the ASUW in the academic year, 1914-15. In the fall of 1922, he replaced Ed Leader as the crew coach. He coached the varsity eight to its first IRA championship in 1923 and two more championships in 1924 and 1926. His 1925 crew finished second to Navy and the 1927 team came in second to Columbia. The junior varsity teams won three consecutive IRA titles starting in 1925. After the 1927 season, he left Washington to coach at Pennsylvania. His salary was the highest in rowing history to that point—$15,000—considerably more than the $6,600 he was getting at Washington. After 27 years at Penn, he became the head coach at Navy. His 1952 varsity eight won the 1952 Olympics in Helsinki, Finland.

Husky List

Washington has had many football players who were selected to the first team All-Conference and/or Pacific Coast teams for more than one year:

George Wilson, 1923-25, HB
Chuck Carroll, 1927-28, HB
Paul Schwegler, 1930-31, T
Max Starcevich, 1935-36, G
Vic Markov, 1936-37, T
Ray Frankowski, 1940-41, G
Hugh McElhenney, 1950-51, FB
Don Heinrich, 1950, 1952, QB
Chuck Allen,1959-60, G
Don McKeta, 1959-60, HB
Charlie Mitchell, 1961-62, HB
Rick Redman, 1962-64, G, LB
Junior Coffey,1962-63, LB
Steve Thompson, 1966-67, DT
Calvin Jones, 1970-72, DB
Gordy Guinn, 1971-72, DL
Skip Boyd, 1973-74, P
Michael Jackson, 1977-78, LB
Nesby Glasgow, 1977-78, CB
Jeff Toews, 1977-78, OT
Doug Martin, 1978-79, DT
Chuck Nelson, 1980-82, PK
Ron Holmes, 1983-84, DT
Reggie Rogers, 1985-86, DT
Mike Zandofsky, 1986-87, OG
Steve Emtman, 1990-91, DT
Donald Jones, 1990-91, LB
Dave Hoffman, 1991-92, LB
Napoleon Kaufman, 1992-94, TB
Mark Bruener, 1993-94, TE
Lawyer Milloy, 1994-95, FS
Olin Kreutz, 1996-97, C
Benji Olson, 1996-97, OG
Jason Chorak, 1996-97, DT

Husky Lore

GEORGE ZELL McCLELLAND, an outstanding two-miler on the track team, won every interclass cross country race during his four college years, 1911-1914. Washington did not have an intercollegiate cross country team then. His winning times in the four-mile cross country events were:

1911	22:41.6
1912	22:12.2
1913	21:31
1914	21:18.4

1915 Tyee

1915 W 1916

Husky Moment

Ninth Unbeaten Season

The 1915 Washington football team completed Washington's ninth unbeaten season (1895, 1908-1915) outscoring its opponents 274-14 and finishing with seven wins and no losses. Former Washington quarterback Wee Coyle coached Gonzaga in a game against Washington in Spokane on Oct. 23. Washington won 21-7. Gonzaga's only score was a forward pass to Captain Tom Berry, the first time a Washington team had given up a passing touchdown. On Nov. 6, Washington crushed California in Berkeley 72-0. It was the first time the two football teams had met since 1904. Washington scored 11 touchdowns with Cy Noble and Allan Young each scoring three touchdowns. A week later on Denny Field, the two teams met again with a much closer contest. California's defense was so strong that Washington gained yardage only eight times during the entire game. Washington scored with eight minutes to go to break a scoreless tie. The scoring drive featured a long pass from Hap Miller to George Smith and several good line smashes. Walt Shiel scored on a short off-tackle dive and Miller kicked the extra point. California tied the game moments later on a 55-yard touchdown pass, Sharpe to Gianelli, and a successful conversion. In the last minute of play, Miller raced 30 yards to California's five-yard line. On the next play, Noble plunged over for the touchdown and a Washington victory, 13-7. Washington rooters carried California's Roy Sharpe off the field on their shoulders for his brilliant running, passing, and leadership. Washington closed the season with a shutout win over Colorado, 46-0, in the first game ever played against the Boulder school.

Washington beats Cal and records its ninth unbeaten season.

1916 Tyee

Husky Spotlight

The Washington crew won another Pacific Coast championship. On April 7, 1916, they beat Stanford, a boat with almost the same oarsmen who had finished second the year before at the Intercollegiate Rowing Association race at Poughkeepsie. Washington took a boat length lead at the mile mark and kept steadily increasing the lead to seven boat lengths at the finish. On May 27, California came to Seattle. Bucking heavy winds, Washington finished in 17:41 thrashing Cal by 16 lengths.

The Washington wrestling team won the Northwest Conference championship by defeating the Oregon Agricultural College team, 19-12, on March 4 and Washington State College, 12-8, a week later in Pullman. The WSC match featured Captain Van de Bogart winning two consecutive matches—the 175 pound and the heavyweight events.

Husky Highlight

After the 1915 football season ended, the Pacific Coast Conference (PCC) was formed. The conference was founded at a meeting on Dec. 15, 1915, at the Oregon Hotel in Portland. The initial members were California, Oregon, Oregon Agricultural College, and Washington. Conference play began in 1916. One year later, Washington State College was admitted; Stanford joined in 1918. In 1922, the PCC expanded to eight teams with the admission of the University of Southern California and Idaho. Montana joined in 1924, and UCLA in 1928. In 1950, Montana resigned from the conference and in 1959, the PCC was dissolved and the Athletic Association of Western Universities was formed with five members—California, Stanford, Southern California, UCLA, and Washington. Washington State joined in 1962, and Oregon and Oregon State joined in 1964. In 1968, the name, Pacific-8 Conference, was adopted. Ten years later, the conference became the Pacific-10 with the admission of Arizona and Arizona State.

1916 Tyee

Husky Legend

Ray Hunt

Ray "Mike" Hunt starred on four Gil Dobie teams (1912-1915). He was a great defensive end and pass receiver and was captain in 1915. In the 10-0 win over Oregon in 1914, Hunt battled on sheer nerve in a very rugged game. After the game, Gil Dobie, in rare praise of an individual player, told Hunt: "Mike, I wouldn't take you out if both your legs were broken. I've got that much confidence in you." Hunt made the All-Northwest football teams in 1914 and 1915 and was selected to the all-time Washington team up to 1930.

HUSKY LIST

Washington's 72-0 win over California, in 1915, was one of the most lopsided wins in Washington history. The top 10 all-time scoring victories are:

Opponent	Score	Year
Whitman	120-0	1919
Willamette	108-0	1925
Whitworth	100-0	1913
College of Puget Sound	96-0	1924
Fort Worden	90-0	1911
Whitman	77-0	1931
College of Puget Sound	80-7	1925
College of Puget Sound	73-0	1929
California	72-0	1915
West Seattle Athletic Club	66-0	1932
Oregon	66-0	1974

HUSKY LORE

ON March 17, 1915, the Board of Regents elected Dr. Henry Suzzallo as president of the University of Washington. Raised in California, he received his B.A. from Stanford and his Ph.D. from Columbia. He had a brief tenure as an assistant professor of education at Stanford. From 1909 to 1915, he was a professor of the philosophy of education at the Teachers' College of Columbia University. He served as Washington's president from 1915 to 1926. Suzzallo had a vision of a "university of a thousand years" and one of his dreams was to have a splendidly equipped library as the campus centerpiece. On the completion of the library's first phase in 1926, its collegiate-Gothic presence surely met Suzzallo's ambitions. Originally named the University of Washington library, it was renamed the Suzzallo Library in 1933.

The First Century at Washington

Suzzallo Library

1916 W 1917

Husky Moment

First Ever Pacific Coast Conference Football Championship

On Nov. 30, Washington beat California, 14-7, before 9,000 fans, the largest crowd up to that point to attend a Washington game. Fighting through four periods of heartbreaking football, Washington completed its ninth successive unbeaten season and won the first ever Pacific Coast Conference championship. Captain Louis Seagrave expressed the essence of the game after entering the Cal dressing room. He gripped the hand of Cal Captain "Bud" Montgomery and said: "Bud, you've got a hard, clean, fighting football team and we feel we have been honored in meeting you." The game was Gil Dobie's last as the Washington coach. It was the end of his hardest season. Seven key starters, on the 1915 team, had graduated and three others were National Guardsmen stationed at American Lake near Tacoma. They could only attend workouts on an irregular basis. An early season win (37-6) over Whitman resulted in the loss of two of Washington's most dependable running backs. The climax came when Bill Grimm, the star left tackle and the youngest of the heralded Grimm brothers, was barred from the Cal game because of examination irregularities. This action provoked a two-day player's strike and eventually led to President Suzzallo's dismissal of Coach Dobie. His era had ended. Dobie's 58-0-3 record had brought national prominence to the Washington football program. The record of 63 games without a defeat (one win prior to and one win after Dobie's Washington career) is still the NCAA all-time unbeaten streak.

1917 Tyee

President Suzzallo at football game in 1916.

Husky Spotlight

Gil Dobie had worked under a yearly contract, presumably because he wanted to keep his options open. In 1915, he officially tendered his resignation and the Board of Regents accepted it. President Suzzallo and other key faculty leaders persuaded Dobie to stay. In 1916, the situation was much different. When Bill Grimm, the star tackle was suspended for examination irregularities, the student committee on discipline recommended that Grimm's suspension begin on Dec. 1, after the Cal game on Thanksgiving. The faculty set the date at Nov. 20, thus keeping Grimm out of the game. Grimm's teammates hotly resented the faculty decision. For two days, the players went on strike, refusing to practice and threatening to end the season. Suzzallo stood firmly behind the faculty; Dobie backed the players. The strike ended after prominent alumni met with the players urging them to abandon their protest. The Cal game was played without Grimm and Washington won 14-7. In early December, four of the five members of the Washington faculty athletic committee opposed the renewal of Dobie's contract. On Dec. 8, Suzzallo issued this statement: "Mr. Dobie will not be with us next year. That is now final. The chief function of the University is to train character. Mr. Dobie failed to perform his full share of this service on the football field. Therefore, we do not wish him to return next year." So Gil Dobie left.

Husky Highlight

Gil Dobie's teams never were invited to a postseason bowl game—partly because there were not many bowls in those days and partly for other reasons. In 1915, the Tournament of Roses' officials reinstituted football as the major sporting event to defray the expenses of the annual New Year's floral festival. The first Rose Bowl game was in 1902 when Michigan thrashed Stanford 49-0. The next year, no West Coast team wanted to take on powerful Michigan, and so the festival reverted to holding other sporting events. Between 1903 and 1915, football was replaced by contests such as polo, chariot racing, tent pegging, and even a race between an elephant and a camel. In 1916, Washington State restored the honor of the West by defeating Brown, 14-0. Both Washington State and Washington were unbeaten but Washington State was chosen because it had beaten Oregon Agricultural College 29-0. OAC had defeated Michigan State 20-0, who in turn had defeated Michigan 24-0. Comparative scores meant something in those days. In 1916, Dobie's last season, Oregon got the Rose Bowl bid. Again both Oregon and Washington were unbeaten. They played in a scoreless tie game during the season. Oregon was chosen because the railroad fare from Eugene to Pasadena, for the entire team, was $250 cheaper than from Seattle. Oregon beat Pennsylvania in the 1917 Rose Bowl, 14-0.

1916 tyee

Husky Legend

Louis Seagrave

Louis Seagrave was Washington's first All-America first-team selection. He was selected as a guard on Walter Camp's Football Foundation team in 1916. He played on four unbeaten teams (1913-1916) and was the captain of Gil Dobie's last Washington team in 1916. The four teams recorded 26 wins, no losses, and two ties and outscored their opponents 971-63. He was selected to the Northwest Conference teams in 1915 and 1916. He led the 1916 players in a two-day strike after Bill Grimm, the star left tackle, was barred from further season play after examination irregularities. Seagraves was selected to the all-time Washington team covering the years 1892-1930.

Husky History

Many Washington football players have been named first-team All-Americans. Only 18 have been consensus All-Americans—players receiving a majority of votes at their respective positions. Currently, a player must be a first-team selection by the following selectors—*Associated Press,* Football Coaches, Football Writers, *Football News, Sporting News,* and the Walter Camp Football Foundation.

Year	Player	Position
1925	George Wilson	Running Back
1928	Chuck Carroll	Running Back
1936	Max Starcevich	Guard
1940	Rudy Mucha	Center
1940	Ray Frankowski	Guard
1941	Ray Frankowski	Guard
1963	Rick Redman	Guard
1964	Rick Redman	Guard
1966	Tom Greenlee	Defensive Tackle
1968	Al Worley	Defensive Back
1982	Chuck Nelson	Place Kicker
1984	Ron Holmes	Defensive Lineman
1986	Jeff Jaeger	Place Kicker
1986	Reggie Rogers	Defensive Lineman
1991	Steve Emtman	Defensive Lineman
1991	Mario Bailey	Wide Receiver
1991	Lincoln Kennedy	Offensive Lineman
1995	Lawyer Milloy	Defensive Back
1996	Benji Olson	Offensive Lineman
1997	Olin Kreutz	Offensive Lineman

Husky Lore

CLARA KNAUSENBERGER was the 1916-1917 president of the Women's Athletic Association, captain of the 1917 basketball team, and active in many women's athletic activities. In the spring of 1916, she established two world records in track and field—4-10 in the high jump and 11.1 seconds in the 100-yard dash.

1917 Tyee

Husky Moment

Hiram Conibear Leaves A Rowing Legacy

On the morning of Sept. 10, 1917, at the age of 46, Hiram Conibear was picking plums from a tree in his yard. He slipped and fell head first to the ground. He broke his neck in the fall and was killed instantly. In his 10 years as Washington's crew coach, he implemented a rowing stroke that lifted Washington into the national limelight. His innovations would eventually spread internationally as former Washington rowers coached by Conibear became coaches at other leading institutions. Ed Leader, who rowed under Conibear in 1913 and 1916, replaced Conibear as the head crew coach. Because of the United States' entry in World War I, intercollegiate rowing was suspended. In the spring of 1918, the Washington program consisted of interclass and interclub races.

1918 Tyee

Husky Spotlight

The impact of World War I was significant on intercollegiate athletics. Many student-athletes enlisted in the armed services. There was no Pacific Coast Conference competition. The football and basketball teams played limited schedules. Baseball was discontinued. Tennis and wrestling squads competed on a limited basis. Track and field held interclass competition. Not a single sport had more than one letter winner from the previous season competing. President Suzzallo refused to abandon intercollegiate athletics and directed that the intramural sports program be expanded to ensure every male student be engaged in some athletic activity. Claude Hunt was hired as Gil Dobie's replacement for the 1917 football season. He graduated from DePauw University in 1911 and had three unbeaten seasons at Carleton College in Minnesota before coming to Washington. He was responsible for supervising all Washington sports, except crew, and coached the 1918 basketball team.

Husky Highlight

Washington's unbeaten streak of 63 football games—the longest ever in NCAA history—came to an end on Nov. 3, 1917, when the team lost to California in Berkeley, 27-0. The streak started with a scoreless tie with Idaho on Nov. 28, 1907, and ended with a 14-6 victory over Whitman on Oct. 20, 1917. Gil Dobie coached the teams in 61 of those games. They compiled a record of 58 wins, no losses and three ties. During that period, Washington had a 39-game winning streak, the third longest in NCAA history.

1918 Tyee

Husky Legend

Mayme McDonald

Mayme McDonald was probably the best all-around woman athlete in the Northwest. She was president of the Women's Athletic Association in 1917-1918. She participated in baseball, basketball, field hockey, tennis, and track and field. Here is a list of some of her accomplishments as reported in a *Seattle Star* newspaper article:

- Baseball - Throws ball 190 feet. Expert pitcher and plays skillfully in any department of the game.
- Basketball - Star forward on All-Star Varsity Honor team at University of Washington for three years.
- Hockey - Member of University of Washington championship women's team for three years.
- Tennis - Northwest women's champion in doubles; Inland Empire champion in singles and doubles.
- Track and Field - runs 100-yard dash in 12 seconds; 50-yard hurdles in 8.5 seconds; throws eight-pound shot 31 feet; hurls javelin 87 feet; high jumps 4 feet 6 inches.

Husky List

One of the ways by which Hiram Conibear's rowing influence continued was through the many Washington crew alumni who became rowing coaches at universities across the United States. Following is believed to be a complete list (in the order of the years at Washington).

Ed Leader - Washington and Yale
Rusty Callow - Washington, Pennsylvania, Navy
Ky Ebright - California
Russ Nagler - California
Chuck Logg - Rutgers
Don Grant - Yale
Fred Spuhn - Princeton
Jim Matthews - Pennsylvania
Al Ulbrickson - Washington
Stork Stanford - Cornell
Norm Sonju - Cornell, Wisconsin
Tom Bolles - Washington, Harvard
Ellis MacDonald - Marietta
Loren Schoel - Syracuse, Cornell, Marietta
Harvey Love - Harvard
Walt Raney - Washington, Columbia
Bob Moch - Washington, MIT
Jim McMillin - MIT
Delos Schoch - Princeton
Gene Melder - Clark
Mike Murphy - Wisconsin
Gosta Ericksen - Washington, Syracuse
Charles Jackson - Washington, MIT
Stan Pocock - Washington
Fil Leanderson - Washington, MIT
Al Stocker - Western Washington
Ron Wailes - Yale
Lou Gellerman - Washington, Navy
John Bisset - Washington, UCLA
Dick Erickson - MIT, Washington
John Lind - Washington, Loyola
Jerry Johnson - UCLA
Rick Clothier - Washington, Navy
Doug Neil - Cornell, Wisconsin
Bob Diehl - Western Washington
Bruce Beall - Harvard, MIT
Fred Schoch - Harvard, Navy
Chris Allsopp - New Hampshire
Gil Gamble - Washington

Husky Lore

TWO important professional schools were established at Washington in 1917. Librarianship, which had its beginnings in courses offered in 1911 to meet the needs for professionals in public and institutional libraries, became a separate graduate school program in 1917. In that same year, the program in commerce, which had been separated from the Department of Political and Social Sciences, was established as the College of Business Administration. The college's head, Professor Carleton Parker, formerly of the University of California, built his staff by recruiting faculty from Harvard, Stanford, and Wisconsin. The college developed a close liaison with the business community. It also formulated its own entrance requirements to encourage students in high school commercial programs to seek admission. These students were not previously eligible to enter the College of Arts and Sciences.

1918 W 1919

Husky Moment

Pacific Coast Championship in Baseball

The Washington baseball squad completed its second consecutive undefeated season after World War I curtailed the sport in 1917. The 1918 team won six games. The 1919 team won 10 games and won Washington's first Pacific Coast Conference baseball championship. It was the first team to win the conference championship with an undefeated season. The toughest game was a home contest, on May 15, with Oregon. The Ducks went up, 3-1, after the first inning and 4-1 after three innings. Washington tied the score, 6-6, in the bottom of the sixth. The score remained the same until Oregon went ahead in the top of the 10th, 7-6. Washington knotted the score in the bottom of the 10th. Oregon took the lead for the third time in the top of the 13th inning—9-7.Washington came right back and tied the game in the bottom of the 13th. In the bottom of the 15th inning, Washington's Percy Chamberlain, a star pitcher, blasted a curve ball for a home run and a 10-9 victory. It was the second longest game played on University Field. It was Coach Dode Brinker's last season as a coach, compiling a 55-23 career record (a .705 winning perecentage) over six seasons.

1917 Tyee

Dode Brinker, coach of Washington's first Pacific Coast Conference baseball championship.

Husky Spotlight

Washington won the Pacific Coast championship in crew by beating California and Stanford on May 3, 1918, on the Oakland Estuary. California got off to a very good start, leading their rivals by half a boat length. After the first minute, the lead increased to one boat length over Washington; Stanford began to drop back. It was a two-team race with Cal up by a boat length with 300 yards to go. Washington upped the stroke to 34 to close Cal's lead. Now, it was bow-to-bow with the Bear boat. Washington edged ahead to win by four feet, the closest race ever staged on the Pacific Coast. The winning time was 16:44, a second faster than Cal. Stanford finished a distant third in 17:32. The time was remarkable considering the tide and a headwind all the way down the three-mile course.

Husky Highlight

Until Armistice was signed on Nov. 11, 1918, the fall quarter opened with the campus still studded with military barracks and many Washington student-athletes in service. A Student Army Training Corps football team was formed and coached by Tony Savage, a former Washington star athlete and a Lincoln High School coach. He took over for Coach Claude Hunt who was in the service. Only two games were played—one at home against Oregon Agricultural College (a 6-0 victory) and the other away at Oregon (a 7-0 loss).

Husky Legend

James Arbuthnot

1922 Tyee

Coach James Arbuthnot became Washington's wrestling coach in 1918. He graduated from Kansas State University in 1912 and then was an Instructor of Physical Education at Oregon Agricultural College. He joined Washington as an Assistant Professor of Physical Education in 1918. He was the acting chairman of the department for one year when Chairman David Hall went into military service. He became department chair again in 1923, when Hall became the University's Health Officer. Arbuthnot was regarded as Washington's most versatile coach. He was the only individual in Washington history to coach four different sports. He guided the wrestling team for eight seasons (1918, 1919, 1921-1926) compiling an 18-11 record. He was named head tennis coach in 1919 and, during his 10-season tenure, he compiled an outstanding match record of 24 wins, six losses, and three ties. His players won three individual Pacific Coast Conference championships. He coached Wallace Scott who captured the 1924 National Collegiate singles title. He was the head hockey coach in 1923. When Washington dropped wrestling in 1926, Arbuthnot was selected as the head boxing coach.

Husky List

Top Winning Percentages of Washington Baseball Coaches (Minimum Three Seasons)

Coach	Overall Record	Pct.	Conference Record	Pct.
Dode Brinker (1906, 1909, 1910, 1916, 1918,1919)	55-23	.705	19-5	.792
Ken Knutson (1993-2000)	285-185	.606	130-77	.628
Dorsett (Tubby) Graves (1923-1946)	209-182-2	.602	168-122-1	.579
Dale Parker (1957-1960)	68-48	.590	27-29	.482
Bob McDonald (1977-1992)	422-322-7	.566	162-183-1	.470

DURING World War I, the University continued to maintain most of its programs despite a 30 percent drop in enrollment—only 207 civilian men were enrolled in autumn quarter. President Suzzallo was appointed chairman of the State Defense Council which supervised war loans and bond sales, food conservation, dissemination of war propaganda, and settled labor disputes. More than 1,500 students and faculty served in the military. The University provided accommodations for 2,000 men registered in the Student Army Training Corps, a naval training unit, and a Marine Corps unit. Barracks were erected on campus and the men were fed in the Commons dining room in the Home Economics building. Washington was the only institution on the West Coast conducting instruction in three branches of the armed services.

1919 W 1920

Husky Moment

The Rout

Enjoying a 30-pound advantage per man, Washington recorded its biggest football win in school history, on Oct. 25, 1919, with a 120-0 drubbing of Whitman at Denny Field. Washington sprinted to a school-record 19 touchdowns, seven of which were scored by halfback Ervin Dailey. On his TDs alone, Dailey amassed 350 yards rushing, which would have been a school record if official statistics had been kept. Two of Dailey's scores were long-distance runs of 85 and 70 yards. He also had a non-scoring run of 80 yards. Washington had four other scoring runs of 60, 40, 25 and 20 yards. The game featured one notable amusement—in the second half, Gus Pope, Washington's big guard, tore a big hole in his pants. The game was halted, and first-year trainer, Clarence (Hec) Edmundson, hurried on the field to stitch the pants back together. Washington finished the season with five wins and one loss—to Oregon, 24-13. The team tied for first in the Pacific Coast Conference. The final game, a 7-0 win over Cal, was the last Thanksgiving Day game played on Denny Field. A crowd of 19,000 attended the game, the largest total to that time. Despite the successful season, Coach Claude Hunt resigned on Jan. 20, 1920. Ray Eckman, a halfback on the team, recalled that the football situation was practically impossible for a coach. "The reason was because Washington alumni and citizens here were used to Washington winning nine years in a row. If a ball game was lost, it was 'well, what's wrong?'"

1920 Tyee

Ervin Dailey scored seven touchdowns in a single game.

Husky Spotlight

Irving Cook was Washington's first two-time All-Pacific Coast Conference selection—in 1919 and 1920. As a guard, he played three varsity seasons—1918-1920—and was captain in 1919 and 1920. He was a great defensive player and provided outstanding overall leadership. In 1920, he became Washington's first All-America basketball selection.

1918 Tyee

Irving Cook

Husky Highlight

The Pacific Coast Relays meet was one of the innovations introduced by the new track and field coach, Hec Edmundson. The event was the first relays meet on the West Coast. On April 24, 1920, seven colleges from the four Northwest states entered the meet. Oregon State won with 20 points, followed by Washington with 14. Other schools participating were Idaho, Montana, Montana Wesleyan, Oregon, and Whitman. The event was held each year until 1928 when it was discontinued because visiting teams requested that all expenses be guaranteed.

Husky Legend

Clarence S. "Hec" Edmundson

In 1919, Hec Edmundson became the head track and field coach and trainer at Washington. A native of Moscow, Idaho, he graduated from high school in 1908 and entered the University of Idaho. He was an outstanding runner for Idaho and participated on the U.S. Olympic team in the 1912 Stockholm Olympic Games. He placed sixth in the 800 meters. He also competed in the 400 meters. After graduating from Idaho, Edmundson immediately entered the coaching profession. He became the head basketball and track and field coach at Idaho in 1914. Five years later, he came to Washington to start an outstanding career that ended in 1954. His track and field teams won three Pacific Coast Conference championships and seven Northern Division titles. His teams finished second in the NCAA in 1929 and 1930; third in 1927; fourth in 1928, and fifth in 1921. Edmundson became Washington's head basketball coach in 1921, a position he held until 1947. In his 27 seasons, his teams won three Pacific Coast Conference titles and 10 Northern Division championships. He directed Washington to third place in the 1936 U.S. Olympic Trials tournament and the school's first NCAA tournament appearance in 1943. Edmundson's overall winning percentage in basketball was 71.5 percent, 488 wins and 195 losses. His number of wins and winning percentage are the best in Washington basketball history. He was selected to the Helms Foundation Hall of Fame in both basketball and track and field. His team helped dedicate the Washington Pavilion on Dec. 27. 1927, when Washington defeated Illinois, 34-23. On Jan. 16, 1948, the building was renamed the Clarence S. "Hec" Edmundson Pavilion. He is remembered by his athletes and associates as a great coach and person. He was elected as a charter member of the Husky Hall of Fame in 1979.

HUSKY LIST

In 1919, Washington's lopsided win over Whitman set a record for most points, most rushing touchdowns, and most touchdowns in a single game. Other offensive team records in a single game include:

Rushing yards—559 vs. San Jose State, 1996
Rushing attempts—80 at Washington State, 1956
Rushing yards per attempt—9.0 vs. San Jose State, 1996
Passing yards—428 vs. Arizona State, 1989
Passing attempts—68 at UCLA, 1998
Pass completions—35 at USC, 1998; 35 at Maryland (Aloha Bowl), 1982
Touchdown passes—6 vs. UCLA, 1970
Field goals—5 vs. Houston, 1985
First downs—33 vs. Idaho, 1956
Rushing first downs—27 vs. Idaho, 1956
Passing first downs—20 at USC, 1970
Interceptions made—9 vs. Oregon, 1952
Total offensive yards—734 vs. San Jose State, 1996
Total offensive attempts—98 at USC, 1998
Total offensive average per attempt—11.1 at Washington State, 1950 (Spokane)
Punt returns—9 vs. Montana, 1951
Punt return yards—166 vs. California, 1998
Punt returns for touchdowns—2 vs. Oregon, 1984
Kickoff returns—10 at UCLA, 1973
Kickoff return yards—258 vs. UCLA, 1998
Kickoff returns for touchdowns—1 on 20 occasions; the last by Paul Arnold against Air Force in 1999.

HUSKY LORE

WASHINGTON'S teams were nicknamed the "Sun Dodgers" starting in November 1919. For a short period in 1921, Washington's teams were nicknamed the Vikings. The name came about when an alumni committee, analyzing complaints of the "Sun Dodgers" label, suggested the name "Vikings" be used. Newspapers started to use it despite campus communications that the name was unofficial. In January 1922, a joint committee of students, coaches, faculty, alumni, and business leaders was appointed to come up with a new name. By February 1922, the name, "Huskies," was adopted.

1920-29

1920 W 1921

Husky Moment

Husky Stadium

During the 1919 football season, Denny Field was deemed inadequate for fans attending a Washington football game. Thousands were turned away for the 1919 Thanksgiving game with California—a 7-0 victory. Graduate ASUW Manager, Darwin Meisnest, suggested a new stadium at a student assembly on Nov. 10, 1919. Thus was born an idea resulting in unequaled cooperation between University officials, students, and Seattle citizens. After University president Dr. Suzzallo endorsed Meisnest's plan, a committee was formed, contracts were let and, on April 19, 1920, a state-wide campaign to raise funds began. About 500 student salespersons sold small bronze plaques to those supporters who bought season tickets. The price was $50 for two years and $100 for five years. Most of the $250,000 raised prior to the 1920 season resulted from sales to about 3,500 plaque holders. They received favorable seating in the new stadium. On May 17, 1920, ground was broken for the 30,000-seat stadium. Six months later, the stadium was completed at a cost of $577,000. The stadium area, near Lake Washington, was displaced by high pressure water using a unique method called sluicing. Puget Sound Bridge and Dredging Company cleared about 230,000 cubic yards of earth using 687,000 gallons of water. Student fees, ticket sales, and the sale of bonds financed the first sizable stadium on the West Coast. The first game in the new stadium was played on Nov. 27, 1920, against Dartmouth. 24,500 spectators watched the Big Green roll for four touchdowns and beat Washington 28-7. The stadium became the venue for many University and community events. In several stages, the stadium became larger and now seats 72,500.

The first game was played at Husky Stadium on Nov. 7, 1920.

UWMsSCUA

Husky Spotlight

Hec Edmundson's athletes took fourth in the first NCAA track and field championship meet held on June 17 and 18, 1921, in Chicago. Washington's Gus Pope won the shot and discus events. Vic Hurley took fifth in the 100-yard dash. Reg Pratt was fourth in the 440, and Chuck Frankland tied for fourth in the high jump. Washington won the Pacific Coast Conference title beating Oregon Agricultural College 60-48. Hurley won three events—the 100, 220, and 120 yards low hurdles—and Pope won the shot put and discus throw.

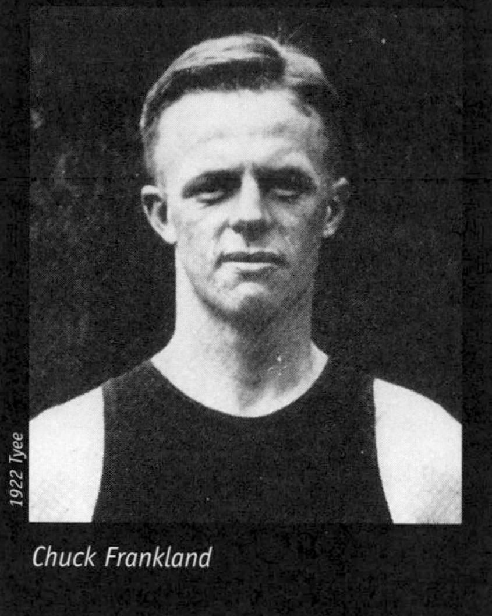

1922 Tyee

Chuck Frankland

Husky Highlight

Bob Abel, Washington quarterback and ASUW president, scored the first touchdown in the new stadium. After receiving the opening kickoff, Dartmouth began a drive that stalled at the Washington 15-yard line. After six minutes of play, Dartmouth attempted a field goal. Abel tore through the line and blocked the kick. The ball bounced into Abel's hands and he rambled 63 yards for the historic touchdown. Washington's coach was Leonard "Stub" Allison. He was the only head coach in Washington history to guide three sports in a single calendar year. In 1920 he coached the basketball, baseball, and football teams. He left to coach the California football team in 1921. After his career at Cal ended in 1944, the "Most Inspirational Player Award" was created and named the Stub Allison Award.

1923 Tyee

Husky Legend

Gus Pope

August "Gus" Pope was Washington's first track and field athlete to win an Olympic medal. Gus was Washington's only entrant in the 1920 Antwerp Olympics. Pope received the bronze medal in the discus with a throw of 138′ 2½″. He took fourth in the discus throw in the 1924 Paris Olympics. He earned three letters at Washington in track and field (1919-1921). He was team captain in 1921. As a senior, Pope won the discus throw and shot put titles at both the Pacific Coast Conference and NCAA championships. He established school records in the shot put and discus throw and an American record in the discus in 1920—146′ 3″. He won the American Amateur Union (AAU) discus throw titles in 1920 and 1921. He achieved a personal best in the discus throw of 152′ 7″. Pope was elected to the Husky Hall of Fame in 1983.

HUSKY LIST

Starting with Gus Pope, 18 Washington track and field athletes have won events in National Collegiate Athletic Association (NCAA) championship meets.

Year	Athlete	Event and Mark
1921	Gus Pope	Shot put - 45′ 4½″
		Discus throw - 142′ 2¼″
1925	Jim Charteris	880 run - 1:55.4
1927	Herman Brix	Shot Put - 46′7⅜″
1928	Rudy Kiser	Mile run - 4:17.6
1929	Steve Anderson	220 low hurdles - 23.5
	Ed Genung	880 run - 1:55.0
1930	Steve Anderson (tied world record)	120 high hurdles - 14.4
	Paul Jessup	Discus throw - 160′ 9⅜″
1963	Brian Sternberg	Pole vault - 16′ 4¾″
1971	Cary Feldman	Javelin throw - 259′ 0″
1975	Keith Tinner, Jerry Belur, Pablo Franco, Billy Hicks	Mile relay - 3:05
1976	Scott Neilson	Hammer throw - 216′ 8″
	Borys Chambul	Discus throw - 202′ 3″
1977	Scott Neilson	35 lb. weight throw - 68′ 10¼″*
		Hammer throw - 228′ 4″
1978	Scott Neilson	35 lb. weight throw - 68′ 7¾″*
		Hammer throw - 237′ 5″
1979	Scott Neilson	35 lb. weight throw - 71′ 5½″*
	Scott Neilson	Hammer throw - 237′ 3″
	Tom Sinclair	Javelin throw - 261′ 3″
1986	Mike Ramos	Decathlon - 8,261 (meet record)
1998	Ja'Warren Hooker	55 meters dash - 6.13*

*indoor NCAA meet

HUSKY LORE

IN 1920, Washington Stadium, later renamed Husky Stadium, had a seating capacity of 30,000. 10,000 seats were added around the rim of the structure in 1936. In 1950, at a cost of $1.7 million, roof-covered stands were built on the south side, adding approximately 15,000 more seats. In 1968, the stadium capacity jumped from 55,000 to more than 59,000 when 3,000 seats were added to the north rim and portable bleachers were installed beyond the east end zone. AstroTurf replaced the grass field in 1968. In 1987, the capacity increased to 72,500 when an upper deck on the north side was added. Also, a glass-enclosed reception and entertainment area (now called the Don James Center) was built below the new upper deck. The 1987 improvements cost $17.7 million In the summer of 2000, synthetic field turf was installed to replace the AstroTurf. It was a gift from Paul Allen, the Seattle Seahawks owner. The Seahawks played at Husky Stadium in 2000 and 2001 while their new stadium was being built.

1921 W 1922

HUSKY MOMENT

Crew Breaks World Record, Loses to Navy at IRA

1922 marked an outstanding year for the Washington rowing program. Coach Ed Leader's varsity crew, stroked by Captain Mike Murphy, won three important races. The first was an overwhelming defeat of California on Lake Washington on April 22, 1922. The second was a decisive win over Wisconsin on June 14. The third was a memorable race on June 26 at Poughkeepsie in which Washington broke the world's record over a three-mile course. The Cal race was postponed for two days because of bad weather. Starting late in the afternoon, Washington initially trailed Cal but then recovered to win by more than 10 lengths. The Huskies recorded the then-fastest time over the three-mile course—15:58.6. After the race, Washington was invited to compete in the Intercollegiate Rowing Association regatta at Poughkeepsie. $7,300 was raised by the Board of Rowing Stewards, organized by Hiram Conibear in 1916, to send the Husky crew to the IRA event. On route to Poughkeepsie, Washington stopped in Madison, Wisconsin, to race the Badgers. Washington won by eight lengths over the three-mile course on Lake Mendota—the time was 15:58. At the IRA regatta, Washington forced a great Navy crew to smash the world's record. The Midshipmen won by three-quarters of a boat length in a time of 13:33.6. Washington was clocked in 13:35.2, also besting the former world record.

The 1922 crew finishes second to Navy in the national championship regatta.

1923 Tyee

Husky Spotlight

Enoch Bagshaw, former Washington football captain, was named Washington's head coach in 1921. He compiled a 63-22-6 record over nine football seasons. Bagshaw coached Washington teams in their first Rose Bowl appearances in 1924 and 1926. The 1921 season was mediocre—three wins, four losses, and one tie. The last game featured Penn State, the East's best team. Penn State won 21-7. Washington's only touchdown was scored by Ray Eckman, a 150-pound halfback. After returning a Penn State punt 30 yards to midfield, Eckman carried the ball every yard but one, on Washington's 80-yard scoring drive.

HUSKY HIGHLIGHT

The Husky baseball team won the Pacific Coast Conference title with 15 wins and only three losses. The team averaged 9.4 runs per game. Perhaps the outstanding feature of the 1922 season was the team's extraordinary base running. The Huskies recorded 88 stolen bases in 91 attempts—a staggering .967 percent. The Husky track and field team again won the Pacific Coast Conference championship. Vic Hurley won conference titles in the 100-yard dash, the 220, and the 220 low hurdles. He won the 100 after being placed six yards behind the starting line after two false starts. Hamilton Greene was the first black person to earn a varsity letter at Washington. He lettered in football.

UWMsSCUA

Husky Legend

Ray Eckman

Ray Eckman was one of the finest athletes in Husky history. He was a star halfback for three seasons—1919-1921—and was the 1921 team captain. He received honorable mention All-America honors in 1921. He was a sprinter on the track and field team. Ray was an assistant football coach from 1922 to 1928. In 1936, Eckman was named Washington's Athletic Director and he served until 1943. University president, Henry Suzzallo stated that "Ray Eckman has given me a new ideal. I have watched him for three years. He has driven his 150-pound body against bigger and stronger men through those years, taken their counter attacks and come up smiling...I don't mind telling you that Ray Eckman is my ideal as a man, a sportsman, and a player and will remain such until another youth comes along and surpasses this lad, if such be possible." Eckman was elected to the Husky Hall of Fame in 1982.

HUSKY LIST

In Husky football history, the top rushing records for a career, a season, and a single game are:

Category	Player	Year	Record
Most yards rushing			
Career	Napoleon Kaufman	1991-94	4041 yards
Season	Corey Dillon	1996	1555
Game	Hugh McElhenny	1950	296 (against WSU)
Most 100 yard games			
Career	Napoleon Kaufman	1991-94	17 games
Season	Greg Lewis	1990	9 games
Most 200 yard games			
Career	Napoleon Kaufman	1991-94	4 games
Season	Napoleon Kaufman	1994	3 games
Rushing yards per game			
Career	Napoleon Kaufman	1991-94	91.8 yards per game
Season	Corey Dillon	1996	141.4 yards per game
Rushing touchdowns			
Career	Napoleon Kaufman	1991-94	33 touchdowns
Season	Corey Dillon	1996	22 touchdowns
Game	Ervin Dailey	1919	7 (against Whitman)

HUSKY LORE

THE University officially accepted the nickname Huskies for its athletic teams on Feb. 3, 1922. The announcement was made at half-time of the basketball game with Washington State. The nickname was selected by a joint committee of students, coaches, faculty, alumni and business leaders. Students and fans did not like the old name of "Sun Dodgers." Football captain-elect, Robert Ingram, presented the "Huskies" nickname at half-time. As he made his speech, large white placards were hoisted in the section occupied by varsity letter winners. The cards read "The Husky stands for fight and tenacity, character and courage, endurance and willingness."

1922 Tyee

Robert Ingram

1922 W 1923

HUSKY MOMENT

First National Champioship

On June 28, 1923, the Husky varsity crew crossed the finish line at the Intercollegiate Rowing Association regatta, a winner by a length and a half over the defending champion Navy. It was the first national championship won by a Husky athletic team. The Huskies were led by first-year coach, Rusty Callow. In April, Washington shocked the Pacific Coast by beating California by more than seven lengths. Many asked: "How could such a young coach turn out a championship eight?" Callow stepped into a system under which he rowed (the Conibear system) and he blended his coaching style into that system. The crew beat Wisconsin on Lake Mendota on the way to the IRA race in Poughkeepsie. Three days before the race, Dow Walling, the Husky stroke, got blood poisoning from a boil on his knee and could not practice. At the start, with Walling back in the boat, Washington got off well and settled into its regular 34 stroke. Rowing in a driving rain storm, the Husky crew had a boat length lead over Columbia and Navy at the two-mile mark. At the two and a half-mile mark, Navy had just about pulled even. At that point, coxswain Don Grant raised his small red flag so that every crew member could see. It was a signal to "Give it all you got." That they did, crossing the finish line with open water over Navy. The Washington crew from bow to stern included: Pat Tidmarsh, Max Luft, Charles Dunn, Rowland France, Fred Spuhn, Captain Sam Shaw, Harvey Dutton, Dow Walling, and coxswain Don Grant. The winning time was 14:03.2. This first Husky national championship team, was elected to the Husky Hall of Fame in 1990. The freshmen, rowing for the first time in the IRA, finished second to Cornell—losing by two-tenths of a second. Al Ulbrickson was the stroke of the freshmen crew.

The 1923 crew wins Washington's first national rowing championship.

UW Media Relations

Husky Spotlight

Victor Hurley established an incredible three-year record as a sprinter for the Huskies in 1921-1923. He was the team's captain in 1923. He won nine Pacific Coast Conference titles helping Washington win Conference team titles in 1921 and 1922 and finish second in 1923. His nine championships—three each in the 100, the 220, and the 220 low hurdles—still stand as a Husky record. After his graduation in 1923, he continued to race. In the 1924 Washington Relay Carnival, he competed, in the 100-yard dash, against Charlie Paddock. Paddock, the 1920 Olympics 100 meters champion and world record holder, won in the slow time of 10.1 seconds.

1922 Tyee

Victor Hurley

HUSKY HIGHLIGHT

Jim Bryan was one of the most versatile athletes to attend Washington. He earned eight letters in three sports—football (1920, 1922, 1923), basketball (1921-1923), and track and field (1921,1922). As a guard on the Huskies' 1924 Rose Bowl team, he caught a pass on a trick play that gave Washington a 14-14 tie with Navy. He was the basketball captain and an All-Pacific Coast Conference selection in 1922. He entered the Husky Hall of Fame in 1981. Chuck Frankland earned five letters—two in basketball (1921, 1923) and three in track and field (1921-1923). He established school records in the high jump (6' 1 7/8") and the 120-yard high hurdles (16.0). In 1922, he won Pacific Coast Conference titles in the two events. He finished in a tie for fourth place, in the high jump, in the 1921 NCAA meet. Frankland served as Athletic Director from 1933-1935 and was a member of the Board of Regents from 1951 to 1957. He was elected to the Husky Hall of Fame in 1981.

Husky Legend

Dorsett "Tubby" Graves

1924 Tyee

In 1923, Tubby Graves became the Husky head baseball coach. Coach Graves attended the University of Missouri from 1905-1909 and played professional baseball after graduation. In 1911, he became Director of Athletics at the University of Alabama where he coached football, basketball and baseball. In 1915, he became the assistant football coach and head baseball coach at Texas A&M. There, he met Hec Edmundson, who was the A&M track coach. They became close friends and vowed to coach together in the Northwest. Graves became the Director of Athletics and head baseball and football coach at Montana State before following Edmundson to Washington. He headed the Husky baseball program from 1923-1946. Over his 24 seasons, his record was 209-182-2, the third most wins and the third best winning percentage in Husky history. His teams won four consecutive Northern Division titles (1929-1932) and seven during his coaching career. He also served as assistant football coach for 24 years and coached freshmen basketball players under Hec Edmundson until 1945. He retired from coaching in 1946 to serve as special assistant to the athletic director from 1946 to 1960. The athletic administration building was named in his memory in 1963. He was elected to the Husky Hall of Fame in 1980.

Husky History

The Intercollegiate Rowing Association (IRA) regatta is the oldest collegiate rowing championship in the country and remains the premier event for men's national rowing honors. The first IRA regatta was in 1895, a four-miler won by Columbia. The IRA consists of five eastern schools—Columbia, Cornell, Navy, Pennsylvania, and Syracuse—and all other schools participate as invited guests. Washington varsity crews have won 11 IRA championships; the junior varsity, 17; the freshmen, 15. The varsity won championships in:

1923, 1924, 1926
1936, 1937
1940, 1941, 1948
1950, 1970, 1997

Washington first rowed in the IRA in 1913. Since then, Cornell is the only school with more IRA varsity victories—12—than the Huskies.

Husky Lore

OTHER sports, sometimes called minor sports, began in the 1920s. Ice hockey and boxing started in 1921; golf in 1923. Boxing became an intercollegiate sport in 1924. Fencing competed in an intercollegiate schedule starting in 1929. Before the 1920s, Washington's football mascot was a three-and-a-half foot wooden statue named Sunny Boy. When Washington changed its mascot to a Husky in 1923, Sunny Boy disappeared. The statute was found in South Bend, Indiana and was returned in 1948 to University officials at the Notre Dame game in South Bend. It has resided ever since at the UW Alumni Association.

Husky Moment

First Rose Bowl for Huskies

The 1923 season was a memorable one—Washington ended the season with 10 wins, finishing second in the conference to California. California turned down the Rose Bowl invitation, so the Huskies were chosen to be the western representative against Navy. The Midshipmen dominated the first quarter with a spectacular passing game. They scored on a 22-yard pass. On their next possession, Washington tied the score on a 23-yard run by Wilson. Les Sherman, a reserve quarterback, came into the game to try the extra point. He wore a size 12 shoe instead of his normal eight, to protect a broken toe. His toe held up and the kick was perfect. Navy scored again, just before half-time, on a 78-yard drive. The conversion was good, and Navy led 14-7. There was no scoring in the third quarter. With about six minutes left in the game, Navy had the ball on its 30-yard line. A center snap sailed through the backfield, and Roy Petrie, the Huskies' right tackle, fell on the ball on the Navy 10. In three plays, Washington lost two yards. With fourth and 12, Coach Bagshaw called a time-out to call a special play. The Huskies lined up in an unbalanced line with fullback Elmer Tesreau on the line and the end in the backfield. This formation made weak side guard, Jim Bryan, an eligible receiver. The Middies put eight men on the line and nobody covered Bryan who delayed on the line and then slipped into the end zone and caught Fred Abel's pass for the touchdown. Sherman again hobbled on to the field and calmly kicked the extra point to tie the score, 14-14. With about three minutes to play, Chalmers Walters intercepted a Navy pass and returned it to the Navy 44. Wilson took a short pass from Abel and raced to the 21. On fourth down, Leonard Ziel attempted a field goal from the 32-yard line. It was high enough and long enough, but it went wide right by about two feet. The game ended two minutes later—Washington 14, Navy 14

1924 Tyee

Husky Spotlight

Washington won its second consecutive Intercollegiate Rowing Association championship at Poughkeepsie on June 18, 1924. Stroked by sophomore Al Ulbrickson, the Husky crew defeated Wisconsin by two boat lengths. Washington's time over the three-mile course was 15:02. 1924 was an Olympic year and the Husky coaches and oarsmen preferred to pass up the IRA race for the Olympic Trials and a shot at the Olympic Games in Paris. The Trials were held three days before the IRA regatta. A faculty committee voted against sending the crew to the Trials arguing that Washington should defend their IRA title and that going to the Trials would require more time away from the classroom. Yale's eight, coached by former Husky oarsman and coach, Ed Leader, won the Trials and the Olympic gold medal.

Husky Highlight

The 1924 Husky basketball team, led by Captain Dick Frayn, won the Northern Division title and had an overall record of 12-2 before meeting California in the Oakland Auditorium in the Pacific Coast Conference playoffs. In a best two-out-of-three format, California won the first game in overtime, 32-31. Washington led 30-29 with 30 seconds to play in regulation. In the second game, California won, again in overtime, 28-25. The teams were not separated by more than three points throughout the whole game. The Huskies led at half-time, 13-11, and 24-23 with about 30 seconds in regulation. In overtime, the Bears clinched the game and the conference championship on two long field goals, while Washington could only muster one free throw.

Husky Legend

Wallace Scott

UW Media Relations

Wallace Scott played tennis for the Huskies for only one year, 1924, and it was a historic one. Scotty won the interfraternity championship the year before. The lefty vaulted to the top spot on the tennis team in early season contests. He led Washington to the Pacific Coast Conference team championship by winning the singles title and teaming with Bob Hesketh to win the doubles title. Both Hesketh and Scott went on to the National Intercollegiate tournament held at the famed Merion Cricket Club in Haverford, Pennsylvania. In the final round, on June 28, 1924, Scott beat Yale's Arnold Jones in straight sets—6-2, 6-2, 7-5. Thirty minutes after the singles match, Scott joined Hesketh in the doubles final. The two started the day by beating a Yale doubles team, 6-3, 7-5. So, the doubles finals was the third match for Scott. Understandably tired, he and Hesketh lost to a Harvard duo, 6-4, 8-6. In his career, Scott won many other titles, including the Pacific Northwest, Pacific Coast, International Canadian, and Inland Empire championships. He is the only Husky ever to win a National collegiate singles championship. He entered the Husky Hall of Fame in 1990.

HUSKY LIST

Washington has appeared in 14 Rose Bowl games, winning seven, losing six, and tying Navy, 14-14, in its first Rose Bowl appearance.

Year	Opponent	Score	Huskies Selected Most Valuable Player
1924	Navy	14-14 Tie	None
1926	Alabama	20-19 Loss	George Wilson, HB (Co-MVP)
1937	Pittsburgh	21-0 Loss	None
1944	Southern California	29-0 Loss	None
1960	Wisconsin	44-8 Win	Bob Schloredt, QB George Fleming, HB
1961	Minnesota	17-7 Win	Bob Schloredt, QB
1964	Illinois	17-7 Loss	None
1978	Michigan	27-20 Win	Warren Moon, QB
1981	Michigan	23-6 Loss	None
1982	Iowa	28-0 Win	Jacque Robinson, RB
1991	Iowa	46-34 Win	Mark Brunell, QB
1992	Michigan	34-14 Win	Steve Emtman, DT Billy Joe Hobert, QB
1993	Michigan	38-31 Loss	None
2001	Purdue	34-24 Win	Marcus Tuiasosopo, QB

ROSCOE "TORCHY" TORRANCE was known as Mr. Everything in Seattle. The University of Washington never had a more loyal, devoted alumnus than Torchy. His love affair with Washington began in 1918 when he enrolled as a freshman student. He played baseball for four years. He became the University's property manager and assistant trainer after graduation. In 1922, he was appointed freshmen baseball coach and ASUW assistant graduate manager. After leaving the University in 1924 to pursue business interests, he continued his active support of the Husky program. He was an avid recruiter, raised funds, and found jobs to help athletes through school. His fund raising efforts led to the formation of the Greater Washington Advertising Fund, used to help athletes with expenses. This activity caused the Huskies to be put on a two-year probation by the NCAA in 1956. For his many positive contributions to athletics, Torchy was elected to the Husky Hall of Fame in 1980.

1924 W 1925

Husky Moment

National Champion in the Half-Mile Run

The Husky track and field team had six outstanding performers who participated in the NCAA championship meet in Chicago—Captain-elect Web Augustine, Jim Charteris, George Clarke, Captain Percy Egtvet, Bill Maginnis, and Drum Wilde. They earned the trip to the nationals by their overall season and Pacific Coast Conference performances. In the PCC meet:

- Augustine was second in the 220-yard low hurdles
- Charteris won the half-mile in a record time of 1:56.5
- Clark was second in the 100
- Egtvet placed in four events—second in the high jump; fourth in the shot put, broad jump, and discus throw
- Maginnis won the two-mile run in a record time of 9:37.5
- Wilde won the mile in record time of 4:24.5
- Al Nardin, who did not compete in the NCAA meet, tied for first place in the pole vault, clearing 12 feet

At the National meet in Chicago on June 12 and 13, 1925, Clarke, Maginnis, and Wilde all finished sixth in their events. In the half-mile run, sophomore Jim Charteris was in last place with two-hundred yards to go. Then, he started his finishing kick, passing every runner, and winning by five yards.

1926 Tyee

The 1925 track team—four scored in the NCAA meet.

Husky Spotlight

Percy Egtvet, track captain in 1925, came to Washington to play football but was unable to play because of a heart condition discovered by the university's Health Services examiners. He was authorized to compete in track and field events and he became one of the highest dual meet scorers in Husky history. He frequently won all four field events in which he participated—the shot put, the discus throw, the broad jump, and the high jump. After graduating in 1925, he became a Husky trainer and, in 1937, the assistant track and field coach—a position he held until 1958.

Jack Westlund won the Northwest Conference golf championship in 1925. In Montclair, N.J., on June 26, 1925, Westlund beat Yale's Frank Wattles in the semi-finals of the National Intercollegiate golf tournament The next day, he finished second to Fred Lambrecht of Tulane University.

Husky Highlight

The Junior Varsity eight-men crew won the Intercollegiate Rowing Association regatta in 1925. The varsity eight was unsuccessful in its attempt to win a third straight IRA championship. Navy beat the varsity by three-quarters of a boat length.

The 1924 Husky football team led the nation in scoring with 355 points and finished the season with a 8-1-1 record. They lost to Oregon, 7-3, and tied California, 7-7, and finished third in the Pacific Coast Conference. George Wilson was selected as a second team All-America halfback.

UW Media Relations

Husky Legend

Jim Charteris

Jim Charteris won every half-mile race in which he participated in Husky Stadium during his three-year varsity career, 1925-1927. As a sophomore, he won the NCAA championship, setting a new meet record of 1:55.4. He finished fifth in the national meet in 1926 and second in 1927. He won the Pacific Coast Conference half-mile event in 1925 and 1927, placing second in 1926. In 1927, Jim won every dual meet and open meet he entered—except one. His only defeat of the season was in the NCAA meet when Johnny Sittig of Illinois beat him by three inches, setting a meet record of 1:54.2. Charteris' exciting fast-finish style of racing thrilled the fans and helped make track and field an exciting spectator sport in Husky Stadium. He normally ran in last place for the first 600 yards of a half-mile race and then he would turn on his finishing kick to overtake his opponents. He was team captain in 1927 and was elected to the Husky Hall of Fame in 1986.

HUSKY LIST

The top Husky teams, in points scored during the regular season, are listed below.

Year	Points in Regular Season	Points in Bowl Games	Overall Total	Overall Record	Top 20 National Ranking
1991	461	34 in Rose Bowl win (34-14)	495	12-0-0	1
1925	461	19 in Rose Bowl loss (19-20)	480	10-1-1	3
1990	394	46 in Rose Bowl win (46-34)	440	10-2-0	5
1986	372	6 in Sun Bowl loss (6-28)	378	8-3-1	18
1996	370	21 in Holiday Bowl loss (21-33)	391	9-3	On Probation
1997	369	51 in Aloha Bowl win (51-23)	420	8-4	18
1971	357		357	8-3-0	19
1924	355		355	8-1-1	
2000	353	34 in rose Bowl win (34-24)	387	11-1-0	3
1970	334		334	6-4-0	
1984	324	28 in Orange Bowl win (28-17)	352	11-1-0	2

THE Washington women's rifle team won its second consecutive intercollegiate championship in 1924 and placed third in 1925. This was the only sport in which women's intercollegiate competition was allowed. Competition was done by means of simultaneous shooting and telegraphing the results. Roberta Bellazzi was the team's best markswoman. The men won three consecutive titles (1923-1925). Winning both the men and women's national titles in the same years (1923 and 1924) had never been done before in the nation. In those two years, the combined teams won 32 of 35 dual meets.

1925 Tyee

Roberta Bellazzi

1925 W 1926

Husky Moment

Undefeated Football Season—Second Rose Bowl

In 1925, Washington won the conference title by beating all its conference opponents, posting a 10-0-1 season, and earning a trip to the Rose Bowl. The Huskies were ranked third in the nation and, for the second consecutive year, led the nation in scoring with 461 points. This regular-season scoring total is tied for the best in Husky history—the 1991 team also scored the same number of points. Alabama was the opponent in the Rose Bowl. George Wilson was sensational in leading Washington to two touchdowns in the first half. The first came on a 54-yard drive with Harold Patton diving the final yard. George Guttormsen's extra point kick failed. The second scoring drive featured a 36-yard run by Wilson, the longest run of the day, and a 20- yard touchdown pass—Wilson to Johnny Cole. Guttormsen's kick again failed, and Washington led 12-0 at half-time. Midway in the second quarter, Wilson was knocked unconscious and was carried off the field on a stretcher. Alabama scored three touchdowns in the third quarter with Wilson on the bench. With two successful conversions, the Crimson Tide led Washington at the end of the third quarter, 20-12. Then Wilson reentered the game and engineered an 88-yard scoring drive, featuring a 27-yard touchdown pass, Wilson to Guttormsen. Gene Cook's extra point was good to bring the Huskies within one point of Alabama, with eight minutes to play. The Huskies mounted one last drive from their 11-yard line. However, Wilson's pass was intercepted on the Washington 35. Two plays later, the game ended. With Wilson in the lineup, Washington gained over 300 yards and scored 19 points. Wilson rushed for 134 yards and completed five of 11 passes for 77 yards and two touchdowns. During his 22 minutes off the field, Washington gained 17 yards, was held scoreless, and gave up 20 points. George Wilson was voted the game's Most Valuable Player, along with Alabama's Johnny Mack Brown. The game, regarded by many as the greatest ever Rose Bowl, was the first radio broadcast of the Pasadena contest.

A Husky tackler closes in on an Alabama runner in the 1926 Rose Bowl.

1926 Tyee

Husky Spotlight

Washington battled Stanford on Nov. 7, 1925. Stanford was led by their great All-America fullback, Ernie Nevers. The Huskies won, 13-0, and stopped Nevers in several critical moments in the game. In the third quarter, Stanford began a drive that featured Nevers carrying the ball on almost every play. He was hit hard by Husky tacklers. On a burst through the line, Nevers broke into the open for what might be a long gain. Suddenly, he was hit by Elmer Tesreau and George Wilson. The Washington players' tackles lifted Nevers off the ground and knocked him flat. The crushing impact could be heard throughout the whole stadium. The hit on Nevers caused Stanford president Wilbur to criticize Washington for illegal roughness and the officials for not enforcing the rules for illegal play. Tesreau was not only an outstanding football player for three years (1923-25) but a three-year letterman in baseball. As a Husky pitcher, he did not lose a game during his career (1924-26). He was voted the top Washington fullback for the first 50 years of the century and was elected to the Husky Hall of Fame in 1985.

Husky Highlight

Captain Al Ulbrickson stroked the Washington varsity eight to another Intercollegiate Rowing Association championship on June 28, 1926. They beat Navy by about 10 feet, a bare second over the four-mile course. The winning time was 19:28.6. The junior varsity eight also won in the three-mile race, beating Pennsylvania by almost four lengths in a time of 15:40.5. It was the first time that both the varsity and junior varsity crews won the IRA championships.

Husky Legend

George Wilson

UW Media Relations

George Wilson played halfback for three seasons (1923-1925) and was a member of the first two Husky Rose Bowl teams (1924 and 1926). He was selected as Co-Most Valuable Player in the 1926 Rose Bowl even though he played only 38 minutes because of an injury in the second quarter. He led Washington to two touchdowns in the first half and another in the fourth quarter when he reentered the game. He generated virtually all of Washington's offense. In the minutes he played, Washington scored all of its 19 points. When he was not on the field, Alabama scored all of its 20 points to win the game, 20-19. Wilson is one of three Husky football players to have his jersey number (33) retired. He was a three-time All-Coast selection (1923-1925) and a second-team All-America selection in 1924. He became Washington's first consensus first-team All-American in 1925. In that year, he was the Guy Flaherty Award winner as the Huskies' most inspirational player. He was considered the best player of the first 50 years of Husky football. Wilson is the co-leader in most career touchdowns (37) in Husky history. He is tied for fifth in career scoring (224 points). He was first Husky to be elected in the College Football Hall of Fame (1951) and he entered the Rose Bowl Hall of Fame in 1991. Wilson became a member of the Husky Hall of Fame in 1980.

HUSKY LIST

Washington varsity crews have won 11 Intercollegiate Rowing Association regatta championships, the junior varsity 17, and the freshmen 15. The 1926 season marked the first time that both Husky varsity and junior varsity eights won the IRA regatta. Below are the years of the double victories and triple victories.

Double Victories (varsity and junior varsity)	Triple Victories (varsity, junior varsity, and freshmen)
1926	
1936	1936
1937	1937
1940	
1948	1948
1950	1950
1997	1997

Washington's five sweeps (triple victories) are the most for any school in IRA history. Cornell and Navy are second with two apiece and four schools have one sweep each.

HUSKY LORE

ART LANGLIE earned three letters in baseball (1924-26), two while attending law school. He played shortstop and second base. As a undergraduate, he received three letters in tennis (1921-23). In 1923, he was the team captain and won the Pacific Coast Conference doubles title with Bob Hesketh; he lost to Hesketh in the singles final. After graduating from law school, Langlie applied his leadership abilities in the political arena. He was elected first as a Seattle city councilman (1935-38), then as Seattle's mayor (1938-41). He served as Washington's governor for three terms (1941-45, 1949-57). Langlie was inducted into the Husky Hall of Fame in 1984.

1923 Tyee

Art Langlie

1926 W 1927

Husky Moment

Huskies Lose Nationals in Track and Field by One and Two-Tenths Points

Illinois and Texas barely edged Washington for the 1927 NCAA track and field title. Dean Anderson, Herman Brix, captain Jim Charteris, Ed Peltret, and Bill Shelley paced the Huskies to a Northwest Conference title and third place in the Pacific Coast Conference meet, won by Stanford. In the PCC meet, the Huskies had two winners—Peltret won the 440 and Charteris the 880. Brix did not have a good day. He finished fifth in the shot put and did not place in the discus throw. In Chicago, on June 11, 1927, it looked as if Washington would stand at the top of the nation. Brix won the shot put with a heave of 46′ 7 3/8″ but did not qualify for the finals in the discus throw. Anderson finished second in the 100-yard dash. Shelley was fourth in the 220 low hurdles and Peltret finished sixth in the 440. All Washington needed to win the national title was Jim Charteris' victory in the 880. Running his last race for Washington, he turned on his famous finishing kick and was edged, by three inches, at the tape by Illinois' Johnny Sittig. The winning time was 1:54.2, a meet record, breaking the old record of 1:55.4 set by Charteris in 1925. Illinois won the race and the meet by the margin of a chest thrust.

1928 Tyee

Captain-elect Dean Anderson finishes second in the 100 and helps the Huskies to a third-place finish in the nation.

Husky Spotlight

The junior varsity crew captured its third straight Intercollegiate Rowing Association championship on June 29, 1927. Rowing on the Hudson River's three-mile course, the crew set a new IRA junior varsity race record, 15:12.8. The crew shattered the old course record by 27.4 seconds. The varsity eight finished second to Columbia by a boat length. After the IRA regatta, Coach Callow accepted the coaching position at Pennsylvania, receiving the then highest salary offered a crew coach in the nation. In his five coaching years at Washington, he entered ten crews in IRA events—winning six and taking second four times. His varsity crews won three national championships (1923, 1924, and 1926). After Callow resigned, Al Ulbrickson, captain and stroke of the 1926 varsity eight, became the head coach. He had been appointed assistant crew coach at the beginning of the 1927 season.

Husky Highlight

The Husky football team had an 8-2-0 season in 1926, closing the season with a 10-6 home win over Nebraska. The team placed fifth in the Pacific Coast Conference with a 3-2-0 record. They lost conference games to Washington State and Stanford. Nebraska played at Washington for the first time. It was Nebraska's first game west of the Rockies. Washington scored in the first quarter on a pass from Louis Tesreau to Captain George Guttormsen. Nebraska's star running back, Blue Howell, scored in the second quarter to come within one point of the Huskies. With about a minute to go in the first half, Gene Cook, a Husky guard and leading kicker on the West Coast, booted a 40-yard field goal to put Washington up, 10-6. In the closing minutes, Nebraska swept to the Husky one-yard line. With time for one more play, Nebraska's Howell dashed around the center pile-up. Harold Paton, the Flaherty Award winner that year, nailed him for a four-yard loss to preserve the victory.

UW Media Relations

Husky Legend

Herman Brix

Herman Brix was one of the most outstanding track and field athletes in Husky history. He competed for Washington from 1926-1928. He was the team captain in 1928. He won the NCAA shot put title in 1927, with a mark of 46′ $7\frac{3}{8}$″. In 1928, he set a world record in the event—51′ 8″—in the Amsterdam Olympic Games. Moments later, an Olympic teammate, John Kuck, bested Brix's mark by about five inches to win the gold medal. Brix won the silver medal. He was a star tackle on the Husky football team for three seasons (1925-1927). After graduation, he competed for the Los Angeles Track Club. He won four consecutive American Amateur Union (AAU) shot put titles (1928-1931). Brix set his second world record in the shot put in 1932 with a heave of 52′ $8\frac{5}{8}$″. After retiring his spikes, with the assistance of Douglas Fairbanks, Brix began a career in motion pictures that spanned over 150 films. Brix appeared in such classics as "The Treasure of the Sierra Madre", with Humphrey Bogart. He was best known as the pre-Johnny Weissmuller Tarzan. At the age of 94, Brix returned to the Husky football scene when he visited one of Washington's practices in preparation for the 2001 Rose Bowl. Wearing his Husky Hall of Fame (1980) jacket, he entertained members of the media and fans on the sidelines with his keen recollections of his Washington playing days and experiences as a actor. Husky head coach Rick Neuheisel had Brix address the team, and he briefly wished them well and emotionally pointed out that, 75 years later, he still vividly recalled playing in the Rose Bowl. Later in the week, Neuheisel used Brix's comments to motivate his team. "Seventy-five years later, and he still gets choked up talking about playing in the Rose Bowl," Neuheisel told his players. "If that does not get you fired up to play in this game, nothing will."

Husky List

Washington's first home football game with Nebraska was in 1926. The series started with a 6-6 tie at Nebraska in 1925. The Huskies have played seven games with Nebraska.

Year	Location	Score
1925	Lincoln, Nebraska	6-6 tie
1926	Seattle	10-6 win
1967	Seattle	17-7 loss
1991	Lincoln	36-21 win
1992	Seattle	29-14 win
1997	Seattle	27-14 loss
1998	Lincoln	55-7 loss

Husky Lore

HUSKY Stadium was built, in 1920, at a cost of $577,000 and partially financed by the sale of bonds. The last of the bonds were repaid and burned on Oct. 23, 1926, during the half-time of the Washington State football game. In 1927, a new Women's Physical Education Building was constructed to replace the original gymnasium. It was renamed to honor Mary G. Hutchinson and her years of University service (1919-1947), including 11 years as head of the physical education department. Washington was admitted to the National Collegiate Athletic Association (NCAA) at its December 1926 convention and President Suzzallo was notified in a letter dated Jan. 4, 1927.

1932 Tyee

Hutchinson Hall

1927 W 1928

Husky Moment

Silver Medals at the 1928 Olympic Games

After leading the Husky track and field team to a Pacific Coast Conference championship and fourth place in the NCAA meet, three Husky athletes competed in the Olympic Trials in Boston on July 6 and 7, 1928. Herman Brix, after finishing third to two Stanford throwers at the NCAA meet, beat them and everybody else to win the shot put (50′ 11¾″). Steve Anderson ran away from everybody in the 110-meter high hurdles. In winning, he equaled the world record of 14.8. Rudy Kiser, who won the NCAA mile run in 4:17.6, finished sixth in the 1500 meters at the Olympic Trials. Anderson and Brix went on to the Olympic Games in Amsterdam. On July 29, Brix set a world record, 51′ 8″, in the 16-pound shot put early in the competition. On his next to last throw, Brix's Olympic teammate, John Kuck, beat Herm's mark by about five inches to set a new Olympic and world record (52′11/16″) and win the gold medal. Brix took the silver medal. On Aug. 1, Steve Anderson, the favorite to win the 110-meter high hurdles, led the event until the final hurdle. Sydney Atkinson, a South African hurdler, nosed Anderson. Both men were clocked in a new Olympic record time, 14.8. This time also equaled the world record for the event. Anderson brought home the second silver medal for Washington athletes.

Steve Anderson, nipped at the tape, takes the silver medal in 1928 Olympics.

UWMssUCUA

Husky Spotlight

The University of Washington Pavilion was dedicated on Dec. 27, 1927. Hec Edmundson's team played Illinois in the first event in the new building. Washington beat the Illini, 34-23. Alfie James made the first field goal in the Pavilion. Illinois won the second game, 33-24. Washington won the third and decisive game, 32-26. The Pavilion cost $663,000. It was financed by ASUW funds, bond sales, and a state appropriation of $100,000. A swimming pool, costing $209,400, was attached to the east of the building, in 1939. The Pavilion was renamed the Clarence S. "Hec" Edmundson Pavilion, on Jan. 16, 1948, to honor Hec for his long-time coaching career in basketball. The 1928 basketball team finished the season with a 22-6 record to win the Northern Division title. The University of Southern California beat the Huskies in two games for the Pacific Coast Conference championship. Both games were played in the Los Angeles Olympic Auditorium. USC won the first game in overtime—53-50—and captured the title by winning the second game, 27-26. Captain Alfie James was selected as an All-American at the end of the season. James was inducted in the Husky Hall of Fame in 1989.

Husky Highlight

The Husky boxing team won the Pacific Coast title in 1928 by winning four of seven individual titles. Army Seigas won the bantam event and Dave Walker won the featherweight title. Captain Emery Arnett had three knockouts in the lightweight bouts leading up to his decisive win in the final match. Bill Broz won the heavyweight event.

Husky Legend

Al Ulbrickson

UW Media Relations

Al Ulbrickson was raised on Mercer Island and graduated from Franklin High School. To get to Franklin, he rowed across Lake Washington. In 1924, as a sophomore, he was the varsity stroke. He rowed in that spot in the varsity eight for two more years. He was the crew captain in 1926. Twice he stroked the Huskies to the Intercollegiate Rowing Association championship—1924 and 1926. He rowed in the 1926 IRA win with a shoulder muscle torn halfway through the four-mile race. In his senior year, Ulbrickson was elected to Phi Beta Kappa, the scholastic honorary. In 1927, he became assistant crew coach under Rusty Callow. When Callow departed to coach at Pennsylvania, Al became the Husky head coach at age 25. Over 31 seasons, he compiled an extraordinary record. During his career both as an oarsmen and coach, Washington won more IRA varsity eight championships than any other school. His varsity crews won six IRA championships—he also won two as an oarsman—took five seconds and eight third-place finishes. His junior varsity crews won ten IRA races and finished second five times. His freshmen boats won 12 IRA titles and took second three times. Several of his greatest coaching triumphs were on the world scene. His varsity eight won the 1936 Berlin Olympics gold medal. His oarsmen won the gold medal in the four-oared, with coxswain, event in the 1948 London Olympics. Another four with coxswain, captured a bronze medal in the 1952 Helsinki Olympics. This boat included his son, also named Al. In the last race of his coaching career, his 1958 varsity eight staged one of the greatest upsets in rowing history by beating Russia's Trud Rowing Club, on Moscow's Khimkinsko Reservoir. The Trud Club crew had beaten Washington in the first round of the 1958 Henley (England) regatta and went on to win Henley's Grand Challenge Cup. Nine crews coached by Ulbrickson are in the Husky Hall of Fame. He was Washington's Athletic Director from 1943 to 1946. Ulbrickson was elected as a charter member of the Husky Hall of Fame in 1979.

Husky History

In 1928, Hec Edmundson's basketball team won Washington's third Northern Division title. Hec's teams won 10 division titles and three Pacific Coast Conference championships during his 27 years of coaching. Below is a list of Husky Pacific Coast Conference basketball titles.

Year	Coach	Season Record	NCAA Record
1931	Hec Edmundson	25-3	The NCAA tournament did not begin until 1939
1934	Hec Edmundson	20-5	
1943	Hec Edmundson	24-7	Lost to Texas and Oklahoma in the Western Regionals
1948	Art McLarney	23-11	Lost to Baylor and beat Wyoming in the Western Regionals
1951	Tippy Dye	24-6	Beat Texas A&M in first round, lost to Oklahoma State in the second round, beat BYU in consolation game
1953	Tippy Dye	28-3	Beat Seattle University and Santa Clara in Western Regionals, lost to Kansas in semi-finals of Final Four, beat Louisiana State in consolation game to place third in the nation
1976	Marv Harshman	25-5	Lost to Missouri in first round
1984	Marv Harshman	24-7	Beat Nevada Reno in first round, beat Duke in second round, lost to Dayton in third round

Husky Lore

WITH the new Women's Physical Education Building constructed in 1927, the Women's Athletic Association greatly expanded its programs. The Women's "W" Club awarded W sweaters for interclass competition in 13 sports—archery, baseball, basketball, canoeing, field hockey, golf, hiking, horseshoes, riding, riflery, swimming, tennis, and volleyball.

1927 Tyee

Women's W Club

1928 W 1929

Husky Moment

Track Team Second in Nation

In 1929, the Huskies were favored to win the NCAA track and field championship. They had depth with 11 men participating in the meet. They had swept the Northern Division championships with six athletes winning seven events. Crosby Pendleton won the 220; Eddie Genung the 880; Rufus Kiser in the mile; Robert Reed in the two miles; Steve Anderson won both the 120-yard high hurdles and 220 low hurdles; and Paul Jessup was a victor in the shot put. Anderson equaled the world record of 14.4 seconds in the high hurdles. There was no Pacific Coast Conference meet in 1929. At the NCAA meet, a number of upsets resulted in Ohio State winning the title with the Huskies taking second. Rufus Kiser finished third in the mile and Paul Jessup was beaten in the discus throw by an Oregon thrower he had bested several times during the season. Steve Anderson finished third in the high hurdles, after getting his arm entangled with another hurdler. He won the 220 low hurdles in 23.5 seconds and Eddie Genung provided the Huskies with another first place by winning the half-mile in 1:55.

1930 Tyee

Husky athletes finish second in the NCAA track and field meet.

Husky Spotlight

The 1929 Husky basketball squad posted an 18-2 record winning all 10 Northern Division games. They met unbeaten California, the Southern Division champions, in the Pavilion for the Pacific Coast Conference championship. On March 1, 1929, the Bears won the first game 43-31. On March 2, before a packed Pavilion, the Huskies trailed at half-time, 21-6. The Huskies outscored the Bears 21-8 to come within two, 29-27, with only a few minutes left. Cal then held the Huskies scoreless and added a free throw to preserve the victory, 30-27, and win the Conference title. Captain Monty Snider was chosen All-Northern Division, along with teammates Hal McClary and Percy Bolstad. McClary was a Pacific Coast Conference first team selection.

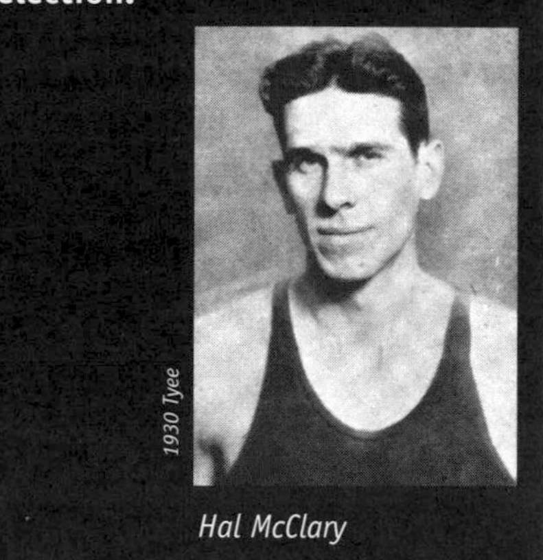

1930 Tyee

Hal McClary

Husky Highlight

The Husky crew was not considered a serious contender in collegiate rowing circles in the 1929 season. In April 1929, California beat Washington by six boat lengths. By June, the Huskies had improved significantly and were prepared for the Intercollegiate Rowing Association regatta. They beat Wisconsin on their way to Poughkeepsie. On race day, June 24, 1929, the water was very rough. After two false starts, the crews swept down the course. Cal's boat sunk and Cornell's shell broke in two. Columbia finished first, beating Washington by two lengths. Washington's baseball team won the Northern Division title, the first of four consecutive championships (1929-1932).

UW Media Relations

Husky Legend

Charles Carroll

Chuck Carroll was a consensus All-America selection in 1928. He was one of the most outstanding football players in Husky history. He could run through and around his opponents with great speed and shiftiness. He was an excellent passer and punter. Carroll was also a punishing linebacker. During his three seasons (1926-1928), he led the Huskies to a 24-8 record, scoring 36 points against Puget Sound in 1928. This scoring mark still stands as the second best in Husky history. His 104 points in 1928 ranks him fourth best in Husky history. Carroll's 195 points are ninth all-time. During the 1928 season, he racked up 17 touchdowns, a total that is second best in Husky history. His 32 career touchdowns are fifth all-time. After Carroll's brilliant play in a Husky loss, 12-0, at Stanford, Pop Warner, the Stanford coach, said: These old eyes have never seen a greater football player." President Hoover, a Stanford alumnus, acclaimed Carroll as "the captain of my All-America team." In 1927 and 1928, he led the Pacific Coast Conference in scoring and was second in the nation in 1928. In the six conference games of the 1928 season, he played all but six minutes. The only minutes he did not play came near the end of the Montana game, with Washington ahead, 25-0. He won the Flaherty Award as the most inspirational team player in 1928. His jersey number two was retired after his last game. Carroll was inducted into the National Football Foundation Hall of Fame in 1964. He was elected as a charter member of the Husky Hall of Fame in 1979.

Husky List

The Husky football top 10 career scoring leaders are:

Player	Years	TD	PAT	FG	Total Points
Jeff Jaeger, kicker	1983-86	0	118	80	358
Chuck Nelson, kicker	1980-82	0	94	59	271
Hugh McElhenny, HB	1949-51	35	23	0	233
Travis Hanson, kicker	1990-93	0	124	35	229
Joe Steele, RB	1976-79	37	1*	0	224
George Wilson, HB	1923-25	37	2	0	224
Steve Robbins, kicker	1974-77	0	108	35	213
Napoleon Kaufman, RB	1991-94	33	0	0	198
Chuck Carroll, HB	1926-28	32	3	0	195
John Wales. kicker	1994-96	0	85	36	193

* Two- point conversion

Husky Lore

IN 1928, Professor Vernon Parrington won the Pulitzer Prize for the first two volumes of "Main Currents in American Thought," a study that marked a fresh approach to American history and literature. He was a professor of English at Washington from 1908 to 1929 and the first person in the State of Washington to win the Pulitzer. He was, presumably, the first former football coach to win the prize. After three years as a quarterback for the College of Emporia, Kansas, he coached the University of Oklahoma. His coaching record was 9-2-1 during the five seasons, 1897-1901. Parrington Hall was named to honor him in January 1931. The building is listed in the State Register of Historic Places and was originally named the Science Hall. Parrington once said that it was "the ugliest (building) I have ever seen." After renaming the building, the university's Board of Regents chose to have it remodeled for the English Department.

1929 W 1930

Husky Moment

Two World Track and Field Records

For the second consecutive year, the 1930 Husky track and field team was second best in the NCAA meet, losing only to USC, 55-40. The team was led by Captain Steve Anderson, Paul Jessup, and Rufus Kiser. Anderson again equaled the world's record (14.4) in taking first in the 120-yard high hurdles and getting third in the 220 lows. Jessup set a new meet record in the discus throw (160′ 9 3/8″). Kiser lost by three yards to get second place in the mile run. In August, Anderson, Eddie Genung (half-mile), Jessup, and Kiser traveled to Pittsburgh for the 55th American Amateur Union meet, with the best athletes in the country competing—both those in college and those who had graduated. Three Huskies—Anderson, Jessup, and Kiser—had graduated and were competing for the Washington Athletic Club. On Aug. 23, 1930, Anderson again equaled the world's record (14.4) in breaking the tape first in the 120 high hurdles. Jessup shattered the world's record in the discus throw with a mark of 169′ 8 7/8″, bettering the old mark by more than six feet. Genung won the 880, setting a meet and American record of 1:53.4. Former Husky, Herm Brix, competing for the Los Angeles Track Club, set a new American record in the shot put (52′ 5 3/4″), two inches off the world record. Kiser finished third in the mile. And all of this on a cold, damp, bleak gray afternoon at the University of Pittsburgh stadium.

1931 Tyee

The 1930 track and field team—second in the nation.

Husky Spotlight

Paul Jessup entered Washington in the fall of 1926 standing six feet, seven inches. Coach Edmundson remarked that "Paul looked like a new born colt." By the time he graduated in 1930, he weighed 240 pounds and had established a record that would stand for a long time in Husky history. He played tackle on Enoch Bagshaw's last three teams and was the captain in 1930. He earned most of his recognition for his accomplishments in track and field. He won the 1929 Northern Division shot put title. He was a double winner in the 1930 meet—the shot put and the discus throw. He won the 1930 NCAA title in the discus throw. In the summer, after his graduation, he set the world record (169′ 8 7/8″) in the discus throw at the AAU meet in Pittsburgh. This mark stood as the Husky record for more than 30 years. Jessup competed in the 1932 Los Angeles Olympics. He was elected to the Husky Hall of Fame in 1982. He is fifth from the left in the bottom row of the 1930 team picture.

Husky Highlight

The Husky baseball team won its fourth Northern Division championship under Coach Tubby Graves. In Graves' first 10 years of coaching, his teams won six championships. Wilson Gaw was the leading hitter over his three-year career (1928-1930) as a first baseman and outfielder. He was captain in 1930 and selected to Graves' all-time team in 1942 as a first baseman. Gaw was elected to the Husky Hall of Fame in 1983.

Husky Legend

Steve Anderson

UW Media Relations

"Stepping Steve" dominated the high hurdles event on the national and international scene during his Husky career (1928-1930). He equaled the world record of 14.4 in the 120 high hurdles five times during his career. International success came at the end of his sophomore year. At the 1928 Olympic Trials in Boston, he won the 110-meter high hurdles, equaling the world record of 14.8 seconds and qualifying for the U.S. Olympic team. At the 1928 Stockholm Olympic Games, he led the field in the 110 hurdles final until the last barrier when South African's Sydney Atkinson edged him at the tape for the gold medal. Both men were timed in 14.8, tying the world record and breaking the Olympic record. Anderson won the silver medal. He led the Huskies to a second-place finish at the NCAA meeet in Chicago, in 1929 and 1930. He won the 220 low hurdles event in 1929; the high hurdles in 1930. He won the 120 high hurdles titles at the AAU meets in 1928, 1929 and 1930. He established a world record (9.8) for the indoor 80-yard high hurdles in the first ever indoor meet held in the Northwest—on March 28, 1929, in the Pavilion. He was inducted as a charter member of the Husky Hall of Fame in 1979.

HUSKY LISTS

There have been five Husky track and field athletes who have set or equaled the world record in their events:

1928	**Steve Anderson, 120-yard high hurdles, 14.4 (equaled four more times in 1929 and 1930)** **Steve Anderson, 110-meter high hurdles 14.8**
1928	**Herman Brix, Shot put, 51′ 8″**
1929	**Steve Anderson, 80-yard high hurdles (indoor), 9.8**
1930	**Paul Jessup, Discus throw, 169′ 8 7/8″**
1932	**Herman Brix, Shot put, 52″ 8 1/2″**
1963	**Phil Shinnick, Long jump, 27′ 4″ (never ratified)**
1963	**Brian Sternberg, Pole vault, 16′ 8″**

AS the stock market soared in 1927 and 1928, students became very interested in common stocks. In 1929, the College of Business Administration introduced a course on the Stock Exchange. In that same year, the market started to decline and the depression started in the following year. The Washington chapter of Gamma Epsilon Pi, the women's national commerce honorary, won the national cup awarded annually to the chapter having the highest scholarship in the country.

Super Legend

Hec Edmundson

In his 35 years as a coach at the University of Washington, Clarence S. "Hec" Edmundson had a knack for building champions. Many called him the father of "race-horse" basketball. Most called him "Uncle Hec" with more than a touch of reverence. He was the coach who made it to the Helms Foundation Hall of Fame not once, but twice. He was the man who loved to run so much he made it an essential of his adopted second love, basketball.

In the Idaho Palouse, Clarence dashed down the road in his first makeshift track shoes—a castoff pair of his mother's rubbers. At frequent intervals, he criticized his own efforts with an "Aw, heck." Hec raced through high school and the University of Idaho. As a Vandal, he ran the quarter mile, the half, the mile, and anchored the mile relay—all in the same meet. As a U.S. Olympian, he participated in the 400 meter and 800 meter events in the 1912 Stockholm Olympics, finishing sixth in the 800.

He began his coaching career at Washington in 1919 as head trainer and track and field coach. He started to build champions. Gus Pope won a bronze medal in the discus throw in the 1920 Olympics and was the 1921 NCAA champion in the shot put and discus throw. Six other NCAA champions followed—Jim Charteris in the 880 (1925); Herman Brix in the shot put (1927); Rufus Kiser, the mile in 1928; Steve Anderson, the low hurdles in 1929 and the high hurdles in 1930; Paul Jessup in the discus throw in 1930; and Eddie Genung, in the 880 in 1931. Anderson equaled the world record in the 110 yard high hurdles five times from 1928 to 1930. Brix established the world record for the shot put in 1928 and again in 1932. Paul Jessup shattered the world record in the discus throw in 1930. Seven of his athletes participated in the Olympic Games and three—Anderson, Brix, and Pope—won medals. In his 35-year track and field coaching career, his teams won three Pacific Coast Conference titles and finished second in the NCAA meet in 1929 and 1930. In 1927, the Huskies were third, fourth in 1928, and fifth in 1921.

Starting in 1921, he built champions in basketball. In his 27 years as head coach, he gained more national recognition than in track. His teams won three Pacific Coast Conference championships and 10 Northern Division titles, including five straight from 1928 to 1932. Six of his players won All-America honors. He recorded more wins—488—than any other coach in Husky history. He won 71.5 percent of the games he coached, giving him the highest winning percentage among Husky basketball coaches. At the time of his selection to the Helms Foundation Hall of Fame, Edmundson was the only coach to be inducted in two sports. He was selected to the Husky Hall of Fame as a charter member in 1979.

Edmundson introduced several major innovations in the game of basketball. His love of running led to fast paced "race horse" basketball style. It was made possible by his remarkable talent for training athletes. "Get them in condition and let them run and wear out the other fellow," was the by-word of Hec's teams. He was the first coach to teach the one-hand shot. He and Husky baseball coach, Tubby Graves, established the Washington State high school basketball tournament. He also originated the "hands-in-the-huddle" of the starting five just before the tip-off of a game, a show of teamwork used universally now.

Besides the championships and his athletes' records and honors, Edmundson is remembered for his personal philosophy. He considered athletics the means to an end. In a speech at a high school athletic banquet, he said: "Long after you leave school, your coach will be following you with the very same interest that he has shown while he has taught you. He'll be very proud of your achievements—in athletics, in business, in home life. And most important he'll be greatly disappointed should you ever fail in citizenship."

As great a favorite as Edmundson was with Husky athletes, colleagues, and fans, a Portland sportswriter, Marlowe Branagan believed "...(Hec) belongs to all who appreciate keen and honest competition." Any wonder they renamed the Washington Pavilion the Clarence S. "Hec" Edmundson Pavilion on January 16, 1948.

Super Legend

Al Ulbrickson

"The Huskies are sprinting and pulling away. They've got open water." That's how Keith Jackson, then KOMO sports director, called the finish of the last race Al Ulbrickson coached. On July 19, 1958, the Huskies beat the powerful Trud Club of Leningrad on the Khiminskoe Reservoir outside of Moscow.

"Open water," could be used to describe many of the races won by Ulbrickson coached crews. Dick Erickson, a member of the victorious 1958 crew and Husky head coach from 1968-1987, said: "Hiram Conibear gets credit for developing the Washington stroke but Al Ulbrickson is the guy who made it work." Ulbrickson forged a record unequaled in not only Husky history but in collegiate history. In 31 seasons as head coach, his Husky varsity crews won six Intercollegiate Rowing Association national championships; the junior varsity crews won 10; freshmen boats 12. Washington crews won all three events in the regatta in 1936, 1937, 1948, and 1950. Only Navy and Cornell swept the three races during Ulbrickson's coaching career but managed to do it only once. In the annual dual regatta against traditional rival California, Ulbrickson's varsity crews won 21 of 28 races.

Ulbrickson's love for rowing started when he was in high school. His family had moved to Mercer Island and there was no high school on the island at the time. Lake Washington had no floating bridge. So young Al set out each morning in a row boat to cross the lake and walk a mile to catch a trolley to Franklin High School in Seattle. He entered Washington in the fall of 1922 and decided to turn out for Rusty Callow's crew program. When he stroked the Husky freshmen crew to a second-place finish at the IRA regatta in 1923, he showed a hint of his brilliant future. The next year, as the stroke of Rusty Callow's varsity crew, he led the Huskies to the IRA championship. In his senior year in 1926, he showed his determination and fortitude. In the last half of the IRA varsity race, he tore a shoulder muscle but kept rowing on to stroke the Washington boat to another national championship.

At the end of his undergraduate days, he had distinguished himself as a student-athlete and was elected to the scholastic honorary, Phi Beta Kappa. After graduation in 1926, he immediately started his coaching career. Callow hired him as the freshmen crew coach. After Callow resigned in 1927 to go to the University of Pennsylvania, Ulbrickson, at the age of 25, was named Washington's head coach. He was the youngest person to be named as a head crew coach. He would later become the first living coach to be admitted to the Helms Foundation Rowing Hall of Fame.

His first years of head coaching met with little success. He faced two huge hurdles. First, his style was not his own. It was basically what Callow had taught him—in essence the style remembered by Conibear's oarsmen. Second, he gained little authority because of his age. Changes were needed. Ulbrickson, with the advice of his freshmen coach, Tom Bolles, and boat builder and counselor George Pocock, began to make changes to the Washington Stroke. Over the five-year period, starting in 1931, the record of Washington's crews steadily improved, culminating in the gold medal victory in the 1936 Olympics. Ulbrickson was honored as the 1936 Seattle's Sports Man of the Year.

His biggest triumphs came on the international scene. In addition to the 1936 victory, his oarsmen won the gold medal in the four-oared, with coxswain, event in the 1948 London Olympics. Another four with cox, including his son Al, captured a bronze medal in the 1952 Helsinki Olympics. In the last race of his coaching career, his 1958 varsity eight staged one of the greatest upsets in rowing history by beating the powerful Trud Rowing Club of Leningrad, on the Khiminskoe Reservoir outside of Moscow. This victory was the one Ulbrickson enjoyed the most.

Ulbrickson retired at the age of 55, a decision that was very difficult after 31 years of coaching. The man who demanded perfection in others was retiring because he could no longer demand perfection of himself. After Ulbrickson died in 1980, Dick Erickson summed up Ulbrickson's career very well when he said: "Al Ulbrickson will remembered in rowing the same as Vince Lombardi in football and John Wooden in basketball." No wonder he led the balloting among the nine individuals and his 1936 crew who were charter members of the Husky Hall of Fame.

1930-39

Husky Moment

First Pacific Coast Conference Basketball Championship

On March 9, 1931, Washington won its first PCC basketball title by beating California in a hard-fought three-game series. All games were played at the Pavilion. On March 6, the Huskies easily won the opener, 41-25. The next night, the Bears were victors, 36-34. Washington won the decisive third game, 42-30. The Huskies took an early lead, 13-4, with John "Shoveling" Fuller hitting a variety of underhand, overhand, side arm and backhand shots. Cal scrambled back to tie the score at half-time, 20-20. In the second half, Washington opened up the lead to 38-26, with six minutes to go. Cal was whistled for 19 fouls to the Huskies' three. Washington converted 14 foul shots to seal the margin of victory. Fuller led the Huskies with 17 points and Ned Nelson played the game of his career at guard. Captain Henry Swanson, Ralph Cairney, and Kline Swygard rounded out the starting five on this history setting team. Swanson and Cairney were chosen to the All-Pacific Coast Conference team. The low scores, in the 1930s and before, were due, in part, to a center jump after each field goal.

1931 Tyee

The 1931 basketball team, Washington's first Pacific Coast Conference champions.

Husky Spotlight

Ralph Cairney was a six-time letterwinner—three in basketball (1930-32), two in track and field (1930, 1932) and one in football (1930). He set a Washington record in the javelin throw (185' 10"). In basketball, he earned national recognition. As a guard, he was a two-time (1931, 1932) All-Pacific Coast Conference selection and an All-America in 1932. He was team captain in 1932 and led the Huskies to three straight Northern Division championships and to their first Pacific Coast Conference title in 1931. Cairney was the only Husky selected on the all-time PCC first team, selected in 1948 by the Helms Foundation. He was elected ASUW president, as well as the most popular man on campus, in the spring of 1932. He was selected the outstanding student in the College of Business Administration. Cairney became a member of the Husky Hall of Fame in 1984. (He is third from the left in the top row of this 1931 team picture).

Husky Highlight

Talbot Hartley, the 1931 track captain, ran the fourth fastest time, 48.8, in the world in the 440 yard dash in 1931. In the same year, he finished fourth in the NCAA meet and third in the national AAU meet. Hartley was elected to the Husky Hall of Fame in 1998. There were only sufficient funds to send the varsity and freshmen crews to the IRA. championship. On June 26, 1931, the frosh boat won Washington's first Freshmen IRA title. For the first three miles, the Husky varsity shell rowed a beautiful race. Because of a late start, the tide from the Atlantic Ocean began to come in, changing the currents of the Hudson River. In the last part of the course, Navy was aided by more favorable water. The river was flowing downstream and down the middle of the course where Navy was rowing and upstream near the shore where Washington was positioned. Navy closed to win the four-miler; Cornell nosed the Huskies for second.

Husky Legend

Paul Schwegler

UW Media Relations

Paul Schwegler was a three-time football letterman (1929-31). From Raymond, Washington, he initially went to Northwestern University in his freshman year but returned to Washington after a very brief stay. The Huskies were glad he returned, because he became one the best tackles in Washington history. He was a two-time All-America tackle in 1930 and 1931. He was also an All-Pacific Coast Conference selection in those years. Stanford's Pop Warner rated Schwegler as one of the four best tackles in the country. In 1931, he was the Husky captain and won the Flaherty Award as the team's most inspirational player. Schwegler played in the East-West Shrine game and was picked as the contest's defensive star. He was elected to the National Football Foundation College Hall of Fame in 1967, and became a member of the Husky Hall of Fame in 1983.

HUSKY LIST

There are 20 basketball players who were selected two or more times to All-Conference (Pacific Coast Conference and its successors) or All-Coast teams.

Irving Cook	1919, 1920	Guard
Henry Swanson	1930, 1931	Forward
Ralph Cairney	1930, 1931	Guard
Hal Lee	1933, 1934	Guard
Bob Galer	1934, 1935	Forward
Bill Morris	1943, 1944	Guard
Jack Nichols	1947, 1948	Center
Sammy White	1948, 1949	Forward
Frank Guisness	1951, 1952	Forward
Bob Houbregs	1951, 1952, 1953	Center
Dean Parsons	1954, 1955	Forward
Doug Smart	1957, 1958, 1959	Center
Bill Hanson	1960, 1961, 1962	Center
James Edwards	1976, 1977	Center
Detlef Schrempf	1984, 1985	Forward
Chris Welp	1985, 1986, 1987	Center
Eldridge Recasner	1988, 1989, 1990	Guard
Mark Sanford	1996, 1997	Forward
Todd MacCulloch	1998, 1999	Center
Deon Luton	2000	Guard

HUSKY LORE

CAPTAIN and third baseman, Bill Hutchinson led the Huskies to their third consecutive Northern Division baseball title in 1931. The Pacific Coast Conference did not have Conference playoffs between the Northern and Southern Division champions until 1947. After playing for the San Francisco Missions of the Pacific Coast League, Hutchinson was invited to try out for the Pittsburgh Pirates. He chose medical school instead and became a very successful surgeon. He started the Pacific Northwest Research Center in 1955. Almost 20 years later, he opened the larger Fred Hutchinson Cancer Research Center. The center was named after his brother, the famous Detroit Tiger pitcher. Bill Hutchinson was elected to the Husky Hall of Fame in 1995.

1932 Tyee

Husky Moment

Fifth Consecutive Northern Division Basketball Title

On Jan. 8, 1932, over 6,500 fans turned out in the Pavilion to see the defending Pacific Coast champions open their conference schedule. Oregon State, coached by Slats Gill, beat the Huskies in overtime, 26-24. The Huskies led, 23-22, in regulation when OSC's lanky Ed Lewis let fly well beyond midcourt with a wild shot that went in. Husky Captain Ralph Cairney tied the score, 24-24, with a foul shot in the closing seconds. In the overtime session, Howard Merrill looped one through the net in the final minute to clinch the OSC win. Washington rebounded with a win the next night, 30-27. On Feb. 26 and 27, Washington met Washington State, led by captain and All-Coast guard, Art McLarney, in the final Northern Division games to determine the title. WSC led the division by one game. Washington won the first game, 32-25, before the largest crowd—10,500—ever assembled, to that point, in the Pavilion. The Huskies' fast-breaking style took the fire out of Coach Friel's WSC squad, who employed a slow, deliberate style of play. Winning their 13th straight conference game on the next night, 44-38, the Huskies won the Northern Division title for the fifth consecutive year. On March 4 and 5, 1932, they lost a chance to gain their second straight PCC title by losing to California, in the Oakland Auditorium, 22-21 and 36-24. In the first game, Cal's Jack Reed hit a shot with 15 seconds left. In the second game, Cal was up 22-8 at half-time and breezed to the victory. The Huskies missed 15 foul shots during the game. Ralph Cairney and Ned Nelson played all 80 minutes in their final games as Huskies.

The 1932 basketball team, wins Washington's fifth straight Northern Division title.

1932 Tyee

Husky Spotlight

Merle Hufford was a three-year halfback on the 1929-31 football teams. He was outstanding on Coach Bagshaw's last team in 1929—a dismal 2-6-1 season. He starred on Coach Jim Phelan's first football team in 1930. Hufford was named All-Coast and All-America in 1929. He was elected to the Husky Hall of Fame in 1990.

In 1931, Ned Nelson became the first Husky baseball All-America. As Washington's first baseman, he led the Huskies to three straight Northern Division titles (1930-32). He was a three-year starter on the basketball team and a member of Washington's first Pacific Coast Conference championship team in 1931. He was elected to the Husky Hall of Fame in 1989.

UW Media Relations

Ned Nelson

Husky Highlight

Led by Captain Lloyd Nordstom, the 1932 Husky tennis team was unbeaten against collegiate opponents. Nordstrom was a three-year letter winner. With his brothers, Elmer and Everett, Nordstrom developed a shoe store, started by his father, John, into a major fashion clothing chain. The Nordstrom Tennis Center, north of Husky Stadium, was built by a very generous gift of the Lloyd Nordstrom family. It was dedicated on June 1, 1989.

1932 Tyee

Lloyd Nordstrom

UW Media Relations

Husky Legend

Edwin Genung

Eddie Genung was an outstanding middle distance runner for Hec Edmundson's nationally ranked track and field teams in 1929-1931. He was captain in 1931. With Steve Anderson and Paul Jessup, Genung helped the Huskies achieve their best national finish ever—second in 1929—in the NCAA meet. He was the national collegiate 880 champion in 1929. He won three straight national American Amateur Union 880 titles (1930-32). In the AAU meet in 1931, he set a new American record of 1:53.4. He was the top American 800-meter runner in the 1932 Los Angeles Olympics. Genung finished fourth in 1:51.7, missing the bronze medal by two-tenths of second. The first two finishers—Hampton of Great Britain and Wilson of Canada—cracked the 1:50 barrier. Genung was elected to the Husky Hall of Fame in 1982.

Husky List

Pac-10 (and its predecessor conferences) Top 10 All-Tme Winningest Coaches
(based on number of wins in conference games only through the 2001 season)

Coach (school, years)	Wins	Losses	Pct.
John Wooden, UCLA, 1949-75	304	74	.810
Amory "Slats" Gill, Oregon State, 1929-64	276	241	.534
Clarence S. "Hec" Edmundson, Washington, 1921-47	266	146	.646
Lute Olson, Arizona, 1984-present	253	71	.781
Jack Friel, Washington State, 1929-58	232	257	.474
Ralph Miller, Oregon State, 1971-89	204	106	.658
Clarence "Nibs" Price, California, 1924-54	192	138	.582
Marv Harshman, Washington State, 1959-71, Washington, 1972-85	176	177	.499
Mike Montgomery, Stanford, 1986-present	170	100	.630
George Raveling, Washington State, 1973-83, USC,1987-94	140	178	.440

Husky Lore

THE nation's depression plunged higher education institutions into a serious crisis. Shrinking tax collections diminished tax receipts for the University of Washington operating funds by over $300,000 in the academic year, 1931-32. President Spencer declared the University was going on "bread and water rations." Subsequently, the Board of Regents slashed salaries and wages by 32 percent. Athletic activities were adversely affected, particularly the minor sports and some of the major sports. For example, there were no Pacific Coast Conference track and field championships from 1929-1935. Some freshmen and minor sports were only sustained through volunteer services of coaches and managers.

Husky Moment

Crew Wins National Sprint Championship

In 1933, Husky crews were unbeaten. In seven races, no varsity, junior varsity, or freshmen crew failed to finish first. The depression was at its worst and the annual Intercollegiate Rowing Association regatta was canceled. On April 8, 1933, on the Oakland Estuary, the Husky crews swept Cal in all three races. The varsity won by seven lengths over a three-mile course. In the most exciting race of the day, the junior varsity edged Cal by a few feet. The freshmen won the two-mile event, beating the Cal yearlings by two-and-a-half lengths. A week later, at Long Beach, California, the Husky varsity and frosh crews raced over the 1932 Olympics' 2000-meter course, defeating Cal and UCLA. The varsity won in 6:30; the freshmen in 6:50.2. A Washington four-oared crew, rowing in a Japanese shell left from the Olympics, won a third event. On July 8, Long Beach was the site of the national intercollegiate sprint championship and Yale was favored to win. Its crew was coached by former Husky oarsman and coach, Ed Leader. Yale had a slight lead at 1000 meters. Washington upped its stroke to 34-35 and, at about the 1500-meter mark, gained a slight lead. In front of the finish stands filled with a screaming crowd, Yale and Washington raced bow to bow. Then the Huskies, with a bit more power in their stroke, edged inches ahead, then a few feet ahead, and finally by six feet to beat Yale, in 6:38.8. Cornell finished third and Harvard fourth.

1934 Tyee

The 1933 crew wins the national sprint championship.

Husky Spotlight

In its first year of intercollegiate competition and participating as a minor sport, the Husky men's swimming team beat Idaho, Washington State, and the Bremerton Swim Club. Washington lost only to the nationally acclaimed Washington Athletic Club Swim team, coached by Ray Daughters. The team trained in a pool in the women's physical education building and traveled to their meets in private cars. Charles Mucha, a standout football player, from 1932-1934, was the team's leading swimmer.

John Cherberg lettered in football for three seasons (1930-1932), playing halfback, fullback, and quarterback. He was the Flaherty Medal winner, as the team's most inspirational player, in 1932. He served as a Husky assistant football coach, from 1946 to 1952, and head coach from 1953 to 1955. Cherberg was elected as the state's Lieutenant Governor in 1957 and served for 32 years, spanning five governors. He was elected to the Husky Hall of Fame in 1981.

Husky Highlight

On Dec. 10, 1932, Washington played in a football game for charity. A group of former college players, banded together as the West Seattle Athletic Club Yellowjackets, challenged the 5-2-2 Huskies to a "city championship" game. Over 3,200 fans paid to see this event, with all proceeds going to needy families. The day before the game, the stadium field had turned into an ice rink because of freezing temperatures. Washington's coach Jim Phelan went out and bought tennis shoes for all his players to provide better traction than football cleats. Phelan had his troops warm up in football shoes. Just before the kickoff, the players put on the tennis shoes. The Huskies rolled up a 66-0 half-time lead as the Yellowjackets went slip sliding all around the field. During the half-time break, the West Seattle outfit rounded up some tennis flats. In a shortened second half, both teams went scoreless.

Husky Legend

Dave Nisbet

UW Media Relations

Dave Nisbet was a first-team All-America end in 1932. He was selected for his blocking, defensive skills, and punt blocking abilities. He was an All-Pacific Coast Conference selection in 1931 and 1932. He was a second-team All-American in 1931. Players on the national championship Southern California team, selected him to their all-opponent's team in 1931. He played in the summer 1933 East-West All-Star game, on Soldier's Field in Chicago, and blocked two punts. In the second quarter, he blocked his first punt, off the foot of Ohio State's Wes Fesler, scooped the ball up and ran 15 yards for the only West touchdown. Husky teammate, Merle Hufford, rushed for 20 yards in a substitute role. The East won 13-7. In 1950, he was picked on the all-time Husky football team, for the first 50 years of the 20th century, receiving the third highest number of votes. Only George Wilson, from the mid-twenties, and Walt Harrison, who played in 1940-42, got more votes. Nisbet was elected to the Husky Hall of Fame in 1988.

HUSKY LIST

In Husky football history, the top passing records for a career, a season, and a single game are:

Category	Player	Years	Record
Most passsing yards			
Career	Brock Huard	1996-98	5,742
Season	Cary Conklin	1989	2,569
Game	Cary Conklin	1989	428 against Arizona State
Passing yards per game			
Career	Sonny Sixkiller	1970-72	196.3 (5,496 yards in 28 games)
Season	Cary Conklin	1989	233.5 (2,569 yards in 11 games)
Pass completions			
Career	Steve Pelluer	1980-83	436
Season	Steve Pelleur	1983	213
Game	Brock Huard	1998	33 against USC
	Tim Cowan	1982	33 against Maryland
Completion percentage			
Career	Tom Flick	1976-80	.603 (252 out of 418)
Season	Steve Pelleur	1980-83	.672 (213 out of 317)
Game	Tom Flick	1980	.941 (16 out of 17) against Arizona
Most touchdown passes			
Career	Brock Huard	1996-98	51
Season	Brock Huard	1997	23
Game	Chris Rowland	1973	5 against California

HUSKY LORE

IN 1933, minor sports enjoyed one of their most successful years. The wrestling, swimming, fencing, rifle and golf teams made a clean sweep of all but two events included on their collective schedules. Captain Don Cook won the National Intercollegiate individual rifle title for the second consecutive year. Fencing was recognized as a minor sport in 1933. A Washington fencing team had competed intercollegiately in 1929. Coached by August Auernheimer, his teams captured 13 consecutive Northern Division titles and won 36 of 39 matches. Fencing was discontinued in 1941. The men's rifle team again won the national championship against 500 universities and colleges.

1934 Tyee

1933 W 1934

Husky Moment

Second Pacific Coast Conference Basketball Title

Led by Captain Hal Lee and Bob "Goose" Galer, Washington recorded a 14-2 conference record to win the Northern Division. They faced Southern California in the Los Angeles Olympic Auditorium for the Pacific Coast Conference title. The stronger and taller USC squad was heavily favored. On March 9, 1934, USC took the opener, 27-25. USC was led by center Lee "Rubber Legs" Guttero who scored 17 points. Washington's tallest player, center Clyde Wagner, was sick before the game and could only defend Guttero for a few minutes before leaving the game. The next night, Washington, with a weakened Wagner playing only a few minutes, won the second contest, 43-41, in overtime. Guttero scored 19 points but fouled out just before the overtime session. The Huskies led in regulation, 37-35, but USC's Foss sank a field goal at the buzzer. Galer led all Husky scorers with 16. On March 12, Lee and Galer put on a dazzling display of offense and defense in leading the Huskies to a 34-30 win in the third game. The Trojans led at half time, 16-9. With Wagner back in the lineup and holding Guttero in check, the Huskies battled back to tie the score, 24-24, with a little more than seven minutes to go. Then Wagner fouled out and Captain Lee moved to the center position. Galer hit a spectacular overhead shot to put the Huskies up, 26-24. It stayed close in the final minutes with Washington going up 30-27 with about four minutes to play. With 90 seconds to play, USC came within one point, 31-30. Then, Lee hit a foul shot and in the last 30 seconds. Galer captured an offensive rebound and put a shot right back up to put Washington safely ahead, 34-30. Galer and Lee finished with 13 points a piece, Wagner held Guttero to nine, and Washington won its second Pacific Coast Conference championship.

Jack Hanover passes to Bob Galer as Huskies beat USC for the Pacific Coast Conference championship.

1934 Tyee

Husky Spotlight

Hal Lee played on the Husky basketball teams in 1932-1934. He was an All-Pacific Coast Conference selection in 1933 and 1934. He was an All-America basketball guard in 1934, the only West Coast player selected. As a centerfielder, he earned three letters, consistently batting over .300, in 1932 and 1933, and hitting .400 in his senior year. He was captain of the 1934 Pacific Coast Conference basketball champions. Lee was the first recipient of the Hec Edmundson most inspirational player award in 1934. He was inducted in the Husky Hall of Fame in 1987.

Husky Highlight

Bill Smith was an end on the Husky football team from 1931-1933. In 1933, he was team captain and earned All-Pacific Coast Conference and All-America honors. On the 1933 team that went 5-4-0 and ended up seventh in the conference, Smith was the second leading scorer in the conference. He scored 36 points as an end and place kicker. Smith handed Stanford a 6-0 loss in 1933 by kicking two field goals. It was Stanford's only regular-season loss in three seasons (1933-1935). The starting Husky 11 played the entire Stanford game. Smith was elected to the Husky Hall of Fame in 1991.

UW Media Relations

Husky Legend

Bob "Goose" Galer

Bob Galer broke the Northern Division season scoring record in 1934. His mark of 176 points—before the center jump after each field goal was discontinued—broke the old record set in 1933 by Ed Lewis of Oregon State. In Galer's three years (1933-1935) as a starting forward, he was a two-time All-Coast selection and an All-America in 1935. He was the 1935 team captain and received the team's Hec Edmundson most inspirational award that year. Galer was named to the second team on the all-time Pacific Coast Conference selections by the Helms Foundation in 1948. He was a Marine Corps fighter pilot in World War II and received the Congressional Medal of Honor for his heroic conduct in the Solomon Islands in the Pacific. Galer was inducted into the Husky Hall of Fame in 1981.

HUSKY LIST

There have been 12 Husky basketball players selected to All-America teams.

Irving Cook	**1920**	**Guard**
Alfie James	**1928**	**Guard**
Ralph Cairney	**1931**	**Guard**
Hal Lee	**1934**	**Guard**
Bob Galer	**1935**	**Forward**
Bob Egge	**1936**	**Guard**
Bill Morris	**1943**	**Guard**
Jack Nichols	**1948**	**Center**
Bob Houbregs	**1953**	**Center (only consensus All- America, NCAA Player of the Year)**
Steve Hawes	**1971, 1972**	**Center**
Louie Nelson	**1973**	**Guard**
James Edwards	**1976**	**Center**

THE Husky Marching Band featured a jazz program, for the first time, in Washington's football game against Oregon on Oct. 14, 1933. During half-time, they played "The Tiger Rag," featuring two outstanding drummers. On the night before, the students staged a torchlight rally parade that swept up University Avenue. Flares went off at 6:30 p.m. to herald over five hours of celebration, ending with the final strains of an eight-piece orchestra playing at a football mixer in the women's gymnasium. The parade featured the Husky band and a police escort of eight cars of dignitaries, including the mayors of Seattle and Portland. Evidently, the rally, the dance, and the jazz performance were the best part of the weekend. The Huskies lost, 6-0.

1934 W 1935

Husky Moment

Husky Swimmer Sets World Records

Jack Medica established world records in the 440-yard and 1500-yard freestyle races and won the 220-yard race as well. These performances by the Husky co-captain gave Washington a second-place tie with Yale University in the NCAA meet in late March 1935. He swam the 440 in a world mark of 4:42.5. He set the world record of 18:59.3 in the 1500 freestyle and established an NCAA record (2:11.5) in winning the 220. At the conclusion of the meet, Medica was acclaimed by the National Coaches Association as the greatest college swimmer in the nation. Later in the year, Medica, at the national AAU indoor meet in New York, set a world record—5:16.3—in the 500-yard freestyle, bettering his own world record by more than 10 seconds. He set a new AAU indoor record—2:10.8—in winning the 220 event. In the 1934 national meet, he also won the 220, 440, and 1500 freestyle events. Medica's performances in 1934, along with Peter Dix's sixth place in the 150-yard backstroke, earned Washington a third-place tie with Yale in the NCAA meet. In 1934, Medica and Charles Mucha led Washington to its first Northern Division title besting Oregon, 44-30.

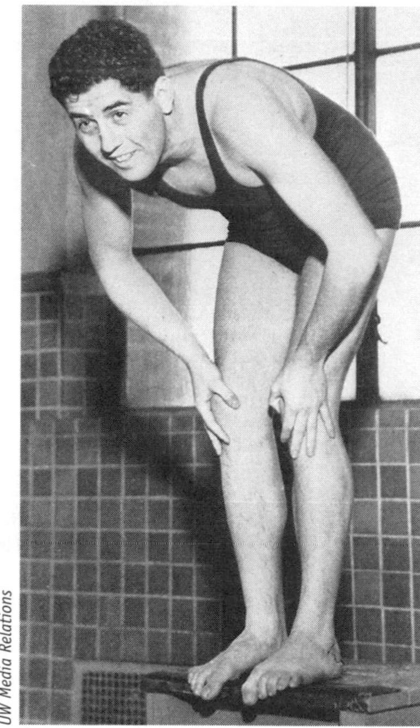

UW Media Relations

Husky Spotlight

After four mediocre seasons, the 1934 football team finished 6-1-1 and third in the conference, losing only to Stanford (24-0) and playing a scoreless tie with Washington State. In Los Angeles, they beat USC for the first time since 1923, 14-7. Ice hockey returned, as a minor sport, after a ten-year absence. Washington won its first intercollegiate series beating the University of British Columbia ice men, two games to one (3-4, 2-1, 8-4). The team was coached by Donald MacKenzie, a business school faculty member. The Business School's administration and faculty building was named after him in 1960.

In the inaugural University of Washington Invitational Ski Tournament, Husky skiers easily defeated competitors from the University of British Columbia and the College of Puget Sound.

Husky Highlight

Three Washington crews rowed in the Intercollegiate Rowing Association regatta in 1935. For the fourth time at Poughkeepsie, a Husky junior varsity crew won, beating Navy by two lengths over the three-mile course, in 14:58.8. For the third time, a Washington freshmen crew won. The frosh beat Cal by more than a length in 10:29 over the two-mile course. The varsity, after leading throughout much of the four-mile race, could not withstand the terrific finish of Cal and Cornell. Cal won, Cornell was second, and Washington third. Cal's time was 18:52 over four miles, the second fastest time in IRA history, up to that point.

1936 Tyee

Husky Legend

Jack Medica

Jack Medica was Washington's first All-America swimmer and first Olympic gold medalist in an individual event. He is the only athlete in Husky history to win three Olympic medals—one gold and two silvers. Medica earned All-America recognition nine times as an unbeatable NCAA freestyle champion. He won NCAA individual titles in the 220-yard freestyle, the 440, and the 1500 events in the NCAA Swimming Championships in 1934, 1935, and 1936, and was voted the most outstanding swimmer in all three NCAA meets. In addition to his collegiate honors, he won 12 national indoor and outdoor American Amateur Union titles from 1933 to 1939, 11 while in college. Medica won titles in six freestyle events—150 meters, 220 yards, 440 yards, 500 meters, 880 yards and one mile. He was co-captain of the 1934 Husky swim team, captain in 1935, and by the end of his collegiate career, he held every school record from 100 yards on up to the mile event. He established collegiate records in the 220, 440, and 1500 meters, and world records in the 440-yard and 1500-meter events and national records in the 220. In the 1936 Berlin Olympics, he won the gold medal in the 400-meter freestyle. Japan's Shumpei Uto had a length lead after 300 meters. Medica cut the lead to about three feet with 50 meters to go and then unleashed a powerful sprint to set an Olympic record, 4:44.5. He took the silver in the 1500 meters. Medica also won another silver medal as a member of the U.S. 800-meter freestyle relay team. He was the only U.S. swimmer to win a gold medal in the 1936 Olympics. In 1958, he was inducted into the Helms Foundation Swimming Hall of Fame. In 1981, he was elected to the Husky Hall of Fame.

HUSKY LIST

Six Husky swimmers have won Olympic medals. All competed for the United States.

Swimmer	Year	Event	Medal
Jack Medica	1936	400 M Freestyle	Gold
		1500 M Freestyle	Silver
		800 M Freestyle Relay	Silver
Lynn Colella	1972	200 M Butterfly	Silver
Rick DeMont	1972	400 M Freestyle	Gold*
Doug Northway	1972	1500 M Freestyle	Bronze
Robin Backhaus	1972	200 M Butterfly	Bronze
Rick Colella	1976	200 M Breaststroke	Bronze

*** Medal taken away because DeMont took a prescribed asthma medication that included a banned substance.**

HUSKY LORE

LEE SIEG began his 13-year tenure, as president of the University of Washington, on Aug. 1, 1934. He and his family took up residence in the presidential mansion on Thirty Sixth Avenue in Madison Park. Built in 1906 and named Hillcrest, it was the home of Mr. and Mrs. Edwin Gardner Ames and Mrs. Ames' parents, Mr. and Mrs. William Walker. Hillcrest was bequested, by the Walker Ames families, to the University in 1931, for the president's residence. In March 1932, University President Lyle Spencer and his family moved into the beautiful, brick colonial home. Remodeled at various times, it has been the home of University presidents ever since. Many university functions are held there each year. It can handle up to 400 guests comfortably in standup parties.

1935 W 1936

Husky Moment

Husky Crew Wins Olympic Gold

Washington's varsity eight won the gold medal in the 1936 Berlin Olympics. On Aug. 12, in Grunau, Germany, outside of Berlin, rowing in the "Husky Clipper," Washington started off by setting a world record for 2000 meters—6:00.8. The victors had to hold off a great British boat to win by about 20 feet. On Aug. 14, 1936, six boats lined up in the finals. Germany and Italy were put in the favorable lanes, protected from strong quartering winds for the first half of the race. Don Hume, the stroke, had been confined to bed for several days before the preliminary heat. He had a cold so severe it was close to pneumonia. Gordon Adam, number three oarsman, also had a very bad cold. So with a sick man in the stroke's seat, a stiff cross wind, and the coxswain's inability to hear the starter's call because of the wind, the Huskies started in last place. In the first quarter of the race, the Italians and German crews jumped out to a substantial lead. Bob Moch, the Husky coxswain, tried to get the ailing Hume to raise the stroke. It was apparent that Hume, in his weakened condition, could not hear Moch's exhortations and could not respond to Moch's commands. With about 600 meters remaining, Washington was behind the Italian and German boats by about a length—almost an impossible situation. Then, the leaders faced the winds and Hume miraculously responded. The stroke beat went higher and higher. The Husky crew passed the Brits, then the Swiss, then Hungary. Then they passed the German crew, much to the dismay of the screaming Nazi crowd. As the Italian and U.S. boats swept into the last 50 meters, Bob Moch rapped furiously on the side of the shell with the handles of the tiller ropes, shouting "now, now, now." The stroke went to 40 and the exhausted Italians could not match the punishing pace. With about five strokes left, the Husky crew passed the Italians and won the gold by about eight feet!

UW Media Relations

The 1936 crew winning the gold medal in the 1936 Olympics.

Husky Spotlight

The 1936 Husky basketball team placed higher than any collegiate team in the U.S. Olympic Trials. After losing the Pacific Coast Conference playoff to Stanford—led by Hank Luisetti—Washington was invited to the Olympic Trials regional tournament. Washington first beat USC, the Southern Division runner-up, 41-27, and Oregon State, second in the Northern Division, beat Stanford, 33-23. On the following night, March 26, Ed Loverich and Captain Ralph Bishop led Washington to victory over Oregon State, 35-29. Next was the final round in New York's Madison Square Garden to determine the team to represent the U.S. in the 1936 Olympics. Four college teams and four AAU squads were in the finals. In the first round, the Huskies beat Chicago's Depaul University, 54-33. Washington was the only college team to make it to the second round where they faced the National AAU champion, McPherson Oilers (from Kansas). The Huskies lost 48-30. They then beat Wilmerding (Pennsylvania), for third place, and won 48-33. Universal Pictures, the AAU runner-up, from Hollywood, won the tournament by edging McPherson, 44-43. The U.S. Olympic team included seven from the victorious Universal team, five from McPherson and one collegian, Husky center, Ralph Bishop. The U.S. team won the gold medal in the 1936 Olympics, defeating Canada in the title game, 19-8. The Huskies' Bob Egge was selected to the All-Pacific Coast Conference team and was an All-America first team guard. He was elected to the Husky Hall of Fame in 1988.

Husky Highlight

Byron Haines scored all the points in the football game against USC on Dec. 7, 1935, in Los Angeles. On the opening kickoff, the Trojan's Jim Sutherland, booted the ball short and it took some crazy bounces down to the Husky one-yard line. Haines picked the ball up, fumbled it, and picked it up again. Haines took off along the goal line to evade the horde of maroon jerseyed giants sweeping in on him. He was tackled in the end zone and USC had two quick points. In the second period, Washington took over on the USC 42-yard line after a Trojan punt went out of bounds. After getting a first down on the 25, Haines scampered through left guard for a Husky touchdown. On the day he was selected to the All-Coast team, Haines scored all eight points in the 6-2 Husky victory.

Husky Legend

1936 Varsity Crew

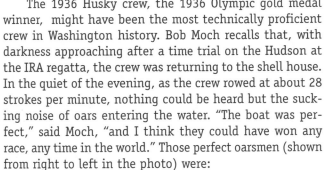

UW Media Relations

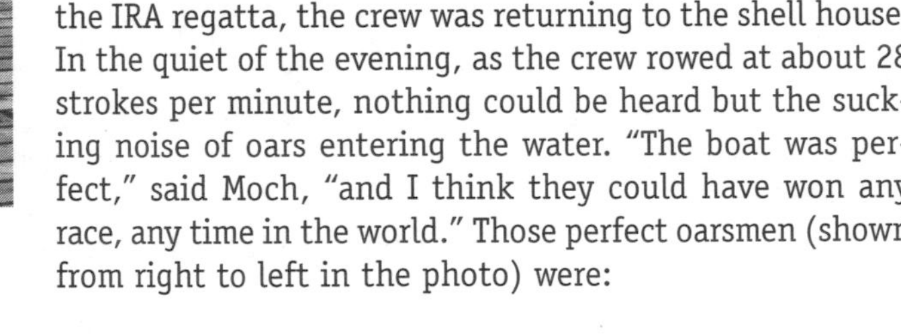

The 1936 Husky crew, the 1936 Olympic gold medal winner, might have been the most technically proficient crew in Washington history. Bob Moch recalls that, with darkness approaching after a time trial on the Hudson at the IRA regatta, the crew was returning to the shell house. In the quiet of the evening, as the crew rowed at about 28 strokes per minute, nothing could be heard but the sucking noise of oars entering the water. "The boat was perfect," said Moch, "and I think they could have won any race, any time in the world." Those perfect oarsmen (shown from right to left in the photo) were:

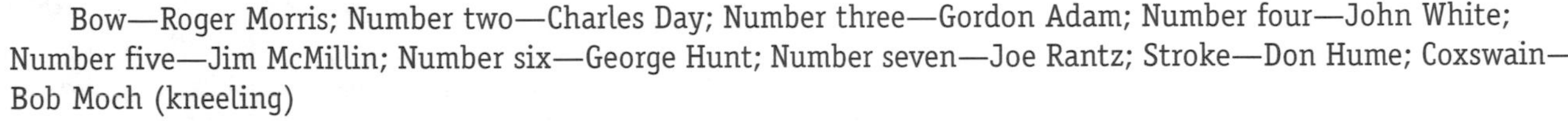

Bow—Roger Morris; Number two—Charles Day; Number three—Gordon Adam; Number four—John White; Number five—Jim McMillin; Number six—George Hunt; Number seven—Joe Rantz; Stroke—Don Hume; Coxswain—Bob Moch (kneeling)

The 1936 Olympic Gold Medal crew was the first team inducted in the Husky Hall of Fame in 1979. All the oarsmen were charter members, along with their coach, Al Ulbrickson.

Husky List

Husky oarsmen have won medals in the 1936, 1948, 1952, 1960, 1964, 1984, and 1996 Olympics. Their names and last year in which they rowed for Washington are:

1936 Eight —Gold medal
Gordon Adam, 1938
Charles Day, 1937
Donald Hume, 1938
George Hunt, 1937
James McMillin, 1937
Robert Moch, coxswain, 1936
Roger Morris, 1937
Joseph Rantz, 1937
John White, 1938

1948 Four with coxswain — Gold medal
Gordon Giovanelli, 1949
Robert Martin, 1948
Allen Morgan, coxswain, 1950
Warren Westlund, 1950
Robert Will, 1949

1952 Four with coxswain Bronze Medal
Phil Leanderson, 1953
Carl Lovsted, 1952
Albert Rossi, coxswain, 1952
Alvin Ulbrickson, 1952
Dick Wahlstrom, 1953

1960 Four without coxswain —Gold Medal
John Sayre, 1958

1964 Four with coxswain —Bronze Medal
Ted Mittet

1984 Four with coxswain Silver Medal
Al Forney, 1982
Ed Ives, 1983
John Stillings, 1978

1984 Eight —Gold Medal
Blair Horn (Canada), 1983
—Silver Medal
Charles Clapp, 1981

1996—Bronze Medal
Mark Schneider, lightweight four without coxswain, 1995

NOTE: Beginning in 1960, with the exception of the Navy eight in 1960, all oarsmen in U.S. Olympic boats were selected, in competition, from rowing clubs and national rowing teams. Generally, the oarsmen had completed their collegiate rowing career.

ON June 26, 1936, the Husky crews did what no crews had ever done before—they won all three Intercollegiate Rowing Association titles. It was the first time in the history of the IRA, that one university's crews won all three races. The freshmen boat won by one length over Cal in the two-mile race (10:10.6); the junior varsity by almost three lengths over Navy in the three miler (14:42.2). The varsity won the four-mile race in 19:09.6. They came from behind—to the cheer "Here Comes Washington"—to beat Cal by one length. In the U.S. Olympic Trials, over a 2000-meter course, they beat Pennsylvania, in an American record time of 6:04.8.

1936 W 1937

Husky Moment

Third Rose Bowl

Washington's football team won the Pacific Coast Conference title in 1936, compiling a 7-1-1 record. The only loss, 14-7, was in the season opener with Minnesota. The Huskies tied Stanford, 14-14, midway in the season. The team recorded five shutout victories leading up to the final regular season contest with Washington State. The winner would capture the conference title and a berth in the Rose Bowl. A Husky Stadium record crowd of almost 41,000 watched Washington race to another shutout win, 40-0. As Rose Bowl hosts, Washington, ranked fifth in the nation, could select its opponent. Most Rose Bowl officials and enthusiasts wanted Louisiana State, the top team in the South and ranked number two nationally, in order to set up a very prestigious bowl game. Coach Jim Phelan wanted Pittsburgh because he wanted to beat the great Pitt coach, Jock Sutherland. On New Year's day, Washington was favored over the Panthers, but Pitt scored a decisive victory, 21-0, in a game that was not nearly as close as the score indicated. Pitt's Bobby LaRue rushed for 118 of the Panther's 254 yards. Pitt held Washington to 57 yards on the ground and 96 in the air. Pitt scored in the first quarter on a 65-yard drive. In the third quarter, Pitt put together a 74-yard scoring march, featuring a 44-yard run by LaRue. Pittsburgh's final touchdown came in the fourth quarter, when All-America end, Bill Daddio, intercepted an attempted Husky lateral and ran 67 yards into the end zone. Daddio booted all three extra points. Washington's only serious scoring threat was in the second quarter when Fritz Waskowitz threw to Byron Haines for a 42-yard gain to the Pitt 20-yard line. The Huskies could go no further.

The Huskies line up before the 1937 Rose Bowl game against Pittsburgh.

1937 Tyee

Husky Spotlight

The Husky crews won all three Pacific Coast and Intercollegiate Rowing Association titles for the second consecutive year. At Poughkeepsie, on June 22, 1937, the freshmen crew led off with a victory over the two-mile course. It was the fourth straight IRA win for a Husky freshmen boat. For the third consecutive year, a Husky junior varsity crew won the IRA. In the three-mile race, the Huskies recorded a course record—13:44—shattering the old record by 34.2 seconds. The varsity crew included all the men who had won the Olympic gold medal in 1936, except for the coxswain, Bob Moch. Navy commanded the varsity race until the two and a half mile mark. Rowing perfectly, the Huskies swept past everybody by the three-mile mark and the race was for second place. Washington finished three lengths ahead of Navy, followed by Cornell, Syracuse, Cal, Columbia, and Wisconsin. Washington set a course record—18:33.6—2.2 seconds faster than the 1928 California crew that won the Olympic gold medal in Amsterdam.

Husky Highlight

Vic Palmason, the Ballard Beauty, won the 880-yard run in the 1937 Northern Division meet, setting a meet and school record. His mark of 1:51.5 was almost two seconds faster than Eddie Genung's former school record of 1:53.4. Palmason also won the Northern Division title in 1935. In the 1936 Pacific Coast Conference meet, the first held since 1928, Palmason finished inches behind Russ Bush of USC. Both runners were timed in a new meet record, 1:52.7. In 1936, he was one of the four best half milers in the country and was headed to the Olympic Trials. Unfortunately, he contracted a severe case of flu and could not make the Trials. In the 1937 PCC meet, he again finished behind USC's Bush, the Trojan runner lowering the meet record to 1:52.3.

Husky Legend

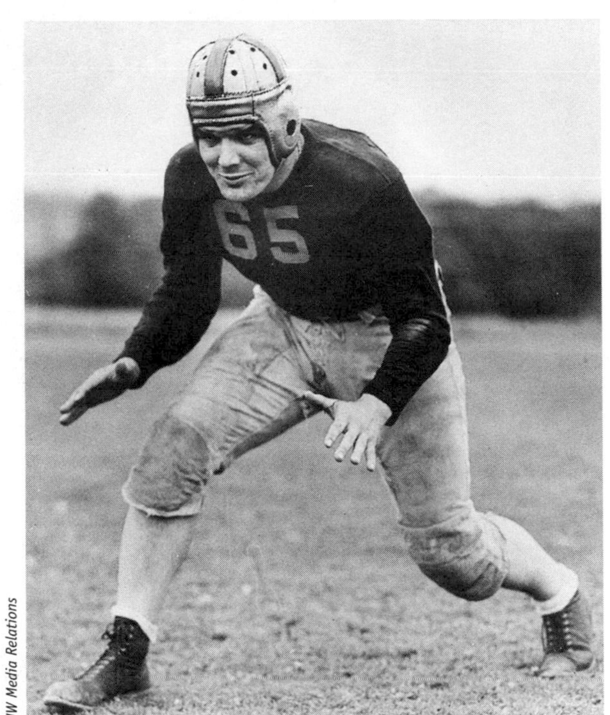
UW Media Relations

Max Starcevich

In 1936, Max Starcevich became Washington's third consensus football All-America. He was an All-Pacific Coast Conference selection in 1935 and 1936, despite only playing one year of high school football. He worked in a steel mill in his hometown, Duluth, Minnesota, after high school until he encountered job difficulties brought on by the depression. He decided to enter college and chose Washington with the help of Washington alumnus, Dr. Strauss. In his first Husky season, he played fullback and then switched to guard in 1935 and 1936. He played in the fourth Chicago All-Star game (1937) that pitted the defending NFL championship team against recently graduated college stars. The collegians were the first all-star team to beat the professionals. They downed the Green Bay Packers, 6-0. Starcevich was elected to the National Football Foundation College Football Hall of Fame in 1990 and the Husky Hall of Fame in 1989.

Husky List

At the end of the 1999 basketball season, the top 15 basketball programs (based on number of wins) among U.S. major schools were:

School	Year Started	Seasons	Won	Lost	Percent-age
Kentucky	1903	96	1745	537	.765
North Carolina	1910	89	1733	608	.740
Kansas	1899	100	1687	723	.700
Duke	1905	94	1583	755	.677
St. John's (NY)	1907	97	1579	714	.689
Temple	1894	103	1517	823	.648
Syracuse	1900	99	1498	703	.681
Pennsylvania	1902	97	1476	837	.638
Oregon State	1902	97	1469	1004	.594
Indiana	1901	98	1452	777	.651
UCLA	1919	80	1449	622	.700
Notre Dame	1898	94	1441	792	.645
Princeton	1901	98	1406	850	.623
Washington	1896	97	1403	906	.608
Utah	1908	91	1403	736	.656

Husky Lore

GLEN HUGHES joined the Washington faculty in 1919 and later became the head of the Drama Department. One of the first dramatic producers in the country to explore the possibilities of a circular theatre, Hughes and his drama students performed in the penthouse of the Meany Hotel. The name stuck when the Penthouse Theatre, the first building in the country designed as a theatre in the round, was built in the late 1930s. It was relocated east of the Observatory, near the old Denny Field, in 1992, and renamed the Glen Hughes Penthouse Theatre.

1939 Tyee

1937 W 1938

Husky Moment

Huskies Win Pineapple Bowl

In 1937, Washington had a regular-season record of 5-2-2 and finished third in the conference. In the last four games, the Huskies recorded three wins and a tie. They played number-one ranked California to a scoreless tie on Nov. 6, in Berkeley. Cal finished 9-0-1 and beat Alabama in the Rose Bowl. After the regular season ended, Hawaii beckoned with an invitation to play in the Pineapple Bowl on New Year's Day against the University of Hawaii. In front of 13,500 fans, Washington rolled to a 53-0 lead before Husky reserves mercifully allowed the Islanders two touchdowns late in the final period. The final score was 53-13. Washington scored four times in the opening quarter. The first score featured left halfback Jimmy Johnston's 15-yard run followed by a lateral to center Bud Ericksen who went the remaining 32 yards for the score. Johnston threw a 35-yard pass to end, Merle Miller, for the second touchdown in as many possessions. Minutes later, Johnston returned a punt 70 yards to the Hawaii two. Miller scored his second touchdown with a plunge up the middle. The Huskies' fourth score, in the first period, was set up by Johnston's 30-yard run to the one-yard line. Reserve fullback, Don Jones plunged over for the score. At the end of the first quarter, the Huskies had put the game out of reach, 26-0. In the second quarter, the Huskies' sixth touchdown featured halfback Joe Dubsky's 39-yard punt return to the Hawaii 11 where he lateraled to tackle, Rich Worthington, who rumbled for the touchdown. Washington led at half-time, 39-0. On Jan. 6, The Huskies completed their season with another win in Hawaii, a 35-6 rout of the Honolulu Townies. The game featured Al Cruver's three touchdowns and two conversions.

UW Media Relations

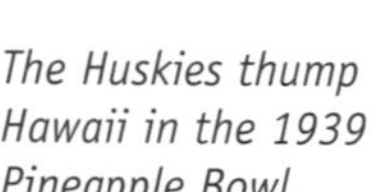

The Huskies thump Hawaii in the 1939 Pineapple Bowl.

Husky Spotlight

The 1938 basketball team finished one game behind Oregon in the Northern Division race and missed out on the Pacific Coast Conference playoffs. Oregon lost to Stanford, led by the great Hank Luisetti. Stanford finished the season with a 21-3 record. The Huskies finished the regular season with a 22-7 record. On spring vacation, they toured Hawaii, playing six games against weak opponents, outscoring them 415-126. In a seventh game, they beat the Luke Field Army All-Stars, 79-43. In two other games, not recorded in the season totals, they played multiple teams in each game. In one, they played a different team each half, winning 82-9. In the other, they played four teams—one each quarter—outscoring the diverse groups, 143-22.

Husky Highlight

The longest winning streak—26—in Husky basketball history started on Feb. 14, 1938, with a 37-29 win over Oregon State, in the Pavilion. The streak ended with a 30-20 home victory against Oregon State on Jan. 21, 1939. The streak started right after Oregon beat the Huskies, 56-53, on Feb. 8, 1938, in a game played in Eugene. Oregon was also the team that beat the Huskies, 57-49, in Eugene, on Jan. 31, 1939, to halt the run at 26 victories. Oregon completed its season by winning the first NCAA basketball championship. They beat Ohio State 46-33.

UW Media Relations

Husky Legend

Vic Markov

Vic Markov was a three-year letterwinner on Jim Phelan's football teams from 1935-1937. He played in the 1937 Rose Bowl and the 1938 Pineapple Bowl. He was considered the premier tackle on the West Coast during his career. He made the All-Pacific Coast Conference team in 1936 and 1937 and was an All-America in 1937. Markov improved his strength by wrestling, qualifying for the NCAA heavyweight finals. In 1936, he competed in the shot put and discus throw for Hec Edmundson's track and field team. For the 1938 College All-Star team, Markov received the second highest number of votes and was selected captain. The collegians faced the Washington Redskins, on Aug. 31, at Soldier's Field in Chicago, Markov's home town. The All-Stars beat the Redskins, led by quarterback Sammy Baugh, 28-16. In 1976, Markov was inducted into the National Football Foundation College Hall of Fame in 1976. He entered the Husky Hall of Fame in 1980.

Husky List

A total of 14 Husky players and coaches have been inducted into the National Football Foundation College Football Hall of Fame

Player	Seasons	Year Inducted
George Wilson, halfback	1923-25	1951
Chuck Carroll, halfback	1926-28	1964
Paul Schwegler, tackle	1929-31	1967
Vic Markov, tackle	1935-37	1976
Hugh McElhenny, halfback	1949-51	1981
Don Heinrich, quarterback	1949, 50, 52	1987
Bob Schloredt, quarterback	1958-60	1989
Max Starcevich, guard	1934-36	1990
Rick Redman, guard	1962-64	1995

Coach		
Gil Dobie	1908-16	1951
Jim Phelan	1930-41	1973
Darrell Royal	1956	1983
Jim Owens (inducted as a player)	1957-74	1982
Don James	1975-92	1997

ALFRED "DOC" STRAUSS earned letters in football (1902 and 1903) and baseball (1903) at Washington. After graduation and attending several medical programs, he became one of the nation's most respected surgeons and a pioneer in cancer research. He received the University's highest alumni award—Alumnus Summa Laude Dignatus—in 1951. He lived in Chicago and actively recruited athletes from the Midwest. Five of them earned All-America honors—Max Starcevich, Vic Markov, Ray Frankowski, Rudy Mucha, and Jay MacDowell. He also supported the Husky crews by providing a workout site and accommodations in Chicago on the crew's train trips to Poughkeepsie. Strauss was elected to the Husky Hall of Fame in 1981.

UW Media Relations

Dr. Alfred Strauss in 1968 christens a Husky shell named for him.

1938 W 1939

Husky Moment

Huskies Lose Northern Division Title to NCAA Champs

The 1939 basketball season ended with the first NCAA national championship game. The center tip, after every score, had been eliminated the year before, and scoring increased significantly. The Huskies' first big games were on Dec. 22 and 23, 1938. They beat Ohio State, 43-41 and 51-37. The Huskies were in the thick of the race for the Northern Division title right down to the final series with Oregon. They took a 13-0 record into Eugene for two games against the Ducks, on Jan. 31 and Feb. 1. They lost both, 57-49 and 58-42. Oregon was led by two All-America players, Lauren "Laddie" Gale and Urgel "Slim" Wintermute. Washington split two games with Oregon State in Corvallis a few nights later. On Feb. 17, 1939, Husky forward, Roy Williamson, established a new Husky single-game record, scoring 25 points in a Husky win, 62-52, against Washington State in Pullman. In early March, Washington had a record of 20-3, trailing division leader, Oregon, by one game. The Ducks came to town for the last two games of the conference season. Before sellout crowds, Oregon swept both games, 39-26 and 54-52. Oregon went on to win the Pacific Coast Conference title, beating California, 54-49 and 53-47, in Eugene. In the western regional championship tournament, Oregon beat Texas and Oklahoma. They met Ohio State, the eastern regional winner, in the first NCAA championship game. In Northwestern University's field house, on March 27, 1939, Oregon beat Ohio State, 46-33.

1939 Tyee

Oregon beats the Huskies for the Northern Division title, and goes on to win the first NCAA championship.

Husky Spotlight

USC met a fired up Husky eleven on Nov. 12, 1938. On a damp, dreary day in Seattle, the ninth-ranked Trojans, unblemished in Conference play, soon saw halfback Jimmy Johnston race 55 yards for a Husky touchdown in the first quarter. Johnston cut back over USC's left guard, spun out of the arms of four Trojan tacklers and eluded the safety man like a "ghost dancing through a grave yard." Don Jones, kicking because both regular booters were injured, converted his first extra point since high school in Sedro Wooley. Except for a few minutes in the second quarter when USC's Grenny Lansdell returned a punt 70 yards for a score, the Huskies were in control of the game. As the game ended with the Huskies up 7-6, Washington had the ball inches away from the USC goal line. It was the Huskies fifth straight victory over USC. The Huskies finished 3-5-1 in Coach Phelan's ninth season.

Husky Highlight

A new pool was built at the east end of the Pavilion and dedicated on March 24, 1939, during the Northern Division championship meet, won by Washington. The pool cost about $209,000, and was financed from Washington's share of the 1937 Rose Bowl proceeds augmented by state and federal grants. In 1937, after a four-year struggle, Husky swimmers and Coach Jack Torney requested Athletic Director Ray Eckman to recognize swimming as a major sport. They also wanted jobs for the varsity swimmers to pay for some of their expenses and a men's pool on campus. Husky men were allowed in the women's pool only three times a week. They had to wear gray, wool, one-piece women's -type swim suits to comply with the rules of the women's physical education department.

Husky Legend

Jack Torney

UW Media Relations

Jack Torney entered Washington as a student in 1923. As an undergraduate, he was a star swimmer when the sport was barely a minor one. He earned three varsity letters in track and field (1925-27). After graduating with a BS in Physical Education, he received a master's degree from Columbia in 1930. He returned to Washington in the fall to join the faculty in the Department of Physical and Health Education. Torney organized the first Washington swim team in the fall of 1932. Through his efforts, swimming became a major sport in 1938 and a men's swimming pool was built. In his 27 years as head swimming coach, his teams won 19 Northern Division titles. He compiled a 142-11-2 dual meet record that included 54 consecutive dual meet victories against collegiate competition. He saw 17 of his Huskies selected to All-America teams. He was elected to the Helms Foundation Swimming Hall of Fame in 1963. He coached the men's tennis team for nine years (1934-41, 1946), winning eight Northern Division titles. He entered the Husky Hall of Fame in 1981.

Husky List

Husky basketball's top five single-game, single-season, and career scoring leaders are:

Single game Player	Year(s)	Games	Average	Points
Bob Houbregs	1/10/53	Idaho		49
Bob Houbregs	3/13/53	Seattle University		45
Bob Houbregs	3/18/53	Louisiana State		42
George Irvine	12/26/69	USC		41
Bill Hanson	3/3/62	California		40
Season				
Player				
Bob Houbregs	1953	33	25.6	846
Chris Welp	1987	35	20.8	729
Louie Nelson	1973	29	23.0	668
Chris Welp	1986	31	19.4	601
Steve Hawes	1971	26	21.8	568
Career				
Player				
Chris Welp	1984-87	129	16.1	2073
Bob Houbregs	1951-53	91	19.5	1774
Todd MacCulloch	1996-99	115	15.2	1743
Eldridge Recasner	1987-90	117	14.5	1700
James Edwards	1974-77	105	14.7	1548

SIX major men's sports had been established at Washington at the end of the 1938-39 academic year—baseball, basketball, crew, football, swimming, tennis, and wrestling. There were also several minor sports—fencing, golf, ice hockey, skiing, and volleyball. Hockey was dropped in 1939; fencing in 1941; and volleyball in 1943. Boxing, which started in 1924, was dropped in 1931. Skiing continued until 1970. In the decade ending with the 1939-40 season, Husky ski teams won Pacific Coast championships in 1936, 1937, 1938, and 1939. Golf teams won Northern Division titles in 1937, 1938, and 1940.

1941 Tyee

Carl Neu, member of the 1938-40 Husky ski teams.

Husky Moment

Sixth National Championship for Husky Crew

Through the gathering dusk, eight varsity shells glided with their "phantom-like prows piercing the inky waters" of the Hudson. Fiercely challenged at the finish by Cornell, the Husky crew claimed Washington's sixth IRA victory. The winning time was 22:42.0 over four miles. It was the youngest Husky boat that ever represented Washington at Poughkeepsie—four sophomores, three juniors, and one senior (Fred Colbert, the coxswain, was also a senior). The varsity rowed in the "Loyal Shoudy" shell built by George Pocock and financed by Dr. Shoudy. A former Washington football player in the Gil Dobie era, Shoudy was a great supporter of Husky athletics. For many years, he would travel to the IRA races to support the Husky crews. Poor race conditions during the regatta forced the junior varsity race to be rowed in the dark of night. The JV crew beat Navy by five lengths over three miles, winning Washington's eighth IRA JV title. Coach Ulbrickson related that once the 15 crews were away from the starting line, they disappeared into the night. He said: "We couldn't see a thing so we all listened for our coxswain's voices. I could hear Vic Fomo's voice getting farther away fastest so I was pretty sure we were out in front." The finish line was illuminated by a searchlight on a Naval ship moored on the far river bank. As Washington's crew crossed the finish line, the white-tipped blades gleamed briefly in the searchlight and the shell disappeared in the darkness once again. In broad daylight, both Washington crews were guests at the World's International Exposition. The Husky oarsmen raised the Purple and Gold flag to the top of the victor's pole at the fair. Since the 1940 Olympics were not held because of World War II, the Husky crew could not defend their Olympic title. The 1940 varsity crew was elected to the Husky Hall of Fame in 1986. Its members were John Bracken, Fred Colbert (coxswain), Dallas Duppenthaler, Al Erickson, Ted Garhart, Chuck Jackson, Gerald Keely, Paul Soules, and Dick Yantis.

UW Media Relations

Husky Spotlight

The Washington swimming team won its second straight Northern Division title by edging Oregon by one point. Before the next-to-last event, Oregon led 56-53. In the 440-yard freestyle race, Husky Mark Bockman won, Peter Goldberg was second and Leo Sheehan gained a precious point in fifth place. The Huskies now led, 64-61, with the 400-yard freestyle event to decide the title. Oregon won, to earn 10 points, but Washington's second-place finish gave them eight points and the title. The victorious Huskies were also led by George Athans' first place in diving and Goldberg's first in the 220-yard freestyle.

Husky Highlight

The Huskies won the annual Northwest intercollegiate ski championship held in Sun Valley during the 1939 Christmas vacation. Carl Neu won the slalom event and Harold Gjolme won the ski jumping title. Gjolme won the overall title by also taking second in the downhill, fourth in the cross country race, and sixth in the slalom. Gjolme's brother, Reida and Neu tied for third in the overall competition. Washington's Bill Redlin became the first Husky skier to win a national championship. In March 1940, he won the International Ski Federation (FIS) downhill championship in the Wasatch Mountains near Salt Lake City. In the 1941 FIS meet held at Aspen, Colorado, he took third—he was the top collegiate competitor—in the downhill.

Husky Legend

Jim Phelan

UW Media Relations

Jim Phelan learned his football from the legendary Knute Rockne. He was a quarterback at Notre Dame from 1915 to 1917. After military service in World War I and an assistant coaching tenure at Missouri, he became Missouri's head football coach in 1921. A year later, he went to Purdue. His Boilermakers were 35-22-5 in his eight seasons. In 1929, his Purdue team won the Big Ten championship. In 1930, he started a 12-year head coaching career at Washington, compiling a 65-37-8 record. His winning percentage—.627—is the fifth best in Husky history. His 1936 team was ranked fifth in the country and played against third-ranked Pittsburgh in the 1937 Rose Bowl. His Huskies lost, 21-0. The next year, Phelan coached Washington to its first bowl victory, a 53-13 win over Hawaii in the Pineapple Bowl. He was inducted into the College Football Hall of Fame in 1973 and the Husky Hall of Fame in 1986.

HUSKY LIST

The leaders in Husky football history in pass receptions, pass reception yards, touchdown receptions, and longest receptions are:

Pass receptions		
Career	Paul Skansi, 1979-82	138
Season	Jerome Pathon, 1997	69
Game	Dane Looker vs. Arizona State, 1998	12
Pass reception yardage		
Career	Mario Bailey, 1988-91	2,093
Season	Jerome Pathon, 1997	1,245
Game	Dave Williams vs. UCLA, 1965	257
Touchdown receptions		
Career	Mario Bailey, 1988-91	26
Season	Mario Bailey, 1991	17
Game	Mario Bailey vs. Oregon State and Toledo, 1991	3
	Brian Slater vs. Washington State, 1986	3
	Anthony Allen vs. Maryland, 1982	3
	Al Mauer vs. UCLA, 1965	3
	Dave Williams vs. UCLA, 1965	3
	Roland Kirkby vs. Kansas State, 1950	3

Longest receptions

84 yards (TD) Willie Rosborough (from Tom Flick) vs. Air Force, 1980
83 yards (TD) Todd Elstrom (from Marques Tuiasosopo) vs. California, 1999
83 yards (TD) Corey Dillon (from Brock Huard) vs. San Jose State, 1996
80 yards (TD) Harrison Wood (from Tom Menke) vs. Air Force, 1967
80 yards (TD) Jim Houston (from Steve Roake), lateral to Corky Lewis vs. USC, 1955
80 yards (TD) George Black (from Don Heinrich) vs. Stanford, 1952
80 yards (TD) Merle Miller (from Fritz Waskowitz) vs. Washington State, 1937

HUSKY LORE

"TENNIS is a sport where one participant slams a globule over the net and out of reach of a skittering foe across the court ...when it is not raining." Despite the weather, the Husky tennis team captured its sixth Northern Division championship in seven years. These seven teams, coached by Jack Torney, compiled a 41-1 record in dual matches.

1940 Tyee

1940 Tennis Team

1940-49

1940 W 1941

Husky Moment

"I've Never Seen a Gang with Such Sockeroo"

On June 25, 1941, the "Flying Forty-One" won the Intercollegiate Rowing Association regatta. Three rowers had been in the 1940 championship crew—John Bracken, Ted Garhart, and Chuck Jackson. Coach Al Ulbrickson described them "as great a crew as I've had. I've never seen a gang with such sockeroo." The Huskies led for the first mile. Then, Cal started to move and led by the point of the bow at the two-mile mark. The coxswain, Vic Fomo, lowered the beat to 29, and Ted Garhart, the stroke, smoothed out the rhythm, and the run of the boat between strokes was nothing short of fantastic. Washington increased its beat first to 32, then 34, and finished with a sprint at 36. The Huskies finished the four-mile course two and a half lengths ahead of California in a time of 18:53.3. Earlier in the year, Washington defeated Cal by almost four lengths over a three-mile course on the Oakland Estuary. The crew established a course record—14:28. This record has never been broken. Former Washington oarsman and coach, Rusty Callow called the Huskies "the best, strongest and fastest Washington crew I've ever seen. None has more power in the engine room." He did not change that opinion during the remaining 20 years of his life. Rusty said: "This is not a picture crew inboard, but they have obviously rowed so far together that they can and do trust each other enough that they can row with abandon and still have a steady keel under them." The 1941 crew—John Bracken, Vic Fomo (coxswain), Doyle Fowler, Ted Garhart, Chuck Jackson, Bill Neill, Paul Simdars, Tom Taylor, and Walt Wallace—was elected to the Husky Hall of Fame in 1991. Bracken, Garhart, and Jackson were also elected to the Husky Hall of Fame as members of the 1940 crew.

UW Media Relations

The "Flying Forty-One," national championship crew.

Husky Spotlight

The Huskies had three All-America football players in 1940. Guard Ray Frankowski was a consensus selection and together with center Rudy Mucha, another consensus All-America in 1940, formed one of the game's most feared interior lines. Mucha was the first Husky center to be an All-America. He played that position for three years (1938-1940). He also handled the kick-off duties. Mucha was a star guard for the 1946 Chicago Bears, the National Football League champions. He was elected to the Husky Hall of Fame in 1990. Jay MacDowell played end on Jim Phelan's teams in 1938-1940. As a senior, at age 19, he earned All-America and All-Coast honors. Both he, Mucha, and teammate Dean McAdams played in the 1941 East-West Shrine Game. The East featured 1940 Heisman Award winner, Michigan's Tom Harmon. MacDowell was admitted to the Husky Hall of Fame in 1991.

Husky Highlight

The 1940 Husky football team had a 7-2-0 record and finished second in the Conference. Washington lost to Minnesota, 19-14, in an away game to open the season. On Nov. 9, Washington played Stanford. Both teams entered the contest unbeaten in conference play. The Indians were led by All-America quarterback, Frankie Albert. The Huskies scored first on a drive in which two plays did the damage—a 56-yard run by fullback Jack Stackpool and a 33-yard touchdown pass from Dean McAdams to Earl Younglove. Johnny Mizen kicked the extra point and added a field goal midway in the third quarter to put the Huskies up, 10-0. Just before the third quarter ended, Pete Kmetovic intercepted a Husky pass on the Washington 41-yard line. Two plays later, Albert hit Kmetovic on a 44-yard scoring strike. On the next Washington series, Stanford intercepted a pass deep inside Washington territory to set up a Hugh Gallarneau one-yard scoring plunge. Kmetovic's second interception iced the game when he returned it 32 yards for Stanford's third tally. Stanford won 20-10 and finished the season unbeaten, ranked number two in the nation. The Indians beat Nebraska in the Rose Bowl, 21-13. The Huskies finished 10th in the nation, their highest ranking since 1936. The team also recorded five shutout victories, including a 41-0 victory over UCLA in Los Angeles. Bruin running back Jackie Robinson rushed for 66 yards and passed for 129 in the game. Robinson would later become the first black to play in Major League Baseball with the Brooklyn Dodgers.

Husky Legend

UW Media Relations

Ray Frankowski

Ray Frankowski was a consensus All-America selection in 1940 and 1941. He was acclaimed as the best guard in the nation during his college career. He was picked on every All-Opponent team in 1940 and 1941. Frankowski earned three letters in football (1939-1941) and was a two-time All-Coast selection (1940 and 1941). He was a two-time letterman in wrestling (1940 and 1941) and was the only Husky matman to capture a Northern Division title in 1940. He won the heavyweight class. He gained a sixth letter as a member of the fencing team in 1941. Frankowski was recruited by alumnus Dr. Alfred Strauss out of the Midwest. He joined four other Strauss' "boys" in his generation to be selected an All-America—Max Starcevich (1936), Vic Markov (1937), Jay MacDowell (1940), and Rudy Mucha (1940). After graduation, Frankowski played professional football for the Green Bay Packers (1945) and the Los Angeles Dons (1946-1948).

HUSKY LISTY

Husky Teams Ranked in the Top 20 in the Football Polls

Year	AP	UPI	Year	AP	UPI	USA Today/ CNN
1936	5		1981	10	7	
1940	10		1982	7	7	10
1943	12		1984	2	2	2
1950	11	15	1986	18	17	19
1959	8	7	1989		20	
1960	6		1990	5	5	5
1963		15	1991	2	1	1
1971	19		1992	11	11	10
1977	10	9	1996	16	16	15
1979	11	11	1997	18		18
1980	16	17	2000	3		3

HUSKY LORE

EMMETT WATSON, a long-time sports writer and features columnist for the *Seattle Post-Intelligencer* was a three-time letterman catcher on coach Tubby Graves' baseball teams from 1940 to 1942. He won the Torrance Award as the team's most inspirational player in 1942. He was likened to the physique of Bill Dickey, the great New York Yankees' catcher—tall and streamlined like a hurdler. Watson went to Franklin High School where he caught the pitches of Fred Hutchinson. Hutchinson would go on to star as a Detroit Tigers' pitcher.

1941 Tyee

1941 W 1942

Husky Moment

First Basketball Eastern Trip Against Collegiate Opponents

Hec Edmundson's 1940 and 1941 basketball teams recorded two of the three losing conference seasons in Edmundson's 27-year career. In 1942, the Huskies were 18-7 overall, and 10-6 in the Pacific Coast Conference. The season featured two intersectional series. The first was held on Dec. 19 and 20, 1941, in the Pavilion. Washington State and Washington were co-hosts to two Big Six teams—Kansas State and Missouri. The Cougars crushed Missouri, 62-23, and the Huskies beat Kansas State, 45-31, on the first night. On the second, Washington beat the Tigers, 52-31, and the Pullman squad handled the Wildcats, 47-22. A week later, after a cross country train ride to Philadelphia, the Huskies beat Temple, 64-36. Washington was led by Chuck Gilmur's 18 points. On Dec. 30, they met the New York University Violets in Madison Square Garden before almost 13,000 fans. In the first 10 minutes, Washington raced to a 20-2 lead. The Huskies broke the Garden's single-game field goal and scoring record by wilting the Violets 72-38. Norm Dalthorp led the Huskies with 15 and Wally Leask scored the record-breaking field goal as the horn sounded to end the game. The last stop, before returning home, was East Lansing, Michigan. On Jan. 2, 1942, the Huskies beat Michigan State, 45-42, paced by Bob Lindh's 12 points.

The Huskies break the Madison Square Garden scoring record.

Husky Spotlight

Jim Phelan, Husky football coach, was fired by Athletic Director, Ray Eckman, after a 5-4-0 record in 1941. Phelan took on the head coaching job at St. Mary's College in California. Assistant Coach, Ralph "Pest" Welch, replaced him.

Bob Odman, tennis captain in 1942, led Washington to its ninth Northern Division championship and its eighth in nine years. In late June, Odman journeyed to New Orleans and played in the NCAA tournament. In the second round, he lost to the eventual winner, Stanford's Ted Schroeder, in a grueling match, 8-6, 6-1. On July 6, 1942, in Montclair, NJ, Odman, using slashing forehand shots, beat Princeton's tennis captain, Dick Bender, 6-3, 6-2, to win the Eastern Intercollegiate singles championship.

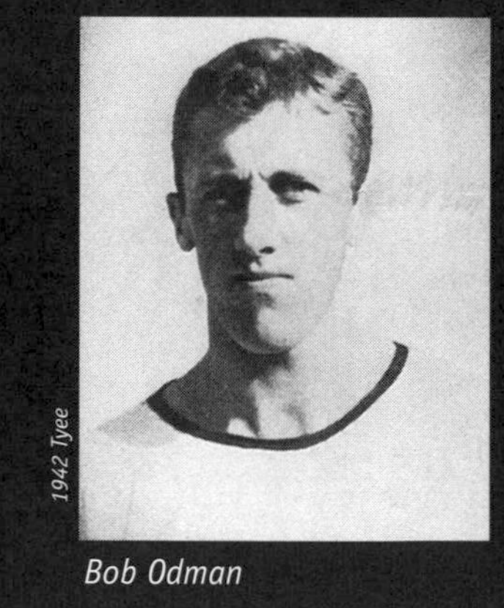

1942 Tyee

Bob Odman

Husky Highlight

The 1942 Husky golf team won the Northern Division championship, beating runner-up Oregon State by 34 strokes. Washington, as a team, was only one over par and smashed the Northern Division record by nine strokes. Harold "Toss" Gjolme, an outstanding Husky skier, was the Husky captain and number-one Husky golfer. He and his golfing partners—Bart Taro, Jack Hazlett; and Keith Welts—went to the NCAA tournament in South Bend, Indiana in late June. They went on their own because of University travel expense restrictions and unofficially represented Washington. They did pretty well, taking fourth place as a team behind Stanford, LSU, and Northwestern. Gjolme reached the semi-finals before bowing out to the eventual winner, Stanford's Frank Tatum. The Husky track team won the Northern Division title for the first time in 10 years. Scoring in 13 of the 15 events, the Huskies beat runner-up Idaho, 50-30. Gene Swanzey won the Pacific Coast Conference title in the 880, in 1:55.5.

Husky Legend

Ted Garhart

Selecting an individual oarsman as a Legend is highly unusual because, arguably, crew requires the greatest team work of any sport. Every rower in a shell must be pulling his or her weight every second. Ted Garhart was an oarsman with extraordinary abilities and accomplishments. His coach, Al Ulbrickson, gave this praise in 1942 to his three-year varsity stroke. "In all my rowing experience, I have never seen as fine an oarsman or as fine a stroke. Without hesitation, I rate him number one." Garhart graduated from Garfield High School in Seattle where he participated in track as a high hurdler. A university freshman in 1938, he turned out for crew, and in the spring of 1939, he rowed in the freshmen boat that won the Intercollegiate Rowing Association regatta. In 1940, he stroked the youngest boat ever to compete at the IRA to victory. As a junior, he was the stroke in the victorious "Flying Forty One" boat that some observers claim was the fastest shell in Husky history. Garhart believes the 1940 crew was better. "They were bigger, stronger men aboard. We were better balanced as well." Because of World War II, the 1942 IRA regatta was not held, thus preventing Garhart from stroking a fourth national championship. The war also took away a possible opportunity for Garhart and the Husky crew to represent the United States in the Olympics. During his four years at Washington, Garhart was in a Husky boat that never lost a race. He was selected as Husky co-athlete of the year in 1942 and also received the Lauer Trophy, annually awarded to the man who has done most for the university. Garhart also was selected as *Seattle P-I's* 1942 "Man of the Year" in sports. He was inducted in the Helms Foundation Rowing Hall of Fame and he entered the Husky Hall of Fame twice—the first time in 1986, as the stroke of the 1940 men's varsity eight; again, in 1991, as the stroke of the 1941 varsity eight.

Husky List

Men's and Women's Husky Golf Coaches

Men's Coaches	
Bill Jefferson	1935-41
Bill Jefferson, Jr.	1942-43, 1946-1956
Ray Bennet	1956-1969
Bill Tindall	1969-76
Ron Hagen	1976-83
Bill Tindall	1983-92
John Krebs	1992-95
O.D. Vincent	1995-present

Women's Coaches	
Edean Ihlanfeldt	1975-81
Jan Lanphere	1981-82
Lesley Hobert	1982-83
Mary Lou Mulflur	1983-present

WORLD War II significantly impacted the Husky athletic program. All Pacific Coast Conference football rosters were limited to 28 players. The crew had to go back to the old Leschi-Madison Park course because of military restrictions near the Sand Point Naval Station. No IRA regattas were held for five years (1942-1946). Jack Torney, tennis and swim coach, entered the Navy at the close of the 1942 swim season. Other coaches followed. Over 100 faculty members and many more students served in the armed forces. A Navy V-12 unit was established on campus, and the Applied Physics Laboratory was created to do Navy anti-submarine research. It was the first special contract research agency established on campus. A number of university departments took an active part in war-related training and research programs. During the war, civilian enrollment decreased by more than 3,500 students. More than 100 faculty members took leaves of absence to enter the armed services or some special branch of government. The university's existing academic programs continued. New ones were established. For example, the Far Eastern Department developed intensive programs to study the culture and languages of China, Japan, Russia, and Korea.

Husky Moment

The 1943 Husky basketball team was 24-7 and won 10 of its last 11 conference games to capture the Northern Division title, the ninth under Hec Edmundson. Pre-conference play featured the first and only game with the Harlem Globetrotters. On Jan. 19, 1943, Washington beat the Trotters, 49-30. They finished the conference race at home by defeating Oregon State, 53-33 and 44-35. They met the Southern Division champs, Southern California, in the Pavilion for the Pacific Coast Conference title. On March 12, 1942, the Huskies beat the Trojans, 53-51, on a one-handed push shot by sophomore reserve guard, Bill Taylor, with seven seconds left in the game. The score was tied 11 times and the lead changed nine times. Husky guard Bill Morris led all scorers with 16 points. On March 13, Washington won the second game, 52-45. The score was tied 43-43 with eight minutes left. Then the Huskies made a 9-2 run to take the PCC title. Captain Wally Leask and USC's Jim Seminoff led all scorers with 18 points a piece. Washington made its first NCAA basketball tournament appearance in the four-team Western Regional in Kansas City, Missouri. The winner would face the Eastern Regional champion for the NCAA title. In the first game, on March 26, 1943, the Huskies faced Texas and led at half-time, 33-28. With six minutes left in the game, Texas had rallied to take a 53-52 lead. The Huskies regained the lead at 55-53 with two minutes remaining. Freshman Roy Cox scored three field goals down the stretch to give Texas the victory, 59-55. Johnny Hargis, the outstanding Longhorn forward scored 30 points. Morris led the Huskies with 22. The next night, in the consolation game, the Oklahoma Sooners, paced by the 18 points of All-America, Gerald Tucker, beat Washington, 48-43. At one point in the second half, the Sooners were up 43-30. Taylor had 16 points for Washington. Wyoming beat Texas to win the Western title and beat Georgetown for the NCAA championship.

1941 Tyee

Husky Spotlight

Ralph "Pest" Welch's first season, as the Husky head football coach, ended with a 4-3-3 record. All the losses were to California schools—a 19-6 loss to Cal, 20-7 to Stanford, and 14-10 to UCLA. The Bruins won the conference title and lost to number-two ranked Georgia in the 1943 Rose Bowl, 9-0. Husky center, Walt Harrison, was elected honorary captain at the end of the season. During his career as a Husky, he played every position but guard and halfback. He was the Flaherty Medal winner, as the team's most inspirational player, in 1941. A three year letter winner (1940-42), he was voted All-Coast in 1942. Harrison received the second most votes, behind George Wilson, for the all-time Husky Team for the first 50 years of the 20th century. Harrison entered the Husky Hall of Fame in 1999.

1942 Tyee

Walt Harrison

Husky Highlight

The 1943 Husky swimming team splashed through the season undefeated and captured the Northern Division championship for the fourth time in five years. Bob Buckley took over the coaching duties when Jack Torney entered the Navy in the spring of 1942. It was Buckley's first and last season as head coach as he left for Naval duty after the 1943 season. Co-captain Pete Powlinson was a double winner in the 50 and 100 in the Northern Division meet. Co-captain George Athans won his third straight ND diving title. Powlinson and Athans competed in the NCAA meet in Columbus, Ohio. Powlinson was third in the 50 and fourth in the 100 freestyle. Athans failed to place in the meet but later went on to New York where he took third in the National AAU indoor meet. Washington tied for 10th in the NCAA meet won by host, Ohio State. Powlinson was an All-America in 1943 and again in 1947, after returning from military service. The Husky track team again won the Northern Division title and finished eighth in the NCAA meet held at Northwestern University. Five Huskies scored points in the meet—Tom Kamm, a freshman, took third in the long jump; Bill Kydd fourth in the javelin throw; Dick Yantis fourth in the discus throw; Bob Smith fifth in the 220; and captain Gene Swanzey sixth in the 880.

Husky Legend

Arnie Weinmeister

UW Media Relations

Arnie Weinmeister entered Washington in 1941 and became a starting end on the freshmen football team. He starred as an end on the 1942 varsity before entering the military service. He returned to Washington in the fall of 1946 and became the Huskies' starting fullback. In 1947, he was shifted to tackle and earned his third varsity letter. He played in the 1948 East-West Shrine Game and on the College All-Stars team in Soldiers Field in Chicago. The College All-Stars were coached by Notre Dame's Frank Leahy and lost to the defending NFL champion Chicago Cardinals, 28-0. Weinmeister played professional football for the New York Yankees in the All-America Conference—in 1948 and 1949—and was Rookie of the Year in 1948. He starred for the National Football League's New York Giants for four seasons (1950-53). As an All-NFL selection in 1950, Weinmeister started in the First Pro Bowl game in 1951 and in the Pro Bowls of 1952, 1953, and 1954. He was the Seattle Man of the Year in Sports in 1953. Weinmeister was admitted to the National Football League Hall of Fame in 1984—one of only two Huskies to be selected; Hugh McElhenny is the other. Weinmeister entered the Husky Hall of Fame in 1982.

HUSKY LIST

There have been 25 former Husky players who have been on the roster of a Super Bowl participant. (through Super Bowl XXXV in 2001)

Player	Super Bowl and Team
Anthony Allen	XXII, Washington
Eric Bjornson	XXX, Dallas
Dennis Brown	XXIX, San Francisco
Dave Browning	XV, Oakland
Mark Bruener	XXX, Pittsburgh
Blair Bush	XVI, Cincinnati
Hillary Butler	XXXII, Denver
Tony Caldwell	XVIII, Los Angeles Raiders
Rich Camarillo	XX, New England
Chris Chandler	XXXIII, Atlanta
Ernie Conwell	XXXIV, St. Louis
DeMarco Farr	XXXIV, St. Louis
Jamal Fountaine	XXIX, San Francisco
Kevin Gogan	XVII, XVIII, Dallas
Brian Habib	XXXIII, Denver
Ron Hadley	XXIII, San Francisco
Dana Hall	XXIX, San Francisco
Ron Holmes	XXIV, Denver
Ray Horton	XXIII, Cincinnati XXVII, Dallas
Joe Kelly	XXIII, Cincinnati
Ray Mansfield	IX and X, Pittsburgh
Lawyer Milloy	XXXI, New England
Benji Olson	XXXIV, Tennessee
Dave Pear	XV, Oakland Raiders
Ray Pinney	XIII, XIV, Pittsburgh
David Richie	XXXII, Denver
Steve Thompson	III, New York Jet
Jeff Toews	XVII, XIX, Miami

THERE were many acts of heroism by Washington students and graduates serving in the armed services in World War II. On Sept. 29, 1942, Lt. Fritz Waskowitz, Husky football captain in 1937, became the first outstanding Husky athlete to be killed in action. Major Robert Galer, Husky basketball captain and All-America in 1935, received the highest military award, the Congressional Medal of Honor, in 1943. Galer led his Marine Corps fighter squadron against Japanese forces in the Solomon Islands area. His superb airmanship, his outstanding flying skills and personal valor resulted in his shooting down 11 enemy bombers and fighters during a 29-day period. He and his squadron shot down 27 Japanese planes.

1937 Tyee

Fritz Waskowitz

1943 W 1944

HUSKY MOMENT

Fourth Rose Bowl

Because of war-time travel restrictions, the 1944 Rose Bowl invited the Pacific Coast Conference Northern and Southern Division champions to play each other. Washington won the Northern Division title by default when other conference schools in the Northwest failed to field teams. Washington's record was 4-0, with wins over Whitman and service teams. The Huskies had not played a game since Oct. 30, when they routed the Spokane Air Command team, and two of their first-string running backs had been called to service. Washington controlled the first period, twice driving deep into the Trojan's territory but failing to score. Late in the second period, USC turned to the air, negating Washington's size advantage with quick passes to their fleet ends. With 40 seconds in the half, the Trojans had fourth down on the Washington 11-yard line. Troy quarterback Jim Hardy tossed to halfback, George Callahan, who made a final move at the goal line for the touchdown. Dick Jamison kicked the point-after, and the Trojans had a 7-0 lead at half-time. USC scored midway through the third quarter on another Hardy-to-Callahan hookup, and Jamison converted to put USC up, 14-0. Late in the third period, Hardy tossed his third touchdown pass, this time to his other end, Gordon Gray. Gray scored again in the fourth quarter on a throw from left-handed substitute quarterback, Ainslie Bell. The Trojans added a safety by blocking an Everett Austin punt into the end zone that was recovered by the Huskies' fullback, Wally Kramer. The final score was 29-0. One oddity in the game involved Bill McGovern, the only substitute tackle the Huskies had. On Thanksgiving Day, 1943, McGovern played for Stadium High against Lincoln in Tacoma's annual cross-town turkey fest. On Dec. 10, he enrolled in one of the service programs at Washington that made him eligible

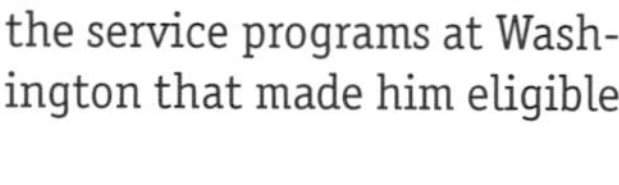

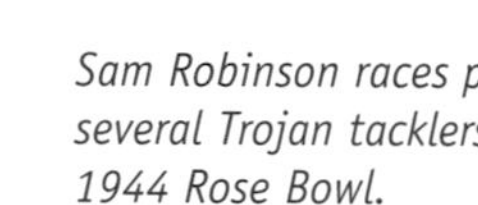

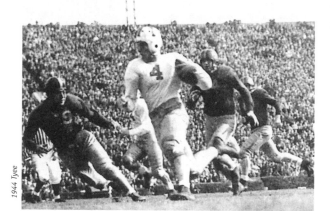

1944 Tyee

Sam Robinson races past several Trojan tacklers in the 1944 Rose Bowl.

Husky Spotlight

The Huskies won their 10th Northern Division basketball title. There were no conference playoffs because of W.W. II restrictions. Washington posted a 15-1 conference record, 26-6 overall. The only conference loss was to Idaho, 55-53, in the next-to-last game of the season. The team had a very unusual makeup. War-time trainees enrolled at Washington made up the "service squad," and regular students made up the "civilian squad." Freshmen were allowed to play. The service unit included 1943 All-America guard, Bill Morris. Morris was playing his fourth year under war-time eligibility rules. Freshman Jack Nichols started on the civilian unit. The civilian team played mostly road games and a combined team, led by some of the trainees, played in games, in the Pavilion. The civilians included the first Chinese player for Washington, the diminutive Al Mar. In a game on Feb. 11, 1944, against Washington State, Mar led all scorers with 22 points. He had several other double-digit scoring games.

HUSKY HIGHLIGHT

Husky guard Bill Morris set the Northern Division single-game scoring record by rolling up 30 points in a 69-55 victory against Idaho, on Feb. 22, 1944. On March 1, Washington State's Don McMillan surpassed Morris' week-old record by four points, pouring 12 field goals and 10 free throws through the basket.

The Washington swimming team swam in only two meets, beating a Sand Point Naval Station team, 60-10 and 52-20. Four members of the Husky team—Park Gloyd, Bill Flagg, Gordon Sherwood, and Don MacLane—won the National indoor junior AAU championship in the 200-yard freestyle relay.

1943 Tyee

Husky Legend

Bill Morris

Bill Morris earned four varsity basketball letters—three as a regular Washington student in 1941-43 and one as a Navy V-12 trainee in 1944. Morris had very quick hands as evidenced in a game against the Harlem Globetrotters on Jan. 18, 1943. One of the Globetrotters extended the ball to him in one of their classic tricks. Normally, the ball was quickly pulled back as the opposing player went after it, and the Globetrotter reached forward with his other hand to shake it with his foe. Morris, however, swiped the ball cleanly and went down the court for an uncontested layup. The Globetrotters tried again to foil Morris; once more Morris stole it away and made the basket. It was no trick that he was a three- time (1942-44) All-Northern Division selection as a guard and on the All-Pacific Coast Conference team in 1943—there were no All-PCC teams from 1944 until 1956. Morris was a Helms Foundation All-America in 1943. The next year, he was an All-Coast selection and made the Converse All-America team. Morris was co-captain of the 1944 team and received the Hec Edmundson Most Inspirational Player award in that year. He led the Huskies to the Pacific Coast Conference title and their first NCAA appearance in 1943. He established the single-game Northern Division scoring record—30 points—in 1944. Morris became the Husky freshmen coach for one season under Hec Edmundson (1947) and continued under Art McLarney (1948-50), and Tippy Dye (1951-59). He was elected to the Husky Hall of Fame in 1988.

Husky List

Washington's NCAA Appearances in Men's Basketball

1943 West Regional (Kansas City, Mo.)
Texas 59, Washington 55; Oklahoma 48, Washington 43

1948 West Regional (Kansas City, Mo.)
Baylor 64, Washington 62; Washington 57, Wyoming 47

1951 NCAA Regional (Kansas City, Mo.)
Washington 62, Texas A&M, 40; Oklahoma State 61, Washington 57; Washington 80, Brigham Young 67

1953 West Regional (Corvallis, Ore.) Washington 92, Seattle U 70; Washington 74, Santa Clara 62
Final Four (Kansas City, Mo.) Kansas 79, Washington 53; Washington 88, Louisiana St., 69

1976 Midwest Subregional (Lawrence, Kan.)
Missouri 69, Washington 67

1984 West Subregional (Pullman, Wash.) Washington 64, Nevada-Reno 54; Washington 80, Duke 78
West Regional (Los Angeles, Calif.)
Dayton 64, Washington 58

1985 West Subregional (Salt Lake City, Utah)
Kentucky 66, Washington 58

1986 Midwest Subregional (Dayton, Ohio) Michigan State 72, Washington 70

1998 East Subregional (Wash. D.C.) Washington 69, Xavier 68
East Regional (Greensboro, N.C.) Washington 81, Richmond 66; Connecticut 75, Washington 74

1999 Midwest Subregional (New Orleans, La.)
Miami (Ohio) 59, Washington 58

Husky Lore

THERE are eight known football players who suited up for both Washington and Washington State athletic teams. These "Couskies"— Al Akins, Tag Christensen, Wally Kramer, Vern Oliver, Jay Stoves, Bill Ward, Hjalmer "Jelly" Andersen, and Jim Thompson—all began their college careers at Washington State. During World War II, the Navy and Marines transferred new enlistees to Washington for the equivalent of officer candidate training. WSC's football program, already depleted by military call-ups, was curtailed until 1945. The first six players listed above played for Washington in 1943, after wearing the Crimson and Gray in the previous season. All, but Akins, played Cougar football. Akins lettered on WSC basketball teams in 1940 and 1941. He started in the Husky backfield in the 1944 Rose Bowl. Anderson and Thompson lettered in 1942 for Washington State and played for the Huskies after the war ended.

1944 W 1945

Husky Moment

Huskies Maul the Bears

Led by their captain, Flaherty Medal winner, Seattle's 1944 Sports Man of the Year, and star guard Jim McCurdy, Washington played a limited conference football schedule in 1944. The Huskies played two conference contests—both away—against USC, in a Monday night game and California. On Oct. 23, the Trojans routed the Huskies, 38-7. Five days later in Berkeley, Washington trounced Cal, 33-7. The Huskies received the opening kickoff and drove 65 yards for a touchdown in 17 plays. Keith Decourcey carried the ball the last 10 yards in two plays over right and left guard. Muir's pass, at the beginning of the second quarter, was intercepted by Dick Ottele on the Cal 41-yard line. Ottele was the workhorse on the second touchdown drive and scored on a one-yard plunge to put Washington up, 13-0. After a Cal fumble on the Washington 42, Washington scored in six plays. The touchdown came on a five-yard pass from Ottele to Hagen. Washington led at the half, 20-0. The Huskies scored on the opening drive of the third quarter, capped off by Decourcey's 18-yard touchdown run. Cal scored its lone touchdown in the third quarter and Washington added its last tally in the fourth quarter, ending a 70-yard drive. The rest of the season featured a home-and-away series with both Whitman and Willamette. The Huskies won all four games, outscoring the two teams, 247-12. In two of the games, Washington shut out Whitman and Willamette by identical scores, 71-0. The Huskies lost their last two games of the season to service all-star teams. The 4th Air Force Flyers from March Field shut out Washington, 28-0, on Armistice Day. The 2nd Air Force Super-bombers from Spokane destroyed the Huskies, 47-6, to close the 5-3-0 season.

1945 Tyee

Huskies trounce Cal 33-7 in Berkeley.

Husky Spotlight

Washington played its longest basketball schedule in the school's history—40 games—in the 1945 season. The team recorded 22 wins overall. It was Hec Edmundson's 25th season as head coach. Unfortunately, his silver anniversary season team could only manage to win five of 16 conference games. The conference record—.312—was the worst in Edmundson's 27-year coaching career. Fourteen of the non-conference wins came in games against service teams, AAU squads, and non-conference collegiate opponents. Again, the Huskies had a team made up of regular students and military trainees.

Husky Highlight

Head crew coach, Al Ulbrickson, became Washington's Athletic Director from 1943-1945. The Husky crew program lay practically idle during the period, 1942-1945. In the spring of 1945, the Husky track team was divided into two units—a civilian team and the other made up of military trainees. In one of the two meets of the season, the trainees posted 62 points, the civilians 41, and Washington State 28. In a four-school Northern Division championship held in Pullman, a combined Washington team captured the title.

Husky Legend

Earl "Click" Clark

UW Media Relations

In Earl "Click" Clark's role as Husky Athletic Trainer, he assisted more athletes than anybody in Washington history. As a freshman, Click played end on Gil Dobie's 1912 team that was undefeated (6-0) and rolled up 190 points to its opponent's 17. After one year at Washington, he transferred to Montana where he was a starting end for three years. Clark joined the Husky staff as an assistant football coach under Enoch Bagshaw. After two years (1927 and 1928) as an assistant, he became the head trainer and began his 32-year ministry (1929-61) to athletes in all Husky sports. He was known for his modest and unobtrusive manner, his wide grin, clever wit, and ability to take a joke. At the 1953 Final Four before the practice prior to the Kansas-Washington game, Clark began the required ankle taping of the players. One by one, he opened the tubes normally filled with rolls of tape only to find each tube packed with sand. Two Husky players, Joe Cipriano and Doug McClary, were cackling in the background before they revealed what they had done and recovered the missing tape. Clark was honored as the 1941 *Seattle Post-Intelligencer's* "Man of the Year" in sports and elected to the Husky Hall of Fame in 1990.

Husky List

Washington's First Team All-Americans Through 1949

1916	**Louis Seagraves, end**
1925	**George Wilson, halfback ***
1928	**Chuck Carroll, halfback ***
1929	**Merle Hufford, halfback**
1930	**Paul Schwegler, tackle**
1931	**Paul Schwegler, tackle**
1932	**Dave Nisbet, end**
1933	**Bill Smith, end**
1936	**Max Starcevich, guard ***
1937	**Vic Markov, tackle**
1940	**Jay MacDowell, end**
	Ray Frankowski, guard *
	Rudy Mucha, center *
1941	**Ray Frankowski, guard ***

*** Consensus All-American**

THE Husky Winter Sports Club was organized in the fall of 1944. The club provided discounted ski passes, gave ski instruction and even had its own private lodge in the Cascades purchased by the ASUW. It was sold in 1962. The first university bowling leagues were organized in the winter of 1944-45. Three leagues played a 10-week schedule at the "U" Bowling Alleys on 25th below the campus. The Log Rollers captured the men's league crown; the Goon Squad took top honors in Women's League I and the Kidwell Kids won Women's League II.

Husky Moment

The Husky football team played only conference teams during the 1945 season. They opened with a home win over Oregon, 20-6, and lost a week later to Cal in Berkeley, 27-14. Two shutout victories followed the Cal loss—6-0 win over Washington State and a 13-0 triumph over Oregon State. On Oct. 27, 1945, in Seattle, the Huskies met 20th-ranked USC. Washington opened the scoring, shortly after the second quarter began, when freshman quarterback, Joe Stone, hit Marv Hein with a perfect strike behind the Trojan secondary. Hein ambled the remaining 16 yards to the goal line untouched. Wally Dash's kick was wide, low and just awful. USC countered with a crushing 77-yard scoring drive. They converted to go ahead, 7-6. With just over nine minutes left in the game, the Huskies had the ball on the USC seven-yard line, fourth and goal. From the bench came place-kicking specialist Dash to line up for the field-goal attempt. The center snap did not go to the holder, substitute quarterback, Jesse Standish, but directly to Dash. Then Dash, who had never thrown a pass or attempted a run as a Husky, surprised everyone by spiraling a beautiful pass to Gordie Hungar in the end zone. Dash kicked the point-after to complete a storybook ending. Unfortunately, the 13-7 win was the high point of the season. The next week, the Huskies shut out Oregon, 7-0, on a soggy, muddy Multnomah Stadium field, but two losses in their last three games dashed their hopes for another Rose Bowl.

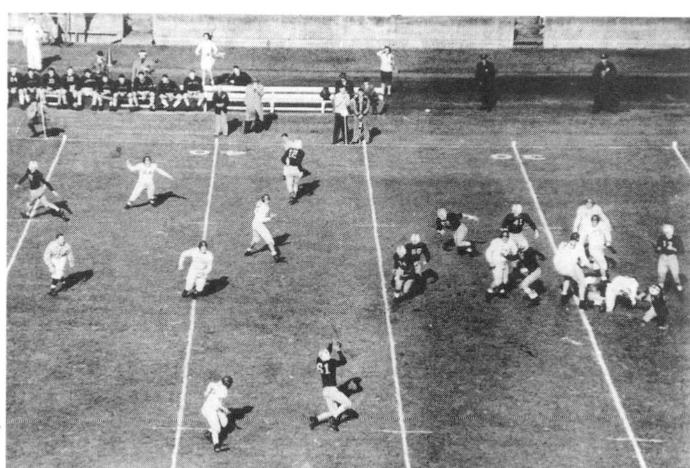
1946 Tyee

The Huckies upset USC 13-7.

Husky Spotlight

Tubby Graves retired after the 1946 baseball season. He coached Husky baseball teams for 24 years, compiling the third best winning percentage in Husky history— .602—and the third highest number of wins, 209. On June 21, 1946, the first Lake Washington International Regatta was held in Seattle. The feature event was a 2000-meter race with eight boats represented—Cal, Cornell, Harvard, MIT, Rutgers, University of British Columbia, Washington and Wisconsin. The boats raced from the Seattle Tennis Club to Madronna Beach. All shells were provided by Washington. The Huskies took an early lead and held it for 1500 meters. Then Cornell came roaring down the inside lane, with a powerful 37 beat, to win in a time of 7:19.7. MIT inched ahead of Washington to finish second. All boats rowed "uphill" into a very stiff wind. Most boats swamped on the return to Union Bay. Cornell was coached by Stork Stanford who rowed with Husky coach Al Ulbrickson on the 1926 national championship crew. Just before the start of the race, about 30 aircraft of all sizes soared upward to herald the biggest rowing event ever staged in Seattle.

Husky Highlight

Don Wold finished second in the mile run at the 1946 NCAA track and field meet in Minneapolis. He was in fourth place coming into the final stretch. Starting his sprint a little late, he was able to pass two runners and almost nipped Illinois' Bob Rehberg at the tape. Coach Edmundson thought he would have won if he had started his kick a little earlier since Wold had a lot left at the finish. Jack Torney returned from the Navy to coach his last tennis team. His netmen won 26 of 28 individual team matches. He also coached the swim team to its fifth Northern Division title in his then 11-year tenure. Husky swimmers set three Pacific Coast Conference records. George Heaney (backstroke), Bud Hill (breaststroke), and Pete Powlinson (freestyle) set the 300-yard medley relay record, 2:59.3. Powlinson set the 100 freestyle mark at 51:8 and Heaney established a record—1:30.1—in the backstroke.

UW Media Relations

Husky Legend

Jack Nichols

Jack Nichols had an outstanding varsity basketball career at Washington. He lettered as a freshman in 1944, and in 1947 and 1948. In 1945 and 1946, he lettered at USC where he was registered as a Navy trainee. Because of his five varsity years, the NCAA had to rule on his eligibility to play in the NCAA tournament in 1948. He was a three-year selection on the All-Northern Division team (1944, 1947 and 1948) and a two-year pick on the All-Southern Division unit in 1945 and 1946. Nichols probably is the only player in Pacific Coast Conference history to be selected to five all-star teams. He earned All-America honors in 1948 when he led the Huskies to their first NCAA tournament victory, 57-47, against Wyoming. In the NCAA Western Regional, he led all scorers with 39 points in two games. Also in 1948, Nichols set the Pacific Coast Conference single-game scoring record, with 39 points against Idaho. That year, he established the single-season record in the PCC—265 points. Both records stood up until 1953 when Washington's Bob Houbregs broke them. His 39 single- game total is still seventh in Husky history. He was the Huskies' co-captain in 1944 and the 1948 captain. He was the second Husky to play in the National Basketball Association, playing for nine seasons, including five with the Boston Celtics. He was a member of the 1957 Celtics when they won the NBA title. Nichols was elected to the Husky Hall of Fame in 1980.

Husky List

Huskies in the National Basketball Association

Charles Dudley—Seattle, 1973; Golden State, 1975-78; Chicago, 1979

James Edwards—Los Angeles Lakers, 1978, 1993-94; Indiana, 1978-83; Phoenix, 1983-87; Detroit, 1989-91; Los Angeles Clippers, 1991-92; Portland, 1994-95; Chicago, 1995-96

Chuck Gilmur—Chicago 1947-50; Washington 1950-51

Petur Gudmundsson—Portland, 1982-83; Los Angeles, 1986-87

Lars Hansen—Chicago, 1976; Seattle, 1978; Kansas City, 1980

Steve Hawes—Cleveland, 1972; Houston, 1975-76; Portland, 1976; Atlanta, 1977-83; Seattle, 1983-84

Bob Houbregs—Milwaukee, 1954; Baltimore, 1954-55; Boston, 1955; Fort Wayne, 1955-57; Detroit, 1958

George Irvine—Virginia Squires, 1971-75 (ABL); Denver, 1976

Todd MacCulloch—Philadelphia, 2000 to present

Rich Manning—Vancouver, 1996-97; Los Angeles Clippers, 1997-98

Louie Nelson—Capital Bullets, 1974; New Orleans Jazz, 1975-76; San Antonio, 1977; Kansas City, 1978; New Jersey, 1978

Jack Nichols—Washington, 1949-50: Tri-Cities, 1950-51; Milwaukee, 1953-54; Boston, 1954-58

Mark Pope—Indiana, 1997-1999

Eldridge Recasner—Denver, 1995; Houston, 1996; Atlanta, 1997-98; Charlotte, 1999-2000

Lorenzo Romar—Golden State, 1980-83; Milwaukee, 1984; Detroit, 1984-85

Mark Sanford—Miami, 1998; Sacramento, 1999

Detlef Schrempf—Dallas, 1986-89; Indiana, 1989-93; Seattle, 1994-99; Portland, 2000

Chris Welp—Philadelphia, 1988-89; San Antonio, 1990; Golden State, 1990

Phil Zevenbergen—San Antonio, 1988

Husky Lore

THE Husky golf team swung through Northern Division competition unbeaten and untied. After winning the title, Washington sent four golfers to represent the University, for the first time, at the NCAA championship in Princeton in late June. The four were Harold "Tass" Gjolme, Joe Greene, Jack Hazlett, and Vern Burks. Gjolme finished eighth overall.

1947 Tyee

Harold Gjolme

1946 W 1947

Husky Moment

Phelan Returns to Beat Huskies

Former Husky coach Jim Phelan brought his highly touted Gaels of St. Mary's (California) to Husky Stadium, on Sept. 28, 1946, for the season's opener. St. Mary's edged the Huskies, 24-20, in one of the most exciting football exhibitions held on the stadium gridiron. Most of the 41,000 fans were stunned when All-America halfback "Squirmin" Herman Wedemeyer skirted around end and raced 53 yards for the initial score. Washington countered with a 50-yard drive capped off by Dick Ottele's quarterback sneak. The kick was good, and Washington led, 7-6. A few minutes later, the Huskies scored again when halfback Larry Hatch intercepted a Denis O'Connor pass and ran it back 63 yards to the St. Mary's one-yard line. Two plays later, right halfback Whitey King wedged through to the end zone to put Washington ahead, 14-6. In the second half, disaster struck quickly when fullback Arnie Weinmeister fumbled on the Washington six-yard line, setting up St. Mary's second score. Wedemeyer's pass for the extra point was knocked down by Husky defenders. Late in the third quarter, Weinmeister raced 57 yards to the St. Mary's one, and two plays later, he plunged in for Washington's final score. Early in the fourth quarter, St. Mary's got a first down when Washington was penalized for delay of the game. From the Husky 43, O'Connor hit Hank Van Gleason on a "stutter" pass for 13 yards and he covered the remaining 30 yards for a touchdown. After Wedemeyer's kick went wide, the Huskies still led, 20-18. After receiving the kickoff, the Huskies drove to the St. Mary's 47. On the next play, Gonzalo Morales intercepted Ottele's pass on the 25-yard line and lateraled to Johnny Johnson who was knocked out of bounds on the Washington 20. After two plays, Halfback Jack Verutti hit O'Connor with a 13-yard pass for the go ahead touchdown. Verutti's kick was wide. The Huskies threatened two times in the final minutes. An intercepted pass ended one drive on the Gaels' 30-yard line. On the second drive, Bob Nelson could not quite handle Ottele's pass in the end zone. The game ended with the Gaels outscoring Washington, 24-20. The Huskies ended the season with a 5-4-0 record.

1947 Tyee

Husky Spotlight

Fred Provo received the Flaherty Medal as the football team's most inspirational player. He led the Huskies in rushing in the 1946 season. Husky fans knew him as a hard driver with the speed of a gazelle. Few knew that he sustained an injury in the Battle of the Bulge in late 1944 and was told he would never play football again.

The 1947 Husky baseball team was 9-7 in Art McLarney's first year as baseball coach, succeeding Tubby Graves. McLarney was a former Washington State baseball and basketball star. The Huskies finished second to WSC in the Northern Division race. First baseman Sammy White was the team's leading hitter and finished second in the Division with a batting average of .377. White made the All-Northern Division first team.

In the NCAA track meet held in Salt Lake City, three Huskies placed—Jack Hensey was fifth in the 880, Bill Steed was fifth in the two-mile event, and Lyle Clark finished sixth in the 120-yard high hurdles won by world record holder, Harrison Dillard.

Husky Highlight

All three Husky crews were back in the IRA regatta on June 21, 1947. The regatta was not held from 1942-1946, due to World War II. The freshmen won the two-mile event in 9:40.3. The junior varsity finished fourth, and the varsity was third. Right after the races, Coach Al Ulbrickson nominated the freshmen crew, except for number-six oarsman, Bill Works, to row in the second annual Lake Washington regatta on June 28. A total of 12 boats were in the race, the largest number of crews ever to row on the lake. Over 100,000 spectators lined the Seward park 2000-meter course. With perfect conditions, Yale jumped to an early lead. Half-way, five boats were still in contention—Yale, Harvard, Washington, Cornell, and Pennsylvania. At the 1500 mark, it was Yale, Harvard and Washington. In the final drive, Harvard swept to the finish first. Yale staved off the Huskies to take second, a quarter of a boat length ahead. The victorious Harvard crew was coached by Tom Bolles, another former Husky oarsman who rowed in the 1926 national championship boat.

Husky Legend

UW Media Relations

Sammy White

Sammy White graduated from Lincoln High School in Seattle in 1945 and led the Lynx to the 1945 state high school basketball championship. As a Husky, White was an outstanding baseball and basketball player. He earned more recognition during his Washington years as a basketball player because of the Huskies success in the Pacific Coast Conference and the NCAA tournament. He was an All-Northern Division forward selection in 1948 and 1949 and All-Coast in 1948 (there was no PCC team selected while White was playing for the Huskies). In 1949, he was picked for the All-West team, the selections made by the National Association of Basketball coaches. The other PCC selections were USC's Bill Sharman and Stanford's George Yardley. White, along with Jack Nichols, led Washington to its first NCAA tournament win, 57-47, against Wyoming in 1948. He played varsity baseball for the Huskies in 1947 and 1948 and was the team's leading hitter in both years. After graduation, he played with the Pacific Coast League's Seattle Rainiers from 1949 to 1951. He then started an 11-year career in major league baseball, starring nine years as a catcher with the Boston Red Sox from 1951-59. He finished his career with Milwaukee (1961) and Philadelphia (1962) in the National League. White was elected to the Husky Hall of Fame in 1984.

HUSKY LIST

Huskies in Major League Baseball

Rick Anderson (1978) — **New York Mets, 1986**
Pitcher — **Kansas City Royals, 1987-88**

Mike Blowers (1986) — **New York Yankees, 1989-91**
Third baseman — **Seattle Mariners, 1992-95,1997**
Los Angeles Dodgers, 1996
Oakland Athletics, 1998

Dode Brinker (1905) — **Philadelphia Phillies, 1912**
Outfielder, Third baseman

Scott Brow (1991) — **Toronto Blue Jays, 1993-94, 1996**
Pitcher — **Arizona Diamond Backs, 1998**

Chet Johnson (1939) — **St. Louis Browns, 1946**
Pitcher

Ron Johnson (1980) — **Kansas City Royals, 1982-83**
Second baseman — **Montreal Expos, 1984**

Aaron Myette (1996) — **Chicago White Sox, 1999**
Pitcher

Royal Shaw (1905) — **Pittsburgh Pirates, 1908**
Infielder

Sean Spencer (1996) — **Seattle Mariners, 1999**
Pitcher

Kevin Stocker (1991) — **Philadelphia Phillies, 1993-97**
Shortstop — **Tampa Devil Rays, 1998-2000**
Anaheim Angels, 2000

Sammy White (1948) — **Boston Red Sox, 1951-59**
Catcher — **Milwaukee Braves, 1961**
Philadelphia Phillies, 1962

HUSKY LORE

HEC EDMUNDSON completed his last year as Washington's head basketball coach with a 1947 overall season record of 16-8, finishing third in the Northern Division, with an 8-8 conference record. His career record of 488-195 is the best in Husky history. In conference wins, he ranks third among all who have coached in the Pacific Coast Conference (and its successors). The Washington Pavilion was renamed the Clarence S. "Hec" Edmundson Pavilion on Jan. 16, 1948. Edmundson continued as track and field coach through the 1954 season. Art McLarney, the Husky baseball coach and former Washington State baseball and basketball star, succeeded Edmundson. He coached for three seasons before resigning for health reasons.

1949 Tyee

Art McLarney

1947 W 1948

HUSKY MOMENT

Washington wins its First NCAA Tournament Game

Washington's basketball team went through a hectic 1948 season. At the end of the Northern Division race, Oregon State and Washington were tied with 10-6 records, one game ahead of Washington State, at 9-7. A one-game playoff to determine the ND champion was played at Oregon's McArthur Court. The Huskies easily handled the Beavers, 59-42, and then journeyed to Berkeley to meet the Southern Division winner, California, on March 12. Cal won the first game, 64-51. The Huskies stormed back to take the second, 64-57, led by forward Sammy White (21 points) and center Jack Nichols (18 points). In the third game, Washington overcame a six-point half-time deficit (30-24) to win the PCC title, 59-49. Representing the Far West in the Western Regional NCAA tournament at Kansas City, Missouri, the Huskies fell victim to the Baylor Bears. The Huskies opened up a 34-17 lead in the first half and were up 37-26, to start the second half. The Baylor five, led by guard Bill Taylor, came out strongly and narrowed the lead to 50-46 with 10 minutes left. Baylor took the lead at the seven-minute mark, 55-53, but Washington regained the lead, 60-58, with about four minutes to go, on a great shuffle pass from White to Nichols for the lay-up. In the closing moments, Baylor forged ahead to win, 64-62. Taylor led all scorers with 20 points, and Nichols paced the Huskies with 17. Baylor beat Kansas State, 60-52 to win the western crown and go on to the NCAA finals. They lost to Kentucky at Madison Square Garden, 58-42. The Huskies met the Wyoming Cowboys in the Western Regional consolation game. Jack Nichols poured in 22 to lead Washington to a 57-47 victory, their first in NCAA tournament history. The Huskies led 32-24 at half-time and increased the lead to 47-29 with 12 minutes to go in the second half. Jack Nichols held Wyoming center Jerry Reed to two points. Nichols topped all tournament players with 39 points and White was seventh with 25.

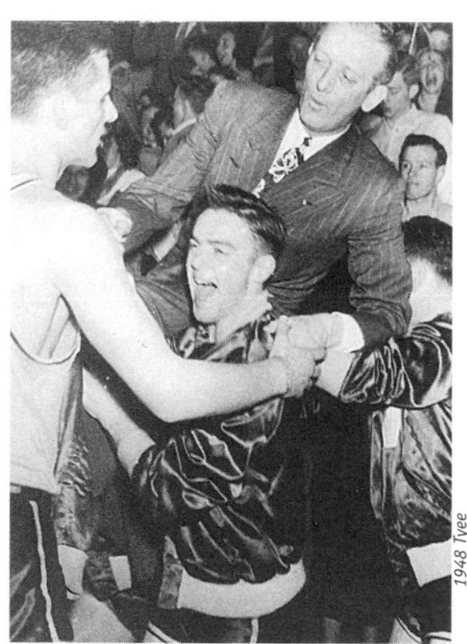

1948 Tyee

Center Jack Nichols and Coach Art McLarney celebrate Washington's Pacific Coast Conference title.

Husky Spotlight

Washington crews again swept all races in the Intercollegiate Rowing Association regatta on June 22, 1948, in Poughkeepsie. It was the third time that Washington boats scored a sweep. In the freshmen race, Washington's Ken Brockman jumped his slide in an attempt to put something extra in the first pull of the oar. He landed on the track and ripped the back of his leg open. He rowed on—he required nine stitches after the race—to help the Huskies overcome a poor start to beat favored Navy by two lengths in 9:46.9, over two miles. In the junior varsity race, Washington beat Cal by three lengths, covering the three- mile course in 14:28.6. The varsity finished the sweep by beating Cal in the three-miler in 14:06.4. In the Olympic Trials, over a 2000-meter course on Princeton's Lake Carnegie, the Huskies lost to Cal in the semifinals, on July 2. Cal led by more than a boat length at the 1500 mark. Then Washington started its sprint and closed rapidly on the fading Cal boat. The Bears had just enough to hold off the furious Husky finish to win by six inches in a time of 5:58.0. On July 3, Cal became the U.S. Olympic eight, beating Harvard and Princeton in the finals, in a time of 6:02.2. In the 1948 London Olympic games, Cal beat the rest of the world and won the Olympic gold medal.

HUSKY HIGHLIGHT

Jack Nichols scored 39 points, on March 5, 1948, to lead the Huskies to a win over Idaho, 77-37. It was the best single-game total in Pacific Coast Conference history. He also set the single-season record of 265 points. Nichol's teammate, Sammy White, led the 1948 Husky baseball team in hitting for the second straight season. His batting average was .367. The Husky swimming team won the Northern Division championship—its eighth in nine years—and finished 10th in the NCAA championship event.

Husky Legend

UW Media Relations

The 1948 Olympics gold medal four surround coxswain Allen Morgan. From left, Warren Westlund, Bob Martin, Bob Will, Gus Giovanelli.

After the Huskies swept all three races at the Intercollegiate Rowing Association regatta in June 1948, Coach Al Ulbrickson entered his varsity eight in the Olympic Trials in Princeton, N.J. Ulbrickson also selected the four oarsmen from the stern of the junior varsity eight, along with the coxswain, to enter another event—the four-oared with coxswain. The five men—Gordon Giovanelli, Bob Martin, Allen Morgan (coxswain), Warren Westlund, and Bob Will—had never rowed in a four-oared event before. The crew won the Olympic Trials to become the U.S. Olympic team representative in the four-oared event. George Pocock was the crew's coach in the 1948 London Olympics. The rowing events were held on the Thames River in Henley. Pocock was a great choice not only because of his rowing knowledge, but because he had lived in England as a boy and rowed on the Thames. Pocock suggested to Ky Ebright, a former Husky coxswain and coach of the Cal varsity eight, that they go down river to Marlow and less-congested conditions to train. Back at Henley for the preliminary event, the Huskies drew the Great Britain crew out of the field of 16 boats. On Aug. 5, 1948, they embarrassed the home crew, winning by four lengths, in a time of 6:48.8. On Aug. 7, they had to row two races. They beat Finland in the quarterfinals and France by two lengths in the semifinals. On Aug. 9, the European crews got off to good starts and the Huskies were soon trailing the Swiss by about two lengths and the Danes by one. Halfway through the race, Washington had pulled even with the crew from Denmark and was only a half length behind the Swiss. At the three-quarter mark, the Huskies upped the beat to 42-44 and Pocock, watching from the shore, said he could see the bow elevated out of the water. The Husky crew representing the United States won the gold medal, beating the Swiss by about two lengths in a time of 6:50.3. They returned home with the gold medal, the second in Husky rowing history. The victory is the only time a U.S. crew has won the four with coxswain event. The crew was inducted in the Citizens Savings Athletic Foundation Hall of Fame in 1976 and the Husky Hall of Fame in 1981.

Husky List

First Team All-Conference Baseball Selections Since 1958 (more than one year)

Don Daniels, 2b, 1958, 59
George Grant, SS, 1959, 60
Phil Swimley, P, 1960, Of, 1961
Ray Price, P, 1973, 74
Ron Johnson, 2b, 1978,79, Dh, 1980
Jeb Best, Of, 1981, 82
Bob MacDonald, Coach, 1981, 85, 90, 92
Timo Donahue, 2b, 1987, If, 1989
Kevin Stocker, SS, 1990, 91
Brandon Newell, P, 1992, 93
Randy Jorgenson, 1b, 1992, 93
Joe Trippy, Of, 1994, 95
Ryan Soules, 1b, 1996, 97
Brett Merrick, P, 1994, 95
Kevin Miller, SS, 1996*, 97*, 98
Chris Magruder, Of, 1996, 97, 98
Ken Knutson, Coach, 1997, 98
***Conference Player of the Year**

ONE of the most significant campus developments after the war years was the establishment of the Health Sciences School incorporating medical and dental instruction. In 1945, the State Legislature appropriated $3,750,000 for a building and $450,000 for operations. University President Sieg reached retirement age during the war but continued in office until the Board of Regents could appoint a successor. They wanted a person to lead the university in the post war era and with knowledge of the health sciences. They found Dr. Raymond B. Allen, the head of the University of Illinois' Chicago campus and dean of the university's medical school. He became Washington's president in September 1946.

1948 W 1949

Husky Moment

The Husky tennis team won Washington's 14th Northern Division title in 1949 and its 10th straight championship. They also recorded a perfect season, winning every match. Lefthanded Jim Brink won his third consecutive Northern Division singles title. In late June, four Washington players went to the 1949 NCAA tennis tournament in Austin Texas—Jim Brink, Fred Fisher, Jack Lowe, and Wally Bostick. Brink and Fisher advanced to the third round of the singles division before being eliminated. Lowe and Bostick lost in the first round. The four players were also in the doubles division. Neither pair was seeded. In the first round, Lowe and Bostick were eliminated. Brink and Fisher won their first-round match against UCLA's Glenn Bassett and Jack Shoemaker, 6-1, 6-2. They won the next day's second round by trimming Stanford's Bob Lewis and Kirk Mecham, 6-0, 7-5. Next, they advanced to the quarterfinals against a duo from Rollins College, Buddy Behrens and Gardner Larned. The Floridians could not handle the Husky pair, losing 5-7 and 4-6. Brink and Fisher were on to the semifinals. Host Texas pinned their hopes on the Longhorn team of Felix Kelley and Bobby Goldfarb. Now, the Husky duo had to win three matches to get to the finals. Brink and Fisher easily dispatched the Texans in straight sets, 6-2, 6-3, 6-4. In the finals, on June 25, they met a University of San Francisco pair that they had defeated earlier in the Seattle doubles championship. USF's Alf Larsen and Sam Match won the first set, 6-4. Then Brink and Fisher scooted around the court to make impossible recoveries. Fisher switched from his usually tame game to slaughtering every ball on which he got his racket. The team's superior volleying and Fisher's great service game powered them to a four-set victory, 4-6, 6-3, 6-3, 6-3. Washington took second place in the team standings behind San Francisco.

1950 Tyee

Jim Brink

Husky Spotlight

In 1948, new facilities for the rowing program were built. On June 28, 1947, the Board of Regents named it the Hiram Conibear Shellhouse and approved construction plans in February 1948. It was the first building designed and built for Washington crews. The two-story building cost $325,000. It contained a 100-foot long dining and social room leading to a tiled terrace deck overlooking Lake Washington. The upper deck also included coaches' offices and a study hall. George Pocock's shell-building shops occupied the rest of the upper deck of the building. On the lower deck were lockers, shower rooms and storage space for 42 shells. The freshmen and junior varsity crew won the Intercollegiate Rowing Association regatta and the varsity finished second. Washington won the Poughkeepsie Regatta Trophy for the second time since the award originated in 1947. The trophy was awarded to the school accumulating the highest number of points in the varsity, junior varsity, and freshmen races.

Husky Highlight

Howard O'Dell started his five-year football coaching tenure at Washington in 1948. He came from Yale where he compiled a .700 winning percentage over a six-year career. Shortly after arriving at Washington, he was confined to bed with a kidney ailment. Reg Root, a Yale graduate, expanded his duties as line coach and took over the head coaching responsibilities in Odell's absence. The Huskies did not help speed Odell's recovery as they went through a dismal 2-7-1 season. The season was marked by the deaths of two players—Henry "Mike" Scanlon and Al Kean. Mike received the Flaherty Medal in 1948. On Nov. 27, 1948, Washington played its first football game with Notre Dame. The Irish were coming off a 1947 national championship season and ranked number two in the nation. Coached by Frank Leahy, Notre Dame won the 1948 game, 46-0, before 52,000 fans in South Bend.

Husky Legend

Jim Brink and Fred Fisher

1950 Tyee

Fred Fisher

Jim Brink and Fred Fisher won the NCAA tennis doubles title in 1949. They are two of the three Huskies in Washington history to win an NCAA tennis championship—Wallace Scott won the singles title in 1924. Brink earned three varsity letters in 1947-49 and was the Northern Division singles champion in those years. He won the Northern Division doubles title in 1947 and 1948 with partner, Jack Lowe. The 1949 doubles final was cancelled because of rain. In the 1948 NCAA tournament, the Husky duo was eliminated in the second round. Brink cruised through to the singles semi-finals. He lost in four sets to Henry Likas of the University of San Francisco—4-6, 1-6, 7-5, and 3-6. Likas beat top-ranked Vic Seixas in the finals. In 1949, Brink reached the quarterfinals in the national amateur singles tournament. He lost to Poncho Gonzales, the nation's number-one ranked amateur netman. Fred Fisher only played for Washington in 1949. He attended the U.S. Naval Academy for two years. He was the Midshipmen's number-two player in 1946 and number one in 1947. Next year, he attended Washington but had to sit out the 1948 season because of NCAA transfer rules. Fisher became Brink's doubles partner right before the NCAA tournament. He and Brink advanced to the third round of the NCAA singles division before being eliminated. In the doubles, they swept all the competition away. Brink and Fisher won their first-round match, 6-1, 6-2. They won the next day's second round, 6-0, 7-5. Next, they advanced to the quarterfinals, winning 7-5 and 6-4. In the semifinals they beat a Texas team in straight sets, 6-2, 6-3, 6-4. In the finals, on June 25, they lost to USF's Alf Larsen and Sam Match in the first set, 6-4. Then, the Huskies' superior volleying and service game powered them to a four-set victory, 4-6, 6-3, 6-3, 6-3. Brink and Fisher were elected to the Husky Hall of Fame in 1989.

Husky List

Husky Men and Women in National Collegiate Tennis Championships (quarterfinals or better)

Men's Singles

1924 Wallace Scott—National Collegiate Champion
1948 Jim Brink—Lost in NCAA semifinals
1952 Bill Quillian—Lost in NCAA quarterfinals
1953 Bill Quillian—Lost in NCAA quarterfinals
1954 Bill Quillian—Lost in NCAA quarterfinals
1955 Bill Quillian—Lost in NCAA finals

Men's Doubles

1949 Jim Brink and Fred Fisher—NCAA champions
1953 Bill Quillian and Don Flye—Lost in NCAA quarterfinals

Women's Singles

1971 Trish Bostrom—Lost in AIAW quarterfinals
1972 Trish Bostrom—Lost in AIAW quarterfinals
1998 Kristina Kraszewski—Lost in NCAA quarter finals

Women's Doubles

1971 Trish Bostrom and Janis Metcalf (Redmonds College)—Won the AIAW mixed college championship

ALTHOUGH the 1948 Washington-Notre Dame game in South Bend was a disaster on the football field, the Washington Alumni Association was pleased to recover Sunny Boy, Washington's mascot before the 1920s. Sunny Boy's portrait appeared on the masthead of the *Sun Dodger,* the lusty campus humor magazine in 1919. The three-and-a-half foot wooden statue was meant to be a symbol of "Joe College"—books under one arm, a football under the other. In 1923, Sunny Boy was removed from the trophy room of a university fraternity house as a prank and shipped to South Bend to keep it in hiding. Curly Harris, the Alumni Association director, mentioned the legend of the statue to Midwest sportswriters prior to the Notre Dame game. A farmer, living outside of South Bend, read the story and matched the description of the mascot with one gathering dust in his barn. Sunny Boy was presented to university officials at the football game and has resided ever since at the UW Alumni Association offices.

1949 W 1950

Husky Moment

Hugh McElhenny's Record Breaking Kickoff Return

Coach Howard Odell was able to coach for the entire 1949 football season, after fully recovering from a kidney ailment that sidelined him during most of the 1948 schedule. The Huskies finished seventh in the conference with an overall record of 3-7-0. Two sophomores—Don Heinrich and Hugh McElhenny—broke on the scene and began to rewrite Husky football records. In the second game at Minnesota, on Sept. 24, 1949, over 58,000 fans had just settled in their seats. The suddenness of what happened next shocked the Gopher rooters. McElhenny, with the long graceful sweep of his arms, gathered in the opening kickoff on his four-yard line, cut sharply to his right and faked a hand-off to Roland Kirkby. He then set straight for the Minnesota goal line. Not a Gopher hand touched him as Husky teammates cleared his path. At midfield, McElhenny was in the clear and he raced the last 50 yards not even deigning to look back at his pursuers. The 96-yard return established a Husky record and still stands as the sixth longest kickoff return in Husky history. Unfortunately, Minnesota swung into action behind a huge offensive line, powered by All-America Leo Nomellini and Clayton Tonnemaker. They rolled to a 35-7 half-time lead and won 48-20. One week later, Notre Dame made its first trip to Seattle. Led by All-America Leon Hart (who would receive the Heisman Trophy in 1949—the only lineman to ever receive the award), the Irish fell behind, 7-0. The Huskies scored when Don Heinrich threw a perfect 40-yard strike to Roland Kirkby who had outraced the Notre Dame secondary. He caught the pass on the Notre Dame 15 in full stride and sped across the goal line. Jim Rosenzweig kicked the extra point. With 83 seconds to go in the first half, Irish quarterback Bob Williams hit Hart on a 20-yard scoring play. Powered by another All-America, halfback Emil Sitko, Notre Dame rolled over the Huskies in the second half to win, 27-7, enroute to their fourth national championship between 1943 and 1949.

1952 Tyee

Hugh McElhenny

Husky Spotlight

The scene of the 1950 Intercollegiate Rowing Association regatta changed to the Ohio River in Marietta, Ohio. On race day, June 17, 1950, a prolonged rainstorm caused the river to rise, and conditions became hazardous. The races were all shortened to two miles, but the conditions did not disrupt Husky dominance in national competition. For the fourth time in IRA history, the Huskies won all three races. No other crew, up to that point, had been able to achieve the feat once. The freshmen crew won the opener over even a shorter course—about a mile and a half—beating Navy by a half length. The junior varsity boat turned in the surprise of the day, beating a very strong Cal boat by more than one and half lengths, in 8:10.4. In the varsity race, Washington got off to a slow start, and Stanford and Wisconsin took an early lead. At the three-quarter mile mark, Washington demonstrated its tremendous power by taking the lead. At the halfway point, Washington had a half boat lead. Navy had misfortune when its number-six man broke his oar on a marker buoy. True to the Navy tradition, the seven other oarsmen rowed the rest of the race. With a quarter of a mile left in the race, Washington had a length and a half lead. Then Cal made a terrific move to pass all the other boats and trailed only Washington. Washington finished almost three lengths ahead of Cal. The time was 8:07.5. In the victorious Washington boat was a sophomore, Al Ulbrickson, who knew the Husky coach very well.

Husky Highlight

The Husky ski team finished third in the National Intercollegiate championships at Arapahoe Basin, Colorado. Gustav Raaum led the Huskies by winning the ski jumping event with leaps of 140 feet and 138 feet; his teammate and Norwegian countryman, Gunnar Sunde, was second. Raaum finished ninth in the cross country race to win the combined nordic and ski jumping title. The Huskies scored 1435.54 team points to trail Dartmouth (1483.84) and Denver University (1442.56) and finish third in team standings.

Husky Legend

Gustav Raaum Collection

Gustav Raaum

Gus Raaum was born in Norway and came to the United States in 1947 as a member of the Norwegian Ski Jumping Team. In 1946, he won the Junior Division of the Homenkollen ski jumping competition, in Oslo Norway. Homenkollen is often referred to as the world's premier ski jumping event. Raaum entered Washington in 1947 and competed for three years on the Husky ski team. In 1948, he won the Pacific Northwest and California-Nevada ski jumping championships. In 1950, he added another Pacific Northwest title and won the National Collegiate ski jumping and nordic combined (jumping and cross country) ski championships at Arapahoe Basin, Colorado. He served for 28 years on the Ski Jumping Committee of the International Ski Federation (FIS). During that period, he was one of the three U.S. delegates to the International Ski Congress. Raaum chaired the FIS jumping committee for 16 years. He was Chief of Ski Jumping events at the 1980 Lake Placid Winter Olympics. In 1980, he was elected to the U.S. National Ski Hall of Fame. Rauum entered the Husky Hall of Fame in 1992.

Husky List

All-Time Husky Football Team First 50 Years of the 20th Century

Player (Year Graduated)	Position	Number of Votes
Bill Smith (1933)	End	7,370
Dave Nisbet (1932)	End	7,812
Vic Markov (1937)	Tackle	7,051
Paul Schwegler (1931)	Tackle	5,115
Bill Wright (1927)	Guard	6,620
Steve Silvinski (1938)	Guard	4,824
Walt Harrison (1942)	Center	9,246
Wee Coyle (1911)	Quarterback	5,717
George Wilson (1925)	Halfback	10,282
Chuck Carroll (1928)	Halfback	7,658
Elmer Tesreau (1925)	Fullback	7,180

THE significant growth in the student body and related activities after World War II ended, which led to the construction of the first phase of the Husky Union Building (HUB) in 1949. It cost $1,265,000. Its present configuration resulted from seven additional phases of construction costing almost $6 million. The HUB houses a full range of student services as well as facilities for the general campus community—eating places, entertainment, a bookstore branch, barber shop, meeting rooms, and student-government offices.

1950 Tyee

George Wilson

George Wilson was one of the best all-around college players in the United States, a fact recognized by Grantland Rice who made All-America selections for *Collier's Magazine.* In 1925, Rice named Wilson to his first-team All-America backfield along with Illinois' Red Grange and Stanford's Ernie Nevers. Wilson was the first consensus All-America in Husky history.

His selection was even more noteworthy when taking into account the impact and bias of the Eastern sportswriters on football coverage in Wilson's playing days. Damon Runyan, a New York sportswriter, actually saw Wilson play in the 1926 Rose Bowl against Alabama. Runyan described Wilson as "one of the finest players of this or any other time." In 1969, the Centennial of college football, Wilson was named to the all-time Western All-Star football team. In the backfield were Nevers, Morley Drury of USC and the Trojans' O.J. Simpson.

Wilson was a high school star in Everett on a team coached by Enoch Bagshaw who became Washington's head football coach in 1921. In 1923, Wilson's sophomore year, he was a major reason for Washington becoming one of the most formidable teams on the West Coast. As a triple-threat back, he could dictate games from either side of the line of scrimmage. It was Wilson's running, passing, and tackling that led to a shutout of heavily favored USC, 22-0, a 10-1 regular season and Washington's first trip to the Rose Bowl. Wilson was the Huskies' offensive star in the Jan. 1, 1924, tie with Navy, 14-14.

In 1924, Wilson led Washington to an 8-1-1 record and was a second-team All-America selection. He ran, he threw passes, he caught passes. He blocked and tackled. He was the team's punter. He was fast and quick and utterly fearless. He was a quiet man who did not talk very much and did not assume anything for himself. He had a terrific stiff arm and he used it on many of his runs. Harold Patton, the right halfback on the 1925 team remembers Wilson knocking five opponents off their feet, stiff-arming his way to a touchdown. He was becoming a legend.

In 1925, his 14 touchdowns and 85 points led Washington to an unbeaten regular-season record, 10-0-1. The team outscored its regular-season opponents 461-39 and led the nation in scoring. Only the 1991 Husky national championship team has scored as many points in a regular season. Wilson climaxed his brilliant career in the Rose Bowl against Alabama, a game called by many as the greatest Rose Bowl game. Alabama won 20-19 primarily because Wilson was out of the game with injuries for 22 minutes. During the 38 minutes that he played, Washington scored three touchdowns and accounted for 300 yards. Wilson passed for two touchdowns and set up the third with his great running. He was voted the game's co-Most Valuable Player along with Alabama's Johnny Mack Brown.

A review of Washington's record before Wilson's career showed the impact he had on the Husky football program. In the three years before Wilson joined the varsity, Washington had a combined 10-10-2 overall record and a 4-7-2 Pacific Coast Conference record. During Wilson's three varsity years (1923-25), the Huskies won 28 of 34 games (28-3-3), lost only two conference games and outscored their opponents 1135 to 141. They played in two Rose Bowls and led the nation in scoring in 1924 and 1925. More than anyone, he attracted fans. Attendance for regular-season games increased from 95,900 in 1922 to 186,000 in 1925.

Was Wilson better than Red Grange, reputedly the best player of Wilson's day? Two weeks after the 1926 Rose Bowl, Wilson played his first professional game. It was in the Los Angeles Coliseum. Wilson kicked off to Grange and hit the "Galloping Ghost" so hard that Grange became a groggy ghost. Wilson gained 128 yards to Grange's 30. A week later he again outplayed Grange. A San Francisco newspaper report read: "Wilson plainly showed that he is a great football player, as great if not greater than Harold "Red" Grange."

Wilson was elected to the College Football of Fame (1951), the Rose Bowl Hall of Fame (1991), and the Husky Hall of Fame (1980).

Hugh McElhenny

No football player in Washington history has made more people say: "I don't believe that" or "Did you see that move?" than Hugh Edward McElhenny. He still is the most spectacular single offensive force in Husky football history.

John Jarsted was the radio voice of the Huskies when McElhenny was playing at Washington. "I know everything that was written about him, and none of it was adequate. Hugh was always doing the impossible." Jarsted said: "He drove tacklers batty. The idea that Hugh was a great runner because of how he practiced was garbage. He was a free spirit, often goofed off during the week and was called on the carpet. What he did on Saturdays wasn't taught. It came straight down from heaven."

McElhenny had great speed and hurdling ability. In addition to his extraordinary football skills, he was a brilliant track and field performer at George Washington High School in Los Angeles. In 1947, McElhenny was unbeaten in the long jump and both the high and low hurdles and won the California high school state championship in those events. He tied the existing high school world record for the 120-yard high hurdles and ran the 100 yard dash in 9.7 seconds.

McElhenny attended Compton Junior College in the fall of 1948 where he scored 23 touchdowns, a dozen of them on runs of more than 30 yards. In the spring of 1949, he married Peggy Opthand and entered Washington in the fall of 1949.

In the second game of the 1949 season, an away contest against Minnesota, McElhenny electrified everybody when he took the opening kickoff 96 yards for a touchdown. It was the first of his many exciting runs. In the home opener in 1950, he ran 91 yards for a touchdown in the Huskies' 33-7 victory over Kansas State. In the same season, in a game against Oregon State, he slogged 59 yards to the end zone and then scored twice more to turn a close game into a 35-6 rout. In the final game of the 1950 season against Washington State in Spokane, McElhenny ran for a school record of 296 yards and set a Pacific Coast Conference season rushing yardage record of 1,107. He scored five touchdowns, the last one an 84-yarder.

The next year, his senior year, McElhenny established another school record with a dazzling 100-yard touchdown punt return against USC. In the California game, he scored 22 of the Huskies' 28 points, six coming on a 65-yard touchdown run from scrimmage. He finished the season with 936 rushing yards, 24 catches for 339 yards, and 17 touchdowns. His 17 touchdowns, together with 23 points after touchdowns, gave him a season scoring total of 125 points. His season points total came within one of the nation's leader, San Francisco's Ollie Matson. His point total was 34 more than Chuck Carroll's previous Husky record of 91 set in 1927. He is the only Husky to have a punt return, a kickoff return, and a run from scrimmage, all over 90 yards and all for touchdowns.

"He was the darnest animal," said UCLA coach Red Sanders. "He ran around you, through you, and if the situation demanded it, right over you."

In one home game, he was pinned on the sideline as a defender approached him. McElhenny leaned his upper body as far to the boundary marker as possible as if attempting to put off the inevitable tackle. Just before the opponent made contact, Hugh swung his whole body toward the defender and knocked him head over heels and raced on for a touchdown.

An All-America selection in 1951, McElhenny was eighth in the balloting for the Heisman Trophy, won by Princeton's Dick Kazmaier. McElhenny was named Seattle's Man of the Year in Sports for 1951. He played in the 1952 East-West Shrine game, Hula Bowl game, and College All-Star game. McElhenny was selected to the National Football League Hall of Fame, the College Football Hall of Fame, and was a charter member of the Husky Hall of Fame.

1950-59

1950 W 1951

Husky Moment

Pacific Coast Champions in Dye's First Year

Coach Tippy Dye's first year as Washington's head basketball coach was a great one because of the scoring of junior Frank Guisness and sophomore center Bob Houbregs and the hustle and floor leadership of senior Louie Soriano. The team compiled a 24-6 season and was ranked fifth in the nation at the end of the campaign. The Huskies reeled off 10 straight wins to start the season before losing the next four of five. They won the Northern Division title by winning nine of the last 10 games and headed into the Pacific Coast Conference playoff with UCLA at Edmundson Pavilion. Behind 11-1 during the opening minutes of play, the Huskies rallied to trail by three at half-time, 33-30. They held the Bruins to 18 points in the second half and bombed in 40 to win easily, 70-51. Guisness led all scorers with 21. In the second game, Washington won, 71-54, with Guisness again on top with 22. In the Western Regional tournament in Kansas City, Missouri, the Huskies were seeded fourth in a field of eight teams and first faced Southwest Conference winner, Texas A&M. Washington led 27-15 at half-time and were up 48-40 with six minutes left. They held the Aggies scoreless the rest of the game and won 62-40. In the second round, Washington met Oklahoma A&M. The team shot horribly in the first half and trailed 36-23. In the second half, Washington closed to within one point, 50-49, eventually losing 61-57. In the consolation game, the Huskies trounced BYU 80-67. Houbregs racked up a tournament-high 53 points and was selected to the all-tournament first team.

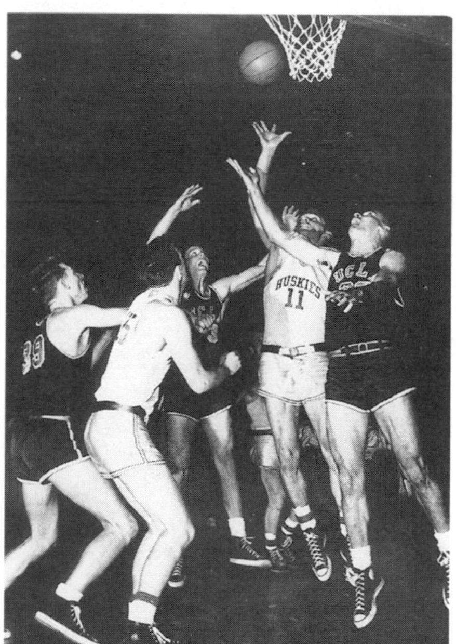

1951 Tyee

Frank Guisness (No. 11) and Bob Houbregs hit the boards as the Huskies beat Cal enroute to the Pacific Coast Conference title.

Husky Spotlight

Dick Sprague was a three-year letter winner in football (1950-52) and played varsity basketball in 1952. He was an All-America defensive back in 1950. He and teammate Don Heinrich were the first sophomores in Husky history to earn All-America honors. Sprague made seven interceptions in 1950, a total that ranks him tied for fourth all-time in Husky record books. Despite a back injury that limited his action in his senior year, he had 13 career interceptions and he is tied for third all-time in that category. His speed and athleticism enabled him to play several positions during his career. He played offensive halfback and was selected to the All-Pacific Coast Conference first team in 1950. He performed the punting duties in 1951 and returned punts and kickoffs in his three years as a Husky. He recorded the longest Husky kickoff return (56 yards) in 1951. Sprague was the Husky captain in 1952 and received the 101 Club's Scholarship Award in that year. Sprague was selected to the Husky Centennial team in 1990. He entered the Husky Hall of Fame in 1995.

Husky Highlight

The Husky football team finished with an 8-2 record and was ranked 11th in the nation. The key conference game was on Nov. 4, when a record crowd (55,245) watched the Homecoming game against California. Both teams were unbeaten in the conference with the winner on the inside track to the Rose Bowl. Late in the first quarter, Dick Sprague intercepted a Jim Marinos pass on the Cal 45 and returned it four yards. Don Heinrich's pass to Bill Earley and Roland Kirkby's 12-yard run put the ball on the Bears' two-yard line as the quarter ended. On the second play of the new quarter, Earley spun into the line and scored. Jim Rosenzweig converted and the Huskies led 7-0. Cal responded quickly. They went 65 yards in 12 plays to even the score. In the second half, Washington got an early break. Husky linebacker Bill Peterson recovered a Cal fumble on the Bears' 33. On fourth and eight, the Cal defense swarmed all over Heinrich as he attempted to pass, and the Bears took over on their 35-yard line. Cal then went 65 yards for a touchdown to go ahead, 14-7. The Huskies had two more scoring opportunities late in the fourth quarter. With fourth and goal on the Cal two-yard line, Heinrich called an audible for a short pass. His target, Tracy King was stuffed at the line of scrimmage—some observers said he was tackled. Heinrich hesitated when King went down. Richter, the huge All-America linebacker, jumped over the middle of the offensive line and batted the ball out of Heinrich's hands. Cal recovered the fumble. Three plays later, Cal's great running back, Johnny Olszewski, fumbled, and Washington recovered on the Bear nine. The Bear defense again rose up and stuffed the Husky offense to snuff out Washington's bid for the conference title and the Rose Bowl.

Husky Legend

Don Heinrich

UW Media Relations

Don Heinrich finished his Husky career as one of the greatest quarterbacks in college history. After he led Bremerton High School to a state football championship, he entered Washington in 1949. As a sophomore in his first varsity season in 1950, he was named to the Associated Press' All-America and all-coast teams. In that year, he completed a NCAA-record 134 passes (60.6 completion percentage). In 1951, Heinrich suffered a shoulder separation in pre-season practice and did not play at all in the season. In 1952, he again led the nation in passing with 137 completions and finished his Husky career with a school record 4392 yards and 33 touchdowns. He still ranks sixth in Husky history in career passing yards and sixth in total offense. His 80-yard touchdown pass to George Black in the 1952 Stanford game ranks third all-time. He was an all-conference, all-coast, and All-America selection in 1952 and finished ninth in the Heisman Trophy balloting in that year. Heinrich played seven seasons in the National Football League with the New York Giants and Dallas Cowboys. The Giants' teams on which he played were in three NFL championship games. The 1956 team won the title, beating the Chicago Bears, 47-7. Heinrich capped his career by being selected to the National Football Foundation College Hall of Fame in 1987 and the Husky Hall of Fame in 1981.

HUSKY LIST

Don Heinrich's College Records

Year	Games	Passes Att	Comp	Yards	TDs	Ints	Pct.	Total Offense
1949(#)	10	119	64	899	6	7	.538	807
1950	10	221	134*	1846	14	9	.604	1806
1951	Did not play							
1952	10	270	137*	1647	13	17	.507	1652
Totals	30	610	335	4392	33	33	.549	4265

 # Freshmen team totals—freshmen could not play on the varsity team then
*** First in Nation**

ON Nov. 25, 1950, Washington beat Washington State, 52-21. The game was not memorable because of the score but because of the bizarre finish. With under two minutes left, Washington was leading 45-14. Earlier it had been announced that Don Heinrich had set a national single-season pass-completion record. So the Huskies went to the ground game to help Hugh McElhenny set a Pacific Coast Conference single-season rushing record. Then, it was discovered that Heinrich had only tied the record. One problem—the Cougars had the ball. Clyde Seiler, a Husky defensive tackle, rushed on the field, yelling to let the Cougars score. On the next play, Dick Sprague allowed Dick Rowley to catch a pass from Dick Gambold and run into the end zone untouched. With 50 seconds to go, the Huskies went to work to get both records. Roland Kirkby took the kickoff and ran straight out of bounds. Heinrich's pass to Joe Cloidt was incomplete. The next one was the record-breaker—a short pass in the flat to Kirkby. Quickly they huddled to call a rushing play, and it was a very good one. Heinrich pitched out to McElhenny who broke loose for 84 yards and his fifth touchdown of the day. The run gave Hugh 296 yards for the game (still a Husky record) and 1107 for the season—a new PCC record. At the end of the season, at the urging of his teammates, Cassill retired Kirkby's jersey number 44. Many believed Kirkby was the best all-around Husky player during his three-year career, 1948-1950.

Husky Moment

The Punt Return Everybody Remembers

When you ask observers of Hugh McElhenny about his most memorable moments, they recount his 100-yard punt return Oct. 6, 1951 against USC. USC, featuring their great running back, Frank Gifford, scored first and led 7-0. Washington knotted the score only to have the Trojans score again. This time Gifford's kick was no good and USC led at half-time, 13-7. In the fourth quarter, with fourth down and nine on the Washington 48, the Trojans' Des Koch punted the ball to the goal line in the northwest corner of the field. All the coaches were yelling at McElhenny to let it go. "I thought I was between the five- and 10-yard line. It was probably stupid, but it's sort of a runner's feeling that you go for it." Sidestepping the first tackler, the King shook off another and began to step up the north sideline in easy strides. Suddenly with a burst of speed and Husky blockers upending Trojan defenders all over the field, a clear path opened up down the field to the goal line. McElhenny turned on the throttle. "It was like a touchdown out of a cornball movie...only it was real," Gifford said. McElhenny's return still is the longest in Husky history. Oh, the Huskies missed the extra point and the Trojans scored again to win the game, 20-13. On that day, few remember the score, but everybody remembers the punt return.

1952 Tyee

Hugh McElhenny heads up field on his 100-yard punt return.

Husky Spotlight

Two oarsmen from the 1952 varsity eight and two others and the coxswain from the junior varsity were selected for the four-oared with coxswain event in the 1952 U.S. Olympic Trials. The lineup was Carl Lovsted, bow; Captain Al Ulbrickson and son of the Husky coach, number two; Dick Wahlstrom, three; Fil Leanderson, stroke; and Al Rossi, cox. After four rounds of racing on Lake Quinsigamond in Worcester, MA., the crew won the right to represent the United States in the 1952 Olympic Games. In the finals of the Trials, they beat a Navy four and a crew representing Seattle's Washington Athletic Club. The WAC crew included several members of the Husky four that won the 1948 Olympic gold. On the Baltic Sea near Helsinki, Finland, the Husky four put on a terrific finish in the last 50 meters to beat the Leander Club of Great Britain in the first heat. They won the semi-final heat with a sprint in the last 500 meters and now faced Czechoslovakia, Finland, Great Britain, and Switzerland in the finals. On July 23, 1952, the Huskies battled the Czechs and the Swiss for the medals. Czechoslovakia won by more than three seconds with the Swiss crew taking second by four tenths of a second over the Washington crew. Husky oarsmen had captured their third medal in the last three Olympic Games. The bronze medalists were inducted in the Husky Hall of Fame in 1998.

Husky Highlight

Pete Salmon was a three-time All-America swimmer. In 1949, he earned national honors as a member of the 300-yard medley relay. Salmon swam the breaststroke leg, followed by George Heaney in the backstroke, and Dick Campbell in the freestyle. In 1950, he competed for Canada in the British Empire Games. In 1951, he rejoined the Huskies and was an All-America in the 50-yard freestyle and 150-yard individual medley event. In the medley, Salmon was the NCAA champion and helped the Huskies to a ninth place national finish. As a senior in 1952, he earned All-America honors in the 50-yard freestyle and 150 individual medley, an event in which he was fourth in the NCAA meet. Salmon was admitted to the Husky Hall of Fame in 1990.

UW Media Relations

UW Media Relations

Husky Legend

Hugh McElhenny

Hugh McElhenny has been acclaimed as the greatest running back in Washington history. In the book, *Celebrating 100 Years of Husky Football,* McElhenny is described as "...the wildest football imagination come to life....He was the kind of runner who could make more magic, write more stories and paint bigger pictures in the span of five yards than practically anybody else could do in 30, 40, or 50 yards." The story continues. "In all the history of football, perhaps only Red Grange before McElhenny and Gayle Sayers after him made open-field running such a spectacle." Considering he played only 20 games as a Husky, his records are even more remarkable. He still ranks first in four categories and in the top five in six other categories. He won many honors. He was first team all-coast in 1950 and 1951 and first team All-America in 1951. He finished eighth in the Heisman Trophy balloting in 1951 and was voted Seattle's Man of the Year in Sports. He played in the 1952 East-West Shrine game, the Hula Bowl, and the College All-Star game. He played 13 seasons in the National Football League. He was Rookie of the Year in 1952, named All Pro four times and played in six Pro Bowls. He was inducted in the National Football League Hall of Fame in 1970 and the College Football Hall of Fame in 1981. McElhenny was elected as a charter member of the Husky Hall of Fame in 1979.

HUSKY LIST

In his 20 games as a Husky, Hugh McElhenny established many records. Below are some of his records and where they rank in Washington history.

Category	Record	All-Time Ranking
Rushing Yards		
Career (1949-51)	2499	5th
Season (1950)	1107	6th
Game (1950)	296 against Washington State	1st
Points by a Running Back		
Career	233	1st
Season (1951)	125 (second in nation)	2nd
Touchdowns		
Season	17	2nd(tie)
All-Purpose Yards		
Career	4234	2nd
Season (1951)	1678	5th
Kick-off Return Yards		
Career	747	9th
Game (1949)	96 against Minnesota	6th
Longest Punt Return	100 against USC in 1951	1st
Best Rushing Average		
Career	5.5 yards per game	3rd
Season (1950)	6.2	2nd
Game (1950)	14.8 against Washington State	1st

HUSKY LORE

AS Husky athletes and teams gained national recognition, so did Washington's athletic facilities. Under the leadership of Athletic Director, Harvey Cassill, an upper deck was constructed on the south side of Husky Stadium. 15,000 seats were added with a cost approximating $1.7 million. The NCAA swimming championship was held at Washington in 1947. Edmundson Pavilion was the site of the 1949 and 1952 basketball Final Four. The 1951 NCAA track and field championships were held in Husky Stadium. Washington's George Widenfelt took second in the high jump in the meet. Competing for Sweden, he finished fourth in the decathlon in the 1952 Olympic Games. Cassill served as Athletic Director from 1946 until early 1956 when he resigned over the football team's revolt against Coach John Cherberg and the discovery of a fund to pay expenses of some players. Cassill was elected to the Husky Hall of Fame in 1992.

1952 W 1953

Husky Moment

Final Four—Third in the Nation

Before the words "March Madness" hit the collegiate scene, the 1953 Washington team stirred up a basketball frenzy in the Pacific Northwest. The Huskies ended the regular season with a 23-2 record and a chance to win the national championship. The postseason started in Edmundson Pavilion in the Pacific Coast Conference playoff with the California Bears. In a two-out-of-three series, the Huskies shut down the Bears, 60-47, on March 6, 1953, and again the next night, 80-57, to advance to the NCAA Western Regional tournament in Corvallis. On March 13, they faced off against Seattle University led by All-America Johnny O'Brien, in a much awaited contest between the two Seattle schools. The fan furor and press coverage leading up to the game was unmatched in Seattle sports history. KING-TV carried the game; it was the first live out-of-state telecast of an athletic event by a local station. Unfortunately, the game didn't match the hype. From the first whistle, Washington led. With about three minutes to go, Bob Houbregs had 43 points, and Washington was up 90-59. The Husky fans then shouted to Tippy Dye to put Houbregs back in to break the NCAA tournament record. With 2:09 to go, big Bob hit a field goal to set the record and immediately left the game. The Huskies won 92-70. The next night, Santa Clara fans suffered pain as Houbregs hit a two-handed shot from halfcourt to put the Huskies up 53-51 at the end of the third quarter. They won the tournament final, 74-62. The following day, the team flew to Kansas City for the Final Four. Houbregs and others believe that the team never recovered from the Seattle University victory and were not mentally prepared for the first game, on March 17, against Kansas. The Jayhawks employed a relentless pressing defense that produced 14 steals. Houbregs fouled out with 2:46 gone in the third period. With seven minutes to go in the final period, Kansas was ahead 69-47 and won 79-53. Washington came back the next night and blew out Louisiana State, led by All-America Bob Pettit. Houbregs scored 42 to help the Huskies take third place in the nation, the highest national ranking in Husky history.

UW Media Relations

Doug McClary, Bob Houbregs, Charlie Koon, Joe Cipriano, Mike McCutheon (kneeling); the starting five on the 1953 team that finished third in the nation.

Husky Spotlight

William Henry Harrison "Tippy" Dye was Washington's basketball coach from 1951-1959. Dye graduated from Ohio State lettering three years in football, basketball, and baseball. He quarterbacked the Buckeyes to one conference title and two second place finishes and was an All-America basketball selection in 1936. After serving in the Navy during World War II, he returned to Ohio State as an assistant football coach and head basketball coach. His three year (1947-1950) basketball record was 53-34 including a 22-4 mark in his last season. At Washington, Dye compiled a 156-91 record, the third most wins in Husky history and the second best winning percentage—.632. Under his leadership, his teams won the Pacific Coast Conference championship in 1951 and 1953 and finished second in 1952, 1956, 1957 and 1959. His Huskies finished third in the Western Regional tournament and fifth in the nation in 1951. Dye's 1953 team compiled the best season record—28-3— in Husky history, advanced to the Final Four for the only time in Washington history, and finished third in the nation. Dye resigned from Washington after the 1959 season to become Athletic Director first at Wichita State, then Nebraska, and finally Northwestern, the program from which he retired. Dye was elected to the Husky Hall of Fame in 1996.

Husky Highlight

Washington's crews won the 1953 national team championship at the Intercollegiate Rowing Association regatta held on Lake Onondaga near Syracuse. The freshmen crew finished well ahead of the other boats in the two-mile race. The junior varsity swept to a five-length victory. The three-mile varsity race had Cornell, Navy, and Washington matching stroke for stroke for much of the race. Near the end, Navy powered to the lead and finished one and a quarter lengths ahead of Cornell who edged the Huskies for second. With two firsts and a third, Washington received the team trophy. After a 7-3-0 football season and a third place conference finish, Coach Howie Odell was fired and John Cherberg was selected to head the Husky football program. Odell finished his Washington career with a 23-25-12 record.

UW Media Relations

Husky Legend

Bob Houbregs

Bob Houbregs graduated from Queen Anne High School and entered Washington in 1949. He played on the 1950 freshmen team that compiled a 21-1 record. As a sophomore, he led the Huskies to a Pacific Coast Conference title and a fifth-place national ranking. In 1953, Houbregs had the most outstanding year of any basketball player in Husky history. He was a consensus All-America (the only one in Washington's history), the Helms Foundation National Player of the Year, and the leader of the Husky squad that finished third in the NCAA Final Four. He was Washington's leading scorer in each of his three varsity seasons. He established Husky records in numerous categories. With an unstoppable and accurate hook shot, he still owns the top three single-game scoring totals, topped by a school-record 49 points against Idaho in 1953. Houbregs also earned letters in baseball in 1951 and 1952. A first-round draft choice of the Minnesota Hawks, Bob played five years in the National Basketball Association with Milwaukee, Baltimore, Boston, Fort Wayne, and Detroit. He was inducted in the College Basketball Hall of Fame in 1987 and was a charter member of the Husky Hall of Fame in 1979. Houbregs is the only Husky basketball player to have his jersey number (25) retired.

HUSKY LISTS

During his three-year Husky career, Bob Houbregs established many basketball records. Listed below are some of his records and where he ranks in Husky history.

Category	Record	All-time Ranking
Points Scored		
Game	49 against Idaho in 1953	1st
Season	846 in 1953	1st
Career	1774 (1951-53)	2nd
Field Goals Made		
Game	20 of 35 against Seattle University in 1953	1st
Season	325 out of 604 in 1953	1st
Scoring Average		
Game	25.6 in 1953	1st
Career	19.5	2nd
Rebounding		
Game	22 against Utah in 1952	Tied for 5th
Season	381 in 1953	2nd
Career	971	5th
Most Wins		
Season	28	1st
Career	98 (including his freshman year)	1st

HUSKY LORE

PERHAPS the family with the greatest Husky athletic accomplishments is the McClary clan. Doug McClary was a three-time letter winner in basketball (1951-53) and earned three more letters as an end on the football team. His father, Hal, was a Husky center in 1928-1930 and an all-conference selection in 1929 and team captain in 1930. Doug's mother Roberta (Bellazzi) was a 1926 Washington graduate. She was the school's best markswoman on the 1924 national championship women's rifle team and set the American discus throw record in 1925. Doug's younger brother, Dave, earned letters in baseball in 1954 and 1955. And finally, Doug's daughter Carlin earned four letters in Husky basketball (1979-82), was captain in 1982, and established Husky scoring and rebounding records. She still ranks second all-time in career rebounding and seventh in career scoring. She holds the record for most points scored in a women's basketball game in Edmundson Pavilion—38 points against Seatle University in 1980.

1953 W 1954

Husky Moment

Hec Edmundson Retires

Clarence S. "Hec" Edmundson retired after the 1954 track and field season, completing his outstanding Husky coaching career. He coached Washington basketball teams for 27 years (1921-47) and track and field for 35 (1919-54). In Edmundson's last track season, the Huskies produced the best team point performance in his career, swamping the Vancouver Olympic Club, 110-21. They also scored more points than had ever been scored in dual meet competition with Idaho, beating the Vandals, 98-33. In the Northern Division meet, the Huskies were determined to make a good showing for their beloved coach. Washington led throughout the entire meet until the last event—the mile relay. Oregon won the event and edged the Huskies by one point for the title. In the Pacific Coast Conference meet, the Huskies finished seventh, far behind the victorious USC squad. The meet was held at Husky Stadium on May 28 and 29, 1954. On May 28, PCC coaches, former athletes and friends and colleagues gathered to pay tribute to this wonderful man.

1955 Tyee

Hec Edmundson retired after coaching 35 track and field seasons.

Husky Spotlight

Bob Fornia, Denny Meyer, and Darrold Skartvedt were the last Pacific Coast champions coached by Hec Edmundson. Fornia won the mile run in 1953 in 4:12.3. Meyer captured the two mile event in the 1954 meet in a record time of 9:9.1. Skartvedt leaped 23′ $8\frac{7}{8}$″ to take the long jump title in 1953. In the NCAA meet in 1953, Skartvedt took fourth in the long jump and Meyer finished sixth in the two mile race.

Bill Stuht, Husky third baseman, was selected to the Northern Division first team in 1952. Hitting .333 and displaying airtight glovework, he was first team NCAA District 8 (West Coast) in 1953. He was the team captain and shortstop in 1954.

UW Media Relations

Bill Stuht

Husky Highlight

John Cherberg began his first season as head football coach. Cherberg became an assistant coach under Ralph "Pest" Welch in 1946. He was retained as freshmen coach by Howie Odell in 1948. During his five seasons as freshmen coach, his teams won 22 of 23 games, losing only his first game as frosh coach to Oregon, 25-24. His 1953 varsity team went 3-6-1 and finished seventh in the conference. He coached for two more years, going 2-8-0 in 1954 and 5-4-1 in 1955. His overall record of 10-18-2 produced the lowest winning percentage—.344—in Husky history among coaches whose careers were at least three years long.

UW Media Relations

Husky Legend

Milt Bohart

Milt Bohart was a three-year letterwinner in football (1951-53). After starting as a linebacker and defensive guard, he moved to offensive guard in 1953. In that year, he was selected first team All-America by *Look Magazine* and second team by the Associated Press and United Press. In 1953, Bohart received All-Pacific Coast Conference and all-coast honors. He was the Associated Press National Lineman of the Week for his play in the Huskies 13-13 tie with seventh-ranked USC on Oct. 10, 1953. Bohart received the Flaherty Medal as the most inspirational player in 1953. He played in the East-West Shrine Game and the Hula Bowl in 1954.

Husky List

Hec Edmundson's Coaching Summary

Basketball (1921-1947)

- **Three Pacific Coast Conference championships (1931, 1934, 1943)**
- **10 Northern Division titles, including five straight from 1928 to 1932**
- **First Husky appearance in the NCAA tournament (1943)**
- **11 of his teams won 20 or more games; only 10 other Husky teams have done that**
- **Winningest coach in Husky history—488-195 record with a winning percentage of .715**
- **Third most wins in conference history**
- **508-204 career record (including four seasons at Idaho)**
- **Career winning percentage ranks him 38th all-time among NCAA coaches**

Track and Field (1919-1954)

- **Three PCC championships**
- **Eight Northern Division titles**
- **Six Top 10 NCAA team finishes (including second place finishes in 1929 and 1930)**
- **Coached athletes who won seven NCAA individual titles and set four world records. Seven of his athletes competed in the Olympics and three won medals**

Husky Lore

THE University of Washington significantly improved its academic standing in the late 1940s and early 50s. Many joining the faculty in the period received their formal academic training in prestigious universities and a high proportion held Ph.D. degrees. Faculty performance resulted in many honors and awards. In 1953, Professor Theodore Roethke became Washington's second Pulitzer Prize winner with his book, *The Waking*. Dr. Robert Rushmer won national recognition for his cardiovascular research. Many received Ford Foundation, Fulbright, and Guggenheim awards and others hosted conferences of noted scholars and scientists. Overall, the University was nationally recognized by being invited to become a member of the Association of American Universities. This association included the most outstanding academic institutions in the nation.

Husky Moment

Great Comeback Against UCLA Falls Short

The Husky football team was 2-8 in 1954 and finished tied for last in the Pacific Coast Conference. The Huskies beat only Utah and Oregon State. In the second game of the season, Washington played its first home game against Michigan and lost 14-0. On Oct. 9, the Huskies faced number-two ranked UCLA and Red Sanders' single-wing offense featuring All-America Bob Davenport. In the first quarter, the Bruins scored on a 61-yard drive in 10 plays. Davenport went in for the touchdown on a 10-yard run over right guard. In the second quarter, the Huskies stopped the Bruins on the 15, on the five and on the three-yard line. Leading 7-0 at half-time, UCLA scored quickly in the third quarter after recovering a Husky fumble on the kickoff. An interception set up the third Bruin score, and with five minutes left in the third quarter, UCLA had a commanding lead, 21-0. Then the Huskies went to work. Starting on their own 36-yard line, Washington scored in eight plays. The big play was a 33-yard touchdown pass from sophomore quarterback Bob Cox to another soph, Dean Derby. Then the Huskies recovered a fumble on the Bruin 25. On fourth and two on the five-yard line, Cox threw a perfect strike to the wide open Corky Lewis. Bob Dunn's kick was wide and the Huskies trailed by eight. Again UCLA fumbled and Lewis recovered on the Bruin 41. Cox tossed his third touchdown pass, a nine yarder to sophomore Bud Green. Dunn's kick brought the Huskies within one. They then tried an onside kick. It failed, and the Huskies were called for unnecessary roughness on the play. The Bruins now had the ball on the their 36. Again they fumbled, and Lewis recovered on the UCLA 40. Cox tried two passes to Derby, one of which was just deflected away from his waiting arms in the end zone. With less than a minute remaining and on fourth down, the Huskies completed a screen pass that fell short of a first down, and the Bruins took over and ran out the clock for a 21-20 victory.

1955 Tyee

Bob McNamee runs for yardage as number-two ranked UCLA edges Washington 21-20.

Husky Spotlight

Stan Hiserman succeeded Hec Edmundson as the Husky track and field coach in 1955 to begin his 14-year tenure. He graduated from Stanford in 1939. At the Farm, he was captain and a member of a world record-setting 880-yard relay team. After serving in the military during World War II, Hiserman became the head coach at Idaho in 1946 and continued there until 1954. His 1955 Husky team finished just $2^3/_4$ points behind the victorious Oregon squad in the Northern Division meet. Jim Hilton won the second of his three Northern Division titles (1954, 1955, 1956) in the pole vault. The Husky swim team won its fifth straight Northern Division title and eleventh in thirteen years. The team's 116 points were 57 ahead of second place Washington State.

UW Media Relations

Stan Hiserman

Husky Highlight

Gordon McAllister was a four-year letterman in the small bore rifle team. He was the Northwest Intercollegiate rifle champion in 1955 and led the Huskies to three Northwest titles. McAllister was an All-America second team selection in 1953 and 1954 and a first team pick in 1955. He was the national Naval Reserve Officers Training Corps champion in 1953. McAllister was selected to the Husky Hall of Fame in 1997.

1955 Tyee

Husky Legend

Bill Quillian

UW Media Relations

Bill Quillian entered Washington in 1951 after graduating from Queen Anne High School. While there, he won four Seattle city tennis championships. He was a member of the U.S. Junior Davis Cup team (18 and under) for three years. Quillian was a Husky four-year letter winner (1952-1955) and was team captain in 1955. He never lost in regular-season dual-match collegiate competition and won four Northern Division singles titles and four doubles titles. Bill competed in the NCAA tennis championships in each of his four years. He reached the quarterfinals in 1952, 1953 and 1954 (held at the Seattle Tennis Club). In the 1955 NCAA tournament, Quillian breezed through the first four rounds without losing a set. In the semifinals on June 24, he beat USC's Pancho Antreras, 6-4, 4-6, 3-6, 6-0, 6-1. In the finals on June 25, Tulane's Pepe Aguero, a Brazilian Davis Cup member, was the victor in four sets, 6-1, 4-6, 6-1, 6-0. Quillian competed in almost every major U.S. amateur tournament and was ranked ninth in the country in 1957. He won seven Washington State singles championships. Bill competed internationally, including matches at Wimbledon and the French Open. He was a member of the 1958 Davis Cup team. He became the Husky tennis coach in 1966, and during his eight-year coaching career amassed a 63-39 record and winning percentage of .618. Both his number of wins and winning percentage are the fourth best in Washington history. After his untimely death in 1984, the varsity courts were named in his honor. Quillian was admitted to the Husky Hall of Fame in 1985.

HUSKY LIST

Football Series with Michigan

Year	Location	Score
1953	Ann Arbor, Michigan	50-0 loss
1954	Seattle	14-0 loss
1969	Ann Arbor	45-7 loss
1970	Seattle	17-3 loss
1978	Rose Bowl	27-20 win
1981	Rose Bowl	23-6 loss
1983	Seattle	25-24 win
1984	Ann Arbor	20-11 win
1992	Rose Bowl	34-14 win
1993	Rose Bowl	38-31 loss

HUSKY LORE

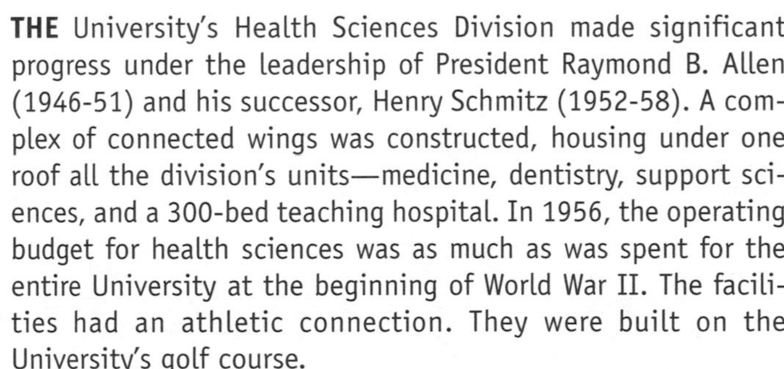

THE University's Health Sciences Division made significant progress under the leadership of President Raymond B. Allen (1946-51) and his successor, Henry Schmitz (1952-58). A complex of connected wings was constructed, housing under one roof all the division's units—medicine, dentistry, support sciences, and a 300-bed teaching hospital. In 1956, the operating budget for health sciences was as much as was spent for the entire University at the beginning of World War II. The facilities had an athletic connection. They were built on the University's golf course.

Husky Moment

Team Mutiny

The 1955 football season opened very positively with four straight wins including shutouts of Minnesota and 10th-ranked USC. Then the situation began to unravel. Key players felt they could no longer play for Coach John Cherberg, citing his short fuse and harassment of assistant coaches and players. Shortly before the last game against Washington State, some Husky players called Torchy Torrance, an avid Husky booster and head of the Washington Advertising Fund. They wanted to voice their displeasure with Cherberg, but Torrance told them to see Athletic Director Harvey Cassill. After a 27-7 win over the Cougars, 30 players met with Cassill. The meeting was supposedly held in secret, but news leaked to the media, and for several months, the feud monopolized the headlines in the sports pages. In early December, the ASUW's Board of Control voted 12-2 against rehiring Cherberg. Three days later, the Board of Regents rehired him on the condition that Cherberg restore unity. In the Jan. 24, 1956 *University Daily,* an editorial called for Cherberg's resignation, because nothing was being done to bring about harmonious relations. Out of all this turmoil, three major actions took place. First Cassill fired Cherberg on Jan. 27, 1956. In retaliation, Cherberg went public to tell his side of the story, and soon everybody knew that the Washington Advertising Fund was paying players far above the amount allowed by the Pacific Coast Conference. The Feb. 20 issue of *Sports Illustrated* had an article entitled: "Boosters Mess It Up at Washington." Soon, a Washington State Legislature review began along with investigations by the Pacific Coast Conference and the NCAA. Next, Cassill resigned on Feb. 9. Finally, on May 6, all Washington athletic teams except crew were put on a two-year probation by conference officials when investigations disclosed that 27 football players had received an average of $60 per month over the allowed $75. The PCC ruling prevented any Washington team from winning any conference championships, the football team from appearing in the Rose Bowl and the basketball team from competing in postseason games. All other sports, except crew, could not compete for any championships.

UW Media Relations

Coach Cherberg was fired in early 1956 and the Huskies put on probation for excess player payments.

Husky Spotlight

Bruno Boin was a three-year basketball letter winner (1956, 1957, 1959). Boin was named a third team All-America, all-conference second team and all-coast first team in 1959. He was the team's co-captain in 1957 and captain in 1959. He received the 101 Club Scholarship Award (the top student-athlete) in 1956, 1957, and 1959. Boin was the Hec Edmundson Most Inspirational Player Award winner in 1959. A great hook shooter and rebounder, Boin still ranks in the top 10 all-time in several categories—career scoring percentage (17.1 per game), career rebounds (832), and free throws in a game (13 for 13). He was elected to the Husky Hall of Fame in 1992. Walt Taulbee won the 1956 NCAA championship in the downhill ski event at Winter Park, Colorado. His teammate, Peter Birkeland, was second. The Husky team, coached by Karl Stingl, finished eighth overall.

Bruno Boin

UW Media Relations

Husky Highlight

Washington beat 10th-ranked USC 7-0, on Oct. 8, 1955. The only score of the game featured one of the most spectacular plays in Husky history. With 6:20 to play in the game, the Huskies had the ball on their 20-yard line. Quarterback Steve Roake threw a 20-yard pass to right end Jim Houston on a crossing pattern, right to left. After running five yards, Houston was hit. Coming up from the left side to block was the other Husky end, Corky Lewis. As Houston was falling on the Husky 45-yard line, he lateraled the ball to Lewis in full stride. Corky raced past a would-be tackler and headed straight downfield 55 yards for the game's only touchdown. He reached the goal line just before the Trojans' C.R. Roberts, one of collegiate football's fastest players, closed in for the tackle. To gain the victory, Washington rebuffed Jon Arnett, Roberts and company four times inside the 19-yard line. It was the Huskies' first win over USC in Seattle since 1945.

1956 Tyee

Washington beats 10th-ranked USC 7-0 on an 80-yard pass and lateral play.

UW Media Relations

Husky Legend

Eric Hughes

Eric Hughes became Washington's first gymnastics coach in 1956. He grew up in Victoria, British Columbia, and captained the gymnastics team at Victoria High School. He entered the University of Illinois in 1939 and was a member of the 1941 Illini NCAA championship gymnastics squad. After serving two years in the Royal Canadian Air Force, he returned to Illinois and was a letterwinner on the school's 1946 NCAA championship track team. Hughes received a B.S. and M.S. degree in physical education from Illinois and came to Washington in 1950 as a doctoral student. He also worked in the intramural sports department and started a gymnastics club. In 1955, he received his doctorate in Education Administration and established a gymnastics program in the 1955-56 school year. Hughes' teams compiled a 146-31-1 record, dominating Pacific Northwest competition and gaining national recognition. During his career, the Huskies appeared 15 times at NCAA championships and finished second in 1965. Hughes' teams placed in the top 10 in the country four other times. He coached eight NCAA individual champions; five are in the Husky Hall of Fame. Hughes was the head coach of a U.S. team that toured Europe. He was the manager of the 1972 U.S. Olympic gymnastics team. His Husky Gymnastics Club, composed of current and former Husky gymnasts, won the Amateur Athletic Union (AAU) national championships in 1968 and 1969. Hughes was elected to the Husky Hall of Fame in 1989.

Husky List

Pacific Coast Conference (and successor conferences) Top 10 Single-Season Scoring Leaders

Name	School	Points	Season
Lew Alcindor	UCLA	870	1967
Khalid Reeves	Arizona	848	1994
Bob Houbregs	Washington	846	1953
Harold Miner	USC	789	1992
Mel Counts	Oregon State	775	1964
Reggie Miller	UCLA	750	1986
Gary Payton	Oregon State	746	1990
Terrell Brandon	Oregon	745	1991
Gail Goodrich	UCLA	744	1965
Sean Elliott	Arizona	743	1988

Husky Lore

WHEN the Pacific Coast Conference put the Husky athletic program on probation in May 1956, the crew program was exempted. The NCAA subsequently declared all Washington athletic teams ineligible to participate in postseason and national championship events. The Intercollegiate Rowing Association, while not a part of the NCAA, enforced the ban because its member schools—Columbia, Cornell, Navy, Pennsylvania, and Syracuse—were also NCAA members and felt obligated to follow the NCAA decision. Some critics of the IRA member schools' decision to enforce the ban, and thereby keep Washington out of the IRA regatta, observed that probation was the only way those schools could beat the Huskies. The Washington State Senate sent a letter to the NCAA and the IRA urging them to drop "the unreasonable, uncalled for and unwarranted indictment" of the Washington crew program. The two associations held to their decision, and the Husky crews were banned from rowing in the IRA regatta in 1957 and 1958. The irony of the decision was that a much larger venue awaited the Husky varsity eight in 1958.

1956 W 1957

Husky Moment

Wilt Chamberlain Comes to Town

The 1957 Husky basketball team opened with three games on the road and returned to face Wilt Chamberlain and the rest of the Kansas Jayhawks on Dec. 14 and 15, 1956. Before 11,700 fans in the Pavilion, Wilt scored 32 points to lead Kansas to a 77-63 victory. He also sent a message to the young Huskies by blocking Bruno Boin's first hook shot. The Huskies tried a sagging defense to stop Wilt, leaving Maurice King open to hit outside set shots from outside. King scored 18 of his 24 points in helping Kansas take a 41-24 lead at half-time. Boin was able to get his other shots off and finished with 16. Sophomore Doug Smart had 15 to go along with his 11 rebounds. The next night, an overflow crowd of 12,000 saw Kansas race to a 50-41 half-time lead and beat the Huskies 92-78. Kansas scored the most points in Husky history, up to that point, by a visiting team. Wilt again showed his extraordinary skills in racking up 37 points and 28 rebounds. Smart scored 33 points to go along with his 17 rebounds, to break the sophomore record (32) set by Boin the year before. Kansas played in the NCAA championship game to end its season, losing to North Carolina, 54-53, in three overtimes. Chamberlain was the tournament's MVP. The Huskies finished second behind California in the Pacific Coast Conference.

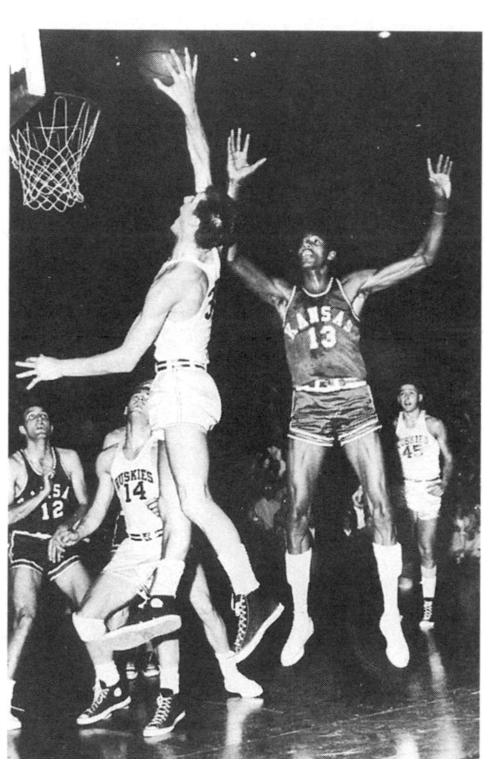

1957 Tyee

Bruno Boin dunks on Wilt as Chamberlain leads the Kansas Jayhawks in two wins over the Huskies.

Husky Spotlight

George Strugar earned letters in football in 1955 and 1956 as a tackle. In his senior year, he was named to the Coaches' All-America team and was a second team All-America selection by United Press International. He was the first Husky to play in the Senior Bowl (1957). Strugar played seven years in the National Football League—five with the Los Angeles Rams, one with the Pittsburgh Steelers, and the last year with New York Jets. Strugar entered the Husky Hall of Fame in 1988.

Terry Tobacco was a three-year letterman (1955-57) in track and field. In 1956, he anchored the Canadian 1600 meter relay team to a fifth place finish in the Melbourne Olympic Games. He also represented Canada in the 400 meter dash in both the 1956 and 1960 Olympic Games. He won the 440 yard dash in the 1957 and 1958 Pacific Coast Conference meets and took second in 1959. He ran the anchor leg on the Husky mile relay team that won the PCC title in 1959, establishing a new Washington record of 3:14.2. Later that year, he placed third in the 440 in the NCAA meet, setting a new Husky record of 46.6.

Husky Highlight

George Briggs was hired as Athletic Director after Harvey Cassill resigned in early February 1956. Briggs was an assistant athletic director at California. His initial tasks were to stop the funding of players' expenses and find a new football coach. He established the Tyee Club that accepted contributions from boosters that could be used for grant-in-aid to athletes, under the NCAA rules, in exchange for the purchase of football and basketball season tickets in favorable viewing locations. Briggs wanted a football coach who was tough on conditioning and discipline and could win games in the fourth quarter. He offered the job to three of the best—Michigan State's Duffy Daugherty, Texas A&M's Bear Bryant and Bud Wilkinson of Oklahoma. Wilkinson suggested Darrell Royal, his former quarterback and the head coach at Missouri State. Royal agreed to come to Washington and signed a four-year contract for $17,000 a year, one of the highest coaching salaries in the nation at that time. He only coached one season, and his record was 5-5-0. Texas came calling. Royal was able to get out of his contract and start a long career with the Longhorns. He was the first Washington football coach to leave the program voluntarily since Victor Place left in 1908 to coach at Notre Dame.

Husky Legend

UW Media Relations

Doug Smart

Doug Smart was an outstanding student-athlete and a three-year letterman on Husky basketball teams from 1957-59. As a forward/center, he led the Pacific Coast Conference in field-goal percentage and was second in scoring and rebounding in 1957. In the next year, he was the conference's leading rebounder and was second in field-goal percentage and scoring. In his senior year, he was first in field-goal percentage and rebounding and second in scoring. Smart was a third team All-America in 1959 and was first team all-conference and all-coast in each of his three years. In his two appearances against Wilt Chamberlain and the Kansas Jayhawks he scored 48 points. Smart ranks in the top 10 in Husky history in career scoring, single-season rebounds, and season rebounding average per game. He holds Husky records for career rebounds (1051) and career rebounding average (13.5 per game). Smart was elected to the Husky Hall of Fame in 1994.

HUSKY LIST

Washington's Basketball Record Against Pac-10 Opponents (through the 2000 season)

	Overall Record	Home Record	Away Record	Neutral Site Record
Arizona	15-30	11-11	4-18	0-1
Arizona State	18-29	11-12	6-17	1-0
California	67-63	43-23	24-40	0-0
Oregon	170-94	100-32	67-62	3-0
Oregon State	138-129	93-37	42-91	3-1
Stanford	53-57	38-16	14-40	1-1
UCLA	28-79	23-28	5-50	0-1
USC	55-57	32-24	21-33	2-0
Washington State	160-88	92-31	67-55	1-2
Total	704-626	443-214	250-406	11-6
Percentage	52.9%	67.4%	38.1%	64.7%

HUSKY LORE

BAND Day at Husky football games was originated in 1950 by band director Walter C. Welke as a means of honoring cities loyal to the University and its activities. High school bands from the cities joined the Husky Marching Band for the half-time performance. Now high schools from across the state participate. Each band is introduced and plays during pre-game warm-ups. The bands then join the Husky Band for the playing of the national anthem and the half-time show.

1950 Tyee

Husky Moment

The Huskies Against the USSR

The Husky crew could not go to the Intercollegiate Rowing Association regatta and compete for the national championship in 1957 and 1958. The reason was the ban on postseason competition resulting from the discovery of the Washington Advertising Fund used to pay football players. The Husky varsity crew was a very good one. They were unbeaten in West Coast competition in 1957. Supporters indicated that if they went unbeaten in 1958, they would raise the funds to send them to the Royal Henley regatta on the Thames River in England. All season long, the cry "On to Henley" spurred the crew. They won each race leading up to the last hurdle—a 2000-meter race on May 31 against Oregon State and the University of British Columbia crews. After the Huskies' one-length victory over UBC, funds poured in from the people of Seattle and the Northwest to send the crew to Henley. Before arriving in England, the U.S. State Department made arrangements to send the Washington eight to Moscow, as the first team to go behind the Iron Curtain as part of a cultural exchange program. At Henley, because of the narrowness of the course, only two shells could race at a time. It was necessary to draw for the pairings. Washington drew the co-favorite—the Trud Club of Leningrad, Russia. The race was held in a downpour of England's famous rain, and the Huskies lost by a length and a quarter. Trud went on to win the Grand Challenge Cup. Fifteen days later, on July 19, 1958, on the choppy waters of Khiminskoe Reservoir outside of Moscow, the Huskies lined up against four Russian crews, including Russia's best, the Trud Club. Keith Jackson, the KOMO sports director, broadcast the race live—the first sports broadcast from the Soviet Union. The Soviet Army crew jumped to an early lead. By the 500-meter mark, the Huskies had passed the Army boat and pulled even with the Trud crew. At 1000 meters, Washington had nearly a length lead and soon, Jackson bellowed forth to his listeners: "The Huskies are sprinting and pulling away. They got open water." As they passed the roaring grandstand crowd, the oarsmen were swinging powerfully, riding the waves like bronco-busters. They glided across the finish one and three quarter lengths ahead of the Leningrad crew in one of the greatest upsets in the annals of rowing.

1959 Tyee

The Husky crew that staged one of the biggest upsets in collegiate crew history in Russia.

Husky Spotlight

The Husky men's pool was the venue for the Northern Division swimming and diving championships. Oregon State led after the first night's events, 82-75. On the second night, the Huskies got a big boost when four of their swimmers gained 16 of the 21 event points by finishing one-two-three and sixth in the 200 yard breaststroke. Harold Tauscher won the event to add to his victory in the 100 breaststroke. Going into the final event—the 400-yard medley relay—the Huskies led by four points and had to win the relay to assure victory. Dale Griffith in the opening backstroke leg and Bob McMahon in the breaststroke built up a one-second lead. Then Tim Thornton added six more seconds in the butterfly segment to send Ken Gage home easily in the freestyle to seal the championship. Coach Jack Torney was given a dunking for leading his Huskies to Washington's 16th Northern Division swim championship in his 23 years as coach. Emory Bundy, ASUW president and team captain, was chosen as the Northern Division swimmer of the year—he won the 50, 220, and 440 freestyle events.

Husky Highlight

In Jim Owens' first season as Washington's football coach, the Huskies were 3-6-1 and finished sixth in the Pacific Coast Conference. The highlight of the season was a 13-6 win over the Rose Bowl-bound Oregon Ducks in Eugene. The key to the victory was the running of Luther Carr, Mike McCluskey, Jim Jones, and Dick Payseno. Carr rushed for 52 yards, McCluskey 51, and Jones 46. Washington's first scoring drive started when Bruce Claridge cracked through the Oregon line and knocked a pass off target and into the hands of teammate Marv Bergmann on the Ducks' 25-yard line. Seven plays later, Bobby Dunn plunged over for the touchdown and then kicked the extra point. On the third play of the second half, Oregon's quarterback, Jack Crabtree, hit Pete Welch on a 76-yard touchdown play for the Ducks' only score. Early in the fourth stanza, McCluskey made two sizable gains in the Huskies' 67-yard scoring drive. With the Ducks on the Husky 16, Duane Lowell intercepted Crabtree's pass to end the game.

Husky Legend

Jim Owens

UW Media Relations

Jim Owens played football for Oklahoma in 1946-49, after serving two and a half years in the Navy Air Corps during World War II. Owens was the Sooners' captain and leading receiver in 1949 when the team went 11-0. He earned All-America honors that year. After graduating in 1950, Owens played one season for the Baltimore Colts while also serving as a part-time assistant at Johns Hopkins University. Owens became an assistant to Paul (Bear) Bryant, first at Kentucky (1951-53) and then at Texas A&M (1954-56). Owens became the Husky head coach in 1957 at the age of 29. At Washington, he was 99-82-6 during his 18 seasons. His teams won three Athletic Association of Western Universities titles and went to three Rose Bowls, including the Huskies' first ever Rose Bowl win in 1960—the stunning 44-8 defeat of Wisconsin. After the second Rose Bowl victory over Minnesota in 1961, the Helms Foundation ranked Washington the number-one team in the nation. In 1959, United Press International selected him as the coach of the year on the West Coast. Owens was ranked sixth in the balloting for Associated Press' Coach of the Year and was named to the All-Wilkinson team at Oklahoma. He was runner-up for coach of the year in 1960. He served as Washington's Athletic Director from 1960-69. Owens was inducted as a player in the National Football Foundation College Football Hall of Fame in 1982. He was elected as a charter member of the Husky Hall of Fame in 1979.

HUSKY LIST

The 1958 Washington crew that won in Moscow was elected to the Husky Hall of Fame in 1984. Its members were:

Chuck Alm (Captain) - number five
John Bissett - coxswain
Dick Erickson - two
Lou Gellermann - six
Phil Kieburtz - four
Andy Hovland - seven
Roger McDonald - three
John Sayre - stroke
Bob Svendsen - bow

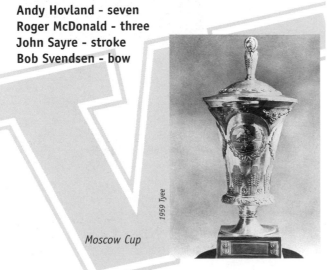

1959 Tyee

Moscow Cup

AFTER the Husky crew's victory in Moscow, the oarsmen were in a hurry to get back to their hotel and prepare for the grand reception and dinner hosted by the Moscow Sports Committee. As they were ready to leave the race course, the Russian championship women's eight asked if they might take a ride in the Husky shell, the Swiftsure. So the American men took the boat off the rack, carried it back to the water, presented it to the Soviet women, and bid them a good row. In the evening, the hospitality was even more cordial as the Huskies were feted to Russian food and drink and presented photo albums of Moscow. They then spent two days sight-seeing in Moscow with Russian news media and photographers following the oarsmen's every move. In a gesture of goodwill, after a call to boat-builder George Pocock, Coach Ulbrickson presented the Swiftsure to the Soviet Rowing Federation.

Husky Moment

Al Ulbrickson Retires

After the fall crew drills, Al Ulbrickson retired after 32 years of coaching the Husky rowing program. His extraordinary record included 21 victories in the 28 California-Washington regattas; six firsts, five seconds, and nine thirds in the varsity eight events of the Intercollegiate Rowing Association regattas; four sweeps at the IRA; an Olympic championship crew in 1936 and 1948; a bronze medal crew in 1952; and the stunning victory in Moscow in 1958. On May 5, 1959, Ulbrickson was honored at a banquet at the Olympic Hotel. More than 600 former oarsmen and friends of the Husky rowing program attended. Many wrote personal notes to Al in tribute to their association with him. "... With your uncompromising way of life as an example, your honest urging to give the best that's in us—stressing the need for teamwork...this lasts much longer and sinks much deeper into the lives of the men you have touched. Perhaps our reflection and practice of these values gained and crystalized under your example is the greatest tribute we can give." Fil Leanderson succeeded Ulbrickson as head crew coach. He was an oarsman at Washington and stroked the four-oared crew that won the bronze medal in the Helsinki Olympics in 1952. Leanderson was an assistant coach at MIT for two years before joining Washington as an assistant in 1955. John Bissett, the coxswain of the 1958 varsity eight became the assistant coach.

UW Media Relations

Husky Spotlight

Washington again finished second in the Pacific Coast Conference in basketball—the third time in four years. Cal won the conference title for the third straight year and nipped West Virginia, led by the MVP Jerry West, to win the NCAA championship in 1959. The Huskies went into the last two games of the season trailing Cal by one game. They lost both in Los Angeles—one to UCLA, 56-55 and the other in overtime to USC, 80-74. Doug Smart set a career conference scoring record of 956 points, a record that was never broken because the Pacific Coast Conference was dissolved at the end of the academic year. It was replaced by the Athletic Association of Western Universities with five original members—Cal, Stanford, UCLA, USC, and Washington. The 1959 season was the last for Tippy Dye who resigned to become Athletic Director at Wichita State. He compiled a 156-91 record at Washington and the second best winning percentage (.632) in Husky history. John Grayson replaced Dye. Grayson came from Idaho State, where he had a three-year record of 69-17, including three appearances in the NCAA Far West regional tournament.

Husky Highlight

Playing their football first game at Ohio State, the Huskies went up against a heavily favored Buckeye squad. Ohio State was the 1958 Rose Bowl champion—they defeated Oregon 10-7. Before 82,900 fans on Oct. 4, 1958, Washington gave Ohio State all they could handle. Washington scored first. Ohio's Bob White slid a punt off his foot and out of bounds on the Ohio State 31. The Huskies' Don McKeta ripped off a 14-yard gain and then 12 more for the score. George Fleming's kick was good. Late in the first quarter, the Buckeyes scored on a 28-yard drive set up by White's interception of a Phil Borders' pass. The conversion failed, and the Huskies led at half-time, 7-6. In the fourth quarter, Ohio State got another break when fullback, Bob Schloredt, went back to punt on the OSU 46. He had trouble handling the snap and then kicked it. Blocked by a wave of Buckeye defenders, the punt was recovered by Jim Marshall. Seven plays later, the Buckeyes scored to win 12-7. As Don McKeta recalled, even though the season ended 3-7, they played several close games against tough opponents. Jim Owens and his Huskies looked forward to 1959.

Husky Legend

The 1959 Husky baseball team

JW Media Relations

The 1959 baseball team was the first Husky nine to play in post-season competition.

The 1959 Husky baseball team, coachd by Dale Parker, had Washington's best season in almost three decades. They finished with a 21-12 season record and won the Northern Division title by one game over Oregon. They played USC for the Pacific Coast Conference title and lost two straight games to the Trojans, 17-3 and 9-0. Because USC was ineligible to go to the NCAA tournament because of NCAA rules violations, the Huskies went on to their first postseason competition as the PCC representative. Washington met Fresno State in a two-out-of-three series in the NCAA District 8, held in Seattle's Sick's Stadium. Fresno won the opener, 3-2. The Huskies came back to win the second game, 5-4. In the third contest, Fresno State beat Washington 10-5 and went on to represent the West Coast in the eight-team NCAA College World Series.

Husky List

The 1959 Washington baseball team was inducted in the Husky Hall of Fame in 1996. Its members were:

Daryl Burke
Don Daniels
George Grant
Peter Hanson
Floyd Harlington
Bob Hofeditz
Earle Irvine
Ken Jacobson
Bob Johnson
Carlton Olson
John Pariseau
George Pitt
Dick Reiten
Don Rhodes
Gary Snyder
Jim Stjerne
John Swinehart
Jerry Thornton (captain)
Jack Walters
Ernie Wheeler
Robert Wyman

Husky Lore

DR. CHARLES E. ODEGAARD was appointed President of the University of Washington in 1958. A man of outstanding intellectual and leadership capabilities, he led Washington through its greatest period of growth. Odegaard and his administration also had to deal with campus problems brought about by the civil rights movement, the Vietnam War, and demonstrations of activist, anti-war groups emerging in America. Dr. Odegaard joined Washington from the University of Michigan where he was Dean of the School of Arts and Sciences, the youngest ever to head the school.

1961 Tyee

Husky Moment

Rose Bowl Five—A Smashing Victory

Coach Milt Bruhn's Wisconsin Badgers arrived in Pasadena with the expectation of continuing the Big Ten's dominance over West Coast teams in the Rose Bowl. They quickly discovered they were in trouble with the faster, more agile Huskies. Quarterback Bob Schloredt and halfback George Fleming paced Washington to a 17-0 lead before the Badgers made a first down. On the Huskies' second drive of the game, Washington had fourth down on the Wisconsin six. Schloredt gave the ball to Don McKeta who ran in for the touchdown. Minutes later, Washington recovered the first of four Wisconsin fumbles and Fleming booted a 36-yard field goal. Later in the first quarter, Fleming returned a punt 53 yards for a touchdown and added the extra point for a 17-0 lead. In the second quarter, Wisconsin scored its only touchdown and passed for a two-point conversion to trail 17-8. Washington responded quickly when Fleming returned another punt for 55 yards down to the Badger 23. Then, in the game's most spectacular play, Schloredt threw the ball into the hands of the stretched-out Lee Folkins in the end zone. The Huskies went into the locker room, up 24-8. Washington scored in the third quarter behind the running of fullback Ray Jackson. The Huskies stopped the Badgers on four consecutive plays inside the Washington ten and took over on the seven yard line. 10 plays later, Schloredt capped off a 93-yard drive with a three-yard keeper to boost the score to 38-8. The final score came on a three-yard lob from Bob Hivner to Don Millich. The Huskies' 44 Rose Bowl points were the most in Rose Bowl history (broken in 1984 by UCLA in its 45-9 victory). Fleming and Schloredt were named co-MVPs.

1960 Tyee

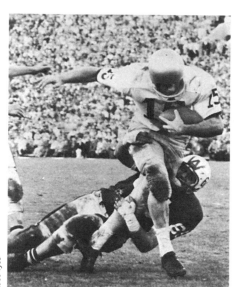

Bob Schloredt on a rollout in the Huskies' smashing victory over Wisconsin in 1960.

Husky Spotlight

Don McKeta was the heart and soul of the Husky teams in 1958 to 1960. Don's varied skills perfectly fit the single platoon football of his era. He was just as good defensively as he was on offense. He intercepted passes and made tackles as well as he ran and caught the ball. He made numerous key plays to bring Washington victories. One of his most memorable came near the end of the Washington State game in 1960. At half-time of the game, 10 stitches were required to close a gash in his leg. With the Huskies down 7-0, McKeta put aside the pain and did the bulk of the running on a fourth-quarter scoring drive of 53 yards. Washington needed the two-point conversion to win the game and ensure its second straight Rose Bowl appearance. Again, the Huskies went to McKeta who caught Bob Hivner's pass for the one-point victory, 8-7. He was the 1960 Seattle Sports Man of the Year and earned All-Coast and All-Big Five honors in that year. In 1998 McKeta received the All-American Football Foundation's "Unsung Hero" award. He was elected twice to the Husky Hall of Fame—first as an individual inductee in 1984 and again as a member of the 1959 football team in 1994.

Husky Highlight

The Huskies finished the 1959 regular football season with a 9-1-0 record and first in the AAWU. Washington started the season with four straight wins and then met seventh-ranked USC on Oct. 17. On a bright, crisp fall day, this game had everything that combines to make a classic one—power plays, stirring defenses, well-designed strategy, artfully executed passes, and a minimum of errors. USC scored on its second possession and again in the second stanza, to lead 14-0. The Huskies rallied. Quarterback Bob Schloredt rolled out for a score. George Fleming's kick was good and the Huskies trailed at half-time, 14-7. With about 10 minutes to go in the game, Schloredt, operating from the Bug I formation again, scored from the five-yard line and then rushed for two points and Washington led 15-14. The Trojans reclaimed the lead four minutes later after Willie Wood engineered an 80-yard touchdown drive and a two-point conversion and a 22-15 USC victory. A week later in Eugene, Washington spotted the Ducks a 12-0 lead. The Huskies scored in the second quarter and again in the third to go ahead 13-12. With three minutes left, Oregon drove to the Husky 22. Then Schloredt catapulted through the air to intercept what looked like an Oregon touchdown pass. The Huskies closed out the season with four more victories. On the final weekend of play, UCLA beat USC, 10-3, and Washington finished first in the AAWU standings among the teams in the old Pacific Coast Conference. The PCC standings decided the Rose Bowl representative, and the Athletic Directors of the former PCC schools voted unanimously to send the Huskies to the Rose Bowl.

Husky Legend

The 1959 Football Team

1960 Tyee

Co-MVPs of the 1960 Rose Bowl, George Fleming and Bob Schloredt, receive the Key to the City from Seattle Mayor Gordon Clinton at a huge welcome back rally.

Only two football teams in Husky history have been inducted in the Husky Hall of Fame—the 1959 and the 1991 teams. The 1959 team captured the imagination of Husky fans everywhere and perhaps like no other in Husky football. The whole area got behind them in a day when no professional sports were on the scene to compete for fan commitment and media attention. Also, the team brought respect back to the West Coast by becoming only the second to beat a Big Ten opponent since 1947 when the two conferences had agreed to square off in the Rose Bowl. USC defeated Wisconsin in 1953.

Husky List

The members of the 1959 Washington football team were:

Ricardo Aguirre
Chuck Allen
Lee Bernhardi
Barry Bullard
Tim Bullard
Don Carnahan
Jim Carphin
Stan Chapple
Larry Clanton
Pat Claridge
Keith Cordes
Mike Crawford
Gary Dasso
Ben Davidson
Dick Dunn
Bob Echols
Dave Enslow
Jim Everett
George Fleming
Lee Folkins
Carver Gayton
Kurt Gegner
Serge Grant
Bob Hivner
Sam Hurworth
Ray Jackson
Joe Jones
Kermit Jorgensen
Bill Kinnune
Gary Kissell
Roy McKasson
Don McKeta
John Meyers
Don Millich
John Nelson
Ed Peasley
George Pitt
Jim Quessenberry
Bob Schloredt
Jerry Schwarz
Jim Skaggs
Barney Therrien
Jack Walters
Dan Wheatley
Bob White
John Wilson
Brent Wooten

DON McKeta won the Flaherty Award as the team's most inspirational player in 1959 and 1960—only the second player in Husky history to receive the award twice. The other football player to be so honored was Tom Wand in 1911 and 1912. McKeta's teammates selected him as co-captain in the 1960 and 1961 Rose Bowl games. McKeta is the only football player in Husky history to twice lead Washington teams in the Rose Bowl.

1953 Men's Basketball Team

Five men from the state of Washington were starters on the best men's basketball team in Husky history. All graduated from Western Washington high schools. Joe Cipriano, a 5'11" guard from Nooksack Valley; Charlie Koon, another 5' 11" guard from Bremerton; Bob Houbregs, the 6' 7" center from Queen Anne; Doug McClary, a 6' 8" forward from Olympia; and Captain Mike McCutcheon, 6' 1" forward from Garfield. All were seniors and, except for Koon who had transferred from Olympic Junior College in his junior year, all had played together for three years coming into the 1953 season.

They were recruited by head coach Art McLarney in 1949. They played on the 1950 freshmen team coached by former Husky All-America Bill Morris and had a 21-1 record. As sophomores, they joined Duane Enochs, Frank Guisness, Lou Soriano, and captain LaDon Henson to capture the Pacific Coast Conference title. Their 24-6 season record included two NCAA tournament wins. In 1952, McCutcheon, co-captain with senior Guisness, led the team to a 25-6 record. Because they lost the conference title to UCLA in a best two-of-three playoff in the small UCLA gymnasium, they did not make the regional playoffs and watched the NCAA Final Four in Edmundson Pavilion.

They enjoyed one another. They loved to practice together. They went out to movies, and parties, and on dates together. Bill Ward, the 1953 Hec Edmundson Most Inspirational Award winner, contributed much to the team's unique chemistry. As Seattle University's 1953 All-America John O'Brien said: "They were good people."

Coach Tippy Dye had instituted a center-oriented offense built around Houbregs. Dye taught him the hook shot, a shot Houbregs had never used in high school. As individuals, they had skills that fit the team's style that featured the scoring and inside game of Houbregs. The guards were quick and put defensive pressure on their opponents. Cipriano played defense with his hands, poking at his opponent like a little animal, tugging on pants or jerseys. He was a pest. Koon was a real student of the game, a fine shooter, and a terrific passer who was very effective at getting the ball inside. McClary could jump out of the gym and was a great rebounder. McCutcheon was very strong, got great rebounding position, and played outstanding defense.

In 1953, with a 23-2 record, they met California for the Pacific Coast Conference title and the conference berth in the NCAA Western Regional. At Edmundson Pavilion, they won two straight against the Bears, 60-47 and 80-57. Next came the much awaited game with Seattle University in the first game of the regional in Corvallis. Although it was not a close game—the Huskies won 92-70—it might have been the most emotional game Washington had played all season. The following night, they beat a very good Santa Clara team in a closely contested game to go to the Final Four.

In that year, only two days separated the regional final and the first Final Four game. The Huskies beat Santa Clara on Saturday, March 14, flew to Kansas City on Sunday in a propeller driven plane, practiced Monday, and met Kansas on Tuesday evening, March 17. Houbregs felt the team never recovered from the high of the regional. Click Clark, the Husky trainer who was normally upbeat and positive with the athletes, was upset after observing the team's practice and said: "You guys are not ready to play." Coach Dye felt Kansas had the only defense that could upset the Huskies defensively. The Jayhawks' guards put pressure on Cipriano and Koon and made it difficult to get the ball into Houbregs and the forwards. Houbregs was called for four fouls in the first half and fouled out with over 17 minutes to play. After losing to Kansas 79-53, the Huskies came back the next night to take third in the tournament by beating Louisiana State 88-69.

Cipriano, Koon, Houbregs, McClary and McCutcheon and their teammates—Don Apeland, Will Elliott, Roland Halle, Dean Parsons, Steve Roake, Don Tripp and Bill Ward—were the best men's basketball team in Husky history.

- Most wins in a season—28 in 1953
- Best overall record in a single season—28-3—and best winning percentage (90.3%)
- Best varsity record (three years)—77-15—and the best winning percentage (83.7%)
- The highest finish of any Husky basketball team—third in the nation
- The only basketball team in Washington's history to be included in the Husky Hall of Fame (1985)

Jim Owens

Jim Owens and His 1959 Purple Gang

Bear Bryant, the legendary coach at Kentucky, Texas A&M, and Alabama had a direct impact on the success of the Husky football program. It came in the form of one of Bear's boys—Jim Owens.

A charismatic young coach, Owens brought hard-nosed, smash-mouth intensity to Seattle. When he arrived in 1957, Owens brought a bevy of assistant coaches from the Southwest—Tom Tipps, Chesty Walker, and Bert Clark to teach football—Bear Bryant style.

Owens' 1959 team was forged out of very demanding conditioning drills and what players called the "death march"—a run-till-you-drop workout in which players started in a three-point stance, ran 15 yards and repeated the drill for several lengths of the field. In Owens' first year in 1957, the team had lack of depth and inexperience at key positions. Of the 53 players who turned out for fall practice, only 20 were letterwinners. Although the season ended 3-6-1, clearly something was happening. The coaches stressed character, courage, discipline, persistence, teamwork, and the will to excel. In 1958, 28 of the 50 who started the pre-season practices were sophomores; four others were juniors who had not played a minute of varsity football. None of the five candidates for quarterback had taken a varsity game snap. Some sophomores had played on the unbeaten 1957 freshmen team—Chuck Allen, Barry Bullard, Stan Chapple, Pat Claridge, Lee Folkins, Kurt Gegner, Bill Kinnune, Bob Schloredt and Brent Wooten. They were joined by junior college transfers George Fleming, Bob Hivner and Don McKeta, a 24-year-old Navy veteran who grew up in Pennsylvania. Many of these sophomores were starters. They played one-platoon football, both offense and defense. The 1958 season ended 3-7 but included wins over Minnesota, Oregon, and a very close loss, 12-7, to the Rose Bowl champion and seventh-ranked Ohio State, in Columbus, Ohio. The Huskies couldn't wait for 1959.

Washington started the 1959 season with four straight wins and then met seventh-ranked USC. On a bright, crisp October day, the game had everything. In a classic struggle, the Huskies lost in the final minutes, 22-15. A week later in Eugene, they edged eleventh-ranked Oregon, 13-12. They closed out the season with wins over UCLA, Oregon State, California and Washington State to win the conference title, a 10-1 season record, and a Rose Bowl invitation. On New Year's day in Pasadena, they faced Wisconsin, the Big Ten champion, billed as bigger and stronger than the Huskies. Wisconsin was favored by 10 points and most thought the Badgers would continue the dominance of Big Ten teams in the Rose Bowl. Since the pact between the Big Ten and the Pacific Coast Conference schools was formed in 1947, only one Pacific Coast school had won the Rose Bowl. In the other 12 games, Big Ten schools not only won but in four games, their teams had won by more than 26 points.

Jim Owens and his staff were brilliant in their preparation of the Husky team. They stressed teamwork, the will to win, and mental toughness. The Badgers quickly discovered they were in trouble with the faster, quicker Huskies. Quarterback Bob Schloredt and halfback, George Fleming, paced Washington to a 17-0 lead before Wisconsin made a first down. The final score was 44-8 and the Huskies' scoring total broke the Rose Bowl record for most points scored by a team. Owens recalled: "It would be hard to find a club anywhere, anytime, that played a 60-minute period better than that team did that day."

The 1959 team captured the imagination of Husky fans everywhere and perhaps like no other in Husky football.

"We had a coach that took his players and molded them into a winner," said Don McKeta, the heart and soul of the team and a two-time winner of the Guy Flaherty Award as the team's most inspirational player. "No one expected us to do anything. We changed Husky football. We changed the way football was played on the West Coast."

The whole area got behind the Huskies in a day when no professional sports were on the scene to compete for fan commitment and media attention. The next year, they stayed together, lost only to Navy en route to another 10-1 season. In the 1961 Rose Bowl, the Huskies faced Minnesota, the number-one ranked team in the nation at the end of the regular season. Again they won 17-7. The Huskies were voted the number-one team in the nation by the Helms Foundation, the only poll in those days taken after all the bowl games had been played.

In 1994, members of the 1959 football team were inducted in the Husky Hall of Fame—the first football team in Husky history to be selected.

1960-69

1960 W 1961

Husky Moment

1961 Rose Bowl

Despite being the defending Rose Bowl champions and sporting a 9-1 record, Washington entered the 1961 bowl game as decided underdogs. The Big Ten's representative, Minnesota entered the game ranked number one in the national polls. But just like the favored Wisconsin Badgers a year earlier, the Gophers left with a 17–7 setback courtesy of an explosive Husky start and a determined second-half defensive effort. Washington used its superior quickness to offset Minnesota's size advantage in the early going. George Fleming kicked a 44-yard field goal, putting Washington on the scoreboard first and himself into the Rose Bowl record book with the longest field goal kick in its history. Quarterback Bob Schloredt, who missed the second half of the season with an injury, entered the game in the first quarter, replacing starter Bob Hivner. He directed a drive that culminated with a three-yard scoring pass to halfback Brent Wooten early in the second quarter to increase the Huskies' lead to 10-0. Schloredt relied on his feet later in the quarter to set up Washington's third score. On second-and-two from just inside midfield, he scrambled 31 yards to the Gophers' 18-yard line. Four plays later he scored from the one-yard line to build the Huskies' advantage to 17-0 at the half. Minnesota's only scoring drive came during the third quarter after the Huskies fumbled the ball away on their own 32-yard line. Washington's defense managed to intercept three Gopher passes to kill drives. Schloredt was named the game's MVP for the second consecutive year, a first in Rose Bowl history. After the game, the Helms Foundation awarded Washington its national championship trophy. Although not as highly respected as the wire service polls, the Helms Foundation was the only organization at the time to pick its national champion ... AFTER the bowl games were played.

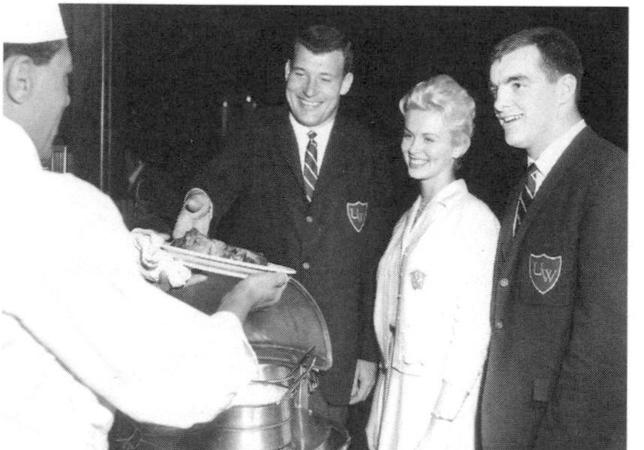

1960 Tyee

The Huskies enjoy prime rib at Lowry's for the Rose Bowl's annual Beef Bowl with the Rose Bowl queen.

Husky Spotlight

Roy McKasson

At 6-1 and 205 pounds, Roy McKasson was considered undersized by the standards in 1960 when he piled up numerous honors as the center on the Huskies' victorious Rose Bowl team. He earned All-America honors from the Associated Press, *Look Magazine,* the American Football Coaches, Newspaper Enterprise Association and ABC Sports. He appeared in Washington's back-to-back Rose Bowl victories in 1960 and 1961 and was selected by coach Jim Owens as a game captain during his senior season. McKasson went on to play in the Hula and All-American Bowls and was inducted into the Husky Hall of Fame in 1987.

Husky Highlight

George Fleming was an all-purpose player for the Husky football team and a vital cog in Washington's back-to-back Rose Bowl victories in 1960 and 1961. As a running back, Fleming saw limited time as a senior, gaining 293 yards. It was his special teams play that set him apart. In 1960, he earned all-conference and All-Coast honors when he converted 23 of 24 PATs and led the team in scoring with 65 points. That same year he averaged a robust 14.8 yards per punt runback. He finished his career as the all-time leader in punt return average at 10.9 yards per return on 44 runbacks. In the 1961 Rose Bowl he booted a 44-yard field goal to get the Huskies rolling toward a 17-7 victory against Minnesota. His kick also sent him into the Rose Bowl record book with the longest field goal in the game's history. A year earlier, as a junior, Fleming shared the Rose Bowl's MVP award with Husky quarterback Bob Schloredt. Fleming sparked the Huskies to their 44-8 victory against Wisconsin with a 57-yard punt return for a score and a 64-yard pass reception to set up another score. A transfer from East Los Angeles Junior College, the Dallas native went on to play for the Oakland Raiders in the now-defunct AFL, for one season. Fittingly, he set a field-goal record in his only year with the Raiders.

Husky Legend

Bob Schloredt

UW Media Relations

One of the key components to Washington's back-to-back Rose Bowl victories in 1960 and 1961 was quarterback Bob Schloredt. The tough-nosed two-way player, who was born in Deadwood, South Dakota, is one of the most popular players in modern Husky football history. Schloredt drew national attention for the fact he played with very limited vision in his left eye as a result of a childhood accident when he was seven years old. His story of being a "One-Eyed Quarterback" was featured in a 1960 issue of *Sports Illustrated,* making him the first Husky athlete to grace the cover of the fabled sports publication. Schloredt entered his junior season as a backup to Bob Hivner, but found himself in the starting role after just one game due to an injury to Hivner. He proceeded to lead the '59 Huskies to a 10-1 record that included a 44-8 victory against Wisconsin in the Rose Bowl. The victory was Washington's first Rose Bowl victory. Schloredt passed for 102 yards, rushed for 81 yards, threw one touchdown pass and ran for another to earn the bowl's MVP honors. Schloredt was named the Associated Press' first-team All-America quarterback in 1959 and picked up second-team honors from the Hearst Newspaper chain. Schloredt's senior season was slowed when he suffered a broken collarbone at mid-season against UCLA. He did not return to the lineup until the Rose Bowl, when he again was named the game's most outstanding player after rushing for 68 yards, and one score, and passing for 16 yards in the Huskies' 17-7 victory against Minnesota. He became the first player to win back-to-back MVP honors in the Rose Bowl's history. A multi-talented player who was also a starting defensive back, Schloredt set a UW record in 1959 with his punting average (40.0) and held the record for longest punt from 1958 to 1975 thanks to a 71-yard boot against Oregon State in 1958. Following his senior season, Schloredt appeared in the Hula and All-American Bowls. He played two seasons with the British Columbia Lions in the Canadian Football League before returning to Jim Owens' staff as an assistant coach from 1963-73. He was inducted into Washington's Hall of Fame in 1981 and the Rose Bowl Hall of Fame in 1991.

Husky List

Washington's Bowl MVPs (Announced by Bowl Committee)

Year	Bowl	Player of the Game	Score
1926	Rose	George Wilson, rb	Alabama 20, Washington 19
1960	Rose	Bob Schloredt, qb	Washington 44, Wisconsin 8
		George Fleming, rb	
1961	Rose	Bob Schloredt, qb	Washington 17, Minnesota 7
1978	Rose	Warren Moon, qb	Washington 27, Michigan 20
1979	Sun	Paul Skansi, wr	Washington 14, Texas 7
		Doug Martin, dt	
1982	Rose	Jacque Robinson, rb	Washington 28, Iowa 0
1982	Aloha	Tim Cowan, qb	Washington 21, Maryland 20
		Tony Caldwell, lb	
1983	Aloha	Danny Greene, wr	Penn State 13, Washington 10
1985	Orange	Jacque Robinson, rb	Washington 28, Oklahoma 17
		Ron Holmes, dt	
1985	Freedom	Chris Chandler, qb	Washington 20, Colorado 17
1986	Sun	Steve Alvord, dl	Alabama 28, Washington 6
1987	Independence	Chris Chandler, qb	Washington 24, Tulane 12
1989	Freedom	Cary Conklin, qb	Washington 34, Florida 7
1991	Rose	Mark Brunell, qb	Washington 46, Iowa 34
1992	Rose	Steve Emtman, dt	Washington 34, Michigan 14
		Billy Joe Hobert, qb	
1997	Aloha	Rashaan Shehee, tb	Washington 51, Michigan State 23
1998	Oahu	Brock Huard, qb	Air Force 45, Washington 25
2001	Rose	Marques Tuiasosopo, qb	Washington 34, Purdue 24

Note: Jacque Robinson is the only player to win MVP honors in both the Rose and Orange Bowls.

A MEMBER of Washington's 1960 and 1961 Rose Bowl championship teams, Chuck Allen stands as one of the greatest linemen in school history. Named to the Huskies' Centennial Team, Allen was a two-time all-coast and all-conference performer. He played 12 years of professional football with San Diego, Pittsburgh and Philadelphia. As a rookie for San Diego in 1961, he was named to the all-AFL team. He was enshrined into the Chargers' Hall of Fame in 1984 and named to the Husky Hall of Fame in 1994. He began his coaching career at Washington in 1973 and later served as an administrator for two decades with the Seattle Seahawks.

Husky Moment

Basketball Upsets No. 4 USC

The times did not look promising for the Husky basketball team in early January of 1962. Washington had lost senior guard Lyle Bakken with a torn Achilles tendon, and coach John Grayson was forced to juggle his starting lineup for the first time during the season. The Huskies were struggling, having lost three in a row and four of five after a 59-49 defeat to top-ranked Ohio State at the Los Angeles Classic. USC's fourth-ranked Trojans were in town for back-to-back dates on Jan. 12 and 13 and were heavy favorites to extend UW's losing streak. The Trojans were led by All-American center Johnny Rudometkind, who entered the series averaging 20.8 points per game. But it would be his Husky counterpart, UW center Bill Hanson, who would steal the show. Hanson, who was averaging 20.2 points per contest, scored 37 during the Friday night series opener to lead the Huskies to a surprising 85-67 rout of USC. With the game tied at 42-42, Hanson scored 12 points in a four-minute span to help the Huskies to a 63-48 lead. Hanson also contributed nine rebounds in the victory. He became just the third Husky player to ever eclipse the 30-point mark in a game. Hanson was not Washington's only standout. Keith Brown, who replaced Bakken in the lineup, had nine points and nine rebounds. The next night, Hanson kept up his torrid scoring pace, blitzing USC for 32 points, but it was not enough as the Trojans rebounded for a 78-64 victory. The loss ended an eight-game winning streak for the Huskies on their home court. Despite dropping its next game at Stanford, Washington finished the season strong, winning nine of their final 12 games. The victory against the fourth-ranked Trojans equaled the highest rated team Washington had ever defeated. In 1951 the Huskies upset a fourth-ranked St. Louis squad.

UW Media Relations

Ed Correll grabs a rebound in Washington's upset of fourth-ranked USC.

Husky Spotlight

Ray Mansfield

Ray Mansfield is probably better known for his football playing career after he left the University. He lettered for the Huskies from 1960-62 as a 6-3, 220-pound center. Sidelined part of the 1960 season due to a neck injury, Mansfield emerged as a consistent force on the offensive line during his junior season. He was recognized as a second-team all-conference and all-coast player in 1961. The Kennewick native earned third-team Associated Press All-American honors as a senior in 1962. The Philadelphia Eagles selected him in the second round of the 1963 NFL draft and used him on both offense and defense. He played just one season there before moving on to the Pittsburgh Steelers where he gained legendary status until his retirement in 1976. He was a member of the Steelers' Super Bowl Championship team in 1975 and 1976. When he retired he owned Pittsburgh's record for consecutive games played with 198 appearances. Mansfield had the privilege of playing for the 1963 College All-Star team that defeated Vince Lombardi's Green Bay Packer squad 20-17. A native of Kennewick, Mansfield died in 1996 at age 55 while hiking in the Grand Canyon. He was inducted into the Husky Hall of Fame in 1995.

Husky Highlight

Bill Hanson was a three-time All-AAWU selection for the Husky basketball team from 1960-62. When he concluded his career, Hanson's 20.8 scoring average was second in school history behind Bob Houbregs' average of 25.6 points per game. The 6-8 Husky center from Mercer Island came to Washington with the reputation of a scorer. He led the state of Washington in that area as a prep standout as both a junior and senior. After averaging 20.0 points for the Huskies' freshman team, Hanson lit up the hoops as a sophomore, averaging 16.4 points per game. In 1962, he poured in 40 points against California to become the only Husky player besides Houbregs to score that many points in a game. He had back-to-back 37- and 32-point outings against USC as a senior in 1962. Hanson was also an accurate shooter. Of the top 25 scorers in UW history, he is one of just four players to shoot better than 50 percent in each of their varsity seasons.

UW Media Relations

The Husky band performs during pregame ceremonies.

Washington quarterback Marques Tuiasosopo runs the option.

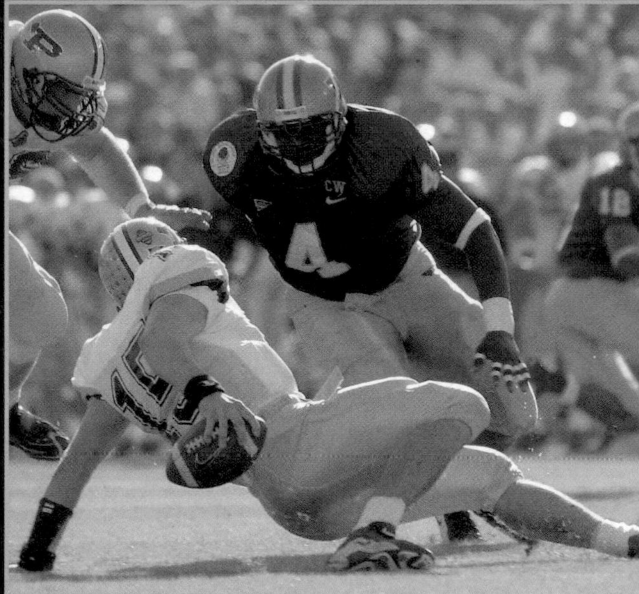

Jeremiah Pharms moves in on Purdue quarterback Drew Brees.

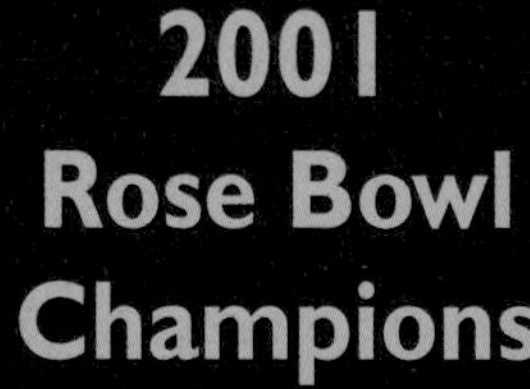

2001 Rose Bowl Champions

Washington coach Rick Neuheisel acknowledges the crowd.

Linebacker Derrell Daniels, fullback Pat Conniff and quarterback Marques Tuiasosopo celebrate the Huskies victory.

All photos courtesy of the University of Washington

Husky Legend

Charlie Mitchell

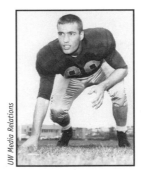

UW Media Relations

Just when Husky fans thought there would never be another Washington running back to rival Hugh McElhenny, along came Charlie Mitchell. A product of Seattle's Garfield High School, Mitchell was a speedy back who burst on the scene in 1960 when he led the team in rushing with 467 yards. His average of 6.3 yards per carry was the best among all AAWU running backs. Mitchell picked up numerous football honors for his performances in 1961. He was tabbed all-coast, all-conference and a second-team All-American by ABC-TV. He holds the distinction of being the first Husky player named to a Playboy All-America squad. As a senior, he led the Huskies in receiving with nine catches for 108 yards. He finished his career with 2,539 all-purpose yards. His rushing total (1,362) was second only to McElhenny. Mitchell was especially elusive on kickoff return teams. He led Washington in that category all three years he played and ran back kicks for scores of 90 yards vs. UCLA (1961) and 85 yards vs. Idaho (1960). He averaged 32.6 yards per return on the 17 kicks he ran back during his playing days. Mitchell also excelled on the defensive side for coach Jim Owens' teams. After graduation, Mitchell went on to play in the East-West Game, the Hula Bowl, and he was the leading rusher on the College All-Star team that defeated the Green Bay Packers in the All-Star game. He played professional football with the Denver Broncos from 1963-67 and with Buffalo in 1968. A strong proponent of higher education, Mitchell earned his masters in education from Seattle University and a Doctor of Education degree from BYU. He went on to serve as the president of Seattle Central Community College. He was inducted into the Husky Hall of Fame in 1992.

HUSKY LIST

Ed Corell Sets Rebounding Mark

Few records can stand the test of time the way Ed Corell's single-game rebounding total has. It was almost four decades ago that "Easy Ed" set a Husky rebounding standard that might never be eclipsed. The 6-6, 210-pound junior from Alameda, California, led the Huskies to a 67-49 victory against Oregon on Feb. 24 in Hec Edmundson Pavilion by scoring 23 points and grabbing 30 rebounds. The Huskies outrebounded the Ducks, 66-46, during the game. "Everything just seemed to be going the right way," said Corell after breaking Dean Parson's previous mark of 26 rebounds set vs. Idaho in 1955. Corell, who led Washington in rebounding as a sophomore and junior, would go on to earn second-team All-AAWU honors that season. To help put his record in perspective, consider that over the next 38 seasons, Washington only had 11 games where a Husky collected at least 20 rebounds.

Top UW Rebounding Games

30	Ed Corell vs. Oregon, 1962
28	Steve Hawes at Stanford, 1972
26	Dean Parsons vs. Idaho, 1955
22	Bob Houbregs vs. Utah, 1953
22	Jim Coshow vs. Iowa, 1955
22	Steve Hawes vs. Stanford, 1972

HUSKY LORE

UW Media Relations

JOHN MEYERS was always trying to find a way to help the Huskies. Meyers, a native of Richland, was a high school basketball All-American, leading his team to the state championship. Also an outstanding football end, Meyers decided early in his college career to play both sports at Washington. Meyers lettered in football from 1959-61 and was a member of the Huskies' back-to-back Rose Bowl championship teams. He played on the freshman basketball squad and for the varsity in 1959-60 as a sophomore. A large player (242 pounds) for his time, he held the distinction of being the lone sophomore starter on the '60 championship football squad. As a senior, he earned all-coast and honorable mention All-American honors playing tackle on both sides of the ball. His teammates honored him by naming him the recipient of the Guy Flaherty Inspirational Award. Drafted by the Los Angeles Rams, he spent his NFL career playing for the Dallas Cowboys (1962-63) and the Philadelphia Eagles (1964-67). After his playing career, he was always close to the Husky athletic program. He served as the president of the Tyee Club and was the vice president for Husky Fever. He was responsible for a seat cushion program in Husky Stadium that helped to endow a scholarship each year.

1962 W 1963

Husky Moment

Basketball Upsets UCLA

The Washington basketball team ended a five-game losing streak to UCLA's highly regarded Bruins by handing coach John Wooden's team back-to-back losses at Hec Edmundson Pavilion on Jan. 4-5. The Huskies won the series opener 62-61 thanks to a stingy defense that held the Bruins' leading scorer, Fred Slaughter, to just two points, 13 below his season average. UCLA only shot 24.7 percent from the floor, but still managed to hold a 47-41 lead with 14:24 to play. At that point, the Huskies scored 19 of the game's next 20 points to seize a 60-48 lead. The Huskies then experienced a nine-minute scoring drought but managed to survive for the one-point win. Dale Easley, the Huskies' 6-7 center, led Washington with 25 points and 11 rebounds. Saturday's game was almost a replay of Friday's effort. The Huskies held a 12-point lead and had to fend off another Bruin rally to claim a 67-63 victory. Ed Corell provided the double-double with 19 points and 13 rebounds. Slaughter was once again held in check, scoring only five points. UCLA led 59-57 before the Huskies scored eight consecutive points to pull off the win. Walt Hazzard led all scorers by topping the Bruins with 20 points. The following season the Bruins would win the first of 10 national championships over 12 years.

UW Media Relations

Dale Easley

Husky Spotlight

Phil Shinnick

When is a world record performance not a world record? That is a question that Phil Shinnick wishes he never had to answer. Shinnick was a three-time letterwinner for the Husky track team from 1963-65. The Spokane native competed in the high jump, triple jump, sprints, 400-meter relay and the high hurdles. He collected 186 points in his career, the most ever by a Husky performer. But it was the long jump where he truly excelled. On May 25 in 1963, at the Modesto Relays, Shinnick unleashed a jump of 27-4 to eclipse the world record mark of 27-3¼ held by the Soviet Union's Igor Ter-Ovanesyan. Less than 10 minutes later, Husky teammate Brian Sternberg toppled the world pole vault mark. By the end of the day, only one of them still held the distinction of being an "official" world champion. There was no wind gauge monitoring Shinnick's leap and therefore the mark was not submitted as a world record. Amazingly, prior to that day, Shinnick's previous best jump was 25-5. Despite the fact track officials refused to verify his mark, Shinnick went on to have one of the top careers of any Husky performer. In 1964 he was a NCAA All-American and represented the United States at the 1964 Olympics in Tokyo. In 1992 he was elected into the Husky Hall of Fame.

Husky Highlight

When wrestling finally returned to the Husky campus in 1958, no one knew exactly what to expect. It had been 17 years, since grapplers competed for the Purple and the Gold. By the 1962-63 season, the Huskies showed the first sign they would have an impact on the sport. That season, Rich Bell qualified for the NCAA championships. Bell did not stop there. He finished fourth at the NCAAs to become the first placewinner in wrestling in school history. It would be another five years before Washington qualified another wrestler for the NCAAs and six seasons before another Husky would finish as a placewinner.

SID Files

Husky Legend

Brian Sternberg

Brian Sternberg stands as one of the most outstanding, inspirational, and courageous athletes in Washington history. His father, Harold, a former pole vaulter at Seattle Pacific College, introduced Brian to the sport as an eighth grader. In 1961, as a senior at Seattle's Shoreline High School, he drew national acclaim with a vault of 14-3¾ inches. With the aid of the introduction of the fiberglass pole to the sport, Sternberg began his record-setting career at Washington. As a 19-year-old sophomore, he set the American indoor record in March in Milwaukee with a clearing of 16-3½. He achieved even greater heights by setting the world record at the 69th Annual Penn Relays in 1963 with a soaring 16-5 performance. Unfortunately, he held the mark for just three days. Not to be outdone, on May 25 in Modesto, California, Sternberg reclaimed the world title with a leap of 16-7. That time the mark lasted for five days. Later that season, in June, he reset the mark with a 16-8 mark at the Compton Relays. He was the youngest athlete to better the 16-foot mark and he was only the fourth Husky to hold the distinction as a world record holder. Almost overshadowed in his record-setting efforts was the fact Sternberg won the NCAA pole vaulting title that same year with a mark of 16-4¾ that stayed a record until the 1967 nationals. An outstanding athlete, Sternberg also lettered for the men's gymnastics team. In 1963, he was voted the University's athlete of the year and named the co-winner of the *Seattle Post-Intelligencer's* Man of the Year. Tragically, that was also Sternberg's last year as a competitor. A trampoline accident in July ended his athletic career and left him paralyzed. Sternberg was inducted into the Husky Hall of Fame in 1983.

Husky List

Norm Dicks

As a Pac-10 Medalist in 1963, it should not come as a surprise that Norm Dicks would go on to serve his home state in Congress. The Bremerton native lettered for the Huskies in 1961 and 1962 as a 195-pound guard and linebacker. He led the team in tackles in both 1961 and 1962 and was named to the AAWU All-Academic team following his junior season. Dicks is one of 19 Husky football players who has been honored as a Pac-10 Medalist. Here's a look at the list:

1961	Barry Bullard	1983	Chuck Nelson
1963	Norm Dicks	1984	Steve Pelluer
1974	Joe Tabor	1985	Dan Eernissee
1975	Dennis Fitzpatrick	1988	David Rill
1976	Ray Pinney	1989	Brett Wiese
1978	Blair Bush	1990	Greg Lewis
1980	Bruce Harrell	1991	Ed Cunningham
1981	Mike Reilly	1993	Jim Nevelle
1982	Mark Jerue	1995	Ernie Conwell
		1996	Dave Janoski

Husky Lore

UW Media Relations

THE term "coaching legend" is used so often it has become a cliché. But not when it is applied to Dr. Norm Kunde. Few coaches can equal the tenure Kunde had with Husky athletics. In 1933, Kunde started the men's volleyball program at the University. He held that position for 35 years. His teams won 90 percent of their dual collegiate matches and he produced 21 all-district players. His teams won 21 of 25 Northwest Collegiate Championships and six Class A District Open titles. Only once in his tenure, 1958, did the Huskies suffer a losing season. He was inducted into the Helms Foundation's Hall of Fame in 1957. Ironically, the year after Kunde retired, the NCAA recognized his sport. He later served a five-year term on the NCAA's volleyball tournament committee. From 1928 to 1931 Kunde coached the Husky boxing squads and tutored 11 Pacific Coast Champions.

1963 W 1964

Husky Moment

1964 Rose Bowl

The Huskies entered their third Rose Bowl in five years in a familiar position as an underdog. Coach Pete Elliott's Illinois team had a 7–1–1 regular-season record and was ranked third in the country, while the Huskies had overcome a 0–3 start to finish the year 6–4. Washington featured a hard-driving ground game led by quarterback Bill Douglas, fullback Junior Coffey, and future pro halfbacks Ron Medved and Dave Kopay. The defense earned its reputation as a hard-hitting group, which was almost impossible to run against, anchored by a future Husky head coach, end Jim Lambright. The Illini featured perhaps the most famous alumnus of the 1964 Rose Bowl, linebacker Dick Butkus. The Huskies' opening drive proved to be costly. Already without Coffey, due to a foot injury, Washington lost starting quarterback Bill Douglas to a knee injury after moving the Huskies to the Illini 26-yard line. Backup quarterback Bill Siler entered the game and completed the first pass he attempted but left end Al Libke fumbled on the Illini six-yard line. The Huskies held tough and used an Illinois fumble in the second quarter to set up the game's first score. Kopay took a pitch and scored from the six-yard line to give the Huskies their only score. After holding the Illini inside the 10-yard line, the Husky offense again fumbled the ball away. This time Illinois capitalized with a 32-yard field goal. Illinois converted another Washington turnover into points early in the second half when Siler was intercepted at midfield. The ball was returned to the Washington 32 where Illinois started its second scoring drive. The Illini scored in six plays for a 10–7 lead, helped by a Washington piling-on penalty. Washington had a chance to go ahead at the end of the third quarter, but on a third-and-seven, Siler's pass was picked off on the Illinois four-yard line. Illinois responded with the only full drive of the day, moving from the Husky 15-yard line, 85 yards for the touchdown. Almost as important as the points was the fact that Illinois ate up eight minutes of the final quarter on the drive and went on to win 17-7.

UW Media Relations

Dave Kopay

Husky Spotlight

Bill Douglas

The script was going exactly as Bill Douglas had in mind during the 1963 football season. Douglas, a three-year letterman from 1962-64, had quarterbacked the Huskies from a 0-3 start to the Rose Bowl. Douglas was well on his way to directing the Washington to an early lead in their matchup against Big Ten Champion Illinois when he suffered a knee injury in the first quarter that forced him from the game. A product of Wapato High School in eastern Washington, Douglas posted the best total offense marks by an UW signal caller since Don Heinrich. He had 1,242 yards of total offense, the best production since Heinrich put up 1,652 total offense yards in 1952. A solid passer and deceptive ball handler, he was a multiple threat for opposing defenses. As a junior, Douglas won all-conference and second-team all-coast honors. He overcame the knee injury to again lead Washington in passing as a senior, but his production was down nearly 600 yards to a total of 360 yards. Douglas was a National Football Foundation Scholar-Athlete in 1964 and a Big Six medalist in 1965. Douglas never played professional football. Instead, he returned to eastern Washington and prospered in the construction business.

Husky Highlight

A member of Washington's powerful backfield in 1963, Ron Medved sparked the Huskies to a 19-11 victory against Stanford thanks to an 88-yard touchdown run. At the time, it ranked as the fifth longest run from scrimmage in UW history. Medved, a Tacoma native, was known for his powerful blocking and running. He also played in the defensive secondary and handled place kicks and kickoffs. Jim Owens selected him as a game captain in 1963, the first time a sophomore earned that honor under Owens' watch. He became a team captain in 1965 when he was honored by his teammates as the Flaherty Award winner. Medved lettered in 1963-65 and went on to play in the East-West Shrine game and the Hula Bowl. He played professionally for the Philadelphia Eagles as a defensive back from 1966-70.

UW Media Relations

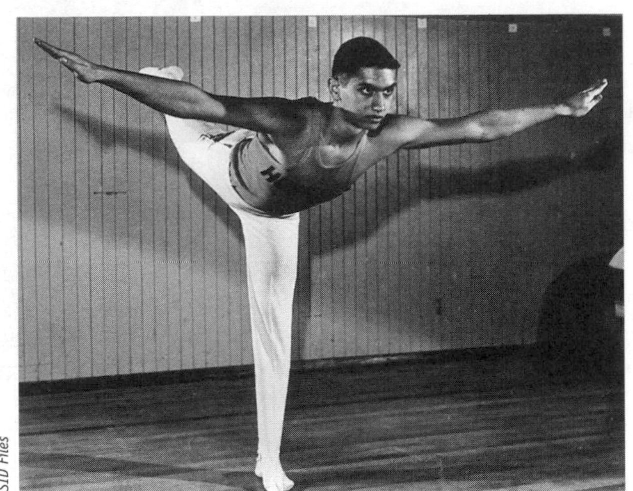
SID Files

Husky Legend

Jim David

Jim David was a two-time All-American who helped the Washington gymnastics team to its highest team finish (second in 1965) in school history. He placed third nationally in the floor exercise as a senior. In 1964 he was named the Washington Athlete of the Year and helped Washington win the conference championships in 1963, 1964 and 1965. As a junior, he finished second in tumbling and fourth in floor exercise at the NCAA Championships. That season the Huskies recorded a fourth-place team finish. During his sophomore campaign, David placed in three events, finishing fourth in tumbling, fifth in floor exercise, and 10th on trampoline, to help Washington to a ninth-place showing. As a junior he was second in tumbling and fourth on floor. During his senior season he finished third on floor exercise. The Huskies were fourth as a team in 1964 and second in 1965. In addition to his outstanding routines at the NCAAs, he won four AAWU championships during his career. In 1966, he competed on a team that won the New Zealand and Australian national championships. The Seattle native attended Blanchet High School and returned to Washington to receive his MBA in 1970. He was inducted into the Husky Hall of Fame in 1987.

HUSKY LIST

Top Passing Games in UW Bowl History

Tim Cowan,
1982 Aloha Bowl vs. Maryland —350 Yards
Mark Brunell,
1993 Rose Bowl vs. Michigan—308 Yards
Tom Flick,
1981 Rose Bowl vs. Michigan—282 Yards
Brock Huard,
1998 Oahu Bowl vs. Air Force—267 Yards
Chris Chandler,
1987 Independence Bowl vs. Tulane—234 Yards
Cary Conklin,
1989 Freedom Bowl vs. Florida—217 Yards
Brock Huard,
1996 Holiday Bowl vs. Colorado—203 Yards

HUSKY LORE

Wariboko West Finishes Fourth at Olympics

MOST of the focus, from a Husky point of view, at the 1964 Olympic long jump competition focused on Phil Shinnick. The one-time Washington record holder in the event, hopes were high that he might break through with a medal-winning performance. Instead, it was his UW teammate, Wariboko Queen Boy West, who nearly stole the show. West was a triple jumper at Washington who set the school record in the event with a mark of 49-4¾ at the Far West Relays during the 1964 collegiate season. Instead of competing in that event at the Olympic Games, the coaches of his native Nigerian team entered him in the long jump. The wet, rainy conditions, that left puddles on the runways at Tokyo's National Stadium, were far from ideal. Still, West turned in a leap of 24-11¼ to place fourth in the event.

1964 W 1965

Husky Moment

Men's Gymnastics Places 2nd at NCAAs

The 1964-65 Husky men's gymnastics team proved to be the most successful in school history. After rolling to a perfect regular-season record,coach Eric Hughes' team won the Northwest College Invitational by scoring a whopping 213.5 points to runnerup Eastern Washington's 86.5 points. The Huskies then used strong performances by Bob Hall and Jim David to capture the AAWU title by outscoring second-place California by five points (160-155). Hall won the all-around, side horse and horizontal bar titles, while David took home top honors in floor exercise. Next stop was the NCAA championships. The Huskies walked away with individual finishes of second, third, fourth, fifth and ninth place. As he had done all year, Hall led the Huskies with a second-place finish on side horse and a fourth-place showing in the all-around. David placed third in floor exercise while Mark Buckingham was fifth on the horizontal bar. Mike Lovell finished ninth in the all-around. Under a new format that lasted one season, Penn State advanced through a bracket of dual meet competitions to face each other in the finals. The Nittany Lions won the NCAA title by a score of 68.5 to 51.5.

UW Media Relations

Eric Hughes

Husky Spotlight

Junior Coffey

As a fullback at Washington, Junior Coffey would often be categorized as a thoroughbred thanks to his powerful running style. How ironic that description would turn out to be. Considered one of the top high school running backs in the nation out of Dimmitt, Texas, Husky coach Jim Owens relied on his Lone Star State connections to lure Coffey to Washington. He easily lived up to his billing. In 1962, as a sophomore, Coffey led the AAWU in rushing with 581 yards, averaging 5.9 yards per carry. Named to the all-conference and all-coast teams, his future looked bright. Foot troubles sidelined Coffey on and off as a junior. After the team started 0-3 without Coffey, his return helped to spark the Huskies to win six of their final seven games and return to the Rose Bowl. Another foot injury kept him out of the game that Washington lost to Illinois. Coffey rebounded as a senior and again led Washington with 581 rushing yards and eight scores. In his first year of professional football, Coffey played for the 1965 Green Bay Packer squad coached by Vince Lombardi that defeated the Cleveland Browns for the NFL title. After his football career faded, Coffey raised thoroughbred race horses at Seattle's Longacres Race Track until the facility closed.

Husky Highlight

It was the summer of 1964 and Lynn Nance found himself in Los Angeles, waiting for his basketball career at UCLA to begin after transferring from Southwest Baptist Junior College. A native of tiny Granby, Mo., Nance did not feel comfortable in the sprawling metropolis. So, before he ever played a game for the Bruins, he elected to transfer to Washington. Nance was a two-year starter for the Huskies and led the team in scoring (17.5 ppg.) and rebounding (9.4 rpg.) as a senior, earning honorable mention All-America honors. The St. Louis Hawks of the NBA drafted him, but a knee injury delayed his reporting to rookie camp. After flirting with a coaching career, Nance went to work for the FBI and later the NCAA before returning to coaching. In 1984, he led Central Missouri State to the NCAA Division II national title. In 1989 Nance realized a lifelong dream when he returned to be the head coach at Washington. He was the first former basketball player to come back and coach the Huskies. He recorded 50 victories during his four-year tenure.

UW Media Relations

Husky Legend

Rick Redman

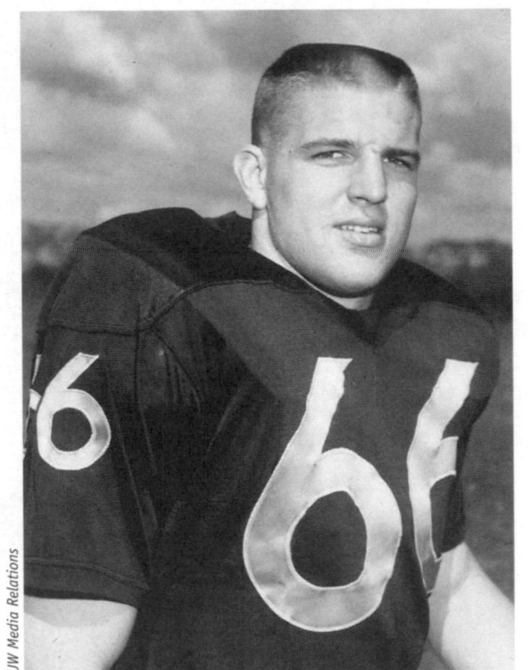

UW Media Relations

Coming out of Blanchet High School in Seattle, Husky fans could not wait for Rick Redman to join the lineup. A three-year letterwinner from 1962-64, Redman is one of Washington's most decorated athletes, claiming All-American recognition in three seasons. He was a consensus All-American in both 1963 and 1964. He typically produced between 12-15 tackles a game and was also the team's punter, averaging 37.6 yards on his 134 career punts. Redman was the team's L. Wait Rising Award winner as the top lineman in 1964 and was the *Detroit Sports Extra* Lineman of the Year in 1963. He was a co-captain as a senior and went on to earn lineman of the game honors during the 1965 East-West Shrine Game. Redman also participated in the Hula Bowl. The majority of his professional football career was played in San Diego. In his first season with the Chargers, the team was the AFL's Western Division Champions. He served as a player-coach his last two years with the franchise. In 1974, he played with the Portland Storm of the World Football League. Redman went on to become chairman and CEO of Sellen Construction, a firm that handled the renovation of Hec Edmundson Pavilion from 1999-2000. He was inducted into the College Football Hall of Fame in 1995 after joining the Husky Hall of Fame in 1982.

HUSKY LIST

Washington Finishes at the NCAA Skiing Championships

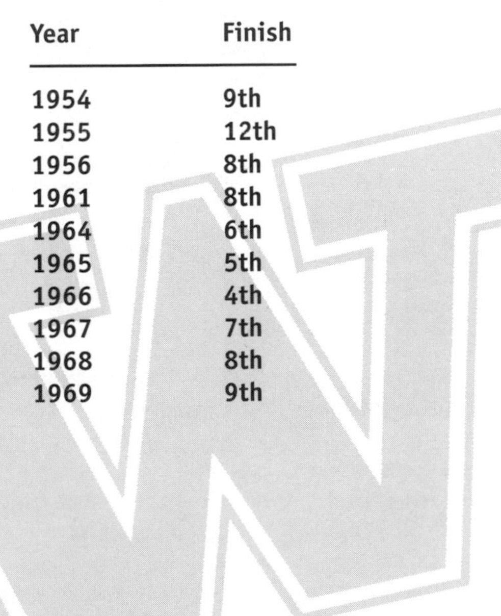

Year	Finish
1954	9th
1955	12th
1956	8th
1961	8th
1964	6th
1965	5th
1966	4th
1967	7th
1968	8th
1969	9th

Huskies Host NCAA Skiing Championships

FOR the first time in the event's 12-year history, the University hosted the NCAA Skiing Championships at Crystal Mountain. The Huskies managed a fifth-place finish while Denver won the team title for the ninth time in 12 years. Washington had a remarkable run of success at the NCAAs during the 1960s. Between 1961 and 1969 Washington placed in the top nine at the event seven times, highlighted by a fourth-place finish in 1966 at Crested Butte. In 1963 Tom Nord won the NCAA Championship in jumping. Husky alpine skier Joe Jay Jalbert was the skiing double for Robert Redford in the movie, "Downhill Race."

1965 W 1966

Husky Moment

Williams Sets Receiving Record

Dave Williams was an outstanding athlete for both the Husky football and track teams. He turned in four top-seven finishes at the NCAA track championships in 1965 and 1966, but his most memorable showing came on the football field. It was on a day the Huskies lost 28-24 at UCLA in 1965, that Williams was at his best. That day, Williams set the Husky receiving record with 257 yards. It would be another 22 years before another Washington receiver would even top the 200-yard receiving mark in a game. Williams' efforts in 1965 were unparalleled in school history. He set the single-game receptions mark twice with 10 grabs against both Stanford and UCLA. He also set records for single-season receiving yards (795) and touchdown receptions in a game (three vs. UCLA). His 10 touchdown catches also established a new Husky mark. Williams finished the season with 38 total receptions. He was named a second-team All-American by the Associated Press.

UW Media Relations

Dave Williams' single-game receiving record stood for 33 years.

Husky Spotlight

Bob Hall

UW Media Relations

Bob Hall was an integral part on Washington's gymnastics team that placed second at the 1965 NCAA Championships. The Husky team captain, Hall placed fourth in the all-around and second in the side horse, winning All-America honors along the way. Earlier in the season he won the conference championship in the all-around. As a junior, in 1964, Hall placed fourth in the side horse at the NCAAs to win his first All-American honor. During his three-year Husky career, Washington won the AAWU conference title each season. Following his graduation, Hall competed internationally for a number of United States national teams. In 1966, he placed fourth in the all-around at the North American Gymnastic Championships. In 1988 he was inducted into the Husky Hall of Fame.

Husky Highlight

Despite the loss of graduated All-Americans Jim David and Bob Hall, the Husky men's gymnastics made a return trip to the NCAA Championships at Southern Illinois where Washington posted a seventh-place finish. The Huskies compiled 177.9 points at the nationals while Southern Illinois won the crown with 187.2 points. Rock Fonceca proved to be Washington's top individual finisher with a seventh-place effort on the trampoline. Washington finished the season second at the AAWU Championships behind California. The Huskies could not better the Bears at the Western District Championships, again placing second to Cal. The Bears would go on to finish second at the NCAAs. Mike Fransaas led Washington by winning titles at the Pacific Northwest (all-around, parallel bars), AAWU (parallel bars) and Western District Championships (long horse).

Husky Legend

Steve Bramwell

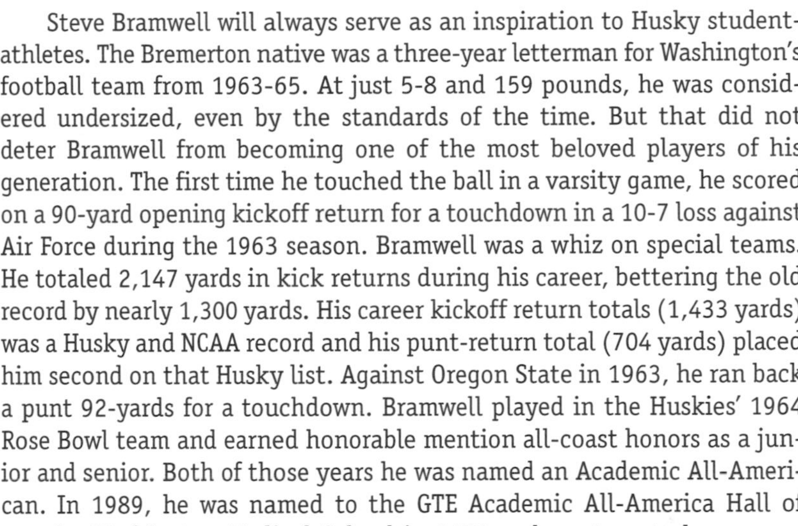

UW Media Relations

Steve Bramwell will always serve as an inspiration to Husky student-athletes. The Bremerton native was a three-year letterman for Washington's football team from 1963-65. At just 5-8 and 159 pounds, he was considered undersized, even by the standards of the time. But that did not deter Bramwell from becoming one of the most beloved players of his generation. The first time he touched the ball in a varsity game, he scored on a 90-yard opening kickoff return for a touchdown in a 10-7 loss against Air Force during the 1963 season. Bramwell was a whiz on special teams. He totaled 2,147 yards in kick returns during his career, bettering the old record by nearly 1,300 yards. His career kickoff return totals (1,433 yards) was a Husky and NCAA record and his punt-return total (704 yards) placed him second on that Husky list. Against Oregon State in 1963, he ran back a punt 92-yards for a touchdown. Bramwell played in the Huskies' 1964 Rose Bowl team and earned honorable mention all-coast honors as a junior and senior. Both of those years he was named an Academic All-American. In 1989, he was named to the GTE Academic All-America Hall of Fame. Bramwell graduated with honors from the Washington Medical School in 1971 and went on to become an orthopedic surgeon. For many years he served as a team physician for the Huskies' athletic program.

Washington's Football Academic All-Americans

1955	Jim Houston, 1st team
1959	Mike Crawford, 1st team
1960	Bob Hivner, 1st team
1963	Mike Briggs, 1st team
1965	Steve Bramwell, 1st team
	Ron Medved, 2nd team
1966	Cliff Coker, 3rd team
1967	Don Martin, 2nd team
1970	Bob Lovlien, 2nd team
1971	Dick Galuska, 2nd team
1972	Steve Wiezbowski, 2nd team
1979	Bruce Harrell, 1st team
1981	Mark Jerue, 1st team
	Chuck Nelson, 1st team
1982	Chuck Nelson, 1st team
	Mark Stewart, 2nd team
1986	David Rill, 1st team
1987	David Rill, 1st team
1990	Ed Cunningham, 2nd team
1991	Ed Cunningham, 1st team
1994	Eric Bjornson, 2nd team
1996	Dave Janoski, 2nd team

HUSKY LORE

Coach Ray Bennett directed the Husky golf team to four NCAA appearance in the 1960s.

Husky Golfers Enjoy Four-Year Run at NCAAs

THE Washington golf team enjoyed its best multi-year showing at the NCAA Championships during the mid-1960s. The Huskies finished 10th in 1963 with a score of 597, tied for 15th in 1964 with a 619, placed 11th with a 602 in 1965 and turned in a 22nd-place showing in 1966 with a 624. It marked the only time in the Huskies' history that Washington made four consecutive appearances at the nationals.

1966 W 1967

Husky Moment

Basketball Upsets No. 3 Houston

Ranked third in the country and sporting a 14-1 record, the Houston Cougars were heavy favorites to dispose of a 7-8 Washington team when the teams collided on Jan. 28, 1967 in Hec Edmundson Pavilion. Earlier in the season, the Cougars had defeated the Huskies 87-65 in Houston with a lineup that included collegiate all-stars Elvin Hayes, Melvin Bell and Don Chaney. But the Cougars traveled to Seattle at a time in their schedule that did not see them play a game for two weeks due to a semester break. Houston did not look rusty in the early going, grabbing a quick 11-6 lead. The Huskies fought back and climbed ahead 18-14. Washington maintained the lead and went into halftime ahead 46-34. Twice in the second half the Huskies upped the lead to 14 points and held a 73-60 advantage before the Cougars scored six straight points. Leading by five with a minute to play, Washington saw Houston score the game's next four points to close the gap to 79-78. Rick Slettedahl netted a pair of free throws and sealed the win for the Huskies. David Hovde led five Huskies who scored in double figures with 17 points and added 17 rebounds. David Carr added 14 points for UW. Hayes (19), Bell (13) and Chaney (12) combined for 44 points. Washington won the game by outshooting the Cougars 55 percent to 40 percent. The Huskies went on to post a 13-12 record, the program's first winning record in five years.

UW Media Relations

David Hovde had 17 points and 17 rebounds to lead the Huskies' upset of third-ranked Houston.

Husky Spotlight

Records Fall at UW-WSU Track Meet

Washington distance runners Dave Roberts and John Celms made Husky history on May 6 when the UW track team defeated cross-state rival Washington State 88-57 in a dual meet in Husky Stadium. Roberts upset the Cougars' Gerry Lindgren in the mile by besting his own school-record time (4:05.4) with a mark of 4:01.7. That also set a record for Husky Stadium and the meet. After turning in a half-mile time of 2:04.5, the duo picked up the pace and Roberts managed to out-sprint Lindgren in the final 300 yards to win by seven-tenths of a second. An hour later, in the two-mile race, Lindgren managed a win against the Huskies, but it took the best time in the world that year to achieve the victory. Lindgren won the two-mile against Celms with a time of 8:37.3. Celms' 8:40.1 clocking crushed the old Husky mark of 8:52.6.

Husky Highlight

When 7-0 UCLA came to Husky Stadium as the third-ranked team in the nation on Nov. 5, the Huskies were two touchdown underdogs as they sought to improve their 4-3 record. The Bruins had their eyes set on the Rose Bowl. UCLA led the conference in five statistical categories and topped the nation in scoring at 36.3 points per game. Quarterback Gary Beban and halfback Mel Farr were the stars for the high-powered Bruins. The Huskies had one key factor playing into their favor. The conditions for Washington's homecoming game were nothing less than a quagmire. UCLA, on the other hand, had practiced in near 100-degree temperatures in Los Angeles the week of the game. Washington got on the scoreboard first thanks to Don Martin's career-best 42-yard field goal. After UCLA evened the score with its own field goal, the Huskies took control of the game. Jim Sartoris returned the Bruins' kickoff 82-yards to the 11-yard line. Three rushing plays later, Jeff Jordan found the endzone for the Huskies. In the second quarter, Washington put the game away when Frank Smith returned an interception 29 yards for a score. The Husky defense preserved the 16-3 victory with two gallant stands in the second half. With UCLA on the Huskies' 20-yard line, Steve Thompson broke through the line, sacked Beban and caused a fumble that Washington recovered. In the fourth quarter, with UCLA on the 11-yard line, Washington again shutdown the Bruins' high-powered offense. UCLA's loss, combined with USC's 35-9 victory against California, gave the Trojans the conference championship.

Husky Legend

Tom Greenlee

UW Media Relations

Tom Greenlee earned his reputation on Montlake as a hard-nosed player who would fly to the ball and display a penchant for making big defensive plays. Despite his size (6-0, 195-pounds), he played defensive end as a senior, where he earned consensus All-America honors in 1966 under coach Jim Owens. Greenlee began his career as a running back on the freshman squad and then moved to the defensive secondary and also returned kicks as a Husky. A native of Seattle and a graduate of Garfield High School, Greenlee was twice voted All-AAWU and all-coast. He was named an honorable mention All-American as a junior. The Huskies' team captain his senior season, he was named the squad's L. Wait Rising Award winner. The three-time Husky letterwinner participated in the East-West Shrine Game and the Hula Bowl and was chosen in the fourth round of the NFL draft by the Chicago Bears. His older brother, Pete, also played for Washington. Greenlee was inducted into the Husky Hall of Fame in 1987.

HUSKY LISTS

Washington's National Football Foundation Scholar-Athlete Award Winners

Year	Player
1960	Barry Bullard
1963	Mike Briggs
1964	Bill Douglas
1966	Mike Ryan
1972	Bill Cahill
1979	Bruce Harrell
1984	Dan Eernissee
1985	Hugh Millen
1987	David Rill
1993	Jim Neville

Mike Ryan

THE term "student-athlete" truly applied to Mike Ryan. A three-year starter for the Husky football team as an offensive guard, as a senior, the 6-0, 220-pounder was one of four Rhodes Scholarship finalists from the University. An economics major, Ryan came from a very athletic family. His father, John, was a 190-pound All-America tackle for the University of Detroit. His older brother, Joe, also played for Washington and was a member of the Huskies' 1964 Rose Bowl team. While he did not get a chance to play in a Rose Bowl, Mike Ryan had a decorated Husky career, both on and off the field. As a senior, he was a member of the University's Board of Control. The Associated Men's Students voted him the University's top senior. He was the recipient of a National Football Foundation postgraduate scholarship. A standout at Wenatchee High School, Ryan attended the UW on an academic scholarship. That did not prevent him from being a solid contributor for the Husky football team. In fact, his teammates dubbed him with a nickname (The Beast) that befitted his athletic prowess more so than his academic standing.

1967 W 1968

Husky Moment

Crew Wins Western Sprints

There were not a lot of highlights on the Husky athletic scene during the 1967-68 academic year. In fact, the student newspaper, *The Daily,* listed the top sports story of the year as the report issued by Jim Owens which called for an end to discrimination within the athletic department. Basketball coach Mac Duckworth resigned after a 12-14 season, and the Husky football team lost four of its last five games. Washington did have one outstanding display of athletic prowess on May 20 when the Husky Varsity eight crew team won the Western Sprint Regatta at Seward Park in Seattle. It was a sign that Dick Erickson's reign as the Washington crew coach would be a successful one. The Huskies rowed a blistering pace in the calm waters and established a course record with their time of 5:56.7. Stanford and UCLA tied for second place in 6:00.4. The conditions were so favorable the Huskies smashed the old course record by more than 30 seconds. The Husky crew included stroke Mike Viereck and oarsmen Fred Mann, Brad Thomas, Howie Wallace, Lars Anderson, Glen Bowser, Rick Cole, Brian Miller and coxswain Bob Moch, the son of the coxswain of the 1936 gold medal-winning crew.

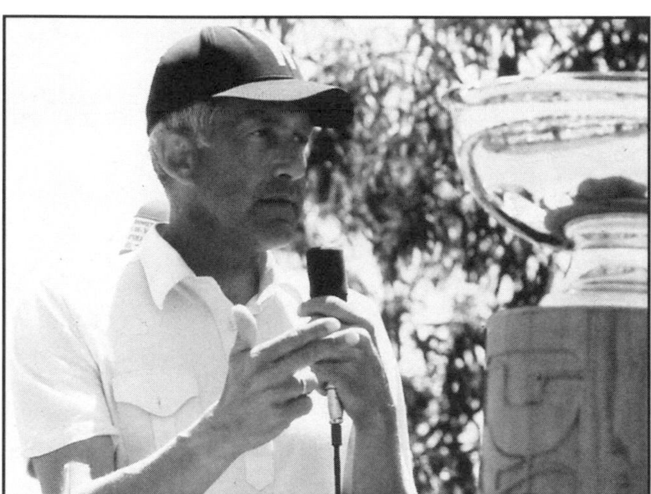

UW Media Relations

Head coach Dick Erickson led the Husky rowers to the Western Sprint Regatta Championship in his first year.

Husky Spotlight

When the Washington crew program needed someone to breathe new life into it, the Huskies turned to an alumnus to get the job done. Dick Erickson was a member of Washington's 1958 eight-oared shell that traveled to Moscow and defeated the famed Trud Rowing Club of Leningrad. Erickson was a member of the varsity eight teams as a junior and senior, lettering from 1956-58. He later earned a master's degree from Harvard before returning to Montlake to coach the Husky freshmen from 1964-67. His first year the frosh squad won every race except for a second-place finish at the IRAs. During his four-year tenure coaching the UW freshmen, the Huskies lost just one dual meet race. In 1968, Erickson was named as the head coach of the rowing program. His first varsity eight team went on to place second at the IRA. By year three under his direction, the Huskies captured their first IRA varsity eight title in 20 years. Erickson coached the Husky crews from 1968-87, leading his teams to 15 Pacific Coast titles. He was inducted into the National Rowing Hall of Fame in 1992 and was brought into the Husky Hall of Fame in 1994. Erickson saw his crews compete internationally in England and Egypt. His 1977 Huskies won the Grand Challenge Cup and Visitor's Challenge Cup at the Henley Royal Regatta. From 1972-76 he served as a member of U.S. Olympic Rowing Committee. After retiring from coaching, Erickson worked as a member of the athletic department's events and facilities staffs.

Husky Highlight

Perfection put Dave West into the spotlight during the 1967-68 Husky basketball season. That year, West put together a streak of 28 consecutive free throws to set a Husky record that would stand for 23 years. West, a three-time letterwinner, was a guard on the 1968 team that posted a 12-14 record. West's streak was highlighted by his 10-for-10 effort in a 64-52 victory against California on Feb. 19. That tied the school record for single-game accuracy and made him only the fifth Husky player to make at least 10 straight free throws in a game. At the conclusion of his career, he owned the all-time free-throw shooting title having made 98 of 120 attempts (81.7 percent). His 72-for-86 (.837) free-throw shooting in 1968 stood as a single-season record for 10 years. It was not until 1989, when Eldridge Recasner made 33 straight free throws, that West's record was toppled.

UW Media Relations

Husky Legend

Steve Hawes

UW Media Relations

A native of nearby Mercer Island, Steve Hawes was a three-year letterwinner for the Huskies from 1970-72. He was the first Husky hoopster to be named a two-time All-American, earning the distinction for his play during his junior and senior seasons. Hawes finished his Husky career as the school's all-time leader in scoring average (20.8 points per game). He averaged 21.7 points as a senior, 20.3 points as a junior and 20.0 points as a sophomore. Hawes' record-setting resume also included marks for rebounds in a single season (386) and single-season rebounding average (14.8). His dominance is reflected in the fact that he led the Huskies in scoring in 52 of the 73 games he played and topped the team in rebounding 62 times. The 6-10 Husky center led Washington to records of 17-9 (1969-70), 15-13 (1970-71) and 20-6 (1971-72). He missed seven games as a sophomore due to a broken leg, but still managed to earn honorable mention All-Americ honors from the Associated Press. That same season, the *Basketball News* tabbed him as one of the top 10 sophomores in the country. His senior season, the Huskies posted a 10-4 record in the Pac-8 and finished as runners-up to UCLA, which went on the win the NCAA title behind the play of Bill Walton. During his Husky career, Hawes played for three different coaches. George Davidson directed his freshman team in 1968-69. He played for Tex Winter from 1969-71 and in Marv Harshman's first season (1971-72) with the Huskies. Coming out of Washington, Hawes was picked in the second round of the NBA draft by the Cleveland Cavaliers and chosen in the fifth round of the ABA draft by the Dallas Chapparels. Hawes began his professional career in Venice, Italy, where he played two years. He then returned to the states and enjoyed a 10-year career in the NBA, spending time with Houston (1974-75), Portland (1975-76), Atlanta (1976-83) and Seattle (1983-84). After he ended his playing career, he worked as an assistant basketball coach in Italy for one year and then returned to the Puget Sound to coach for Seattle University and Washington. Hawes was inducted into the Husky Hall of Fame in 1987.

Husky List

Men's Basketball All-Conference Selections by Team (through the 2000-2001 season)

1. UCLA	98
2. Washington	77
3. California	74
4. USC	73
5. Stanford	64
6. Oregon State	57
7. Oregon	50
8. Washington State	38
9. Arizona	34
10. Arizona State	18

Husky Lore

George Irvine ... Washington's NBA Connection

WHEN George Irvine was a basketball player at Washington, he dreamed of a career in the sport. Little did he know that he would accomplish that, but not primarily as a coach. Irvine lettered for the Huskies from 1967-70. He started all three years at forward and scored 1,314 career points, averaging 16.8 points per game over 78 contests. Following his graduation, he signed with the Virginia Squires of the ABA. He played six years professionally before a knee injury forced him out of the lineup. He joined Larry Brown, a teammate on the Squires, in Denver as an assistant coach. Irvine's NBA career was spent primarily with the Indiana Pacers. He worked for the franchise as a scout, assistant coach, coach (twice) and vice president. Irvine's Husky ties were always strong. His brother, Earle, also played at Washington and his nephew, Brandon, was a member of the Husky baseball squad. In 2000 he was named the head coach of the Detroit Pistons.

1968 W 1969

Husky Moment

Men's Gymnastics at NCAAs

In 1968 an eight-man team from the Husky Gymnastics Club won the National AAU Championship. One of the stars of that squad was junior Mauno Nissinen, who placed second on side horse, third on parallel bars and the all-around, fourth in horizontal bar and seventh in long horse. For the native of Oulu, Finland, his performances at the AAU Championships proved to just be a warmup. In 1969, Washington played host to the NCAA Championships in Hec Edmundson Pavilion and Nissinen made sure the home fans went home happy. After helping to guide Washington to a 10-0 regular-season record, Nissinen won the all-around, the side horse and the horizontal bar at the Pac-8 Championships. At the NCAAs, in front of a home crowd, he became the first Washington gymnast to win a national title when he won the all-around competition. He also placed third on the horizontal bar and was fourth on side horse. His teammate, Sho Fukushima, finished fifth in the all-around and on the horizontal bar. Later that year, the Huskies, behind Nissinen's all-around title, won their second straight AAU title. Both Nissinen and Fukushima earned All-American honors. Nissinen was inducted into the Husky Hall of Fame in 1991.

UW Media Relations

Mauno Nissinen won the all-around competition at the 1969 NCAA championships.

Husky Spotlight

Tex Winter

Who would have known in 1968, when Tex Winter was named the head basketball coach at Washington, that someday he would go on to be an integral part of one of the greatest sports dynasties in history? Winter's arrival in Seattle was a shock at Kansas State, where he had just won his eighth Big Eight title with the Wildcats during a 15-year career. Winter took over a Husky program that had experienced only one winning season in six years. He led his first group of Huskies to a 13-13 record, improved that to 17-9 in year two and 15-13 in his third year. Overall, Winter accomplished a 45-35 record at Washington before leaving to take over as the head coach of the NBA's San Diego Rockets in 1971. Winter's collegiate coaching record included 454 wins he collected while at Marquette (1951-54), Kansas State (1954-68), Washington (1968-71), Northwestern (1974-78) and Long Beach State (1979-83). Winter joined the Chicago Bulls staff in 1985 and is credited with introducing the triangle offense that helped the Bulls win six NBA World Championships. In 1999, when he joined coach Phil Jackson's staff with the Los Angeles Lakers, he had been active in coaching for 52 seasons, the longest tenure of any college Division I or professional coach. In 1958, he was named the NCAA national coach of the year.

Husky Highlight

Randy Berg stands as one of the most outstanding and decorated wrestlers in the Washington program's history. During the 1967-68 season, Berg won the 123-pound division of the Pac-8 Championships as the Huskies posted a second-place finish behind Oregon State. The following season, Berg repeated as the 123-pound conference champion. That season he led the Huskies to a 13th-place finish at the NCAA Championships, the best showing in school history. Berg's third-place finish at the nationals was the highest finish by a Husky grappler. In 1969-70, as a senior, Berg again won the Pac-8 title as the Huskies again placed second to the Beavers. Berg and the Huskies went on to place seventh at the NCAAs, improving six spots on the previous best showing by a Husky squad.

UW Media Relations

Husky Legend

Al Worley

UW Media Relations

They say that records are meant to be broken. It will take a Herculean effort for someone to topple the mark that Al Worley etched into the college football annals in 1968. That season Worley intercepted a NCAA record 14 passes. He did it during a time when the Huskies played just 10 games. Worley also set a Husky single-game record with four interceptions against Idaho. No wonder the Wenatchee native was known as "The Thief." Worley finished his three-year career at Washington with 18 interceptions to establish himself as the school's career leader in that category. For his unprecedented accomplishments, Worley drew All-American honors from the Associated Press, United Press International, American Football Coaches Association and *Football News.* Besides his numerous All-American accolades, Worley was decorated as a second-team *Sporting News* All-American, a first-team All-Pac-8 pick, a first-team UPI All-Coast selection and the KING-TV Most Improved Player. He ended his collegiate career by participating in the Hula Bowl where, appropriately, he made an interception. He also appeared in the East-West Shrine Game and the All-American Game. Worley was named Washington's athlete of the year for 1968-69. He continued his football career briefly as a member of the Seattle Rangers semi-professional team from 1969-70. He was inducted into the Husky Hall of Fame in 1992.

Husky List

NCAA Single-Season Interception Leaders

Al Worley, Washington	1968	14
George Shaw, Oregon	1951	13
Terrell Buckley, Florida State	1991	12
Cornelius Price, Houston	1989	12
Bob Navarro, Eastern Michigan	1989	12
Tony Thurman, Boston College	1984	12
Terry Hoage, Georgia	1982	12
Frank Polito, Villanova	1971	12
Bill Albrecht, Washington	1951	12
Hank Rich, Arizona State	1950	12

Husky Lore

UW Media Relations

DICK KNIGHT became the first NCAA All-American in the history of the Husky tennis program. He manned the number-one spot for coach Bill Quillian's teams from 1968-70. In 1969, he went undefeated in Pac-8 competition. The following season, he captained the Huskies to a fourth-place finish in the Pac-8, the only time a northern division school had finished ahead of a southern divisional school. That year he reached the fourth round of competition. Knight competed in the U.S. Open while a player at Washington. He qualified for and competed in the 1972 Wimbledon Championships. While enrolled at Washington, Knight played in one non-collegian tournament that lasted more than five hours with a final outcome of 32-30, 3-6, 19-17. It was one of the matches that helped to bring about the modern tiebreaker in tennis.

1969 W 1970

Husky Moment

Yoshi Hayasaki

When Husky gymnastics coach Eric Hughes attended the 1964 Olympic Games in Japan, he did so with a purpose. In addition to watching the Games, he developed contacts that allowed him to recruit Japanese high school gymnasts. One such person was Yoshi Hayasaki. In 1966, Hayasaki came to America as an exchange student at Issaquah High School. In his final two years (1970-71) at Washington, Hayasaki won back-to-back NCAA titles in the all-around competition. He was the first Husky student-athlete to garner back-to-back national titles. He was also the first to be honored as the athlete of the year twice and to receive All-America honors three years in a row. The native of Osaka took home eight Pac-8 titles and four AAU championships during his collegiate career. In 1967, he enrolled at Washington, and by the end of his freshman year he had placed second in the all-around at the National AAU Championships. Hayasaki also dominated the U.S. Gymnastics Federation's national championships in 1968, winning the all around, second in floor excercise and long horse and sixth on side horse. A devastating Achilles tendon injury caused Hayasaki to miss the entire 1969 collegiate season, but he recovered in time to compete in the AAU nationals as an unattached entry and won the parallel bars. He later went on to coach the men's gymnastics team at Illinois and led the Illini to the NCAA team championship in 1989. He was inducted into the Husky Fall of Fame in 1983.

UW Media Relations

Yoshi Hayasaki won back-to-back NCAA gymnastics titles in the all-around in 1970 and 1971.

Husky Spotlight

Not considered one of the top teams in the field, the 1970 Husky Varsity eight rowing team sparked Washington to top honors at the 1970 National Collegiate Rowing Championships on June 13. The varsity rowers upset three-time defending champion Pennsylvania to claim their first IRA championship in 20 years. Thanks to a second-place showing by both the freshmen and junior varsity boats, Washington brought home the Ten Eyck Trophy for the best overall performance at the IRAs. It was Washington's first all-around victory since 1964. Penn began the varsity race like it would win its unprecedented fourth straight title. The Quakers rowed as high as 47 beats a minute, would taper off, and then sprint again. The strategy worked for more than half the race as Penn built up a one-length lead. With 800 meters to row, the Huskies started to close the gap. Washington pulled even with 500 meters to go and then poured it on to win by one and one-half lengths. Penn faded terribly down the home stretch and finished fifth. The Huskies' winning time, rowing into a strong headwind, was 6:39.1. Wisconsin placed second in 6:44.9. The Husky crew was comprised of stroke Cliff Hurn and oarsmen Rick Copeland, Mike Viereck, Chad Rudolph, Brian Miller, Brad Thomas, Larry Johnson and Greg Miller. Jim Edwards directed the team as coxswain. On the trip back from Syracuse, the Huskies stopped in Manhattan, Kansas, and raced the team from Kansas State, beating the Wildcats by six lengths.

Husky Highlight

Rafael Stone knew how to make his teammates on the Husky basketball team look good. Get them the ball. The 5-9 Stone was a starting guard for Washington from 1967-70, never averaging more than 6.6 points per game. But he was masterful at setting up scores. Playing during an era when assists were not as highly regarded, Stone set Washington's single-game assists record with 16 at California on Feb. 20, 1970. Three decades later, the mark still stood as a Husky record. Stone is without a doubt one of the top setup men in Washington history. On the list of top single-game assist leaders, Stone is the only player with at least four 12-assists games. Stone's flashy play led long-time *Seattle Post-Intelligencer* Royal Broughan columnist to exclaim: "he has more moves than Bobby Fischer." It was no wonder that Stone's teammates referred to him as "Wonder Boy." Stone also excelled in the classroom, earning Academic All-America honors.

UW Media Relations

Husky Legend

Larry Owings

UW Media Relations

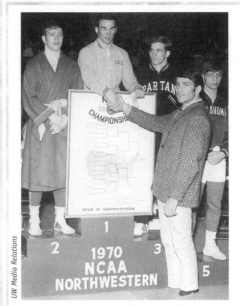

Larry Owings stands tall on the victor's stand after winning the NCAA title. Iowa's Dan Gable is pictured on the far left.

Simply put, Larry Owings shocked the world. The setting was Northwestern's McGaw Hall, jam-packed with a capacity crowd of 8,500. The event was the 142-pound finals at the 1970 NCAA Wrestling Championships. The opponent was Iowa State's Dan Gable. If ever an athlete was considered invincible in a sport, it was Gable. The Cyclone senior entered his final collegiate match against Owings with a string of 181 consecutive victories. He had never lost a match during his combined high school and collegiate career. The streak included 108 victories by pin, including all five of his NCAA matches prior to the finals. Just a 19-year-old sophomore, Owings entered the match with an impressive 33-1 record. During the season, he wrestled primarily in the 150- and 158-pound weight classes. He trimmed down to the 142-pound division thinking that was his best chance for victory. It was also a chance to get another shot at Gable, who defeated Owings at the 1968 Olympic Trials. Owings jumped out to an early lead in the match thanks to a first-period takedown. Trailing 10-9 with 25 seconds remaining, Owings had a near pin and a takedown to win the match. An eight-minute video of what many consider to be the greatest moment in collegiate wrestling is on permanent display in the Wrestling Hall of Fame in Stillwater, Oklahoma. Owings became the first Husky to win an NCAA wrestling championship. He was also named the event's overall outstanding wrestler. His victory helped the Huskies to a seventh-place finish in the team standings. During his career, Owings won the Pac-8 Championship in 1970, '71 and '72. He went on to reach the NCAA finals as both a junior and senior and placed second at the 1972 Olympic Trials. During his career he defeated four NCAA champions, 10 Olympic champions, two Olympic placewinners and two world champions.

Husky History

Washington's Men's Gymnastics NCAA All-Americans

Year	Gymnast	Event
1964	Jim David	Tumbling
1965	Bob Hall	Pommel Horse
	Jim David	Floor Exercise
1968	Yoshi Hayasaki	Parallel Bars
	Yoshi Hayasaki	All-Around
1969	Mauno Nissinen	All-Around *
1970	Yoshi Hayasaki	Rings
	Yoshi Hayasaki	Parallel Bars
	Yoshi Hayasaki	Horizontal Bar *
	Yoshi Hayasaki	All-Around*
	Hide Umeshita	All-Around
1971	Yoshi Hayasaki	All-Around *
1972	Rich Gaylor	Vaulting
1977	Steve Wejmar	Vaulting *
	Melvin Cooley	Horizontal Bars
1978	Melvin Cooley	Horizontal Bars *

* NCAA Champion

Husky Lore

THE 1969 football season proved to be a disruptive year for the Husky football program. When a group of black football players wanted to discuss unfair treatment on the team, head coach Jim Owens questioned every player regarding their commitment to the team. Unhappy with the responses of four players, Owens suspended Ralph Bayard, Greg Alex, Lamar Mills and Harvey Blanks. The incident caused an uproar and gained national media coverage. In protest, the other black players on the team boycotted the team's game at UCLA. Owens relented and three of the four players were reinstated for the final two games. Facing the prospects of a winless season, the Huskies defeated Washington State 30-21 with Bayard scoring a pair of touchdowns. "We put all of our frustration and anger into that game," he said years later. The effects spilled over into the 1970 season, but some of the tension was erased by the Huskies' 6-4 record. Bayard, who led Washington in receiving in 1969 with 13 catches for 290 yards, graduated from Washington in 1971 and later, returned to receive his master's degree. After a career with the state's high school athletic association, Bayard joined the UW athletic staff as an associate athletic director.

Super Legend

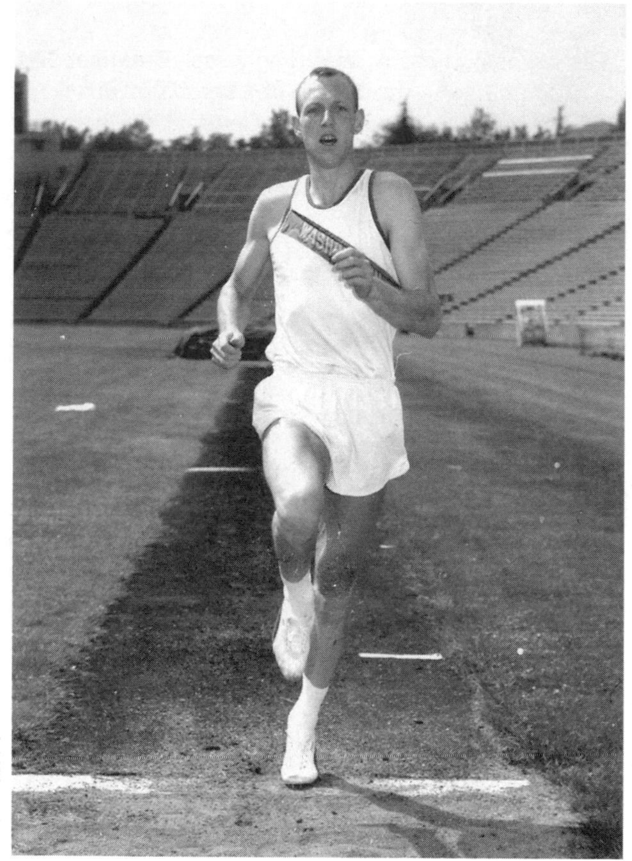

UW Media Relations

Phil Shinnick

Phil Shinnick and Brian Sternberg

Shinnick and Sternberg, their lives and athletic performances will always be intertwined, because on May 25, 1963, these two Washington sophomores broke world records and then suffered tragedy.

Phil Shinnick was a three-sport star—football, basketball, and track and field—at Gonzaga Prep in Spokane. He set city records in the high jump and long jump and was the state long jump champion in 1960 and in 1961 as a senior. Brian Sternberg grew up in the Normandy Park area of Seattle and took up pole vaulting in the eighth grade. His father, a vaulter at Seattle Pacific University, put a cedar pole in his hand. They built a vaulting box in a hole in the ground in the nearby woods and with a string for a crossbar, young Brian soon was clearing about 8′ 6″. The family moved to the Shoreline area and Brian continued his vaulting at Shoreline High School. In his senior year (1961), he finished second in the state championship meet, at 13′ 4″, and later recorded the highest high school vault in the nation at 14′ 3³/₄″. At that time, he was vaulting on a metal pole as the fiberglass pole had not yet been introduced. He also participated in gymnastics that contributed greatly to his vaulting technique and ability.

As Washington freshmen, Shinnick and Sternberg soon became good friends and shared their goals and dreams. Brian was also helped by Husky junior, John Cramer, who had mastered the metal pole. Cramer was ranked fifth in the world in 1962 and recorded the highest vault in the world on a metal pole that year. In the spring of 1962, Sternberg and Shinnick participated in a limited number of meets on the freshmen team. They looked forward to varsity competition in 1963. Sternberg's success came quickly when he won the NCAA indoor championship and established a new American indoor record of 16′ 3¹/₂″. Then he stunned the track and field world when he set the outdoor world record—16′ 5″—at the Penn Relays in Philadelphia. Phil signaled his capability to the track and field world when he set a new meet record of 25′ 2″ in the dual meet with Oregon. A week later, he won the Far West meet championship with a leap of 25′ 5″.

Both athletes eagerly awaited the AAWU conference championships in Berkeley, California on May 25. Shinnick's desire was to set a new conference record and jump farther than anyone opposing him. The great long jumpers—Jesse Owens, Ralph Boston, and the current record-holder, Russia's Igor Ter-Ovanesyan, were imprinted in his mind from the film clips that he used to analyze each step of their jumps. Sternberg had transformed the pole vault into a gymnastics event. He expanded the boundaries of jumping, twisting, and thrusting his body upward in flight with the new fiberglass pole. The two Huskies seemed to defy gravity and the forces limiting speed, strength, and power in their events.

Neither athlete performed at his best in the AAWU meet. Wind conditions did not favor the jumping events. Sternberg won the vault at 15′ 9″. Shinnick did not even qualify for the final round of the long jump. He fouled on his first two jumps and then popped a big one over 26′. However, the official raised the red flag and exclaimed Shinnick had left the jumping pit out of balance. Such an exit from the pit was not a violation of any long-jumping rule but it did not matter. What did matter was that the now angry and frustrated Husky had only one more jump left in the preliminary round. After talking with Coach Stan Hiserman, Shinnick placed his take off mark two feet behind the board and came down the left side of the runway. On his fourth and last jump, he took off well behind the board and landed in the hard pan on the edge of the pit. His feet skidded under him, and he landed on his back and shoulder with a mark of 21′ 5″. He was out of the competition before it really had started.

Near the end of the meet, Hiserman rounded up some of his best athletes and told them that they could compete in the evening at the Modesto Relays, one of the biggest meets on the West Coast. Some of the world's best track and field athletes would compete. Former world record holder 1960 Olympic champion, Ralph Boston, was in the long jump. The great New Zealand middle distance runner, Peter Snell, beat a very fast field in the mile in 3:54.9, five tenths of a second off his world record. The world's fastest sprinter, Bob Hayes, was featured. Shinnick and Sternberg, warmed by the valley heat, were excited to jump again. As the Husky contingent approached Modesto, it stopped to eat a great training meal of hamburgers and old fashioned milkshakes. They then walked onto the field. Shinninck and Sternberg were put in the flight of jumpers that were the best in the competition. On his first jump of the competition, Ralph Boston opened with a 26′ leap. Shinnick followed with a 26′ 8″ jump but fouled. He felt something big was going to happen. On his next jump, he sprinted down the runway in the warmth of the sun setting in the west and the moon rising in the east. It was a fair jump, the right foot planted in the pit at 27′ 10″ and the left foot at 27′ 5″. Boston was beside the pit and said, "Phillip, you have the world record." By the time the officials tugged and pulled on the tape measure and stretched it across the take off board, they finally announced a distance of 27′ 4″, three quarters of an inch beyond the Russian's world record.

Meanwhile, the competition in the pole vault was heating up. John Pennel, who had set a new world record of 16′ 6¾″ a few weeks earlier, matched Sternberg's clearances until the cross-bar was raised to 16′ 7″. Sternberg cleared the bar and then watched as Pennel missed his three attempts at the new world-record mark.

The two Husky sophomores walked in the Modesto night arm-in-arm, joyful and triumphant. They could not at that moment envision tragedy. For Sternberg, it would come soon after he set the world record at 16′ 8″ at the Compton Relays on June 8 and win the NCAA title a week later. On June 28, he beat Pennel to win the national AAU championship and head up the American vaulting team to compete in Russia in late July. On July 2, 1963, Sternberg was going through a gymnastics routine on the trampoline. After attempting a full twist, double back somersault, he landed on his head and broke his neck. As he lay there, he told gymnastics coach, Eric Hughes, that "he got lost in the air and didn't know where he was in relation to the ground." He was released from University Hospital in the spring of 1964 and has lived as a paraplegic, physically bound to a bed and wheelchair. Emotionally, he is the same character who dared to dangle at the end of a fiberglass pole.

UW Media Relations

Brian Sternberg

For Shinnick, the tragedy was not physical. It was mental frustration and torment arising from officials' errors on that warm May evening in Modesto. There was no wind gauge monitoring Shinnick's jump. The two officials, whose only duty was to place the wind gauge on the long jump runway and watch it to make sure the wind was blowing at less than the allowable limit, were not paying attention. So, Shinnick's mark could not be submitted as a world record. Increasingly, Phil found his jump in Modesto to be an albatross, not an accomplishment. "It always came across as 'Here's this guy who stumble-bummed into a meet and he broke the world record,' " Shinnick observes.

Sternberg was honored as the co-winner of Seattle's Man of the Year in Sports in 1963, linked with mountain climber, Jim Whittaker, who was the first American to reach the summit of Mt. Everest in May 1963. Sternberg was chosen by the Helms Foundation as North America's Athlete of the Year for 1963 and received the Helms World Trophy with five other athletes representing five other continents. He was admitted to the Husky Hall of Fame in 1983.

Shinnick still holds the Husky record in the long jump, the mark set in Modesto. He finished sixth in the 1963 NCAA meet (25′ 4″) and third in 1964 (25′ 7¼″). He was a member of the US Olympic team in 1964 and finished twenty-second in the Tokyo competition. He placed fourth in the 1968 U.S. Olympic Trials with a jump of 26′ 6½″ and went to Mexico City as an alternate on the U.S. Olympic team. He was admitted to the Husky Hall of Fame in 1992.

1970-79

1970 W 1971

Husky Moment

Cary Feldman Wins NCAA Javelin Title

Junior Cary Feldman had the perfect setting for his second appearance at the NCAA Track and Field Championships—Husky Stadium. Feldman was a competitor in the javelin competition when the 1971 NCAA Championships were held in Seattle. It marked the first time since 1951 that the Huskies had played host to the event. With 12,650 in attendance for Sunday's final on June 19, Feldman pulled the upset by winning first-place honors with a toss of 259 feet. Arizona State's Mark Murro was the favorite entering the event. He was the American record holder in the event having recorded a throw of 300-0 in 1970. During Thursday's trials, Murro accidentally jabbed his big toe with the javelin. Murro placed second with a toss of 257-1. Feldman became Washington's first NCAA Champion since Brian Sternberg won the pole vault in 1963. The meet proved to be a huge success as 16 stadium records were set. Highlighting the final day of competition was Villanova's Marty Liquori, who won his third straight mile title with a time of 3:57.6, the first sub-four minute mile in Husky Stadium history. Feldman was an unlikely success story when he arrived on the Montlake campus. A native of Bellingham, he only placed fifth in the javelin at the state championships as a senior. Feldman simply proved to be a late bloomer. By his sophomore season, Feldman had placed third at the NCAA Championships. He did not return to the NCAAs for his senior season due to a groin pull, but he did recover in time to place seventh at the Olympic trials. As a graduate student in 1973, he recorded a toss of 298-4, the second best mark by an American at the time and the seventh best mark in the world. That effort would have eclipsed the gold medal winner's finish at the 1972 Olympics. Feldman's resume included a gold medal at the 1971 Pan American Games.

UW Media Relations

Husky Spotlight

Steve Hawes Sets Season Rebounding Record

UW Media Relations

Despite playing with a sore left knee, Steve Hawes had the best rebounding year in Husky basketball history as a junior. That season he pulled down a total of 386 rebounds in 28 games for an average of 14.8 per game. That total was good enough to rank him 15th in the nation in that statistic. Twice that season, Hawes pulled down 20 rebounds in a game. He had 20 against city rival Seattle University on Dec. 4 and eight days later equaled that number against Montana. Hawes came close to matching his record total as a senior when he pulled down 365 rebounds. Only Doug Smart, who had 373 rebounds in 1958-59, and Bob Houbregs with 381 in 1952-53 have surpassed the 350 rebound total in a season at Washington.

Husky Highlight

Louis Nelson Starts Stellar Hoops Career

When it comes to judging outstanding players in the Husky basketball program, one of the best began his career during the 1970-71 season. Nelson started his UW career by averaging 15.9 points per game as a sophomore. The native of Compton, Calif., went on to average 23.0 points per game as a senior in 1972-73 to lead Marv Harshman's team to a 16-11 record. Nelson finished his career with 1,504 points, the third highest total in UW history at the time, trailing only Bob Houbregs (1,774) and Steve Hawes (1,516). The 668 points that Nelson scored in 1973 were the second best single-season mark in Husky history. A three-year starter at guard, Nelson averaged 15.1 points per game as a junior. He scored over 30 points five times during his career, highlighted by a 36-point effort vs. Grambling during the 1972-73 season. He also had 35 points against Oregon as a senior. Nelson was named to the All-District and All-Pac-8 squads following his senior season. Baltimore chose him as the first pick in the second round of the 1973 NBA draft.

Husky Legend

UW Media Relations

Lynn Colella

While women's swimming was not a varsity sport at the University when Lynn Colella was an undergraduate, she certainly ranks as one of the top performers in the school's history. After just missing out on a spot for the 1968 Olympic team by three-tenths of a second. Colella was going to make sure she represented the United States in Munich in 1972. Competing for the Cascade Swim Club, she placed second at the Olympic trials in 1972 in the 200 butterfly, turning in a time of 2:17.3 that bettered the existing world record. Karen Moe, who won the trials, would go on to reset the world record at the Olympics with a time of 2:15.6 and Colella placed second (2:16.34) to take home the silver medal. Colella had to sprint past Stanford's Ellie Daniel in the final 20 meters after all three swimmers came off their final turn virtually even. Moe, a UCLA student, gave the Pac-8 schools a sweep of the medals in the contest. All three swimmers bettered the existing world record during the race. Colella, who called herself the "Old Woman" of the team, was the co-captain of the U.S. Olympic swim squad. Colella's swimming career was filled with numerous AAU and international championships. She won both the 200 breaststroke and 200 fly, and finished third in the 100 breaststroke at the 1971 Pan American Games. Her younger brothers, Steve and Rick, also swam at Washington. She shared the 1971 *Seattle Post-Intelligencer* Sportsman of the Year award with Rick. An electrical engineering major at Washington, she later came back to help coach the women's club team and tutored standout Irene Arden. Colella was inducted into the Husky Hall of Fame in 1980.

Husky List

UW Crew Dominates West Coast Rowing

In 1971 the Husky men's crew team began a dominant run of eight straight West Coast/Pacific Coast Conference rowing championships. The Huskies would equal that win streak from 1990-1997 capturing eight Pac-10 titles. Here's a look at Washington's dominance in the event:

Year	Site	Winner	Year	Site	Winner
1960	Long Beach	California	1981	Redwood Shores	Washington
1961	Montlake Cut	Washington	1982	Redwood Shores	California
1962	Long Beach	Washington	1983	Redwood Shores	Washington
1963	Redwood City	Washington	1984	Lake Natoma	Washington
1964	Mission Bay	California	1985	Lake Natoma	Washington
1965	Montlake Cut	Washington	1986	Lake Natoma	California
1966	Mare Island	Washington	1987	Lake Natoma	UCLA
1967	Long Beach	UCLA	1988	Lake Natoma	UCLA
1968	Montlake Cut	Washington	1989	Lake Natoma	UCLA
1969	Mission Bay	Washington	1990	Lake Natoma	Washington
1970	Long Beach	UCLA	1991	Lake Natoma	Washington
1971	Montlake Cut	Washington	1992	Lake Natoma	Washington
1972	Long Beach	Washington	1993	Lake Natoma	Washington
1973	Los Gatos	Washington	1994	Lake Natoma	Washington
1974	Lake Burnaby	Washington	1995	Redwood Shores	Washington
1975	Long Beach	Washington	1996	Redwood Shores	Washington
1976	San Pablo	Washington	1997	Lake Natoma	Washington
1977	Redwood Shores	Washington	1998	Lake Natoma	California
1978	Montlake Cut	Washington	1999	Lake Natoma	California
1979	Redwood Shores	California	2000	Redwood Shores	California
1980	Redwood Shores	Washington			

Economic Shortcomings Hit Athletic Department

A dark shadow extended over the Husky athletic department during the summer of 1970. At that time, athletic director Joe Kearney announced that the general operating budget would be reduced by $180,000 and that 35 scholarships would be dropped. The cut in scholarships saved the department $50,000, thus sending the athletic department into the 1970-71 academic year with $230,000 less funds than the previous year. Of the 35 scholarships lost to the program, 12 came from football, eight from skiing, and three from baseball. Basketball, golf, swimming, tennis, track and wrestling each gave up two. The eight scholarships cut from skiing were all that program had. In addition, budgets were reduced for the Husky marching band and the cheerleaders. Despite the cuts, University officials kept the policy intact that student fees would not support the athletic department. Washington remained the only team in the Pac-8 that was not supported by student fees.

1971 W 1972

Husky Moment

Husky Wrestlers Upset No. 1 Iowa State

One of the high points for coach Jim Smith's Washington wrestling program came on Jan. 21, 1972 when the Huskies upset top-ranked Iowa State 17-16 in front of a crowd of 8,148 at Hec Edmundson Pavilion. The large turnout almost forced athletic department officials to drop the price of admission from $1.50 to $1.00 for adults because they feared they would not have enough change for the ticket kiosks. The Huskies did not get off to a great start when Mike Downer, wrestling at 118 pounds, suffered a shoulder injury and lost to Dan Mallinger 6-5. The Huskies rebounded thanks to a 158-pound win by Don Pleasant to grab a 14-9 lead with three matches remaining. Bill Murdock, wrestling at 177 pounds, managed a take down with 26 seconds remaining to register a win and increase the lead. Coach Jim Smith considered those victories the turning point, since both of those Husky wrestlers had lost during the previous season's matchup in Ames, Iowa. At 190 pounds, Washington's Randy Corn lost but managed to avoid a pin to defending NCAA champion Ben Peterson. That meant the Cyclones would need a pin or 10-point victory in the final heavyweight match, to avoid the upset. Washington's 230-pound sophomore Don Dunham was a prohibitive underdog against Iowa State's massive 390-pound Chris Taylor. Still, Dunham managed a pair of escapes on takedowns and was able to avoid a pin, which gave Washington the win. It snapped the Cyclones 33-match winning streak. Afterwards Dunham said: "I didn't know I could lose and still feel like a winner." Iowa State coach Harold Nichols had another point of view of the upset. "The turning point was when they hired the referee," he said.

UW Media Relations

Don Dunham

Husky Spotlight

Purdue Football Game

There have been many thrilling games played in Husky Stadium, and the Huskies' 1971 matchup with Purdue ranks right up there with the best of them. In a seesaw affair, the Huskies came from behind four times to earn a 38-35 victory before a crowd of 58,927. The two teams battled back and fourth in the third and fourth quarters with Washington taking a 31-28 lead on an 18-yard touchdown pass from Sixkiller to Jim Kreig. It took just one play for the Boilermakers to retake the lead. when Gary Danielson connected with Darryl Stingley for an 80-yard scoring bomb with 3:39 to play to put the Boilermakers back ahead 35-31. The Huskies refused to surrender. Sixkiller used a third-down, 31-yard pass to Scott, from the Huskies' 29-yard line, to get Washington past midfield. He then connected with Scott for a 33-yard touchdown with 2:29 to play to put UW ahead 38-35. Husky linebacker Rich Huget sealed the win when he intercepted a pass from Danielson with 1:49 to play. Sixkiller finished the game with 387 passing yards on a 24 for 48 performance, including three interceptions. Danielson was 11 of 23 for 183 yards and ran 43 yards on a keeper to give the Boilers their first lead at 14-7. Purdue's hard-running Otis Anderson had 121 yards on 19 carries. Washington was bolstered by Jerry Ingalls' fine rushing effort of 91 yards on 22 carries. The Huskies piled up 575 yards of total offense to 383 for the Boilermakers.

Husky Highlight

Bill Murdock, NCAA Wrestling Champion

In 1972 Bill Murdock was simply perfect. A four-year letterman on the Husky wrestling team, the highlight of Murdock's career came during his junior season when he swept three major college events and posted a perfect 38-0 record. He won the Triple Crown for west coast wrestlers by capturing the West Coast Invitational, the Pac-8 title and the 177-pound weight class at the NCAA Championships. He became Washington's second NCAA wrestling champion, following in the footsteps of Larry Owings. Murdock's finish helped the Huskies to a fourth-place showing as a team. He became the first Washington state high school wrestling champion to win a national championship for the Huskies and, at the time, was just the third to win a NCAA title at any university. Murdock, who was also a golden gloves boxing champion, was a state champion wrestler while attending Kent-Meridian High School. He wrestled at Washington from 1970-73, serving as a team captain during his senior season when he repeated as conference champion. He compiled a career record of 77-25-2 (.750). Murdock continued his wrestling career as an assistant coach at UNLV. He was killed in an automobile accident in California in 1981. Ten years later he was inducted into the Husky Hall of Fame.

UW Media Relations

Husky Legend

Sonny Sixkiller

When you consider the great, romantic names linked with college football, you have to include Sonny Sixkiller. But Sixkiller had more than a highly recognizable name to stand apart from other college quarterbacks of his era. He had a cannon for an arm. Sixkiller's first season at Washington, he had to wonder what he had gotten himself into. While he played with the freshman team, the varsity, relying on an option rushing game, went 1-9, picking up the only win at season's end against Washington State. The next season, with Sixkiller at quarterback, the scenery changed 180 degrees. He led the team to a 6-4 finish, the best turnaround in the nation that season, and topped the country in passing. The team tied for second in the Pac-8 race that season. At the time, the passing champion was based on completions per game, and Sixkiller led the nation in that category with an average of 18.6. He was also fifth in total offense at 225.8 yards per game. That year he set five Husky game records and six season marks. Thanks to his early success, Sixkiller became an idol in the Northwest. There was a hot-selling record about him, "The Ballad of Sonny Sixkiller." There were "6-Killer" tee shirts and a "6-Killer" fan club sponsored by a local radio station. As a junior and senior, Sixkiller guided the Huskies to back-to-back 8-3 records, finishing third in the Pac-8 both seasons. He finished his Husky career as the all-time passing leader in yards (5,496), attempts (811), completions (385) and total offensive yards (5,288). Sixkiller was featured on the cover of both *Sports Illustrated* and *Boys Life*. After playing two years in the World Football League, he entered into a career in sales. He joined the television crew for Washington's football replays on Fox Sports in 1994. That was not his first exposure in the entertainment business. He appeared as a player in the Burt Reynolds movie "The Longest Yard." He was inducted into the Husky Hall of Fame in 1985.

HUSKY LIST

Washington's 20-Win Basketball Seasons

Year	Record	Coach
1928	22-6	Hec Edmundson
1930	21-7	Hec Edmundson
1931	25-3	Hec Edmundson
1933	22-6	Hec Edmundson
1934	20-5	Hec Edmundson
1936	25-7	Hec Edmundson
1938	29-7	Hec Edmundson
1939	20-5	Hec Edmundson
1943	24-7	Hec Edmundson
1944	26-6	Hec Edmundson
1945	22-18	Hec Edmundson
1948	23-11	Art McLarney
1951	24-6	Tippy Dye
1952	25-6	Tippy Dye
1953	28-3	Tippy Dye
1972	20-6	Marv Harshman
1976	23-5	Marv Harshman
1984	24-7	Marv Harshman
1985	22-10	Marv Harshman
1987	20-15	Andy Russo
1998	20-10	Bob Bender

Marv Harshman Takes Over Basketball Program

WHEN Tex Winter decided to leave Washington on May 14 of 1971 and accept the position of head coach with the NBA's San Diego Rockets, the Husky brass did not have to look far to find his replacement. On June 5 Washington tabbed Marv Harshman to take over the program. Husky athletic director Joe Kearney picked Harshman among a field of candidates that included Central Washington's Dean Nicholson, Ohio State's Fred Taylor, Illinois State's Will Robinson and Grambling State's Fred Hobdy. It was his third head coaching position in the state. The former standout athlete at Pacific Lutheran had coached his alma mater from 1946 to 1958, compiling a 241-121 record. He joined the Washington State staff in 1959 as the head coach and directed the Cougars to a 155-181 record, including winning seasons in five of his last six seasons. Harshman, who was 53 at the time of his hiring, would go on to have a 14-year career at Washington that produced a 246-146 record.

1972 W 1973

Husky Moment

Rick DeMont Wins Gold in Olympic Swimming

Rick DeMont was not even old enough to get his driver's license when he plunged into the pool at the United States Olympic Trials. The 15-year-old DeMont, a native of San Rafael, California, and a future Husky, had no problems blowing by the field to move on to the Games in Munich. While Mark Spitz grabbed the majority of the headlines at the swimming venue, claiming seven gold medals, DeMont made a little history himself. He rallied from last place to win the 400-meter freestyle with an Olympic record time of 4:00.26. It was the first gold won by an American swimmer in Munich besides Spitz. Unfortunately, DeMont's victory did not last very long. As he prepared for the start of the 1,500 freestyle, Olympic officials informed him that he had to forfeit the medal after failing a drug test. At the time of the meet, DeMont was taking a prescribed asthma medication called Marax, which included the banned substance ephedrin. He thought he had been cleared to swim, since the substance was for a medical condition. His appeal, before a review board, narrowly failed. DeMont was the first gold medalist, under the new doping regulations, to be stripped of a medal. Years later, he would sue the U.S. Olympic Committee because he felt they did not adequately support him during his appeal process. DeMont became one of three high school students who competed at the Olympics whom Husky coach Earl Ellis recruited to Washington. The others were Robin Backhaus, who won the bronze medal in the 200 butterfly, and Doug Northway, the bronze medalist in the 1,500 meter freestyle. Following his Olympic effort, DeMont gained some gratification at the World Swimming Championships in Belgrade where he won the 400 meters in a world-record time of 3:58.18. He became the first man to ever break the four-minute barrier. In 1973, *Swimmers World* tabbed him as the World Swimmer of the Year. DeMont swam two years at Washington, but left the team in 1975 when the program's funds were severely cut due to budgetary constraints.

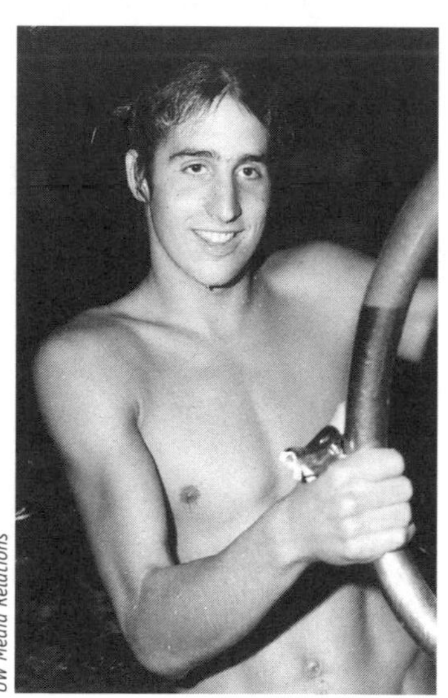
UW Media Relations

Husky Spotlight

Laurel Anderson wins AIAW Vault Title

Few gymnasts have made the comeback that Laurel Anderson did during her sophomore season. She placed fourth in the all-around competition at the 1972 AIAW championships, with second-place marks in the vault, a third-place finish on bars and an eighth-place effort on floor exercise. She had high hopes of better finishes in 1973, but she broke a toe in the season's first meet. Anderson actually competed in some meets with a cast on her foot, but at season's end, she was unable to achieve a qualifying standard at the Northwest Regional Championships. She did have one option that she exercised. She petitioned for a spot in the nationals and her request was granted. She traveled to the championships at Grand View College in Des Moines, Iowa in April and promptly won the vault title competing for the UW Gymnastics Club and Gymnastics Inc. A few weeks later, she competed in Hec Edmundson Pavilion against several member of the U.S. national team at the U.S. Gymnastics Federation's National Elite Championships. A year earlier, she won the Washington state open championship at the elite level and went on to place third in the all-around at the YWCA National Championships.

Husky Highlight

Tom Scott Catches On

UW Media Relations

While Sonny Sixkiller was getting most of the attention for flinging the football all over Husky Stadium, someone had to do the dirty work of catching all of those passes. In a pass-oriented offense, that person was Tom Scott, and he could not have been happier with his job description. A transfer from San Mateo Junior College, Scott wasted little time making a name for himself on the Husky squad. As a junior in 1971 he earned all-coast and All-Pac-8 honors. He led the league with 820 receiving yards, setting a Husky single-season record along the way. His 35 receptions ranked fourth in the conference and was the fourth best season in Husky history. Scott proved to be a versatile player, rushing 32 times for 221 yards. He averaged 13.2 yards on punt returns and 20.5 yards on kickoff returns. He had a total of 1,366 all-purpose running yards as a junior. While Scott did not have as successful a senior year, recording just 11 catches for 284 yards, he kept up his big-play reputation by averaging nearly 26 yards per catch.

Husky Legend

Trish Bostrom

UW Media Relations

Trish Bostrom was a trailblazer for Husky athletics. From 1969-72 she dominated the collegiate tennis scene in the northwest. She became the first Washington player to reach the quarterfinals of the AIAW National Collegiate Tennis Championships in both 1971 and 1972. An adept doubles player, she won three national doubles championships during her collegiate and amateur career. She won the 1971 U.S. National Collegiate Mixed Doubles Championship, the 1972 U.S. National Amateur doubles Grass Court title, and the 1972 U.S. National Amateur Doubles Clay Court title. Bostrom was the first player in UW history to be the number-one ranked player for four consecutive years (1969-72). She was also the first player to win the Pacific Northwest Collegiate Championship (1970 and 1972) and to capture a Pac-8 singles title (1972). She appeared on the National Junior Wightman Cup Team from 1970-72 and served as a co-captain for that team in 1972. Bostrom graduated Phi Beta Kappa and Magna Cum Laude from Washington in 1973 with a degree with distinction in political science. In 1983, she received her Juris Doctorate degree from the SMU Law School. As a professional, she was ranked as high as No. 5 in the world in doubles (1978) and 35th in the world singles rankings (1977). Her career included appearances at such prestigious events as Wimbledon, the United States, French, Japan and Australian Opens. She played in the World Team Tennis Professional League from 1974 to 1979. She was inducted into the Husky Hall of Fame in 1987.

Husky History

Husky Basketball Victories Against Top-10 Opponents

Date	Score
Dec. 19, 1951	#8 Washington 58, #4 St. Louis
Dec. 12, 1952	#4 Washington 53, #7 UCLA 49
Dec. 27, 1955	Washington 76, #6 Iowa 71
Feb. 9, 1957	Washington 90, #5 UCLA 74
Dec. 30, 1957	Washington 71, #8 Michigan State 69
Jan. 6, 1961	Washington 58, #9 UCLA 45
Feb. 18, 1961	Washington 61, #8 USC 55
Jan. 12, 1962	Washington 85, #4 USC 67
Feb. 17, 1962	Washington 73, #6 Oregon State 61
Jan. 4, 1963	Washington 62, #9 UCLA 61
Jan. 5, 1963	Washington 67, #9 UCLA 63
Feb. 1, 1963	Washington 49, #7 Stanford 48
Jan. 28, 1967	Washington 81, #3 Houston 78
Dec. 8, 1967	Washington 98, #7 Purdue 87
Dec. 14, 1974	Washington 74, #9 Kansas 64
Feb. 20, 1975	Washington 89, #10 USC 88
Feb. 22, 1975	Washington 103, #2 UCLA 81
Feb. 12, 1977	Washington 78, #2 UCLA 73
Feb. 22, 1979	Washington 69, #1 UCLA 68
Dec. 23, 1982	Washington 55, #6 Missouri 48
Jan. 3, 1991	Washington 70, #4 Arizona 56
Jan. 16, 1992	Washington 62, #7 Arizona 60
Feb. 2, 1997	Washington 92, #10 Arizona 88
Feb. 4, 1999	Washington 90, #10 Arizona 84

AT 5-8 and 170 pounds, Calvin Jones was considered by some as too small to excel on a football field. Jones had an outstanding football career at Washington from 1970-72. He was a three-time all-coast and All-Pac-8 Conference selection and was named to the AP (first) and UPI (second) All-American teams following his senior season. He was named the winner of the Flaherty Award and the KIRO Player of the Year as a senior. Jones' story was quite remarkable. In November of 1970, he left the University, along with three other black players, due to the turmoil that had embroiled the Husky program. He enrolled at Long Beach City College with plans to transfer to Long Beach State and resume his playing career. Instead, he returned to Seattle the following August and rejoined his Husky teammates. Jones saw signs of progress in the hiring of a black assistant athletic director and the addition of a black coach on the Washington football staff. Jones captained the Huskies as a senior and went on to play in both the Hula and East-West All-Star games. He was drafted in the 15th round by the Denver Broncos and played there from 1973-76. Jones graduated from Washington with a degree in social welfare and often turned media interviews into discussions regarding world social affairs. The son of a pastor, in 1982 Jones graduated from Harvard's Divinity School and went on to work as a director of youth services at the City Mission Society in Boston. He was inducted into the Husky Hall of Fame in 1983.

Husky Moment

Unknown Chris Rowland Sets Passing Mark

As Washington prepared for its Oct. 6 football game with California in Berkeley, Husky coach Jim Owens predicted: "I think they will throw the ball 30 or 40 times." With Vince Ferragamo calling the signals for the Bears, it was a sure bet Cal would pass the pigskin. But, as the afternoon unfolded, it turned out the usually run-oriented Huskies would be the ones really tossing the ball around. In the Pac-8 opener for both teams, the Bears jumped all over the Huskies in the early going and pulled away to a 37-7 lead and went into the locker room at halftime ahead 37-14. Even when Ferragamo went down in the second quarter with an injury, Cal backup quarterback Steve Bartkowski came off the bench and promptly tossed a 75-yard scoring pass on his first play. Meanwhile, Husky quarterbacks Dennis Fitzpatrick and James Anderson could not rally the Huskies. Instead, Owens went deeper on his bench and called on Chris Rowland. The sophomore did not let his lack of experience bother him. He came out throwing, and throwing, and throwing. Trailing 44-14, Rowland's rally brought the Huskies to within nine points (44-35) with 8:16 left to play. What might have been the greatest college comeback up until that point came to an end when Cal's Mark Bailey ran 48 yards for a score and then the Bears kicked a field goal to up their lead to 54-35. Still, Rowland kept throwing. He tossed two more scoring passes to bring the Huskies to within 54-49 at the final gun. Rowland set a Husky and Pac-8 record with his five touchdown passes. He also established an NCAA mark with 31 pass attempts in the fourth quarter. That mark would stand until the 1985 season. Rowland's final numbers were 17 of 43 for 311 yards. Despite his efforts, the Husky defense could not stop Cal and star running back Chuck Muncie. He rushed for 126 yards as the Bears totaled 625 yards of total offense. Rowland's touchdown total eclipsed the old Husky record of four scoring tosses set by Don Heinrich in a 1950 game against Washington State. The next week Rowland would earn his first start against Oregon State. The Cal game stands in the Husky record books for the most points scored in the series with the Bears and the most points scored in a loss by Washington.

UW Media Relations

Chris Rowland

Husky Spotlight

At a time when swimming prospered at Washington, Rick Colella was one of the most popular swimmers in the program, thanks to his local ties and his older sister, Lynn, who had blazed a trail as one of the region's top competitors. Colella was a Seattle native who attended Nathan Hale High School. As a freshman, he won the Pac-8 championship in the 200-yard breaststroke. He also won the 400 intermediate relay at the event and repeated that title in 1973. In 1971, Colella won the 200 breaststroke and placed second in the 400 intermediate relay at the 1971 Pan American Games in Cali, Columbia. His victory in the breaststroke was an upset of Mexican Olympic hero Felipe Munoz by one tenth of a second. In 1972, he placed fourth in the 200 breaststroke at the Olympics with a time of 2:24.28, missing a silver medal by just .61 seconds. In 1973 he was named the AAU's Outstanding Male Swimmer. After he graduated from Washington, he earned a bronze medal at the 1976 Olympics in the 200 breaststroke. He was a member of the 1973 and 1975 World Championships teams. Colella was a four-year finalist at the NCAA championships, earning All-America honors 15 times. He held four school records during his career and was inducted into the Husky Hall of Fame in 1982. Colella served as a member of the U.S. Olympic Committee from 1975-81. Rick and his sister shared the *Seattle Post-Intelligencer's* Sportsman of the Year Award in 1971, marking the first time the honor was voted to a brother-sister combination.

Husky Highlight

Gibson Runs Sub-Four Minute Mile

The sub-four minute mile has always been a romantic mark in track circles. On Feb. 18, 1974, Husky sophomore Greg Gibson became the first Washington runner to beat that magical mark. A native of small Connell, Wash., Gibson ran a time of 3:59.1 to place third at the San Diego Indoor Games. North Carolina's Tony Waldrop won the race with a time of 3:55.0. Gibson's quarter mile splits were 1:00, 2:00.4, and 2:59.8. "When I heard my time after three laps, I knew this was it," Gibson said after the race, which was only his second mile of the indoor season. His previous best mile was a time of 4:04.5. Gibson set the UW 880 record as a freshman with a time of 1:48.4.

UW Media Relations

UW Media Relations

Husky Legend

Irene Arden

Irene Arden is one of the most decorated swimmers in Washington history. During her Husky career she was honored as an All-America on 19 occasions. A specialist in the butterfly, she was also an outstanding competitor in the backstroke, individual medley and relay events. She was an All-American in all four events. She had a pair of second-place showings at the 1973 AIAW Championships in the 50 fly and the 100 fly and was fifth in the 200 IM. In 1973, at the World Student Games, she won gold medals in the 100-meter butterfly and the 400 medley relay. She was among the first women to receive an athletic scholarship to the University. As a senior she was recognized as the team's most valuable swimmer. Arden, a native of Vancouver, Washington, went on to earn a master's degree from Seattle University in 1981 and began a career as a teacher. She was inducted into the Husky Hall of Fame in 1985.

HUSKY LIST

Skip Boyd ... Punting Ace

In the windy confines of Husky Stadium, life as a punter can be difficult. That's what sets Skip Boyd apart from his Husky counterparts. In 1973 Boyd set Washington's single-season punting record for average kick at 43.0 yards per punt. The following season, he almost equaled it, averaging 42.2 yards per punt. Boyd ranks second on Washington's career punt average list with a 41.17 average, just behind Jeff Partridge's record of 41.19 he set from 1981-82. Boyd tried 86 more punts than Partridge and kicked one more season. In 1999 he was named to the all-time Washington football team by the *Seattle Times*. Here's a look at the top five punting seasons in UW history.

1. Skip Boyd, 1973	**43.0**
2. Skip Boyd, 1974	**42.2**
3. Jeff Partridge, 1982	**42.1**
4. Thane Cleland, 1986	**41.2**
5. Channing Wyles, 1990	**41.0**

AT the time Don Smith was hired as an assistant athletic director at Washington in 1971, black activist professor Harry Edwards called him "a spook to sit outside the door." Edwards' derogatory remark turned out to be way off base. Smith proved to be a valuable administrator and friend to student-athletes of all colors and sexes for more than two decades. After being on the job for a year he was elevated to associate director in charge of all areas of administration. In 1989 he was promoted to senior associate director and oversaw most of the support areas in the department. Smith graduated from Iowa State in 1959 following a four-year stint in the Air Force. He worked as a sports editor in Ames, Iowa and moved to Seattle in 1963 to work for the *Seattle Times*. In 1966 he went to work for AT&T as a public relations specialist. Smith's hiring came during a time when 40 black organizations, in coalition, said hiring a black administrator would not do any good for the athletic department's image and race problems. At the time of his hiring, he told *Seattle Times* sports editor George Meyers, "The day is going to come when you're 65 and no use to anybody else, and you look back over your life and say: 'What did I do to try to make this a better place for all of us to live in?' This is my first real opportunity. It may be that I may not be the man for that kind of job. I'd like to find out—at least to say that I gave it a try." Smith did more than that. He probably did more to smooth out the department's racial problems than anyone else.

Husky Moment

Basketball Defeats UCLA in Wooden's Last Loss

In a game that turned out to be the final loss in famed UCLA basketball coach John Wooden's career, the Huskies defeated the Bruins 103-81 in Hec Edmundson Pavilion. The victory ended a long string of futility against UCLA, a team the Huskies had not beaten since the 1963 season. Even sweeter, the Huskies avenged a 100-48 loss, the worst in the program's history, suffered against the Bruins a year earlier in Seattle. Ranked second in both wire service polls, the Bruins had defeated Washington 92-82 earlier in season, but the Huskies had momentum going into the rematch. On the Thursday prior to the game, Washington upset 10th-ranked USC 89-88. The Huskies grabbed the upper hand in the UCLA game when James Edwards and Larry Jackson scored back-to-back baskets to give the Huskies a 32-28 lead. Washington built that into a 52-44 halftime advantage, despite being outscored 16-0 from the free throw line. Jackson wound up leading all players in scoring with 27 points. Husky fans were nervous at the half with the 6-11 Edwards saddled with four fouls and 6-10 Lars Hansen with three personals. In the second half the Huskies kept pulling away and played tough defense that limited UCLA to just 36.6 percent shooting from the field for the game. Washington converted 55.2 percent of its attempts. UCLA All-American Dave Meyers scored just 11 points. The game marked the fourth time the Huskies eclipsed the 100-point mark during the season and just the sixth time a team had reached the century mark against the Bruins. UCLA would go on to defeat Louisville to win the NCAA Championship in San Diego.

UW Media Relations

Larry Jackson

Husky Spotlight

Mile Relay Team Wins NCAA Title

The Husky men's track program won its first NCAA relay title at the 1975 championships in Provo, Utah. Washington turned in the fastest time in the world during the year to capture first place. In a well run, highly competitive race, the Huskies' Billy Hicks gave Washington its first lead in the final straightaway, passing Baylor's Tim Son and Kansas' Clifford Wiley on the outside to break the tape with a time of 3:05.1. The time broke the UW school record and also established a new mark for BYU's stadium. The Husky relay team had already laid claim to both of those marks earlier in the meet when they clocked a time of 3:05.55 in the semifinal heat. Freshman Keith Tinner started the race for Washington by running his lap in 46.7, his fastest 440 time ever. Jerry Belur then took the handoff and turned in a lap of 47.4 seconds. Pablo Franco got the Huskies back in contention on the third leg by turning in his fastest quarter mile with a time of 45.1 seconds. Trailing by five yards when he took the baton, Hicks ran his lap in 45.9 seconds to give Washington the victory.

Husky Highlight

They say revenge is a dish best served cold. After an embarrassing 58-0 loss to the Ducks in Eugene the previous season, the UW football team counted the days before Oregon returned to the Husky schedule. Washington got its revenge, whipping the Ducks 66-0 at Husky Stadium. For motivation, head coach Jim Owens brought in a handful of players who were on the Husky squads in 1969 and 70 that lost to UCLA 57-14 only to rebound for a 61-20 victory the next season. Dennis Fitzpatrick, directing the Huskies' veer offense, rushed for 105 yards and passed for 57 more. Washington's 240-pound fullback Robin Earl pounded the Ducks for 61 yards and a pair of scores. Washington finished with 508 total yards to 55 for the Ducks. The Huskies had 30 first downs to just two for Oregon. After jumping out to a 24-0 halftime lead, the Huskies scored 28 points in the third quarter. Then Chris Rowland scored on a two-yard keeper on fourth down to make it 58-0. The crowd roared as placekicker Steve Robbins booted the PAT to make it 59-0, bettering the margin the Ducks had won by. Robbins ended the day with nine PATs to set a Husky record. Washington added a late score when the team drove 90 yards on 15 rushing plays. The victory ended a four-game losing streak for the Huskies and was the team's first conference victory in 11 outings. After the game, Owens was asked what adjustments he made at halftime. "I sat down and subtracted 24 from 59 and got 35," he said with a grin.

Husky Legend

Dennis Fitzpatrick

UW Media Relations

Dennis Fitzpatrick may be one of the lesser-known "Legends" in the rich annals of Washington's athletic program, but his one feat, on two feet, certainly is deserving of the honor. It is ironic that a football program, known for producing top-notch passing quarterbacks, would have one of the best rushing days ever credited to a quarterback. Fitzpatrick earned that distinction in 1974 when he led the Huskies to a 24-17 Apple Cup victory against Washington State by piling up 249 rushing yards on 37 attempts. Washington, which had adopted an option rushing attack, defeated the Cougars to finish the season 5-6. As it turned out, that would be head coach Jim Owens' last game. He resigned shortly afterwards. Fitzpatrick had hoped to be new UW coach Don James' first quarterback, but he lost his redshirt year as a sophomore in 1972 when he appeared in one mid-season game. Fitzpatrick lettered for Washington in both 1973 and 1974. Fitzpatrick never led Washington in passing, but he did top the team in rushing in 1974 with 697 yards, a single-season UW record for a non-running back. As a senior, he was voted the team's Guy Flaherty Award winner as the most inspirational player. While Fitzpatrick missed out on an opportunity to play in the Rose Bowl as a Husky, he came very close during his professional career. After graduating, he began a long career in hotel management by starting as a cashier at the old Olympic Hotel (now the Four Seasons) in downtown Seattle. He eventually worked as the general manager of the Pasadena Doubletree Inn, in the shadow of the Rose Bowl, a team host hotel for the annual bowl game.

Husky List

Best Men's Swimming Team Finishes at the NCAAs

Year	Finish
1973-74	4th
1972-73	5th
1971-72	6th
1946-47	7th
1974-75	7th
1970-71	7th
1977-78	9th
1950-51	9th
1972-74	10th
1947-48	10th

WITH Title IX of the federal Education Amendments Act of 1972 legislation ready to start, the University organized an ad hoc committee to examine the issue of competitive women's sports programs. The result was a recommendation to establish a women's intercollegiate athletic program. Previously run through the intramural department as club sports, women's athletics joined the men's athletics program starting in the 1974-75 academic year. Programs in basketball, crew, golf, gymnastics, swimming, tennis, track and field and volleyball began to receive additional funding. The budget for those women's programs was increased from $40,000 to $200,000 in one year, but they were far from equal partners with their men's counterparts. Foremost, there were no scholarships awarded to female athletes. Secondly, their facilities were almost nonexistent. There were no women's locker rooms, instead the athletes used the general locker room in the intramural building. Teams shared equipment, and the first women's athletic director, Jeanne Holm, worked only part time. The first year of women's varsity athletics was not much more than improved club teams. The Huskies did get off to a good start when the volleyball team defeated Washington State in mid-October in its first match. Success, and changes, would come soon. Two years after gaining varsity status, 25 women athletes would receive grants-in-aid. However, the scholarships were on a "Come and See" basis, where coaches did not award them until after the athlete had competed for one year and demonstrated her qualifications.

1975 W 1976

Husky Moment

Huskies Shock Cougars With Late Rally

Poor Don James. What was the new Husky coach going to have to do to have his first Apple Cup measure up to any future affairs? In one of the most popular games for Husky fans, and worst memories for Cougar loyalists, Washington literally snatched (twice) victory away from cross-state rival Washington State. Leading 27-14 with just three minutes to play, WSU head coach Jim Sweeney elected to go for it on fourth-and-one with the Huskies pinned on their own 14-yard line. Cougar quarterback John Hopkins tossed a pass in the direction of tight end Carl Barschig for a sure score. However, Husky defensive back Al Burleson had read the play and stepped in front of Barschig and raced 93 yards for a touchdown. Washington forced the Cougars to punt on the next series and took over on the Husky 22-yard line. On the Huskies' first offensive play, Warren Moon, who was just three-for-21 at that point, rolled right and threw a pass toward Spider Gaines. The pass was woefully short, and Washington State defensive back Tony Heath appeared to have the interception, but the rain-slicked ball popped into the air and Gaines grabbed it from between two Cougar defenders and used his sprinter speed to race into the endzone for the score. It was Gaines' second big touchdown reception from Moon in the game. Late in the first half, also following an interception of a Hopkins pass, Gaines had scored on a 29-yard throw to cut the Cougars' lead to 24-7. Washington State had jumped out to an early lead, scoring four times following Husky turnovers. The Cougars had just 84 yards of offense in the first half. Sweeney's decision to go for it on fourth down late in the game was partially due to the fact that, in the second half, Washington State had drives end on Washington's three-, 28- and 21-yard line only to see placekicker Chuck Diedrick miss field-goal attempts of 20, 45 and 38 yards. Afterwards Sweeney told the press: "It was a riverboat gambler's call, and we just shouldn't have done it."

UW Media Relations

Spider Gaines

Husky Spotlight

Don James Hired as Football Coach

Christmas came early for Husky fans in 1974. On Dec. 23 athletic director Joe Kearney hired Don James as the Washington football coach to replace Jim Owens. The 1975 season started a 18-year run that saw the Huskies post a 153-57-2 record and appear in bowl games in 13 of his final 14 seasons. The 41-year-old James came to Washington after a four-year stint at Kent State during which the Golden Flashes compiled a 25-18-1 record. Kearney announced a four-year contract for James that started with an annual salary of $28,000. James was the last of four candidates who interviewed for the vacated position. The others were Mike White of California, Douglas Porter of Howard University and Darryl Rogers of San Jose State. In typical Don James style, within 90 minutes of being offered the job, he was on the telephone with Husky recruiting coordinator Mel Thompson arranging recruiting visits. He had already made up territorial recruiting assignments for two of his assistant coaches, even though he did not know who they would be. That type of organization was one of the things that most impressed the selection committee who selected him for the job. Included in that group was junior cornerback Frank Reed, who accurately predicted: "Given the right situation, I think you're going to hear a lot about this guy." As it turned out, Washington was the right situation for Don James.

Husky Highlight

Scott Neilson and Borys Chambul win NCAA Track Titles

Scott Neilson and Borys Chambul gave the Washington track program its first pair of NCAA track champions since the 1930 season when Steve Anderson (120-yard high hurdles) and Paul Jessup (discus) won dual titles. Neilson, competing as a freshman, won the first of his four consecutive hammer throw championships with a toss of 216 feet and eight inches. Chambul took the discus throw with a toss of 202 feet and three inches. He was the first Husky discus thrower to better the 200-foot mark. Both Neilson and Chambul came to Washington from Canada. Neilson was a native of New Westminister, British Columbia and Chambul was from Scarborough, Ontario.

UW Media Relations

Borys Chambul

UW Media Relations

Husky Legend

Robin Backhaus

Robin Backhaus was one of the last outstanding swimmers for the Husky program in the mid-'70s. He was a two-year star for the Huskies before transferring to Alabama to complete his collegiate career. Before Backhaus ever got wet in the Husky pool, he had established himself as one of the world's top swimmers by winning a bronze medal at the 1972 Summer Olympic games in Munich. He won back-to-back NCAA Championships in the 200 butterfly in 1973 as a freshman and in 1974 as a sophomore. Backhaus became Washington's first NCAA champion. He swam the event in a time of 1:47.048 in 1974 and turned in a time of 1:47.168 time as a sophomore. In all, he was honored as an All-American 11 times in six different events. He set the school records in the 500-yard freestyle and the 200-yard freestyle. He won nine Pac-8 swimming titles in his two-year Husky career. Backhaus was involved in one of the most memorable races in Husky history. During the 1973 season, in a dual meet with Stanford in the Husky Pool, Backhaus narrowly edged Stanford Olympian Mike Bruner in a dramatic 100-yard freestyle race. Backhaus eventually moved to Hawaii where he worked as a commercial diver and later a secondary school teacher. He continued his athletic career there by taking up open canoe paddling and masters swimming. Backhaus was inducted into the Husky Hall of Fame in 1991.

HUSKY LIST

Chester Dorsey Tops UW Assists List

A four-year letterman for the Huskies, Chester Dorsey made outstanding passing marks both on and off the court. His 466 all-time assists is nearly 100 more than the second closest UW player. As a senior, the four-year letterman was honored for having the team's top grade point average. He helped the Huskies to a 71-36 record during his four-year career, averaging 6.4 points per game during his career. A native of Indianapolis, Dorsey was nicknamed "Chet the Jet" during his Husky career.

Player, Years	Assists
1. Chester Dorsey, 1974-77	466
2. Eldridge Recasner, 1987-90	376
3. Kim Stewart, 1975-78	343
4. Donald Watts, 1996-99	310
5. Alvin Vaughn, 1981-84	292
6. Jamie Booker, 1994-97	289
7. Detlef Schrempf, 1982-85	284
8. Don Vaughn, 1978-81	269

Women's Basketball Begins Winning Streak

UW Media Relations

Kathy Neir

AFTER going 11-11 in its first season as a varsity program in 1974-75, the Husky women's basketball team, under the direction of coach Kathy Neir, put together its first winning season in 1975-76. Washington produced a 17-11 record that included a third-place finish in the regional tournament. In the Huskies' first season, under coach Christine Burkhart, the team produced an 11-11 record and also placed first at the NCWSA Area Playoffs. The Husky program began with a 78-49 loss to Western Washington on Jan. 8, 1975. The student newspaper, *The Daily,* did not even give the team a write-up for the contest. Washington won its first game on Jan. 17 when the Huskies defeated Puget Sound 36-23. Winning was synonymous with the program. The Huskies put together a string of 24 consecutive winning seasons from 1976-1999.

1976 W 1977

Husky Moment

Men's Crew Wins Henley

Rarely has the national championship in crew been decided in foreign waters, but for all practical purposes, that's what happened in the summer of 1977. Determining the best collegiate shell was not very clear cut. That season, Washington declined to row in the IRA championships after winning the Pac-8 title. Cornell went on to finish first at the IRAs, but many observers felt they were not even the best eastern team. Harvard, which raced in the Eastern Sprints, was also absent from the IRA. Ironically, all three crews would be in Great Britain to compete at the Royal Henley Regatta. On the first day of racing, Washington and Cornell drew byes and Harvard was eliminated by the Garda Siochana Boat Club, Ireland's national squad. In the semifinals, Cornell fell to the British national team, leaving only the Husky crew to represent the Stars and Stripes. Washington, facing the Garda boat, almost never made it to the finish line. Midway through the semifinal race, a pair of teenagers, rowing a dingy, were directly in the path of the Husky crew. Luckily, the dingy slipped out of the way and UW coxswain John Stillings kept the unsuspecting team on course as Washington went on for the upset. In the finals the Huskies never let the British get into the race. Washington grabbed a deck-length lead at a quarter mile, stretched their advantage to one-third at the mile and won by a length. It marked the first time since 1959 the Americans had captured the Grand Challenge Cup race. In addition to Stillings, the team was comprised of Mike Hess, Jesse Franklin, Terry Fisk, Mark Miller, Mark Umlauf, Ross Parker, Mark Sawyer and Ron Jackman. Seven of those rowers would go on to compete for the U.S. team at the World Rowing Games a month later. After Henley, the Huskies stayed in Europe to race in the Lucerne International Rowing Regatta and finished sixth in the lightweight eights, fourth in the four-with-coxswain and a disappointing ninth in the heavyweights. Husky coach Dick Erickson called the win at Henley, "My biggest thrill." The 1977 crew was inducted into the Husky Hall of Fame in 1999. Hess and Stillings would go on to row with the U.S. team at the 1976 Olympics.

UW Media Relations

Husky Spotlight

Steve Wejmar Wins NCAA Vault Title

As a freshman competing at the NCAA gymnastics championships, Steve Wejmar figured he was a bit of a long shot to win a national championship. Ranked second in the event, he did not have the "big meet" experience of many of the other competitors. As the last competitor on the floor, Wejmar needed a nearly perfect vault to capture the national title. "On my first vault, a handspring full, I got a 9.5. That meant I had to score a 9.65 on the double front, so I kind of relaxed because there was no way I could do that. Just before the second vault, I decided I might as well go for broke. It was the best vault I had ever done." Wejmar scored a 9.75 on his final attempt to literally leap past the competition into first place. His score also set a Washington school record. Wejmar's title made him the first freshman gymnast to earn All-American honors. As a result of his victory in Tempe, his hometown, Kent, Washington, proclaimed April 5, 1977 Steve Wejmar Day. He became the first Husky gymnast to win an NCAA title since Yoshi Hayasaki captured the all-around and high bar titles in 1971. Earlier in the season Wejmar won the Pac-8 title in the vault.

Husky Highlight

Women's Crew Wins West Coast Sprints

The Husky women's crew team swept its first major regatta in 1977 when Washington won all four races at the West Coast Sprints, later known as the Pacific Coast Championships. The light eight won in a time of 3:53.1 and the open eight took first place in a time of 3:40.18 on the 1,000-meter course. The Huskies also claimed wins in the Light Four and Open Four races. The event was held in Redwood Shores, California and marked the first time all eight conference schools participated together. After losing earlier in the season to California, the Huskies upset the Bears in the semifinals by two lengths to gain a spot in the finals. There the Huskies defeated UCLA by almost four seconds.

Husky Legend

James Edwards

UW Media Relations

James Edwards was one of the Bad Boys and that was a good thing if you were a Detroit Pistons fan in the late 1980s. Edwards proved to be a key addition by Pistons' head coach Chuck Daly that helped Detroit to a pair of NBA Championships in 1989-90. Dubbed the "Bad Boys" for their bruising style of play, Edwards was a solid force on a team that featured Isiah Thomas, Joe Dumars, Dennis Rodman and Bill Laimbeer. It was ironic that Edwards was a "Bad Boy" considering how often his college coach, Marv Harshman, called him a "nice young man." The 7-1 Edwards was a four-year letterman at Washington from 1974-77. He was named an All-American as a senior while also receiving all-coast accolades. He was an All-Pac-8 selection as both a junior and senior. Edwards finished his Husky career with 1,548 points, the second best total in UW history at the time. He also had 792 rebounds. Washington won 72 games during his playing career, highlighted by a 23-5 record in 1975-76 that included a return to the NCAA tournament for the first time since 1953. As a senior, Edwards was a team captain and led Washington with a 20.9 point scoring average and 10.4 rebound average. A Seattle native, Edwards guided Roosevelt High School to a state championship. He was the first alternate for the 1976 United States Olympic basketball team. He was taken in the third round (46th overall) of the 1977 NBA draft by the Los Angeles Lakers. His 19-year NBA career saw him play for eight different teams. He appeared in more games than only eight other players at the time of his retirement. In addition to his championship rings at Detroit, he was a reserve center for the Chicago Bulls 1996 World Championship team.

HUSKY LIST

Scott Phillips Sets Receiving Marks

When Sonny Sixkiller completed his playing career in 1972, the Husky passing game seemed to disappear with him. But, ironically, the next three seasons produced one of the most sure-handed receivers in Husky history in Scott Phillips. He is the only player to lead Washington in receiving for three consecutive seasons. He had 34 catches in 1974, 33 in 1975 and 26 in 1976. Here is a look at Washington's top career receivers:

Player	Receptions	Yards
1. Paul Skansi, 1979-82	138	1723
2. Mario Bailey, 1988-91	131	2093
3. Vince Weathersby, 1985-88	130	918
4. Jerome Pathon, 1995-97	125	2063
5. Scott Phillips, 1973-76	111	1866

AFTER coaching the Colorado State football team from 1962-70, Mike Lude was fired from his post with Colorado State. Lude took on the challenge of becoming the athletic director at Kent State, shortly after several of the University's students were shot by national guardsmen during a demonstration. Lude built the Kent State athletic program into one of the best in the Mid-American Conference. Along the way, he hired a football coach named Don James to resurrect the program. When Lude replaced Joe Kearney as the athletic director at Washington in 1976, it began a 15-year tenure that saw the Husky program grow and expand and become a model for financial stability. Ironically, James was already the football coach at Washington when Lude joined the staff. The two worked to make the Husky football program one of the best in the nation, laying the groundwork for Lude to expand the overall department. Among his accomplishments were the 13,000-seat addition to the north side of Husky Stadium that brought the total capacity up to 72,500. The Tyee Center (later renamed the Don James Center) was added to the stadium and provided an instant boost to fundraising efforts. Other additions under Lude included the three-story Graves Annex, including a new weight room, the Nordstrom Indoor Tennis Center and the team assembly room in Husky Stadium. Lude was a native of Kalamazoo, Michigan, and a graduate of Hillsdale College. He was inducted into the Husky Hall of Fame in 1998.

Husky Moment

Washington Wins the Rose Bowl

In his third season as head coach at Washington, Don James knew there were some doubters. After going 6-5 and 5-6 in his first two seasons, the Huskies struggled to a 1-3 start at the beginning of the 1977 season. Things looked gloomy after back-to-back losses at Syracuse (22-20) and Minnesota (19-17). Playing their conference opener on the road at Oregon, the Huskies put together one of the most pivotal wins in the program's history. The Huskies blasted the Ducks 54-0 and went on to win six of their final seven games. The only loss, to UCLA, was later forfeited by the Bruins. In late November, the Huskies upset 14th-ranked USC 28-10 in monsoon-like conditions at Husky Stadium to vault to the top of the Rose Bowl race. Washington's Pasadena appearance was the program's first since the 1963 season. With quarterback Warren Moon calling the plays, the 13th-ranked Huskies upset fourth-ranked Michigan 27-20. Moon led Washington 49 yards on the team's first possession, and scored on a two-yard run to give the Huskies a 7-0 lead. Moon then hooked up with the speedy Spider Gaines for a 62-yard completion to set up a field goal and a 10-0 lead. Moon added another one-yard scoring run to finish off a 60-yard drive and send Washington into the locker room with a 17-0 lead. Early in the third quarter, Moon tossed a 28-yard touchdown strike to Gaines, and the Huskies looked like they would rout the Wolverines. Two plays later, Michigan finally broke its scoring drought when Rick Leech found Curt Stephenson for a 76-yard score. The Huskies managed another field goal to close out the third quarter with a 27-7 lead. Michigan rallied for a pair of fourth-quarter scores, but lost its momentum when Gregg Willner missed the extra-point conversion on the second score, leaving the Huskies with a 27-20 cushion. The Huskies needed a pair of interceptions in the final minutes to hold on for the win, including a pickoff by Michael Jackson at the Husky three-yard line. Moon was voted the game's most valuable player after completing 12 of 23 passes for 188 yards. Joe Steele led the Husky rushing game with 77 yards. The success of the 1977 team allowed James to recruit the players that proved to be the nucleus of the 1981 and 1982 Rose Bowl teams.

UW Media Relations

Warren Moon

Husky Spotlight

When critics said that, at just 6-0 and 210 pounds, Michael Jackson was too small to play inside linebacker for the Huskies, they overlooked one important aspect of his game ... his speed. Jackson became a consummate playmaker on the Husky defense from 1975-78 as a four-year letterman. He started his career at safety, but a rash of injuries in the linebacking corps early in the 1975 season forced him into the lineup at inside linebacker. He never left. After four years of play he had an amazing 524 tackles to show for his efforts. The 210 tackles he racked up in 1977 stands as a Washington record that may not fall. Jackson's biggest play that season was not a tackle, but an interception. It was his late pickoff of a Rick Leach pass, at Washington's three-yard line, that preserved the Huskies 27-20 Rose Bowl victory. Jackson felt slighted after his junior season when neither major wire service named him to their All-America teams. They did not make that mistake during his senior season. He was tabbed a second-team All-American by both the AP and UPI in 1978. That season he amassed 168 tackles, a total that also ranks on Washington's top-10 single-season list. His list of honors includes all-coast and all-conference selections in both 1977 and 1978. Jackson went on to play eight seasons for the Seattle Seahawks and then briefly entered into a television career as both a broadcaster and actor. In 1999 the Seattle Times named him to the all-Washington team for the century.

Husky Highlight

Husky Crew Sweeps PCC Races

Racing at home on the Montlake Cut, the Washington men's crew team put on a dominant performance to sweep all five races at the Pac-8 Championships. The Huskies racked up wins in the Frosh 8, Junior Varsity 8, Varsity 4, Lightweight 8 and Heavyweight 8. The Varsity 8 defeated California by three-tenths of a second to complete the sweep. The season took on a bit of historic perspective when Carolyn Patten became the first female coxswain for the Husky men's team. A native of San Diego, Patten was a member of the Husky junior varsity team. Patten was a member of the Husky women's crew program before an injury cut short her rowing career. She worked as a coxswain for 18 months before coach Dick Erickson inserted her into the lineup for the opening Class Day races. Her junior varsity eight squad went on to win that race and claim the George M. Varnell Trophy.

Husky Legend

Warren Moon

As a senior at Washington, Warren Moon completed an athletic questionnaire by answering "Career Plans?" with the answer "Professional football." He sure had that right. Almost a quarter century after he played his last game at Washington, Moon was still quarterbacking teams in the NFL. A native of Los Angeles, Moon transferred to Washington after a one-year junior college career. Moon's first two years at Washington were tough. He beat out Husky favorite Chris Rowland for the starting quarterback slot in 1975, Don James' first year as head coach, and started the first six games of the season before being replaced by Rowland. With Rowland lost to graduation, Moon took over the starter's spot again as a junior. Some Husky fans though he was inconsistent and questioned if he could lead the team. When Moon told James that he thought the criticism might be because he was black, James responded with: "No, it is because you are the quarterback." As a senior, Husky fans understood what James saw in Moon. He completed 113 of 199 passes (56.8 percent), for 1,584 yards, threw 11 touchdowns and rallied Washington from a 1-3 start to a Rose Bowl berth. There, the 13th-ranked Huskies upset fourth-ranked Michigan 27-20. Moon finished his three-year Husky career with 3,277 passing yards. He was the co-Player of the Year in the Pac-8 as a senior and also took home Rose Bowl MVP honors that year. He began his professional career with Edmonton in the Canadian Football League in 1978, opting to sign there before the NFL draft. He guided that team to five consecutive Grey Cup titles during a six-year stay before heading to the NFL in 1983. Moon's NFL career included several teams, including the Seattle Seahawks, but he truly made himself a solid Hall of Fame candidate with his longest stint as quarterback of the Houston Oilers. Moon ranks among the top 10 on the NFL's all-time passing list with over 47,000 yards. When combined with his CFL stats, Moon has passed for more yards than any professional player. He joined the Husky Hall of Fame in 1984.

Husky History

Huskies Start Win Streak Against Bears

When Washington' football team defeated California 50-31 in Berkeley in 1977, no one knew that it would start a Husky win streak in the series that would extend into the next Millennium. The victory was the first of 18 straight the Huskies would record by the 2000 season. The streak is one of the longest in NCAA history between two teams.

1977 — UW 50, CAL 31 (Berkeley)
1979 — UW 28, CAL 24 (Berkeley)
1981 — UW 27, CAL 26 (Berkeley)
1982 — UW 50, CAL 7 (Husky Stadium)
1984 — UW 44, CAL 14 (Husky Stadium)
1985 — UW 28, CAL 12 (Berkeley)
1986 — UW 50, CAL 18 (Husky Stadium)
1988 — UW 28, CAL 27 (Husky Stadium)
1989 — UW 29, CAL 16 (Berkeley)
1990 — UW 46, CAL 7 (Husky Stadium)
1991 — UW 24, CAL 17 (Berkeley)
1992 — UW 35, CAL 16 (Husky Stadium)
1993 — UW 24, CAL 23 (Berkeley)
1994 — UW 31, CAL 19 (Husky Stadium)
1997 — UW 30, CAL 3 (Berkeley)
1998 — UW 21, CAL 13 (Husky Stadium)
1999 — UW 31, CAL 27 (Berkeley)
2000 — UW 36, CAL 24 (Husky Stadium)

Melvin Cooley Wins NCAA Gym Title

RARELY have Oregon fans cheered on an athlete from the University of Washington, but Melvin Cooley did not give them much of a choice. Cooley, a senior on the Husky men's gymnastics team turned in a spectacular final routine to capture first place in the horizontal bar at the 1978 NCAA Championships. Cooley was so impressive that he received a standing ovation from the pro-Oregon crowd in Eugene. A second-place finisher at the NCAAs as a junior, Cooley was the heavy favorite to take home first-place honors. He was fresh off a top showing at the Pac-8 Championships that earned him Gymnast of the Year honors. Cooley jumped out to first place in the competition during Thursday night's compulsory round by scoring 9.6. Bart Conner, a future Olympian, was close behind with a score of 9.5. The two were even after Friday's preliminary optionals when Cooley allowed his hand to touch the mat on his dismount, earning him a score of just 9.4. At Saturday's finals, Cooley turned in a score of 9.7 to clinch the top prize. Later that year he would go on to add an AAU national championship to his impressive string of victories. The two-time All-American was named to the Husky Hall of Fame in 1994.

1978 W 1979

HUSKY MOMENT

Husky Hoopsters Topple Top-Ranked Bruins

It did not seem very probable that Washington could upset top-ranked UCLA when the Bruins visited Hec Edmundson Pavilion near the close of the 1979 campaign. Coach Marv Harshman's Huskies were 11-16 and headed for their first losing season under his guidance. Washington had lost six of nine games, and the Bruins were on a six-game winning streak. But with two victories against UCLA in the Bruins' last four trips to Seattle, Hec Edmundson Pavilion was becoming a tough place for the Southern Californians to win. Little did they know a giant from Iceland would be their undoing. Petur Gudmundsson, a 7-2 center on the Husky team, proved to be the cornerstone of Harshman's plan in upsetting the Bruins. Early and often Washington got him the ball, and he scored seven of the Huskies' first 11 points. UCLA coach Gary Cunningham had his defense sag back on Gudmundsson and double team him, and that left Washington's outside players open to shoot. The Huskies built leads of 23-12 and 50-38, thanks in part to sound defense by guard Lorenzo Romar, and solid rebounding. Earlier in the season, in an 86-61 loss to the Bruins at Pauley Pavilion, UCLA had outrebounded Washington by a wide 46-24 margin. All-American David Greenwood had 16 rebounds alone while also scoring 24 points in that game. But with Gudmundsson playing inspired ball, the Huskies kept even with the Bruins in the rebounding department in the rematch. A late run gave UCLA a 68-67 lead with 20 seconds to play. After a timeout, Harshman had his players look for Gudmundsson inside, but the Bruins double teamed him, leaving junior forward Stan Walker open to hit a 17-foot jump shot with three seconds to play to give the Huskies a dramatic 69-68 victory. Gudmundsson led the Huskies with 17 points on seven-for-13 shooting. Ironically, the Huskies lost their next game, to USC, on a tip-in basket with two seconds to play.

UW Media Relations

Petur Gudmundsson

Husky Spotlight

Winning NCAA titles was becoming second nature for Husky senior hammer thrower Scott Neilson and he did not disappoint anyone when he claimed his fourth straight title at the 1979 NCAA Track and Field Championships in Champaign, Illinois. Neilson bettered the field with a top throw of 237 feet and three inches. But the fact Washington came home with two NCAA champions was a bit of a shock. Tom Sinclair, competing in the javelin competition, even surprised himself by taking top honors at the event. At 6-0 and 180 pounds, Sinclair was usually one of the smaller competitors during meets and that held true at the NCAAs. Sinclair was used to that, but he was not accustomed to the new and slick runway he found at the Illini track. Since the surface was new, Illinois officials requested the competitors to wear shorter spikes so as not to damage the runway. That took away what Sinclair felt was his best asset, a powerful plant before throwing. As a result, he barely qualified for the finals, placing 10th among the 12 finalists. After several coaches challenged the shorter spikes, meet officials relented and allowed the finalist to switch to their regular one-half inch spikes. That was all Sinclair, a Gig Harbor native, needed. He uncorked a throw of 261 feet and three inches in the finals to take first-place honors. The throw was a personal best for Sinclair. The Huskies almost had a third champion when shot putter Steve Summers placed second with a school record toss of 65-11.

HUSKY HIGHLIGHT

Husky Hall of Fame Starts

Thanks to the efforts of the University's Alumni Association, its Big "W" Club and the athletic department, a Husky Hall of Fame was started in 1979. The Husky Hall of Fame was created to honor and preserve the memory of those athletes, teams, coaches and members of the athletic department staff who have contributed in an outstanding and positive way to the distinction of the Washington athletic program. An annual banquet is held each year to induct the newest members. The gala has switched between the fall and spring during its existence. Members were honored with plaques. The Hall of Fame room is located in the west end of the renovated Hec Edmundson Pavilion. The first Hall of Fame class included Steve Anderson (Track, 1928-30), Chuck Carroll (Football, 1926-28), Hiram Conibear (Crew, 1907-17), Gil Dobie (Football, 1908-16), Hec Edmundson (Basketball, 1921-47; Track, 1919-1954), Bob Houbregs (Basketball, 1951-53), Hugh McElhenny (Football, 1949-51), Jim Owens (Football, 1957-74), Al Ulbrickson Sr. (Crew 1927-58) and the 1936 Men's Eight-Oared Crew. Legendary UCLA basketball coach John Wooden was the speaker at the inaugural Hall of Fame dinner.

UW Media Relations

Husky Legend

Scott Neilson

Scott Neilson's performances at the NCAA championships from 1976-79 make him the most successful thrower in the Washington track program's history. A native of New Westminster, British Columbia, Neilson won a total of seven NCAA titles, including four straight in the hammer throw at the outdoor championships and three in the 35-pound weight throw at the indoor event. At the time, he was just the second collegiate competitor to claim four consecutive NCAA titles in the same event. The other was Oregon's Steve Prefontaine, who won four straight three-mile/5000 meter races. Neilson never lost a meet in 40 competitions during his college career. As a freshman in 1976, Neilson served notice that he would be the man to beat in the Pac-8. In a dual meet at Oregon he recorded a throw of 213 feet and four inches to break the conference record by four feet. He won the NCAA title with a throw of 216-8. During his sophomore season, he had the eight best throws for all collegiate competitors. He won the NCAAs with a toss of 228-4, bettering his previous best mark by five feet. He took the NCAA title in 1978 with a toss of 237-5. A bonze medalist for Canada at the 1975 Pan American Games, Neilson won the gold medal there in 1979. He won the NCAAs his senior season with a mark of 237-3. His top throw as a collegian was a distance of 238-8 at Oregon as a junior. That effort established a school, field, Pac-8 and collegiate record. In 1979 he was named a winner of the NCAA's Top-Five student-athlete award. He graduated with a 3.69 grade point average and went into a career in medicine. Neilson was inducted into the Husky Hall of Fame in 1986.

HUSKY LIST

Two of Washington's long-time programs enjoyed the best seasons in their history during the spring of 1979. The Husky men's tennis team compiled a 30-4 record, setting a school record for wins in a season. The team pieced together a 24-game win streak, bettering the old school record by 14 victories. Junior Chris Romney set a single-season win record with his 27-6 mark and he also won a record 17 straight matches. The Husky baseball team was equally successful, smashing 34 school records while compiling a 37-13 record. The victory total was a school record that featured a 19-game winning streak.

Pac-8 Becomes Pac-10

ON July 1 of 1978, the Pac-8 ceased to exist, and the Pac-10 Conference came into existence. It was not an expansion that was exactly greeted with open arms. In a vote in December of 1976, the eight presidents of the Pac-8 schools voted to allow Arizona and Arizona State to join the league. Arizona and Arizona State had been members of the Western Athletic Conference. It took two key agreements, forced by the northwest schools, to pave the way for the agreement. First, changes in revenue-sharing matters would have to be approved by a three-fourths vote of the University presidents. Secondly, revenue from football games would continue to be divided 50-50. Historically, the football teams at Oregon, Oregon State and Washington State did not draw as well as the rest of the league and therefore splitting gate receipts equally would benefit the northern schools. There were strong rumors that, if the expansion deal fell through, USC would withdraw from the conference.

1979 W 1980

Husky Moment

Stolp Earns First Harrier All-America Honors

Washington senior Bill Stolp became the first Husky cross country runner to earn All-America distinction when he competed at the 1979 NCAA Championships in Bethlehem, Pennsylvania. While Stolp placed 45th in the competition, only United States citizens were designated as All-Americans. Removing the foreign runners from the field and Stolp stood as the 23rd best finisher. He ran the race in a time of 30:09.7. Washington's State's Henry Rono took home top honors with a time of 28:19.6. Stolp was Washington's top finisher in every meet during the season, including a ninth-place showing at the West Region Championships. Stolp's finish was the best by a Husky at the event until Curt Covin placed 17th at the 1986 championships. Stolp was a native of Lynnwood.

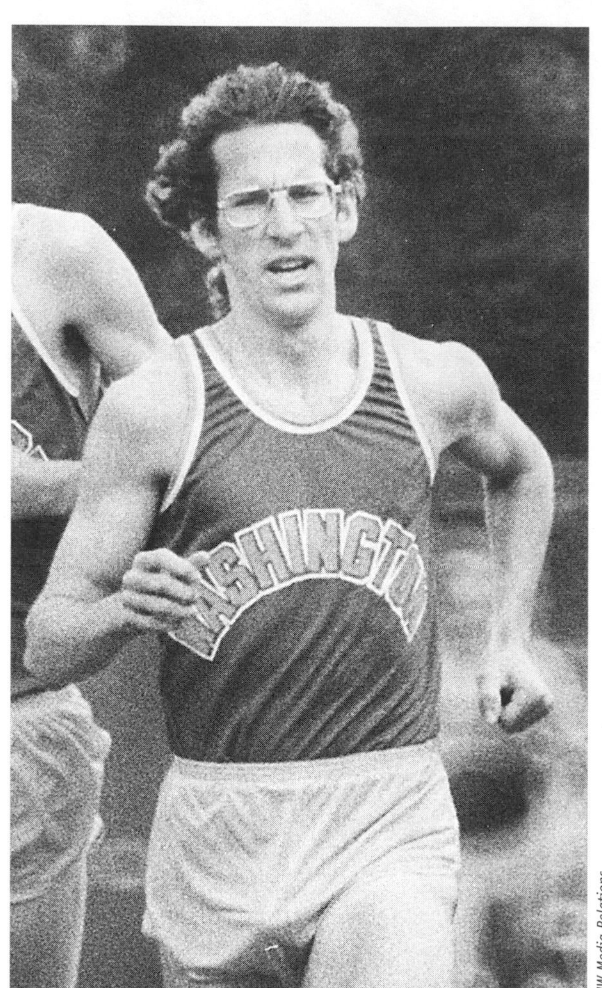

UW Media Relations

Husky Spotlight

The economic problems that caused athletic director Joe Kearney to strip away scholarships at the start of the decade resurfaced at the close of it as well. On June 9 of 1980, Husky athletic director Mike Lude announced that Washington would not compete in the sports of wrestling or men's gymnastics in the next season. Neither sport ever returned to varsity status. Lude said that by dropping the sports the athletic department would directly save $100,000. Washington was facing a deficit of $762,110 for the 1980-81 academic year. Lude cited the fact that there were fewer than 20 gymnastics teams in the state's high school ranks to feed the Husky program. He said wrestling was selected to be dropped because four Pac-10 schools no longer offered the sport and the opportunity for conference competition had lessened. Six years earlier Washington had announced that it was dropping men's skiing as a varsity sport due to budget cutbacks and a lack of area competition. When department-wide cutbacks were made in the mid-70s, Husky swimming coach Earl Ellis urged that the men's program be dropped so that swimmers could transfer to more competitive programs without having to sit out a year. While there were cutbacks in support of swimming, it was never dropped below its varsity status.

Husky Highlight

Doug Martin proved to be the first of several outstanding defensive linemen who played for the Huskies during Don James' tenure as head coach. Martin, who started for three-and-a-half seasons, lettered four times from 1976-79. At 6-3 and 253 pounds, his speed and agility made him a tough foe for opposing offensive lines to block. Based on his tackling totals, they did not accomplish that very often. Martin had 99 tackles as a sophomore, 107 as a junior and 66 as a senior. His numbers took a dip in 1979, his final Washington season, due to an off-season knee injury that he suffered during spring drills. Despite the setback, Martin needed only four months of rehabilitation to return for the Huskies opener his senior season. He went on to earn second-team All-America honors from the Associated Press, United Press International and the Newspaper Enterprises Association. *Playboy Magazine* also tabbed him to appear with its preseason all-star squad. Despite being confined to a wheelchair, Martin made the appearance for the famous Playboy photo shoot. Martin earned all-coast and all-conference honors as a junior and senior. He was a member of the Huskies' victorious Rose Bowl (1978) and Sun Bowl (1979) teams. He won lineman of the game honors in the Sun Bowl for his 10-tackle effort in a 14-7 win against Texas. In 1980 Martin was taken in the first round of the NFL draft by the Minnesota Vikings. He played his entire nine-year professional career there. Martin's older brother, George, played at Oregon and professionally for the New York Giants.

UW Media Relations

Husky Legend

Joe Steele

It was ironic that Washington State would be the opponent when Joe Steele had a chance to break Hugh McElhenny's 28-year-old single-season Husky rushing record. Ironic because it was McElhenny's 296-yard rushing effort against the Cougars in 1950 that allowed "The King" to become the first Washington ball carrier to eclipse the 1,000-yard rushing mark. McElhenny finished that season with 1,107 yards. Steele, on his last carry of the season, raced 28 yards for a score and toppled McElhenny's long-standing mark by finishing his junior season with 1,111 yards. It took a huge effort by Steele that day, 193 yards, to even put himself into a position to threaten McElhenny's mark. In the first game of his senior season, Steele broke McElhenny's career rushing record and would go on to set UW's all-time rushing mark with 3091 yards. At the time, that total ranked him seventh on the Pac-8 Conference's all-time rushing list. It was not until 1990, when Greg Lewis rushed for 1,279 yards that Steele vacated his crown as the single-season rushing leader. Four years later, Napoleon Kaufman toppled his career rushing mark with 4,401 yards. Steele's career rushing marks should have been higher, but a knee injury against UCLA in the eighth game of his senior season cut his playing career short. Despite a lengthy rehab, the Seattle Seahawks drafted the hometown product in the fifth round of the 1980 draft. He was cut from the team during preseason drills. The following year he signed a contract with Edmonton in the Canadian Football League, but an ankle injury led to his departure during his first season. Steele rushed for 421 yards as a freshman, including a 157-yard effort against Oregon. He had 865 yards as a sophomore, 1,111 as a junior and 694 as a senior. A versatile player, he caught 62 passes for 473 yards and returned a kickoff 89 yards for a score as a freshman.

Husky Lists

Washington kick return specialist Mark Lee ran himself into the record book during the 1979 season when the senior returned three punts for touchdowns. His last, a 64-yard runback, gave Washington a 28-24 victory against California. In 1990 Beno Bryant would equal Lee's mark with three punt returns for scores. Bryant added another one in 1991 to claim the school record for punt returns for touchdowns with four. Here's a look at Lee's and Bryant's punt returns for scores:

Mark Lee

1979	**53 yards vs. Oregon (UW 21-17)**
	62 yards vs. UCLA (UW 34-14)
	64 yards vs. California (UW 28-24)

Beno Bryant

1990	**52 yards vs. San Jose State (UW 20-17)**
	82 yards vs. Arizona State (UW 42-14)
	70 yards vs. Arizona (UW 54-10)
1991	**53 yards vs. Kansas State (UW 56-3)**

The Olympic Boycott

WHEN the United States Olympic Committee voted by a 2-1 margin on April 12, 1980 to support President Jimmy Carter's boycott of the 1980 Summer Olympic Games in Moscow, it cost several Huskies an opportunity to compete internationally. Men's assistant rowing coach Bob Ernst was set to direct the women's crew teams at the Olympics, which included Jan Harville, the future Husky women's head coach. Ernst felt his team had a chance to medal in four of the six rowing events. Several other current or former Husky athletes were also scheduled to appear in that Summer's games, including Chris Allsopp (rowing),Duncan Atwood (track and field), Hope Barnes (rowing), William Buchan (sailing), Rod Ewaliko (track and field), David Kehoe (rowing), Scott Neilson (track and field), Kristi Norelius (rowing) and Chris Wells (rowing). Several other Husky athletes, such as high jumper Maggie Garrison and shot putter Caryl Van Pelt, had taken a year off from school just to train for the Olympic Trials.

Super Legend

Larry Owings

Wrestling is no longer a varsity sport at the University of Washington but the legend of Larry lives on. On March 28, 1970 at Northwestern University in Evanston, Illinois, Larry Owings, a Husky sophomore, gave us what the *Chicago Tribune* trumpheted as "one of the most unforgettable moments in the history of sport and possibly all sport."

Growing up on the Owings' small farm near Hubbard, Oregon, Larry attended Canby High School, winning two state championships—one at 136 pounds as a junior; the other at 138 pounds as a senior. Owings chose Washington on the basis of an excellent architectural program and the enthusiasm of three-year Husky coach Jim Smith, who was building a strong wrestling program. Owings' success at Washington came quickly. Freshmen could not compete at the varsity level in Pac-8 competition but could compete as varsity members at the NCAA tournament. Cutting his weight 20 pounds to compete in the 130-pound event, Owings advanced to the NCAA quarterfinals. Weeks later, Owings entered the initial national championship competition of the newly-formed U.S. Wrestling Federation—in both Greco-Roman style wrestling and the freestyle tournament. Owings won championships in both styles in the 149.5 pound classification and was named the outstanding wrestler in the Greco-Roman competition.

In his sophomore year (1969-1970), Owings had a 19-1 record going into the Pac-8 tournament. He beat former Canby teammate, Kim Snider of Oregon State, to win the title. Owings' non-stop action technique, his endurance honed from very hard training, and his high pain tolerance resulted in his number-two seeding in the 142-pound class at the NCAA tournament. The number-one seed was Iowa State's Dan Gable, a two-time NCAA champion. Gable was a senior competing in his final college tournament. He was undefeated in seven years and 181 matches of high school and college wrestling. Owings had wrestled Gable in the 1968 Olympic Trials. Although he lost to Gable, 13-5, Owings almost pinned Gable in the match and felt he had improved considerably since his senior year in high school and knew how he could beat his extraordinary opponent. At the weigh-in before the match, Bud Palmer, a commentator for ABC's Wide World of Sports, asked Owings why he would drop to a weight class that would be impossible to win because he would face Gable. Larry's eyes flashed. He was silent at first. "I'll beat him," he stated in the most determined tone imaginable. The usually smooth Palmer was dumbfounded.

In the five preliminary NCAA matches, Gable had notched five pins to record an average of 4:26 minutes to complete an eight-minute match. Owings recorded four pins in four matches in an even quicker 4:03. The showdown was at hand. The first round ended with Owings up 3-2. In the second period, Owings electrified the crowd by driving the fireman's carry low and deep until he suddenly lifted Gable into the air and unto the mat. The noise level was described as "comparable to Niagara Falls during the spring thaw." Gable came back to score four points before the second period ended with Owings up 8-6.

Owings was in the top (ride) position as the final stanza started. Gable scored another two points on a reversal to tie the score. He also was adding to his almost two minutes of ride time which would give him two addtional points at the final buzzer. With a minute to go, Owings summoned all his strength and determination and miraculously escaped from Gable's grasp and went ahead 9-8. With less than 30 seconds remaining, Owings shot at Gable's legs and then lifted him straight up and dropped him awkwardly on his buttocks for two more points. After Gable escaped a near pin predicament, he was awarded one point and Owings another two for getting Gable into the near pin position. As the pair slowly edged off the mat, the referee, Pascal Perri, whistled them out of bounds with three seconds to go. On the whistle, Owings drove in to try for a takedown and then it was over. The final score was 13-11. Gable sagged to one knee. He had lost.

Owings was acclaimed the outstanding wrestler of the tournament. Many claim that the match was the greatest in collegiate wrestling history; certainly the most publicized. Owings triumph was the first Husky NCAA wrestling title. He would win Pac-8 titles in his junior and senior years and reach the finals in the NCAA tournament in both years. Gable would never lose again on his way to winning the gold medal in the 1972 Munich Olympics. He met Owings one more time in the 1972 Olympic Trials and won 7-1.

Scott Neilson

Scott Neilson was the epitome of the student athlete when he competed in the hammer and 35-pound weight throws at the University of Washington. A son of a New Westminster, British Columbia doctor, he majored in chemistry and pre-med. Neilson may be one of the best examples of an athlete on a major college level who believed gymnasiums and athletic fields are attached to schools and not the reverse. He chose Washington not only for the advantages it offered athletically but more importantly, in his view, what it offered academically.

Neilson also reached an athletic performance level achieved by no other athlete in Husky history. In the hammer throw, he won four NCAA outdoor titles (1976-79) and established the NCAA meet record in 1978 with a throw of 237′ 5″. He set the collegiate record—238′ 8″—in 1978 in a dual meet with Oregon. Neilson entered the NCAA indoor 35-pound weight event in his sophomore year and won three NCAA titles in that event (1977-79). Up to 1979, he was one of one of two male athletes to win four outdoor NCAA titles—Oregon's middle distance runner Steve Prefontaine was the other.

The hammer throw gets its name from a 16-pound metal ball attached to one end of a single steel wire with a handle on the other end. The thrower picks the handle up, gives the chain and ball two winds to gain momentum, then spins his body three or four times and lets the ball, chain, and handle go. Neilson, always the academic analyst, estimated that, at the distance he was throwing, the hammer was traveling at close to 60 miles per hour generating about 550 pounds of pull at release. The weight throw consists of throwing a 35-pound ball attached by two chain links to a triangle held by the thrower. People who throw the hammer and the weight are big.

Neilson first began throwing the shot and discus in eighth grade. His coach supplied him with his first hammer, one the coach made in his metal shop. In high school, he had a goal of 150 feet but soon he was throwing 200 feet and had no serious competition. So, he developed the discipline of competing against himself. So dominating was Neilson after he came to Washington that he was never beaten in collegiate competition. At Washington, he joined a very select group of throwers coached by one of the best in the nation, Husky coach Ken Shannon. In 1976, four Husky throwers won Pac-8 titles—Borys Chambul in the discus throw, Rod Ewaliko in the javelin throw, Russ Vincent in the shot put, and Neilson. Both Chambul, another Canadian, and Neilson won NCAA titles. Soon Duncan Atwood and Tom Sinclair joined the group to give Washington one of the best unit of throwers in the country. Neilson won his first NCAA championship with a throw of 216′ 8″. In his sophomore year, he took up the 35-pound weight event and won the first of his three NCAA indoor championships in that year. He established school and Pac-8 records in winning his second NCAA title with a throw of 228′ 4″. In his junior year he again established Husky and Pac-8 marks and set a collegiate record of 238′ 8″ in a dual meet with Oregon on April 1, 1978. In June, he won his third NCAA hammer title with a new NCAA meet record of 237′ 5″. He ended his Husky career with his fourth NCAA title (237′ 3″) and became the only athlete in Husky history to win seven national championships in track and field or any other sport.

His excellence in the classroom was honored as well. With his 3.69 grade point average, he was chosen as the Pac-10's 1979 Medalist and was named one of the NCAA's Top Five student athletes in 1979. After graduation, this gentle mighty man won the 1979 Pan-American Games. He entered the University of British Columbia's medical school in the fall of 1979 and was a member of the Canadian Olympic team which boycotted the 1980 Olympic Games. He now practices as an anesthesiologist in Nanaimo, B.C.

You can help write the next chapter of Great Husky Moments

Nearly all the great Husky moments chronicled in this special book were made possible, in part, by the generous contributions of Husky fans like you. The University of Washington Department of Intercollegiate Athletics is self-sustaining and supports 21 varsity teams and over 650 student-athletes. This means the next generation of Husky achievers is depending on your support to help them realize their goals and dreams... on the field, in the classroom, and beyond.

For information on how you can support Husky Athletics, through contributions, ticket purchases or other opportunities, please contact us at 206/543-2210.

There are hundreds more great Husky moments just waiting to happen....we hope you'll want to be a part of them.

1980-89

Husky Moment

The 1981 Rose Bowl

Washington, finishing the regular season with a 9-2 record and ranked 16th nationally in both polls, met Big Ten champion Michigan, the fifth-ranked team in the country, in the Rose Bowl under circumstances reminiscent of their 1978 meeting at the same venue. The Huskies again entered the Pasadena Classic as decided underdogs, but this time they could not pull off the upset. Rather than the drama of the 27-20 victory over Michigan just three years earlier, Washington suffered a disappointing 23-6 defeat despite outplaying the winners for the first half. The Huskies came out impressive, but there was a sense that nothing would go their way. On the third play of the game, Tom Flick found Aaron Williams over the middle, but only after the ball was tipped into his hands. The play went for 52 yards, but was called back due to offensive pass interference. On Washington's second possession, Flick marched the club 63 yards to just inside the Wolverine one-yard line. But on fourth-and-one from point-blank range, Toussaint Tyler was stopped for no gain. Although one official prematurely signalled a touchdown, he was overruled by the linesman. The Huskies again appeared to have scored a touchdown when center Mike Reilly snared Kyle Stevens' mid-air fumble midway through the second period, and ran it into the end zone, but the play was ruled dead. While Washington was outplaying its rival—the Huskies led in total offense 269-133—Michigan led 7-6 going into the locker room at half. The second half was a different story, i.e., all Michigan. The Huskies were held to just 10 third-quarter plays while Michigan scored 16 second-half points.

UW Media Relations

Tom Flick

Husky Spotlight

Washington's standout quarterback, Tom Flick, finished his career as the holder of Washington's all-time pass completion percentage record. He completed 252 of 418 passes—an accuracy rate of 60.3 percent. Flick took over the starting quarterback role late in the 1979 season and guided the Huskies to four wins in five games, including a victory against Texas in the Sun Bowl. During the 1980 season he passed for 2,178 yards, the second highest total in school history, trailing only Sonny Sixkiller's record of 2,303. He tossed 15 scoring passes that year to tie the Husky record also held by Chris Rowland (1973) and Sixkiller (1970). Flick passed his way into the record books early in the season when he connected with Willie Rosborough for an 84-yard score in a 50-7 rout of Air Force. His 316 passing yards against the Falcons would prove to be his career-best passing day. His most accurate passing day came as a senior against Arizona when he missed on only one try in 17 attempts, throwing for 230 yards. Flick guided the Huskies to the 1980 Pac-10 Championship and the Rose Bowl, wrapping up the berth with a 20-for-32 performance for 311 yards against Washington State. Flick was taken in the fourth round of the 1982 NFL draft by the Washington Redskins and would go on to play five years as a pro.

Husky Highlight

The Washington baseball team pieced together a six-game win streak, to finish the 1981 season as the Pac-10 Northern Division Champions. It marked the first time the diamondmen had won a championship since the 1959 season. The Huskies posted a 33-20 season the third-straight 30-win season under coach Bob MacDonald. Washington had to sweep a three-game series from Washington State, the 13-time defending league champions, to lay claim to the championship. Sporting a 10-6 (.625) league record, the Huskies felt they had won the title against the 11-7 Cougars (.611). However, Pac-10 commissioner Wiles Hallock ruled that two cancelled games with Oregon would have to be played because they could have an impact on the final league standings. Ironically, Oregon had announced it was dropping its baseball program and had concluded its season. The Huskies traveled to Eugene, needing to win both games to claim the title. A split would mean a three-way playoff in Corvallis involving Washington State and Oregon State. The Huskies beat the "lame" Ducks 5-4 in extra innings in the first game and 5-1 in the second game to again clinch the pennant. With no rest, the Huskies returned to Seattle to meet Southern Division runner-up Stanford a best-of-three playoff. If UW won, it would go on to meet Southern Division champion Arizona State. A Stanford win gave the Sun Devils the title outright. Led by right fielder John Elway, the Cardinal took the mini-series with 10-8 and 10-6 victories.

Husky Legend

Al Forney

Edmonds native Al Forney is considered one of the most successful rowers in the modern history of the sport at Washington. Much of Forney's acclaim was earned on international waters as a rower on several U.S. national teams. As a freshman at Washington, he was a member of the Huskies' Pac-10 championship team. He would go on to row for the 1980 team that toured Egypt, the 1981 crew that claimed the collegiate national championship and the Grand Challenge Cup at the Royal Henley Regatta. A swimmer and football player at Woodway High School, he did not start rowing until he enrolled at the University. As a senior, he was the team's co-captain and the president of the Varsity Boat Club. Forney was a member of the U.S. four-oared crew that won the gold medal at the World Championships in Lucerne, Switzerland. Many considered that the top international regatta of the year since the Soviet Union and East Germany would boycott that summer's Olympic Games in Los Angeles. Notably absent, however, from the World Championships was the team from New Zealand. The U.S. squad would encounter them at the Olympics finishing second to the Kiwis by a boat length for the silver medal. It was the first medal for the U.S in the straight fours since 1960. The 6-4 Forney rowed the stroke for the U.S. team at the Olympics. Forney almost did not make the Olympic squad. He had to win an ergometer test to gain the final position on the team. Forney's national-team stint included rowing in the eights for the U.S. at the 1982 and 1983 World Championships after serving as an alternate in 1981. Forney was inducted into the Husky Hall of Fame in 1996.

Husky List

Shutouts in Rose Bowl History

When Washington shutout Iowa 28-0 at the 1982 Rose Bowl, it marked the first time in 29 years a team did not score during the game. Up until the 2001 Rose Bowl, there had not been another shutout, making the Huskies' defensive effort the only one in 470 games.

Year	Team	Score	Year	Team	Score
1902	Michigan	49	1936	Stanford	7
	Stanford	0		Southern Methodist	0
1916	Washington St.	14	1937	Pittsburgh	21
	Brown	0		Washington	0
1917	Oregon	14	1938	California	13
	Pennsylvania	0		Alabama	0
1919	Great Lakes Navy	17	1940	USC	14
	Mare Island Marines	0		Tennessee	0
1921	California	28	1943	Georgia	9
	Ohio State	0		UCLA	0
1922	California	0	1944	USC	29
	Washington & Jefferson	0		Washington	0
1931	Alabama	24	1945	USC	25
	Washington State	0		Tennessee	0
1933	USC	35	1948	Michigan	49
	Pittsburgh	0		USC	0
1934	Columbia	7	1953	USC	7
	Stanford	0		Wisconsin	0
			1982	Washington	28
				Iowa	0

THE blades of the Washington men's crew team have cut through many bodies of water across the world, but probably no place as famous as the Nile in Egypt. In 1980 the Huskies returned to the Mideast to compete in the "Festival of Oars" on Dec. 23 and then move on to row in the 10th annual Nile River International Rowing Regatta on Dec. 28. The trip marked the fourth straight year the Huskies had traveled to Egypt. Washington made its first trip in 1977 after being invited as the champions of the Grand Challenge Cup at the Royal Henley Regatta. In 1980, head coach Dick Erickson, assistant coach Bob Ernst and 12 oarsmen and a coxswain made the trip from Seattle. Competing for Washington were John Christiansen, Mike Crustolo, Gary Dohrn, Al Erickson, Gary Evans (cox), Al Forney, Gregg Hoffman, Blair Horn, Jan Janjnic, Dave Lauber, Guy Lawrence and Charles Van Pelt. Erickson had to be careful in his selections because the boats they would row in were constructed for smaller bodies. Racing only in an eight-oar race, the Huskies competed against teams from Canada, Ireland, Great Britain, West Germany and Egypt. The Huskies placed second to a U.S. national team while Harvard's third-place showing gave the American a sweep of the top three spots. In Cairo, the U.S. national team took first place again in the eights but by just two-tenths of a second. The Husky fours finished second to an Egyptian team. The Huskies returned to Egypt again in 1982. In 1981 a crew made up of rowers from two Egyptian club teams rowed in the Opening Day races.

1980 W 1981

Husky Moment

Ernst Takes Over Women's Crew

After working as the men's assistant crew coach for seven years, at age 34, Bob Ernst took over the Washington women's program in 1980. He replaced John Lind and immediately began to mend some rifts that had developed in the program from rowers who had quit due to training tactics they questioned. It was not Ernst's first experience coaching women's teams. He coached the U.S. Olympic team in 1980 that competed in Switzerland and Amsterdam during the boycott of the games in Moscow. His stint with the U.S. women's national team began in 1976 when he was named an assistant coach. Ernst had developed a successful reputation with the Husky men's team. His freshmen scullers won the Pac-10 title all seven years he coached them. Ernst's plans for the women's program included the open boat classification and de-emphasizing the lightweight program. He was also a proponent of weight training to develop power. He was so committed to the program that he lived in an apartment in the Conibear Shellhouse the first year he coached the UW women. His philosophies worked as Washington went on to completely dominate the collegiate rowing scene during the decade. Ernst grew up in California and broke into the rowing profession at UC Irvine. His 1974 team placed second to Washington at the Western Sprints, prompting Erickson to offer him the vacated assistant men's coaching position. Ernst will forever be a part of the athletic tradition at UC Irvine. As an undergrad, he and several friends helped to give the school its unique nickname of the Anteaters.

UW Media Relations

Husky Spotlight

Lisa Baughn, Volleyball All-American

Lisa Baughn became the first volleyball player at Washington to earn All-America honors. In 1980 she led the Huskies from her middle blocker position to a 25-9 record that included a 12-0 mark in the Northwest Women's Volleyball League. The team was ranked ninth in the preseason poll and lived up to those expectations by winning its first-ever regional championship. Baughn and four other Husky players competed for the University Club team that qualified for the United States Volleyball Association Junior Nationals. Ranked as high as eighth during the season, Washington placed 10th at the 1980 AIAW national championships. A year earlier the Huskies finished 11th in the tournament. At just 5-10, Baughn was considered short for her position. She came to Washington after earning prep honors at Montlake Terrace High School and attending Edmonds Community College as a freshman. In 1981, as a senior, Baughn saw her chances as repeating as an All-American cut short when she missed a third of the season due to a stress fracture in her right shin. Her sister, Cheryl, also played volleyball at Washington. Baughn was named to the *Seattle Times* all-century volleyball team.

Husky Highlight

Joyce Caps Impressive Freshman Season

Regina Joyce showed in April of 1981 that she would be the person to beat in the 3,000 meters at the AIAW national championships. Competing at the Northwest College Women's Sports Association meet, she took first place with a time of 8:59.39 to become the first American collegian to break the nine-minute mark. North Carolina State's Julie Shea held the old record of 9:02.6. Joyce was never really challenged at the AIAW nationals in Austin, Texas on May 30. She led from wire to wire in the 3,000 meters to become Washington's first women's national champion in track. She won in a time of 9:02, breaking the meet record by more than seven seconds and bettering her victory in the qualifying heat by 34 seconds. Joyce never lost a 3,000-meter race during the season. The meet capped off a tremendous freshman year for Joyce. She had run the fastest 1,500-meter time (4:13.2) in the nation that season, but bypassed the event at the AIAW nationals to concentrate on the longer distance. During the fall she placed sixth at the 1980 AIAW Cross Country championships to become the first All-American for the Huskies in that sport.

UW Media Relations

Husky Legend

1981 Women's Crew

The 1981 Washington's women's crew team will long be remembered for laying the foundation of success that would stretch into the next millennium. Armed with a newfound enthusiasm for the sport, boosted by first-year coach Bob Ernst, the Huskies shocked the rowing world that spring. The first sign of Washington's resurgence came during the Opening Day races when the Huskies upset California, the defending national champions. The Bears' shell had five returning rowers from its championship squad. It marked the first time the Huskies had defeated Cal in Seattle and UW did it convincingly, winning all three races. Washington beat Stanford to win the Pacific Coast Championship and then did its part to insure a legitimate national championship would take place on Oakland's Lake Merritt. Several days before the Eastern Sprints were to be held, the Washington team sent a telegram to the Yale women's squad that said: "Fellow oarswomen: We just want to give you our support at the upcoming Eastern Sprints. We'd love to see you beat Princeton." Princeton, the favorite to win the Eastern Sprints, was not scheduled to row at the nationals. Yale pulled off the upset, setting up a true national championship race. During the preliminary heats the Huskies defeated Yale and Boston University with a time of 3:21.3 on the 1,000-meter course. In the finals, Washington crossed the finish line first in a time of 3:20.8 while Yale was second in a time of 3:22.9. The Husky junior varsity rowers defeated Wisconsin to give the Huskies a sweep of the top two races. The Huskies finished fourth in both the novice eight and four-with-coxswain races. The varsity eight shell was rowed by Shyril O'Steen, Kristi Norelius, Peg Achterman, Karen Mohling, Susan Broome, Madeline Hanson, Debbie Moore, Jane McDougall (stroke) and Lisa Horn (coxswain).

Husky Lists

Volleyball All-Americans

1980 - Lisa Baughn, AIAW First Team
1988 - Laurie Wetzel, AVCA First Team
1988 - Melinda Beckenhauer, AVCA Second Team
1989 - Melinda Beckenhauer, AVCA First Team
1996 - Angela Bransom, AVCA First Team
1997 - Makare Desilets, AVCA First Team

AVCA - American Volleyball Coaches Association
AIAW - Association of Intercollegiate Athletics for Women

EDEAN IHLANFELDT is the woman responsible for launching the women's golf team at Washington, and she never took a dime for the job she loved so much during her coaching career. When Washington expanded its athletic lineup to include women's sports, Kit Green hired Ihlanfeldt, one of the area's top players, to coach the Huskies. Armed with an envelope of names and addresses of women who signed up to play, she started the program in 1974 before retiring eight years later in 1981 at the age of 50. During her eight-year coaching career, Ihlanfeldt never accepted payment for her coaching duties. Instead, she donated her salary back for scholarships. Three of Ihlanfeldt's teams and five individuals qualified for the AIAW championships. During her tenure, Washington was the only northwest team to qualify for the nationals. Two of her players, Robin Walton and Mary Lou Mulflur went on to appear on the professional tour and several others became club pros. Ihlanfeldt was no stranger to championship golf. Her list of victories included five PNGA titles, six Montana State championships, three Washington State titles, four Seattle City championships, the Trans-Mississippi title and the Canadian Open Championship. The Washington women's golf program named its fall golf invitational in her honor. She was inducted into the Husky Hall of Fame in 1989.

1981 W 1982

Husky Moment

The 1982 Rose Bowl

Washington, 9-2 in regular-season play, entered the 1982 Rose Bowl in a familiar position—as underdogs. For the fourth time in four postseason appearances, the Huskies' bowl opponent was rated the favorite, and for the third time, Don James' club ignored the odds. Washington recorded the first Rose Bowl shutout in 28 years, a 28-0 whitewash of Big Ten champion Iowa. The two clubs battled to a scoreless tie after one quarter, although Washington did get inside the Hawkeye 30-yard line twice thanks to the Husky kicking game. First cornerback Ray Horton returned an Iowa punt 48 yards to the Iowa 29, then punter Jeff Partridge was roughed in the act to keep another drive going until it stalled at the Hawkeye 28. Eventual Rose Bowl MVP Jacque Robinson broke the scoring ice early in the second period, bulling over from one yard out to cap a 65-yard drive. Robinson romped for 34 yards on seven carries during the drive. Washington upped its lead to 13-0 just 0:19 before the half when fullback Vince Coby smashed over from a yard out to climax a 60-yard march. Iowa made its deepest penetration in the third period—to the Husky 29—but was stymied by a Ken Driscoll interception. Robinson took over again in the final stanza, gaining 66 yards on three carries, including the final 34 yards on a nifty run up the right side to cap a 69-yard drive that put the Huskies ahead 21-0. The UW onslaught ended with quarterback Tim Cowan's three-yard reverse with 7:13 to go. Washington took advantage of two Iowa fumbles and picked off three Hawkeye passes to turn the tide in its favor. Robinson gained 142 net yards on just 20 carries to pace the ground game, and quarterback Steve Pelluer completed 15-of-29 passes for another 142 yards. Inside linebackers Mark Jerue (13) and Ken Driscoll (11) led the stop troops. Driscoll and defensive backs Vince Newsome and Derek Harvey each grabbed an enemy pass.

UW Media Relations

Jacque Robinson scores Washington's first touchdown in a 28-0 victory against Iowa.

Husky Spotlight

The 1981-82 Husky men's basketball team became the first to win a postseason game since the 1953 season when Washington reached the NCAA Final Four. Coach Marv Harshman's 11th edition of Husky basketball featured forwards Dan Caldwell and Brad Watson, center Kenny Lyles and guards Steve Jackson and Steve Burks. Caldwell led the team in both scoring and rebounding with 13.6 and 6.9 averages. The team also featured a freshman named Detlef Schrempf. The Huskies looked like they might be a contender for a spot in the NCAA tournament when they put together a 10-game win streak winning 14 of 15 games at midseason. However the Huskies lost their last five regular-season games to boast an 18-9 record heading into the NIT. The Huskies were picked in the preseason Pac-10 poll to place ninth, but they eventually climbed as high as 19th in the national polls. At one point the team was 17-3 overall and 10-1 in the conference. The Huskies had to play five of their final seven regular-season games on the road. The Huskies finished fourth in the Pac-10 with an 11-7 record. In the NIT, the Huskies defeated BYU 66-63 in the opening round of play. The Huskies trailed by 12 at halftime, but the Cougars came out cold at the start of the second half, scoring just two points in six minutes. Burks shook off a late-season scoring slump to lead the Huskies with 23 points. In the second round Washington played host to Texas A&M and lost 69-65.

Husky Highlight

Washington Defense Sets Record

Pacific did not figure to pose a serious threat to the Husky football team when the two faced off in Husky Stadium in 1981. The Huskies broke out to a 24-0 lead and coasted to a 34-14 victory that saw the Washington defense hold the Tigers to a school-record -50 rushing yards. Pacific quarterback Sander Markel was accountable for most of the lost yardage on numerous sacks. He still managed to connect on 23 of 36 passes for 222 yards and a pair of scores. Pacific had 31 rushing attempts and gained 39 gross yards but suffered 89 yards of lost yardage. Markel lost 52 yards on nine attempts. Tony Caldwell and Ray Cattage led the Husky effort with three sacks apiece. The rushing total set a Pac-10 record for fewest rushing yards. The old mark was -43 rushing yards by Portland in a game against Oregon State in 1946.

Husky Legend

Marv Harshman

UW Media Relations

In 1971 Marv Harshman became the 14th head basketball coach in the Washington program's history. During his Husky coaching career, his teams compiled 246 wins, placing him second on the school's all-time coaching victories list. He ended his career with a record of 246-146, a winning percentage of .628. Harshman still ranks among the 20th winningest Division I coaches of all time with 654 career victories combined at Washington, Washington State and Pacific Lutheran. He coached in 1,090 collegiate games, the third-highest total in Division I history behind only Dean Smith (1,133) and Henry Iba (1,105). Harshman directed the Huskies to four 20-win seasons, with five teams competing in postseason play including three trips to the NCAA tournament. He garnered many honors while at UW, including induction into the National Basketball Hall of Fame and a stint as the president of the National Association of Basketball Coaches. Harshman taught over 500 athletes the game of basketball while coaching at Washington as well as Pacific Lutheran and Washington State. He concluded his Washington career with back-to-back Pac-10 championships in 1984 and 1985. Harshman attended Lake Stevens (Wash.) High School and was an undergrad at Pacific Lutheran in Tacoma, Washington where he was a two-time All-America basketball selection. He graduated in 1942 with a degree in biological science and then joined the U.S. Navy in which he served until 1946. Harshman began coaching at his alma mater, PLU where he served 13 years (1946-58) and compiled a 241-121 record. He spent the next 13 seasons at Washington State where he posted a 155-181 record from 1959 to 1971.

Husky List

Washington's Morris Trophy Winners

The Morris Trophy is awarded annually to the top offensive and defensive linemen in the Pac-10 Conference. What makes the award unique is its voting system. The league's offensive players vote on the top defensive lineman and the defensive players select the top offensive lineman. The annual presentation is made during the Rose Bowl Hall of Fame ceremonies in Pasadena.

Year	Player, Position
1981	Fletcher Jenkins, defensive tackle
1984	Ron Holmes, defensive tackle
1986	Reggie Rogers, defensive tackle
1989	Bern Brostek, center
1990	Steve Emtman, defensive tackle
1991	Steve Emtman, defensive tackle
1991	Lincoln Kennedy, offensive tackle
1992	Lincoln Kennedy, offensive tackle
1993	D'Marco Farr, defensive tackle
1996	Bob Sapp, offensive tackle
1997	Olin Kreutz, center
2000	Chad Ward, guard

The Wave

DESPITE claims by others, the Wave can trace its origin back to Husky Stadium. It was Oct. 31, 1981 when former cheerleader Rob Weller (yes, the same Rob Weller who once co-hosted Entertainment Tonight) was back on the sidelines and instructed the Washington crowd to start in one section and make a human wave that rolled around Husky Stadium. The original Wave saw Husky fans remain standing until the a full circle was completed in the stadium. Weller's original idea—working with former Husky band director Bill Bissell—was to have the crowd stand rapidly from the lowest seats to the highest. But they could not effectively coordinate the attempts. The Wave is believed to have started in the third quarter as the Huskies reeled off 28 points en route to a 42-31 win over the John Elway led Stanford team. Weller was a yell-leader at Washington from 1969 to 1972 and was extremely popular with the student section.

1981 W 1982

HUSKY MOMENT

Women's Crew National Champs

The Washington women's crew team had to overcome several challenges to win its second straight national rowing title. First, the distance of the race was extended from 1,000 meters to 1,500 meters, a length the eastern crew programs were more used to rowing. It was a move that did not sit well with Husky coach Bob Ernst since most international races were contested at 1,000 meters. Second was the weather. Racing on Lake Waramug in Kent, Connecticut, the event was almost swamped by the stormy conditions. On June 5, during the heat races, the Huskies had to contend with gale winds and six inches of rain that dropped in the area during the day. The powerful Husky varsity eight crew ignored the weather and steamed past Brown University for a five-second victory. Ernst had his team practice on Friday during similar stormy conditions just in case the storm front stayed in the area throughout the weekend. It did and Ernst's decision paid off. On Sunday, the race officials decided to push back the 10 a.m. start time to 5:30 p.m. By race time the conditions were actually worse, and the direction of the course was reversed due to the gusty winds that reached 25 knots. The Huskies grabbed the lead by the 500-meter mark and stretched that out to three-quarters of a length by the 1,000-meter mark. The Huskies won their second national title with a time of 4:56.4 while Wisconsin grabbed second place with a time of 4:59. Boston University was third followed by Yale, Stanford and Cornell. "This time they expected us to win and we were happy to accommodate them," Ernst said. "We proved to them we can beat them at their own distance. Last year we won by two seconds, this year it was by twice that margin. If they put on another 500 meters we'll win by twice that distance." For the second year in a row, the junior varsity boat also took first-place honors by defeating Boston University 5:08.7 to 5:14.7. The Husky varsity eight rowers were: Loren Smith, Karen Mohling, Susan Broome, Peg Achterman, Margie Cate, Kristi Norelius, Julie Baker, Jane McDougall and Lisa Horn (cox).

Husky Spotlight

The emerging Washington women's gymnastics program was represented at the 1982 NCAA championships by sophomore Suzie Sun. The Portland native finished 19th in the all-around competition at the national meet. Sun's career at Washington almost did not happen. She was ready to retire from the sport at age 18, but former Husky coach Ed Zimmer talked her into continuing while she was concluding her club career. Sun's career at Washington was almost cut short during her freshman season when she suffered a sever knee injury that eliminated her chances of competing at the NCAAs and threatened her career. She returned to the NCAAs as a senior in 1984 and placed 36th as the Husky team posted an eighth-place finish. Sun concluded her career as the school record holder in the all-around and floor exercise.

UW Media Relations

HUSKY HIGHLIGHT

Jeb Best was one of the key components in the Husky baseball team's resurgence early in the decade of the 1980s. He lettered at Washington from 1979 to 1982 and earned All-Pac 10 Northern Division honors three times. He was honored as a third baseman in 1979 and as an outfielder in 1981 and 1982. During his four-year career the Huskies compiled a 126-75-1 record and won the Pac-10 North title in 1981. Best, who played all three positions in the outfield, went four-for-seven in his final plate appearance to bat .401 as a senior. That allowed him to post back-to-back .400 batting averages for his final two Husky seasons. When he finished his career, Best was truly the best. He owned career marks for at bats (673), runs (155), hits (264), runs batted in (157) and doubles (40). He had tied the career marks for games played and home runs. Almost 20 years later, Best still ranked in the top 10 of nine of Washington's 12 career hitting categories. After he concluded his Husky career, Best signed with the Seattle Mariners.

UW Media Relations

Jeb Best

Husky Legend

UW Media Relations

Carlin McClary

When Carlin McClary played for the Husky women's basketball team from 1978 to 1982, she was continuing a long family tradition of athletics at Washington. McClary's father, Doug, was well known as a forward for Washington's basketball team from 1951-53, helping the Huskies to a pair of Pacific Coast championships. He started for the 1953 team that placed third in the NCAA tournament. McClary's grandfather, Hal, was a dominating center for Hec Edmundson's teams from 1928-30. He was twice named to the Coast League North Division all-star team. But McClary's family tradition did not stop there. Her uncle, Dave, lettered in baseball at Washington, and her grandmother, Roberta, participated in a number of sports as an undergrad and at one point held the national record for the discus. Carlin proved early on that she would make her family proud. As a freshman she averaged 17 points and 10.9 rebounds per game. Although her scoring average dropped slightly in every subsequent season (16.0 as a sophomore, 11.6 as a junior and 9.0 as a senior), she became the first Husky player to score 1,000 points in a career. She finished her career as Washington's all-time leading scorer with 1,508 points and the all-time rebounding champion with 982. She held that record until 1999 when Amber Hall concluded her UW career with 1,003 rebounds. McClary started in 109 of the 112 games she played in. As a sophomore she scored 38 points in a game against Seattle University to set a Husky scoring record. That mark stood up for 11 years until Shaunda Green had a 39-point game, in double overtime, in 1991. McClary set a freshman scoring record with a 31-point game against Seattle University.

HUSKY LIST

Winningest Men's Soccer Seasons

Despite posting a 17-3-1 record, the Husky men's soccer team was passed over for a berth in the 1981 NCAA soccer tournament.

Year	Record	Pct.
1982	18-2-1	.881
1977	14-2-1	.853
1983	17-3-1	.833
1981	17-3-1	.833
1976	15-2-3	.825
1996	15-3-1	.816
1980	17-4-0	.810
1997	15-3-2	.800
1984	14-3-2	.790
1992	15-3-3	.786
1974	15-3-3	.786
1973	15-4-4	.739

WHEN *Seattle Post-Intelligencer* artist Bob McCausland first began a Washington football cartoon in 1959, his main character didn't have a name, walked on all fours and looked a little ferocious. That soon changed as his main character, the skinny, upright Hairbreadth Husky sporting a booster hat and a large letterman's jacket appeared each week during the football season for the next 22 years. The newspaper carried two Hairbreadth cartoons weekly, one before and one after each game. Those cartoons were enjoyed by coaches, team members, fans and even opposing teams until 1981 when the P-I stopped carrying Hairbreadth Husky. A collection including 240 of McCausland's best cartoon was published in a 1982 book entitled *Hairbreadth Husky*.

1982 W 1983

Husky Moment

Men's Crew vs. Harvard at Nationals

While the Washington men's varsity eight did not bring home the gold medal from the 1983 national championship regatta, the Huskies brought home memories of participating in one of the greatest collegiate races in modern history. Contested on Lake Harsha, just outside of Cincinnati, the race featured the Huskies, Harvard, Brown, and Yale. There would be no preliminary heat races or repechages scheduled. It was a one-race dash for the national title. It was truly a Final Four of rowing. Harvard had won the Eastern Sprints, Brown took first place at the IRA regatta, Yale returned five oarsmen from its 1982 team that won the inaugural Cincinnati regatta and the Huskies had won the Pacific Coast Rowing Championship. Not everything at the regatta was smooth sailing. The Huskies found themselves on the water for 72 minutes before the race started. First, a motor launch got its propeller entangled in a buoy line. Then, a seat popped lose on the Brown boat that required repairs. When the race finally began, the Huskies grabbed the early lead as coach Dick Erickson had instructed his team to do. The Huskies found themselves with a three-quarters length lead with 500 meters to go, when Harvard began a strong move. The two boats crossed the finished line virtually even. Two race officials using hand-held stopwatches compared their times and decided Washington was the winner. However, after a 15-minute review of a video tape, Harvard was declared the winners by two feet. It was the Washington varsity eight's first loss of the season. Officially the Crimson was clocked at 5:59.6 and the Huskies at 6:00. "We hadn't really had to sprint in any of our races, and we really didn't pull it off smoothly," said Husky coxswain Lee Miller. "We raced a really good race, I thought, but they just taught us how to wind it up. Brown finished third and Yale was fourth. Interestingly, Harvard rowed in the only wooden boat at the event. The other three teams used the more modern carbon-fiber shells.

Husky Spotlight

When it comes to catching footballs, few Washington players did it with as much flair as Paul Skansi. As a prep player from Gig Harbor, Skansi had a hard time convincing the Huskies he was worthy of a scholarship. Just six games into his freshman season, Skansi was a starter in the Husky lineup. That season he went on to earn Most Valuable Player honors for Washington in the Huskies' 14-7 Sun Bowl victory against Texas. He had five receptions in that game. Skansi would go on to become the all-time leading receiver in Washington history with 138 catches, breaking Scott Phillips' six-year-old record of 111 catches. Skansi led Washington in receiving in three of his four seasons. He was a team captain as a senior in 1982 and was named to the all-Pac-10 team in addition to earning honorable mention All-America honors. Skansi appeared in four bowl games as a Husky, including a pair of Rose Bowls, catching passes for quarterbacks Steve Pelluer and Tim Cowan. He caught 10 passes in Washington's 21-20 Aloha Bowl victory against Maryland. At just 5-9, Skansi was not the prototype college receiver. He was considered even more of a long shot as a professional player. He once again proved those critics wrong. Pittsburgh drafted him in the fifth round and he played one season with the Steelers before being cut. He then signed with the Seattle Seahawks where he played for nine seasons.

Husky Highlight

When Arizona upset Arizona State, costing the Sun Devils a shot at the Rose Bowl, that moved Washington out of the Fiesta Bowl and into the inaugural Aloha Bowl in Honolulu. It was the first time in 35 years a bowl game was played on the Hawaiian Islands. Tim Cowan's brilliant passing performance (33-53-0-350) brought Washington back from a 20-14 deficit for a 21-20 victory over Maryland in the game. Twice during Washington's final drive Cowan ran for first downs on fourth-down situations and found Anthony Allen for a first down on yet another fourth-down call. With third down on the Maryland 11 with 0:12 left, Cowan looked into the left corner of the end zone and found Allen free for the tying touchdown. Chuck Nelson's extra point gave Washington the 21-20 victory. Cowan's 33 completions and 363 yards in total offense were both UW historical bests (bowl games not officially included in Husky records) and his 350-yard passing performance had been bettered only three times. Allen also had an exceptional game with eight catches for 152 yards. Cowan was voted offensive MVP while Husky linebacker Tony Caldwell was named defensive MVP. The final drive was all Cowan as the senior quarterback either ran or passed the ball on 15 of 16 plays in marching the Huskies down the field. The victory enabled Washington to finish 10-2 and be ranked No. 7 in both wire service polls.

Husky Legend

Chuck Nelson

UW Media Relations

At the age of nine, Chuck Nelson finished sixth in the national Punt-Pass-and-Kick competition. In 1982 Nelson, a placekicker on the Washington football team, capped a terrific Husky career by being named a first-team All-American by the *Associated Press, United Press International,* the Walter Camp Football Foundation, the *Football News* and the Football Writers Association. He was Washington's first consensus All-American in 16 years. In addition to all of his national honors, Nelson was also recognized by the *Everett Herald* and the *Seattle Post-Intelligencer* as the region's athlete of the year. He finished his senior season as the owner of eight NCAA records, 14 Pac-10 records and 14 Washington records. Over his junior and senior seasons Nelson booted 30 consecutive field goals to crush the old NCAA record of 16 shared by Ish Ordonez of Arkansas (1978-79) and Dale Castro of Maryland (1970). As a senior he made 25 of 26 field goals (.962) with his only miss coming in the Apple Cup against Washington State. Nelson scored 109 points as a senior to give him 271 in his career to better Hugh McElhenny's career scoring mark of 233 points he set between 1949-51. During his three-year Husky career, Nelson made 92 of 95 PATs and 59 of 72 field goals. His career accuracy for field goals (81.9 percent) was one of his NCAA records. During his last two years he made 41 of 46 (.891) field goal attempts. He was far more accurate than such highly regarded collegiate kickers as Tony Franklin (.554) and Russel Erxleben (.628) and Nelson had to do much of his kicking in the windy conditions of Husky Stadium. Nelson's career did not get off to a great start. In his first game against Air Force he missed his first extra-point conversion, ending a streak of 111 straight by UW kickers, and also misfired on two field goal attempts. Husky coach Don James gave him another chance at the end of the first half, and Nelson booted a 46-yard field goal that launched his successful career. Nelson also excelled in the classroom where he earned Pac-10 All-Academic honors from 1980-82. He was an Academic All-American in 1982, the recipient of an NCAA post-graduate scholarship and the Pac-10 Medalist in 1983.

Husky List

Chuck Nelson's NCAA Records

Category	No.
Consecutive field goals	30
Field goals in a half	4
FGs per game, career	1.79
3 or more FGs per game, season	5
3 or more FGs per game, career	9
Field goals, three seasons	59
FG-PAT pct., season	.983
Points per game, career	8.21
Points kicking, career	271

Husky Lore

IN 1999 Whitepaw's Arlut Spirit of Gold Dust ("Spirit") made his debut as Washington's sideline mascot . He was the 10th Alaskan Malamute to serve as the Husky mascot. The Husky mascot leads the team out of the tunnel before every home game and wanders the sidelines during the contest accompanied by trainer Kim Cross and several of Cross' children, who act as handlers. The previous mascots were Frosty I (1922-29), Frosty II (1930-36), Wasky (1946), Wasky II (1947-53), Ski (1954-57), Denali (1958), King Chinook (1959-68), Regent Denali (1969-80), Sundodger (1981-91), King Redoubt (1992-97) and Prince Redoubt (1998). The Sigma Alpha Epsilon fraternity acquired the first dog, Frosty I, and acted as its handlers. In 1959 Harry Cross, a professor of law at the University, took over the dog handler duties with King Chinook. Chinook's first appearance was the Idaho game that season. Cross' son, Kim, watched the dog on the sidelines.

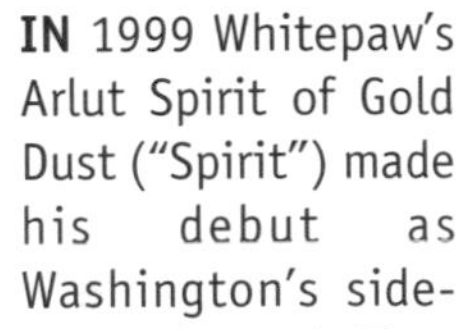

UW Media Relations

1982 W 1983

Husky Moment

Women's Crew National Champs

The national women's collegiate rowing championships were quickly becoming the Husky Invitational, and 1983 Washington team only added to that legacy. Racing on Lake Wingrd in Madison, Wisconsin, the Huskies won their third straight national titles in both the varsity eight and junior varsity shells. Both teams won by one and one-half lengths on the 1,000-meter course in rainy conditions. The Husky varsity rowed the course in 4:57.1 to better second-place Dartmouth's 5:03.02 effort. The host school, Wisconsin, challenged the Huskies in the first 500 meters before placing third in a time of 5:03.06. The anticipated battle between the Huskies and Eastern Sprint champion Boston University never transpired. The Terriers did not win their heat race and had to qualify for the finals through the repechage. In the finals, Boston University placed a disappointing fifth. The junior varsity turned in a winning time of 5:17.40 to beat Wisconsin to the finish line by 5.5 seconds. The victorious varsity shell, named Bodacious, was rowed by Julie Baker, Eleanor McElvaine, Sara Nevin, Ellen Pottmeyer, Jan Fulton, Karen Mohling, Maureen King, Loren Smith and Betsy Beard directed the team as the coxswain. It was Mohling's third national title. The 24-year-old fifth-year student from Chicago served as the team captain. Baker and Smith both rowed in their second consecutive championship shell.

Husky Spotlight

The Husky men's soccer team capped a one-loss regular season with an invitation to the NCAA championships in 1982. It was Washington's first post-season appearance since 1978 and would be the last until the 1989 campaign. The Huskies lost in the opening round of the tournament 3-2 to San Francisco when the Dons outscored Washington 4-1 in a shootout. San Francisco's scoring total was uncommon for a UW opponent. as the Huskies outscored their opponents 62 to 11. Washington recorded 14 shutouts during its 20 regular-season games behind the stellar goaltending of Mark Schuur. He had 56 saves during the year and registered a goals against average of just .056 per game. Schuur was credited with all 14 shutouts. Offensively the Huskies were led by Mike Enneking's 16 goals and John Klein's nine assists. A total of five Huskies were named to the All-Northwest Collegiate Soccer Conference team. Enneking and Schuur were joined on the squad by midfielder Mike Park, defender Steve Englebrick and forward Tad Willoughby. Washington was undefeated in league play, posting a 6-0-1 record. The Huskies finished the year with an overall record of 18-2-1. Simon Fraser (1-0) was the only other team to defeat the Huskies. Frank Gallo, the conference coach of the year, resigned in February after posting a 51-9-2 record in three seasons. Gallo was only a part-time coach earning $3,000 a year and could no longer afford the time commitment based on his salary.

Husky Highlight

Regina Joyce Second at NCAA Cross Country Championships

The fact junior Regina Joyce finished second at the 1982 NCAA women's cross country championships in Bloomington, Indiana was not a shock to running enthusiasts. The fact the Husky team placed 14th overall at the competition was. The Huskies surprised the field at the NCAA regional championship by bettering California for the third and final spot at the national meet. Joyce's second-place finish marked the fourth time in her Husky running career that she was named an All-American. She ran the 5,000-meter course in a time of 17:07, trailing only Virginia's Lesley Welch, who won the national title in a time of 16:30.7. Joyce placed higher than Stanford's Ceci Hopp, who defeated her at the regional championships. "Regina ran the best race she's ever run," said Washington coach Al Bonney after the meet. Bonney changed Joyce and the Huskies' training routine in preparation for the season, focusing on longer distances during their practice sessions.

Husky Legend

Regina Joyce

UW Media Relations

Regina Joyce will long be remembered as the first great women's long distance runner at Washington. Ironically, she traveled a great distance just to be a Husky. A native of Sussex, England, she gave up running for three years after she turned 17 only to take up the sport again to lose some weight. She enjoyed running so much she decided to return to competitive racing. The summer before her freshman year at Washington, she won the United Kingdom's 3,000-meter championship at London's fabled Crystal Palace in a time of 9:13.8. Thanks to several coaching connections, she selected Washington over Clemson as her American college of choice and enrolled in 1980 as a 23-year-old freshman. Regina, which means Queen in Latin, truly ruled the Husky track scene. She placed sixth at the 1980 AIAW cross country championship to become the Huskies' first female All-American in the sport. That spring she won the 3,000 meters at the AIAW championships, establishing herself as the first UW woman to win a national title. Records tumbled at Joyce's feet. She set national records in several events. As a freshman, while winning the NCWSA regional championship, she set the national collegiate record in the 3,000 meters with a time of 8:59.39. That same year she turned in the nation's top 1,500-meter mark with a time of 4:12.7 She helped the Washington women to break the American collegiate record in the distance medley relay with a time of 11:05.8 at the Martin Luther King games at Stanford in March of 1981. Joyce was 12th at the 1981 NCAA cross country championships and placed second in the 1982 event. She finished fifth at the 1983 NCAA 10,000 meters and she won the first marathon she entered—the 1983 Fiesta Bowl Marathon—running the 14th fastest race in history with a time of 2:32.56. Joyce had been sidelined that spring by a series of freak accidents, including a broken collarbone she suffered in a road race and a bruising encounter with a car in another. In 1984 she opted to run the marathon at the summer Olympic Games for Ireland, the homeland of her parents. She was joined on the Irish national team by her sister Monica.

Husky List

Washington and the Final Four

The University of Washington has played host to the men's Final Four five times during the history of the tournament. As of 2000, the time when the Kingdome was demolished, only three other cities, Kansas City (10), New York (7) and Louisville (6) had hosted the event more than Seattle.

Year	Champion	Score	Runner-Up	Attendance	Site
1949	Kentucky	46-36	Oklahoma State	10,600	Edmundson Pavilion
1952	Kansas	80-63	St. John's	10,700	Edmundson Pavilion
1984	Georgetown	84-75	Houston	38,471	Kingdome
1989	Michigan	80-79 OT	Seton Hall	39,187	Kingdome
1995	UCLA	89-78	Arkansas	38,540	Kingdome

IN track lingo, it is known as a "blanket finish." When so many competitors cross the finish line at the same time it requires a true photo finish to reveal the winner. That's what took place at the 1983 NCAA track and field championships in the 400-meter relay race that featured Washington's quartet of Sterling Hinds, Byron Howell, Dennis Brown and LaNoris Marshall. The quartet was better known as the "Atomic Dogs." Brown ran the first leg and got the Huskies out to the early lead. However, Washington's second baton exchange between Hinds and Howell was not clean and cost the team precious hundredths of a second. Marshall ran the last leg and faced the daunting task of holding off Tennessee's world-class sprinter Willie Gault. Trailing by seven yards on the final exchange, Gault reeled in the field and forced the photo finish. The final determination was Tennessee edged the Huskies for first place by three-hundredths of a second. The Volunteers' winning time was 39.22 to 39.25 for the Huskies. Georgia placed third with a time of 39.27. Washington's time established a school record. The Husky team was an interesting mix of athletes molded by first-year sprint coach Clyde Duncan. Brown and Hinds were recruited to play football at Washington while Howell was a member of the basketball team. Washington was not expected to be a serious challenger for the NCAA title after placing eighth at the conference championships. Allergy problems had slowed Hinds during the Pac-10 competition.

1983 W 1984

HUSKY MOMENT

Men's Basketball Wins Pac-10 Championship

Marv Harshman's best Washington basketball team came during his 13th season when the Huskies posted a 24-7 record, tied Oregon State for first in the Pac-10 with a 15-3 mark, and advanced to the Sweet 16 of the NCAA tournament. The conference championship was the first by a Washington squad since 1953 and the win total was the best in 31 years. The Husky lineup was made up of forwards Detlef Schrempf and Paul Fortier, center Christian Welp and guards Shag Williams and Alvin Vaughn. Schrempf led the team in both scoring (16.8 points per game) and rebounding (7.4 rebounds per game). After opening the season with a victory against Texas Tech, the Huskies lost their next two games to No. 12 LSU and New Mexico before going on a tear. Washington won 12 of its next 13 contests and proved to be tough in close games, winning three overtime affairs, including two that took three extra periods to decide. By the end of the season, the Huskies found themselves ranked 15th in the final basketball rankings. Ironically, the Huskies were sent to Pullman, where Harshman coached Washington State for 13 seasons, for their NCAA matchup with Nevada. Behind Schrempf's 23 points and 13 rebounds, Washington dispatched the Wolfpack 64-54, setting up a second-round game with 14th-ranked Duke. The Huskies found themselves trailing the Blue Devils 43-35 at halftime, but Harshman and his staff told the team to be patient and take advantage of opportunities when they presented themselves. Washington went on a 10-2 scoring spurt to start the second half and tie the game. The Huskies stretched that into a 16-to-four scoring run to grab a 51-47 lead. Shooting a school-record 77.8 percent (31 of 44) from the field, Washington held off Duke down the stretch for an 80-78 victory. Schrempf hit 11 of 14 shots to lead the team with 30 points. With the Final Four scheduled for the Kingdome, the Huskies found themselves just two games away from playing for the national championship in their own back yard. Against Dayton in the Sweet 16, Washington's shooting turned cold, and the Flyers ended the Huskies' championship run with a 64-58 defeat. Roosevelt Chapman keyed the Dayton upset with 22 points while Schrempf scored 18 points and added 11 rebounds for Washington. At the conclusion of the season, Harshman was named the Kodak Division I coach of the year. With the announced retirement of DePaul's legendary coach Ray Meyers, Harshman assumed the role of the active winningest coach in the nation with 620 victories.

Husky Spotlight

Growing up in Mississauga, Ontario, Canada, Sterling Hinds was a good enough hockey player to rise to the Junior B level, just one step from the professional ranks. As much as he enjoyed the sport, it is a pretty safe bet that Hinds' chances to compete in the Olympic Games were as a track sprinter. It was also his best chance to gain recognition in his hometown. Mississauga had already produced hockey great Wayne Gretzky. Hinds came to Washington on a football scholarship and was a three-year letterwinner at tailback from 1981-83, playing on the Huskies' back-to-back Rose Bowl teams in 1980 and 1981. A Canadian Junior sprint champion, Hinds was a stellar sprinter for Washington. In 1982 he ran the second fastest 100-meters in Husky history with a time of 10.27, just .01 off the all-time school mark. That same year he also ran the second fastest 200 meters in Washington history with a 20.61 showing. He ran the second leg on Washington's 1983 400-meter relay team that finished second at the NCAA championships. That summer he anchored Canada's relay squad to a silver medal at the World University Games. At the 1984 Olympics in Los Angeles, Hinds helped Canada to a bronze medal in the 400-meter relay with a time of 38.70. The United States team, featuring Carl Lewis, set a world record in the race with a time of 37.83. Jamaica placed second at 38.62. Hinds' brothers, Doug and Jerry, competed at Lamar and also raced on the Canadian national team.

HUSKY HIGHLIGHT

Husky Rowers win National Title

At the 1984 national rowing championships on Lake Harsha in Cincinnati, the Husky men's crew team claimed its first national championship since 1970 by defeating Yale in the finals in a wire-to-wire victory. Washington was the heavy favorite to win, and the Huskies did it convincingly by rowing the course in a time of 5:51.0 despite the 90-degree temperatures. Yale finished in a time of 5:55.35. "It was a big burden," said coach Dick Erickson. "We should've won, we had to win, and we did win." Up a length after the first 500 meters, the Huskies were determined not to let a repeat of the previous year happen when Harvard came from behind to catch Washington at the finish line. Washington would go on to row in Europe, finishing second twice to the Soviet national team in the Netherlands Rowing Championships in Amsterdam. In England, at the Royal Henley Regatta, the Huskies placed second to the British national team in the Grand Challenge Cup. The varsity eight shell was comprised of Brad Clancy, Pat Gleason and coxswain Mike Teather, Jon Norelius, David Zevenbergen, James Snody, Mike Feltin, Jim Dahl and Chris Pugel.

Husky Legend

Detlef Schrempf

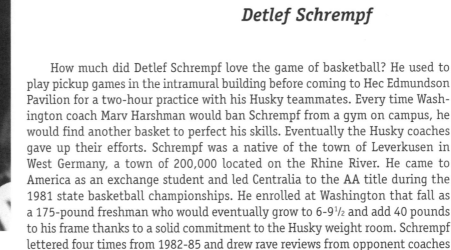

UW Media Relations

How much did Detlef Schrempf love the game of basketball? He used to play pickup games in the intramural building before coming to Hec Edmundson Pavilion for a two-hour practice with his Husky teammates. Every time Washington coach Marv Harshman would ban Schrempf from a gym on campus, he would find another basket to perfect his skills. Eventually the Husky coaches gave up their efforts. Schrempf was a native of the town of Leverkusen in West Germany, a town of 200,000 located on the Rhine River. He came to America as an exchange student and led Centralia to the AA title during the 1981 state basketball championships. He enrolled at Washington that fall as a 175-pound freshman who would eventually grow to 6-9½ and add 40 pounds to his frame thanks to a solid commitment to the Husky weight room. Schrempf lettered four times from 1982-85 and drew rave reviews from opponent coaches for his ability to play any position on the court. As a junior he led the team in scoring and rebounding and was second in assists and steals, earning District VIII player of the year honors. He helped Washington to back-to-back Pac-10 titles and NCAA appearances as a junior and senior, acting as team captain in 1984-85. Schrempf finished his career with 1,449 points and ranked sixth on Washington's all-time scoring list. He averaged 16.8 points as a junior and 15.8 as a senior. His final career averages were 11.9 points per game and 6.2 rebounds per game. He was drafted by the NBA's Dallas Mavericks and went on to play professionally for Indianapolis, Seattle and Portland. In 1991 and 1992 he was the league's Sixth Man of the Year. Schrempf competed on the West German Olympic team in 1984.

Husky List

Pac-10 Football MVPs

In 1983 Steve Pelluer became the second Husky player to be named the Pac-10 Conference's Offensive Player of the Year. Pelluer won the award after completing 213 of 317 (.672) passes for 2,212 yards and 11 touchdowns. At the time, his passing total was the second best in Washington history behind Sonny Sixkillers' record of 2,303 yards in 1970. Here's at a look at the Husky players, through the 2000 season, who were honored as Pac-10 Players of the Year:

Year	Player, position
1977	Warren Moon, quarterback
1983	Steve Pelluer, quarterback
1990	Greg Lewis, tailback
1990	Steve Emtman, defensive tackle
1991	Mario Bailey, wide receiver
1991	Steve Emtman, defensive tackle
1992	Dave Hoffmann, inside linebacker
1994	Napoleon Kaufman, tailback
1996	Jason Chorak, outside linebacker
2000	Marques Tuiasosopo, quarterback

Note: Don James was named the Pac-10 Coach of the Year in 1980, 1990 and 1991.

Tom Hansen Named Pac-10 Commissioner

TOM Hansen a 1959 Washington graduate, took over as the commissioner of the Pac-10 Conference on July 1 in 1983. He succeeded Wiles Hallock as the fifth commissioner of the conference. Previously, Hansen was an NCAA administrator for 16 years, preceded by seven years as the director of public relations for the Pac-10 (then the Athletic Association of Western Universities). During his tenure as Pac-10 commissioner the league inaugurated women's sports programs, created two football television programs, added promotional emphasis on the conference's men's and women's basketball programs and expanded television coverage of the sport. Hansen is prominent in NCAA affairs, serving on a number of major committees. He served for two years as President of the Collegiate Commissioner's Association and for four years on the Board of Directors of the National Association of Collegiate Directors of Athletics.

1983 W 1984

Husky Moment

Women's Crew National Champs

The theme was "Number Four in '84" when the Husky women's rowing team went about the business of defending their national championship in Seattle at the 1,000-meter Green Lake course. As the three-time defending champions and the host school for the event, the Huskies were once again the favorites to win the gold medal. But this year's crew had a different look. Only two Washington rowers, Eleanor McElvaine and Sara Nevin, returned from the Huskies' 1983 varsity eight crew. Also missing was head coach Bob Ernst, who was on a leave of absence to coach the United States women's Olympic team. In his place, John Squadroni took over as the interim coach. The Huskies also used the race to debut their new ultra-light carbo-fiber Empacher racing shell named "The Eagle." The only other time the boat had been raced was at the 1983 World Championships by the silver medal U.S. squad. The most serious challenger again appeared to be Wisconsin, the winner of the Eastern Sprints. The Husky varsity eight breezed into the finals with a convincing win in its heat race, but then the team watched in dismay as the junior varsity eight was upset by Yale to end a streak of three straight national crowns in that division. Rowing into a gusty headwind, the Huskies' varsity eight nearly experienced disaster on their opening strokes when the boat almost went off course. Coxswain Jeannie Bucko got the team back under control and the Huskies pulled even with Wisconsin and Radcliffe in the first 500 meters. With just under 200 meters remaining to race, the Washington powered up its stroke rate and pulled away for the victory in a time of 3:29.48. Radcliffe placed ahead of the Badgers for second-place honors. "With about 250 meters to go, we got four seats up on Wisconsin and Radcliffe, and that fired us up," Bucko said afterwards. "We just took off." The windy conditions, that were not as favorable in the lighter Empacher shell, caused the Huskies to row 11 seconds slower in the finals than they did during the heat races. In addition to McElvaine, Nevin and Bucko, the Washington varsity eight crew consisted of: Gail Stewart, Liz White, Liese Hendrie, Cherie Gawley, Chris Campbell and Kristi Stingl.

UW Media Relations

Husky Spotlight

The Washington women's gymnastics team turned in its best showing at a national meet at the 1984 NCAA Championships when the Huskies placed eighth. The meet was staged in Los Angeles. The NCAA meet was only the fourth time the national governing body had sanctioned a national tournament in the sport. Washington had made appearances at the AIAW gymnastics championships between 1975 and 1977 with a best finish of 13th at the 1976 competition. The Huskies entered the NCAA meet ranked ninth in the nation. Washington's lineup included five all-arounders, gymnasts who competed in all four events—vault, balance beam, uneven bars and floor exercise. The Husky lineup included Wendy Gangwer, Wendy Goya, Suzie Sun, Christi Robell, and Nancy Rhinesmith. Sun had earned Northern Pacific Athletic Conference gymnasts of the year honors during the season. Gangwer proved to be Washington's most successful competitor at the NCAA meet, scoring 35.95 to place 30th in the all-around.

Husky Highlight

A trio of former Huskies earned gold medals for the victorious women's rowing team at the 1984 Summer Olympic Games in Los Angeles. The U.S. squad, under the direction of Washington women's coach Bob Ernst, won its first gold in the event. The Husky rowers who helped the eight squad to victory were Kristi Norelius, Shyril O'Steen and coxswain Betsy Beard. All three had won national championship while at Washington. Norelius was a member of the 1980 United States team that missed the Moscow Olympics due to America's boycott of the event. She was 27 years old for the 1984 games while O'Steen was 23 and Beard was just 22. Rowing on the flat water of Lake Casitas just north of Los Angeles, the U.S. team found itself trailing by the length of a boat deck at the midway point of the final race. Beard called for a power 20 stroke and the Americans drew even with 200 meters left to race. As the Romanians began to falter, the U.S. squad raised its stroke rate to a furious pace and won by less than half a length in a time of 2:59.8. Romania was timed on the 1,000-meter course with a finish of 3:00.87. Holland was a distant third at 3:02.92. "It was stroke for stroke the whole way," O'Steen said. "I don't think we won it until the last 10 strokes or so." Ernst credited his coxswain for driving the team to victory. "Without Betsy, we don't win," he said. "She was the difference."

UW Media Relations

Husky Legend

Karen Murray

Reviewing her career numbers, it is hard to believe that women's basketball player Karen Murray was known as a "reluctant shooter" during her Husky playing days. At 5-10, Murray played both guard and forward at Washington. As a freshman, she moved into a starting role in just her third game and went on to average 13.3 points per game and 6.2 rebounds per game while also leading the team in assists with four per outing. She earned second-team All-Northwest Women's Basketball League honors in her first year with the Huskies. As a sophomore, averaging 15.5 ppg., she was named to the AIAW Region IX team. Murray continued to pile up honors as a junior when she averaged 19.7 ppg. She was named a third-team All-American by the American Women's Sports Federation and selected to the All-Nor-Pac team and the league's all-tournament squad. That season she set the school records for free-throw shooting by making 48 of 58 (82.8 percent) and for field-goal accuracy (53 percent). The Pasco, Washington, native finished her career as the school's all-time scoring leader with 1,745 points. Her senior season, when she averaged 17.0 ppg., she shot 84 percent from the charity stripe to finish second nationally in that category. Murray met her future husband, Michael Hodgins, during a pickup game in the intramural building. After graduating from Washington, she played professionally in Europe and was eventually coached by her husband. Murray is the only Husky player to lead the team in both field goal and free throw shooting all four years of her career. She scored in double figures in 84 percent of the games in which she appeared. She left the Husky program as the career and single-season leader in scoring, field goal and free-throw percentage. In 1992 she became the first Washington's women's basketball player inducted into the Husky Hall of Fame.

Husky List

Husky Rowing Medalists at the Olympics

Name	Year	Event	Medal
Marc Schneider	1996	Lightweight four without coxswain	Bronze
Betsy Beard	1984	Eight	Gold
Charles Clapp	1984	Eight	Silver
Al Forney	1984	Four with coxswain	Silver
Blair Horn	1984	Eight (Canada)	Gold
Ed Ives	1984	Four with coxswain	Silver
Kristi Norelius	1984	Eight	Gold
Shyril O'Steen	1984	Eight	Gold
John Stillings	1984	Four with coxswain	Silver
Ted Mittet	1964	Four with coxswain	Bronze
John Sayre	1960	Four with coxswain	Gold
Phil Leanderson	1952	Four with coxswain	Bronze
Carl Lovsted	1952	Four with coxswain	Bronze
Alvin E. Ulbrickson	1952	Four with coxswain	Bronze
Richard Wahlstrom	1952	Four with coxswain	Bronze
Albert Rossi	1952	Four with coxswain	Bronze
Gordon Giovanelli	1948	Four with coxswain	Gold
Robert Martin	1948	Four with coxswain	Gold
Allen Morgan	1948	Four with coxswain	Gold
Warren Westlund	1948	Four with coxswain	Gold
Robert Will	1948	Four with coxswain	Gold
Gordon Adam	1936	Eight	Gold
Charles Day	1936	Eight	Gold
Donald Hume	1936	Eight	Gold
George Hunt	1936	Eight	Gold
James McMillin	1936	Eight	Gold
Robert Moch	1936	Eight	Gold
Roger Morris	1936	Eight	Gold
Joseph Rantz	1936	Eight	Gold
John White	1936	Eight	Gold

Ernst Guides U.S. Rowers to Olympic Gold

WASHINGTON crew coach Bob Ernst was the head coach of the United States Olympic rowing team that won the gold medal in the eights competition at the 1984 Summer Games in Los Angeles. It marked the first time the American women had captured the top prize at the Olympics. Ernst had three former Huskies in the winning shell. Betsy Beard served as the coxswain and she was joined by Kristi Norelius in the number-six seat and Shyril O'Steen in the bow position. Ernst continued his Olympic tenure in 1988 when he returned as the head of the women's team and in 1992 when he served as a commentator for NBC Sports for the rowing competition.

1984 W 1985

Husky Moment

Orange Bowl Win

Ranked either third or fourth in the major national football polls, the Washington football team felt it needed a significant victory against Oklahoma in the 1985 Orange Bowl to unseat top-ranked BYU for the 1984 national championship. The Huskies got the victory, but wound up second in all of the major polls behind the undefeated Cougars. BYU's top ranking was questioned by some pollsters since it played a relatively easy schedule and defeated a 6-5 Michigan team in the Holiday Bowl. Despite the disappointment of not claiming the national title, the Orange Bowl helped to put Washington coach Don James and his Huskies on the national map. Oklahoma entered the game ranked first in the nation in rushing defense, allowing an average of just 68 yards per game. James devised a system of trap plays that capitalized on the Sooners' aggressive defense to pull off the 28-17 victory. Washington rolled up 311 yards, including 192 rushing yards, led by game MVP Jacque Robinson's 135-yard effort. The game was close entering the final quarter when the Sooners took a 17-14 lead on a 35-yard field goal by Tim Lashar with 6:15 to play. Washington quarterback Hugh Millen, who came off the bench to relieve starter Paul Sicuro, marched the Huskies 74 yards in seven plays to take the lead on a 12-yard touchdown pass to his Roosevelt High School teammate Mark Pattison. Oklahoma's Buster Rhymes fumbled the ensuing kickoff out of bounds at the two-yard line. Several plays later the Huskies' Joe Kelly intercepted an Oklahoma pass at the 10-yard line to set up Washington's final score. Rick Fenney slammed into the endzone on a six-yard run with 4:48 to play to give the Huskies a 28-17 lead. Washington was in control early in the game when the Huskies took a muffed OU punt and scored first on a touchdown pass from Sicuro to Danny Greene. After another defensive stop, Sicuro led Washington on a 72-yard, 14-play march that Robinson capped with a one-yard scoring run. Oklahoma rallied for a pair of second quarter touchdowns, including a 61-yard pass play at the end of the half, to tie the game. Forced to sit in the lockerroom for a 40-minute halftime show, the Huskies took the time and regrouped for the second half comeback. Oklahoma, which gained 286 yards in the game, was hurt by six fumbles, including two it lost to the Huskies.

Husky Spotlight

The 1984-85 men's basketball season was the last for legendary coach Marv Harshman. His 14th Husky team made it a memorable year by winning the Pac-10 title, but it came down to the last day of play to secure the championship. Ranked in the top 10 in several preseason polls, the Huskies won their first five games of the season and carried an 8-2 record into their Pac-10 opener. The conference race turned into a wild affair as the Huskies eventually tied USC for first place with dual 13-5 league marks. A mid-February loss at Oregon appeared to knock the Huskies out of the conference race. They were 8-5 in Pac-10 play and needed to sweep their final five games and hope for some upsets. That is exactly what happened. First Washington upset No. 18 Oregon State, the Huskies first win in Corvallis in eight years. Then they easily handled Washington State 68-55 at home on Marv Harshman Appreciation Night. The Huskies turned back No. 19 Arizona 60-58 to climb into a tie for second place before finishing up conference play with road wins against the Bay Area teams. Washington needed league-leading USC to lose on the road in the final weekend to gain a share of the title and that happened when Oregon State upset the Trojans in overtime. By virtue of a better overall record, the Huskies received the Pac-10 automatic bid to the NCAA tournament where they were eliminated by Kentucky 66-58.

Husky Highlight

Football News National Champs

While Washington did not finish first in any of the major wire service polls following the 1984 football season, the Huskies were recognized by one publication as the national champions. *The Football News,* a widely read weekly football tabloid, picked Washington as the top college team in the nation. The Huskies were second in the CNN-*USA Today* poll with 751 points while BYU collected 789 points. BYU picked up 26 of the 32 first-place votes. Washington also finished second in the *Associated Press* writer's poll with 1,140 votes to 1,160 for BYU. The Cougars picked up 38 first-place votes to 16 for Washington and six for Florida. *The New York Times,* which ranked its standings on a computer-generated point system, tabbed Florida as the top team with 1,000 points while Washington was fifth with 910 points and BYU figured just 10th with 826 points.

UW Media Relations

Husky Legend

Jacque Robinson

Washington standout Jacque Robinson sandwiched a four-year career with two of the greatest performances by a running back in Husky bowl game history. As a freshman playing in the 1982 Rose Bowl, he picked up game MVP honors by rushing for 142 yards and a pair of touchdowns in the Huskies' 28-0 rout of Iowa. As a senior, playing his final collegiate game, he helped Washington to a 28-17 victory against Oklahoma in the 1985 Orange Bowl. Robinson earned MVP honors with 135 rushing yards and two scores against the nation's toughest defense against the run. Robinson became the first player to earn MVP honors in both the Rose and Orange bowls. In between those two seasons, injuries and battles with his playing weight hampered his Husky career. Robinson started only 17 times during his 58-game career. As a sophomore Robinson led the Pac-10 with 926 rushing yards and earned first-team all-conference honors. He only started the final five games that season. Injuries limited him to only 296 rushing yards as a junior. He returned to his top form as a senior when he placed fifth in the league in rushing with 909 yards. He led the Pac-10 that season with 13 touchdowns and was named a second-team all-conference performer. Robinson's single best rushing game came during the 1982 season when he ripped Texas Tech for 203 yards in a 10-3 Husky victory. He became just the sixth UW player to crack the 200-yard rushing mark in a game. Robinson finished his career with 2,300 rushing yards which was fourth on the all-time list at the time. Robinson remembers his Orange Bowl victory as his most memorable moment. He started that game and the team went on to finish second in the national polls. Remarkably, his effort in the 1982 Rose Bowl came after he sat on the bench for most of the first two quarters.

Husky List

Washington's Top Rushing Games in Bowl Games

Name	Bowl	Opponent	Yards-Touchdowns
1. Rashaan Shehee	1997 Aloha Bowl	Michigan St.	193-2
2. Jacque Robinson	1982 Rose Bowl	Iowa	142-2
3. Corey Dillon	1996 Holiday Bowl	Colorado	140-2
4. George Wilson	1926 Rose Bowl	Alabama	139-0
5. Jacque Robinson	1985 Orange Bowl	Oklahoma	135-1
6. Greg Lewis	1991 Rose Bowl	Iowa	128-0
7. Greg Lewis	1989 Freedom Bowl	Florida	97-0

Husky Lore

The Sooner Schooner Penalty

EARLY in the fourth quarter of the 1985 Orange Bowl, Washington was involved in one of the strangest spectacles in college football history. After Tim Lashar kicked a 22-yard field goal to give Oklahoma a 17-14 lead, a penalty was called on the Sooners which nullified the score. That was followed by another penalty on Oklahoma's mascot, the Sooner Schooner, a Conestoga wagon powered by two tiny ponies. The Sooner Schooner's driver, Rex Harris, apparently did not see the flag and charged on the field for a brief celebration. The officials promptly called a 15-yard unsportsmanlike conduct penalty on the Sooner Schooner and tacked it on to the other penalty. The 20-yard setback made Lashar's next attempt a 42-yarder, which was blocked by Washington's Tim Peoples. Inspired by the momentum swing, Washington went on to score two touchdowns in less than 60 seconds around the five-minute mark, and won the game, 28-17.

Husky Moment

Women's Crew Dynasty Grows

By winning its fifth straight national rowing championship in 1985, the Husky women's crew program truly established itself as a dynasty in sports. After whipping top challenger California by 13 seconds at the Pacific Coast Championships, Washington traveled to the National Collegiate Rowing Championships in Arlington, Virginia in early June to defend its national title. Washington had raced just three times during the 1985 season, at the San Diego Crew Classic, at Seattle's Opening Day Regatta and at the PCCs. The Huskies had suffered a rare loss during the season, falling to the University of Victoria, a team comprised primarily of Canadian national team members, in San Diego. The Lake Occoquan course was set for a 2,000-meter race, a new distance for the nationals, but it had to be trimmed back due to high water on the lake. The top contenders to challenge the Huskies were Wisconsin, Princeton and Dartmouth, but all three found themselves in the same heat race with the Tigers coming out on top. Racing at 1,800 meters, Washington won its heat by two lengths over second-place Minnesota in a time of 6:29.2. The Huskies did not let up in the finals, covering the 1,750-meter distance in a blistering time of 5:28.4. Wisconsin placed second and Minnesota a surprising third, shutting out the traditional eastern powers from the top three spots. Earlier in the season coach Bob Ernst had had Washington's favorite shell, "The Eagle" shipped east so his team could compete in its own equipment. The Husky junior varsity shell placed second to Princeton after unsuccessfully filing a protest after it appeared the Tigers left the start line early. Washington's varsity eight crew included: Eleanor McElvaine, Sara Nevin, Chris Campbell, Liese Hendrie, Birgit Ziegler, Lynne Kalina (coxswain), Cherie Gawley, Christy Dotson and Kristi Stingl. McElvaine, a three-time national champion, called the finals "the best race of my life."

Husky Spotlight

As a senior in 1985, Leteia Hughley led the Husky women's basketball team in scoring with an 18.6 average and finished her career with 1,704 points. Hughley trailed only former teammate Karen Murray (1,745 points) on the all-time scoring list. Hughley's senior campaign proved to be one of the best overall seasons of any Washington player. In addition to leading the team in scoring, she also topped the Huskies in assists with 151, steals with 97 and blocked shots with 17. She set a Washington record with 15 20-point games that season and recorded a total of 30 20-point outings during her career. The four-year letterwinner (1982-85) started 105 of the 106 games she appeared in. A 5-7 guard from Flint, Michigan, she was an All-Nor-Pac pick as both a junior and senior.

UW Media Relations

Husky Highlight

Future Husky women's basketball teams will have to be nearly perfect if they are going to better the record of the 1984-85 squad that posted a 26-2 record. The only regular-season loss came against national power Long Beach State. The 1984-85 Husky team also holds the distinction of being the first to qualify for the NCAA championships. Second-year coach Joyce Sake led Washington to both the Northern Pacific Athletic Conference regular-season and NorPac tournament titles. The team was ranked as No. 11 in the nation and pieced together a 21-game winning streak. When the team appeared in the Jan. 7 Associated Poll rankings in the No. 19 position after an 11-1 start, it was another first for the young program. Leteia Hughley and Renee Avelino were the team MVPs and named to the All-NorPac team. The other starters were Kathy Rue, Hilary Recknor and Lisa Oriard. After a 26-1 regular-season, the Huskies drew UCLA in the first round of the NCAA tournament. The popularity of the squad forced the game to be moved from the Pavilion Addition to the main Pavilion. The Bruins, led by future track Olympian Jackie Joyner, dispatched the Huskies 78-62. Sake, who was voted the District 8 coach of the year, shocked her squad after the season by resigning to accept a full-time teaching position at Grossmont College in San Diego. She had spent nine years there as an assistant coach before coming to Washington. Sake's two-year record with the Huskies was 43-10.

Husky Legend

Eleanor McElvaine

UW Media Relations

A three-time national champion for the Washington women's crew program, Eleanor McElvaine established herself as one of the program's greatest rowers, despite a complete lack of experience before she enrolled at college. Like many other successful rowers at Washington, McElvaine was an outstanding high school athlete who was looking for a competitive outlet when she enrolled in college. Despite her lack of rowing experience, McElvaine was such an exceptional and strong athlete, that she was rowing in the varsity eight shell by her sophomore season. She was a part of Washington's national championship crews in 1983, '84 and '85. A native of Everett, she won nine varsity letters in swimming (four), baseball and track (two each) and softball (one) at Cascade High School. During her three-year Husky career, she rowed in only one race that Washington did not win. As a senior in 1985 she was tabbed by the *Everett Herald* as its Woman of the Year. She was named an assistant coach at Washington in 1990 and guided the Husky novice teams to eight straight first place finishes at the Pacific Coast/Pac-10 Championships. She helped to coach the Husky fours to an NCAA title in 1998, the same year the team repeated as national champions. In 1994 she was honored, along with head women's rowing coach Jan Harville, by the U.S. Rowing Association as its Woman of the Year. Her international rowing resume includes a stint as the assistant coach for the U.S. Junior National Team in 1997 and 1998. She managed all the water activities for rowing at the 1998 Summer Olympic Games in Atlanta. Once when she was asked what rowing had meant to her, McElvaine replied: "I learned about making goals, pushing through obstacles, having self-confidence to do it. I can do whatever I want."

Husky List

Top Women's Basketball Records

Year	Coach	Record	Pct.
1984-85	Joyce Sake	26-2	.929
1989-90	Chris Gobrecht	28-3	.903
1976-77	Kathie Neir	22-4	.846
1977-78	Kathie Neir	26-5	.839
1987-88	Chris Gobrecht	25-5	.833
1990-91	Chris Gobrecht	24-5	.828
1985-86	Chris Gobrecht	24-6	.800
1986-87	Chris Gobrecht	23-7	.767
1994-95	Chris Gobrecht	25-9	.735
1993-94	Chris Gobrecht	21-8	.724

Chris Gobrecht Named Women's Basketball Coach

UW Media Relations

ON May 20 of 1985 Chris Gobrecht took over the Washington women's basketball team as the sixth coach in the program's 12-year history. At age 30, she came to Washington after coaching at Cal State Fullerton for six seasons. She posted an 85-92 record there, including a 20-11 mark during the 1984-85 season. Gobrecht was one of only two coaches to be interviewed in Seattle for the Husky opening. The other was Ohio State coach Tara Van Derveer, who accepted the vacated position at Stanford shortly after her Washington interview. Gobrecht took over a UW team that had lost its top three players to graduation and led them to a 24-6 record and the second round of the NCAA tournament in her first season with the Huskies.

1985 W 1986

Husky Moment

Freedom Bowl Win

Sophomore quarterback Chris Chandler passed for 141 yards and ran for 72 more in leading Washington to a 20-17 victory over Colorado in the second annual Freedom Bowl in Anaheim. The win boosted Washington's overall bowl record to 9-6-1, and a 6-2 record in bowls under Don James. The Freedom Bowl was Washington's seventh straight postseason bowl appearance, and eighth in nine years. Chandler, starting only his third game at quarterback, was voted the game's MVP. A Colorado field goal early in the third quarter tied the game at 10-10, but Washington responded to regain the lead. A 36-yard kickoff return by David Trimble gave the Huskies excellent field position on their own 47. Chandler's 15-yard option keeper followed by a 14-yard pitch to Rod Jones were key plays in the drive. Vince Weathersby got 12 yards on a draw play to the Colorado five, and then Tony Covington ran twice and got the score on a one-yard dive. Washington led 17-10. Washington increased its lead to 20-10 on its next possession as the Huskies moved 67 yards on 11 plays. Chandler passes to Lonzell Hill, Tony Covington and David Toy accounted for 36 yards and Chandler added 19 more on another option run. With fourth-and-one at the Colorado one-yard line, Washington opted for a sure three points on Jeff Jaeger's second field goal. Colorado made things interesting midway through the fourth quarter when holder Barry Helton passed 31 yards to Jon Embree for a touchdown on a fake field goal as the Buffs cut Washington's lead to 20-17. Colorado got the ball right back and marched to the Husky seven-yard line but Joe Kelly forced a fumble and David Rill recovered to preserve the win.

UW Media Relations

Chris Chandler

Husky Spotlight

It took less than one full season for Mike Blowers to establish himself as the all-time Husky home run leader in 1986. A transfer from Tacoma Community College, Blowers wound up playing for the Diamond Dawgs because Washington coach Bob MacDonald proved to be a man of his word. Few Division I schools recruited Blowers out of Spanaway because he was considered too slow. MacDonald promised him a chance to play shortstop at Washington and that proved to be the key point in Blowers enrolling at Washington instead of cross-state rival Washington State. Blowers blasted 16 home runs in his first season with the Huskies in 1986. He also set a single-season RBI record that year with 59. He entered professional baseball following the 1986 Husky season and went on to play with several teams on the major league level, including the Yankees, Mariners and Athletics.

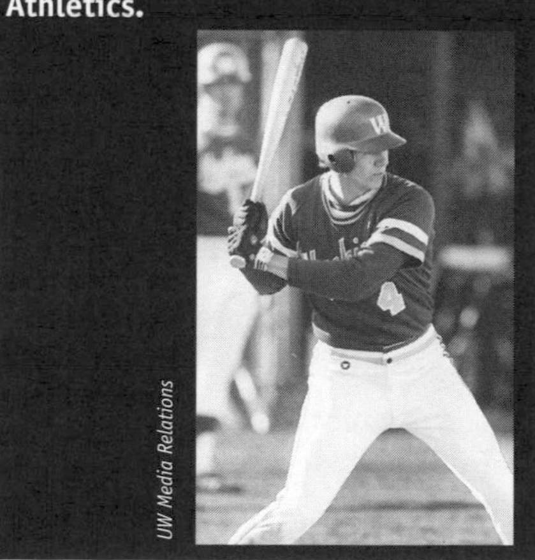

UW Media Relations

Husky Highlight

When Mike Ramos won the NCAA decathlon title in 1986 he did it in impression fashion, setting a meet record with a score of 8,261 points. Ramos became the first male at Washington to win an NCAA track title since 1979. The decathlon is a two-day event. Day one consists of the 100-meters, long jump, shot, high jump and 400-meters. Day two features the 110-meter hurdles, discus, pole vault, javelin and 1,500-meter run. Competitors consider it a type of endurance contest. After the first day, Ramos found himself trailing Southern Mississippi's Sten Ekberg for the lead. Ramos, a native of Missoula, Montana, used personal-best marks in the 110-meter hurdles, the discus and the 400-meters to take first place in the meet. Ramos won Pac-10 titles in the decathlon in 1983, 1984 and 1986 after redshirting the 1985 season. His 1986 Pac-10 title included a collegiate record score of 8,322 points. At that meet he had better marks in six of the 10 events than Bruce Jenner did in setting the American record at the 1976 Olympics. Ramos' efforts at catching Jenner's mark were hampered by a new javelin with a balance point that would not let it go as far as the javelins used in Jenner's day. He won the event at the World University Games in Japan in 1985. He went to the first Goodwill Games in the Soviet Union, but a torn stomach muscle did not allow him to complete the competition.

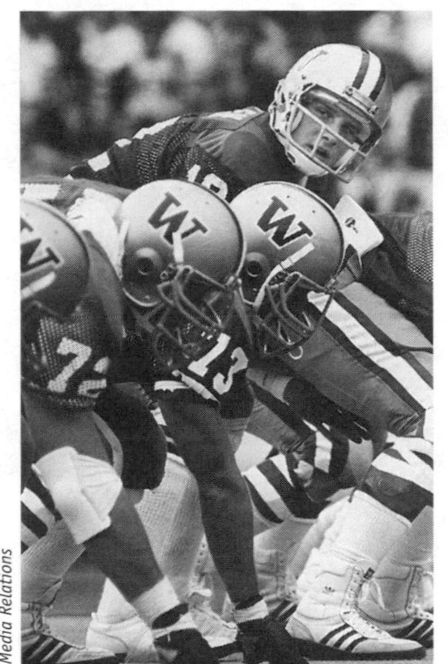
UW Media Relations

Husky Legend

Hugh Millen

Growing up in Ann Arbor, Michigan, Hugh Millen dreamed about playing quarterback for his beloved Michigan Wolverines. In time, he turned into a nightmare for the Big Ten powerhouse. Millen's family eventually moved from the midwest to Seattle and he prepped at Seattle's Roosevelt High School before enrolling at Santa Rosa Junior College. As a sophomore he played just 18 quarters due to an injury and only San Diego State showed any interest in him. A strong student, Millen enrolled at Washington and walked on to the football squad. After redshirting the 1983 season, he became the first walkon quarterback to start for a Don James Husky squad in 1984 when he helped Washington to an 11-1 record and second-place finish in the national polls. Millen passed for 1,051 yards that season and put the Huskies on the national map when he completed 13 of 16 passes for 165 yards and a touchdown in Washington's 20-11 upset of third-ranked Michigan in Ann Arbor. His passing totals included a 73-yard touchdown pass to Mark Pattison, his high school teammate at Roosevelt. That game was just Millen's second start, and it came in front of 103,000 hostile Wolverine fans. In the 1985 Orange Bowl, James called the strong-armed Millen off of the bench for the final quarter of action when the Huskies had to play into a stiff headwind. He completed just two passes, but one capped UW's go-ahead scoring drive in the 28-17 victory against Oklahoma. While he passed for 1,565 yards as a senior, his 1985 season did not live up to preseason expectations. The team finished 6-5 and Millen suffered a shoulder injury in the ninth game of the season that cut short his collegiate career. Millen's senior season did have some highlights. He was named to the District VIII Academic All-America team and a National Football Foundation and Hall of Fame scholar. He was selected by the Los Angeles Rams in the third round of the NFL draft and enjoyed an 11-year NFL career.

Husky List

Washington's First-Round NFL Draft Picks

Name	Year	Team
Dean McAdams	1941	Brooklyn
Rudy Mucha	1941	Cleveland
Dave Williams	1967	St. Louis
Blair Bush	1978	Cincinnati
Doug Martin	1980	Minnesota
Curt Marsh	1981	Oakland
Ron Holmes	1985	Tampa Bay
Joe Kelly	1986	Cincinnati
Reggie Rogers	1987	Detroit
Bern Brostek	1990	Los Angeles Rams
Steve Emtman	1992	Indianapolis
Dana Hall	1992	San Francisco
Lincoln Kennedy	1993	Atlanta
Napoleon Kaufman	1995	Los Angeles Raiders
Mark Bruener	1995	Pittsburgh

Lou Gellerman

THE public address voice at Husky Stadium since 1985 has belonged to Lou Gellerman, a 1958 UW graduate. Gellerman, whose trademark "Hello Dawg Fans" introduction echoes throughout Husky Stadium each gameday during the fall, was a four-year rower at Washington, and is a member of the Husky Hall of Fame as a part of the 1958 crew which rowed against the Soviets in Moscow. Gellerman is assisted on gameday by his two veteran spotters, Rick Smidt and Bob Sifferman.

1985 W 1986

Husky Moment

Helena Uusitalo Wins NCAA Javelin Title

Helena Uusitalo became the first female at Washington to win an NCAA individual track championship in 1986 when she took first place in the javelin. The NCAA began sponsoring a track and field championship in 1982, a year after Regina Joyce won the 3,000 meters at the AIAW championships. Uusitalo, a junior from Sodankyla, Finland, won the national title with a toss of 193-1. Her winning throw came on her second attempt. That proved to be lucky because she sprained her ankle on her fourth try and had to scratch her final two attempts. Uusitalo's throw did not better her personal best that she set at the NorPac Championships when she threw a distance of 197-4. That toss proved to be the seventh best distance ever by a collegiate competitor. At the NCAA championships, Uusitalo defeated Alabama's Iris Gronfeldt, the two-time defending champion. At just 5-5 and 123 pounds,Uusitalo was considered small among the event's competitors. She was a self-taught thrower, taking up the sport after seeing it on television. She practiced alone in a field beside her parents home, which was located just 100 miles south of the Artic Circle. Uusitalo had only been enrolled at Washington for six months when she won the NCAA title.

UW Media Relations

Husky Spotlight

In just two seasons at Washington, Jana Ellis established herself as one of the top swimmers in the program's history. The Husky pool was like a home away from home for her since her father, Earl, was Washington's men's and women's swim coach for 19 years. As a freshman in 1984-85 Ellis qualified as a four-time All-American and finished second in the 200 individual medley at the NCAA championships. She earned All-America honors three times as a sophomore. Following the 1986 season she transfered to Florida to swim for the Gators' more nationally competitive program. Ellis completed her collegiate career as an 18-time All-American. She left Washington as the holder of nine school records. Her older sister Robin and her older brother Duff also swam at Washington. Ellis became the first freshman in school history to earn All-NorPac honors as she qualified for the NCAAs in the 200 IM, the 400 IM, the 200 and 400 breaststroke and the 400 and 800 freestyle relay. She graduated from Florida in 1989 and was a member of the U.S. national team from 1985 to 1989. At one time she was a member of the world record 400 freestyle relay team. In 1995 she returned to Washington to work for her father as an assistant coach for three years.

Husky Highlight

Crew Streak Stopped

Washington's dominance at the national rowing championships finally came to an end in 1986 when the Huskies placed third behind Wisconsin and Radcliffe. Washington had won five consecutive national championships in the varsity eight competition. Rowing on the 2,000-meter Lake Harsha course in Cincinnati, Wisconsin capped an undefeated season by winning in a time of 6:52.28. Washington crossed the finish line in 6:59.84. The race marked the second time the Badgers had defeated the Huskies during the 1986 season. Washington entered the national regatta after capturing its seventh consecutive Pacific Coast rowing title by defeating second-place Stanford by five lengths. Washington's five straight national titles would be a benchmark that no other program would approach. Princeton came the closest, finishing first three consecutive years from 1993-1995.

Husky Legend

Chris Gobrecht

UW Media Relations

Chris Gobrecht was a pioneer for the Washington women's basketball team, lifting it to heights of popularity that made the Huskies one of the most respected programs in the nation. Gobrecht took over as the Huskies' coach after Joyce Sake unexpectedly resigned in 1985 after a 26-2 season that included the team's first NCAA tournament appearance. Gobrecht's successful run started in the first of her 11 seasons at Washington. The Huskies went 24-6 and advanced to the second round of the NCAA championships. An NCAA bid was almost mandated as Washington went to the tournament nine times during her tenure, including four regional appearances. In 10 of 11 seasons her teams recorded at least 17 victories and never suffered a losing season. Washington won three conference titles under Gobrecht, including the Pac-10 championships in 1988 and 1990. She was named the coach of the year following the 1987 and '88 seasons. If the Huskies were not at the top of the Pac-10, they weren't far behind, finishing runner-up in the conference four times (1987, 1989, 1991, and 1995). Gobrecht posted a lot of firsts. She was the first women's basketball coach to lead the Huskies for five consecutive seasons, to win 100 games, and to reach the 300-win milestone in her career. Only Tennessee's Pat Summitt reached 300 wins quicker than Gobrecht. In the summer of 1990, she served as assistant coach for one of the USA Basketball Select teams that traveled to Czechoslovakia and Italy. And in the summer of 1989, she coached the silver-medal winning East Team at the U.S. Olympic Festival. She left Washington to take over the program at Florida State in 1996 and then was named the head coach at her alma mater, USC, in 1997. Gobrecht's 11-year record at Washington was 243-89. Her players were honored 11 times as All-Pac-10 picks and two, Karen Deden and Rhonda Smith, earned All-America honors.

HUSKY LIST

All-Time Pac-10 Women's Basketball Standings
(Through the 2000-2001 season)

	Titles	W	L	Pct.	W	L	Pct.
		Pac-10			Overall		
Stanford	10	228	43	.841	380	90	.809
Washington	3	180	90	.667	300	149	.668
Oregon	2	158	112	.585	274	171	.616
USC	2	158	112	.585	248	187	.570
UCLA	1	149	121	.552	236	204	.536
Arizona	0	112	158	.415	223	215	.509
Oregon State	0	102	168	.378	200	221	.475
California	0	96	174	.356	229	233	.495
Arizona State	1	85	185	.315	179	238	.429
Washington State	0	83	187	.307	177	238	.426

Women's Athletics Joins Pac-10 Lineup

IN December of 1985, Pac-10 school officials voted to integrate women's athletics into the conference. The league officially went co-ed on July 1, 1986. Previously the Pac-10's women's programs had been split into several alliances. Arizona, Arizona State, Stanford, UCLA and USC were members of the Pacific West Conference. California, Oregon, Oregon State, Washington and Washington State competed in the Pacific Athletic Conference. Discussions first began about merging the women's programs into the conference in 1981. The benefits included increased revenue, visibility and media coverage. Recruiting was also expected to improve since the women's programs would be associated with a well-known conference. The NCAA first included women's sports championship programming in 1981. The NorPac, of which Washington was a member, came into existence in 1982.

1986 W 1987

Husky Moment

First Windermere Cup

The face of Washington's annual Opening Day Regatta took a dramatic turn in 1987. That year the Seattle-based Windermere Real Estate Company stepped forward with a sponsorship for the event. The result was an increase in competitive racing that featured some of the best rowing programs in the world making an annual trek to the Montlake Cut to race the Huskies. The 1987 regatta marked the 18th annual Opening Day festivities. On hand to challenge Washington was the powerful Soviet Union national team. The event marked the first time a Soviet crew had rowed in America in 25 years. It also sparked fond memories of the 1958 Husky crew that defeated the Trud Rowing Club just outside of Moscow in one of the most famous races in Washington history. ABC Sports commentator Keith Jackson, who made the radio call of that memorial event, returned to Seattle for the inaugural Windermere Cup broadcast on KOMO-TV. Also on hand were the members of the 1958 Washington crew. Both the Soviet men's and women's teams easily won their races against the outmatched Husky squads. The Soviet men rowed the course in 5:41.16 compared to a time of 5:56.23 by the Huskies. The Soviet women finished in 6:11.73 compared to 6:21.58 for Washington. After the men's race, the two crews pulled side-by-side and four Soviet rowers traded places with men in the Husky shell and then the teams rowed back down the Montlake Cut to a thunderous ovation of the tens of thousands of onlookers. *Seattle Times* columnist Blaine Newnham lit the fire for the event by challenging the Opening Day Regatta to become something more than a Husky intrasquad race when the setting was in place for a major international affair.

Husky Spotlight

Reggie Rogers was a two-sport standout at Washington for both the football and basketball teams. He began his Husky athletic career on the basketball team as a 6-7 power forward. He was a frequent starter during the 1982-83 season and was named to the Pac-10 all-freshman team. He averaged 8.4 points and 5.3 rebounds per game that season. Rogers was moved to center and became a backup as a sophomore when Christian Welp broke into the starting lineup at the post position. That spring he decided to turn out for football drills and return to a sport he had excelled in as a prep player in Sacramento. Although he had not played a full season of football since his junior year in high school, he quickly won a starting role on the Husky defense. Rogers was a member of two Pac-10 championship basketball teams (1984 and 1985) and appeared in the Orange (1985), Freedom (1985) and Sun (1986) Bowls for the Husky football squad. As a senior he anchored a Husky defensive line that allowed just 88.9 rushing yards per game. He was the Morris Trophy winner as the Pac-10's top defensive lineman in 1986 and a first-team All-American. He was the seventh pick in the 1987 NFL draft by the Detroit Lions.

Husky Highlight

Just like the best Husky kicker that played before him (Chuck Nelson), Jeff Jaeger missed his first field-goal attempt at Washington. The miss proved to be a rarity. A four-time letterman from 1983-86, Jaeger went on to set the NCAA record with 80 career field goals. He broke the record with his 80th boot in the 1986 Apple Cup against Washington State. Jaeger also finished his Husky career as the school's all-time scoring leader with 358 points. Jaeger was named a consensus All-American in 1986 after connecting on 17 of 21 field-goal attempts and making all but one of his 43 extra-point attempts. In 1999 the *Seattle Times* named Jaeger to its all-time Husky football team.

UW Media Relations

UW Media Relations

Husky Legend

Christian Welp

Only a week after Christian Welp arrived in Centralia as a West German exchange student, Husky basketball coach Marv Harshman was busy recruiting him. Welp was months away from playing his first prep basketball game and leading Olympic High School to the AA state championship, but Harshman knew all about his abilities. Husky forward Detlef Schrempf had played against Welp in national team tournaments in German and had given the Husky coaches a positive scouting report. Welp committed to Washington after making his first visit and before any other American coaches had a chance to see him play. Welp turned out to be a four-year starter and the all-time scoring leader while playing for the Huskies from 1984-87. As a newcomer in 1984 he was named the Pac-10 Conference's freshman of the year. He averaged 10.6 points and 6.2 rebounds that season while helping Washington to the first of back-to-back Pac-10 titles and three straight NCAA tournament appearances. Welp refined his game in the summers by playing for the German National Team and was a member of that country's 1984 Olympic squad. As a junior Welp averaged 19.4 points and 8.5 rebounds for the Huskies and upped those totals to 20.8 points and 9.0 rebounds during his senior campaign. He earned All-Pac-10 honors in both of those seasons and was voted the conference's player of the year as a junior. Welp broke Bob Houbregs' 34-year-old Husky career scoring record during his senior season against Washington State. Houbregs' old scoring mark stood at 1,774 points. Welp scored 40 points in a 90-80 victory against UCLA in 1986 to become one of four Washington players to achieve that scoring mark. He was picked by the Philadelphia 76ers in the first round of the 1987 NBA draft. Welp went on to a professional career that included stops with San Antonio and Oakland before he returned to Europe to continue his professional career.

Husky List

International Teams Who Have Competed in Windermere Cup

1987	Soviet Union
1988	Australia
1989	Italy
1990	People's Republic of China
1991	Czechoslovakia
1992	Lithuania
1993	Humboldt (Germany)
1994	Dutch National Team
1995	South Africa
1996	Russian National Team
1997	Australian National Team
1998	Nottinghamshire County Rowing Club (England)
1999	New Zealand
2000	Egypt

Volleyball Makes Inaugural NCAA Showing

IN 1986 the Washington women's volleyball team made its first appearance in the NCAA championships. The Huskies, coached by Lindy Vivas, had posted a 22-12 regular-season record and finished 20th in the final poll. Washington was led by captains Jolyn Koppinger and Genne Terry. The Huskies drew number-one ranked BYU in the opening round of the NCAAs. The two teams had met twice during the year and the Cougars had won 3-0 and 3-2. The Huskies did not fair any better in their NCAA match played on BYU's home court. The Cougars won by scores of 15-4, 15-8 and 15-10. Washington would return to the NCAAs in two of the next three seasons.

1986 W 1987

Husky Moment

Women's Crew Regains National Title

It only took one year for the Washington women's crew team to return to the top of the sport. The Huskies exerted their dominance by sweeping all three major races at the 1987 National Collegiate Rowing Championships at Lake Natoma. In the varsity eight finals, Washington got off to an uncharacteristic slow start, but passed Yale and Radcliffe by the 1,000-meter mark and rowed away from the field for a six-second victory ahead of Radcliffe. The Huskies covered the 2,000-meter course in a time of 5:53.8. The win capped an undefeated season for the Husky crew. "The main thing is that they didn't go overboard when they were down at the start," said UW coach Bob Ernst. "They were very controlled, patient and systematic about knowing they could make the boat go faster." The Husky junior varsity team won its race in a time of 6:45.9 to beat second-place Yale to the finish line. Washington's varsity four defeated Princeton by 2.5 seconds in the closest race of any Husky shell. Washington's sweep marked the first time since the event began in 1979 that a team had captured first place in the top three races. The Washington varsity eight team consisted of: Linda Lusk, Heidi Hook, Trish Lydon (coxswain), Alice Henderson, Kris Sanford, Lisa Beluche, Sarah Watson, Fritzi Grevstad and Katarina Wykstrom. The victory was Washington's sixth national championship in seven seasons.

UW Media Relations

Husky Spotlight

In just her sophomore season, Husky gymnast Yumi Mordre became the first NCAA champion in the sport for Washington. And she did it twice. Mordre's performance at the 1987 NCAAs will be hard to top. She won the beam and vault championships, placed fourth in the uneven bars, sixth on the vault and second in the all-around competition. Mordre's all-around finish came at Friday's competition in Salt Lake City and her individual finishes took place during Saturday's event finals. "I didn't even come into the meet thinking about the individual events," she said. "I was thinking more about the team and all-around competitions, so I'm really surprised." Mordre's showing came as a surprise to meet officials who did not invite her to the pre-meet press conference that featured the nation's top all-arounders. Mordre's two individual titles marked the first time one gymnast had taken home two event crowns in the six-year history of the meet. Her place showings gave her the distinction of being a four-time All-American. Mordre's scores helped the Huskies to finish ninth among the 12 teams competing at the championship. Oklahoma's Kelly Garrison-Steve won the all-round with a score of 38.15 while Mordre's point total was 37.85. Her scores in the all-around competition were 9.5 on vault (sixth place), 9.5 on uneven bars (seventh place), 9.45 on beam (fifth place) and 9.4 on floor exercise (11th place). She barely missed qualifying for the floor exercise event in the individual finals.

Husky Highlight

A trio of Huskies came away from the 1987 Pac-10 track and field championships at Oregon State as winners. Dan Bell took first place in the steelplechase, Vicki Borsheim won the high jump and Helena Uusitalo captured the javelin crown. Bell, a Seattle native, broke away from a six-man pack in the final lap to win the event with a personal best time of 8:36.68. That ranked as the fastest time in the nation for collegiate competitors. He would go on to place third in the event at the NCAA championships. Borsheim set a meet and Wayne Valley Field record with a jump of 6-0¾. The victory was one of several outstanding accomplishments for her. Borsheim had previously set the school record in the high jump with a leap of 6-2¾. She qualified for the NCAA championships but did not place. That year she was named an Academic All-American and the *Everett Herald's* Woman of the Year. Uusitalo won the Pac-10 meet with a throw of 180-7, far below her personal best of 202-0. She was bothered by tendinitis in her right elbow that season and had only participated in three meets. Uusitalo went on to finish second at the NCAA's with a throw of 182 feet. The 1987 Pac-10 track championships marked the first time female athletes competed in the meet.

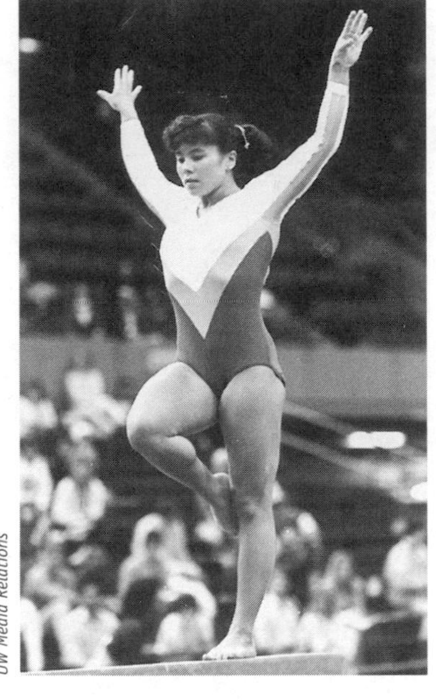

UW Media Relations

Husky Legend

Yumi Mordre

Yumi Mordre's stellar career as a gymnast at Washington almost never got started. At the start of the 1985 season, she suffered a serious knee injury during warmups for a meet. It would have been easy for Mordre to retire from the sport right then. She had already achieved great heights as a gymnast. In 1983 she won two gold medals and one silver medal at the 1983 Pan American Games. A year later she was named the alternate for the 1984 U.S. Olympic team that would go on to medal at the Los Angeles games. Mordre battled back from her injury to become the most decorated gymnast in Washington history. As a redshirt freshman she earned All-America honors by finishing fourth in the balance beam competition at the 1986 NCAAs. Earlier that season she had been honored as the NorPac gymnast of the year. A year later she became the first gymnast to win multiple events at the NCAAs by placing first in the vault and balance beam. She was second in the all-around that season. Mordre earned All-American honors a total of seven times during her four-year Husky career. She helped the Huskies to their first conference championship in 1986 and concluded her career as the school record holder in all four events and the all-around. In 1989 she was named the winner of the American Award honoring the nation's top gymnast. Mordre, whose parents were Norwegian and Japanese, grew up on Vashon Island. She spent much of her teenage years living in Eugene, Oregon, where she could train at the National Academy of Artistic Gymnastics. She eventually moved back home and competed for the Puget Sound School of Gymnastics in Puyallup. Mordre was so proficient at her sport that a move she developed, a one-armed diomidoff, was named after her.

HUSKY LISTS

Top-20 Finishers at the NCAA Women's Gymnastics Championships

Year	Gymnast	Event	Place
1999	Lanna Apisukh	All-Around	13th
1999	Lauren Riesenman	All-Around	13th
1998	Klara Kudilkova	All-Around	3rd*
1998	Tiffany Simpson	All-Around	6th*
1998	Tiffany Simpson	Vault	5th*
1998	Klara Kudilkova	Vault	8th*
1998	Tiffany Simpson	Floor Exercise	4th*
1998	Klara Kudilkova	Floor Exercise	13th*
1997	Tiffany Simpson	Vault	6th*
1997	Klara Kudilkova	Floor	6th*
1997	Tiffany Simpson	Floor	10th
1997	Tiffany Simpson	All-Around	7th*
1997	Jamie Stauffer	All-Around	9th
1997	Amber Edros	All-Around	17th
1997	Klara Kudilkova	All-Around	17th
1988	Yumi Mordre	All-Around	7th*
1988	Yumi Mordre	Balance Beam	2nd*
1987	Yumi Mordre	All-Around	2nd*
1987	Yumi Mordre	Vault	1st*
1987	Yumi Mordre	Uneven Bars	4th*
1987	Yumi Mordre	Balance Beam	1st*
1987	Yumi Mordre	Floor Exercise	11th
1986	Yumi Mordre	Balance Beam	4th*
1982	Suzie Sun	All-Around	19th

*Earned All-America honors.

HUSKY LORE

UNDER the direction of coach Earl Ellis, the Washington swimming programs enjoyed their most successful seasons. Ellis spent 20 years with the Husky program, including 19 as the head coach before retiring in 1998. He directed the men's teams to a record of 215-45 (.827) in dual meets and was responsible for starting the women's team and guiding it to a 206-29-2 (.873) record. Ellis coached 36 men's All-Americans, 25 women's All-Americans, seven Olympians (including three medalists) and six national champions. His biggest thrill might be having all three of his children compete for him at Washington. Ellis grew up in Mount Vernon and stocked the majority of his Husky rosters with swimmers from the state of Washington. His teams won three Pac-10 titles and had seven top-11 finishes at the NCAAs from 1970-78.

UW Media Relations

Husky Moment

UW Golf Team Wins Pac-10 Title

Paced by sophomore O.D. Vincent's first-place finish, the Washington men's golf team won its first conference championship since 1963 by winning the 1988 Pac-10 title. Playing at the Orinda Golf Club in Oakland, the Huskies put together rounds of 366, 369 and 369 for a three-round score of 1,104, six strokes better than second-place Arizona. Vincent fired off rounds of 73, 70 and 71 to finish two strokes under par. He became the first golfer from the northwest to finish first since Oregon's Brent Murray took medalist honors in 1978. The last Husky to place first at the conference championships was Clint Names in 1961. Bill Tindall, who was a sophomore linkster on Washington's 1963 squad, was voted the Pac-10's coach of the year. The team's championship earned the Huskies their first trip to the NCAA championships since 1966. In addition to Vincent, the Husky lineup included Todd Tibke, Scott Whaley, Ted Himka, Mike Swingle and Cameron Smith. Tibke and Whaley finished tied for second at the tournament with matching scores of 218 on the 6,352-yard, par 72 course. Himka fired a 229, Swingle scored 231 and Smith finished with a 234 total.

UW Media Relations

O.D. Vincent

Husky Spotlight

Washington extended its postseason record under head coach Don James to 7-3 with its 24-12 victory over Tulane in the Independence Bowl, in Shreveport's Independence Stadium. Taking a 6-4-1 record into the game, the Husky defense kept the Tulane Green Wave from scoring a touchdown while Washington quarterback Chris Chandler was named the Offensive Player of the Game, passing for 234 yards and two touchdowns. Led by 12 tackles from linebacker David Rill, the Washington defense held college football's 11th-best scoring team 20 points below its season average. Green Wave quarterback Terrence Jones completed 17-of-40 passes for 248 yards, and was intercepted once and sacked three times. Rover Darryl Hall picked off an errant Jones pass on the Wave's first series to set up Washington's first touchdown—a three-yard run by tailback Tony Covington culminating a 61-yard, 10-play drive completed with 7:43 to play in the first period. Tulane scored 10 second-quarter points on a 44-yard punt return by Mitchell Price and a 21-yard field goal by placekicker Todd Wiggins. The Green Wave's only other points came on a safety with seven seconds left in the game. Washington did its share of second-quarter scoring, adding 14 points to its 7-0 first-quarter lead. Both of Chandler's second-quarter touchdowns were five-yard pass completions, with the first going to tight end Bill Ames and the second to split end Darryl Franklin.

Husky Highlight

Ernst Takes Over Men's Crew

When the Washington rowing team took to the waters in 1988 it marked the first time in 20 years that Dick Erickson was not in a Husky launch barking out instructions on Lake Washington. When Erickson began work as a fundraiser at Washington, Bob Ernst took over as head coach of the men's rowing program. Ernst became the first non-Washington graduate to head up the program since Hiram Conibear in 1917. Ernst had served as the assistant men's coach from 1975 to 1980 and directed the women's team to six national championships in seven years from 1981-87. He would successfully return the Husky program to the elite level in college rowing and coach Washington to its 12th national championship in 1997.

UW Media Relations

Husky Legend

Chris Chandler

UW Media Relations

Chris Chandler set plenty of records during his quarterbacking career at Washington. On Jan. 31, 1999, 11 years after he concluded his Husky career, he set another first that he will always call his own. That day Chandler became the first former Husky signalcaller to be the starting quarterback in the Superbowl. Chandler's Atlanta Falcons team went on to lose to the Denver Broncos 34-19 in Super Bowl XXXIII, but it was quite an accomplishment for the journeyman quarterback who was with his sixth professional team. A standout prep player out of Everett High School, Chandler broke into Washington's starting lineup late in 1985, his sophomore season, when Hugh Millen was sidelined by injury. He guided Washington on a late 98-yard scoring drive to defeat USC 20-17. At that season's Freedom Bowl, he earned game MVP honors by passing for 141 yards and rushing for 72 more in the Huskies' 20-17 victory against Colorado. In 1986, as a junior, Chandler led one of the most potent offenses in Washington history. The team set a school scoring record by averaging 33.8 points per game and averaged 382.1 yards per game, the second best mark in school history. Chandler threw for a record 20 touchdowns while passing for 1,994 yards. The Huskies finished 8-3-1 and lost 28-6 to Alabama in the Sun Bowl. The school promoted Chandler for the Heisman Trophy during his senior season, a first for a Don James player at Washington. Injuries plagued him during his final campaign, and he did not meet the lofty preseason expectations. He passed for 1,739 yards but just nine touchdowns. Chandler ended the season on an up note by winning MVP honors at the 1987 Independence Bowl, a 24-12 win against Tulane. He finished his career with 4,161 passing yards, the fourth best total in school history.

Husky List

Craig Beeson Tops Soccer Scoring List

Everett native Craig Beeson recorded a pair of records when he knocked in a goal 1:15 into Washington's 8-0 victory against Seattle University in 1987. The Husky senior recorded his 19th goal of the season to establish a new single-season scoring record. It was also the 53rd goal of his career to put him in the top position on that scoring list.

Player	Seasons	Goals
1. Craig Beeson	1984-87	53
2. Dan Vaughn	1974-77	52
3. Mike Enneking	1980-83	44
4. Erik Penner	1991-94	38
5. John Klein	1981-84	37
6. Jason Boyce	1994-97	36
Ward Forrest	1972-75	36
8. Rees Bettinger	1996-99	30
Mike Park	1980-83	30
10. Eddie Henderson	1985-89	29

Husky Lore

APPROVED by the Board of Regents in April of 1985, an addition to the north side of Husky Stadium was completed in 1987 that boosted the venue's seating capacity by 13,700 to 72,500. The addition would benefit the athletic department in several ways. The additional seats projected an additional $700,000 in annual gate revenue and another $1 million in contributions. It would also make Husky Stadium one of the loudest, and toughest, college stadiums in the nation. In addition to the extra seating, the project also included the 480-seat Tyee Center. Blocks of four tickets for the endzone-to-endzone super suite were $50,000 for a 10-year period. The expansion was funded by $5 million raised by Tyee Center ticket sales, $5 million from a department endowment fund that was established in 1976, and $2.6 million from a ticket surcharge and bank and revenue loans. The project was narrowly finished on time after the first partially completed section collapsed on Feb. 25 during construction. Crews worked feverishly over the next seven months to make up for the lost time. The stadium expansion was just one of several major capital improvements at that time. A three-story office annex was constructed just north of the Husky pool to accommodate Washington's growing athletic program and provide a home for a new weight room. A team meeting room was also constructed off of the tunnel in Husky Stadium and the south grandstands in the arena's lower bowl were refurbished.

1987 W 1988

Husky Moment

Harville Guides Rowers to National Title

A change at the top did not mean a change in results for the Husky women's crew team. When Bob Ernst was named Washington's new men's crew coach, Jan Harville moved up from her assistant coaching position to take charge of the powerhouse Husky women's team. The 10th annual Women's Collegiate Rowing Championships were held in Tioga, Pennsylvania, on Lake Hammond. Sunday's finals had to be postponed a day due to windy conditions that reached 30 knots. The Huskies took the lead from the start and crossed the 2,000-meter course in a time of 6:41.00 to defeat Yale (6:42.37) and Brown (6:42.50). It was Washington's second straight title and the seventh for the program in eight years. The junior varsity program was not as good against their counterparts from Yale, finishing second to the Elis. For the first time the Huskies also won the Sprague Cup, presented to the team with the highest overall point total. The win was especially satisfying for Husky rower Chris Van Pelt. Four years earlier she was diagnosed with cancer of the lymph nodes. She lost 40 pounds while undergoing treatment, but the cancer eventually went into remission. She was joined in the victorious varsity eight shell by Lisa Beluche, Kris Sanford, Sarah Watson, Stephanie Doyle (coxswain), Gail Dorf, Katarina Wikstrom, Fritzi Grevstad, and Trudi Ockenden.

UW Media Relations

Husky Spotlight

Using a balanced scoring lineup, the Washington women's basketball team won its first Pac-10 championship during the 1987-88 season. The five Husky starters averaged between 10.7 and 12.4 points per game. The starting lineup featured Yvette Cole and Jacki Myers at guard and a frontcourt of Lisa Oriard, Traci Thirdgill and Karen Deden. Deden, a prep All-American out of Montana, earned Pac-10 co-freshman of the year honors for the year. Oriard and Cole were named to the All-Pac-10 squad and third-year coach Chris Gobrecht was tabbed as the league's coach of the year. The Huskies finished the regular season with a 24-4 record that included a 16-2 ledger against Pac-10 competition. The season will be remembered as the year the program's attendance took a huge jump up. After averaging 768 fans per game in 1986-87 the Huskies found themselves playing before crowds 10 times that size. When Washington defeated 10th-ranked Stanford 77-60 a crowd of 4,268 showed up for the matchup in Hec Edmundson Pavilion. The 11th-ranked Huskies received a first-round bye for the NCAA tournament, their fourth straight appearance. A sell-out crowd of 7,882 packed Hec Ed when Washington faced No. 18 New Mexico State. A year earlier the Huskies had attracted just 1,700 for the same team in a first-round NCAA matchup. Using its trademark pressure defense, Washington won easily 99-74 to advance to the Sweet 16.

Husky Highlight

Nancy Kessler proved to be one of the most successful golfers in the history of Washington's program while lettering four times between 1984-87. During her career, Kessler played 109 rounds and averaged 79.3 strokes per outing. She won two tournaments and finished in the top 10 nine times. The 1987-88 season was Kessler's most productive. She won both the Edean Ihlanfeldt and BYU Invitationals. Her opening-round score of 69 at BYU proved to be her best single-round score while a Husky. She placed in the top 10 in seven of the events she appeared in that season. In 1988 the Huskies placed third at the Pac-10 Championships at Sahalee Country Club, topping fifth-ranked USC, eighth-ranked Arizona and 19th-ranked Stanford. Kessler finished fourth at the tournament behind a trio of Arizona State golfers. She shot a 72 on the final day of play.

UW Media Relations

Husky Legend

UW Media Relations

Jennifer Ponath

Senior Jennifer Ponath accomplished her top two goals in 1988 by winning the shot put championship at both the Pac-10 and NCAA Championship meets. She just missed on her bid to make the United States Olympic squad. Ponath was the best of a trio of terrific throwers for the Huskies. She won the NCAA title in Eugene, Oregon, with a throw of 54-4½. Her teammates, Shirley Ross and Meg Jones, finished second and fifth, respectively, at the national meet. Their point totals helped the Huskies to a 10th-place team finish, the program's best showing at the NCAAs. Ponath became the third Washington woman to win a track and field national title. Regina Joyce had won the 3,000 meters in 1981, and Helena Uusitalo took first place in the javelin in 1986. Ponath came down with a case of strep throat the week of the NCAAs, but she kept it a secret from her coaches so they would not limit her training or pull her out of the competition. Earlier in her senior year Ponath set the school record in the shot put with a toss of 55-7. She was fourth in the event at the 1988 U.S. Track Championships with a throw of 55-6 and placed eighth at the Olympic Trials with a toss of 54-6¾.

Husky List

Top UW Women's Throwing Marks

Shot Put	
55-7	**Jennifer Ponath, 1988**
52-6	**Shirley Ross, 1988**
51-10¼	**Caryl Van Pelt, 1981**
51-5	**Aretha Hill, 1998**
51-2½	**Meg Jones, 1987**
Discus	
215-3	**Aretha Hill, 1988**
179-3	**Jennifer Ponath, 1988**
175-8	**Cecilia Barnes, 1999**
174-10	**Meg Jones, 1987**
170-7	**Sandy Whitlock, 1990**
Hammer	
169-1	**Rebecca Morrison, 1998**
168-7	**Soozie Shanley, 1996**
168-2	**Aretha Hill 1998**
156-4	**Cecilia Barnes, 1999**
144-3	**Sesilia Thomas, 1999**
Javelin	
197-4	**Helena Uusitalo, 1986**
191-2	**Deanna Carr, 1983**
182-4	**Shelly Sanford, 1989**
173-4	**Tessie Schorr, 1993**
171-10	**Liz Lasater, 1986**

Husky Lore

The Nordstrom Tennis Center

ON March 18 of 1988 ground was broken on the $3.9 million Lloyd Nordstrom Tennis Center. The 51,000-square foot complex featured six indoor courts, a lockerroom, a snack bar and seating for 300 spectators. The building's namesake played varsity tennis at Washington from 1930-32 and was captain in 1932. He was the youngest of the three sons of John Nordstrom, the founder of Nordstrom, Inc. A gift of $2.5 million from his family provided the major funding for the facility. The construction, on a former athletic practice field, began that month and was completed in June of 1989. The center would allow the Husky men's and women's programs to have a first-rate facility for matches and practices. Washington would no longer have to rent space from local tennis clubs and be forced to work around their schedules. In 1988, the year before the building opened, the men's and women's teams combined to play just nine of 54 matches at home due to the difficulties of scheduling court time. As a result of the building's construction, both tennis coaching positions were elevated to full-time status.

Husky Moment

Husky Football Teams Pulls off Miracle Comeback at Cal

Trailing by 24 points in the third quarter, the Washington football team recorded its greatest come-from-behind victory at California to keep its eight-game win streak against the Bears alive. The Huskies entered their matchup with Cal as an 11-point favorite, but the team was reeling after losing to Arizona 16-13 on a last-second field goal. Washington looked listless in the opening 30 minutes. By halftime Cal had rolled up 263 yards of offense and a 24-3 lead thanks to a school-record 55-yard field goal on the final play of the second quarter. In the locker room at halftime, Husky defensive coordinator Jim Lambright gave a fiery talk to his players. It worked. After the Bears added a field goal to take a 27-3 lead in the third quarter, the Huskies kept Cal in check and regrouped on offense. Washington went on to score 25 points in the final 20 minutes of the game to squeeze out a 28-27 victory. Placekicker John McCallum capped the comeback with a 25-yard field goal with just two seconds to play to raise the Huskies' record to 6-4. Washington quarterback Cary Conklin engineered the Husky comeback by passing for a career high 315 yards, completing 24 of 42 pass attempts. Brian Slater was the other offensive star, catching eight passes for 146 yards, including a 33-yard grab to set up Washington's winning field goal. California managed just 115 yards in the second half and could not convert on a short-yardage situation that would have allowed the Bears to run the clock out.

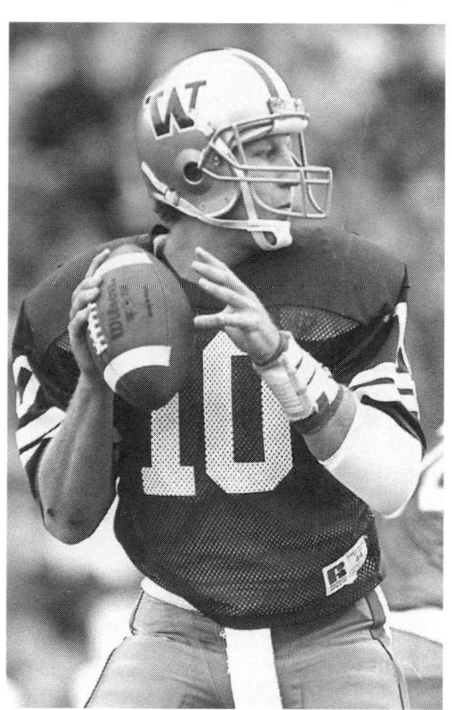
UW Media Relations

Cary Conklin

Husky Spotlight

The Washington men's rowing team showed signs of a revival when it surprised the field at the 1989 national rowing championships with a second-place finish. Harvard, the regatta's heavy favorite, won its third consecutive national title in one of the closest races in the Cincinnati event's history. The Crimson covered the course in 5:36.5 but they had to come from behind to reel in the Husky team which led by two seats at the halfway point on the 2,000-meter Lake Harsha course. Washington's time was 5:38.9. Only seven seconds separated the top six teams in the finals. The Huskies gained a measure of revenge by beating Pac-10 Champion UCLA to the finish line. The Bruins had nipped the Huskies at the Pacific Coast Championship by just .17 seconds. Washington, which had not won a regatta in three years, had to pay its own way to the event. Most of the teams invited were provided with expenses money for the trip to Cincinnati. It was the Huskies' first appearance at the national championships since 1985.

Husky Highlight

In 1989 Eldridge Recasner topped off his Washington career by becoming the first Husky men's basketball player to earn all-conference honors three years in a row since Bill Hanson did it in 1962. Recasner's selection made him one of six UW players to make an all-conference team three times. Recasner's honors were certainly well deserved. He averaged 17.0 points as a sophomore, 18.1 as a junior and 16.2 as a senior. His point total (1,700) was the third best in Husky history when he concluded his career. He also figured second on the all-time assists (367) and steals (115) lists. He was the first three-time captain in Washington history.

UW Media Relations

Husky Legend

Joanie Komura

O.D. Vincent

O.D. Vincent is responsible for reviving the Husky golf program twice, once as a player and later as a coach. In 1988, as a 19-year-old sophomore, he won the 1988 Pac-10 individual championship and guided the Huskies to their first team title since 1963. It was only the third conference title in the program's history. Washington went on to place 15th at the NCAA Championships. That season Vincent averaged 74.7 over 23 rounds of play. He also won the HammondBell Pacific Coast Intercollegiate and set a three-round school record at the Stanford/U.S. Intercollegiate with a six-under score of 210. At the NCAAs, Vincent led the tournament after two rounds before finishing 19th. He redshirted the 1990 season and then returned to earn co-medalist honors, along with teammates Mike Swingle, at the 1991 Oregon Invitational. He finished second at four events that season, including the Pac-10s. In November of 1991, he shot a final round of 67 and became the only American to qualify for the European Tour in 1992. At the 1992 British Open, he was among the leaders after the first two rounds of play. Vincent's father, Orrin II, grew up in Kent and played golf at Seattle University. A course developer, in August of 2000 he opened Washington National, an 18-hole course featuring a Husky theme in Auburn, Washington. O.D. was named the head golf coach at his alma mater in 1996. He guided his 1999 team to a fourth-place finish at the NCAA championships. He was honored as the College Golf Association's National Coach of the Year for the 1999 season.

HUSKY LIST

Football's Greatest Comebacks

Here is a list of the games where Washington rallied from a deficit of 14 points or more to gain a victory:

Deficit	Time	Qtr.	Final	Opponent	Site (Date)
24 (3-27)	9:03	3Q	28-27	California	Seattle (Nov. 12, 1988)
21 (0-21)	12:31	3Q	27-26	California	Berkeley (Oct. 10, 1981)
21 (0-21)	1:41	2Q	22-21	Purdue	W. Lafayette (Sept. 23, 1972)
21 (0-21)	3:42	1Q	28-27	UCLA	Pasadena (Oct. 28, 1989)
20 (3-23)	7:25	3Q	24-23	California	Berkeley (Oct. 9, 1993)
17 (0-17)	9:44	3Q	21-17	Oregon	Eugene (Sept. 22, 1979)
15 (7-22)	4:13	2Q	30-29	Oregon St.	Portland (Oct. 22, 1960)
14 (14-28)	5:30	2Q	42-38	Arizona St.	Tempe (Sept. 5, 1998)
14 (10-24)	14:51	4Q	25-24	Michigan	Seattle (Sept. 17, 1983)
14 (0-14)	3:33	1Q	30-23	Wash. St.	Spokane (Nov. 22, 1980)
14 (0-14)	10:17	2Q	29-20	Oregon St.	Corvallis (Oct. 24, 1970)

IT is safe to say that legendary Husky marching band director Bill Bissell marched to a different beat. He took over the Washington band in 1970 and made it one of the most entertaining units in the country. The Huskies were known for their zany and colorful antics. At the 1979 Sun Bowl the band performed a mock striptease at halftime. In one Apple Cup matchup with Washington State, Bissell had the band spell out SILO TECH while playing the Cougar fight song. The band once saluted California by spelling out BEERS and BARES before finally getting it right with a formation that read BEARS. A native of Dunsmuir, California, Bissell's family moved to Ashland, Oregon when he was 10 years old. That was the same town that produced fabled Husky quarterback Sonny Sixkiller. Bissell graduated from Willamette University in Salem, Oregon, majoring in music education. After earning a master's degree in music from Illinois, he taught and served as the band director for 14 years at Bremerton West High School before joining the Husky staff. Bissell made songs such as "Tequila" and "Louie, Louie," such fan favorites that the latter was proposed as a possible state song. "I love good vaudeville," Bissell once said. "I think I was born at the wrong time. Those older acts intrigue me with the cleverness they show. The surprise element is big. I've always kept that in the back of my mind when planning shows."

Husky Moment

Volleyball Upsets No. 2 Stanford

The Husky women's volleyball team pulled off the biggest upset in the program's history when it toppled second-ranked Stanford in the first round of the 1988 NCAA West Regional at UCLA's Pauley Pavilion. The ninth-ranked Huskies had lost to Stanford twice earlier in the season and were not expected to put up a serious challenge. Washington won the match 15-11, 3-15, 9-15, 15-9 and 15-8. The deciding fifth game was tied at 5-5 before the Huskies reeled off nine straight points to grab a commanding 14-5 lead. Laurie Wetzel led the UW effort with 24 kills, eight blocks and 19 digs. Stanford finished the season with a 28-3 record. The Huskies had a good feeling when they extended Stanford to a fifth game. Washington had not lost all season when going the full five games in a match. The Huskies reached the regional championships after defeating Arizona State in the opening round of the tournament in Hec Edmundson Pavilion. That marked the first time the Huskies had played in the larger Pavilion in seven seasons. The 1988 NCAA tournament was Washington's first postseason appearance since 1986 when the Huskies lost to top-ranked BYU in the opening round of play. UCLA, the No. 1 team in 1988, eliminated the Huskies 3-0 in the third round of the championship. Washington finished the season with a 22-7 record under first-year coach Debbie Buse, a former two-time letterwinner for the Huskies.

UW Media Relations

Laurie Wetzel

Husky Spotlight

Picked to finish ninth in the Pac-10 in the preseason poll, the Husky volleyball team shocked everyone by advancing to the third round of the NCAA Championships in 1988. Heading up Washington's impressive play was All-American Laurie Wetzel. She guided the Huskies to a 22-7 record and a highest-ever ranking of ninth. A native of Puyallup, she led the Pac-10 in both kills and digs as a senior. She ranked ninth nationally in kills with an average of 14.63 per match. She figured 13th nationally in digs with 11.42 per contest. The Huskies finished their Pac-10 slate with a 13-5 record, good for third place in the league standings. An outside hitter, she was the third player chosen in the Major League Volleyball draft in 1989. She finished her Husky career with 505 kills to establish a school record.

Husky Highlight

Women Rowers Dominate Pacific Coast Championships

The Washington women's rowers wrapped up a decade of excellence by winning their 10th consecutive Pacific Coast/ Pac-10 Championship in 1989 in Sacramento. The Huskies defeated Stanford by four seconds, winning with a time of 6:44.64. The Huskies had lost to California earlier in the year and posted a slower time than Stanford at the Stanford Classic earlier in the year. For once, the Huskies were not a strong favorite at the Pac-10 Championship, but they proved their detractors wrong. The Huskies would go on to place fourth at the national rowing championships and the junior varsity squad captured the national title. UCLA would break the Huskies' winning streak at the Pac-10s by claiming the 1990 and 1991 championships.

Husky Legend

UW Media Relations

Yvette Cole

During Yvette Cole's senior season, head coach Chris Gobrecht stated: "She is far and away the single greatest impact player, and she's probably one of the best representatives of what the program's all about, her style of play, where she came from as a person." It was high praise from Gobrecht, but well deserved. As a freshman in 1984-85, Cole was named the NorPac Conference Newcomer of the Year. That season she tied for the team lead in scoring, rebounding and steals and was second in assists. Not bad for a 5-8 player who did not earn a starting role except for six games. Cole would end up leading Washington in scoring in each of her four seasons. She averaged 12.2 points as a freshman, 14.1 as a sophomore, 12.7 as a junior and 15.5 as a senior. She completed her career with 1,681 points, the third highest total at the time. She earned All-Pac-10 honors during her junior and senior seasons. Cole's job was usually to defend the opposing team's best guard—an honor for a Gobrecht-coached team. A product of Wilson High School in San Francisco, she played in the NCAA tournament every year she was a Husky. Washington produced records of 24-6, 23-7, 25-5 and 23-10 during her career. While she was not recruited by Gobrecht, she proved to be one of her most reliable players. As a senior she was forced to play most of the season at small forward because of injuries to the team. Cole appeared in 95 games during her career, but started only 28 times. She was inducted into the Husky Hall of Fame in 1996.

HUSKY LIST

Women's Pac-10 Rowing Championship Results

Year	Site	Varsity 8	JV 8	Novice 8	Varsity 4
2000	Lake Natoma	Washington	Washington	Washington	Washington
1999	Lake Natoma	Washington	Washington	Washington	Washington
1998	Lake Natoma	Washington	Washington	Washington	USC
1997	Lake Natoma	Washington	Washington	Washington	Sacramento St.
1996	Redwood Shores	Washington	Wash. St.	Washington	Mills
1995	Redwood Shores	Washington	Wash. St.	Washington	Washington
1994	Lake Natoma	Washington	Washington	Wash. St.	Washington
1993	Lake Natoma	Washington	Washington	Washington	Pacific Lutheran
1992	Lake Natoma	Washington	Washington	Washington	Washington
1991	Lake Natoma	UCLA	UCLA	Washington	Wash. St.
1990	Lake Natoma	UCLA	UCLA	Washington	UC Santa Barbara
1989	Lake Natoma	Washington	Washington	California	UC Santa Barbara
1988	Lake Natoma	Washington	Washington	Stanford	Washington
1987	Lake Natoma	Washington	Washington	Washington	Washington
1986	Lake Natoma	Washington	Washington	Washington	Washington
1985	Lake Natoma	Washington	Washington	Washington	Washington
1984	Lake Natoma	Washington		California	UCLA
1983	Redwood Shores	Washington	Washington	Washington	Washington
1982	Redwood Shores	Washington	Washington	Washington	Oregon State
1981	Redwood Shores	Washington	Washington	California	Washington
1980	Redwood Shores	Washington	California	Washington	
1979	Redwood Shores	California	California	Washington	Washington
1978	Montlake Cut	California	California	Washington	
1977	Redwood Shores	Washington			Washington

SEATTLE was the center of the college basketball universe late in the decade of the 1980s. Washington played host to back-to-back NCAA Women's Final Fours in 1988 and 1989 at the Tacoma Dome. At the same time the University hosted the NCAA Men's West Regional in 1988 and the Men's Final Four in 1989 at the Seattle Kingdome. The 1988 Women's Final Four drew a crowd of 8,584 and saw Louisiana Tech come from behind to defeat Auburn in a thrilling 56-54 contest. The following year saw Tennessee defeat conference opponent Auburn 76-70 in the finals. It marked only the second time the Women's Final Four had been held in the same city in back-to-back seasons. The first two Women's Final Fours, in 1982 and 1983 were contested in Norfolk, Virginia. In the first overtime game for the national championship since 1963, Michigan defeated Seton Hall 80-79 to win the 1989 Men's Final Four. The 1988 Pac-10 Men's basketball tournament was scheduled to be played in the Tacoma Dome, but a problem with local promotional sponsorships forced the tournament to be moved to Tucson. Washington had played host to the Men's Final Four in 1984 and would do so again in 1995.

1989 W 1990

Husky Moment

Cary Conklin Sets Passing Mark

Coming off a dramatic 28-27 come-from-behind victory at UCLA, Husky quarterback Cary Conklin found himself needing to pull off another miracle finish the next week when he set Washington's all-time passing mark. Conklin and the Huskies trailed the Bruins 21-0 in the Rose Bowl, but answered with a 10-yard touchdown run by Greg Lewis with a minute to play to cap the rally. The next week at home against Arizona State, Washington found itself down 21-7 early in the second quarter. The Huskies managed to rally and tie the game at 24-24 before the Sun Devils pulled away for a 34-32 victory. Conklin was spectacular in the loss. He completed 28 of 42 passes for 428 yards and three touchdowns. He also threw three interceptions in the game. Conklin entered the game with 1,876 passing yards and finished the game with 2,304 yards, one more than Sonny Sixkiller's single-season total he set in 1970. Only Sixkiller, Tom Flick and Steve Pelluer had passed for 2,000 yards in a season before Conklin eclipsed the mark. Andre Riley was Conklin's main target against the Sun Devils. He caught nine passes for 223 yards and two scores. Riley's total's included a 69-yard touchdown catch. Conklin was four-for-six for 89 yards in the first quarter, eight-for-13 in the second quarter for 113 yards, seven-for-10 in third for 72 yards and nine-for-13 for 144 yards in the final period. The old Husky single-game passing record was 387 yards by Sixkiller in a game against Purdue in 1971. Riley's receiving total was the best day by a Husky since the 1968 season. In addition to breaking the passing record, Conklin also established a new mark for total offense with 419 yards, toppling Sixkiller's previous best of 362 yards against Oregon State in 1970. Washington's team passing total was a record, bettering the old mark of 409 yards set in 1970 against UCLA. Turnovers were costly in the defeat for the Huskies. In addition to Conklin's three interceptions, Washington also fumbled the ball away three times, including two that were the result of blindside hits on Conklin. Washington and Arizona State delighted the Homecoming crowd at Husky Stadium with a combined total of 1,020 offensive yards, 527 by the Huskies.

UW Media Relations

Husky Spotlight

The 1989 NCAA cross country championships proved to be the best finishes ever for both the Washington men's and women's programs. Hosted by the U.S. Naval Academy in Annapolis, Maryland, the Husky men figured fourth overall and the women came in 12th place. Al Hjort, a senior from Marysville, turned in a school-best 23rd-place finish for Washington in a time of 30:28. He earned All-America honors for his effort. A year earlier he was 65th at the event. The previous best men's team finish came in 1988 when the harriers placed 18th. Curt Corvin's 27th-place finish in 1986 was the previous best effort by a Husky. The Husky women had won both the Pac-10 and Region VII titles leading up to the national meet. Washington's finish bettered the previous best showing of 13th-place in 1982. Sue Ocken paced the Huskies by placing 39th overall. The other women's finishers were Jennifer Gillett (43rd), Michele Buresh (54th), Jennifer Draughon (73rd) and Stacie Hoitink (77th). Washington's other men's runners were Pat Johnson (35th), Adam Leahy (43rd), Stormy Shouman (91st) and Shawn Anderson (106th). Johnson earned regional Academic All-American honors in 1989.

Husky Highlight

Rick Noji Wins Pac-10 High Jump Title

After tying for second place twice in the high jump at the Pac-10 Championships, Rick Noji finally conquered the event as a senior in 1990. A fifth-year senior, Noji won the conference meet with a jump of 7-2½. The meet took on special meaning for Noji since it marked the final time he competed in Husky Stadium as a collegian. Noji outleaped California's Jeff Rogers for the title. Rogers' best leap was two inches shorter than Noji's winning mark. They were the only two competitors to clear the 7-0 mark. To the delight of the 3,556 in attendance, Noji took one shot at his own Husky Stadium record of 7-4½, but he just narrowly missed tying the mark. Noji, who was also a sprinter on the Husky track squad, was hampered during his senior season by a knee injury that affected his takeoff attempts in the high jump. The Washington coached decided to pull Noji from the 400-meter race to allow him to concentrate on the high jump. Noji's win made him the first Husky to win a Pac-10 title in the event. "It means a lot to win here," Noji said after the winning jump, "I just put the past behind me."

Husky Legend

UW Media Relations

Rick Noji

Few high jumpers in the world could achieve what Washington's Rick Noji did during his track career. While Noji's career best leap was an impressive 7-6$\frac{1}{2}$, it was still quite some distance from the best marks in the world. But then again, at just 5-8, Noji was competing in a sport where most of his competitors were at least four inches taller than he was. On top of that, Noji was also an outstanding sprinter during his college career. Noji first gained acclaim while competing for the Franklin High School track team. As a sophomore he cleared a height of 6-11$\frac{3}{4}$. As a junior he leaped 7-4$\frac{1}{2}$. As a senior he cleared 7-4. That same year he set the Husky Stadium record during at the state meet with a jump of 7-2. Noji discovered he had a natural ability for the sport between his freshman and sophomore years in high school when he leaped 5-8$\frac{1}{2}$ in his first attempt at clearing a raised bar. A Japanese-American, Noji felt that his sprinters' speed helped him to make up for his lack of size. "I'm a speed jumper," Noji said. "It seems like when I'm sprinting well, I'm jumping well. And if I stop sprinting, I usually find my jumping falls off." Noji once finished third in a 60-meter race that featured Canadian Olympian Ben Johnson, the one-time world sprint champion. In Noji's first meet at Washington, he set the school record with a high jump of 7-3$\frac{1}{2}$. He won the 55-meter dash in that same competition. Noji reset the school mark at the World Asian Games in Mexico City when he set a personal best with a jump of 7-5. He went on to equal that height five times during his college career. In 1987 he placed second at the Pac-10s in the high jump and sixth at the NCAA's with a 7-1 clearance. In 1989, while redshirting the track season, he jumped 7-6$\frac{1}{2}$ at a meet in Eugene to set a school record that still existed when he was inducted into the Husky Hall of Fame in 1999. Noji competed at three world championships (1991, 1993 and 1995) and four U.S. Olympic Trials (1984, 1988, 1992 and 1996). He was recognized six times as an All-American during his Husky career. The best measure of how impressive a high jumper Noji was probably comes in a comparison of how much height competitors can clear above their heads. Noji's top effort was 20$\frac{1}{2}$ inches above his head. Only Franklin Jacobs, another 5-8 competitor who once jumped 7-8, leaped higher than Noji.

Husky List

Single-Season Husky Football Passing Leaders

(Based on passing yards)	PA	PC	PCT	TD	YDS
1. Cary Conklin (1989)	365	208	.570	16	2569
2. Damon Huard (1995)	287	184	.641	11	2415
3. Sonny Sixkiller (1970)	362	186	.514	15	2303
4. Billy Joe Hobert (1991)	285	173	.607	22	2271
5. Marques Tuiasosopo (1999)	295	171	.580	12	2221
6. Steve Pelluer (1983)	317	213	.672	11	2212
7. Tom Flick (1980)	280	168	.600	15	2178
8. Marques Tuiasosopo (2000)	323	170	.529	14	2146
9. Brock Huard (1997)	244	146	.598	23	2140
10. Sonny Sixkiller (1971)	297	126	.424	13	2068

Husky Lore

UW Media Relations

WHILE he only played one season for the Husky golf team, Mike Combs has a place in Washington history as the only UW graduate to play in the Masters. After playing his first three seasons at Oklahoma, Combs played his final collegiate season at Washington in 1989-90. A native of Kennewick, Washington, he played in all 37 of Washington's competitive rounds, averaging 73.9 strokes per round. In the summer of 1990, he won the United States Public Links Championship in Portland and earned a spot in the field for the 1991 Masters. In Augusta, Combs was matched with golf legend Jack Nicklaus for the first two rounds. He missed the cut, but shot a second-round 74 while carding a two-day score of 155.

1989 W 1990

Husky Moment

Women's Basketball to Regional Finals

In 1990 the Husky women's basketball team finished its most successful season by reaching the regional finals of the NCAA Championships. Washington and Stanford tied for the Pac-10 title with identical 17-1 records. The Cardinal crushed Washington 102-62 in Palo Alto on Jan. 11 and then a month later the Huskies returned the favor by dumping Stanford 81-78 in Hec Edmundson Pavilion. Washington went into the NCAA tournament as the No. 1 seed in the Mideast Region and ranked third in the nation. The Huskies received a first-round bye and opened the tournament against a 22-9 DePaul squad, who had beaten Western Kentucky in the opening round of play. DePaul was a team that had beaten Washington 61-57 in the Huskies' third game of the season. Playing before a capacity crowd of 8,170 in the Pavilion, the Huskies gained their revenge by dropping the Blue Demons 77-68. Washington advanced to the regional in Iowa City to face South Carolina in the Sweet 16. The Lady Gamecocks were ranked No. 19 nationally and sported a 24-8 record. Washington struggled in the early going and found itself trailing by two when head coach Chris Gobrecht drew a technical foul seven minutes into the contest. That seemed to rally the team, and five minutes later the Huskies went on a 22-2 run to take a 43-24 lead. Behind Karen Deden's 17 points, the Huskies defeated South Carolina 73-61. Jacki Myers added 16 points while Tracy Thirdgill and Amy Mickelson both scored 14 points. The Huskies' pressure defense forced the Lady Gamecocks into 25 turnovers. One game away from the Final Four in Knoxville, the Huskies faced an Auburn squad looking for its third consecutive trip to the finals. Outrebounded 52 to 38, Washington lost to the Tigers 76-50. Deden was the only Husky in double figures with 11 points. Washington finished the season with a 28-3 record. In the NCAA finals, Stanford would defeat Auburn for the national title.

UW Media Relations

Karen Deden

Husky Spotlight

Amy Mickelson broke into the starting lineup for the Washington women's basketball team as a junior and helped the Huskies to back-to-back 23-10 and 28-3 records. Her senior season the 6-3 center helped to guide the Huskies to the regional finals of the NCAA tournament. That season she led the Huskies with a 14.9 scoring average and was the team's most accurate shooter, connecting on 51.2 percent of her field-goal attempts. Her father, George, was the governor of South Dakota during her years as a Husky. Mickelson was known for her trademark hook shot. "If every player does what Amy had done," said coach Chris Gobrecht, "We'll be a top 10 team forever."

UW Media Relations

Husky Highlight

One of the most memorable games in Washington's women's basketball history was played on Feb. 10 in 1990 when No. 2 Stanford visited Hec Edmundson Pavilion. The game drew a capacity crowd of 7,704 and they were treated to a classic. A month earlier the Huskies had been humiliated at Stanford by a 102-62 score. The Cardinal came into the matchup with a 20-0 overall record and a 10-0 mark in Pac-10 play. A victory against the No. 7 Huskies would practically wrap up the Pac-10 title for Stanford. The Huskies played steady and built a 10-point lead in the second half only to see the Cardinal rally and tie the game at 73-73. Laurie Merlino scored the Huskies' final eight points to give Washington an 81-78 victory. The junior guard hit a 15-foot jumper to give UW a 75-73 lead with 1:43 to play. She then converted a layin with 57 seconds left to increase the Husky lead to four points. Katie Steding knocked down a jump shot to bring Stanford within two. Merlino made a pair of free throws with 15 seconds left and then two more when the Cardinal received a technical foul for calling a timeout when it did not have any left. Merlino finished the game with 22 points. Amy Mickelson led the Huskies with 24 points, while Traci Thirdgill, regarded as a defensive specialist, added 15 points. Trisha Stevens topped Stanford's scoring with 21 points while Jennifer Azzi added 18 and Steding 15.

UW Media Relations

Husky Legend

Jan Harville

During her freshman orientation at Washington in 1970, a notice caught Jan Harville's eye. "It was a sign for the women's rowing club," Harville recalls. "It said, `No experience necessary,' so I decided to try it." Women's crew in Seattle may never have been the same if Harville had not decided to give the sport a shot. Harville rowed as an undergraduate from 1970-73 and won the team's most inspirational award as a senior. She continued her rowing career with the Lake Washington Rowing club and later as a member of the U.S. National Team from 1978-84. At the same time she worked as a microbiologist for Northwest Hospital. Harville's hard work and determination paid off in 1980 when she was selected to compete for the 1980 U.S. Olympic Team. That same year she joined the Husky program as the women's freshman coach. Unable to compete at the 1980 Olympic games due to the U.S. boycott, she finally realized that dream when she rowed for the 1984 team at the Los Angeles Games. Her international resume includes a bronze medal at the 1979 World Championships and a gold medal at the 1980 event and silvers in 1982 and 1983. She has also coached numerous national teams in international competition. After working as a Husky assistant coach for Bob Ernst until the 1988 season, she took over as the women's head coach. In her first year she coached Washington's varsity eight to the national championship, the seventh in an eight-year period for the program. In 1996 when the NCAA began to sponsor a championship in rowing Harville was named to the women's crew committee. The Huskies captured the first two NCAA team titles in 1997 and 1998 while also winning the varsity eight championships at those events. In 1991 Harville was inducted into the National Rowing Hall of Fame.

Husky Lists

Top Women's Basketball Attendance Marks

Date	Opponent	Attendance
Mar. 17, 1990	DePaul	8,170
Mar. 11, 1995	Stanford	7,900
Mar. 19, 1988	New Mexico State	7,882
Feb. 10, 1990	Stanford	7,704
Mar. 3, 1990	UCLA	7,392
Jan. 11, 1991	Stanford	7,383
Feb. 12, 1994	Southern California	7,349
Jan. 6, 1994	Stanford	7,238
Jan. 25, 1992	Stanford	7,211
Jan. 23, 1999	Stanford	6,872
Feb. 25, 1995	Stanford	6,857
Mar. 16, 1991	Iowa	6,814
Feb. 26, 1994	Washington State	6,608
Jan. 30, 1993	Stanford	6,452
Feb. 19, 1995	Oregon	6,079

Husky Lore

IN the summer of 1990, Washington and the city of Seattle played host to the second Goodwill Games. The international sporting competition, the brainchild of television executive Ted Turner, included 1,200 athletes from 84 countries competing in 21 sports. It was one of the largest civic events in the city's history. Moscow had hosted the first Goodwill Games in 1986. Those contests featured just 19 events and a "finals only" format. The 1990 Goodwill Games were the largest multisport event in the United States since the 1984 Olympic Games in Los Angeles. Washington's campus was used to house the athletes and Husky Stadium served as the site for the track and field events and the opening ceremonies. Hec Edmundson Pavilion featured wrestling and volleyball competitions. The 17-day event, which started on July 20, was staged at a cost of $60 million. Over 70,000 fans turned out for the opening ceremonies. The high caliber of the track and field participants saw numerous Husky Stadium records fall. In April of 1990 the new King County Aquatics center was opened in Federal Way to host the swimming events. It would later become a part-time home for the Husky swimming team and a frequent site for the Pac-10 Championships.

W Super Legend

UW Media Relations

Lynn Colella

In early 1972, Lynn Colella and her brother, Rick, were honored as the co-winners of the *Seattle Post-Intelligencer's* 1971 Sports Man of the Year. It was special because it was first time that a brother and sister combination ever won the honor. Lynn, after graciously accepting the "Man of the Year" award quipped: "After all, isn't that what every girl dreams of —being Man of the Year?" Maybe Lynn in a subtle way encouraged the award to be renamed to the "Sports Star of the Year" (which it is now called). It was one of her many leadership acts to bring equality to women's athletics.

The Colellas received the award for gold medal wins in the 1971 Pan America Games and other national and international victories. Lynn won a gold in the 200-meter butterfly and 200-meter breaststroke and Rick won the 200-meter breaststroke. Lynn also took a third in the 100 meter breaststroke, and Rick captured a silver in the 400-meter individual medley. He would go on to be a member of the 1972 U.S. Olympic Team and finish fourth in the 200-meter breaststroke. He would win a bronze medal in the 200-meter breaststroke in the 1976 Munich Olympics.

Earlier in 1971, Colella set an American record in winning the 200-yard breaststroke in the National American Amateur Union (AAU) indoor championships. She also won 100-yard breaststroke, was second in the 200-yard butterfly, and finished fourth in the 100-yard butterfly.

After many years of training, the best was still to come. Colella started swimming in 1961 at the age of 10 at the Cascade Swim Club. She was coached initially by John Tallman who two years later became the Husky men's swimming coach. Early on, Colella set her sights high. Her goal was to make the 1968 U.S. Olympic Team. She missed out for a spot on the team by three tenths of a second in the 200-meter butterfly. The 1972 Olympics quickly became her goal. It was not easy keeping her competitive edge when she entered the University of Washington in the fall of 1968. Washington did not have a women's swimming team. She sandwiched two daily workouts around her electrical engineering studies, training during the week with the Husky men's swim team and at the Cascade Swim Club on the weekends.

Colella admitted it was difficult for her to continue competing. "In those days, there was no future in the sport for women in college. Men had athletic scholarships and four years of good competition. Yet there is so much pressure on a woman. You can't be a social butterfly when you're getting up at 6 a.m. on Saturday to swim."

Somehow, she managed to successfully pursue her academic and athletic goals. In January 1972, she set a new American record in the 200-yard butterfly. She set three meet records in the Women's National Intercollegiate swimming and diving championships held in March. One record was in 200-yard freestyle, the other two in the 100-yard butterfly and 100-yard breaststroke events. In April, she won the 200-yard breaststroke and took third in the 200-butterfly in the National AAU indoor championships.

After graduating in June 1972, magna cum laude, with an electrical engineering degree and a Phi Beta Kappa key, she made the U.S. Olympic Team when she finished second in the 200-meter butterfly in the Olympic Trials. She was chosen as the co-captain of the U.S. Olympic women's swim team.

At the 1972 Munich Olympics, it took a world record to keep Lynn from winning the gold medal in the 200-meter butterfly. Colella pushed her teammate, Karen Moe to victory in 2 minutes, 15.6 seconds, bettering the world mark by a full second. Lynn won the silver medal in 2:16.4 and another American, Stanford's Ellie Daniel, took third in 2:16.7. It was a three-women race when Moe, Daniel, and Colella came off the turn at 150 meters virtually together. Moe surged ahead, and Colella moved past Daniel in the last five strokes.

Colella continued her competitive swimming until 1975, winning numerous AAU, national, and international competitions and setting an American record in the 200-yard butterfly and 200-yard breaststroke in 1973. She also competed in the 1973 and 1975 World Championships. She pursued a master's degree in electrical engineering and helped coach the Husky women's club team to a third place national finish in 1973. She was inducted in the Husky Hall of Fame in 1980, the first women to be admitted.

Yumi Mordre

Yumi Mordre is the most decorated gymnast in Washington history. She was the first and only Husky female gymnast to win an NCAA title; the first Husky female to earn All-America honors (achieved seven times); and the first female gymnast in NCAA history to win two individual titles in a single year.

Mordre started gymnastics at the age of seven near her home on Vashon Island.

"I had a lot of extra energy after school," she recalled. "My mother thought gymnastics would be a good way to get body awareness and use my excess energy, and so she enrolled me in some tumbling classes."

Mordre's gymnastics interests took her to the National Academy of Artistic Gymnasts in Eugene, Oregon to train with elite gymnasts from all over the country. She made the U.S. National Team—the top 20 female gymnasts in the nation—in 1981 and was a member for three more years. She moved from Eugene back to the Tacoma area and attended Charles Wright Academy and graduated from Franklin Pierce High School in 1984. She never competed on her high school gymnastics teams but opted to train at the Puget Sound School of Gymnastics in Puyallup. She competed in the 1983 Pan American Games, winning a gold medal in the floor exercise, a silver in the all-around, and a team gold. Mordre finished ninth in the 1984 US Olympic Trials—eight made the team—and was named as the first alternate on the team.

That disappointing experience taught her what she believes is the most important thing she learned from the sport.

"I think athletics helps to teach you that winning is not everything, and that it is OK to come in second or last, as long as you give it your best and that you learn from your mistakes. It is much easier to win than it is to lose and how you handle that and how you actually set out to improve yourself is what athletics provides."

Mordre entered Washington primarily because of its business school and because her parents would be able to see her compete. College gymnastics posed an interesting challenge to her. Elite female gymnasts are young. Usually, they reach their prime between the ages of 15 and 17. By the time they attend college, they often are burned out and worn out on gymnastics. In college, you begin to compete with the lower level of the elite class of gymnasts or the level just below. However, Mordre saw the college competition as a great opportunity. She actually improved some of her routines, particularly in the uneven bar event. She also focused on the academic part of her life.

In her freshman year, Mordre's primary focus was on getting back to a competitive level after reconstructive knee surgery to repair a torn ligament. In addition, she grew over three inches and her timing was off. She did not compete in 1985. As a redshirt freshman in 1986, she became Washington's first All-America gymnast with a fourth-place finish on the balance beam at the NCAA championships. The next two seasons were her best years as a college competitor. In her sophomore year, she was Washington's first female NCAA champion, winning the balance beam and the vault. She finished second in the all-around, fourth in the uneven bars, and 11th in the floor exercise. In 1988, Mordre placed in the top 10 in three events at the NCAA championships—second in the balance beam, sixth in the floor exercise, and seventh in the all-around. In 1989, she said: "My body was just getting old." Unfortunately, she suffered a fracture of her heel in warm-ups on the uneven bars at the NCAA meet to go with a triceps pull suffered earlier in the season. She still competed but did not finish very well.

In Pac-10 conference competition, Mordre was a five-time champion. She won the balance beam in 1988 and 1989 and the floor exercise, vault, and all-around in 1987. In 1987, she was named the University's Female Athlete of the Year. As a senior, she was selected by American Athletics Incorporated as the 1989 National Senior Gymnast of the Year in recognition of her academic, athletic, and community achievements. She was named an Academic All-America in 1989, graduating with a 3.5 grade point average. Mordre was inducted into the Husky Hall of Fame in 1995.

1990-2000

Husky Moment

Rose Bowl Victory

Husky sophomore Mark Brunell passed for a pair of touchdowns and ran for two more to lead Pac-10 Champion Washington to a convincing 46-34 win over Iowa in the 1991 Rose Bowl. Washington and Iowa combined for 80 points, making the 77th Rose Bowl the highest scoring in history. The opportunistic Huskies built a 33-7 halftime lead, with two first-half touchdowns coming courtesy of the UW defense. The Pasadena victory left Washington 10-2 for the season, while Iowa dropped to 8-4. The game marked Washington's 12th bowl appearance in the 16-year coaching reign of Don James, who improved his bowl record to 9-3, including 3-1 in the Rose Bowl. Left-handed Brunell's running and passing skills earned him Rose Bowl MVP honors as he completed 14 of 22 passes for 163 yards. Washington faithful also rejoiced in the return of senior All-America running back Greg Lewis, who spent the month prior to the Rose Bowl rehabilitating an injured knee. Lewis hadn't lost a step, however, as he rushed for a game-high 128 yards on 19 carries. Washington's defense, ranked first in the nation in stopping the run, allowed Iowa just 139 net yards on the ground, recorded five sacks and forced five turnovers (four interceptions) in the game. Iowa also became the sixth team in 1990-91 to surrender more than 40 points to the high-scoring Huskies. The strong tradition of Don James' special teams surfaced early in this game when red-shirt freshman Andy Mason blocked an Iowa punt that was scooped up by junior cornerback Dana Hall, who sprinted for a touchdown. With less than five minutes elapsed, Washington led 10-0. After Iowa closed to 10-7 with 12:39 left in the half, Washington erupted for 23 consecutive points. A 38-yard Travis Hanson field goal, and a 37-yard interception return by senior cornerback Charles Mincy gave Washington momentum. Two touchdowns generated by Brunell, on a five-yard run and a 22-yard pass to Mario Bailey, gave the Huskies their nearly insurmountable 33-7 lead at intermission. Iowa threw a scare into the Huskies as Hawkeye quarterback Matt Rodgers rallied his team for 27 second-half points. Iowa fullback Nick Bell's 20-yard touchdown run with 5:07 to play pulled the Hawkeyes within 13 at 39-26. But Brunell put out the fire on the next possession with a 31-yard scoring completion to Bailey. A late Iowa score made the score 46-34 as Washington held on to claim the Pac-10's second consecutive Rose Bowl win and eighth in the past 10 years.

Husky Spotlight

When Kevin Stocker waited for his named to come up during the 1991 Major League Baseball draft, he figured to go in the fifth or sixth round. He was pleasantly surprised when Philadelphia took him in the second round. It drew even more comparisons between Stocker and the last great Spokane shortstop—Ryne Sandberg. Ironically, Sandberg, an all-star with the Chicago Cubs, also originally signed with the Phillies. Stocker was named a second-team All-American by the American Baseball Coaches Association in 1991. Stocker led the Huskies in batting (.374), hits (77), runs (54) and stolen bases (28). Despite not playing his senior season, Stocker finished his college career ranked fourth all-time in runs (129) and was first in stolen bases (67). Stocker played in the major leagues with the Phillies from 1993-97 before joining the Tampa Bay Devil Rays in 1998.

UW Media Relations

Husky Highlight

You could call Mark Brunell Mr. Rose Bowl. He is the closest thing as a sure bet to one day being admitted as a member of that organization's hall of fame. As a sophomore quarterback, Brunell played like a seasoned veteran in 1990, guiding Washington to a 9-2 regular-season record and the first of three straight Rose Bowls. He was an exceptionally talented quarterback who could scramble as well as he could throw. In his first year as a starter he passed for 1,732 yards and 14 touchdowns. Brunell was honored as the 1991 Rose Bowl MVP after leading the Huskies to a 46-34 victory against Iowa. His play was limited as a junior due to a knee injury, but he saw action as a backup in the Rose Bowl, completing seven of eight passes for 89 yards in the Huskies' 34-14 victory to clinch the national title. Brunell returned to the starters' role for the 1993 Rose Bowl. He passed for 308 yards and almost engineered a dramatic comeback in a 38-31 loss to Michigan. Brunell owned three Rose Bowl records by the conclusion of his third appearance. As a passer, rusher, and even receiver, Brunell accounted for 51 touchdowns during his career. He was also a standout baseball player who was selected by the Atlanta Braves in the 1992 baseball draft, despite the fact he had not played competitively since he was a high school senior.

UW Media Relations

Husky Legend

Greg Lewis

Husky senior tailback Greg Lewis was recognized as the nation's top junior or senior running back in 1990 when he won the inaugural Doak Walker Award. Lewis set a Husky rushing record during the season by gaining 1,279 yards in 10 games. He missed the Apple Cup matchup with Washington State due to a knee injury. He returned to the Washington lineup for the Rose Bowl and darted through the Iowa defense for 128 yards on 19 carries. He was also honored as the Pac-10 Offensive Player of the Year and was named to the Walter Camp Football Foundation and *The Sporting News* All-America teams. As a freshman and sophomore, Lewis patiently waited his turn to play behind starter Vince Weathersby. When he moved into the starting lineup he immediately brought more speed, and a breakaway running threat, to the Husky backfield. In the 1989 season opener he rushed for 133 yards against Texas A&M. The next week he collected 165 yards versus Purdue. Lewis would go on to finish his junior year with 1,100 yards to become the fourth Washington player to run for 1,000 yards in a season. His senior rushing total made him the first Husky to post consecutive 1,000-yard rushing seasons. Lewis gained at least 100 yards in nine straight games in 1990 to set a Husky record. He set his single-game rushing high against California in 1990 with 205 yards. Lewis was always reliable for positive yardage. He had just 71 negative rushing yards in 514 rushing attempts during his final two seasons. His 3,091 career rushing yards ranked as the third highest total in Washington history. He was taken by the Denver Broncos in the 1991 NFL draft. Lewis' efforts were recognized by his teammates who voted him the Guy Flaherty Award winner as the most inspirational player in 1990.

HUSKY LIST

Highest Scoring Rose Bowl

Washington's 46-34 victory against Iowa in the 1991 Rose Bowl was the highest scoring game between the two teams with a combined 80 points. Washington's 46 points were the fourth highest total by a team in the New Year's Day Classic. Here's a look at the top scoring games in Rose Bowl history:

Year	Team	Points
1991	Washington	46
	Iowa	34
1963	USC	42
	Wisconsin	37
1986	UCLA	45
	Iowa	28
1993	Michigan	38
	Washington	31
1999	Wisconsin	38
	UCLA	31
1974	Ohio State	42
	USC	21
1930	USC	47
	Pittsburgh	14

THE 1991 Royal Henley Regatta marked the 152nd time the event was held near the market town of Henley-on-Thames in England. It marked the seventh time the Washington men's crew team participated in the races. "It's like a rowing festival," said Husky men's coach Bob Ernst. "In England they say there are three social events: Henley, the Royal Ascot horserace and Wimbledon. We go to Henley certainly to try to win the event we're in, but also because we feel that it's a tradition of Washington rowers and it's important to stay in contact with that." The Huskies were entered in the Ladies Plate Challenge with 32 international crews, including the other top U.S. collegiate crews —national champion Pennsylvania and Cornell, the fifth-place finisher at nationals. Washington qualified to travel to Henley by virtue of winning the West Coast rowing championships. The Huskies had finished fourth at the national championships. The Huskies made the trip to England without junior Scott Munn, a world-class rower who stayed in the states to compete for a spot on the U.S. national team. At Henley, Washington defeated an Oxford boat but lost in the semifinals to a crew made up of rowers from the University of London and Oxford University. Washington's other trips to Henley had been in 1958, 1973, 1977, 1978, 1981 and 1984.

Husky Moment

Women's Basketball Team Snaps Stanford Streak

When it comes to dramatic, last-second shots to win basketball games, Washington's Laura Moore recorded one of the best. In front of a national television audience on ESPN, and a capacity crowd of 5,141, Moore stunned eighth-ranked Stanford in Maples Pavilion on Feb. 9, 1991 to end the Cardinal 42-game home winning streak. A backup point guard who had seen her playing time diminish over the past month, Moore checked into the game for the first time with just 25 seconds remaining and the Huskies trailing 68-67. Stanford's Sonja Henning had made one of two free throws to give Stanford the late lead and set up the Huskies' final possession. During a time out, Washington coach Chris Gobrecht designed a play to get the ball inside to Husky center Karen Deden. With seven seconds left, Deden got off a short jump shot that bounced off the front of the rim and was deflected out to the top of the key where Moore picked it up and drained the winning 17-foot jump shot. The game was a classic. Trailing 57-50, the Huskies rallied to tie the game. The two teams battled to ties at 59, 61, 65 and finally 67 when Laurie Merlino connected on a jump shot with 59 seconds to play. Stanford's Sonja Henning was fouled with a half a minute to play, but she converted on just one of two free-throw attempts. Merlino finished with 13 points while Deden and Tara Davis paced the Huskies with 14 points apiece. The Husky defense was a key in the game. Washington forced the Cardinal away from the quicker pace they enjoyed into a halfcourt game. The victory improved the Huskies to 17-3 overall.

UW Media Relations

Laura Moore

Husky Spotlight

It seemed like every time freshman Mari Bjone ran the 400-meter hurdles event for Washington she set a school record. Bjone, a native of Oslo, Norway, came to the U.S. as an exchange student. Luckily for Washington, she attended high school at Tacoma's Bellarmine Prep. Bjone's record-breaking season was highlighted by winning the Pac-10 championships in the event with a time of 58.21. It was a school record. It bettered the old mark of 58.69 that she had set a day earlier in the preliminary heats at the conference meet. Bjone qualified for the NCAA championships where she placed seventh.

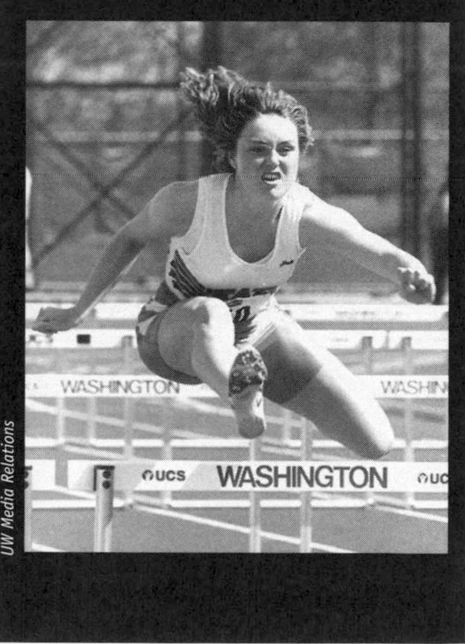

UW Media Relations

Husky Highlight

The only time women's basketball player Laurie Merlino missed a game in her career was because she had to fly to Boston for an interview to graduate school at Northeastern. Merlino was a great role model as a student athlete. A tough-minded, 5-6 point guard for the Huskies, she was also an exceptional student. Following her senior season she was one of 14 women basketball players nationally to receive an NCAA postgraduate scholarship. She was a three-time Pac-10 All-Academic Team member who worked as an undergrad in hospital emergency rooms using sign language to assist deaf patients. Merlino's father was deaf and her mother had lost 85 percent of her hearing. Merlino grew up communicating by sign language and she felt that aided her on the basketball court by giving her quick hands. As a senior in 1991 he earned All-Pac-10 honors after leading the Huskies in steals with 60 while averaging 12.6 points per game.

UW Media Relations

Husky Legend

Karen Deden

UW Media Relations

When Karen Deden signed a national letter of intent to play basketball at Washington it was another sign that coach Chris Gobrecht was building a national power. A highly recruited prep standout from Missoula, Montana, she spurned offers from the University of Montana, where her older sisters Linda and Doris had starred, and several other top programs to become a Husky. Deden was an immediate hit with Husky fans. The 6-4 center/forward started all 30 games as a freshman during the 1988 season and helped the Huskies to a 25-5 finish and an appearance at the NCAA West Regional. She averaged 11.0 points and 7.0 rebounds that season as the Huskies won their first Pac-10 championship. Deden developed into the consummate all-around player at Washington. She was tremendous rebounder, solid scorer, effective shot blocker and great passer. As a junior, she was second on the team with 106 assists, often igniting a Husky fast break with her accurate outlet passes. During her four-year Husky career, she led the team in assists over 20 times. She gave opposing defenses fits with her ability to play both outside and down low in the post. Deden finished her Husky career with 1,596 points, at the time the fourth best total in Washington history. Her 912 rebounds were a school record. Deden's teams compiled a record of 100-23 and won a second Pac-10 title in 1990. She was an All-Pac-10 and District VIII All-American as both a junior and senior. Deden was able to continue her playing career after she left Washington. She competed overseas in professional leagues in Japan and France before playing for the New England Blizzard of the American Basketball League.

Husky List

Husky Women's Tennis Players Appearances at AIAW/NCAA Championships

In 1991 the Husky women's tennis duo of Cindy Olejar and Mary O'Reilly became the first Washington tandem to qualify for the NCAA doubles championships. They lost 6-1, 6-3 in the first round to Julie McKeon and Tonya Fuller of San Diego and finished the season with a 19-6 record. Here's a list of all of the Husky women's tennis players who have participated in either the AIAW or NCAA individual tennis championships:

Singles

Year	Player	Finish
1971	Trish Bostrom	AIAW Quarterfinals
1972	Trish Bostrom	AIAW Quarterfinals
1979	Lisa Moldrem	AIAW First Round
1979	Christi Dorsey	AIAW First Round
1998	Kristina Kraszewski	NCAA Quarterfinals
1999	Kristina Kraszewski	NCAA First Round
2000	Kristina Kraszewski	NCAA First Round

Doubles

Year	Player	Finish
1971	Bostrom/Janis Metcalf	AIAW Mixed College Champions
1979	Moldrem/Gretchen Van Dyke	AIAW First Round
1991	Cindy Olejar/Mary O'Reilly	NCAA First Round
1996	Katherine Costain/Kori Sosnowy	NCAA Second Round
1999	Ilona Kordonskaya/Kraszewski	NCAA First Round

Husky Lore

Women's Soccer and Softball Added to Athletic Lineup

IN December of 1990 the Washington athletic department announced that it would add two sports—women's soccer and softball—to its athletic lineup. The additions raised the number of varsity athletic programs the University offered to 23. The sports were added as a part of a campus-wide gender-equity plan. Women's soccer was scheduled to begin competition in 1991 and softball would field its first team in the spring of 1993. About $700,000 for coaches, scholarships, travel, equipment and other expenses for the two programs would come from tuition waivers, money that previously would have been paid by the athletic department to the state's general fund. The two sports were expected to draw roughly 40 more female student-athletes into the Husky program. The University's commitment came 18 years after the Title IX legislation came into effect. Dang Pibulvech would be named to coach the first women's soccer team and Theresa Wilson was picked to coach the softball team.

1991 W 1992

Husky Moment

Football Wins the National Championship

The seeds of Washington's 1991 national championship season were sown a year earlier in a loss to UCLA. Ranked second in the nation and sporting an 8-1 record, the Huskies stumbled at home to the unranked Bruins 25-22 to cost them any chance of a national title. That loss caused team members to focus even more in the offseason on obtaining their ultimate goal. In 1991, a potent offensive squad and an athletic defense came together to create a team that finished the season with a perfect 12-0 record to give Washington its first football National Championship. Offensively, the Husky running game was powered by Beno Bryant and Jay Barry, who helped Washington to average over 230 yards per game. They were complemented by sophomore quarterback Billy Joe Hobert, whose favorite receivers were All-Americans Mario Bailey or Orlando McKay. Senior center Ed Cunningham, All-American tackle Lincoln Kennedy, and Siupeli Malamala led an offensive line that enabled the Huskies to muster over 470 yards of total offense a game. At the end of the season, five offensive players were named first or second-team All-Pac-10. Consensus All-American Steve Emtman led one of the stingiest defenses college football has ever seen. Washington allowed less than 10 points a game while holding opposing rushers to 67 yards a game. The Huskies' defense swarmed the ball on every play with raw athleticism coming from every angle. En route to the title, the Huskies had several critical victories. They rallied to hand Nebraska one of its worst defeats (36-21) in Lincoln. In a key showdown with seventh-ranked California, Bryant broke off a long scoring run late to secure a 24-17. USC also played Washington tough, but bowed 14-3 in the Coliseum. The Huskies blew past Michigan 34-14 to win the Rose Bowl and pick up the national championship honors from the *USA Today*/CNN Coaches Poll, the UPI/ National Football Foundation, the Football Writers and *Sports Illustrated*. An undefeated Miami team was the top vote getter in the *Associated Press* poll.

Corky Trewin

Husky Spotlight

Trailing by two touchdowns in the second half, the fourth-ranked Huskies rallied to defeated ninth-ranked Nebraska 36-21 in Lincoln. Sophomore quarterback Billy Joe Hobert, starting just his second game, completed 23 of 40 passes for 283 yards and a touchdown to keep Washington's national championship hopes alive. Hobert engineered a comeback that saw the Huskies score 27 unanswered points during a 9:41 span over the third and fourth quarters. Husky coach Don James called it one of the greatest wins during his Washington career. "This has got to be right up there at the top because of who we played and where we played," he said. Nebraska entered the game averaging 573 rushing yards in its first two contests but was held to just 135 yards by the Husky defense. On offense, the Huskies put on one of the greatest performances ever at Memorial Stadium. Washington rushed for 335 yards and finished with a total of 618. Beno Bryant rushed for 139 yards while Jay Barry added 110, including an 81-yard touchdown run in the fourth quarter to put the game away. Washington's total offense was the second most ever against the Cornhuskers. The Huskies' 31 first downs were a record against a Nebraska squad and the 36 points were the most scored by an opponent in Memorial Stadium since 1958. The loss also ended Nebraska's 20-game home winning streak against non-conference opponents.

Husky Highlight

As a freshman forward on the Husky men's basketball team, Mark Pope was honored as the Pac-10 Conference's Freshman of the Year. The Bellevue native averaged 10.3 points and 8.1 rebounds as a first-year player for Washington. He was the third Husky to earn the conference honor. Christian Welp (1984) and Mike Hayward (1988) were also named the Pac-10's top newcomers. Pope was the only Pac-10 freshman to start every game for his team during the season. Following his sophomore season Pope elected to transfer from Washington with the departure of coach Lynn Nance. He enrolled at Kentucky and helped the Wildcats to the 1996 NCAA Championship as a 6-10, 240-pound center. He was selected in the second round of the 1996 NBA draft by the Indiana Pacers.

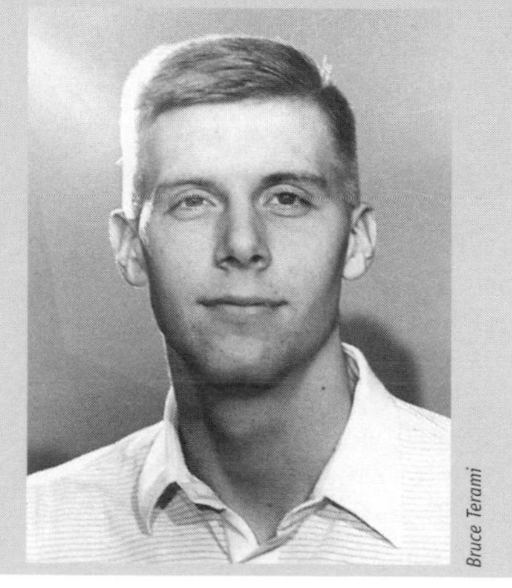

Bruce Terami

Husky Legend

Steve Emtman

Bruce Terami

It is hard to believe, but Steve Emtman, one of the best college football defensive linemen in the game's history, was hardly recruited out of high school. Even supporters in his hometown of Cheney thought Emtman might be making a mistake by going to the Seattle school telling him that it might be too big for him and that he would never play. Emtman's emergence as the nation's best defender was aided by his dedication and hard work and the decision to retool the Husky defense after a disappointing 6-5 season in 1988. Emtman played sparingly as a redshirt freshman in 1989 but became a focal point on Washington's new "attack style" pressure defense as a sophomore. He had 55 tackles in 1990 and helped the Huskies to lead the nation in rushing defense, allowing a stubborn 1.9 yards per rush. In Emtman's junior year, his last at Washington, he drew plenty of national attention and double teams by opposing defenses. He was a unanimous All-America selection, finished fourth in the balloting for the Heisman trophy and won the Lombardi and Outland Trophies presented to the nation's top lineman. Emtman anchored Washinton's all-star laden defense that allowed only 67.2 rushing yards per game and 9.2 points per contest. He registered 60 tackles and led the team with 16.5 tackles for loss. The Huskies posted a perfect 12-0 record, including a 34-14 defeat of No. 4 Michigan in the Rose Bowl. Washington was named the national champion in all but one major poll. Emtman would go on to be the first pick in the 1992 NFL draft by the Indianapolis Colts. In 1999 he was inducted into the Husky Hall of Fame.

HUSKY LISTS

Mario Bailey Sets Receiving Marks

Washington senior split end Mario Bailey had one of the best seasons ever by a Husky pass catcher in 1991. He led Washington with 62 receptions for 1,037 yards and a school-record 17 touchdowns. Bailey was recognized as a first-team All-American by the *Associated Press,* United Press International and the Football Writers Association. Bailey finished the year as the Husky record holder for single-season receptions (62), single-season touchdown catches (17), career receiving yards (2,093), career touchdown receptions (26) and touchdown catches in a game (three). Here's a look at where Bailey and the other top receivers rank on Washington's career receptions list.

Player (Years)	NO	YDS	AVG	TD
1. Mario Bailey (1988-91)	131	2093	15.9	26
2. Jerome Pathon (1995-97)	125	2063	16.5	16
3. Scott Phillips (1973-76)	111	1866	16.8	8
4. Paul Skansi (1979-82)	138	1723	12.5	13
5. Brian Slater (1985-88)	87	1648	18.9	16
6. Lonzell Hill (1983-86)	103	1641	15.9	16
7. Spider Gaines (1975-78)	66	1529	23.2	16
8. Orlando McKay (1988-91)	96	1407	14.7	13
9. Darryl Franklin (1984-87)	92	1393	15.1	6
10. Anthony Allen (1979-82)	99	1372	13.7	11

Hedges Named Athletic Director

THE Washington athletic department broke new ground in July of 1991 when Barbara Hedges was named the athletic director to succeed Mike Lude. She became the first female athletic director at what was considered a major Division I institution. She was the second female athletic director at a Division I football institution. San Diego State hired Mary Alice in 1983, but she remained as the head of the Aztec athletic program for just two years before being fired. Hedges was no stranger to the Pac-10. She earned her bachelor's degree from Arizona State in 1963 and received her master's from Arizona in 1971. She had worked at USC since 1973 before accepting the position at Washington.

Husky Moment

Baseball to Regionals

After a 33-year wait, the Washington baseball team returned to the NCAA tournament in 1992. Washington was the sixth seed in the six-team 1992 West I Regional field at Tucson, Arizona. In their first game, the Huskies upset the host and top seed, beating Arizona 6-5. Starter Chris Berg threw 7.2 innings, allowing only four hits and one run. The Wildcats, led by John Tejcek's two homers, scored four in the bottom of the ninth, but UW's Eric Schmidt came in to close the door on the Wildcats. Game two matched the Huskies with old foe Fresno State and the Huskies came up with a miraculous finish to keep their postseason hopes alive. Trailing 3-2 in the bottom of the ninth, UW got a break when the Bulldog shortstop made a bad throw to first on a grounder by Derrin Doty. Steve Murphy singled Doty to second and Jeff Weible sent him home with another single. The winning run came when Murphy scored when the Fresno State pitcher overthrew third base on a bunt by Ryan Rutz. Jim Riley went the distance for his school-record-tying 10th win. Only two wins away from the College World Series, the Huskies' string of luck ran out with an 11-0 loss to eventual national champion Pepperdine. That was followed by a 9-3 defeat at the hands of Hawaii, a game in which Washington trailed only 4-3 in the eighth inning.

UW Media Relations

Derrin Doty

Husky Spotlight

Husky senior Sonja Forster and junior Mitch Leffler won their respective events at the 1992 Pac-10 Track and Field Championships at Oregon's Hayward Field. Forster won the heptathlon with a school-record performance of 5,266 points. She set three personal marks en route to the title. Originally a walkon to the UW program, she had finished fourth in the event as a junior. During the first day of the two-day, seven-event competition, she set personal bests in the 100 meters (14.15) and the 200 meters (25.65) to grab a seven-point lead. During Saturday's finals she won the long jump (19-10¾), finished seventh in the javelin (101-4) and turned in a career-best time of 2:28.64 in the 800 meters to better Washington State's Ester Medema for the first-place medal. Forster became the first Washington athlete to win the event at the conference championships. She went on to the NCAA championships where she placed 13th with a score of 4,659. Leffler became the first men's Pac-10 champion since high jumper Rick Noji in 1990 by upsetting Oregon's Shannon Lemora in the 800 meters. Leffler, who had lost to Lemora during the regular season, won the race in a time of 1:49.05.

Husky Highlight

Shaundra Greene Sets Basketball Scoring Record

Surprisingly, Shaundra Greene set the Washington women's basketball team's single-game scoring record on a night when she connected on just eight of 22 field-goal attempts. Playing against Northern Illinois in the first round of Iowa's Amana-Hawkeye Classic, Greene scored 39 points in Washington's 101-91 double-overtime victory that was marred by 74 fouls. Greene, a forward, benefited the most by the official's calls. She converted 23 of 27 free-throw attempts to allow her to set the scoring record. Both free-throw totals were career highs and school records. In fact, Greene's previous best scoring effort was just 19 points. Greene capped her outstanding effort by collecting a career-high 13 rebounds.

UW Media Relations

Husky Legend

Women's Soccer Program Begins

Joanie Komura

Rhonda Klein

It did not take long for the newfound Husky women's soccer team to taste success. Less than a year after being added as a varsity program, the Huskies played their first match on Sept. 8 in San Diego where they defeated San Diego State 2-0. Rhonda Klein, a freshman from Puyallup, scored the Huskies' first goal 65 minutes into the contest. Sophomore goalkeeper Tamara Broder was credited with the shutout. On Sept. 14 Washington played its first home game at Everett High School in front of a crowd of 350. The Huskies tied 16th-ranked Portland 1-1 when Melanie Brennan scored the first home goal in school history. The next week, after just four matches, the Huskies found themselves ranked 20th in the nation in the weekly Intercollegiate Soccer Association of America poll. Washington was 2-1-1 after its first four matches and would go on to post a 10-6-2 record under head coach Dan Pibulvech. He was brought to Seattle to guide the Husky program after a very successful eight-year career at Colorado College. He led four of his Colorado College teams to the Women's Final Four. Washington's first roster included 13 freshmen on the 24-player roster. The Huskies routinely started up to eight freshmen.

HUSKY LISTS

Top Individual Scoring Performances in Women's Basketball History

Pts	Name	Opponent (score)	Date
39	Shaunda Greene	N. Illinois (101-91 2OT)	Nov. 30, 1991
38	Carlin McClary	Seattle University (80-73)	March 1, 1980
38	Rhonda Smith	Texas Tech (79-75)	Nov. 22, 1994
36	Sherrie Felton	Washington State (82-69)	March 4, 1978
36	Yvette Cole	California (84-92)	Feb. 12, 1987
35	Megan Franza	Idaho (99-72)	Dec. 18, 1999
34	Jamie Redd	USC (68-69)	Jan. 2, 1997
33	Megan Franza	Stanford (85-83)	Jan. 27, 2000
33	Leteia Hughley	Brigham Young (88-83)	Dec. 5, 1981
33	Jamie Redd	Gonzaga (77-67)	Dec. 9, 1997
32	Margie Nielsen	Seattle Pacific (90-41)	Dec. 2, 1977
32	Amber Hall	California (83-78) (OT)	Feb. 2, 1998
32	Jamie Redd	Texas (64-77)	Dec. 2, 1996
32	Jamie Redd	Kansas (61-76)	Dec. 8, 1996
32	Amber Hall	California (83-78)	Feb. 21, 1998
31	Carlin McClary	Seattle (92-66)	Jan. 23, 1979
31	Liz Chicane	Idaho State (63-50)	Feb. 7, 1981
31	Karen Murray	Portland State (80-57)	Feb. 15, 1983
31	Leteia Hughley	Long Beach State (66-75)	Dec. 8, 1984
31	Rhonda Smith	Oregon (87-74)	Jan. 23, 1993
31	Jamie Redd	UCLA (98-75)	Jan. 4, 1997
30	Carlin McClary	Portland State (106-81)	Jan. 20, 1979
30	Karen Murray	Portland State (110-72)	Feb. 16, 1982
30	Renee Avelino	Brigham Young (92-79)	Dec. 16, 1983
30	Jamie Redd	Stanford (76-106)	Feb. 22, 1997
30	Jamie Redd	Purdue (71-88)	Mar. 14, 1998
30	Meghan Franza	California (69-68)	Jan. 1, 2001

Wilson Named to Head Up Softball Program

WHEN you trace the ultra-successful start of the Husky softball program it can be attributed to Teresa Wilson being named the program's first head coach and the timing of her appointment. Husky athletic director Barbara Hedges picked Wilson to start the Washington program in August of 1991, a full year before she would have her first player enroll for classes. The early hiring provided Wilson with the time she needed to handle all of the administrative duties with starting a new sport, and more importantly, it gave her a full year to recruit a team. She brought some lofty credentials with her to Washington. She was an All-American pitcher who led Missouri to a seventh-place finish in the 1983 College Softball World Series. She was a successful head coach at Oregon from 1985-89, guiding the Ducks to a 54-18 record and fifth-place showing at the 1989 World Series. That year she was honored as the national coach of the year. Prior to her arrival at Washington she led Minnesota to the Big Ten championship.

Super Legend

Don James, Steve Emtman and the 1991 National Championship Team

The Huskies, coming off a 10-2 record and a 46-34 victory over Iowa in the 1991 Rose Bowl, entered the 1991 season ranked fourth in the country.

Offensively, the Huskies had a very balanced attack. The running game was powered by Beno Bryant and Jay Barry. They helped Washington average over 230 rushing yards per game. The passing game averaged over 240 yards per game featuring quarterback Billy Joe Hobert and wide receivers Mario Bailey and Orlando McKay and tight ends Mark Bruener and Aaron Pierce. Center Ed Cunningham, Lincoln Kennedy and Siupeli Malamala led an offensive line that enabled the Huskies to roll up over 470 yards of total offense per game, the best in the Pac-10. They scored 461 points in the regular season to tie the 1925 team for most points.

Steve Emtman anchored one of the strongest defenses in collegiate history. Washington allowed its opponents only 101 points in the regular season, less than 10 points per game. They held their opponents to 67 rushing yards a game. Emtman was the most decorated lineman in Husky history and perhaps received the most honors of any football player in Washington history. He was a consensus All-America, received the Lombardi Award and Outland Trophy as the nation's outstanding defensive lineman and finished fourth in the Heisman Trophy balloting, the highest finish of any player in Husky history. The Husky defense seemed to swarm to the ball on every play and from every angle with speed and athleticism. Brett Collins, Jamie Fields, Chico Fraley, Dave Hoffmann, Donald Jones, and Andy Mason created a wall few backs could penetrate. And when they did, the runners met Walter Bailey, Dana Hall, Shane Pahukoa, and Tommie Smith. The defense ranked first in the nation in turnover margin.

The first two games were away. They held Stanford's Heisman hopeful, Glyn Milburn, to 16 yards and the Cardinal to 238 yards in a lopsided 42-7 victory. Next was Nebraska who had won 20 consecutive home games against non-conference opponents. The Cornhuskers were up 14-6 at half-time and things only got worse when Nebraska scored early in the third quarter after Washington muffed a punt on its own two-yard line. The Huskies showed their poise and strength and reeled off 27 unanswered points, capped off by Jay Barry's 81-yard touchdown late in the fourth quarter. Washington won 36-21 and rolled up 618 yards of total offense against the ninth-ranked Cornhuskers.

Washington returned home for three straight games, piling up 158 points to three for their opponents. They first beat Kansas State 56-3, sending the Wildcats home with negative 17 rushing yards. The Huskies scored in six of their first seven possessions. The game also featured the return of injured quarterback Mark Brunell as a backup to Hobert. Next, they crushed Arizona 54-0, prompting Dick Tomey, Arizona's head coach to say: "Their defense is dominant. Steve Emtman has to be the best lineman in the country. Nobody blocks him, and the folks around him are great football players. Washington is as good a team as the Pac-10 has had, ever." The following week, Mario Bailey hauled in three touchdown passes as Washington recorded another shutout, a 48-0 win against Toledo.

On a warm, sunny day in Berkeley, third-ranked Washington met unbeaten and seventh-ranked California in a nationally-televised game. The Bears struck first on a 27-yard pass play near the end of the first period. Washington answered with a Hobert-to-Bailey touchdown strike to tie the score. After the teams traded field goals, the Huskies scored just before half-time when Barry scored on a nine-yard run. The Bears knotted the score near the end of the third quarter when Lindsay Chapman raced 68 yards for a touchdown. On the Huskies' next possession, Bryant broke up the middle and raced 65 yards for a 24-17 lead. Cal made one last charge, but Washington's cornerback, Walter Bailey, broke up a pass at the goal line on the final play to give the Huskies their sixth straight win.

Washington returned to Husky Stadium for its next two games. They beat Oregon 29-7, holding the Ducks scoreless until the final five minutes and limiting them to 129 yards of total offense. After the game, Oregon Coach Rich Brooks lauded the Huskies. "...Washington is the best team I've seen in this league ever." Next up was Arizona State. The Huskies scored the first 41 points on their way to a 44-16 win and moved up to a tie for second in the polls behind Miami.

On the road again, Washington beat USC 14-3 and then thrashed Oregon State 58-6 to clinch the conference title and a return trip to the Rose Bowl. The Huskies closed out the regular season in Seattle with a 56-21 victory over the Cougars who featured quarterback Drew Bledsoe.

With a shot at the national title, Washington met fourth-ranked Michigan in the 1992 Rose Bowl. The Wolverines had a star-studded lineup featuring Heisman Trophy winner and wide receiver, Desmond Howard, and quarterback Elvis Grbac. Coach Don James emphasized the importance of the game in his talk to the team 48 hours before kickoff.

He first commented on the strength of Michigan's coaching staff and their offense and defense. He next reminded the Huskies of what they had achieved and what was on the line in the Rose Bowl. He repeated the five ingredients of being a good team player:

- 100 percent preparation and performance
- Courage — 11 tough football players on the field at all times
- Mental preparation
- Care — we all owe each other everything
- Loyalty — keep the great team unity

He then told them to get their game face on.

"Get it on as soon as possible. This is the time we cannot be bothered by others. Our total focus is our preparation for Michigan. We stop the levity. The entertainment is over. We will soon be the entertainers. We will be the performers in the biggest game of all of our lives. I mean every man in here. We have to be mentally prepared and not make dumb mistakes...Now is the time to PR (Personal Record). A PR will get us the greatest prize in all of college football. You will be a team marked forever in the eyes of the football fans in the state of Washington. You will cherish this honor for a lifetime."

He closed with these final thoughts:

- You have worked harder than any team I have coached
- You have prepared better during the past 14 workouts than any bowl team I have coached
- Now we count down the hours before the kickoff—48 hours—and we use them to mentally prepare ourselves for the greatest day of our lives.
  — For a PR
  — For a national title
- We need to prove to Michigan and the world that we are number one

Bruce Terami

Steve Emtman

They did not disappoint James, his coaching staff, and the hundreds of thousands of fans who watched and listened to the game. Hobert gave Washington an early lead with a two-yard touchdown run. A Michigan touchdown and pair of Travis Hanson field goals put Washington up 13-7 at half-time. In the third quarter, Hobert found Mark Bruener, running free along the back of the end zone and hit him with a perfect pass. Early in the final quarter, Hobert passed for a touchdown to Pierce, to give Washington a 28-7 lead. Brunell, the 1991 Rose Bowl Most Valuable Player, completed seven of eight passes in the fourth quarter, including a 38-yard touchdown pass to Bailey. Hobert and Emtman shared MVP honors in leading the Huskies to a 34-14 victory.

They knew they were the best in the land. Now they had to wait for the results of the final polls. Early on January 2, James received a phone call informing him the Huskies had been voted the National Champions in the *USA Today*/CNN coaches poll with Miami second. The Huskies were also picked first in the UPI/National Football Foundation, Football Writer's and *Sports Illustrated* polls. Miami was picked first only in the Associated Press poll.

It was Washington's first football national championship. This perfect team would end up with the most points scored in Husky history—495—and be inducted in the Husky Hall of Fame in 1997. Coach Don James completed his 18-year Washington career before the start of the 1993 season. He compiled a 153-57-2 record, giving him the most wins in Husky history. He took his teams to 14 bowl games (six Rose Bowls) and they won 10 of them, including four Rose Bowl wins. James was inducted in the College Football Hall of Fame in 1997 and the Husky Hall of Fame in 1993. Steve Entman was inducted in the Husky Hall of Fame in 1999.

Husky Moment

Huskies Make Third Straight Rose Bowl Appearance

The ninth-ranked Huskies attempted to make history by winning their third straight Rose Bowl, but instead suffered a 38-31 defeat at the hands of seventh-ranked Michigan. Washington led 24-21 at halftime but could not control Michigan tailback Tyrone Wheatley, who ran for 235 yards on just 15 carries, including touchdown runs of 88, 56 and 24 yards. Michigan grabbed an early 3-0 lead on its first drive with a 41-yard Peter Elezovic field goal. Washington answered with a one-yard touchdown run by Darius Turner, capping a nine-play, 80-yard drive to go ahead 7-3. The key play of the drive was a 35-yard pass from senior quarterback Mark Brunell to tight end Mark Bruener across the middle, setting the Huskies up at the Michigan one-yard line. The seesaw first half continued with Michigan taking a 17-7 lead before the Huskies pulled to within three on a 64-yard touchdown pass from Brunell to freshman Jason Shelley. Shelley finished the game with three receptions for 100 yards. Brunell's hot passing continued on Washington's next possession when he again connected with Bruener, this time in the corner of the end zone to put the Huskies ahead 21-17 at halftime. Wheatley broke free again on the first play of the second half, bursting through the middle of the Husky line and racing 88 yards for a touchdown, putting the Wolverines back on top 24-21. Husky sophomore Napoleon Kaufman, who was held to 39 yards rushing on 20 carries, gave the Huskies a boost on special teams when he answered the Wheatley touchdown run by returning the ensuing kickoff 47 yards to the Michigan 46-yard line. Fittingly he would cap the drive seven plays later with a dive over the top for a touchdown and a 28-24 lead. Washington added to the lead on its next possession when Travis Hanson converted a 44-yard field goal for a 31-24 Husky lead. With the field goal, Hanson extended his career Rose Bowl record to five. Two possessions later Michigan took advantage of a Kaufman fumble at the Washington 24-yard line as Wheatley scored on the first play, tying the game at 31. Michigan then scored the only points of the fourth quarter when Wolverine quarterback Elvis Grbac threw 15 yards to tight end Tony McGee for the eventual game-winning touchdown with 5:29 remaining. The loss spoiled what was perhaps Brunell's finest performance in a Husky uniform. The senior quarterback completed 18-of-30 passes for 308 yards and two touchdowns.

Husky Spotlight

At 6-7 and 335 pounds, Lincoln Kennedy had a big impact on the Husky football program. An offensive tackle who flattened numerous opponents, Kennedy was the only unanimous first-team All-America pick among Pac-10 players and the top offensive tackle in the nation his senior season in 1992. The Husky offense averaged 387.6 yards-per-game largely due to his blocking. He was also a two-time first-team All-Pac-10 pick and Pac-10 Morris Trophy winner as the league's top offensive lineman. Kennedy was one of four finalists for the Lombardi Award and a semi-finalist for the Outland Trophy. He allowed only two sacks in his four years at Washington and was the ninth player selected in the 1993 NFL draft as a first-round pick of the Atlanta Falcons.

Bruce TGerami

Husky Highlight

Randy Jorgensen almost traded slap shots for base hits when it came time to choose a college. Jorgensen's family had deep roots in hockey thanks to his Canadian-born father. One of his brothers, Ken, played in the Western Hockey League and another, Casey, was a referee in the league. As a senior in high school, Jorgensen participated in a top all-star game in Boston and hoped to draw the attention of a college scout. He did. Boston University offered him a scholarship for both hockey and baseball. But they were too late. Jorgensen had already made a commitment to play baseball for the Huskies. He proved to be a valuable first baseman for the Washington program, earning All-Pac-10 Northern Division honors as a sophomore and junior. As a sophomore in 1992 he led the team in batting with a .332 average while collecting 74 hits and 58 runs batted in. In 1993 he batted .374 and hit nine home runs while driving in a school record 61 runs. He was a second-team All-America pick by the National College Baseball Writers Association. Four times during the season he was recognized as the conference's player of the week. That spring he was taken by the Seattle Mariners in the 12th round of the Major League Baseball draft.

Husky Legend

Don James

UW Media Relations

Don James was born Dec. 31, 1932 in the football hotbed of Massillon, Ohio. There he played quarterback and defensive back for two state championship teams at Washington High School. He then accepted a scholarship to Miami of Florida where he set five school passing records. James was then commissioned a Second Lieutenant in the US Army where he served two years before resuming his studies at the University of Kansas and doubling as the Jayhawks' freshman football coach. He graduated in 1957 with a master's degree in education. He moved back to Miami where he was head football coach at Southwest Miami High School for two years. He then turned to the college ranks and served as an assistant coach at Florida State (1956-65), Michigan (1966-67) and Colorado (1968-70). In 1971, James was named head coach at Kent State where he stayed four years, compiling a 25-19-1 record and taking Kent State to its first-ever bowl game. Two days before Christmas in 1974, James accepted the head coaching position at Washington. In his 18 years at Washington, James compiled a 153-57-2 record, making him the winningest football coach in Washington history. He took his teams to 14 bowl games (10-4) including a Pac-10 record nine straight from 1979-87. He guided the Huskies to six Rose Bowls and is one of only four coaches to win four Rose Bowl games. His 1991 team finished the season 12-0 and won Washington's first ever national championship. When James retired he had the 10th best active winning percentage, the eighth most victories among active coaches, fourth most bowl victories, fourth best bowl winning percentage and the 12th most bowl appearances. James was named national college coach of the year in 1984 and 1991. He was inducted into the Husky Hall of Fame in 1993 and the College Football Hall of Fame in 1997.

HUSKY LIST

NCAA Most Consecutive Winning Football Seasons

All-time based on a winning percentage of .500 and above

No.	School	Years
46	Penn State	1939-87
42	Notre Dame	1889-1932
40	Texas	1893-1932
38	Alabama	1911-50
37	Nebraska	1962-99
29	Oklahoma	1966-94
29	Texas	1957-85
28	Virginia	1888-1915
27	Michigan	1892-1918
26	Virginia Tech	1894-1919
24	Brigham Young	1974-98
24	Washington	1977-2000
24	Florida State	1977-2000
23	Syracuse	1913-35
23	Ohio State	1899-21

Note: List is through the 2000 season.

IT seems like all great teams have a few characters on them, and Washington's outstanding gridiron teams from the early 1990s were no exception. They had the bruising inside linebacker combination of Dave Hoffmann and James Clifford, known together as Hoff and Cloff. Hoffmann and Clifford were a new brand of strong, quick linebackers who could get to a ballcarrier like a heat-seeking missile. Hoffmann was the more decorated of the two, earning All-American honors as both a junior and senior. He was a finalist for the Butkus Award, presented to the nation's top linebacker, in 1992. Clifford was Mr. Reliable and would also go on to star as a slugger for the Husky baseball team. Several years after they concluded their Husky careers, they acted as a tag-team sideline reporting duo for Washington's football replays. Their insight, mixed with satirical humor, made for some hilarious moments. They co-hosted a segment of the weekly coaches show that had a cult-like following. Instead of doing typical standups from Husky Stadium, they gave their pregame analysis from spots around Seattle, including the popular Dutchess Tavern, with a raucous crowd in the background. Hoffmann went on to a career in the FBI while Clifford worked as a strength and conditioning coach for the Seattle Mariners. Husky fans will always remember them for their smash-mouth brand of football.

1992 W 1993

Husky Moment

Men's Soccer First NCAA Win

The Husky men's soccer team capped off its best season to date by picking up its first-ever victory in the NCAA Championships. The Huskies, despite being the top-seeded team in the west and the fourth-ranked team in the nation, opened the tournament on the road at Portland. Washington, which played half of its games in Husky Stadium, did not have a suitable field to host any NCAA matches. The Pilots surprised the Huskies by taking a 1-0 lead just three minutes into the contest. Washington, behind the brilliant play of junior goalkeeper Dusty Hudock, had surrendered just 11 goals in 19 regular-season games. Hudock led the nation with a 0.43 goals against average. Trailing for the first time all season in the second half, Washington tied the match when Gerd Strom scored four minutes into the second period. With 30 minutes remaining to play, Erik Penner scored his 14th goal of the season to give the Huskies the victory. Penner finished the season as the team's scoring leader with 34 points (14 goals, six assists). Washington's tournament run ended on a muddy field at Indiana when the host Hoosiers handed the Huskies a 2-0 defeat. It marked the only time all season an opponent had scored more than one goal against the Washington defense. For Indiana, it was the Hoosiers' 29th victory in 30 home NCAA tournament matches. Washington finished the season with a 15-3-3 record.

UW Media Relations

Dusty Hudock

Husky Spotlight

After being shunned by the NCAA selection committee in 1992 as a junior, Chet Crile finally made it to the NCAA championships as a senior. Although Crile was eliminated by Georgia's Wade McGuire 6-1, 6-1 in the first round of play, he was named an All-American by virtue of being ranked 20th in the final Intercollegiate Tennis Association singles rankings. McGuire would go on to finish as the runner-up at the tournament. Crile posted a 39-15 record as a senior. Crile was named the Pac-10 Northern Division player of the year three times between 1991-93. As a junior he was ranked 25th nationally with a 30-10 record. As a senior he was named Washington's men's Pac-10 Medal winner.

UW Media Relations

Husky Highlight

Washington senior cross country runner Stacie Hoitink wrapped up her Husky career by earning All-America honors at the 1992 NCAA Cross Country Championships. Hoitink's 30th-place finish helped Washington to place 12th at the event. She became just the third All-American in the cross country program's history. Regina Joyce was an All-American from 1980-82 and Carrie Moller picked up the same honors in 1991. Hoitink ran the 5,000-meter course in a time of 17:57.7, just 56 seconds behind Villanova's Carole Zajac who won the national title. Washington freshman Tara Carlson just missed being named an All-American after finishing 35th overall. Carlson had placed second at the NCAA West Regional to pace the Huskies to the team championship.

UW Media Relations

Husky Legend

UW Media Relations

Kit Green

A lot of the credit for the newfound success of Washington's Olympic sports programs in the 1990s belonged to associate athletic director Catherine "Kit" Green. Green worked diligently to improve the status of Washington's 21 Olympic sports since she joined the athletic department in 1974. She was instrumental in adding women's programs after the passage of Title IX legislation in 1974. She also fought for the proper funding that allowed the Husky programs to grow and to compete on a national level. In 1994 the National Association of Collegiate Women Athletic Administrators honored her for her work in increasing opportunities for women in athletics. Green first came to Washington in 1960 as a women's physical education instructor and coach for the field hockey and women's tennis teams. She stayed for four years before working at Seattle University as an assistant professor of physical education and a coach. Green returned to the UW in 1969 as an administrator. A native of Schenectady, N.Y., she earned her bachelor's degree in physical education from Skidmore College in 1954. After working as a physical education instructor for several years, she enrolled at Colorado and earned her master's degree in 1959. Much of Green's work was done outside of the boundaries of the Washington campus. She served on the boards of numerous community organizations in Seattle and was a committee member on a number of national collegiate councils. From 1965 to 1967 she was president of the Northwest College Women's Sports Association. Green was inducted into the Husky Hall of Fame in 1998.

HUSKY LISTS

Men's Tennis Career Singles Victory Leaders

	NAME	W-L	PCT.	YEARS
1.	Chet Crile	108-48	.692	1990-93
2.	Eric Drew	86-34	.717	1996-99
3.	Ornello Arlati	78-46	.629	1993-96
	Scott Pearson	78-22	.780	1980-83
5.	Randy Lim	69-33	.676	1979-82
6.	Billy Jacobsen	68-22	.756	1982-83, 85-86
7.	Dan Zeratsky	67-30	.691	1980-83
8.	Mark Neubauer	65-42	.607	1981-84
9.	Jeff Parry	64-43	.598	1986-89
10.	Nick Williams	63-31	.670	1995-97

Husky Softball Team Plays Inaugural Season

THE Washington softball team completed its first season with a 31-27 record. The Huskies lost their first game, 7-0, to 11th-ranked Michigan on Feb. 26. Washington rebounded to defeat the Wolverines 4-0 the next day to pick up its first win. Stephanie Burns pitched a five-hit shutout to get the historic victory. The season turned into a year of remarkable firsts. The team consisted of eight freshmen, two sophomores and three junior college transfers. Outfield Angie Marzetta, one of the junior college transfers, led the Huskies in batting with a .472 average. She set a Pac-10 record with 59 stolen bases and earned All-Pac-10 and second-team all-region honors. Infielder Michelle Church was a second-team All-Pac-10 selection. The Huskies won their first Pac-10 game when they defeated 19th-ranked Arizona State. The Huskies would go on to post a 7-18 record in conference play, including a 22-0 and 24-0 doubleheader victory against Stanford, the other first-year program, in the Pac-10. Washington played its home games in Bellevue during its inaugural season at Hidden Valley Field. The season would be the only year in the program's history that the team did not participate in the NCAA tournament.

W Super Legend

Fast Crews

UW Media Relations

Washington's 1997 NCAA Championship Team

George Pocock, the great builder of racing shells, once remarked: "There are no fast boats, only fast crews." Washington has had many fast crews. A total of 12 men's varsity eights have won national championships and nine women's varsity eights have been acclaimed the best in the U.S.

The Intercollegiate Rowing Association (IRA) regatta is the oldest rowing championship in the country and remains the premier event for national rowing honors for college men. The first IRA regatta, on June 24, 1895, was a four-miler between Columbia, the winner, Cornell and Pennsylvania. The IRA consists of five eastern schools—the original three and Navy and Syracuse. Other colleges participate as invited guests. The Huskies competed in the national championships held annually on Lake Harsha in Cincinnati from 1982 to 1994. Washington returned to the IRA for its 100th anniversary in 1995.

Washington won its first IRA national championship in 1923 winning the three-mile varsity eight race in 14:03.2. Washington won again at Poughkeepsie in 1924 (15:02) and over a four-mile course in 1926 (19:28.6). Before the 1936 crew won the Olympic gold medal in Germany, they won the IRA four miler in 19:06.6. The crew set an American record (6:04.1) for 2000 meters in the Olympic Trials and a world record (6:00.8) in the preliminary heat of the Olympic Games. The 1937 crew, with several oarsmen from the 1936 boat, won the IRA in 18:33.6.

The Flying Forty and Forty One crews won back-to-back IRA championships in 1940 (22:42.0) and 1941 (18:53.3). The 1941 crew also set an Oakland Estuary course record in the annual race with California, covering the three-mile course in 14:28.0. The race was permanently shortened to 2000 meters in 1968. The only Husky crew to get near the 1941 crew's time was the 1958 crew who rowed the Estuary course in 14:30.7.

The 1948 crew won Washington's eighth IRA championship in 14:06.4. A few weeks later, they raced over a 2000-meter course in 5:58.1, losing by six inches to California in the semi-final heat of the Olympic Trials. Cal won the trials and the 1948 London Olympics gold medal. In 1950, Washington again won the IRA title, winning the two-mile race in 8:07.5.

It took 20 more years for the Huskies to win another IRA championship. In 1970, Washington covered the 2000-meter course in 6:39.3. Starting in 1983, Washington entered the national championship race in Cincinnati and won the 1984 title, covering the 2000-meter course in 5:51.1. In 1995, Washington returned to the IRA for the regatta's 100th anniversary. In 1997, Washington won its 12th national championship in 5:51.0. This victory came a day before the Washington women's team won the first-ever NCAA Women's Rowing championships. The men's victory, along with those of the second varsity eight and the freshmen eight, gave Washington its fifth sweep in Husky history—three more than any other school in the history of collegiate rowing. Husky coach Bob Ernst summed up the sweep when he said: "I could not be happier right now. This is what we wanted to do. We came in figuring the freshmen and varsity had a pretty good chance to win and with the JVs (second varsity) winning too, everyone goes home with a smile." Princeton's coach Curtis Jordan exclaimed: "The varsity race was superlative. I didn't think Washington was going to be as dominant as they were. There was nobody at their speed. They rowed with a poise I haven't seen in a long time."

Varsity coxswain Sean Mulligan thought the Huskies rowed a perfect race. "From when we took our first few strokes and settled into our base cadence, I knew we were going to win. We had an aggressive start and we just tried to dominate the middle of the race."

Two other Husky crews were fast. The 1958 crew could not row in the IRA regatta because the Washington athletic program was on probation. In the last race Al Ulbrickson coached, the Huskies beat the Trud Club of Leningrad on the Kimkinskoe Reservoir outside of Moscow. It was one of the biggest upsets in the annals of collegiate rowing. Dick Erickson, a member of the 1958 crew and Husky crew coach from 1968-1987, decided to bypass the IRA regatta in 1977 and take his crew to Henley, England. The Husky varsity crew defeated the British National team at Henley-on-the-Thames in the Grand Challenge race, earning the first victory for a U.S. crew at the Henley event in 18 years.

Women's rowing, virtually non-existent following a short period in the early 1900s, returned in the late 1960s. In 1975, it was elevated to a varsity sport. The first women's collegiate championship was held in Oak Ridge, Tennessee, in 1980. The course was 1000 meters. In 1981, the Washington women's varsity eight captured its first national title in 3:20.8, defeating Yale by two seconds. Three members of that Husky Hall of Fame crew rowed on U.S. Olympic teams. Susan Broome was a member of the 1984 and 1988 teams; Kristi Norelius was a member of the 1980 team and the gold medal 1984 eight; Shyril O'Steen was also a member of the victorious 1984 crew.

The Husky women, coached by Ernst (1981-1987), won an unprecedented five straight titles with wins in 1982 (4:56.4 over 1500 meters), 1983 (4:57.1 over 1500 meters), 1984 (3:29.5 over 1000 meters) and 1985 (5:28.4 over 2000 meters). They won again in 1987, Ernst's last year as the women's coach, in 6:33.8. Ernst became the men's coach in 1988, and Jan Harville stepped up from the novice women's coaching position to become the head women's coach. In her first year, the women's varsity crew captured the Husky women's seventh national title in 6:41.0.

In 1997, the Washington women's crews qualified to compete for the first-ever NCAA crew championship. The inaugural event, to which eight schools were invited, was held on Lake Natoma's 2000-meter course in Sacramento. The Washington women knew the Husky men had swept the races the day before. Junior Kari Green said: "We had just finished our last set of heats and had taken the boat out of the water when they announced the men's victories over the loud speaker. It was so exciting to hear and added a little bit of pressure."

Washington entered the varsity eight finals with a slim, five-point lead over Princeton in the team standings. The women's varsity responded, finishing in 6:31.8, more than five seconds ahead of second-place Massachusetts. After the race, Coach Harville said: "To win by open water...well, you don't dream about that. You never know how the race is going to turn out, but I've never had more confidence in a crew that I've coached." The only senior in the boat, Tristine Glick was ecstatic at the end of the race. "I was really confident at about 300 meters to go. I couldn't wait to get across the finish line. To be able to do what we did was the most wonderful experience." With the second varsity eight and varsity four finishing second in their races, Washington won the team title, the first NCAA team championship, in any sport, in Husky history.

In 1998, the Washington women won their second NCAA team title and Washington won their ninth national women's varsity eight championship by beating Massachusetts again in 6:52.0. For the second year in a row, the team title came down to the final race. Going into the final varsity eight event, Washington, Brown, and Virginia were deadlocked for first place with 43 points apiece. Brown finished third in the race, and Virginia was a distant sixth.

UW Media Relations

The 1997 Husky squad won the IRA Championship.

Husky Moment

Baseball at Regional

The Husky baseball team earned an at-large berth to the Midwest II Regional in Wichita in 1994. The fifth-seeded Huskies beat second-seeded Long Beach State in the opener, 10-4. Washington was down 3-0 going into the fourth, but posted six runs in that inning, including three on a home run by Ross Junkin. The following day, Washington was trailing Santa Clara, 7-2, before scoring nine runs in the last three innings, including five in the ninth. Brett Merrick kept the UW in the game, getting out of a bases-loaded, no-outs jam in the bottom of the eighth. In the winners' bracket semifinal Washington lost to top seed Georgia Tech 6-2. Tech All-American Nomar Garciaparra accounted for five RBI with a double and a home run. In the evening game that would decide who would face the Yellow Jackets on championship Monday the Huskies scored five in the fifth, including three on a homer by Sean Linville, to defeat Long Beach State 6-2. In game one of the championship final with Georgia Tech, Brian Loucks' three-run homer, his first HR of the season, in the bottom of the 14th inning gave Washington a 12-9 win and forced another game. Freshman Justin Bice, who had thrown only 12 innings all season, allowed only one hit in 4 2/3 innings for a win. In game two, the Huskies ran out of gas and lost 18-7 despite grinding out 19 hits. Washington fell behind 6-0 in the first and never got closer than five runs. UW right fielder Jon Vander Griend topped a tremendous tournament by hitting for the cycle in the final game of the regional.

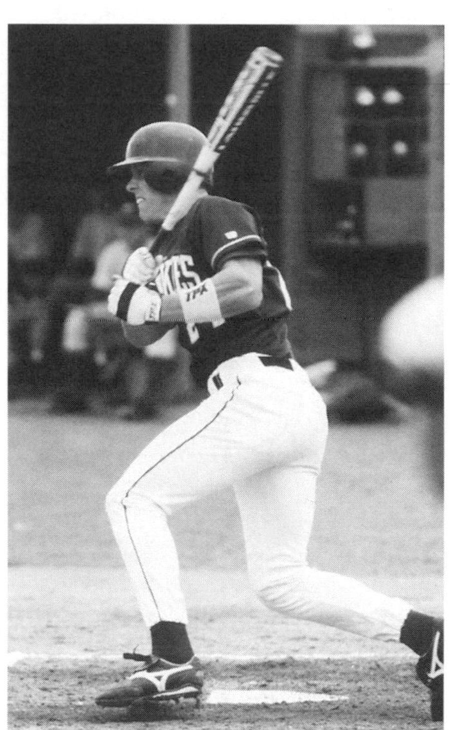

UW Media Relations

Brian Loucks

Husky Spotlight

Powered by Oxford University junior transfer Simon Baines, the Washington men's cross country team won its first Pac-10 championship in 1993. Baines proved to be the difference maker for the Huskies who placed fifth at the 1992 Pac-10 meet. Baines placed fourth in the meet, covering the 5,000-meter course in 24:07. The Huskies did an excellent job of running as a pack to hold off second-place Washington State by three points. David Hughes was eighth, Sam Alexander was 14th, George Barajaz placed 15th and Darren Hunter was 26th. Washington entered the meet ranked 14th in the naton. The Huskies went on to place second at the NCAA regional and eighth at the NCAA championships. Head coach Mike Johnson was honored as the Pac-10 coach of the year.

UW Media Relations

Simon Baines

Husky Highlight

During the 1990s, Arizona was the most dominant men's basketball team in the conference. If the program had an Achilles heel, it might have been playing the Huskies, especially in Seattle. Between 1991 and 1999, the Huskies defeated the Wildcats six times, including five times in Seattle. All five times Washington won at home, the Wildcats were ranked in the top-12 in the nation. The first Husky win in the decade came on Jan. 3 during the 1991 season when they defeated the fourth-ranked Wildcats 70-56 to end a 10-game losing streak to Arizona. Washington played a tight matchup-zone defense that allowed Mike Hayward to record a school-record seven steals. The Wildcats made just three of 22 three-point attempts. Husky forward Dion Brown led all scorers with 21 points. In 1992 the Huskies used a 15-foot jump shot from center Rich Manning at the buzzer to pull off a 62-60 victory against the seventh-ranked Cats. Bob Bender's first Husky team was just 2-15 when it faced 12th-ranked Arizona in 1994. With starting guard Jamie Booker sidelined with the flu, reserve Jason Tyrus scored a career-high 20 points to key the 74-69 shocker against 12th-ranked Arizona. In 1996 Jason Hartman made two free throws with 1.1 seconds left in overtime to give Washington an 80-79 win versus No. 14 Arizona in the Huskies' first win in Tucson since 1984. In 1997 the Huskies shot a blistering 59 percent from the floor and behind sophomore guard Donald Watts' 15 points, defeated the 10th-ranked Wildcats 92-88. Watts was the key man again in 1999, scoring 24 points in a 90-84 upset of Arizona, again ranked No. 10.

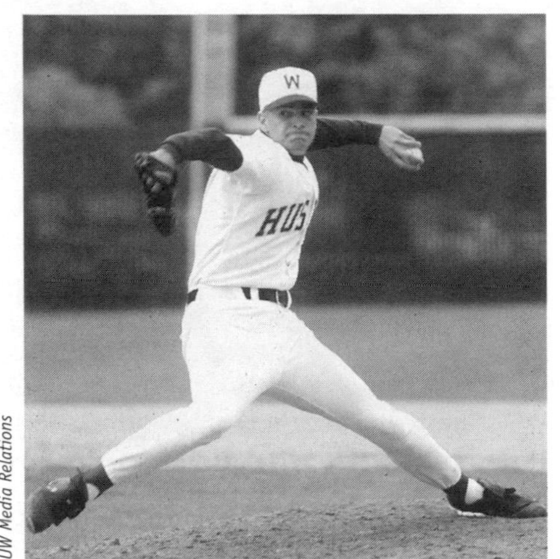

UW Media Relations

Husky Legend

Brett Merrick

When Washington baseball coach Ken Knutson needed to put a game away, he went to his bullpen and reliable lefty Brett Merrick. The hard-throwing Seattle native etched his name into the Husky record books as the most proficient closer in Washington history. In 1994, as a sophomore, Merrick earned first-team All-America honors from Collegiate Baseball after concluding the regular season tied for the national lead in saves with 20. Merrick became the first Husky baseball player to earn first-team All-America honors by any organization. He was also tabbed a second-team All-American by the American Baseball Coaches Association and a third-team All-American by *Baseball America* and the National Collegiate Baseball Writers' Association. Merrick successfully recorded a save in 20 of 22 opportunities. His total was a Pac-10 mark and just three short of the national record. Merrick thrived in pressure situations. During the regular season, only one of his earned runs came in a save situation, and three of six earned runs he surrendered on the year came against Central Washington. Merrick did not waste any time on the mound, throwing fast balls about 90 percent of the time he faced a batter. As a junior Merrick posted just 10 saves because the Huskies did not have as many late-game leads. Still, his double-digit save effort was just the third in school history. After the season Merrick was drafted in the 12th round by the Cleveland Indians. In addition to setting the single-season saves record, Merrick left Washington as the holder of the career record with 30 all-time saves. He pitched in 79 innings his final two seasons, allowing just 55 hits while recording 88 strikeouts. Knutson had high praise for the program's best relief pitcher. "It's easy for me," he said. "When Brett's in, I'm done managing."

Husky List

Husky Baseball All-Americans in the 1990s

Year	Player	Pos.	Yr.	Team(s)
1992	Brett Newell	SS	Fr.	honorable mention (CB)
1992	Ryan Rutz	2B	Fr.	honorable mention (CB)
1993	Randy Jorgensen	1B	Jr.	2nd team (Smith)
1994	Brett Merrick	LHP	So.	1st (CB), 2nd (ABCA), 3rd (BA, Smith)
1994	Brett Newell	SS	Jr.	3rd team (Smith)
1994	Joe Trippy	OF	Jr.	3rd team (Smith)
1994	Ryan Rutz	2B	Jr.	honorable mention (Smith)
1994	Chad Hartvigson	LHP	Sr.	honorable mention (Smith)
1995	Brett Merrick	LHP	Jr.	1st team (CB preseason)
1996	Chris Magruder	OF	Fr.	1st Team (CB)
1996	Kevin Miller	SS	Fr.	honorable mention (Smith),1st team (CB), 2nd (BA)
1997	Kevin Miller	SS	So.	3rd team (CB preseason), 2nd team (NCBWA), 3rd (CB), 3rd (BA)
1997	Jake Kringen	LHP	Jr.	2nd team (NCBWA)
1997	Ryan Lentz	3B	So.	3rd team (NCBWA)
1998	Jeff Carlsen	P	Fr.	1st (CB), 2nd (TSN)
1998	Chris Magruder	OF	Jr.	1st (CB preseason), 2nd (TSN pre season), 2nd (NCBWA), 3rd (BA)
1998	Kevin Miller	SS	Jr.	1st (TSN preseason), 2nd (CB pre season), 2nd (NCBWA)
1999	Jeff Heaverlo	RHP	Jr.	2nd team (USA Today), 3rd team (NCBWA)
1999	Dominic Woody	C	Jr.	3rd team (NCBWA)

Smith - Smith Super Team (NCBWA); CB - Collegiate Baseball; BA - *Baseball America;* ABCA - American Baseball Coaches Association; TSN - *The Sporting News*

Husky Lore

Armitage-Johnson Sails Into History

WHEN Stephanie Armitage-Johnson's husband, Fred, said that he saw something in the newspaper that could change his wife's life, she did not know if she should take him seriously. What he saw was an article about an attempt to form an all-women's crew to compete for the 1995 America's Cup sailing championship. He suggested that his wife submit an application. Armitage-Johnson was not an accomplished sailor. In fact, she had only been involved with the sport on a recreational level for two years. What she was was an accomplished Olympic-style weightlifter and an assistant strength and conditioning coach at Washington. She was the 1990 and 1991 national champion in her division. Armitage-Johnson, 33, was one of 600 women who submitted applications for the team, and thanks to her tremendous strength and stamina, she was selected to be a winch grinder. Under the direction of Bill Koch, the skipper of the victorious 1992 America's Cup team, America3 (America Cubed) became a reality. After eight months of training the team raced against four-time America's Cup champion Dennis Conner in the final American races. While their boat, the Mighty Mary, did not succeed in their effort to race in the America's Cup finals, the team drew a tremendous amount of media attention to the sport and women competing in what was regarded as a male-dominated event.

1993 W 1994

Husky Moment

Husky Softball Reaches NCAAs in Second Season

In only the program's second year of existence, the Washington softball team received a bid to the 1994 NCAA championships. The Huskies traveled to Northridge, California for the regional that also featured 20th-ranked Cal State Fullerton, third-ranked Cal State Northridge and unranked Maine. Washington was ranked 10th heading into its first postseason appearance. The regional was one of eight double-elimination tournaments across the country that would provide the teams for the College Softball World Series. The Huskies drew Fullerton, a team they had beaten three of four times in the regular season, in the opening round. Washington's postseason debut was not very smooth. The Huskies committed an uncharacteristic four errors and stranded 11 baserunners in a 2-1 loss. The Huskies rebounded in the loser's bracket by eliminating Maine 10-0. Washington catcher Jennifer Cline smacked a pair of home runs, including a three-run shot and a grand slam, to provide all the offense the team needed. After a short rest, the Huskies met Fullerton for the second time in the tournament. The results were not much better. The Huskies committed four errors in the early innings and allowed the Titans to grab a 4-0 lead after just two innings. While stinging from the losses, the young Husky squad gained valuable experience that would pay off in the years to come. "We've got kids who are playing in regionals for the first time," said Washington coach Teresa Wilson. "An entire team made up of freshmen and sophomores. They've got to live the pressure before they can understand how to deal with it."

UW Media Relations

Jennifer Cline

Husky Spotlight

In 1992 the Husky women's soccer team played what the NCAA determined to be the nation's toughest schedule. The Huskies played eight ranked teams on the way to an 8-9-2 finish. That slate looked easy compared to the start of the 1993 season. Washington opened by playing its first five games against teams that were ranked among the top six in the nation. The Huskies suffered back-to-back 2-0 losses to No. 2 Portland and No. 6 Stanford. Times looked bleak when Washington played No. 5 Santa Clara in the North Carolina Invitational. After trailing 1-0 Melinda Torre scored on a header on a pass from Tara Bilanski to knot the score. Eight minutes later Torre added another goal and the Huskies upset Santa Clara 2-1. The victory was Washington's first against a top-20 team in 16 tries. In the previous two years of existence the Huskies were 0-13-2 vs. ranked opponents. Washington did not stop there. The Huskies went on to defeat No. 3 Duke 2-0 in the tournament. Melanie Brennan and Emily Thompson scored for the Huskies and Jessica Conrardy recorded the shutout. The Huskies finished off their southern swing by losing to top-ranked North Carolina 2-0. Washington finished the season with a 9-6-2 record and played a total of 10 ranked teams over the course of the year.

Husky Highlight

In the short, but storied history of the Washington women's softball program, Angie Marzetta stands out as its first star. A transfer who helped to lead Central Arizona College to a pair of junior college national championships and a 103-5 record from 1991-92, Marzetta had her pick of colleges but chose the upstart Husky program. After leading the Pac-10 with 59 stolen bases in 1993, Marzetta helped Washington to its first NCAA appearances in 1994. A two-time All-Pac-10 selection, she was a third-team All-American as a senior, batting .364 and helping Washington to a No. 10 national ranking. Marzetta batted .427 for her Husky career. After graduating, she played for the Colorado Silver Bullets women's professional baseball team before starting a career in broadcasting.

UW Media Relations

Husky Legend

Tara Bilanski

UW Media Relations

Wearing jersey number 13 did not prove to be an unlucky experience for women's soccer player Tara Bilanski. When she finished her senior season in 1995 Bilanski, a midfielder, was the all-time leader in every offensive category. She scored 27 goals and added 20 assists for a total of 74 points. She set Washington's single-season record for goals with 12 in 1995, including five that were game winners. She also set single-season records that year with six assists and a total of 30 points. Two times during her career she scored three goals in a game and one time she was credited with three assists. As a junior she helped the Huskies to their first NCAA tournament appearance where they defeated Oregon State before being eliminated by Stanford. Bilanski helped lead the team back to the NCAAs during her senior season. She started 72 of 74 career matches and was voted the team's Player of the Year three times. Her list of honors included being named to the 1995 All-Pac-10 and all-West Region teams. An outstanding student, Bilanski was twice picked to the addidas Scholar Athlete All-American squad and was a three-time Pac-10 all-academic honoree. In 1996 she joined the Husky coaching staff as an assistant coach.

Husky List

Year-by-Year Husky Softball Results

Year	Overall Record	Pac-10 Record	Postseason Finish
1993	31-27	7-18, 7th	None
1994	44-21	14-10, 3rd	NCAA Regional
1995	50-23	17-11, 4th	NCAA Regional
1996	59-9	23-4, 1st	NCAA Runnerup
1997	50-19	16-11, 3rd	NCAA, 3rd
1998	52-15	19-9, 2nd	NCAA, 3rd
1999	51-18	15-12, 3rd	NCAA Runnerup
2000	62-9	17-4, 1st	NCAA, 5th

Husky Lore

MICHELLE Church was a hard-hitting leader of the Husky softball team during her career from 1993-96. She earned first-team All-America honors as a senior and was named a second-team Academic All-American. That same year she was the recipient of an NCAA postgraduate scholarship and named the NCAA's Woman of the Year for the state of Washington. Church batted .335 during her playing days and was a three-time All-Pac-10 pick. She graduated as Washington's all-time leader in at bats (843), hits (282), games played (264) and games started (264). She also held single-game records for runs (five), runs batted in (eight) and doubles (three).

1994 W 1995

HUSKY MOMENT

Huskies Ends Miami's Record Winning Streak

Two-touchdown underdogs, the Washington football team recorded one of the most impressive victories in the team's history by defeating Miami 38-20 to end the Hurricanes' NCAA-record 58-game home win streak. Playing in the hot, humid and muggy Orange Bowl, the Huskies outplayed the Hurricanes by being physically dominant, better conditioned and the team that came up with the big plays. The first half went Miami's way as the Hurricanes grabbed a 14-3 lead when Yatil Green beat Husky cornerback Russell Hairston for a 51-yard touchdown with 13 seconds left to play. At halftime Hairston vowed to his teammates that he would make up for his lapse in the second half. Washington took command of the game in a frantic four-minute period early in the third quarter. First, fullback Richard Thomas took a screen pass and darted through the Miami defense for a 75-yard score. Tailback Napoleon Kaufman, who was held to 80 rushing yards by the Miami defense, delivered a critical downfield block to pave Thomas' way to paydirt. It was the longest pass in Husky quarterback Damon Huard's career and the longest scoring play against the Hurricanes during their nine-year home win streak. On Miami's ensuing possession, Hairston came through on his promise. He intercepted Frank Costa's pass and returned it 34 yards for a touchdown and an 18-14 Husky lead. Washington then recovered a fumble on Miami's kickoff return. The Huskies next score was bizarre. Washington quarterback Damon Huard scrambled toward the endzone but fumbled the ball. Backup sophomore tackle Bob Sapp covered it in the endzone to give Washington a 25-14 victory. There was plenty of time for the high-powered Hurricanes to mount a comeback, but it never happened. The Huskies continually kept drives alive and made critical plays. One of the most memorable came when Husky defensive lineman Mike Ewaliko delivered a crushing tackle to Hurricane wide receiver Jami German that knocked him out for five minutes. Almost lost in the magnitude of the win was the fact Kaufman's rushing total allowed him to pass Joe Steele to become the all-time rushing leader. To recognize Miami's win streak, Hurricane fans had hung cardboard gravestones with the scores of every game in one endzone. A 59th gravestone, with Washington stenciled onto it, was put up at the start of the game. It was taken down as the game wound down and, somehow, came into the possession of the Washington team as a bounty for the victory. In the postage media interview, Sapp came up with the memorable line to sum up the day. "It was," he said, "the whammy in Miami."

Husky Spotlight

In the late 1990s *Sports Illustrated* rated Washington as the top college in the nation when it comes to producing standout tight ends. Of all the great ones who have played at Washington—players like Scott Greenwood, Aaron Pierce, Ernie Conwell and Cam Cleveland—Mark Bruener stands out as the best. Bruener was named an All-American as both a junior and senior, earning first-team honors in 1993 as a junior. That season he pulled in 30 passes for 414 yards and three scores. As a senior in 1994 he raised his reception total to 34 for 331 yards. He finished his four-year UW career with 90 catches for a total of 1,012 yards and four scores. The soft-spoken Bruener was a tough hombre on the field. "I get more of a charge running over guys than running around them," he once told a reporter. "It's so much fun to hit a guy." In addition to being an excellent receiver, Bruener was a devastating blocker who was respected by his teammates for his irreproachable work ethic.

Bruce Terami

HUSKY HIGHLIGHT

When Husky men's soccer coach Dean Wurzberger was assessing the needs of his team in 1993 he knew he needed to add speed to his front line. He found the answer in Jason Boyce, a lighting-quick forward from Corona Del Mar High School in Newport Beach, California. Boyce's announcement to attend Washington was a huge boost to the program. He was a *Parade* All-American and considered the top prep forward on the west coast. In 1994, as a freshman, he led the team with nine assists. It was an accomplishment that Boyce would be readily identified with during his Husky career. Boyce would go on to set UW single-season (13 in 1995) and career assists (34) records. He was honored as the Mountain Pacific Sports Federation Mountain Division player of the year as a junior and senior. In 1997 he was named a second-team All-American, only the third Husky player to be so honored. He led the team in goals as a senior with 15.

Joanie Komura

Husky Legend

Napoleon Kaufman

Joanie Komura

As much as Napoleon Kaufman will be remembered for his exciting runs as a record-setting Husky tailback, he should be equally appreciated for his dedication to the program and his teammates. After the 1993 season, his junior year at Washington, Kaufman faced a tough decision. Turn pro a year early, or return to Washington and face a year where the team was on probation and ineligible for a bowl appearance. Kaufman remained true to his school and as a result, he became Washington's all-time leading rusher. Kaufman ended the 1993 season with 1,299 rushing yards to set a UW single-season record. He needed a 181-yard rushing game against Washington State to better Greg Lewis' old single-season standard by 20 yards. It was Kaufman's second straight 1,000-yard season. He had rushed for 1,045 yards as a sophomore. Washington touted Kaufman for the Heisman Trophy prior to his senior year, calling him the nation's "Most Exciting All-Purpose Player." He certainly lived up to the hype early in the season. He had 252 all-purpose yards in the season opener against USC and followed that up with 211 yards versus Ohio State. He became the program's career rushing leader with 80 yards in the Huskies' upset at Miami to end the Hurricanes' NCAA-record 58-game home winning streak. He followed that up with 227 yards against UCLA and a career-best 254 yards in a game with San Jose State. At the time he was averaging 204.8 rushing yards per game and topping the voting in the straw polls for the Heisman. Unfortunately he suffered a toe injury against the Spartans that would slow him the rest of the year. He topped the 100-yard rushing mark just two times the remainder of the season. His great start allowed him to run for 1,390 yards to break his own single-season rushing record. He completed his career with 4,401 yards. He was just the fifth back in Pac-10 history to piece together three consecutive 1,000-yard rushing seasons and he was only the 40th rusher in NCAA history to eclipse the 4,000-yard mark in a career.

Husky List

Washington's 200-Yard Rushing Efforts

Yards	Name	Opponent	Year
296	Hugh McElhenny	Washington State	1950
259	Corey Dillon	Oregon	1996
258	Credell Green	Washington State	1955
254	Napoleon Kaufman	San Jose State	1994
249	Dennis Fitzpatrick	Washington State	1974
227	Napoleon Kaufman	UCLA	1994
222	Corey Dillon	San Jose State	1996
221	Don Moore	Ohio State	1966
212	Rashaan Shehee	Washington State	1995
211	Napoleon Kaufman	Ohio State	1994
208	Napoleon Kaufman	California	1992
207	Marques Tuiasosopo	Stanford	1999
205	Greg Lewis	California	1990
203	Jacque Robinson	Texas Tech	1982

Men's Tennis Advances to NCAAs

THE Husky men's tennis team celebrated its return to postseason competition in 1995 when Washington received its first invitation to the NCAA tennis championships since the team format began in 1977. Under the direction of first-year coach Matt Anger, the Huskies played a beefed-up schedule and posted a 12-10 regular-season record. Washington lost to UC Irvine in the first-round of the tournament. Scott More, Tori Dapas and Nick Williams all managed singles victories for the Huskies in the match. Washington, led by junior Ornello Arlati, was ranked 37th nationally heading into the match with the Anteaters. The NCAA appearance was not the only highlight of the year. Washington defeated sixth-ranked New Mexico during the season. The Lobos were the highest-ranked team the Huskies had ever beaten.

Husky Moment

Women's Crew Ends Princeton Win Streak

Spectators at the 1995 Opening Day Regatta witnessed one of the greatest, and most dramatic, crew races in the event's 25-year history. They could also claim their own part in the outcome of the women's Windermere Cup that pitted Washington against Princeton and South Africa. Princeton entered the event as the two-time defending national champions and owners of a 59-race win streak in head-to-head competitions. The Tigers had not lost in any race since the finals of the 1992 national championships. No member of the current Husky crew had ever defeated Princeton in a race. The Tigers' streak looked like it might grow to 60 consecutive victories as the two teams entered the Montlake Cut with 700 meters left in the 2,000-meter event. Princeton held a half-boat length lead. Seat-by-seat the Huskies began to reel in the Tigers under the direction of coxswain Joslyn Howard. As the two teams crossed underneath the Montlake Bridge the Huskies began to pull ahead to the loud roar from the Washington fans that packed the two sides of the course. Washington crossed the finish line about 15 feet ahead of Princeton in a time of 6:39.71. The Tigers' time was 6:41.57. "I knew my crew did everything they could," said Princeton coxswain Sarah Hull. "We just weren't quite used to the whole noise and atmosphere. They couldn't hear me at all." Washington stroke Hana Duriusova, who held that seat in the varsity eight for four years summed up the event the best. "There is no race in the world like this," said the member of the Czech Republic national team. "Not the world championships, not the Olympics, not anything." The two teams met again in June in Cincinnati at the national championships. Again trailing in the final 500 meters, the Huskies put on a power move, but came up just short in their upset bid, and the Tigers won their third straight national title. Princeton won in a time of 6:11.98 while the Huskies were clocked in 6:12.69.

Husky Spotlight

As a track star at Seattle's Rainer Beach High School, Tara Davis won five state championships in the long and triple jump events. She enrolled at Washington in 1990 and went on to have an outstanding career for the Husky women's basketball team, becoming the 13th player to score 1,000 points. In 1994, just several weeks after wrapping up her final basketball season, Davis turned out for the Husky track team. It did not take her long to get back into her old form. After a 10th-place finish at the Pac-10 championships, she qualified for the NCAAs and came in 18th. In 1995 she leaped 20-2¼ on her second attempt to win the Pac-10 championship. She bettered California's Crystal Hayes by 1½ inches. Davis' victory marked the first time since 1992 that a Husky woman had won a Pac-10 title. She returned to the NCAA Championships where she placed 15th. Davis also excelled in the triple jump setting a school record with a leap of 41-7¾ in 1995.

UW Media Relations

Husky Highlight

The Huskies returned to national dominance in women's basketball in 1995 when Washington won the preseason National Invitational Tournament and advanced to the Sweet 16 in the NCAA Championships. Playing their trademark brand of oppressive man-to-man defense, the Huskies overcame a poor shooting night to defeat Arkansas 54-50 in the second round of the NCAA tournament. Sophomore guard Laure Savasta keyed the Husky win with six points, including six clutch free throws in the closing moments. Savasta, who turned 21 on the day of the game, scored 10 of Washington's final 11 points. Rhonda Smith added 14 points for the Huskies. Arkansas' point total was its lowest in 70 games. The Huskies led throughout the game but never more than when they achieved a 41-33 advantage with 7:06 to play. Savasta teamed with backcourt mate Shannon Kelly to shutdown the Lady Razorbacks outstanding freshman guard Christy Smith. The Southeast Conference freshman of the year, Smith scored a team-high 14 points, but she was held to three-for-16 shooting from the field. She had just one assist and nine turnovers. Washington met Texas Tech, the team it defeated for the preseason NIT title, in the first round of the regional at Tennessee and lost 67-52. Washington finished the season with a 25-9 record.

UW Media Relations

Husky Legend

Rhonda Smith

Growing up in Seattle, Rhonda Smith used to watch the Husky women's basketball team play games in Hec Edmundson Pavilion and on local television. She idolized the figures who raced up and down the court. "I saw games on TV and I thought those girls were queens on thrones," she said. "They were so far up there." Smith did not realize that one day she would rise above all of them. Smith came to Washington from Franklin High School and, like many freshmen, struggled to adapt to the college game and coach Chris Gobrecht's demanding coaching style. She stuck with her commitment to be a Husky, and it paid off with huge dividends. She finished her career as the all-time scorer and third-leading rebounder leader. She accounted for 1,801 points, breaking Karen Murray's old record of 1,745 she set a decade earlier. Smith was a tiger on the glass, pulling down 803 rebounds. She led the Huskies in that category her last three seasons, the only player up until that point to top the team in rebounding for more than two years. Smith was the Huskies' most accurate shooter every year she played, the only Washington player to do that. As a senior she guided the Huskies to the preseason National Invitational Tournament championship by scoring a career-high 38 points in the finals at Texas Tech. The Huskies' 79-75 victory snapped the Lady Red Raiders' 24-game home winning streak. It tied as the second highest point total in Washington history. A three-time All-Pac-10 pick, Smith was named to the District VIII All-America team as a junior and senior. Her final season at Washington she averaged 17.7 points and 8.5 rebounds to become the first player in the program's history to earn All-America honors.

Husky List

UW Women's Basketball All-Pac-10 Selections (First and Second Team Only)

1986-87	Lisa Oriard (2nd Team)
	Yvette Cole (2nd Team)
1987-88	Yvette Cole (1st Team)
	Lisa Oriard (1st Team)
1988-89	Yvette Cole (1st Team)
1989-90	Karen Deden (1st Team)
	Amy Mickelson (1st Team)
1990-91	Karen Deden (1st Team)
	Laurie Merlino (1st Team)
1992-93	Rhonda Smith (1st Team)
1993-94	Tara Davis (1st Team)
	Rhonda Smith (1st Team)
1994-95	Rhonda Smith (1st Team)
1996-97	Jamie Redd (1st Team)
1997-98	Jamie Redd (1st Team)
	Amber Hall (1st Team)
1998-99	Jamie Redd (1st Team)
	Amber Hall (1st Team)
2000-2001	Meghan Franza (1st Team)

Husky Lore

UNDER the direction of first-year coach Lesle Gallimore, the Washington women's soccer team made its first postseason appearance in 1994. Just getting there was only part of the story. The 18th-ranked Huskies played at 15th-ranked Oregon State in the opening round of the 24-team tournament. Earlier in the season the Beavers had defeated the Huskies 1-0 in Corvallis. Husky forward Emily Thompson, who missed the first game between the two teams due to a knee injury, gave Washington a 1-0 halftime lead when she scored in the 42nd minute of play. Senior defender Melanie Brennan scored at the 58-minute mark and junior forward added a goal in the 74th minute to give the Huskies the 3-0 victory. Washington met third-ranked Stanford, another team that had defeated the Huskies (2-0) in the regular season, in the second round at the NCAA regional in Portland. After regulation and two overtime periods the match remained scoreless. The Cardinal advanced to the regional final when it bettered Washington 6-5 in penalty kicks. The Huskies ended their most successful season with a 13-6-2 record. Washington set a number of standards during the season. The team scored the most goals (41) in the program's history, allowed the fewest goals (17), had the most shutouts (10), and most importantly, won in postseason play.

1995 W 1996

Husky Moment

The 1995 Apple Cup

When it comes to plots and subplots, the 1995 Apple Cup football game between Washington and Washington State had them all. The Cougars were looking for their first win at Husky Stadium in a decade and Washington needed the victory to clinch a tie for the Pac-10 championship. Washington State was set to start redshirt freshman quarterback Ryan Leaf for the first time while Husky senior signal caller Damon Huard was on the verge of becoming Washington's all-time passing leader. The game was a shootout from the start as the teams wound up combining for 909 yards of offense on a wet afternoon before the largest crowd (74,144) to ever see a game in the series. After Washington State led 14-6 at the half, Husky sophomore tailback Rashaan Shehee got UW back into the contest with an 85-yard TD run. He would go on to finish with 212 rushing yards. Leaf, who benefited by the fact Husky standout safety Lawyer Milloy had to leave the game in the first half with a toe injury, was outstanding, throwing for 291 yards. A John Wales field goal gave Washington a 15-14 lead that did not last long when Leaf hooked up with Kearney Adams for a 30-yard score. The Huskies answered with their own big play when Dave Janoski pulled in a 42-yard touchdown pass from between two Cougar defenders to allow Washington to take a 23-22 lead with 10:51 to play. Janoski finished with six catches for 162 yards. Huard finished the game with 5,692 career passing yards to break Sonny Sixkiller's 23-year old yardage mark. Washington scored again to raise the lead to 30-22. The Cougars managed to tie the game at 30-30 with 2:17 to play. Jerome Pathon returned the kickoff 30 yards to the WSU 46-yard line. Shehee ran 21 yards and then Huard hit Pathon for a 14-yard pass. With just over a minute to play, Wales, who was maligned all season for his poor kicking, drilled a 21-yard field goal to give the Huskies a dramatic 33-30 victory.

UW Media Relations

Rashaan Shehee

Husky Spotlight

Washington men's basketball center Todd MacCulloch was redshirted the first season he was on the Husky campus. Husky coach Bob Bender felt the seven-footer from Winnipeg, Canada, needed a year to get stronger, work on his game and get a better feel for the competition at the NCAA level. As a redshirt freshman in 1996, MacCulloch showed Washington fans that it was a worthwhile wait. Against Arizona State on Feb. 29 he scored 22 points and pulled down 20 rebounds. He made all 10 of his field goal attempts to set a single-game field goal shooting record. MacCulloch played only 26 minutes in the Huskies' 75-64 victory. He was the first Husky to record a 20-20 game since Steve Hawes scored 32 points and grabbed 20 rebounds in 1972. The win ended a three-game losing streak for Washington and was the team's first victory against the Sun Devils in 15 meetings. MacCulloch's shooting performance raised his season field goal percentage to 67.5 percent. "I didn't do anything great," said the typically reserved MacCulloch. "The ball was coming to me and I just picked it up and put it in."

Bruce Terami

Husky Highlight

In 1996 Washington's Adam Setliff reached one of his career goals by competing at the Olympic Games in the discus. Setliff came to Washington after starting his collegiate career at Rice. The top prep thrower in the nation as a senior in 1988, Setliff did not feel he was improving at Rice and decided to transfer. He did not know much about Washington, but he read in the *Track and Field News* that the Huskies were the only team with two throwers (Todd Wilson and Pat Feider) who were ranked in the top 20. He figured there must be a good coach and he was right. Setliff contacted Husky track coach Ken Shannon and told him he had thrown 190 feet. Shannon, the Olympic throwing coach in 1984 said to stay in touch. After Setliff improved his marks Shannon offered a scholarship. As a Husky, Setliff finished second twice at the Pac-10 meet and was fifth at the NCAA Championships. As a senior he recorded a throw of 210-3, the top mark in the nation. After completing his college career he continued to improve his marks. Preparing for the 1996 Olympics he upped his personal best to 219-4. At the Olympics, he was one of two Americans to qualify for the finals where he placed 12th. He won the American Olympic trials in 2000 and finished fifth in the competition at the Sydney Olympics.

Husky Legend

Lawyer Milloy

Joanie Komura

Lawyer Milloy had the reputation as a big hitter on the Husky football team. Based on his first and last games as a member of Washington's baseball team, he was a pretty solid hitter on the diamond too. Milloy's career got off to a slow start in 1992 when he suffered a broken foot that forced him to redshirt the football season. By 1994, as a sophomore, he had become the starting free safety and earned first-team All-Pac-10 honors that season, the only sophomore to be so honored. He led Washington with 106 tackles, placing him third among Pac-10 defenders. He was also the first Washington defensive back to top the team in tackling since Tony Bonwell did it in 1972. Milloy had 115 tackles as a junior to again lead the team in that category. He became the first Husky defensive back to lead Washington in tackles in back-to-back seasons. A unanimous All-America selection, he was named the nation's defensive back of the year by the Touchdown Club of Columbus and was one of three finalists for the Jim Thorpe Award as the nation's top defensive back. He was also named to the All-Pac-10 team for a second consecutive season. He declared for the NFL draft after the 1995 season and was chosen by the New England Patriots in the second round. As a rookie, he started in the 1997 Super Bowl. The Patriots were not the only team to draft Milloy. The Detroit Tigers picked him in the 19th round of the Major League Baseball draft in 1995. He played for three years on the Husky baseball team from 1992-1994. His first at-bat as a freshmen resulted in a home run at Kansas State. He blasted two three-run homers as a Husky to help Washington defeat Washington State in his final day as a baseball player. He was a member of the 1993 Washington baseball team that finished 16th nationally and reached the NCAA regional final.

HUSKY LIST

Multiple-Year Leaders in Tackles

Year	Player	Tackles
2000	Derrell Daniels	97
1999	Derrell Daniels	81
1995	Lawyer Milloy, fs	115
1994	Lawyer Milloy, fs	106
1992	Dave Hoffman, ilb	91
1991	Dave Hoffman, ilb	71
1990	Dave Hoffman, ilb	79
1987	David Rill, ilb	176
1986	David Rill, ilb	155
1985	David Rill, ilb	187
1982	Ken Driscoll, ilb	133
1981	Ken Driscoll, ilb	151
1980	Ken Driscoll, ilb	140
1978	Michael Jackson, ilb	168
1977	Michael Jackson, ilb	210
1976	Mike Baldassin, ilb	200
1975	Mike Baldassin, lb	139
1964	Rick Redman	121
1963 *	Rick Redman	82

* Statistics for only seven games.

KEN Shannon single-handedly made the Washington track throwers one of the most respected groups in the nation. Shannon coached the Husky track team for 32 years, including 29 years as the head coach of the program starting in 1969. During his tenure as head coach, the Washington men recorded seven top-12 finishes at the NCAA Championships and had athletes earn 81 All-America certificates. Shannon produced 39 conference champions, 18 NCAA Champions and coached 10 athletes to NCAA record-holder status and seven Olympians. Shannon was selected to be an assistant coach in charge of throwers and decathlon performers for the U.S. team at the 1984 Olympic Games. He was a javelin assistant for the 1976 U.S. Olympic coaching staff.

Husky Moment

Softball Finishes as Runners-up At NCAAs

The heights the Washington softball team reached in its fourth season are almost unimaginable. Washington won its first Pac-10 championship with a 23-4 record and came within one victory of capturing the first NCAA team championship in school history. The Huskies got off to their best start ever, winning nine in a row before falling to second-ranked Arizona 4-1. Washington won its next 15 games to stand 19-1. Later in the season the Huskies would piece together a 19-game win streak to raise the team's record to 53-8. Included in that was a two-game sweep of top-ranked Arizona, 2-1 and 7-0, that sent Washington to the top of the softball rankings for the first time in the program's history. The Huskies defeated Jacksonville State and Oklahoma State (twice) to make their first trip to the College World Series. Washington defeated Princeton (7-1), California (9-7) and UCLA (8-2) to face off with Arizona for the winner-take-all national championship game. The more experienced Wildcats, winners of three national titles in the previous five years, took command of the final game early. All-American second baseman Jenny Dalton tagged Husky All-America pitcher Heather Meyer for a three-run homer in the first inning. Wildcat right fielder Alison Johnsen hit a two-run double in the next inning to push Arizona's lead to 5-0. The Wildcats made it 6-0 in the top of the fourth inning. That is when the Huskies got back into the game. Michelle Church, Mindy Williams and Leah Francis all had RBI hits to bring Washington to within two runs. In the sixth the Huskies threatened again, loading the bases with no outs, but could not score a run. Arizona held on for the 6-4 victory and the national title.

UW Media Relations

Mindy Williams

Husky Spotlight

When Washington's women's tennis doubles team of Katherine Costain and Kori Sosnowy traveled to the NCAA in Tallahassee, Fla., they were not considered one of the contenders for the title. They left, however, with the distinction of being the first Husky competitors to ever register a victory at the event in either the singles or doubles competition. Costain and Sosnowy qualified for the NCAAs after posting a 19-9 regular-season record that had them ranked 19th in the nation. Costain was the Pac-10 Northern Division player of the year in 1996. She had also won that honor as a freshman in 1994. The Husky duo faced Michigan's Sasrah Cyganiak and Sora Moon in the opening round. Playing in 90-degree temperatures, Costain and Sosnowy fought back from a 5-3 deficit in the third set to post a 7-5, 6-7, 7-5 victory in just under three hours. Stanford's doubles team of Kim Shasby and Julie Scott defeated the Husky team 6-7, 6-1, 6-1 in the second round of the tournament. Costain and Sosnowy were the first doubles team in the program's history to be ranked nationally. They only started playing together during the fall, but they upset the fourth-ranked team at the Rolex Regional tournament to jump into the rankings.

Husky Highlight

It will go down as one of the most unusual athletic events in Washington history. It was called the Washington Discus Competition, but it later became known as the Aretha Hill Invitational. A sophomore at Washington, Hill had placed third at the Olympic Trials in the discus event. But, she did not meet the qualifying standard throw of 196-10 to make the team. Washington officials set up a meet that could serve as a qualifying contest for Hill. Competing against three other throwers, in front of about 50 friends, media and meet officials the event was held on the track throwing field just east of Husky Stadium. Hill made all six of her throws but did not reach the qualifying mark. No problem. The Washington Discus Competition II was quickly underway. Hill's first five throws were all short. She knew she could still qualify the next week at a meet in Santa Barbara, but Hill rejected those thoughts and unleashed a toss of 198-6. It was a personal best and also a school record. She had done it. At the age of 19, she was going to Atlanta for the Summer Olympic Games. The Olympics were Hill's first international competition. She threw 183-10 in the preliminaries to place 16th in her session and 35th overall. She did not qualify for the finals, but she made it to the grandest stage for her sport. It sure was a long way from the throwing area behind the scoreboard at Husky Stadium.

Husky Legend

Amber Hall

Joanie Komura

The intangibles are what made Amber Hall one of the most proficient rebounders in Pac-10 history. A raw, gangly player out of Vancouver, British Columbia, Hall evolved from a great athlete playing basketball to a consummate scoring and rebounding threat who was almost impossible to keep away from a missed shot. Despite suffering with tendinitis in both knees, Hall was named to the Pac-10's all-freshman team in 1996. That season she averaged 6.3 points and 6.1 rebounds. A healthier Hall began to blossom as a sophomore. She upped her scoring average to 13.2 points per game and led the Pac-10 in rebounding with an 11.1 average. Unfortunately, she suffered a broken ankle against Stanford and missed the final five games of the season. Hall's junior season was her best at Washington. She scored at a 17.3 average and managed 11.2 rebounds per game. She was known as double-double trouble for opponents. She had 11 more double-figure scoring and rebounding games than the next highest total among conference players. She would go on to have 48 double-doubles as a Husky. That spring she competed for the Canadian National Team that toured Europe and played in the Slovakia Grand Prix. Hall wrapped up her senior season by becoming Washington's all-time rebounding leader with 1,003. That total stood as the fifth highest mark in Pac-10 history. She finished her career with 1,330 points to rank eighth on the Huskies' all-time list. She was only the sixth Washington player to rank in the top 10 for both scoring and rebounding as a Husky. Hall wound up leading the conference in rebounding three years in a row. Hall excelled as a sociology major. She was named to the Pac-10's All-Academic team as both a junior and senior and she was recognized as a regional Academic All-American as a senior.

Husky List

Women's Basketball Career Rebound Leaders

	Player	Years	Games	Rebounds	Avg.
1.	Amber Hall	1995-99	104	1003	9.6
2.	Carlin McClary	1978-82	112	982	8.8
3.	Karen Deden	1988-91	116	912	7.9
4.	Gena Pelz	1994-98	118	820	6.9
5.	Rhonda Smith	1992-95	116	803	6.9
6.	Yvette Cole	1986-89	122	764	6.2
7.	Liz Chicane	1980-83	99	762	7.7
8.	Margie Nielsen	1977-78	51	738	14.5
9.	Jamie Redd	1995-99	114	714	6.3
10.	Lisa Oriard	1985-88	116	711	6.1

Simpson Starts Stellar Gym Career

AS a freshman on the 1996 Husky women's gymnastics team, Tiffany Simpson showed that she would be one of the greatest performers in program's history by breaking the school record in the all-around at her first home meet. She went on to qualify for the NCAA championships where, slowed by an injury and the flu, she placed 40th. Simpson moved on to greater heights as a sophomore. She paced seventh at the NCAAs in the all-around and came away from the meet as a three-time All-American. Simpson won the vault competition at the Pac-10 championships. Her junior season was more of the same as she helped the Huskies to the 1998 West Regional title, where she was the co-champion in the all-around. She also won the floor exercise at that meet. She repeated as a three-time All-American at the NCAAs that season. She finished her career as the only gymnast to record three 10.000 scores as a Husky.

Corky Trewin

Husky Moment

Men's Crew Sweeps at Nationals

The Washington men's crew team staked its claim as the best program in the nation in impressive fashion at the 1997 Intercollegiate Rowing Association championships. All three Husky boats won gold medals to give Washington a sweep of the top three races. The final day of competition on the Cooper River in Cherry Hill, N.J. began when the Washington freshman team crossed the finish line first in a time of 6:07.3 to defeat second-place Wisconsin by 5.5 seconds. The junior varsity team brought home the next national title when it beat Brown with a time of 6:09. It was not an easy title for the j.v. rowers. They had to advance to the finals through the repechage after losing their opening heat race. The first two wins marked the 10th time in Washington rowing history that the freshman and junior varsity boats had claimed national titles in the same regatta. In the varsity race, Brown held a slim lead over the Huskies entering the final 800 meters of the 2,000-meter race. Washington broke away from a tight pack to win in 5:51.0. Four other teams finished within four seconds of the Huskies. The varsity eight boat included coxswain Sean Mulligan, stroke Bob Cummins and Brett Reisinger, Silas Harrington, Andy Tyler, Matt Andersen, Mat Schostak, Aaron Beck and bow Carl Bolstad. After the season, the Huskies raced for the Ladies Challenge Plate at the Royal Henley Regatta in England. Washington lost to the British national lightweight team by just one foot. It was the only time all season the Huskies had suffered a defeat.

UW Media Relations

Husky Spotlight

Jason Chorak had a specialty. He clobbered quarterbacks. A defensive end with Croatian heritage, Chorak had one of the most stellar defensive seasons in Husky history in 1996. He was named the Pac-10 Conference's defensive player of the year after recording a team-record and conference-leading 14.5 sacks and a team-record 22 tackles for loss. Chorak was a third-team All-America selection by the *Associated Press*. He was named to *Playboy's* preseason All-America team in 1997 and went on to be named a second-team All-American by the *Football News* in 1997. He finished his career as a two-time first-team All-Pac-10 performer. He had 59.5 tackles for loss during his career to rank No. 1 on Washington's all-time list. His 25.5 career sacks ranked as the third highest total in Husky history.

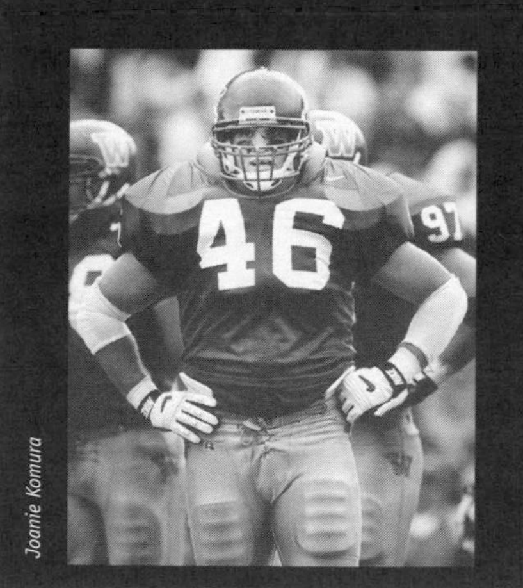

Joanie Komura

Husky Highlight

The 1997 NCAA Mideast baseball Regional was another successful trip for the Huskies as they had two shots to win one game and go to the College World Series, but fell twice to host Mississippi State. Jake Kringen won game one for the Huskies, outlasting SW Louisiana ace Trey Poland for a 5-4 win. In the second game, Washington, playing as the home team, sent 8,364 Mississippi State fans home in shock, scoring four runs in the bottom of the ninth to win, 5-4. Kevin Miller's bases-loaded single tied it, and Ryan Soules' double sent home Kyle Woods for the win. Freshman Jeff Heaverlo allowed four runs in the first, but went the distance for the win. The Huskies beat top-seeded Georgia Tech in game three, 8-4, with Ryan Lentz and Soules each providing three hits. The win sent the Huskies to the championship round and Mississippi State. In the first game, the Huskies gave up seven runs in the second to fall behind. Despite four hits (including two doubles) from Chris Magruder, the UW fell short, 7-5. Rain postponed the final game until the next day when Kringen, the UW ace, faced MSU ace Eric DuBose in front of 10,688 fans. MSU broke a 2-2 tie in the bottom of the eighth and DuBose went the distance for the win. Magruder, who batted .619 for the five games, was a unanimous selection to the all-tournament team, but DuBose was the regional's MVP.

Husky Legend

Todd MacCulloch

UW Media Relations

In the early days of Todd MacCulloch's Husky basketball career, people kept trying to label him with a fitting nickname. The seven-foot post player from Winnipeg Manitoba, Canada was called Big Mac, Big Country, Big Providence, Big Continent. Thankfully, none stuck. If anything, an accurate moniker would have had more to do with his shooting touch than his height. MacCulloch became the second player in NCAA history to lead the nation in field goal percentage in three consecutive seasons. Ohio State's Jerry Lucas also did it from 1960-62. MacCulloch shot 67.6 percent as a sophomore, 65 percent as a junior and 66.2 percent as a senior. He did not qualify as a freshman when he shot 67.5 percent. MacCulloch finished his career having made 702 of 1058 shots, an accuracy rate of 66.4 percent. MacCulloch, like most youngsters in Canada, grew up playing hockey. He didn't begin to concentrate on basketball until he outgrew his favorite sport. The Husky coaches elected to redshirt MacCulloch his first season at Washington, but they brought him on all of the team's road trips so he would know what to expect playing Division I basketball. Husky fans enjoyed watching MacCulloch grow and develop as a player, becoming more physical and dominant in the low post as his career continued. He always played with an even keel, rarely displaying emotion on either end of the court. But, there was the Oregon game. MacCulloch dropped in a late basket against the Ducks and then hustled to the other end of the court to block Oregon's last-second shot. He then erupted in a memorable dance down press row and into the arms of his teammates. MacCulloch was a two-time All-Pac-10 performer who was drafted by the Philadelphia 76ers in 1999. He participated in the NBA Rookie Game during the 2000 All-Star weekend.

Husky List

Records Held by Corey Dillon

On Nov. 16, in a rain-drenched Husky Stadium, Washington junior tailback Corey Dillon ran himself into the Husky record books. Playing against San Jose State, Dillon set several UW offensive records and he did it in just 15 minutes. With the Huskies out to a large lead, Dillon never played after the first quarter. Here's a look at the records he set in 1996:

Single-Season Rushing: 1,555 yards
Rushing Yards in a Quarter: 222 vs. San Jose State
Single-Season Rushing Attempts: 271
Most Rushing Attempts in a Game: 38 vs. Washington State
Most Rushing Attempts in a Quarter: 16 vs. San Jose State
Rushing Yards per Game: 141.4 (1,555 yards in 11 games)
Rushing Touchdowns in a Season: 22

Husky Lore

The Sixth Man

WASHINGTON won the 1997 national championship in basketball. At least, in the movies the Huskies did. Motion picture crews took over Hec Edmundson Pavilion during the spring of 1996 to film "The Sixth Man." In the family-oriented film, college basketball star Antoine Tyler, played by Kadeem Hardison, is about to realize his dream of making it to the NCAA Championship when he dies, leaving his brother Kenny (Marlon Wayans) to lead the Washington Huskies to victory. Kenny loses his drive to win until Antoine's ghost appears to give the team a lift. The film climaxes with the Huskies winning the national championship. Several former Washington players were featured in the production that was released in March of 1997.

1996 W 1997

Husky Moment

Women's Rowing Captures NCAA Championship

The Husky women's crew team won the first NCAA team championship in Washington's history when it captured the 1997 rowing title. The championship, held at Lake Natoma in Sacramento, California, was the first ever administered by the NCAA for women's rowing. Washington was one of eight schools competing for the team championship in the competition which featured races in I Eights (varsity), II Eights (junior varsity) and fours. Hoping for a sweep of all three races, the final day of racing saw Washington's fours and II Eights both place second. Based on the NCAA's scoring system, the Huskies had to finish ahead of Princeton to claim the team title. After the start of the race was delayed by a false start by Brown, Washington, which had not lost any races all season, battled Princeton for the early lead. At about 300 meters, the Huskies showed their dominance and started to pull away. They rowed across the finish line on the 2,000-meter course with open water behind them. Their winning time of 6:31.8 was a boat length and a half ahead of second-place Massachusetts. The Huskies captured the NCAA team title with 201 points while Princeton was second with 184 points and Brown third at 170. Washington's winning varsity eight team included Sabina Telenska, Denni Nessler, Kelly Horton, Katy Dunnet, Annie Christie, Jan Williamson, Tristine Glick, Kari Green and coxswain Alida Purves. A day earlier the Husky men had swept the top three places at the IRA national championships. It marked the first time since 1984 that the Husky men and women were national champs in the same season.

Joanie Komura

Husky Spotlight

Dodie Mazzuca capped a brilliant four-year career on the Husky women's golf team in 1997 when she finished first at the NCAA regional championship. That earned Mazzuca a third straight trip to the NCAAs and helped the Huskies to their second consecutive team appearance at the event. She won three tournaments during her career, tying her coach, Mary Lou Mulflur, as the only Washington player to accomplish that feat. She earned All-Pac-10 and first-team All-America honors as a senior. She holds the distinction of being the first All-American in the program's history. On the final day of the Edean Ihlanfeldt Invitational she shot a Sahalee Country Club record with a sizzling 18-hole score of 65. As a freshman, she shot a 69 on the same course at the same event.

Joanie Komura

Husky Highlight

In 1996, when the two Pac-10 divisional champions met to decide the conference baseball championship, USC defeated Washington 2-1 in the three-game series. In 1997, the 23rd-ranked Huskies found themselves back in the conference championship playoff, this time playing at fifth-ranked Stanford. The Cardinal used a two-run homer in the bottom of the 10th inning in game one of the series to win 7-6. The Huskies pulled off the come-from-behind in the second game, scoring nine times in the sixth inning to win 13-8. In the deciding third game, Washington built an 8-3 lead, gave up six runs in the sixth to fall behind 9-8, then scored three runs in the seventh, with two outs, and held on to win 12-9 and capture the series. A year later the Huskies proved being a southern division opponent for the title was no fluke. Top-ranked Stanford was again the opponent for Washington, who hosted the championship series. Sophomore pitcher Jeff Heaverlo scattered seven hits to get the 16-4 complete game victory in the series opener. The Huskies pounded out 16 hits while handing Stanford its worst loss of the season. Washington's bats remained hot in the second game. After falling behind 3-0 after one-half inning, the Huskies put together a 17-hit assault, including five home runs, to sweep the series with a 12-8 victory. In two days the Huskies had shelled the highly respected Stanford pitching staff for 28 runs on 33 hits.

Joanie Komura

Husky Legend

Sara Pickering

Nobody in college softball history could stroke a ball for a double the way Sara Pickering did during her Husky career from 1994 to 1997. And nobody could stop her from doing it. Despite a nagging shoulder injury, Pickering started all 271 games she played in during her Washington career. During that time she became the program's first two-time All-American and set an NCAA record with 91 career doubles. All four years at UW she played in the NCAA tournament and she guided the Huskies to the 1996 and 1997 College World Series. Her junior season the Huskies advanced to the championship game before falling to Arizona 6-4. Coming out of Corona High School in Corona, California, Pickering had her pick of top college softball programs to choose from. She liked the idea of helping to build the upstart Washington program that would be in only its second year during her freshman season. She brought with her an inside-out swing that mashed balls into the right-center field gap. She later learned to pull the ball and pitchers had little chance of striking her out. Pickering made 842 career plate appearance and struck out only 45 times. She batted .405 as a junior and .413 as a senior to bring her four-year average up to .379. A second baseman, Pickering was a three-time All-Pac-10 performer, named MVP of the 1997 NCAA regional and selected to the College World Series all-tournament team in both of her appearances. In 1999 she joined former Husky assistant John Rittman's staff at Stanford as an assistant coach.

Husky List

Angela Bransom

In 1996 Angela Bransom became the first Husky volleyball player to earn All-Pac-10 honors three years in a row. She also became Washington's third All-American in the sport. Bransom was a senior in 1996 and finished her career as the Washington record holder for career kills (1,676) and single-season kills (546 in 1996). Here's a look at Washington's all-time kills list:

	Kills	Player(Years)
1.	1,676	Angela Bransom (1993-96)
2.	1,580	Laurie Wetzel (1985-88)
3.	1,305	Dragana Djordjevic (1991-95)
4.	1,253	Kristina Laffling (1996-99)
5.	1,240	Makare Desilets (1994-97)
6.	1,146	Leslie Tuiasosopo (1995-98)
7.	1,097	Lisa McGammond (1986-89)
8.	993	Kayley Grim (1986-89)
9.	952	Genne Terry (1982-86)
10.	873	Amy Tutt (1993, 95-97)

Husky Lore

IN the spring of 1997 Washington officials finalized plans for an aggressive fundraising campaign that would result in more than $90 million in capital improvements to the Husky athletic landscape. The Campaign for the Student-Athlete called for the renovation of Hec Edmundson Pavilion, the addition of a 100,000-square-foot indoor practice facility, new playing field and stadium for baseball and men's and women's soccer and the renovation of the Conibear Shellhouse. The Campaign would also increase the endowment for athletic scholarships. The fundraising effort was the result of strategic planning involving University administrators, coaches, student-athletes, community leaders and Husky fans. It was a five-year effort that began July 1, 1995 and concluded June 30, 2000. Private contributions provided the most significant funding portion of the strategic plan. Support came from Washington alumni, Husky fans and supporters, and former student-athletes.

Bruce Terami

The indoor practice facility.

Husky Moment

Cinderella Basketball Team Reaches Sweet 16

The Husky men's basketball team had to come up big in its final three games of the 1998 season if it expected to receive its first bid to the NCAA tournament in 12 years. First, the Huskies buried visiting USC 91-66, setting up a pivotal game with 18th-ranked UCLA. Washington jumped out to a 16-point halftime lead, but Toby Bailey rallied the Bruins by scoring 32 second-half points. Trailing by a point, Washington center Todd MacCulloch was fouled with 1.1 seconds to play. He hit both free throws and the Huskies kept their NCAA hopes alive. Washington finished out the season strong, pounding Washington State 70-51 in Pullman. The Huskies gathered on Selection Sunday in the Hall of Fame room and jumped for joy when their name appeared on the NCAA bracket showing a first-round matchup with Xavier. Playing in Washington, D.C., the Huskies used a patient tempo to disrupt the Musketeers, who liked to play at a quicker pace. Trailing 68-67 with 42 seconds to play, the Huskies worked the clock down and then freshman Deon Luton drained a 17-footer to give Washington the lead. MacCulloch blocked a last-second Xavier shot underneath the basket and the Huskies had their first NCAA win since 1984. Richmond upset third-seeded South Carolina to become Washington's second-round foe. The Spiders had no answers for the 7-0 MacCulloch in the second-round contest. He scored 31 points and grabbed 18 rebounds to lead Washington to an 81-66 victory. The Huskies faced off against the Huskies of Connecticut in the regional semifinals in Greensboro, North Carolina. The Big East Champions were heavy favorites as the No. 2 seed in the East. Connecticut used a seven-point run to grab a 47-39 lead at intermission. UConn looked like it might put the game away when it built the lead to 64-55 with 10:16 to play, but then it went cold, missing three shots and turning the ball over three times. Patrick Femerling hit a jumper with 7:24 to play to bring the Huskies to within 64-63. Washington finally tied the game at 71 with 1:29 left when MacCulloch made one of two free throws. Connecticut's Richard Hamilton scored with 1:01 on the clock to make it 73-71. Washington guard Donald Watts, who played the entire game, then stunned the favorites with a three-pointer with 29 seconds remaining to give the Huskies their first lead of the contest. After UConn missed a series of shots and tip-in tries, Hamilton picked up a loss ball and flipped it into the basket as time expired to give Connecticut a heartstopping 75-74 victory. Washington finished the season with a 20-10 record and had won the hearts of basketball fans across the country with their improbable run in the NCAA tournament.

Husky Spotlight

Ja'Warren Hooker came out of Ellensburg High School as an eight-time state champion and the fastest 100-meter runner in the nation among the prep ranks. He kept that reputation intact in his first season on the Husky track team. After playing football in the fall, highlighted by an 89-yard kickoff return for a touchdown the first time he touched the ball, Hooker hit the track flying. He won the NCAA indoor 55-meter championship, UW's first national title since 1986. He took first place at the Pac-10 Championships in both the 100- and 200-meters, Washington's first-ever double winner. That earned him the conference's Track Athlete of the Year Award. He ran up a win streak of 21 consecutive victories in the 100 meters before placing third at the NCAA Championships.

Joanie Komura

Husky Highlight

In 1997 Washington offensive linemen Benji Olson and Olin Kreutz pulled off a rare accomplishment by both being named first-team All-Americans. Olson was a guard and Kreutz was a center on an offensive line that led the league in sacks allowed and helped the Huskies to an 8-4 record and a lopsided 51-23 Aloha Bowl victory against Michigan State. Olson's selection marked the second consecutive season he was tabbed as a first-team All-American. That made him the first Husky offensive lineman to be dubbed a two-time selection. Kreutz, a native of Hawaii, was also named the Morris Award Trophy as the Pac-10's top offensive lineman. Both players were also two-time All-Pac-10 picks. After the 1997 season, both players entered the NFL draft instead of returning for their senior seasons.

Bruce Terami

Benji Olson

Bruce Terami

Olin Kreutz

Husky Legend

Chris Magruder

UW Media Relations

The numbers back up the fact that Chris Magruder could be considered the greatest offensive player in Washington baseball history. The hard-hitting outfielder was a key component in Washington's three-year success story from 1996-98 that stands as the most prosperous period in the program's history. During that stretch the Huskies posted a 117-65 overall record and a 53-19 mark in Pac-10 play. The Huskies won three Pac-10 North titles and two overall Pac-10 Championships and went on to play in two NCAA regionals. Magruder was a part of a 1996 freshman class that was rated the eighth best in the nation. He emerged from that group when he was tabbed a freshman All-American. In 1997 he began his assault on the Husky record books. Magruder set single-season records for at bats (260), hits (104), runs (97), stolen bases (43) and games played (66). He batted an even .400 to become just the third UW player to reach that lofty batting mark. That summer he earned a spot on the USA national team and was the only American player named to the all-tournament team at the Intercontinental Cup in Spain. In 1998, as a junior, he batted .402 to become the only Husky, besides Jeb Best, to post back-to-back .400 seasons. Magruder was drafted by the San Francisco Giants following his junior season. He finished his Husky career as the all-time leader in at bats (688), runs (225), triples (12), steals (94) and walks. At the time, he was the only Washington player to be ranked in the top 10 of all 12 career offensive lists. He was a first-team all-conference pick each season at Washington and earned All-America honors in 1998. Magruder, a player not even drafted out of high school, was at his best in clutch situations. In the 1997 postseason he batted .571 in eight games. He hit .471 in his last four collegiate games at the NCAA Regional.

Husky Lists

Washington Baseball Career Batting Average Leaders

1.	.392	Jeb Best	1979-82
2.	.375	Chris Magruder	1996-98
3.	.355	Bryan Williamson	1996-99
4.	.353	Dominic Woody	1997-99
5.	.348	Jon Vander Griend	1993-95
6.	.347	Ron Johnson	1978-80
7.	.345	Randy Jorgensen	1991-93
8.	.343	Nick Stefonick	1997-99
9.	.341	Ryan Soules	1995-97
10.	.338	Claude Greene	1978-80

* min. 300 at bats

Washington Baseball Career Hits Leaders

1.	264	Jeb Best	1979-82
2.	258	Chris Magruder	1996-98
3.	229	Kevin Miller	1996-98
4.	221	Joe Trippy	1992-95
5.	218	Derrin Doty	1990-93
6.	205	Ryan Lentz	1996-98
	205	Tom Riley	1978-81
8.	196	Bryan Williamson	1996-99
9.	192	Ron Johnson	1978-80
10.	184	Randy Jorgensen	1991-93

Husky Lore

DONALD Watts did not know it when he enrolled at Washington in 1995, but he started a trend among the several former Seattle Supersonic players. Watts, whose father, Slick, was a flamboyant guard for the Sonics in the 1970s along with "Downtown" Fred Brown, captain of the Sonics' NBA Championship team. Brown's son, Bryan, walked on to the Husky team in 1997. A year later, Marlon Shelton enrolled at Washington and was joined by walkon Michael Westphal as a first-year player. Shelton's father, Lonnie, was a forward for the Sonics' 1979 World Championship team. Michael's dad, Paul, was the Sonics coach at the time and had also played for Seattle during his NBA career. Donald Watts had the best career of any of the Sonics' siblings. A three-year starter, he helped Washington to a 70-45 record and four straight postseason appearances. He finished his career with 1,158 points, to rank 18th on the all-time list. Watts became only the fourth Husky to dish out over 300 assists. At this end of his career, Slick would kid him about their relationship. Someone told Slick, "No one under 30 years old remembers you." "I know," Slick said, "Now they call me Donald's daddy."

Husky Moment

Women's Crew Wins Second NCAA Title

Brown figured to be Washington's stiffest competition at the 1998 NCAA women's rowing championships at Lake Lanier, just outside of Atlanta. Both teams entered the event with undefeated I Varsity (varsity) and II Varsity (junior varsity) teams. Something had to give in the opening heat races when the teams' II Varsity teams were paired together. The Huskies got off to a quick start, but Brown rallied for the victory. Brown entered Sunday's finals with the advantage of racing from the center lane in all three races. In the opening fours race, Washington, racing a team that had competed together just once prior to the NCAAs, held off Williams College for a fourth-place finish. In the II Varsity finals, Virginia pulled away from the field for the victory, and the Huskies rallied in the final 500 meters to nose Brown for second place. As the teams prepared for the I Varsity finals, Washington, Brown and Virginia were all tied in the point standings. The winner would claim the team title. The Huskies made sure it was not even close. After the first 750 meters of the 2,000-meter race, Washington led by three seats. At 1,250 meters, the lead was up to seven seats. Rowing into a head wind, the Huskies finished first in a time of 6:52.0. Massachusetts was second while Brown settled for third. "We didn't know about the three-way tie," said Husky rower Denni Nessler. "Our plan was to have a perfect performance." Washington's winning varsity eight team consisted of coxswain Missy Collins, stroke Sabina Telenska, Nessler, Kelly Horton, Katy Dunnet, Annie Christie, Rachel Dunnet, Vanessa Tavalero and Kari Green.

UW Media Relations

Washington's victorious Varsity Eight.

Husky Spotlight

The 1997 edition of Husky volleyball used the blocking talents of All-American Makare Desilets and the attack skills of All-Pac-10 performer Leslie Tuiasosopo to return to the NCAA tournament for the second year in a row. Ranked 13th in the nation, the Huskies hosted opening round matches that featured Chattanooga, Pacific and Cal State Sacramento. Washington crushed Chattanooga, the Southern Conference champions, in the first round 15-4, 15-3 and 15-2. It was the fewest points scored against the Huskies in a match all season. Desliets broke a 12-year-old Husky record by hitting .923 (12 kills in 13 attempts) to lead Washington. The Huskies jumped out to a quick 7-0 lead against 14th-ranked Pacific in the second round. The Tigers roared back to score 15 straight points and grab the early lead. In the second game coach Bill Neville substituted setter Angie Coma into the contest and the Huskies took off. Washington won the final three games 15-9, 15-10 and 15-10 to advance to the Sweet 16. In the first round of the regional competition, Washington had to travel to top-ranked Long Beach State. The 49ers won handily 15-4, 15-4, 15-13 to run their record to 32-1. Washington finished the season with a 20-10 mark.

Husky Highlight

After placing fifth at the Pac-10 championships, the Washington women's gymnastics team did not look like the favorites to capture the NCAA West Regional championship. Competing on their home floor, Washington did just that, capturing its first regional title. Leading the way were all-around co-champions Klara Kudilkova and Tiffany Simpson. Washington trailed Stanford going into the final rotation, but the Cardinal self-destructed on the beam and the Huskies turned in a strong 49.300 score on floor exercise. Washington won the meet with a season-high score of 196.150. At the NCAA championships in Los Angeles, the Huskies placed seventh in the 12-team field, the best ever showing by a Washington squad. Kudilkova paced the team by placing third in the all-around competition with a score of 39.550. She and Simpson were named All-Americans in the all-around, vault and floor exercise.

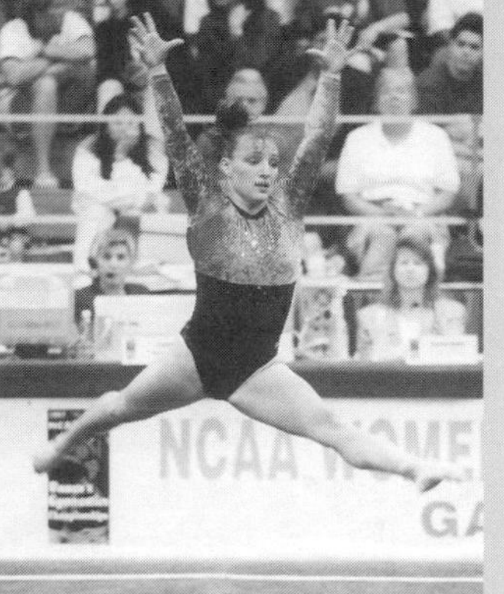

Klara Kudilkova

Husky Legend

Joanie Komura

Aretha Hill

Aretha Hill established herself as one of the nation's top young competitors in the discus during a four-year career at Washington from 1995-98. A Seattle native, Hill began throwing the discus as a ninth grader at Renton High School. She had lost a bet with her physical education teacher, Mark Stewart, a former Husky linebacker, and as a result, she had to try out for the track squad. Stewart thought Hill had the strength, speed and determination to be an outstanding thrower. She did. Her first year competing she placed second in the state AA championships. Hill went on to win three state titles before enrolling at Washington. Her career, and throws, continued to progress. She placed seventh at the NCAAs as a freshman. It was during her sophomore year that her career exploded. She started the season throwing in the low 170s but by the end of the year she won the Pac-10 championship on her final throw with a school-record mark of 195-9. She placed third at the NCAAs with a throw of 189-10. Hill's marks allowed her to qualify for the Olympic Trials where she placed third, but did not register a qualifying mark. Back in Seattle, at a special all-comers meet, she exceeded the qualifying standard to make the Olympic team at just 19 years of age. She went on to place 35th at the summer games in Atlanta, her first international competition. As a junior Hill raised the school record to 196-7 and she was fourth at the NCAAs. As a senior she shattered the UW mark with a toss of 215-3 in a meet at San Diego. The throw was a collegiate record and the second best by an American woman. Hill concluded her senior season by again winning the Pac-10 title and placing second at the NCAA meet. Her chances at a national title were diminished by a late-season foot injury.

HUSKY LIST

Aoki Joins List of Pac-10 Champions

As a sophomore for the Husky women's track team Anna Aoki won the Pac-10 Championship in the 10,000 meters with a time of 35:04.99. She became the ninth Husky to win a conference championship. Her teammate, Deeja Youngquist, placed third in the same race. Here is a look at Washington's Pac-10 champions:

Year	Name	Event	Finish
2000	Kate Bradshaw	10,000 meters	34:41:03
1998	Anna Aoki	10,000 meters	35:04.99
	Aretha Hill	Discus Throw	208-11
1996	Aretha Hill	Discus Throw	195-9
	Soozie Shanley	Hammer Throw	157-10
1995	Tara Davis	Long Jump	20-2¼
1992	Sonja Forster	Hepthalon	5,266 points
1991	Mari Bjone	400-Meter Hurdles	58.21
1988	Jennifer Ponath	Shot Put	55-5¾
1987	Vicki Borsheim	High Jump	6-0¾
	Helena Uusitalo	Javelin Throw	180-7

HUSKY LORE

MAKARE Desilets journey to become an All-American volleyball player at Washington was remarkable. She tells it best. "I grew up in a village that was straight Third World. It was just like something you see in the movies. You've got your pit toilets, your plantation where you get all of your food from, and no running water. You had to go to a stream to get it." Desilets was describing her childhood in a small village in the country of Fiji, where she lived until she was 10. After her mother remarried a Canadian, she moved to Vancouver, B.C. She only began playing volleyball three years before she was recruited to join the Husky team. The sport, however, was in her blood. Her mother, Mereosi, was once a member of Fiji's national team. As a freshman she showed off her specialty early when she set a school record with seven solo blocks in a match with Wyoming. Desilets would go on to become the school's all-time blocks leader by her junior year and finish her career with 677. She earned All-Pac-10 honors as a junior and senior and was honored as an All-American in 1997. She led the nation in blocks that year with an average of 2.04 per game, also a Pac-10 single-season record. That season she guided Washington to a 20-10 record and an appearance in the round of 16 during the NCAA Championships.

Husky Moment

Troy Kelly Leads Husky Golfers to Surprising NCAA Finish

The Washington men's golf team, paced by freshman Troy Kelly, posted a historic finish at the 1999 NCAA Championships at Hazeltine National Golf Club in Chaska, Minnesota. Kelly, a Bremerton, Washington, native, shot a one-under 71 on the final day of competition to complete the tournament with a score of one-under 287 to place second overall. Northwestern's Luke Donald won the individual title with a score of 284. Washington posted its best score (290) of the tournament during its final round to finish fourth as a team. Washington's previous best finish at the NCAAs was in 1988 when the Huskies placed 15th and O.D. Vincent, the coach of the 1999 squad, was 19th in the individual standings. The 1999 tournament marked just the fourth time Washington had qualified for the NCAA Championships. Kelly opened his final round of play with birdies on the second, fourth, seventh and eighth holes and made the turn at three-under 33. The birdie at No. 8 put him at three-under and into a tie with Donald. Kelly, who set the Husky record for stroke average during the season, shot a two-over 38 on the back nine. He bogeyed the 12th and 13th holes and made par on the rest. Georgia won the team title with a score of 1,180 while the Huskies shot 1,189. Fellow Washington freshman Gordy Scutt also had an impressive showing, shooting an even 300 to tie for 23rd place.

Joanie Komura

Troy Kelly

Husky Spotlight

Drew Reaches NCAA Tennis Semis

Senior Husky tennis player Eric Drew was ranked 58th in the nation as he prepared to play in the NCAA championships. By the time he was finished, he had volleyed his way to the semifinals of the event, the best finish by a Washington player since Bill Quillian reached the finals in 1953. Drew, and sophomore teammate Robert Kendrick, were both named All-Americans. Kendrick was ranked 11th in the final college poll, the highest finish ever by a Husky player. Thanks to his showing at the NCAAs, Drew climbed all the way to No. 20 in the final standings. Drew defeated San Diego State's Alex Waske in the first round, Baylor's Johann Jooste in the second round, Florida's Justin O'Neal in the third round and Esteban Carril of Texas Christian in the quarterfinals. Second-seeded Jeff Morrison of Florida defeated Drew 6-2, 6-2 in the semifinals. Drew completed his career with 86 singles victories, the second most in Washington history.

Husky Highlight

When Joe Jarzynka came to the Husky football program as a 5-9 walkon from Gig Harbor, he just hoped to make the team, possibly get some playing time and dreamed of earning a scholarship. He did all of that and more. By his junior season in 1998, Jarzynka had established himself as one of the most versatile players in the nation. He was also a fan favorite at Husky Stadium. That season Jarzynka earned first-team All-Pac-10 honors as an all-purpose player. He developed his reputation for his gutty play as a punt returner who refused to fair catch opponent's kicks. He also ran back kickoffs, played wide receiver and took over the field goal and extra-point kicking duties. He scored his first career touchdown on a Brock Huard pass at Nebraska. He scored his second touchdown on a 91-yard punt return against California. It was the third longest runback in Husky history. He also set a UW and Pac-10 record with 166 punt return yards in that game. Jarzynka took over the kicking duties in the fifth game of the year and successfully made six of eight field goal attempts. He finished the year scoring a total of 61 points. As a senior Jarzynka gave up his kicking duties, but ended his career on a high note by scoring on a 55-yard option pass from Dane Looker against Washington State in the Apple Cup.

Husky Legend

Joanie Komura

Brock Huard

When it comes to athletes being role models, there may not have been a better one than Husky quarterback Brock Huard. The 6-5, 220-pound Huard became Washington's all-time passing leader during his three-year career, throwing for 5,742 yards to better his older brother Damon's record of 5,692 yards he set between 1992 and 1995. Huard's debut in the 1996 season opener at Arizona State is the stuff of legends. With the Huskies trailing 42-21 in the fourth quarter, Huard checked into the game. In the huddle, center Olin Kreutz stated aloud that Washington needed to get into the endzone by the seven-minute mark. Huard said: "You make your block and we'll be there in seven seconds." He then proceeded to throw a 67-yard touchdown pass to Gerald Harris and go on to rally the team to a 42-42 tied before the Sun Devils won on a late field goal. A lefthanded thrower, Huard wore number seven during his Husky career, the same number his older brother wore. His freshman season proved to be the most productive of any first-year Husky quarterback. He became the first UW freshman quarterback to throw for 300 yards in a game when he passed for 311 vs. Arizona. As a sophomore he set a Washington record by passing for 23 touchdowns. He also helped the Huskies set a season passing record with 2,790 yards. Huard finished his junior season as the owner of 22 Husky offensive records, including 51 career touchdown passes. He will long be remembered for his fourth-down, 63-yard touchdown pass to tight end Reggie Davis to beat Arizona State in the season opener. Huard opted to turn pro following the 1998 season.

HUSKY LISTS

Husky Football Career Passing Leaders

Player (Years)	PA	PC	PCT	TD	YDS
1. Brock Huard (1996-98)	776	422	.544	51	5742
2. Damon Huard (1992-95)	764	458	.599	34	5692
3. Marques Tuiasosopo (1997-2000)	761	418	.549	31	5501
4. Sonny Sixkiller (1970-72)	811	385	.475	35	5496
5. Cary Conklin (1986-1989)	747	401	.537	31	4850
6. Steve Pelluer (1980-83)	755	436	.577	30	4603
7. Don Heinrich (1949-52)	610	335	.549	33	4392
8. Chris Chandler (1984-87)	587	326	.546	32	4161
9. Mark Brunell (1989-92)	498	259	.521	23	3423
10. Warren Moon (1975-77)	496	242	.488	19	3277

HUSKY LORE

WASHINGTON athletic director Barbara Hedges surprised everyone when she announced that Rick Neuheisel would succeed Jim Lambright as Washington's 23rd head football coach. He accepted the position on Jan. 9 in 1999 after a four-year tenure at Colorado that produced a 33-14 record. Neuheisel was no stranger to Husky fans. As a quarterback at UCLA, he had set an NCAA record for passing accuracy by completing 25 of 27 passes in a 1983 game that saw the Bruins defeat Washington 27-24. Neuheisel also led his Colorado team to a 33-21 victory against the Huskies in the 1996 Holiday Bowl. Neuheisel was 38 years old when he took over the Husky program. He quickly endeared himself to Washington's fans by bring back the gold helmets to the Husky uniform scheme. His first season Washington was picked to finish in the second half of the Pac-10 race. After getting off to an 0-2 start, the Huskies got hot, winning six of their final eight games, including an emotional matchup with his former Colorado squad. The Huskies controlled the race for the Rose Bowl before suffering a late season, overtime loss at UCLA. Neuheisel became the first Husky coach to lead his team to a bowl game during their inaugural season.

Husky Moment

Husky Softball Teams Finishes Second at NCAAs

The 1999 Washington softball team made another strong run at the NCAA Championship, but wound up one run short. The Huskies, made their fourth consecutive appearance at the College Softball World Series after dominating the regional they hosted in Seattle. Washington surrendered only one run in winning four games from Colgate, Tennessee, Cal State Fullerton and Hawaii. The College World Series turned into a Pac-10 schedule for the Huskies. In the first game, Erin Helgeland's two-run double in the sixth inning propelled Washington to a 4-1 win against Arizona State. In the second round, the Huskies faced third-ranked Arizona, a team that had beaten them in four of five meetings during the season. Washington pitcher Jennifer Spediacci was magnificent in silencing the Arizona bats in a one-hit 3-0 victory. The Huskies blanked California 3-0, getting runs in the first, fourth and fifth innings, to advance to the championship game against top-ranked UCLA. The two teams had split four games during the regular season. The Bruins scored two runs in their first at-bat and took a 3-0 lead in the second inning before the Huskies managed to get on the scoreboard. Helgeland drove in Spediacci in the bottom of the second to bring Washington to within 2-1. UCLA pitcher Courtney Dale kept the Huskies in check until the fifth inning when Amanda Freed took over on the mound for the Bruins. Her changeup handcuffed the Husky hitters, but Washington mounted a comeback in its final at-bat. In the seventh inning, Jamie Graves singled and scored with two outs on an infield single by Kim DePaul. Becky Newbry, the team's lone senior, blasted a ball the UCLA second baseman managed to retrieve and throw for the final out. Washington finished the season 51-18.

UW Media Relations

Jamie Graves

Husky Spotlight

Washington sophomore Kristina Kraszewski became the first Husky player to make back-to-back appearances at the NCAA women's tennis championships in 1999. She would go on to continue her postseason streak with an invitation to the 2000 event. Kraszewski's second trip to the NCAAs was not as successful as her first. She was eliminated at the 1999 tournament in the first round by William and Mary's Delphine Troch 7-5, 6-2. As a freshman, Kraszewski won her first three matches to advance to the quarterfinals, earning All-America honors for her efforts. In the opening round of play at the University of Notre Dame, Kraszewski defeated Duke's Kristin Sanderson 3-6, 6-,1, 6-3 to become the first Husky singles player to win a match at the NCAAs. She fell behind 3-6 in her second round match with Michelle O of William & Mary before rallying to win the final sets 6-2 and 6-4. In the third round, Kraszewski downed Miami's Lioudmila Skavronskaia 1-6, 6-1, 6-1. San Diego's Zuzana Lesenarova finally ousted Kraszewski 6-2, 7-6 in the quarterfinals. Ranked 26th nationally when she entered the tournament, Kraszewski finished the 1998 season with a 31-8 record. During the 2000 season, Kraszewski climbed to No. 1 in the weekly tennis standings for the middle portion of the season before entering postseason competition holding on to the No. 4 spot in the singles' poll.

Husky Highlight

Washington kept its streak of winning an event title at the NCAA women's rowing championships alive with a Fours title in 1999. Powered by a team of freshmen, the Husky Fours won the final race by six seconds with a time of 7:34.50 on the 2,000-meter course. Virginia was the next closest team with a time of 7:40.2. The team consisted of coxswain Mary Whipple, stroke Erin Becht, Anna Mickelson, Kara Nykreim and Kellie Schenk. The Husky varsity eight placed a disappointing fifth in its final race while the junior varsity was fourth in its championship race. Washington placed third in the team competition after winning the event in 1997 and 1998.

UW Media Relations

Husky Legend

Jamie Redd

UW Media Relations

When it was time for someone to take over a game, Jamie Redd gladly accepted that role for the Husky women's basketball team. The most highly touted recruit in the program's history, Redd lived up to all of her expectations during her four-year career from 1996-99. She led the Huskies in scoring all four years, the first player to ever do that at Washington. Her 2,207 career points bettered Rhonda Smith's previous all-time scoring mark by more than 200 points and ranked as the seventh best total in Pac-10 history. The Husky record book practically belongs to Redd. Her accomplishments are almost too numerous to list. She averaged 15.2 points per game as a freshman, 20.5 as a sophomore, 19.3 as a junior and 16.3 as a senior. She loved to push the ball up court on a fast break or pull up for a quick long-range jumper against a foe. She set the Huskies record for three-point shooting with 192 three-point field goals and was such a good athlete that she ranked ninth all-time with 714 rebounds. Redd also accounted for 345 assists. Much of her career she drew the opponent's toughest defender or had to contend with a gimmick defense. Redd was never deterred in her efforts to score. During a pair of back-to-back games at USC and UCLA during her sophomore season she poured in 34 points (her career high) against the Trojans and 31 versus the Bruins. That marked only the second time in Washington's history a player put together consecutive 30-point efforts. Redd grew up in a tough neighborhood in San Francisco and turned to sports to stay out of trouble. She always played with the boys in the neighborhood—basketball, softball, even tackle football. She loved the challenge of tough competition. Following her second year on the basketball team she lettered for the Husky softball team that advanced to the College World Series.

Husky List

Washington's Women's Basketball Career Scoring Leaders

Player	Years	Games	Points	Avg.
1. Jamie Redd	1995-99	114	2027	17.8
2. Rhonda Smith	1992-95	116	1801	15.5
3. Karen Murray	1981-84	107	1745	16.3
4. Leteia Hughley	1982-85	106	1704	16.1
5. Yvette Cole	1986-89	123	1681	13.7
6. Meghan Franza	1998-2001	119	1612	13.5
7. Karen Deden	1988-91	116	1596	13.8
8. Carlin McClary	1979-82	112	1508	13.5
9. Amber Hall	1995-99	104	1330	12.8
10. Laurie Merlino	1988-91	122	1262	10.3

Pavilion Closes for Renovation

FOLLOWING the 1998 basketball season Hec Edmundson Pavilion was shut down for 18 months to undergo a massive transformation. Funded by the Campaign for the Student-Athlete, the 72-year-old building was scheduled for a $43 million renovation and to be reopened in time for the 2000-2001 season as Bank of America Arena at Hec Edmundson Pavilion. The capacity of the building was going to be increased from 7,900 to 10,000 by transforming the arena into a permanent seating bowl. The bothersome support columns, which had hindered spectators' views since the opening of the Pavilion, were removed. Two super trusses were installed to support the building's roof. The renovation would add a number of new features to the Arena. A new Hall of Fame and Founder's Club were located on the west end of the facility. The east end included a year-round practice facility. The men's and women's basketball team received offices in the building for the first time and new locker rooms and meeting rooms were constructed for both programs. The football program also benefited by an expanded lockerroom and breakout meeting rooms. Both the equipment room and athletic training rooms were expanded significantly.

Husky Moment

Marques Tuiasosopo Stuns Stanford

Marques Tuiasosopo led the Husky offense with 207 rushing yards and 302 passing yards as the Huskies rolled up 670 total yards and controlled the clock for 36:31 in a key victory against Stanford. Afterwards, a check of the NCAA record book revealed that no player had ever put together a 200/300 game. That week, Tuiasosopo garnered numerous national honors, and acclaim, for his effort. Prior to his heroic effort, there had only been three Division I quarterbacks to ever rush and pass for 200 yards in game. His 509 yards of total offense ranked as the fourth highest single-game effort in Pac-10 history. Tuiasosopo's totals were incredible, but the fact he played almost the entire game with a severely bruised hip and buttocks made them even more remarkable. On Washington's opening offensive series he was dumped on his backside while completing a rollout pass. His hip started to tighten up and he required in-game treatment to keep him going. The Husky coaches did not let him sit while the offense was off the field. Instead, he continually paced the sideline with quarterbacks coach Steve Axman to keep his hip loose. Tuiasosopo's efforts helped the Huskies to roll up 670 yards against Stanford in a 31-24 victory that put Washington into the lead in the Rose Bowl race. Tuiasosopo carried the ball 22 times during the game and rushed for a pair of touchdowns. He completed 19 of 32 passes including one for a score. "That was one of the most courageous efforts I've ever seen," said Husky receiver Dane Looker. "The guy could hardly stand up in the locker room at halftime. What he pulled off today was miraculous."

UW Media Relations

Husky Spotlight

On July 2, the Washington women's varsity eight crew defeated the University of Victoria (Canada) in the grande final of the inaugural women's open eight race at the Henley Royal Regatta. The Huskies captured the Henley Prize, the first women's trophy awarded since the historic men's regatta began in 1839. In December of 1999, the Henley Stewards decided to elevate the two-year old women's invitational race that had been established to showcase international crews, to a full-fledged open-class prize event. The Huskies covered the 2,112-meter Thames River course in a time of 7 minutes, 29 seconds, crossing the finish line half a boat-length ahead of Victoria. The crews traded the lead all the way down the course and kept it only one foot apart over the last quarter of the race before the Huskies gradually began to break away towards the finish. "This was an awesome race," said Husky head coach Jan Harville. "It's interesting how they keep splits here. At each marker on the course, signs go up saying who's ahead. We were ahead at the first mark by a foot. Then at the second marker, Victoria was ahead by a foot and then we went up again. I told our crew that Victoria had a fast boat and we would have to take the race away from them. We did it in the last 500 meters of the race." The Husky lineup included coxswain Mary Whipple and rowers Sabina Telenska, Nicole Borges, Rika Geyser, Vanessa Tavalero, Anna Mickelson, Lindsey Horton, Theresa Nygren-Birkholz and Nicole Rogers.

Husky Highlight

Washington men's soccer midfielder Wes Hart was named a second-team All-American by both the National Soccer Coaches Association and College Soccer Online. He was a first-team all-academic pick by the NSCAA. Hart, who set the Huskies' single-season assist record with 15 as a junior, scored six goals and added three assists during his senior season. He helped the Huskies to a 15-5-2 record and their fifth straight appearance in the NCAA tournament. Washington lost in the second round at defending NCAA champion Indiana and finished the season ranked No. 12 in the final coaches poll. Hart's career at Washington was only two years long. He transferred to the UW after playing his first two seasons at Wisconsin. In 1999 Hart was named the player of the year for the Mountain Division of the Mountain Pacific Sports Federation. The league also picked him to its all-academic team. Hart owned a 3.45 grade point average as a business major. He was named as one of 15 finalists for the Hermann Trophy, awarded to the nation's top college soccer player, and was chosen to play in the Umbro Select College All-Star Classic following the season.

UW Media Relations

Husky Legend

Barbara Hedges

There was a great trivia question going around the Pac-10 late in the decade of the 1990s. Who was the only conference athletic director who was a college head coach? Interestingly, it was Washington's Barbara Hedges. She coached gymnastics and taught physical education for five years at the University of Arizona before joining the athletic administration at Southern California in 1973. Hedges can proudly claim three conference titles as a college coach. In 1991 she was named the director of athletics at Washington and became the first woman to head up a major Division I athletic department. While there was a considerable amount of attention on Hedges' gender, she always kept her focus on the priorities of building up Washington's overall athletic program. Her first year on the job she saw the Husky football team win its first national championship. In 1997 the women's crew team brought home the school's first NCAA team title. A tireless worker with boundless enthusiasm for her job and working with young student-athletes, Hedges initiated a number of support programs to benefit the Washington program. She also placed an emphasis on building up the Huskies' Olympic sports and rebuilding a struggling men's basketball program. She succeeded in both. Washington made three straight top-25 appearances in the Sears Cup all-sports standings from 1996-99 and the men's basketball team made back-to-back NCAA appearances in 1998 and 1999. Hedges' strategic plan at Washington included the four-year Campaign for the Student-Athlete, a $90 million fundraising effort with an emphasis on capital improvements and scholarship endowments. Hec Edmundson Pavilion was renovated, a new indoor practice facility was built, new homes were constructed for the baseball and soccer programs and the crewhouse was remodeled. Hedges serves on numerous national college athletic committees and was the first woman to serve as president of the National Association of Collegiate Directors of Athletics.

HUSKY LIST

Football Record in the 1990s

Washington's 82-34-1 record in the 1990s is the best among Pac-10 schools. Here's a look, broken down by overall games and Pac-10 games:

	Team	Overall			
		W	L	T	PCT
1.	Washington	82	34	1	.705
2.	Arizona	71	46	1	.606
3.	UCLA	69	46	0	.600
4.	Oregon	69	48	0	.590
5.	USC	68	49	3	.579
6.	Arizona State	61	50	0	.550
7.	Stanford	60	53	2	.530
8.	California	55	59	1	.483
9.	Washington State	53	61	0	.465
10.	Oregon State	29	80	1	.268

WASHINGTON quarterback Marques Tuiasosopo and former softball player Becky Newbry won the top honors at the *Seattle Post-Intelligencer's* Sports Star of the Year Award in February of 2000. Tuiasosopo was named the Seattle-area male athlete of the year from a field that included Seattle Sonics forward Vin Baker, Seattle Mariners pitcher Jamie Moyer, Seattle Seahawks defensive tackle Cortez Kennedy and Atlanta Hawk guard Jason Terry. The other female nominees were Husky athletic director Barbara Hedges, U.S. national team weight lifters Melanie Kosoff-Roach and Lea Forman and American record-setting swimmer Megan Quann. During Newbry's softball career the Huskies finished second at the NCAA championships during her freshman and senior seasons and third as a sophomore and junior. Originally a walkon, she was a first-team All-American outfielder as a senior, batting .436 while starting all 69 games. After her senior season she ranked in the top 10 of practically all of Washington's career offensive categories. Tuiasosopo and Newbry's selections marked the second time since 1994, when the award was presented to both a male and female athlete, that two Huskies swept the honor. In 1994 Napoleon Kaufman and Rhonda Smith were the top vote-getters.

Husky Moment

Softball

A record-breaking season for the Washington softball team ended in bitter disappointment when the Huskies were eliminated by Arizona in the College World Series. Washington finished the season with a 62-9 record, the best mark in the program's eight-year history. After sweeping through the NCAA West Regional by outscoring four opponents by 24-1, the Huskies had high hopes for their first national championship. Washington was the top-ranked team in the nation entering the College World Series in Oklahoma City. The Huskies held the top ranking for the final 13 weeks of the season. Washington defeated unranked DePaul 3-2 in the first round of play before facing Pac-10 rival UCLA in the second round. The Huskies lost 3-2 in a game that had to be continued a day later due to a tornado warning. Later that same day Arizona upset Washington 4-2 in an elimination game that ended the Huskies' season. Washington's roster was loaded with exceptional hitting and pitching. Seniors Jennifer Spediacci and Jamie Graves combined for a 61-9 record and entered the CWS with a combined earned run average of just 0.68, second best in the nation. Redshirt freshman Jenny Topping and true freshman Jaime Clark provided some impressive firepower at the plate. Topping led the nation in home runs with 24 while Clark was right behind her with 23. Clark was named to the all-CWS team. The Huskies shattered their previous team record for homers (39) with 84 during the season. Washington played its first 47 games on the road, posting a 43-4 record.

Joanie Komura

Jenny Topping

Husky Spotlight

The Husky women's crew team placed second overall behind Brown University at the 2000 NCAA Championships. For the fourth year in a row the Huskies won at least one of the final three races when the Varsity Fours took first-place. The Husky Varsity Eight (6:41.10) was second to Brown in the championship race. Brown rowed the 2,000-meter course in a time of 6:37.20. The Huskies and Brown were the top two seeded teams all season. Brown also won the II Varsity Eight (junior varsity) race, beating the Huskies by almost 10 seconds. The Bears and Huskies entered the final race of the day separated by one point (29-28) in the team standings. Brown's victory in the last race gave it a team total of 59 points while Washington finished the day with 55. Virginia was third with 48 points followed by California (38) and Michigan (34) to round out the top five. The Brown Bears, who also won the event in 1999, jumped off the starting line and led wire-to-wire. The Huskies, who were down early, came from behind Virginia and California and made a hard charge over the last 500 meters to claim second place. The victory by the Varsity Four team, comprised of all freshmen, was the second straight national title for Washington in that event.

Husky Highlight

Washington junior women's tennis player Kristina Kraszewski capped off an outstanding season by being named an All-American by the Intercollegiate Tennis Association. She led Washington to a 12-9 record and a No. 30 national ranking by compiling a 28-10 singles record. She was ranked the top singles player in the nation for more than a month after winning the Pac-10 Indoor Tournament in January. She also advanced to the finals of the Rolex National Indoor championships. She became the first Husky to hold the number-one ranking. Kraszewski finished the season ranked sixth in the final individual poll and she participated in the NCAA championships for the third straight season, losing in the first round.

UW Media Relations

Husky Legend

Jennifer Spediacci and Jamie Graves

Joanie Komura

Jennifer Spediacci

Jamie Graves

Washington softball pitchers Jennifer Spediacci and Jamie Graves gave the Huskies a one-two combination that was the best in the nation. When the two seniors finished their careers in 2000, they held all but three of Washington's all-time pitching records. As seniors, they posted almost identical earned run averages to led Washington to a 62-9 record, the most wins in the program's history. Spediacci had a 0.67 ERA while Graves' was 0.69. Spediacci was named the team's MVP after posting a 34-5 record that included 316 strikeouts. She finished her career owning more than 10 Husky pitching marks. Graves was 27-4 in helping the Huskies make their fifth straight College World Series appearance. Spediacci also excelled in the classroom, earning second-team Academic All-America honors. She was a first-team All-American as a pitcher and the Pac-10 Conference's pitcher of the year. Spediacci won 100 games during her career and had 894 strikeouts while Graves was right behind her with 91 victories and 510 strikeouts.

Husky List

Husky Track Stars Earn All-American Honors

A total of seven members of the Washington track and field team earned All-American honors at the 2000 NCAA Championships held at Duke University.

Competitor	Event	Result	Finish
JaWarren Hooker	200 Meters	20.78	Sixth
Jacob Predmore	Decathlon	7,426 points	Seventh
Justin St. Clair	Javelin	223-3	Sixth
Sesilia Thomas	Discus	50-8¼	Eighth
Matt Phillips	Pole Vault	17-4½	Eighth
Anna Aoki	10,000 Meters	34:22.79	Ninth
Ben Lindsey	Discus	191-5	11th

Husky Lore

IN January of 2000 it was announced that Washington National Golf Club, in Kent, would become the official home for the Husky golf program. The course opened in August of 2,000. The first 18 holes constructed at the 36-hole Washington National Golf Club are designated "The University Course" and incorporate a Husky theme, including buildings modeled after landmarks on the University campus. A likeness of Husky Stadium is used for grandstand seating and the primary clubhouse features a resemblance to Hec Edmundson Pavilion. Golf carts at Washington national are purple and gold and special "Husky Tees" are used for championship play. Washington National is part of O.B. Sports, a Kirkland golf development company owned by Orrin Vincent. He is the farther of Washington men's golf coach, O.D. Vincent. The Washington golf program has a dedicated practice facility at the new course and plays its home matches there. Additionally, Washington can also host Pac-10 and NCAA Championship events at Washington National. "The University Course and practice facility will be the finest of its kind in the United States," said Husky coach O.D. Vincent at the announcement. "The course will present us new opportunities to fundraise and give our program and student-athletes tremendous exposure. Most importantly, it will give our players a feeling that they have a home and are not a guest every day that they are out practicing and playing."

Super Legend

Joanie Komura

Aretha Hill

Aretha Hill, a graduate of Renton High School in 1994, quickly established herself as one of the best collegiate discus throwers in the nation. In 1996, after her sophomore year, she was the first Washington African American female athlete to make the U.S. Olympic Team and the youngest (age 19), Washington student-athlete ever to make the U.S. Olympic Team. In 1998, she set an American collegiate record in the discus throw with a mark of 215-3, the second best throw by a U.S. thrower all-time.

Hill did not realize her throwing talent until ninth grade. Her physical education teacher was a former Husky linebacker, Mark Stewart. Stewart noted the strength of Hill's right arm and challenged her to try out for the Renton track team. Initially she became frustrated with her performance and wanted to quit throwing the discus. Her track and field coach, Keith Eager, told her: "...hang with this, you're going to be good at it." Eager saw Hill's potential with her size, strength, and quickness. Aretha did hang with it and soon she was winning meets and having fun.

As a ninth grader, she placed second in the Washington State AA meet. In her three remaining high school years, she won the State AA discus throw title, setting a meet record of 160-9 in her senior year (1994). In the summer of that year, she established a Washington State high school record of 165-9, a distance that was the third best high school mark in the nation in 1994.

Under the tutelage of Husky coach Ken Shannon, one of the premier throwing coaches in the nation, Hill flourished as a collegian. In her freshman year, she placed fourth in the Pac-10 meet and seventh in the NCAA championship meet. In 1996, as a sophomore, Hill experienced what most athletes dream. In April, she hurled the discus 189-6 to break the Penn Relays' record by almost three feet. In May, she won the Pac-10 meet (195-9), took third at the NCAA meet (189-10), and qualified to compete at the U.S. Olympic Trials in June. There she took third with a throw of 190-5 to gain a spot on the Olympic Team, but with one proviso. She had to reach the Olympic qualifying standard of 60 meters or 196-10 by July 16 in a USA Track and Field sanctioned meet.

At the Pacific Northwest Association All-Comers Discus Championship—also dubbed the Aretha Hill Invitational—the competition took place. On a patch of grass behind the Husky football scoreboard, newspaper and television reporters gathered with Aretha's family and friends to watch the event. Each athlete had six throws. Hill's best was her first—195-8. It was not far enough, so another meet began—six more throws. Her next-to-last throw was 191-4, the best of her first five. One last throw for the 1996 Olympic Summer Games in Atlanta. Hill whirled and let the discus fly. It was a long, lovely flying saucer of a toss that flew 198-6. The mark bettered the Olympic qualifying standard by almost two feet, crushed her personal best by almost two feet, nine inches, and sent Hill into ecstasy.

"It feels good to get it and get it good," Hill said. "Now I can say I'm an Olympian. I didn't feel that way at the Trials."

Hill finished 35th at the Atlanta Games with a mark of 183-10. She just missed out on a second Olympic appearance when she placed fifth in qualifying for the 2000 games. In 1997, she again won the Penn Relays, placed third in the Pac-10 and fourth in the NCAA meet. In the summer of 1997, she finished fifth in the World University Games held in Sicily. In her senior year, her talent and hard work took her to a new level. On April 4, 1998, she set the American collegiate record with a throw of 215-3 at the UC San Diego Invitational meet. It was also the second longest throw by an American (the best is 216-10). Of course, that throw established a Husky record. She again won the Pac-10 championship (208-11) and finished second in the NCAA meet (192-5) and was named the Husky Female Athlete of the Year.

Super Legend

Teresa Wilson and Husky Women's Softball

Starting from scratch in 1993, Teresa Wilson, Washington's softball coach, has built one of the best softball programs in the country. At the end of the 2000 season, she had led the Huskies to a 399-141 overall record, an incredible .739 winning percentage.

A fierce competitor, Wilson has been successful in both her playing and coaching careers. She was an All-America pitcher at Missouri and her 14-year coaching record of 603-302 includes stints at Oregon and Minnesota. In only Washington's fourth softball season, the 1996 Husky team won the Pac-10 conference and the NCAA Region-8 championship. They entered the NCAA's Women's College World Series (WCWS) as the number-one seed, sporting a 56-8 overall record.

In the WCWS they advanced to the finals against number-two seed Arizona by beating Princeton, California, and UCLA. During the regular season, the two finalists split their six games. Arizona jumped on top, 3-0, in the first inning on a three-run homer by Jenny Dalton. The Wildcats scored two more runs in the second inning and added another run in the top of the fourth to take a 6-0 lead. Washington scored four runs in the bottom of the fourth on four hits. In the bottom of the sixth, the Huskies loaded the bases on a hit batswomen and two singles with nobody out. In the play of the game, Tami Storseth hit a rocket to third baseman, Kristin Gomez, who threw to home for the force out. Sara Pickering then struck out and Jennifer Cline popped to center to end the inning. Arizona held on to win 6-4.

In 1997, Washington reached the semi-finals of the WCWS, losing to UCLA. In 1998, again they reached the semi-finals, losing to eventual champion, Fresno State. In 1999, they advanced to the WCWS finals against UCLA, the Pac-10 conference champion. The Bruins jumped on Husky pitcher Jennifer Spediacci in the first inning on a two-run single by Julie Adams. Bruin pitcher Courtney Dale led off the second inning with a 250-foot home run to put UCLA up 3-0. Washington scored in the bottom of the second when Erin Helgeland singled home Spediacci. Washington mounted its final rally in the bottom of the seventh and last inning when Jamie Graves led off with a single. She moved to third on two fielder's choices and scored on Kim DePaul's infield single. Senior Becky Newbry hit the ball hard but right at the Bruin second baseman, who flipped to second for the final out and a UCLA victory, 3-2.

In reflection on the first seven seasons, Wilson observed, "We have put ourselves into position to win four times and each time, we haven't gotten the breaks. There are several factors that go into winning a championship. First, you have to have the talent. Second, you have to peak at the right time. Third, you have to stay injury-free. And fourth, you have to be just a little lucky. We've been close to having all four factors in place twice, in 1996 and 1999. We've just not been real lucky."

The factors Wilson looks for in players have never changed. She wants young women who have a respect for the game and give everything they have when they play. She wants student-athletes who are responsible and accountable—people who will always go to class and do good things off the field. On the field, she wants talented athletes with good attitudes about winning and losing. Her players all share Wilson's commitment to hard work, the importance of pulling together, and trusting one another. When interviewed about the program, they readily discuss Wilson's challenge: "You will never work as hard with one group of people to achieve a common goal—that of winning a national championship."

In the 2000 season, it looked like it was the Huskies' year to win the national championship. They played their first 47 games on the road, won six tournaments, finished first in the ultra-competitive Pac-10, and swept four games in the NCAA Region-8 tournament. They were ranked number-one in the nation after the second week of the season. They had the nation's top two home-run hitters—Jenny Topping and Jaime Clark—the second-best earned-run average, and the third-best fielding percentage. With their 61-7 record, the Huskies were the number-one seed in the WCWS. Their dream dissolved quickly after beating DePaul in the first round, 3-2. The defending national champions and third-seeded UCLA, beat Washington 3-2 in a tornado delayed game in Oklahoma City. Arizona, seeded second, ousted the Huskies 4-2 in a loser-out game. UCLA and Oklahoma reached the finals, with the Sooners winning the national championship, 3-1.

2000-2001

Husky Moment

Washington Wins the 87th Rose Bowl— Finishes Third in the Nation

In one of the many press conferences prior to the Rose Bowl, Husky Coach Rick Neuheisel observed that the team that keeps its offense on the field will win. Washington did and beat Purdue 34-24. Passion also helped. After meeting with Curtis Williams, their paralyzed teammate, in the locker room, the offense scored touchdowns on its first two drives. Then, Purdue's quarterback, Drew Brees, took his team on a 90-yard scoring drive. A Purdue field goal near the end of the half made the score 14-10. Both teams scored quickly in the third quarter. On the first play from scrimmage, Rich Alexis took a Marcus Tuiasosopo pitch out and sprinted 50 yards down the left sideline to set up a 47-yard field goal by John Anderson. Just over a minute later Purdue quickly tied the score. The Huskies went ahead for good, 20-17, when Anderson kicked a 42-yard field goal. Then the Husky defense stepped up twice to stop Purdue on three and out possessions. After missing three plays with an injury to his throwing shoulder, Tuiasosopo returned to start the fourth quarter. On fourth and one at the Purdue 35, Alexis bulled for the first down to sustain the scoring drive. It ended with an eight-yard pass to Todd Elstrom to increase the Husky lead to 27-17. Almost five minutes later, Willie Hurst made it 34-17 on an eight-yard touchdown run. The Huskies won primarily because of a dominating second half. Their offense was on the field for over 23 minutes and rushed for 245 yards. Prophet Neuheisel became the first Rose Bowl MVP (1984) to coach a team to a Rose Bowl victory.

UW Media Relations

Willie Hurst

Husky Spotlight

In one of the most remarkable games in Washington history, the Huskies beat Stanford 31-28 in Palo Alto. After going 80 yards in three plays to score the winning touchdown with 17 seconds left, the Husky players and coaches did not celebrate. Instead they walked off the field worried about the condition of teammate Curtis Williams. A senior strong safety, Williams was knocked unconscious after making a tackle on Stanford running back, Kerry Carter, with 2:01 left in the third quarter. Williams joined his teammates in the Rose Bowl from the rehabilitation center in San Jose. When the Huskies walked into their locker room before the game, they found Williams and members of his family waiting for them. It was a very emotional moment for the players and Williams as each teammate filed by. The Tournament of Roses parade grand marshal Tom Brokaw flipped the commemorative coin before the kickoff. Coach Neuheisel asked the NBC news anchor if he would mind giving the coin to Williams. "It would be an honor," replied Brokaw, who did so at half time. After the game, Washington players ran en masse to midfield, looked up to the press box where Williams looked down, raised their helmets and chanted "Cee Dub." A fund has been established to help the Williams family meet expenses.

Husky Highlight

Washington fans had many anxious moments and some great memories from a number of Husky comeback victories. Washington won seven games by a touchdown or less and trailed in eight of its 10 regular-season victories. The games in which they had to overcome the greatest fourth-quarter deficits were against California and Arizona. They trailed the Bears 24-13 going into the last period. Back-to-back turnovers by Cal enabled Washington to score 23 points in a period of about six minutes to go on to win, 36-24. Two weeks later, Washington was down 25-13 to Arizona going into the last quarter. They went ahead 28-25 with over eight minutes to go only to have the Wildcats regain the lead with less than five minutes left. With just over a minute remaining, Washington scored to seal the win, 35-32. In the week after the California game, the most emotional and stunning comeback took place in Palo Alto against Stanford. After a third-quarter spinal cord injury to Curtis Williams, Washington took a 24-6 lead early in the fourth quarter. In less than five minutes left, Stanford scored 22 points to take the lead 28-24 with 53 seconds remaining. Then Marcus Tuiasosopo took over on the Husky 20. He completed three straight passes, the last one a 22-yard strike to freshman Justin Robbins with 17 seconds left. The final score was 31-28 in the 1,000th football game in Husky history.

UW Media Relations

Curtis Williams

Husky Legend

UW Media Relations

Marques Tuiasosopo

Marques Tuiasosopo did not win the Heisman Trophy. He was not named to a single All-America team. But to observers of Husky football from 1997 to 2000, he certainly proved himself one of the greatest quarterbacks in Washington's history. Dubbed "The Somanian Warrior" by legendary ABC broadcaster Keith Jackson, Tuiasosopo was the heart and soul of Washington's offense during his senior year. He guided the Huskies to an 11-1 record, a 36-24 victory against Purdue in the Rose Bowl and only the team's fourth postseason top-five ranking. Tuiasosopo was seemingly the best of all the great Husky signalcallers. He was an efficient passer, outstanding rusher, great field general and unsurpassed competitor. Tagged as a running quarterback, Tuiasosopo quietly passed for more than 5,501 yards during his career, the third highest total in school history. He set a total of 12 Washington offensive records during his career and graduated as the all-time leader in total offense with 6,875 yards, more than 1,000 yards more than the next closest Husky. Still, it was Tuiasosopo's ability to scramble and orchestrate the Husky option offense that made him a lethal threat to opponent defenses. His cool under pressure was invaluable. Eight times during his senior season he led the Huskies from behind for a victory. As a junior, against Stanford, he became the only Division I player to pass for 300 yards and rush for 200 yards in a game. As a senior Tuiasosopo was named the Pac-10's Offensive Player of the Year and became only the third UW signalcaller to earn first-team all-conference honors. He was named the MVP of the Rose Bowl after passing for 138 yards, rushing for 75 yards and passing and rushing for one touchdown each. He was also recognized as the top player on the West Coast when he was presented the 2000 Pop Warner Award.

Husky List

Tuiasosopo Records

Husky quarterback Marques Tuiasosopo finished his UW career as the holder of a handful of school records and one NCAA mark (the only player ever to pass for 300 yards and rush for 200 in a single game). Here is a list of his Husky records:

Career leader total offense—6,875 career yards
Career rushing touchdowns by a quarterback, with 20
Single-season total offense—2,762 in 1999
Single-game total offense—509 yards vs. Stanford in 1999
Total career offensive attempts—1,107
Total offensive attempts in a season—449 in 2000
Single-season total offensive yards per game—251.1 in 1999
Career rushing yards by a quarterback—1,374
Career 200-yard passing games—16
Passing yards by a junior—2,221 in 1999
Bowl game completion percentage—.727 in 2001 Rose Bowl

Led by seniors Megan Franza, Jill Pimley, and LeAnn Sheets, the Husky women's basketball team engineered the greatest season turnaround in Pac-10 history. Coach June Daugherty's Huskies went from ninth place in the conference in 2000 to first place in 2001, sharing the conference title with Arizona State and Stanford. The Huskies entered the first round of the NCAA tournament as the sixth seed in the Western Regional played in Gainesville, Florida. In a very closely contested game, Washington edged 10th seed Old Dominion, 67-65, on Loree Payne's last-second shot. Freshmen Guiliana Mendiola and Andrea Lalum sparked the Huskies to an 86-75 win over No. 3 seed Florida and a return trip to the Northwest for the Sweet 16. Playing in the Spokane Arena, Lalum scored 18 and Franza 17 in the third-round victory over No. 2 seed Oklahoma to reach the Elite Eight. The season ended in a loss (104-87) to No. 5 seed Southwest Missouri State and Jackie Stiles, the NCAA's all-time scoring leader. The Huskies finished 22-10 overall (12-6 in the conference). Franza was selected to the Pac-10 first team for the second year in a row and to the Academic All-America second team. She also established Husky career and single-game records for successful three-point shots. Lalum was selected to the Western Region all-tournament team.

Husky Moment

A Double First—Soccer Teams Win Pac-10 Titles

For the first time in Pac-10 soccer history, both the men's and women's teams from the same university won the Pac-10 title. The Husky men won the first ever Pac-10 conference championship since the season marked the beginning of men's soccer in the conference. Washington won the title with a 7-1 record (13-5 overall) in conference play, Ranked 12th in the nation by NSCAA, the Husky men entered the NCAA championship first round for the fifth straight year. They beat the University of Alabama-Birmingham 1-0 in four overtimes on a goal by Bryn Ritchie. In the second round, they hosted two-time defending national champion Indiana. The Hoosiers won 2-1 to advance to the elite eight. The women became the first Pac-10 champion from outside the state of California by posting an 8-1 conference record. Washington, ranked third in the final regular-season poll, entered the NCAA tournament seeded second. After a first-round bye, the Husky women trounced Montana in the second round 5-0, in the first ever NCAA tournament women's soccer game at Husky Soccer Field. In the quarterfinal round, Portland edged the Huskies 1-0. Washington ended the season with its best ever overall record of 18-3.

UW Media Relations

Kai Carroll

Husky Spotlight

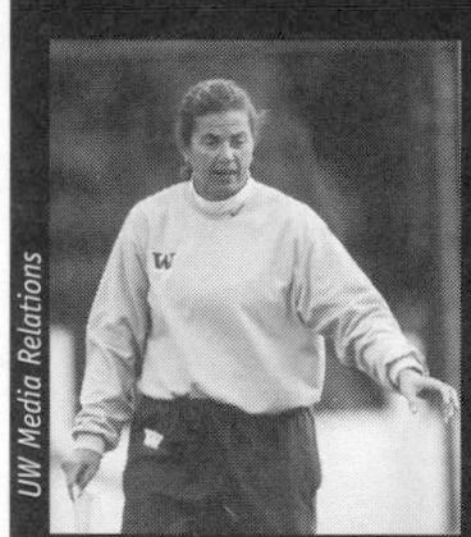

UW Media Relations

Lesle Gallimore has combined her outstanding athletic and teaching skills to rise to the top level of her profession. She has coached Washington to an 80-54-5 (.594) record in seven seasons (1994-2000). Her teams have played in five NCAA tournaments. She led her 2000 team to an 18-3 record, Washington's first women's soccer Pac-10 title, and the Sweet 16 of the NCAA championships. Gallimore was a four-time All-American at California (1982-85) and led the Golden Bears to the national playoffs in three of her four seasons. She was named the University of California's 1976-86 Athlete of the Decade. After graduation, she continued at her alma mater as an assistant women's soccer coach from 1986-89 while also attending law school in San Francisco. In 1990, she became the head women's soccer coach at San Diego State University where her team compiled at 32-25-9 (.533) record over four seasons. She was inducted in the University of California's Athletic Hall of Fame in 1995. Gallimore has been active in the U.S. girl's Olympic development program, serving as a national coach since 1995. She was a member of the board of the National Soccer Coaches Association of American (NCSAA) from 1993-99. For her outstanding record in the 2000 season she was honored as the Pac-10 Coach of the year. A poll of 271 NCAA head coaches named Gallimore as the 2000 National Coach of the Year.

Husky Highlight

Coming out of small Seattle Christian (200 total students), there were some doubters than Tami Bennett could succeed on the collegiate scene at the same level she played as a prepster. Bennett scored a state-record 152 goals during her four-year high school career, including 43 as a senior, and helped Seattle Christian to four consecutive championships. That established her as the state's all-time high school scoring leader, surpassing the total of Olympian Michelle Akers. By the end of her collegiate career in 2000, Bennett had lived up to her reputation as a solid offensive threat. During her Husky career she set school records for career goals (34), career game-winning goals (12), single-season goals (16), single-season game-winning goals (seven) and single-season points (36). Bennett was an integral part in the Huskies' first Pac-10 championship in 2000 and helped the second-seeded Huskies reach the round of 16 in the NCAA Championships. Fittingly, in Bennett's senior season Washington set school records for victories in a season and goals scored.

UW Media Relations

Tami Bennett

Husky Legend

Hope Solo

UW Media Relations

Hope Solo

Hope Solo was a legend before she came to Washington. Playing for Richland (WA) High school, she was the premiere goalkeeper in the nation in 1998. She was a two-time Parade Magazine All-American. Solo was undefeated in goal for the United States' under-18 team at the 1999 summer Pan American Games in Winnipeg, Manitoba. In the gold medal game, she recorded a 1-0 shutout of Mexico. In 1999, her freshman season at Washington, she was a second-team Pac-10 and second-team All-West Region selection. She missed her 2000 spring quarter after being selected to the U.S. National Team and to take part, as one of four goalkeepers, in the 30-player Olympic Residency Camp. She played in two games with the national team. In her 135 minutes of play, she did not surrender a goal. Although she did not make the 18-player U.S. Olympic Team, she was a member of the under-21 national team that won the 2000 Nordic Cup in Germany. As a Husky sophomore, Solo registered six shutouts and an 0.76 goals-against average during the 2000 season. Her goal tending was a very significant factor in leading the Huskies to an 18-3 record, their first women's soccer Pac-10 title, and a spot in the Sweet 16 of the NCAA championships. Solo received first-team All-West honors after being named a second-team All-American. In January 2001, she played in her third National team game. Before 30,000 spectators in Hangzhou, China, Solo played the entire match in a 1-1 tie with the Chinese National team.

Husky List

Washington Women's Soccer All-Time Goals Leaders

1.	Tami Bennett (1997-00)	34
2	Tara Bilanski (1992-1995)	27
	Theresa Wagner (1997-00)	27
4.	Emily Thompson (1992-1995)	21
5.	Melinda Torre (1992-1995)	18
6.	Caroline Putz (1998-00)	17
7.	Casey Dickerson (1995-1998)	15
	Jana Wilson (1996-1999)	15
9.	Kathleeen Juergens (1991-1994)	13
	Melanie Brennan (1991-1994)	13
	Erin Saltzman (1993-1996)	13

Out of the swimming pool and then back into it. The Husky swimming program sinks and then comes up for air 30 days later. On July 27, 2000, Athletic Director Barbara Hedges announced her decision to drop the swimming program after the 2000-2001 season. She did not think there was enough support to build a new training facility and to develop a competitive program. The Washington swimming pool, built in 1937, is only 25 yards long and six lanes and no diving well. During the next 30 days after her announcement, Hedges found a lot of alumni and people throughout the swimming community who were passionate about saving the program. The end result was that Hedges reversed her decision after forming a new partnership with Pacific Northwest Swimming, a group that represents youth swimming throughout the state. A task force was established with specific objectives—to raise $15-20 million to build a new 50-meter practice pool for the Husky team; to enhance swimming opportunities for children; and to help Washington recruit in-state swimmers. Washington could continue to hold major swim meets at the King County Aquatics Center in Federal Way.

Washington Letterwinners

Note: The list of Washington letterwinners is compiled based on records from the University's athletic department as of June 2000. Unfortunately, some sports have incomplete lists of letterwinners. The authors made every attempt to include as many letterwinners as could be documented. They regret the omission of any Husky letterwinners not included within this list.

Baseball

A

Abraham, Martin 1986
Abraham, Nevin 1970
Absher, Tom 1951, 52, 53
Acton, Rick 1966, 67, 68
Agnew, Scott 1979, 80
Agnew, Terry 1974, 75
Aichele, Troy 1989, 90, 91, 92
Akins, Albert 1945
Allan, John 1918,19
Allen 1902
Allen, Robert 1977
Allred, Rod 1970, 71, 72, 73
Alvarado, Tony 1982
Amend, Harry 1968
Anderson, Craig 1976
Anderson, Francis 1932, 33
Anderson, Harris 1943, 45
Anderson, Jelly 1947, 48
Anderson, Kevin 1976
Anderson, Mike 1962, 63
Anderson, Rian 1996, 97
Anderson, Rick 1978
Anderson, Scott 1994
Anderson, Travis 1997, 98, 99
Andrews, Ray 1906
Andring, Bill 1949, 50
Anshutz, Jack 1930, 31, 32, 33
Arnason, Hal 1948, 49, 50
Arney, Ward 1911,12
Arnold, Harry 1927
Arther, Parker 1930, 31
Avery, Jim 1966

B

Baker 1910
Baker, Dick 1935, 36
Baker, Sam 1938, 39, 40
Baker, Tom 1990
Bakke, Bill 1921, 22, 23
Ballard, Jack 1954, 56
Bantz, Burwell 1908
Barberis, Ed 1928, 29, 30
Barlett, Morgan 1941
Barnes, David 1974, 75
Barrett, Ray 1920, 21, 22, 23
Barton, Brian 2000
Basozki, Steve 1972, 73, 74
Batley, Dick 1969, 70
Batt, Harold 1942
Baxter, Lee 1983
Beck, Dillard 1911,12,13
Beckett, Hugh 1924, 25, 26, 27
Beebe, Gene 1911
Beebs, E. 1909
Beem, Aubrey 1916,18,19
Belford 1910
Bell, Bob 1950, 51, 52
Bell, Dave 1966
Bellizzi, Chris 1990
Bennett 1902
Berg, Chris 1991, 92
Bergren, Homer 1933
Best, Jeb 1979, 80, 81, 82
Beswick, Bob 1970, 71, 72
Bice, Justin 1994, 95
Bird, Bob 1942, 48
Bishop, Tim 1995
Biven, Richard 1976
Blondin, John 1945
Blouin, Gary 1984, 85, 86
Blowers, Mike 1986
Boatman 1912,13
Bodman, Lew 1978, 79
Bogart, Dan 1983, 84
Bolstad, Percy 1927, 28, 29
Bomar, Mike 1998, 99, 2000
Boston, Tyson 1998, 99
Boulton, Silas 1934
Boyd, Bob 1924
Brady, Jack 1955, 56, 57
Brakke, Brent 1995
Brand, Denny 1968, 70
Brannan, Claude 1928, 29, 30
Braun, Don 1975, 76, 77
Briggs, Alan 1987, 88
Briggs, Bill 1946, 48, 49
Brinker, Dode 1903, 04, 05
Brink, Bob 1971
Brooks, Greg 1998, 99
Brow, Scott 1988, 90
Brown, A. L. 1908, 09
Brown, Barry 1961
Brown, C. A. 1909,10
Brown, Clint 1993
Brown, Greg 1976, 77, 78, 79
Brown, Keith 1992, 93
Brown, Rick 1981
Brown, Warren 1930, 31
Brucker, Loren 1968, 69
Bruns, Alan 1993
Bryan, Willis 1914,15
Buck, Buddy 1995, 96, 97
Budnick, Lou 1934, 36, 37
Bundy, Ryan 1996, 97, 98
Burke, Daryl 1957, 58, 59
Burke, Howard 1918,19
Burke, John 1991
Burke, Scott 1990
Bussabarger, R.L. 1905
Byler, Butch 1913

C

Cales, Tony 1904, 05
Calhoun, A.P. 1901
Calhoun, Gerald 1927, 28, 29
Call, Michael 1990, 91
Campbell, Tim 1992, 93, 94, 95
Campbell, W.M. 1901, 02, 03, 04
Carey, Michael 1977, 78
Carlsen, Jeff 1998, 99, 2000
Carlson, S. 1909
Carpenter, Derek 1994, 95
Carpenter, Scott 1987, 88
Carroll, Charles 1928, 29
Carson, Todd 1990
Carter, Dwight 1973, 74
Caughlin, Walter 1914
Chamberlain, Percy 1916,18,19
Charouhas, Des 1947, 48
Chorlton, K. 1947, 48, 49
Christiansen, Dick 1964
Christianson, Ray 1957, 58
Churlin, John 1983, 84
Clark, James 1908, 09,10
Clark, Dick 1919
Cleeland, Cameron 1995
Clementson 1908, 09,10
Clifford, Aaron 1990

Clifford, James	1992
Clifford, V.	1909
Cloud, Darrell	1991
Clough, Brian	1987, 88
Codd, J.	1909
Colberg, Roger	1961
Cole, Bob	1964, 65
Cole, Clarence	1903, 04, 05
Colyer, Chris	1984, 85, 86
Cone, Cleary	1947
Connelly, Jerry	1943
Constantino, Frank	1942, 46, 47
Cook, Dick	1933, 35
Cook, Larry	1993, 94
Cook, Ray	1937
Coons	1903
Corbett, G.H.	1902, 03, 04
Core, Whitey	1957
Cornell, Archie	1970
Coultas, Lee	1945
Covey, Duane	1973, 74, 75, 76
Coyle, W.T.	1909,10
Cresap, Ty	1984
Cressap, Ray	1956
Cribby, Ed	1974, 75, 76, 77
Crockett, Jack	1943
Cummins, Bob	1942
Cunningham, Ed	1937
Cusack, Sean	1979, 80

D

Dailey, Don	1956, 57, 58
Dailey, Shawn	1990, 93
Dalthorp, Norm	1941, 42, 46
Daly, Jack	1934, 35, 36
Daniels, Don	1958, 59, 60
Daniels, Zack	1999, 2000
Davidson, Tyler	2000
Davis, Bob	1965
Davis, Glen	1915
Davis, Jack	1969
Davis, Raphael	1927, 28, 29
Davis, Reck	1916
Davis, Robert	1977
Davis, Ryan	1986
Dawes, Roger	1934, 35, 36
Dawson, Terry	1924
Day, Duane	1956
Day, Jamie	1993, 94
Dean, Benji	1995
Dean, Homer	1905, 06
deLisle, Mike	1979, 80
deLisle, Warren	1980, 81
DeDonato, Dave	1938
DeMar, Dwight	1998, 99
Dickison, Chris	1990, 91
Dieni, Dennis	1977
Dignon, Bob	1930, 31
Dillard, David	1981, 82, 83
Dobson, Dave	1938, 39, 40
Dobson, John	1930, 31
Dobson, Tom	1926
Doherty, Steve	1994
Donahue, Timo	1986, 87, 88, 89
Done, Michael	2000
Donovan, Terry	1972, 73
Doty, Derrin	1990, 91, 92, 93
Dow, Dan	1981, 82
Dowd, V.	1909,10,11,12
Downs, Craig	1982
Drake, Justin	2000
Duffy, E.A.	1901, 02
Duffy, Harold	1927
Dumont, Jim	1970, 71
Dunbar, Mike	1972
Dundas, Tom	1970, 72, 73
Durham, Pete	1912,13
Dwyer, Vincent	1986, 87, 88

E

Eakin, Bill	1953, 55
Earley, Bill	1952
Edwards, Dennis	1974
Eicher, John	1967
Eisenlohr, Kermit	1947
Ellis	1908
Engelhart, Jack	1949, 50, 51
Englin, Lance	1980, 81
Enquist, Rudy	1934, 35, 36
Erickson, Ed	1997, 98, 99, 2000
Erickson, Gil	1935
Ernst, Bob	1971
Evans, Rick	1962, 63
Everett, Jeff	1966
Ewing, Ray	1966, 68

F

Faurot, Rod	1956, 57
Feldheger, Gene	1941
Felt, Marion	1930, 31, 33
Fenn, Mark	1975, 76, 77
Ferguson, Ken	1997, 98, 99
Firstenburg, Fred	1935
Fisher	1905
Fisher, Jim	1992
Fitzgerald, Charles	1911,12,13
Foran, Bill	1921
Foran, Ed	1915,18,19, 20
Ford, Doug	1942, 43
Ford, Stewart	1989, 90
Fout, Marion	1932
Fowler, Blair	1996, 97
Fowler, Willard	1941
Franklyn, Mike	1966
Frayn, Dick	1923, 24, 25
Frere, Terry	1957, 58
Freter, Darrell	1983, 84
Frey, Kerry	1962
Friedman, Jeff	1988
Frol, Steve	1974, 75
Frost, Jack	1938, 39, 40
Frostad, Larry	1985, 86, 87

G

Gann, Jake	1999
Gardner, Hal	1925, 26, 27
Gardner, Matt	1998, 99, 2000
Gardner, Osborne	1920, 21, 22, 23
Garner, John	1952, 53
Garthwaite, Jay	2000
Garvey	1905
Gasparovich, Mitch	1934, 36, 39
Gaw, LeMar	1930, 31, 32
Gaw, Wilson	1928, 29, 30
Geiger, Monte	1955, 57
Gelatt, David	1985
Gelliland, Jim	1971
George, Dave	1955
Gibson, Rod	1983
Gibson, Ron	1972, 73
Giertz, Gary	1975
Gies, Matt	1994
Gilbertson, Merlin	1942, 47
Gillespie, John	1998
Ginsberg, Randy	1963, 65
Girard, Jeff	1975, 76, 77
Gissberg, Bill	1942, 43, 47
Glassman, Clyde	1950, 51
Gloot, Al	1947
Goldberg, Bob	1946, 47
Gordon, Dave	1941, 42
Goucher, Robert	1985, 86
Gourley, Bill	1932
Graham, George	1913,14,15
Graham, Robert	1945
Grant, George	1958, 59, 60
Grant, Taylor	1999, 2000
Grassi, Steven	1945
Gray, Dean	1962, 63
Green, Claude	1978, 79, 80
Green, Mickey	1958
Grimm, W.	1909
Grinstead, Loren	1904, 05, 06
Gulin, Chris	1970
Guy, Mel	1970, 73

H

Habenicht, Bradley	1977
Hagerty, Rob	1994, 95
Hagist, Ed	1927, 28, 29, 30
Hall, Bob	1971
Hall, Mike	1966
Hall, Richard	1999
Halle, Roland	1952, 53, 54
Halvorson, Dana	1968, 69
Hammerland	1908
Hammil, Duane	1962
Hampton, Matt	1997, 98, 99
Hannah, Shawn	1996, 97
Hanover, Jack	1933, 34
Hanson, George	1941
Hanson, Pete	1959, 60, 61
Hanzlik, Steve	1970, 71, 72
Harcrow, David	1996
Harlington, Floyd	1958, 59
Harnett, Art	1930
Harper, Elbert	1920, 21, 22, 23
Harryman, Jim	1956, 57
Hartnett, Art	1930, 31, 32
Hartvigson, Chad	1992, 93, 94
Hartvigson, Grant	1994, 95

Name	Years
Hastings, Duane	1985
Hastings, Jim	1968
Hatfield, Shannon	1985, 86, 88, 89
Haugen, Steven	1988
Hazel, Dick	1942, 43
Heaman, Bob	1930, 31, 32, 33
Hearns, Larry	1950, 51, 52
Heath, Larry	1940, 41, 42
Heaverlo, Jeff	1997, 98, 99
Hemingway	1910
Hewson, Willie	1935, 36, 37
Heyamoto, Hiromu	1949, 50
Hickingbottom, H. F.	1909,10,11,12
Hill	1902
Hill, Don	1954, 55
Hilpert, Fred	1960, 61, 62
Hilpert, Adam	1985
Hoag	1918
Hobbs, Jim	1958
Hofeditz, Bob	1959
Holland, Andy	1932, 33
Hollingsworth, Joe	1958
Hollod, Matt	1999, 2000
Holmes, Al	1960, 63
Holmes, Craig	1995
Hoover, J.W.	1904, 05
Hopkins, Sam	1995
Hopper, Buzz	1930, 31
Hopper, Cecil	1930, 32
Hopper, Jay	1969
Hormel, Scott	1982
Horning, Allan	1928
Houbregs, Bob	1951, 52
Howard, Gary	1957
Howard, Lee	1914,15
Howe	1907
Huddle	1908
Hughes, Charles	1907, 08, 09, 10, 11
Huletz, Norm	1955
Hunter, Bill	1942
Hunter, Greg	1977, 78
Hunter, Johnny	1935
Hurd	1912
Hurlbut, Lorne	1951
Huson, Gary	1968, 70
Hutchinson, Bill	1929, 30
Hutchinson, Bill	1966
Hutchinson, John	1932
Hutchinson, Red	1930, 31
Hyllengren, Henry	1924, 27

I

Name	Years
Irvine, Brandon	1994, 95, 96, 97
Irvine, Earle	1959
Isabell, Harry R.	1905, 06, 07, 08
Isotoff, Phil	1966
Izzard, Dick	1940

J

Name	Years
Jackson, Harold	1924, 27
Jackson, Roy	1925
Jacobsen, Ken	1958, 59, 60
Jacobson, Mike	1968
Jahn, Daniel	1998, 99, 2000
James, Mark	1983, 84, 85
Jarvis, Harvey	1953, 54, 55
Jermany, June	1969
John, Jim	1946
Johnson, Bob	1958, 60
Johnson, Bob	1959
Johnson, Bryan	2000
Johnson, Carl	1989
Johnson, Charley	1964, 65, 66
Johnson, Chet	1937, 38, 39
Johnson, Curt	1974, 75, 76, 77
Johnson, Curtis	1986, 87, 88
Johnson, Jack	1911,12,13
Johnson, Joe	1926, 27
Johnson, Kevin	1980, 81
Johnson, Leif	1992
Johnson, LeRoy	1963
Johnson, Ron	1978, 79, 80
Johnson, Tod	1989, 90, 91, 92
Johnston, Reid	1992, 93
Johnston, Scott	1982, 83
Jones, Doug	1975, 76, 77, 78
Jones, Kay	1956
Jonson, Erik	1991
Jorgensen, Cal	1939, 41
Jorgensen, Randy	1991, 92, 93
Jorgenson, Bob	1946, 47, 48
Junkin, Ross	1994, 95

K

Name	Years
Kaber, Shawn	1979
Kafer, Howard	1943, 45
Kallas, Tom	1964, 65
Kanikeberg, Ken	1975, 76
Keiter, George	1946
Kersten, Dave	1973
Kesamura, Joe	1939
Keys, Jeff	1977, 78
Kimmerle, Gerald	1949
King, Art	1941
Kinzer, Mark	1977
Kirner, John	1929
Klekotka, David	1987
Knaplund, Greg	1989, 90
Knight, Brian	1992
Knopf, Howie	1982, 83, 84
Knust, Laurence	1946
Knutson, Ken	1981
Koehler, Jason	1998, 99
Kohl, Alex	1961
Kohls, Bernard	1935, 36, 37
Kohn, Shawn	1999, 2000
Korstad	1902
Kosman, Randy	1971, 72
Kraetz, Earl	1929
Kramer, Wallace	1945
Kringen, Jake	1995, 96, 97
Kriston, Ryan	1994, 95
Kritsonis, George	1957, 58
Kritsonis, John	1982, 83, 84, 85
Kunz, Robert	1945
Kupp, Jake	1963
Kvarnberg, Arnie	1974, 75

L

Name	Years
LaBrache, Wendell	1927, 28
Lajala, Ed	1955, 56, 57
Lambert, Dave	1966
Land, Perry	1918,19, 20, 21
Landner, Guy	1916,18,19
Langan, William	1985, 86
Langlie, Art	1924, 25, 26
Langus, Jim	1963
Lanz, Clinton	1902, 03, 04
Larsen, Marty	1977
Larson, Bob	1939, 40
Leader, Elmer	1914,15,16
Leavers, Leroy	1923, 25, 26
LeBaron, Floyd	1948
Lee, Hal	1932, 33, 34
Lee, Wayne	1996, 97, 98
Leifer, Clare	1968, 69
Leindecker, Gil	1934, 35, 36
Leiser, Herbert	1903, 04
Lentz, Ryan	1996, 97, 98
Leonard, Ralph	1920, 21, 22
Lewis, Dave	1951
Lewis, Fred	1922, 23, 24
Lewis, John	1949
Lewis, Mike	1984
Linarelli, Tom	1998
Lindsay, Ralph	1927
Linden, Todd	1999, 2000
Linville, Sean	1994
Liston, Ed	1922, 23, 24
Lobaugh, Chris	1987, 88
Lockwood, Everett	1910,11
Logan, Hal	1942
Long, Jake	1990
Longfellow, Charles	1903
Lopez, Mike	1980
Loquvam, Henry	1938
Loucks, Brian	1994, 95
Loverich, Ed	1935, 37
Lowry, Don	1956
Lund, Phil	1967, 68, 69
Lundberg, Don	1950
Lutz, Brent	1989, 90, 91
Lynch, Jeff	1996, 97
Lyon, Jack	1964

M

Name	Years
MacDonald, Barry	1980
MacDonald, Bob	1962, 64
Macguire	1910
Magnuson, Dick	1951
Magnuson, Chuck	1952
Magruder, Chris	1996, 97, 98
Mahle, Shawn	1992, 93, 94, 95
Malone, Al	1924
Malone, Coe	1926, 27
Maloney, Gilbert	1920, 21, 22
Manley, Sam	1982, 83
Marcum, Jeff	1976
Marlowe, Paul	1935, 36
Marlowe, Roy	1935, 37
Marriott, George	1920, 21, 22, 23
Martelli, Don	1976

Martin, John	1979, 80
Martin, Ron	1964, 65, 66
Massingale, Matt	1998, 99, 2000
Matheson, Mike	1965
Matlock, Orin	1924, 26
Mattison, Alec	1988
Mattson, W.	1909
Maxwell, R.M.	1945
McAllister, Tim	1963
McCartney, Law.	1949, 50
McClary, Dave	1954
McComas, Stanley	1927
McConnell, F.	1909
McCoy, Cam	2000
McCrosky, Bob	1918,19
McDermott, Paul	1915
McDonald, E.	1901, 02
McDonald, George	1906, 07
McDonald	1924
McFarlane, Bob	1933
McJannet, Roscoe	1914
McKechnie	1907
McKenzie, Ken	1927, 28
McLain, A.	1909
McLain, Bill	1933-34
McLary, Dave	1955
McLaughlin, C.L.	1909
McLean, Archie	1929-30
McMahon, Gordon	1920-22
McManus, J.B.	1901
McNamara, Ed	1981-82
McPherson, K.A.	1901-02
Meagher, W.	1907, 09
Mecca, Greg	1993-94
Menti, Rick	1961-62
Merrick, Brett	1993-95
Muessner, Rod	1979
Meyer	1902
Miles, Hunter	1920, 21, 22, 23
Miller, Doug	1989
Miller, Ben	1999, 2000
Miller, Kevin	1996, 97, 98
Million, Ten	1910
Milliken, Ed	1939
Milloy, Lawyer	1993, 94, 95
Milroy, Walt	1940, 41, 46
Minkler	1902
Mitchell	1903, 04
Mitchell, Chuck	1940
Mitchell, Sam	1951, 52, 53
Moe, Craig	1985
Moen, Bob	1949, 50, 51
Monti, Louis	1941
Moore, Clark	1936
Moore, Dale	1984
Moran, Dugan	2000
Moreland, Tony	1993
Morgan, Al	1924
Moriarty, Edwin	1982, 83, 84, 85
Morreira, Keone	1988, 89
Morrison, Cody	1996, 97, 98
Morrison, Darrell	1927, 28, 29
Morrison, Jim	1951, 52
Morrow, Larry	1956, 57, 58
Morrow, Eric	1991, 93
Mounger, Gary	1966
Mucklestone, Melville	1911
Mueller, Jim	1963, 65
Mueller, Herb	1965, 66, 67
Mullane, Stanley	1927
Mullen, Ron	1950
Mummu, John	1980
Murchy, Dick	1952, 53
Murch, Al	1965
Murphy, Joe	1906
Murphy, Steve	1991, 92
Murray, Matt	1964
Myers, Jeff	1985

N

Na, Jim	1996, 97, 98
Nakagawa, Darin	1997
Nelson, Bob	1970, 71, 72
Nelson, Ned	1930, 31, 32
Nevaril, Roy	1935
Nevins, Willard	1928, 29, 30
Newcomb, Wendell	1936

Name	Years
Newell, Adrian	1996
Newell, Brandon	1991, 92, 93
Newell, Brett	1992, 93, 94
Nichols, Gus	1902, 03, 04, 05
Nichols, Thomas	1988, 89
Nicholson, Ron	1962
Nitsche	1974
Nokes, David	1989, 90, 91, 92
Nollan, Kenneth	1984, 85
Nordvedt, Earl	1945
Noyes, Warren	1943
Nyblod, Russ	1995
Nyquist, Mike	1988

O

Name	Years
O'Brien, Al	1932, 33, 34
O'Brien, Bob	1934
O'Brien, L.	1906
O'Brien, Mike	1991, 92
Oeche, Emil	1928
O'Keefe, Tim	1979, 80, 81, 82
Olson, Carlton	1959, 60, 61
Olson, Randy	1978, 79
Omlid, Brad	1974, 75
O'Neal, A.	1906
Opacich, Andy	1947
Orgill, Pete	1996, 97, 98, 99
Orrico, Frank	1943, 45
Oyler, Bob	1966, 67, 68

P

Name	Years
Pankow, Chip	1969
Pariseau, John	1959
Parker, Bill	1966, 67
Parker, J.B.	1938
Pasatiempo, Don	1976
Pasatiempo, Ed	1974, 75, 76
Pascho, Dave	1982, 83
Pate, Robert	1988, 89
Patten, John	1912,13,14
Patterson, Larry	1974
Pautzhe, Clarence	1930, 31, 32
Pearson, Jim	1971
Pease, Marc	1971
Peltola, Walt	1938, 39, 40
Pennington, Steve	1970
Peterson, Bob	1950, 51
Petterson, Don	1956
Pfeiffer, Norm	1961
Pitt, George	1959, 60
Plouf, Frank	1972, 73
Plummer, Al	1936, 37, 38
Pomfret, Jack	1943
Pope, Jim	1969
Porter, Jamie	1996, 97
Porter, Jeremiah	2000
Powell, Ryan	1995
Pressey, Rod	1954, 55, 56
Prevost, Al	1925, 26
Price, Ray	1971, 72, 73, 74
Prigmore, F.D.	1901, 02, 03, 04
Pripp, Bud	1937, 38, 39
Proo, Gordie	1982, 83
Pugmire, Chris	2000
Pugh, Pat	1964, 65
Puller	1902
Putnam, Ed	1930, 31, 32
Pyfer, Jack	1937, 38, 39

Q

Name	Years
Quickstad, Joe	1930

R

Name	Years
Radosevich, Mike	1970, 71
Railsback, L.G.	1904, 05
Ramseyer, W.	1909
Randall	1902
Randall, Charles	1932
Reams, Bill	1953, 54, 55
Reid, Z.L.	1901, 02, 03, 04
Reimer, Bob	1956, 57
Reiten, Dick	1959, 60
Remington	1902
Rennie, Mike	1977, 78
Reser	1907
Reynolds, Tila	2000
Rice, Ray	1946
Rice, Tim	2000
Rich, Len	1935, 36
Richards	1902
Richards, Bob	1953
Rider, Dave	1993
Rike	1908
Riley, Jim	1991, 92
Riley, Tom	1978, 79, 80, 81
Rittenhouse, Marc	1998, 99, 2000
Robertson, Brent	1999, 2000
Robinson, Ralph	1914
Rode	1920
Rodland, Gordy	1950, 51, 52
Rogers	1902, 03, 04
Rogers, Charlie	1916
Roselli, Lou	1954, 55, 56
Rothaus, Jim	1952
Rourke, George	1931
Routos, Stephen	1985, 86
Russell, Scott	1984, 85
Ruth, Jerry	1966
Rutz, Ryan	1992, 93, 94
Ryan, Don	1946
Ryan, Joe	1927
Ryan, Maurice	1927

S

Name	Years
Sage, Ed	1954
Sager, Stanley	1974
Sampson, Jim	1965
Sasaki, Art	1933
Savage, Anthony	1914
Scalzo, Gerald	1974, 76
Scanlan, Jeff	1980, 81, 82
Scatcherd, Roy	1905
Schmidt, Eric	1992, 93, 94
Schmidtke, Russell	1983, 84, 85
Schock, F.C.	1901
Schoning, Bob	1943, 45
Schreiber, John	1990
Schwindt, Terry	1980
Scott, Jack	1954, 55
Scrivner, Scott	1989
Setzer, Frank	1921, 23
Shafer, Bob	1939, 40
Shaffer, John	1971
Shager, Grant	1926
Shaw, Royal	1905
Sheehan, Eddie	1938
Shepple, Tyler	2000
Sherry, Doug	1964, 65, 66
Sherrick, Lonnie	1964, 65, 66
Shewey, Christian	1993, 94, 95, 96
Shimokawa, Brent	1985, 86, 87, 88
Shindler, Harold	1924, 25, 26
Shoup, David	1988, 89
Siefert, Lawrence	1945
Sieler, George	1904, 05
Sierer, Warren	1938, 39, 41
Sijer, Dan	1978, 79
Sill, Brent	1986, 87
Simonson, Chuck	1971
Skalisky, Cory	1986, 87
Skillingstad, Jeff	1969
Sloan, John	1966
Smith, George	1916
Smith, J.H.	1902, 03, 04
Smith, Luke	1906
Smith, Matt	1993, 94, 95, 96
Smith, Mike	1978, 79, 80
Smith, Ralph	1915,16,18,19
Smith, Walt	1983
Snyder, Gary	1959, 60, 61
Sobottka, O	1987
Solomon, Terry	1969
Soriano, Max	1946, 47, 48, 49
Soules, Ryan	1995, 96, 97
Speidel, Will C.	1902, 03, 04
Spencer, Homer	1939
Spencer, Sean	1994, 95
Sposare, Peter	1985
Squier, Kevin	1981, 82, 84
Staley, Rob	1979, 80
Stallcop, Jack	1936, 37, 38
Stefonick, Nick	1997, 98, 99
Stein, Jim	1980, 81
Stephens, Bob	1949
Stephens, Charles	1948
Stephens, LeRoy	1940, 41
Stephens, Si	1942
Stevenson	1902
Stillwell, Steve	1973
Stjerne, Jim	1960, 61
Stocker, Kevin	1989, 90, 91
Stocker, Steve	1987, 88
Stokes, Spencer	1933, 34
Stone, Girard	1962, 63, 64
Story	1902
Stowell, Ralph	1927
Strauss, Alfred	1903
Strong, Darnell	1974
Strong, Jackie	1973, 74
Stuart	1908
Stuht, Bill	1952, 53, 54
Sturgis, James	1909,10,11

Sullivan, Bob	1930, 31
Sundby, Matt	1997
Swanson, Gordon	1949, 50
Swayne, Donald	1986, 87, 88
Swimley, Phil	1960, 61
Swinehart, John	1959, 61
Swysgood, Bob	1946

T

Tanaka, Brant	1986
Tate, Bob	1946, 47, 48, 49
Taylor, Bill	1943, 48
Taylor, Roy	1915,16,18,19
Teague, Tracy	1988
Teats, Leo	1906, 07, 08, 09, 10
Teats, Ralph	1906, 07, 08
Teats, Roscoe	1901, 02, 03, 04
Tegtmeier, T.	1906, 07
Terhes, John	1989, 90, 91, 92
Tesreau, Elmer	1924, 25, 26
Tesreau, Jeff	1934
Thayer, L.E.	1901
Thayer, Robert	1987, 88, 89
Thiel, Jefferson	2000
Thompson, Casey	1960, 61
Thompson, Guy	1913,14,15,16
Thompson, Harold	1940
Thompson, John	1983, 84
Thompson, Stuart	1962, 63, 64
Thompson, Terry	1967
Thomson, Bill	1969
Thornton, Jerry	1957, 58, 59
Ticen, Kevin	1998, 99
Tjaarda, Pete	1985, 86, 87, 88
Tollefson, Rudolph	1928, 29, 30
Tonkin, Wyatt	1975, 76
Torlai, Kevin	1985, 86
Torlai, Tony	1983, 84
Torrance, Roscoe	1920, 21, 22
Towey, Steve	1986
Tran, Len	1943, 46
Trippy, Joe	1992, 93, 94, 95
Tronson, Derrick	1986
Trout	1902
Tsoukalas, Nick	1975
Tsurouka, Hideki	1982
Tucker, Louis	1949, 50, 51
Turner, Todd	1990, 91

U

Uhlman, Dick	1933, 34
Underwood	1902
Urgubart	1902
Uyehara, Les	1962, 63, 64

V

Vaculin, Frank	1977
Vander Griend, Jon	1993, 94, 95
Vanderplow, Randy	1999, 2000
Vanni, Ralph	1956
Varney, Curt	1987
Vaughan, Don	1953
Velling, Roy	1953, 54
Venable, Steve	1973
Vining, Steve	1972

W

Waite, Malcolm	1951
Wakefield, Greg	1985, 86
Wakefield, Jim	1961
Walby, Gene	1923, 24, 25, 26
Walker, Darcy	1982, 83
Waller	1918
Wallingford, Don	1926
Walsh, Dick	1930, 31, 32
Walters, Jack	1959
Waltz, Bill	1930, 31, 32
Ware, Duane	1981, 82
Warren, Tex	1943
Watson, Ed	1957
Watson, Emmett	1940, 41, 42
Watson, Larry	1953, 54, 55
Watson, Mike	1968
Weber, Joe	1932, 33, 34
Wegener	1912,13
Weible, Jeff	1992, 93
Weiderstrom, Gary	1961, 62
Welts, Robin	1909, 10, 11, 12, 13
Welts, Dick	1920, 21, 22, 23
Wenke, Bob	1943
Wheeler, Ernie	1959, 60
White, C.	1909
White, George	1979, 80, 81
White, Harry	1929, 30
White, Sammy	1947, 48
White, Sean	2000
White, Tom	1966, 67, 68
Whitelaw, Eric	1990
Whitemarsh, Chris	1995, 96, 97, 98
Williams, Dave	1975, 76, 77, 78
Williamson, Bryan	1996, 97, 98, 99
Wilson, Lannie	1965
Wilson, Ross	1915
Wimmer, Matt	1991, 92, 93, 94
Wintermute, Wayne	1932, 33, 34
Wittman, Joe	1939
Wong, Russell	1988
Wood, Michael	1989, 90, 91, 92
Woods, Kyle	1997, 98
Woody, Dominic	1997, 98, 99
Woodward, Troy	1991, 92, 93
Wright, Ken	1966
Wyman, Bob	1959, 60, 61

Y

Yoshino, Jon	1986, 87
Young, Glenn	1943
Young, Harry	1940

Z

Zaepful, John	1956
Zamberlain, Carl	1922
Zech, Bob	1943
Zech, Jerome	1945
Ziegenfuss, George	1937, 38, 39
Zuber, Dan	1978, 79

Mens Basketball

A

Adams, Pete	1993, 94
Akins, Albert	1944
Allen, Sam	1994
Amos, Mike	1995, 96
Anderson, Arthur	1945
Anderson, George	1924, 25
Anderson, Ken	1945
Antoncich, Mark	1933
Antoncich, Pete	1932, 33
Apeland, Don	1953
Arnason, Hal	1948, 49, 50

B

Bakken, Lyle	1960, 61, 62
Ball, Reggie	1971, 72, 73
Balmer, Jess	1916,17
Bantz, Mark	1969
Barge, Bruce	1982, 83
Berenson, Milton	1928, 29
Bergersen, Roberto	1995
Bird, Bob	1942, 43
Bird, George	1948
Bird, Ron	1973
Bishop, Ralph	1934, 35, 36
Blowers, Paul	1945
Boin, Bruno	1956, 57, 59
Bolstad, Percy	1928, 29
Bond, Jason	1992
Bond, Jay	1968, 69, 70
Booker, Jamie	1994, 95, 96, 97
Boston, Bryant	1992, 93, 95, 96
Brady, Eric	1988
Brickner, Bruce	1964, 65, 66
Brigham, Lance	1966, 67
Brobst, Robert	1926, 27, 28
Brooks, Richard	1945, 46
Broom, Gene	1971, 73, 74
Brown, Bryan	1998, 99, 2000
Brown, C.A	1909
Brown, Dion	1989, 90, 91
Brown, Jeff	1990
Brown, Keith	1961, 62
Brown, Webster	1941
Browning, George	1925
Bryan, Bob	1954, 55, 56
Bryan, Jim	1921, 22, 23
Buller, John	1967, 68, 69
Bullock, Larry	1968, 69
Burks, Steve	1979, 80, 81, 82
Bums, Jack	1967
Bye, Van	1970
Byler, Archie	1912,13

C

Cairney, Ralph	1930, 31, 32
Caims, Doug	1919
Caldwell, Dan	1980, 81, 82
Caldwell, Ron	1987
Carey, Senque	1999, 2000
Carmichael, Phil	1973

Canovale, Norm 1945, 47, 48
Carr, Dave 1966, 67, 68
Case, Bruce 1970, 71, 72
Caviezel, Tim 1991, 92
Cipriano, Joe 1951, 52, 53
Clark, Greg 1999, 2000
Clementson, C.C. 1910,11
Coaston, Lou 1957, 58, 59
Cobley, J. Arnold 1925
Codd, John 1944
Coffee, Ben 2000
Cole, Clarence 1903
Colman, T.C. 1909
Cook, A. 1910,11
Cook, Dick 1933, 34, 35
Cook, Erving 1918,19, 20
Corell, Ed 1961, 62, 63
Cornelius, Trent 1991, 93, 94
Coshow, Jim 1954, 55, 56
Crasford, Randle 1921, 22, 23
Creveling, Joe 1945
Crews, Dick 1956, 57, 58
Crowe, Ron 1958, 59
Cummins, Bob 1942

D

Dalquest, John 1926, 27, 28
Dalthorp, Norman 1941, 42, 46
Damon, Clay 1984, 85, 86, 87
Dana, L. 1903
Daniels, Don 1959
Davidson, Jack 1914,15,16,17
Deutsche, Dick 1916
DeWolfe, Jon 2000
Dickau, Dan 1998, 99
Didrickson, Scott 1992, 93, 94, 95
Dixon, David 2000
Dorland, Don 1957, 58, 59
Dorr, Bob 1938, 39, 40
Dorsey, Chester 1974, 75, 76, 77
Dorsey, Pat 1937, 38, 39
Douglas, John 1960, 61
Draney, Ed 1938
Duckering, William 1903
Dudley, Charles 1971, 72
Dunaway 1914
Dunlap, William P. 1901, 02, 03
Duty, Travis 2000

E

Easley, Dale 1961, 62
Eathorne, Les 1946, 47
Eckman, Bob 1947
Eckman, Jim 1949
Edwards, James 1974, 75, 76, 77
Egge, Bob 1935, 36, 37
Elliot, Will 1952, 53
Engstrom, Bob 1948
Enochs, Duane 1950, 51, 52
Evenson, Steve 1985, 86

F

Fahnestock, Rob 1964, 66
Faires, D.E. 1903
Fancher, Jack 1913,14,15
Femerling, Patrick 1996, 97, 98
Fink, Mike 1971
Fisher, Levi 1965, 66, 67
Fleming, Bill 1940
Flilfet, George 1941, 42
Flowers, Bob 1963, 64, 65
Ford, Doug 1942, 43
Fortier, Paul 1983, 84, 85, 86
Frankland, Charles 1921, 23
Frayne, Dick 1923, 24, 25
French, James 1991, 92
Fronk, Bob 1978, 79, 80, 81
Froude, Chester 1924
Fuller, John 1931, 32, 33

G

Galer, Bob 1933, 34, 35
Gannon, Jack 1935, 36, 37
Gardner, Gary 1983, 84
Gardner, Osborne 1923, 24
Getaz, Jack 1944
Gibbs, Rod 1946
Gilbertson, Merlin 1942, 43, 47
Gill, Bob 1945, 46
Gilmur, Charles 1941, 43
Gissberg, Bill 1942, 43
Grant, George 1958, 59, 60
Green, Thalo 1998, 99, 2000
Greer, Jim 1957, 58
Grifn, Andra 1978, 79, 80, 81
Gritsch, Ernest 1929, 30, 31
Gritsch, Tony 1927, 28
Grondsdahl, Dale 1943, 44
Gross, Richard 1926
Gudmundsson, Petur 1978, 79, 80
Guisness, Frank 1950, 51, 52
Gunlach, Ralph 1923, 24

H

Hack, Perry 1927, 28, 29
Hale, Grattan 1925, 26
Hall, Steve 1989, 90
Halle, Roland 1953, 54
Hamilton, Jason 1995, 96
Hanover, Jack 1932, 33, 34
Hansen, Lars 1973, 74, 75, 76
Hanson Bill 1960, 61, 62
Harris, Gordy 1965, 66, 67
Hart, Charlie 1962, 63, 64
Hartman, Jason 1995, 96
Haug, Ron 1944
Hawes, Jeff 1972, 73, 74
Hawes, Steve 1970, 71, 72
Hawken, David 1993 94 95
Hayward, Mike 1988, 89, 90, 91
Heaman, Bob 1932, 33
Heller, William 1910
Henson, LaDon 1946, 9, 50, 51
Hermann, Jim 1964, 65, 67
Hesketh, Bob 1923, 24, 25
Hesketh, L. 1923
Hess, Bart 1977, 78
Hill, Greg 1986, 87
Hill, William 1902, 03,
Holbrook, Paul 1918
Holman, Pete 1991
Hosley, Rex 1911
Houbregs, Bob 1951, 52, 53
Hovde, Dave 1965, 66, 67
Howard, Barry 1988, 89
Howell, Byron 1982, 83
Huguenin, Dave 1967

I

Ide, Wilson 1918,19
Irvine, Earle 1958, 59, 61
Irvine, George 1968, 69, 70
Izzard, Dick 1939, 40

J

Jack, Greg 1975, 76
Jackson, Larry 1975, 76
Jackson, Steve 1980, 81, 82
Jamieson, Cecil 1918,19, 20
Jaloff, Stan 1928, 29, 30
James, Alfred 1926, 27, 28
Jefferson, Keith 1949, 50, 51
Jenkins, Anthony 1988, 89, 90
Jewell, Earl 1925, 27
Johnson, Bob 1965
Johnson, Hall 1927
Johnson, Jerry 1954, 55
Johnson, Michael 1998, 99, 2000
Jorgenson, Bob 1945, 46, 47, 48

K

Kaps, Ryan 1990
Kastner, Walter 1936
Keane, Martin 1993
Keeler, Otis 1912
Kennedy, 1903
King, Richard 1945
Koehler, David 1983, 84
Koon, Charles 1952, 53
Krell, Ken 1972
Kuyper, Tim 1983, 84

L

Larsen, Gary 1968, 69
Lautenbach, Todd 1988, 89, 90, 91
Leask, Wallace 1941, 42, 43
Lee, Dick 1963, 64, 65
Lee, Hal 1932, 33, 34
Leep, Grant 1999, 2000
Leichty, Roy 1903
Lemman, Robert 1945
Lewis, Bill 1977
Lewis, Evan 1921, 22, 23
Lindh, Bob 1940, 41, 42
Lindig, Harry 1903
Lindsay, Brent 1904
Lockhart, Harry 1937, 38, 39
Lombard, Ken 1975, 76
Lopez, Alex 1995
Loube, Fred 1903
Loverich, Ed 1935, 36, 37
Lowe, John 1937

Name	Years
Luton, Deon	1997, 98, 99, 2000
Lyles, Kenny	1979, 81, 82
Lynch, Jack	1964

M

Name	Years
MacCulloch, Todd	1996, 97, 98, 99
Mack, John	1961
Mallory, Jim	1944, 47, 48, 49
Manning, Rich	1992, 93
Mattila, Marty	1981
Mathews, Henry	1964, 65
Matzen, Steve	1977, 78, 79, 80
Mar, Alfred	1944
McClain, Michael	1994, 95
McClary, Doug	1951, 52, 53
McClary, Harold	1928, 29, 30
McCutchen, Mike	1951, 52, 53
McDonald, Bill	1938, 39, 40
McFee, Joel	1913,14,15
McKinstry, Bob	1934, 36
McKnight, John	1973
McMillan, Don	1944, 45
Meekins, Doug	1990, 91, 92
Merrin, Dick	1934
Merritt, Brent	1990, 91
Metzger, Mark	1949
Millikan, Jim	1948
Mitchell, Charles	1940
Mitchell, Darren	1994
Monroe, Mike	1955
Moritz, Andrew	1999, 2000
Morrell, Troy	1985, 86, 87
Morris, Bill	1955
Morris, William	1941, 42, 43, 44
Moscatel, Al	1986, 87
Mossell, Jim	1971, 72
Murphy, Al	1958, 59, 60
Murphy, Emest	1918

N

Name	Years
Nairn, Chandler	1992, 93
Names, Clint	1959, 60, 61
Nance, Lynn	1964, 65
Neff, Jack	1931
Neill, Mike	1976, 77, 78
Nelson, Gary	1955, 56
Nelson, Harry	1940, 41, 42
Nelson, Louie	1971, 72, 73
Nelson, Ned	1930, 31, 32
Nelson, Perry	1944
Nichols, Jack	1944, 47, 48
Nicholson, Leo	1920, 21
Niva, Roger	1960, 61, 62
Nordstrom, Erik	1986
Nordstrom, Lloyd	1931

O

Name	Years
Olsen, Ron	1954, 55, 56
Olsen, Steve	1964, 65, 66
Olson, Oscar	1911,12,13
ONeil, Don	1944
Opacich, Andy	1947, 48, 49
ORailey	1903
Ostenson, Gary	1967, 68
Ostling, Ed	1933

P

Name	Years
Pagett, Brett	1992, 93
Pariseau, John	1957, 58, 59
Parker, Chris	1976
Parsons, Dean	1952, 53, 54, 55
Parthemer, Russ	1949, 50, 51
Paterson, Hunt	1935, 36, 37
Patnoe, Ron	1954, 55, 56
Paul, Ron	1962, 63
Peeples, Clint	1962, 63, 64
Perkins, Doyle	1954, 55, 56
Perkins, Prentiss	1993
Perkins, William	2000
Peny, Virgil	1930, 31, 33
Peters, Albert	1923
Peterson, Arthur	1929, 30
Pope, Mark	1992, 93
Pomfret, Jack	1946
Porter, LaMoyne	1961
Pounds, Larry	1974, 75
Price, Ray	1972, 73, 74
Priess, Newell	1938

Q

Name	Years
Quigg, John	1971, 73

R

Name	Years
Rabel,	1910
Ramsey, Clarence	1974, 75, 76
Randall, George C.	1902
Rashad, Amir (Quentin Youngblood)	1990, 91, 92, 94
Recasner, Eldridge	1987, 88, 89, 90
Reese, Robert	1937, 38
Reiten, Dick	1960, 61, 62
Riddle, Stanley	1916,17
Riva, Blake	1983
Roake, Steve	1953
Roberson, Andy	1993 94, 95, 96
Roberts, Dan	1947
Robinson, Harold	1944
Robinson, Ralph	1913,14,15
Robinson, Tom	1988, 89
Rogers, Reggie	1983, 84, 85
Romar, Lorenzo	1979, 80
Rosenberg, Henry	1935, 36
Rutherford, Eugene	1930

S

Name	Years
St. John, Harold	1925, 26, 27
St. John, John	1909,10,11
Sanford, Mark	1995, 96, 97
Sanor, Jeff	1987, 88, 89
Saunders, Scott	1917
Savage, Tony	1912,13,14,15
Schively, Dick	1915,16
Schlichting, Harold	1939, 40, 41
Schmidt, Warren	1958
Schrempf, Detlef	1982, 83, 84, 85
Schreuder, Otis	1914,15
Schuss, Albert	1925, 26, 27
Schwabe, Eric	1985
Scott, Mark	1975, 76, 77, 78
Seilk, Harry	1919
Seilk, Heine	1921, 22
Sharp, Larry	1961, 62, 63
Sheaffer, Chuck	1943, 46, 47
Sheaffer, Robert	1940
Shelton, Marlon	1999, 2000
Shimer, Pete	1984
Shoudy, Loyal	1902, 03
Sigurdsson, Flosi	1982, 83, 84, 85
Slettedahl, Rick	1967, 68, 69
Smart, Doug	1957, 58, 59
Smith, Al	1974, 75, 76
Smith, Chris	1934
Smith, Don	1957
Smith, George	1916,17
Smith, Ralph	1917,19, 20
Snider, Monty	1927, 28, 29
Sohns, Clinton	1919
Solibakke, Bruce	1956
Soriano, Louie	1949, 50, 51
Staatz, Karl	1911,12
Staatz, Stan	1917
Staatz, V.P.	1920
Stady, Bill	1956, 57, 58
Stewart, Don	1950, 51
Stewart, Kim	1975, 76, 77, 78
Stokes, Curt	1973, 74, 75
Stone, Rafael	1968, 69, 70
Sugg, E.E.	1909,11
Sunitsch, Don	1955, 56, 57
Supper, N.W.	1911
Sutton, Wayne	1912
Swanson, Henry	1929, 30, 31
Swygard, Kline	1931, 32

T

Name	Years
Talbot, Archie	1919, 20, 21
Tanner, Darrell	1983
Taylor, Bill	1943, 44, 47, 48
Taylor, J.D.	1985, 86, 87
Teats, Roscoe	1901, 02
Thompson, Chris	1996, 97, 98
Thompson, Don	1940
Thompson	1903
Tillman, Paul	1970, 71, 72
Tripp, Don	1953, 54
Troyer, Michael	1969, 70, 71
Tuft, John	1956, 57
Tyrus, Jason	1993, 94

V

Name	Years
Vandenburgh, Bill	1945, 47, 48, 49
Vaughn, Alvin	1981, 82, 83, 84
Vaughn, Don	1978, 79, 80, 81
Vidato, Kevin	1984, 85, 86, 87
Voeglin, Karl	1954, 55, 56
Voelker, Bob	1940, 41
Voelker, Jack	1939, 40, 41
Voelker, Richard	1937, 38, 39

W

Name	Years
Wade, Lee	1951
Wagner, Charles	1935, 36, 37

Name	Years
Wagner, Clyde	1934, 35
Walcott, Chris	1997, 98, 99, 2000
Walker, Stan	1977, 78, 79, 80
Wallace, Marc	1970
Waller, Frank	1901, 02, 03
Wand, Tom	1912,13
Ward, Bill	1953
Ward, Jack	1950, 51
Watling, Jeff	1988, 89
Watson, Brad	1980, 81, 82, 83
Watts, Donald	1996, 97, 98, 99
Weber, Joe	1932, 33, 34
Welp, Chris	1984, 85, 86, 87
Welts, Dick	1924
Werner, Ross	1936, 37, 38
West, Dave	1968, 69, 70
West, Harold	1930, 31
West, Mark	1987, 88, 89, 90
Westlake, Doug	1966, 67, 68
White, Sammy	1947, 48, 49
Willenborg, Dave	1969, 70, 71
Williams, Ron	1973, 74
Williams, Shag	1982, 84, 85, 86
Williams	1910
Williamson, Roy	1938, 39
Wilson, Brad	1960
Wilson, David	1985, 86, 87, 88
Wilson, Steve	1962, 63, 64
Woods, Andy	1992, 94
Woods, James	1977, 78, 79, 80
Woods, Maurice	1991, 92, 93, 94
Woolcock, Patrick	1968, 69, 70
Wooten, Jan	1997, 98
Wyman, Don	1934, 35

Y

Youngblood, Quentin (see Rashad)

Z

Name	Years
Zevenbergen, Phil	1986, 87
Ziegenfuss, George	1937, 38, 39

Women's Basketball

A

Name	Years
Adams, Pat	1982, 84
Autrey, Emily	2000
Avelino, Renee	1982, 83, 84, 85

B

Name	Years
Baker, Julie	1979, 80
Bakken Inger	1977, 78
Banks, Pam	1980, 81
Barmore, Jana	1987, 88, 89, 90
Barner, Debbie	1983
Beers, Barbara	1976, 76
Bennett, Mary	1979
Berry, Barb	1977, 78
Bishop, Karin	1985
Bryant, Karen	1991

C

Name	Years
Campbell, Nancy	1975
Carmer, Allison	1987, 88
Caruso, Jenny	1983
Chicane, Liz	1980, 81, 82, 83
Claboe, Amy	1991
Clark, Pam	1984, 85, 86
Coker, Karla	1982
Cole, Yvette	1986, 87, 88, 89
Curry, Karen	1977

D

Name	Years
Davis, Tara	1991, 92, 93, 94
DeCamp, Lori	1977, 78
Deden, Karen	1988, 89, 90, 91
Denman, Karen	1975
Diggins, Tiffany	2000
Djdordjevic, Dragana	1993
Doxsee, Marcella	1997, 98, 99
Duncan, Sarah	1998, 99, 2000

E

Name	Years
Erickson, Aurora	2000
Erickson, Melissa	1998, 99, 2000

F

Name	Years
Felton, Sherri	1978
Foucade, Katia	1992, 93, 94, 95
Franza, Megan	1998, 99, 2000

G

Name	Years
Glover, Juli	1986
Gonsalves, Laura	1992, 93, 94, 95
Grantham, Patty	1979, 80, 81
Gray, Julia	1999, 2000
Greene, Shaunda	1990, 91, 92

H

Name	Years
Hackett, Trish	1979, 80, 81
Hall, Amber	1996, 97, 98, 99
Halpenny, Carli	2000
Hamilton, Kathy	1985, 86
Hanshaw, Carol	1977, 78
Hardwick, Erika	1990, 91, 92, 93
Hart, Kathy	1979
Heliton, Tracy	1987, 88
Higgenbotham, Kathy	1979
Hills, Molly	1996, 97, 98, 99
Hoffmann, Heidi	1993, 94, 95, 96
Hopper, Linda	1975, 76
Hove, Nancy	1983, 84, 85, 86
Hughley, Leteia	1982, 83, 84, 85

J

Name	Years
Jacobsen, Marilyn	1975
Jochum, Leslie	1992
Johanknecht, Mitzi	1979
Johnson, Janet	1977, 78
Johnson, Sherri	1988
Jones, Joyce	1989

K

Name	Years
Kelly, Shannon	1993, 94, 95, 96
Kendrick, Janis	1977
Kerr,Katie	1997
Knoebel, Carol	1987, 88, 89, 90

L

Name	Years
Larsen, Chris	1975
Lewis, Cynthia	1994, 95
Lewis, Veronica	1979
Lewis, Yvette	1981
Lynch, Malinda	1996, 97, 98, 99

M

Name	Years
Malcolm, Nancy	1978
Martin, Molly	1976
McClary, Carlin	1979, 80, 81, 82
McDonald, Chris	1985, 86
McDowell, Nancy	1975
McIntire, Jocelyn	1989, 90, 91
McLean, Jennifer	1984, 85
McManus, Aileen	1985, 86, 87, 88
Merlino, Laurie	1988, 89, 90, 91
Meyer, Shannon	1982
Mickelson, Amy	1987, 88, 89, 90
Miernik, Janie	1975
Moore, Laura	1990, 91, 92, 93
Morrell, Stacey	1994
Motley, Renee	1980, 82
Murray, Karen	1981, 82, 83, 84
Myers, Jacki	1987, 88, 89, 90

N

Name	Years
Nielsen, Margaret	1977, 78
Niemela, Elise	1994, 95, 96, 97
Norton, Joanna	1978, 81, 82
Norwood, Veronica	1979

O

Name	Years
Olsen, Christine	1975, 76
Omodt, Karen	1979, 80
O'Neill, Kelli	2000
Oriard, Lisa	1985, 86, 87, 88

P

Name	Years
Padgett, Terry	1975
Pagano, Chris	1991
Payne, Loree	2000
Percy, Cathy	1980
Pelz, Gena	1995, 96, 97, 98
Perkins, Michelle	1994, 95
Pimley, Jill	1998, 99, 2000

R

Name	Years
Raschkow, Lisa	1984, 85, 86, 87
Rasmussen, Dana	1979, 80
Recknor, Hilary	1984, 85, 86, 87
Redd, Jamie	1996, 97, 98, 99
Reichmann, Heather	1999, 2000
Rogers, Rachelle	1997
Rowe, Charlotte	1975, 76
Rue, Kathy	1982, 83, 84, 85
Russell, Ingrid	1987, 88

S

Name	Years
Savasta, Laure	1995, 96, 97
Seba, Kathy	1981, 82
Shafer, Jo	1989, 90, 91, 92

Sheets, LeAnn 1998, 99, 2000
Shideler, Dana 1981
Smith, Harriet 1976
Smith, Rhonda 1992, 93, 94, 95
Smith, Sherrie 1977, 78, 79, 80
Sorenson, Cheryl 1999, 2000

T

Talmadge, Sarah 1991
Teel, Anne 1994, 96, 98
Thirdgill, Traci 1987, 88, 89, 90
Tilbrook, Margie 1994, 95
Thorlakson, Beth 1976
Tucker, Judy 1984, 85
Tuiaea, Ana 1997, 98

V

Van Pelt, Cathy 1976
Verhulp, Vickie 1976

W

Wade, Wanda 1990
Washington, Dottie 1981
Weber, Cari 1981
Wildhaber, Kelli 1989, 90
Wilkins, Carol Lynn 1977
Williams, Dianne 1991, 92
Williams, Mindy 1997
Wittman, Nancy 1977, 78, 79
Wilson, Julie 1978
Wood, Becky 1983, 84
Wuschnig, Melissa 1993, 94, 95, 96

Y

Yee, Myra 1976

Men's Crew

A

Aarr, Arthur 1908
Accorn, Gerald 1929, 30
Adam, Gordon 1936, 38
Adams, Doug 2000
Adler, Brock 1980
Admundsen, Dave 1963
Ahlstrand, Lucas 2000
Alderson, Ted 1938, 39
Alan, Robert 1986, 88
Allan, Greg 1976
Allen, Grant 1962
Allison, Ryan 1993, 94, 95
Allsopp, Chris 1974, 76
Alm, Charles 1957, 58
Altman, Andrew 2000
Andersen, Lars 1967, 68
Anderson, Ed 1929
Anderson, John 1946, 47
Anderson, Robert 1983
Anderson, Matthew 1995, 97
Andonian, Paul 1954, 56
Andrews, Cam 1991,1992
Argersinger, Ed 1932, 34
Argersinger, Ed 1959
Arneson, Art 1970
Attisha, Raymond 1985, 87
Audett, John 1948, 50

B

Bacher, Hans 1954
Bailey, Kristin 1992, 93
Baird, Roger 1949, 51
Baker, John 1964
Ball, James 1987
Baranski, John 1971
Bargfrede, James 1996
Barker, Andy 1974
Barker, Floyd 1956
Barker, Paul 1978, 80
Barnewt, Bret 1976, 77
Bascom, Thomas 1977, 79
Bates, Walter 1935, 36
Baugh, David 1983, 85
Baze, Randy 1980
Beall, Bruce 1971, 73
Beck, Aaron 1997, 98, 99
Beck, Bruos 1908,10
Beckstead, Jim 1928
Behrbaum, Scott 1992, 93, 94
Beitlers, Girts 1993, 94, 95
Benthin, Bemy 1947
Berghuis, Bob 1976, 77
Berkey, Degraff 1973,1975
Berque, Leroy 1919, 20
Bickford, Paul 1983, 84
Biernacki, Glenn 1985
Billings, Roger 1985
Birkeland, Irar 1952, 53
Bishop, Grant 1946, 47
Bisset, John 1957, 58
Black, Willis 1983
Blanda, Roberto 1993, 94, 95
Blethen, Frank 1926, 27
Boender, Dean 1962
Boeve, Sally 1993
Bogards, Almon 1917,1920
Bolles,Tom 1926
Bolstad, Carl 1995, 97
Bonhey, Parker 1913
Bothel, William 1976
Bowen, Gilbert 1929, 31
Bower, Charles 1956
Bowser, Gren 1967, 69
Bowser, Todd 1999
Bracken, John 1940, 42
Brand, Erik 1996, 97
Brandenthaler, T. 1917,19, 20
Brayshaw, Chuck 1963
Breitenberg, Don 1949
Briggs, Brall 1916,17
Brinsfield, Jim 1973, 75
Brislin, Tim 2000
Brokaw, Clyde 1914,16
Bronson, Mike 1971, 73
Brooks, Winslow 1936
Brossard, Regan 1983
Brown, Chuck 1947, 48
Brown, Harold 1949
Brown, Harry 1964,1966
Bruton, Jason 1994, 95
Burch, Alan 1985
Burkhart, Tom 1970
Burns, Jonathan 2000
Buse, Jon 1971, 73
Buse, Mike 1970
Buvick, Norm 1947, 50
Buwaldo, Paul 1910
Byrd, Bill 1970, 72
Byrd, Joe 1984, 86

C

Caldwell, Hugh 1938
Callaghan, Jim 1951
Callahan, Michael 1994, 96
Callow, Russell 1914,15
Cameron, Bill 1951,1953
Camfield, Roland 1952, 53
Campbell, A.C. 1913
Campbell, Archie 1913
Campbell, Art 1912
Campbell, Greg 1989, 90
Campbell, Charles 1964
Campbell, John 1962, 63
Campbell, Talbot 1919
Campodonico, Gabriel 1993, 94, 95
Canfield, Don 1939
Carey, John 1937, 38
Carrol, Levi 1911
Carter, Scott 1979, 80
Carter, Victor 1934
Cathey, Dick 1955
Catlin, Claude 1909,11,14
Chait, Mike 2000
Chan, Elvis 1991
Charters, James 1989
Chiang, Norm 1970
Chica, George 1938
Christenson, Jim 1959
Christianson, John 1981
Chudzik, Mike 1992, 93
Clancy, Brad 1983, 84
Clapp, Charles 1979, 81
Clark, John 2000
Clark, Newman 1920
Clarke, Dennis 1967
Clarke, Whit 1952
Clay, Chris 2000
Clingan, Wes 1972, 73
Clipson, Vance, II 1987
Clothier, Dick 1964, 65
Coder, Ellis 1939
Cohen, Eric 1980, 82
Colbert, Fred 1939, 40
Colbertson, Terry 1974
Cole, Mike 1972, 74
Cole, Rick 1967, 69
Collins, Melissa 1996
Condon, Hal 1924, 26
Condon, Hal, Jr. 1955, 56
Connolly, Mike 1974
Coon, Carl 1975, 76
Copstead, Rick 1970, 72

Cotler, John	1983, 84
Covey, Dave	1965, 67
Coy, Donald	1936
Crain, David	1994
Crim, Orin	1903, 04
Cummins, Bob	1997, 98
Cushman, Ed	1922
Cushman, Tom	1914,15

D

Dahl, Jim	1982, 84
Damm, Tommy	1977
Davidson, Frank	1979, 81
Davis, Warren	1928, 30
Day, Charles	1935, 37
Day, Herb	1932, 33
Deakin, Matthew	2000
Decker, Jay	1955
Dehn, Bill	1943
Dembicki, Peter	2000
Dempsey, Andrew	1995, 97
Dickhaus, David	1976, 78
Dingwall, Ewen	1938
Dixon, Dave	1947
Dodd, Hugh	1989, 90
Dodd, Lou	1962,1964
Donaldson, Scott	1976, 77
Dohrn, Gary	1980, 82
Dolan, Kevin	1998, 99
Doolin, Lacy	2000
Dowell, George	1997
Doyle, Dan	1987
Doyle, Mike	(Mngr.1993)
Doyle, Phillip	1985, 87
Dressler, Jack	1943
Dunbar, Walt	1907,11,14
Dunn, Charles	1923
Duppenthaler, Dallas	1939, 40
Duppenthaler, Mike	1939, 40
Dutton, H.J.	1923, 25
Dysart, Don	1965, 67

E

Eastabrooks, Sarn	1981, 83
Ebright, Ky	1916,17
Edmundson, Clarence	1932
Edwards, Jim	1969, 70
Efird, Terril	1965, 66
Eldridge, Les	1957
Eng, Rich	1971
Enger, Kyle	1992
Erdly, Bill	1978
Erickson, Al	1940
Erickson, Alan	1980, 82
Erickson, Dick	1956, 58
Erickson, Gus	1937, 38
Ervin, Jack	1943
Estevenin, Perry	2000
Evans, Gary	1979, 81

F

Farrell, Gene	1987
Farrer, James	2000
Felix, Marius	1979, 80, 82
Feltin, Michael	1984, 86
Filippone, Michael	1988, 90
Fish, John	1957, 58
Fisk, Terry	1977, 79
Fix, Charles	1989
Fletcher, Jack	1952
Fletcher, Robert	1948
Flint, Bill	1960
Flint, Ned	1993, 94, 95
Florer, Mark	1978, 80
Fomo, Vic	1940, 42
Fonkalsrud, Eric	1953
Forney, Alan	1980, 82
Fountain, Michael	1977, 78
Fowler, Doyle	1941, 42
Fox, Fred	1974, 76
France, Rowland	1921, 24
Frankland, Jim	1913,14
Franklin, Jesse	1975, 77
French, Doug	1955
Frisch, Stephen	1987, 89
Frost, Ted	1952, 54
Fulton, Dave	1959, 61
Funk, Eric	2000

G

Gagliardi, Dominic	1993, 94
Gallup, John	1938
Gamble, Gil	1974, 75
Garhart, Ted	1940, 42
Garrett, Frank	1985
Gavin, Jim	1962, 64
Gellermann, Lou	1956, 58
Genther, Chet	1975
Gibson, Andrew	1985
Gibson, Ed	1946
Gillespie, Steve	1994, 95, 96
Gilmour, Ross	1980
Ginger, John	1929, 31
Giovanelli, Gordon	1948, 49
Giovanelli, Tom	1973, 74
Gleason, Pat	1983, 84
Glerup, Maruis	1926, 28
Gloster, Dick	1905, 07
Gobler, Arthur	1932
Godfrey, Bill	1909,10
Goodman, Ron	1985
Gordon, Wayne	1939, 40
Graham, Ty	1982, 84
Grant, Don	1922, 24
Grant, Steve	1962
Graybeal, Herb	1938
Green, Bob	1935
Green, Norm	1973
Greif, David	1994, 96
Griffin, Tren	1949, 51
Gruendell, Gordon	1989, 90
Grunboch, Bob	1939
Guiliani, Greg	1978, 80

H

Haak, Dale	1978
Hall, Kevin	1993
Hammer, Paul	1913, 15
Hammond, Whit Haako	2000
Hansen, Kevin	1982
Hansen, Krishan	1998
Hanson, Alden	1964
Hanson, Mel	1973
Harper, Guy	1952, 54
Harr, Adolph	1915,16
Harrah, Bill	1947
Harrington, Silas	1995, 97
Harris, Bob	1947
Harris, Richard	1929, 31
Hart, Art	1954
Hart, Jim	1925, 27
Hart, Jim	1972
Hartman, Charles	1935, 37
Hatch, Merton	1936
Haunreiter, Larry	1964
Hawel, Leo	1937, 38
Hawkins, Christopher	2000
Hearing, Ed	1948, 49
Hedges, Richard	1983, 85
Hedvall, Ed	1992
Helgerson, Warren	1950
Henderson, Steven	1988
Henry, Phil	1992, 94
Henry, Tom	1972, 74
Herness, David	1989, 91
Hess, Michael	1975, 77, 78
Hiatt, Lewis	1978
Hoekstra, Todd	1987, 89
Hoffman, Greg	1981, 82
Holdren, Dale	1983
Holm, Brian	1992
Holmstrom, Ross	1957, 58
Holtz, Benjamin	1987, 88
Holtz, Chuck	1961, 62, 64
Horlsley, Jim	1946
Horn, Blair	1981, 83
Horrocks, Phil	1950
Hovland, Andy	1956, 58
Howay, Jim	1952, 54
Hubbard, Bill	1978, 80
Huey, Jesse	2000
Hughes, Bobbie	1999
Hume, Donald	1936, 38
Hunt, George	1935, 37
Hurn, Cliff	1970, 72
Hurn, Hans	2000
Hutton, George	1913

I

Ingham, Ned	1955, 56
Ingram, Robert	1921, 22
Ito, James	1983, 85
Ives, Ed	1981, 83

J

Jackman, Bill	1992
Jackman, Ron	1975, 77
Jackson, Charles	1939, 41
Jackson, Dylan	1992
James, Daniel	1993, 94
Janjic, Nebojsa	1980, 82
Janjic, Uglesa	1979

Jarvis, Paul 1907
Jensen, Eric 1991
John, Skip 1952, 53
Johnsen, Jerry 1962, 64
Johnson, Bob 1939
Johnson, Joe 1986, 87
Johnson, Larry 1970
Johnson, Michael 1984, 85
Johnson, Rod 1947, 50
Johnson, Stu 1974, 76
Julien, Paul 1972, 73
Jones, Doug 1976, 77
Jordan, Dick 1950

K

Kauffman, Bert 1927
Keely, Gerald 1939, 40
Keely, Skip 1977
Kehoe, David 1978, 79
Kerns, Homer 1924, 26
Ketcham, Stu 1975
Kieburtz, Phil 1956, 58
Kimball, Jared 1989
Kimbrough, Ray 1992
Kinley, Dave 1960, 61
Kirby, Homer 1907, 08
Kitson, John 1984, 85
Knapp, Christopher 1985
Knoll, Chuck 1971
Koehler, Trish 1990
Krause, Greg 1998, 99
Kriefall, Adam 1988, 89
Kroeger, David 1965, 67
Kronfield, Dave 1919, 20
Kueber, John 1991, 93
Kuhns, Rich 1978
Kumm, Ward 1914, 16,17
Kunnen, Steve 1993, 94, 95

L

Lacy, Dick 1953
Lamb, Lynn 1954, 56
Landon, Don 1947, 49
Landwehr, Todd 1982, 83
Lantz, Clint 1903, 04
Lauber, David 1981
Lawrence, Guy 1981, 82
Leader, Ed 1913, 16
Leader, Elmer 1913
Leanderson, Fil 1952, 53
Lee, Bob 1947, 48
Lee, Clint 1913
Lee, Howard 1983
Lee, Tom 1983
Legg, Robert 1975
Leland, Bill 1961
Lethin, Dan 1990
Lethin, Kris 1996
Lethin, Richard 1988, 89
Lewis, Dan 1975
Lewis, Pete 1932
Lewis, Timothy 2000
Liden, Neal 1962
Lind, John 1959
Lisemayer, Kurt 1985
Litchfield, Wally 1929, 30
Logg, Chuck 1920, 21
Loken, Elliott 1943
Long, Ron 1991
Lorenz, Robert 1993
Love, Harvey 1933, 34
Lovejoy, Bart 1907, 09
Lovsted, Carl 1950, 52
Lovsted, Jim 1983
Lowe, Wilbur 1949, 50
Luft, Herman 1919, 21
Luft, Max 1923, 25
Lumpkin, Anna 1992
Lumpkin, Toby 1989, 91
Lund, George 1935, 37
Lund, Philo 1948
Lund, Sydney 1935, 36
Lusher, Doug 1956

M

MacDonald, Ellis 1927, 29
MacDonald, Joseph 1985
MacDonald, Roger 1958
MacDonald, Ron 1983, 84
Magee, David 1978, 79
Magnuson, Charles 1920, 21
Magnuson, John 1960
Malone, Walt 1925
Mann, Fred 1968, 69
Marolick, Frank 1934
Martin, Bob 1947, 48
Martin, Brian 1977, 78
Mason, Lloyd 1922
Matthews, Jim 1925, 26
Maxwell, Jim 1972, 73
May, Charles 1942
McCann, Thomas 1985, 88
McCarthy, C. 1948, 50
McCarthy, Joe 1932
McConacle, Bill 1964
McConihe, Paul 1915,17
McCormick, Gannon 1964
McDaniel, Brian 2000
McDougall, Jim 1975, 76
McElmow, Fred 1903, 04
McFarland, Earl 1964, 66
McFarlane, Bob 1946
McGovern, Brian 1985, 86
McGuinness, Charles 1927
McIntyre, Joe 1951, 53
McKenzie, Dan 1964, 65
McKeown, Mick 1956
McMillin, James 1935, 37
McNeill, Manford 1947
McRory, Ed 1959
Mead, Mark 1984, 85
Mezincescu, Edward 1996
Menefee, John 1980
Michaelson, Victor 1938, 40
Mickelson, Bill 1971, 73
Millar, Mitch 1976, 77
Millar, Norm 1974, 75
Miller, Brian 1968, 70
Miller, Erik 1995, 96
Miller, Ernie 1943
Miller, Lee 1982, 83
Miller, Mark 1977, 79
Miller, Owen 1950
Miller, William 1976, 77
Mills, John 1961
Mills, Tom 1963, 64
Minas, Matt 1990, 93
Mitchell, Fred 1948
Mjorud, Herb 1931, 33
Moch, Bob 1935, 36
Moch, Bob 1967, 68
Moen, Dick 1964, 65
Mohr, George 1909
Molitor, Michael 1989
Monte, Daniel 1978, 79
Moore, Bud 1953, 54
Moore, Chris 1988, 89
Moore, Ed 1934
Moran, Dennis 1985, 86
Morcom, Herb 1925
Morgan, Allen 1947, 50
Morgan, Joe 1912
Morgan, Mike 1975
Morris, Don 1929, 31
Morris, Roger 1935, 37
Morry, George 1935
Mortensen, Art 1943
Moses, Bruce 1985, 87
Mulligan, Sean 1997, 98, 99
Munn, Scott 1990, 91, 93
Murphy, George 1921, 22
Murphy, Virgil 1922
Murray, Bob 1937, 39

N

Naden, Charles 1977
Naden, George 1973, 75
Nagler, Russ 1919, 21
Neal, David 1984, 86
Nederlee, Louis 1920, 21
Neil, Doug 1968
Neill, Bill 1940, 41
Nesbit, Dave 1985, 86
Ness, Ken 1964
Newton, Chuck 1916,17
Nicol, Gorham 1959, 61
Noble, Charles 1931, 32
Nommensen, Gene 1955
Nord, Swan 1920
Nordstrom, John 1957, 58
Norelius, Jon 1984, 86
Norelius, Mark 1972, 74
Northfield, Walt 1919
Norton, John 1984
Nukker, Greg 1970, 71

O

Oates, Kenneth 1984, 85
O'Brien, F.L. 1907, 09
O'Connel, Pat 1983
Odell, Dick 1929, 30
Oistad, George 1928

Olason, Mark 1974, 76
Olmstead, Joel 1927, 28
O'Neal, Arthur 1908, 09
Olsen, Scott 1984
Olson, Rich 1970
Ormond, Pat 1997, 99
Orr, Paul 1928, 29
Orvald, Tucker 1987
Osterman, Garth 1992

P

Panasik, Sasha 1992, 94
Parker, Ross 1975, 77
Parker, Tony 1978
Parkins, Wright 1922, 23
Parrott, Gordon 1931, 33
Parsons, Rich 1996
Paterson, Bruce 1990, 92
Patterson, Brendan 2000
Payne, Bob 1943, 46
Pearce, Bill 1974
Pederson, Mike 1978, 79
Pengelly, Mark 1995, 97
Peters, Bradley 1986, 88
Peterson, Mark 1979, 80
Phillips, Acton 1929, 31
Phillips, Dwight 1969, 71
Phillips, Gene 1958
Pickles, Mike 1986, 88
Pierce, Richard 1985
Pitlick, Bill 1965, 66
Pocock, Stan 1947
Popp, Derek 1989, 91
Powell, Glenn 1984
Pugel, Chris 1983, 84
Pugel, Jim 1979, 80
Pullen, Dan 1903, 05
Pullen, Royal 1910,12
Purnell, Dave 1954, 56
Putman, Mark 1978, 79
Putnam, Roy 1949
Putyrae, Glenn 1993

Q

Quast, Tom 1925, 27
Querubin, Dave 1983
Quinney, Paul 1976, 78

R

Raaum, Scott 1973
Rademacher, Scott 1993
Raney, Fred 1959, 61
Raney, Walter 1933, 35
Rantz, Joe 1935, 37
Rawson, James 1996, 97
Reese, Dave 1972, 74
Reese, Karl 1930
Reisinger, Brett 1996, 98
Rhein, Dirck 1984, 85
Richardson, Otis 1919
Richardson, Robert 1989
Riely, Keith 1952, 54
Roberts, John 1974
Robinson, Rick 1977
Roderick, Dave 1942
Roegner, Kevin 1985
Roesch, Dwight 1973, 75
Rogers, Bob 1955
Rogge, Dan (Edgar) 1996
Rose, Clyde 1914
Rosenkranz, John 1937, 38
Rosequist, Craig 1974
Rossi, Al 1952, 53
Roys, Tom 1985
Rudolph, Chad 1969, 70
Ruggers, Will 1912
Runstad, Jon 1962, 64
Ruthford, Chas 1970, 72

S

Sabo, Steve 1976
Sadler, George 1907
Sanford, Harrison 1924, 26
Sawyer, Mark 1976, 78
Sayre, John 1958
Scales, Don 1976, 78
Schacht, Bud 1935, 36
Schafer, Jamie 1985, 87
Schenck, Earl 1937, 38
Schmaltz, Chris 1995
Schmidt, Henry 1929, 31
Schmidt, Henry 1959, 61
Schneider, Marc 1993
Schoch, Delos 1935, 37
Schoch, Fred 1971, 73
Schock, Brad 1981
Schoel, Loren 1930, 32
Schostak, Matthew 1995, 97
Schluter, Chuck 1967
Schneider, Marc 1994, 95
Schocken, Kara 1994, 95
Schoenberg, Kris 1975, 77, 78
Schoettler, Bob 1928
Schroeder, Carl 1942
Schumacher, Hal 1914
Schwabland, George 1913
Schwartz, Robert 1982
Scott, Jason 1993
Scott, Myron 1927
Seelye, Les 1992
Seifred, Jeff 1992, 93
Sereiva Kestas 1992, 93, 94,96
Sewell, George 1983, 84
Sexton, Larry 1913
Shapiro, Dan 1999
Shaw, Frank 1927
Shaw, Sam 1921, 23
Shepherd, Robert 1987, 89
Shinbo, James 1978, 79
Shinbo, Roberta 1989
Shindler, Dick 1963, 64
Shotwell, Lyman 1910
Silver, Mitchell 1978
Simdars, Paul 1940, 41
Simmons, Preston 1978
Sjaastad, Erik 1994, 95
Skibeness, Al 1922
Slemmons, Wilbert 1917
Smith, Bob 1955
Smith, Craig 1970
Smith, Curt 1955
Smith, David 1994
Smith, Newton 1911
Smith, Steve 1974, 76
Snider, Robert 1933, 35
Snody, James 1983, 84
Snyder, Lani 1994, 95
Soli, Wally 1943
Sommersett, John 1911
Sonju, Norm 1925, 27
Soules, Paul 1939, 40
Spuhn, Fred 1922, 24
Starace, Brent 1996, 97
Steinman, Denny 1974
Stevens, Thomas 1985, 86
Still, Ross 1985
Stillings, John 1977, 78
Stocker, Al 1953, 55
Stoll, Fred 1955, 56
Stromberg, Gage, III 1986, 88
Stuart, Evan 1997, 99
Sundquist, Arthur 1990
Suni, Pete 1971, 73
Svendsen, Bob 1958, 59
Sykes, Colin 1990, 92

T

Taylor, Ed 1912,13
Taylor, Jeffrey 1988, 89
Taylor, Tom 1941, 42
Teather, Mike 1984, 85
Tennesen, David 1973
Thomas, Bob 1955
Thomas, Brad 1968, 70
Thomas, Orwin 1940
Thompson, Dave 1946, 47
Thompson, Dick 1971
Thompson, Don 1938, 40
Thompson, Linc 1983, 84
Thompson, Rex 1970, 71
Thomsen, Ev 1908, 09
Thomsen, Steve 1983, 84
Thomson, Steve 1973, 75
Thorstensen, Bob 1955, 56
Tiedje, Henry 1910,11
Tilten, Guy 1905
Tiomarsh, Pat 1922, 23
Todd, Steve 1997, 98, 99
Towner, Joe 1980
Tuller, Mark 1978
Tupper, Jim 1946, 47
Turay, Norm 1937, 38
Tyler, Andrew 1995, 97
Tzeng, Richard 1996

U

Ulbrickson, Al Sr. 1924, 25, 26
Ulbrickson, Al Jr. 1950, 52
Ulbrickson, Ed 1932
Umlauf, Mark 1975, 77
Umlauf, Robert 1977, 78
Underwood, Julian 1994

Urback, Steve 1975, 76
Urness, Mike 1989, 91

V

Valentine, Jack 1928
Valentine, Stan 1928, 29
Vanbronkhorst, T. 1972, 74
Van Kurhan, Carl 1903, 04
Van Pelt, Charles 1981, 83
Van Schalkwyk, Mark 1985
Vekved, Tim 1987, 89
Venema, Ben 1992
Vernon, Trevor 1992
Viereck, Mike 1968, 70
Vigil, Peter 1986, 88
Vincent, Bob 1940
Voris, Don 1953, 56
Vynne, John 1964

W

Wager, Brian 1960, 61
Wagner, Dana 1975
Wahlstrom, Dick 1952, 53
Wahnsiedler, Alexander 2000
Wailes, Ron 1927, 28
Wailes, Ron, Jr. 1955, 56
Waiss, George 1950
Walker, Bill 1978
Walker, Dee 1970
Walker, John 1987, 89
Wallace, Howie 1966, 68
Wallace, Walt 1941, 42
Waller, Hal 1911,13, 15
Walling, Dow 1923, 25
Walske, Max 1913,14, 16
Walters, Ken 1949, 51
Wand, Walter 1910,11
Ward, Art 1915
Washburn, Wilbur 1933, 34
Waters, Wayne 1955, 56
Watne, Eric 1979, 81
Weight, Mike 1975
Wells, Chris 1974, 76
Welsh, Tim 1979, 80
Wescott, Robert 1938
Westlund, Warren 1947, 50
Wetter, Doug 1955, 56
White, Bob 1933, 35
White, Dave 1969, 71
White, Dave 1992, 94
White, John 1936, 38
Whitney, Karey 1917
Wiberg, Rich 1960, 61
Wilcox, John 1959, 61
Wilkey, Doug 1966, 68
Will, Bob 1948, 49
Will, Clark 1912, 15
Will, Rolfe 1978
Williamson, Don 1931, 32
Willis, Hart 1907, 09
Willite, Harold 1943
Willits, Hal 1943
Wilson, Gregg 1932
Wingard, Phil 1986, 88
Winston, Tim 1978
Witter, Bob 1952, 53
Wohlmacher, Bill 1927, 28
Wolfkill, Ron 1960, 61
Works, Bill 1946, 48
Wright, Larry 1912
Wright, Newell 1912
Wunsch, John 1979
Wuthenow, Art 1925, 26
Wyckoff, Hal 1909,10

Y

Yantis, Dick 1940
Yasutake, Keith 1978, 80
Yeung, Andrew 2000
York, John 1935, 37
Young, Bob 1947, 50
Yount, Paul 1990, 92

Z

Zevenbergen, Dave 1982, 84
Zevenbergen, John 1979, 81
Zimmerman, Hank 1913,15

Women's Crew

A

Achterman, Peg 1981, 82
Alba, Katherine 1991, 93
Anderson, Noelle 1998, 99, 2000
Arnold, Merideth 1992, 94
Athmann, Lynn 1980, 81
Armstrong, Alisa 1985
Armstrong, Lynn 1979, 80

B

Bailey, Betsy 1987, 88
Baker, Denise 1984, 86
Baker, Julie 1982, 83
Baptist, Ruth 1986
Barber, Maili 2000
Barnes, Hope 1977
Bascom, Ellen 1976, 77
Batcheller, Gretchen 1997
Bates, Colleen (Mgr.) 1993
Bates, Jennifer 1990
Beal, Sue 1977
Becht, Erin 1999, 2000
Beluche, Lisa 1986, 88
Biles, Cindy 1986, 87
Bingham, Jennie 1997
Black, Lisa 1977
Bolland, Kristen 1976
Bolz, Laura 1984, 85
Boone, Karen 1986, 88
Borges, Nicole 1998, 99, 2000
Bowers, Amy 1985
Brakke, Laura Leigh 1976, 77
Branesky, Calista 1999
Bray, Paula 1988
Brillon, Alicia 1987, 89
Broadie, Jody 1994, 96
Broome, Susan 1980, 82
Bucko, Jeanne 1984
Bulger, Jeanne 1977, 80
Bulger, Kathy 1976, 78

C

Campbell, Chris 1984, 86
Campbell, Tiffany 1989
Carbonotto, Angella 1977
Carlson, Karin 1989
Cate, Margie 1982
Cerny, Michelle 1985, 86
Chadwick, Becca 1994
Chan, Michelle 1989, 91
Christie, Annie 1997, 98
Clare, Mary Anne 1997
Clark, Jane Louise 1976, 78
Clark, Jane 1979
Cockrell, Kay 1977, 78
Colin, Kathy 1994
Collins, Missy 1998, 99
Cook, Elizabeth 1989
Cox, Linda 1976, 78
Crabtree, Tara 1999
Craig, Penny 1971
Crescenzi, Lynda 1990, 92
Crowell, Liz 1986, 87
Crymes, Kristin 1997, 98
Cullen, Helen 1987, 88

D

Dariusova, Hana 1992, 95
Dauphiny, Lori 1984
Davis, Karen (Mgr.) 1985
Dezwager, Karol 1986
Dicke, Karen 1990, 91
Dion, Laurie 1979, 80
Dorf, Gail 1986, 88
Dotson, Christine 1985, 87
Doyle, Stephanie 1987, 89
Dreyer Sheryl (Mgr.) 1976
Drumheller, Lisa 1978
Dumond, Valerie 1989
Duncan, Jill 1980, 81
Dunnet, Katy 1996, 97, 98, 99
Dunnet, Rachel 1997, 98, 99

E

Ellzey, Sharon 1981, 82
Elmberg, Kari 1986
English, Rachel 1987
Esterly, Jill 1980, 81
Estevenin, Lauren 2000

F

Fairchild, Rebecca 1976, 79
Finholm, Gretchen 1986
Finnigan, Michelle 1987
Fisher, Alice 1984
Flint, Andrea 1979, 80
Fong, Ramona 1997
Freeland, Denby 1992, 93
Freeman, Margaret 1991
Fullerton, Candace 1983
Fulton, Janise 1982, 83

G

Gardner, Julie 1985, 87
Gawley, Cherie 1984, 85
Geary, Maura 1993, 94
Geyser, Adriana 1998, 99, 2000
Gillespie, Megan 1992, 93
Gilliland, Anne Marie 1986, 87
Glick, Tristine 1995, 97
Godwin, Karla 1978, 81
Graham, Rachel 1989
Graves, Gayle 1978, 79
Gray, Tasya 1997, 98
Green, Kari 1996, 98
Grevstad, Fritzi 1987, 89
Guerrero, Melissa 1999
Guyot, Denise 1984, 85

H

Haines, Stephanie 1987, 89
Hamano, Leona 1992
Hamlin, Kathy 1978, 79, 81
Hanson, Madeline 1980, 82
Harder, Anna 1986
Hartman, Mary 1979, 80
Hearing, Tracy 1981
Helde, Carolyn 1989
Helenius, Tina 1988, 89
Henderson, Alice 1985, 87
Hendrie, Liese 1983, 85
Herner, Jennifer 1991
Helsell, Alexa 2000
Hessburg, Anne 2000
Holzrichter, Kim 1991
Hook, Heidi 1987
Horn, Lisa 1981, 82
Horton, Kelly 1996, 98
Horton, Lindsey 1998, 99, 2000
Hou, Anne Marie 1987
Howard, Joslyn 1994, 95
Hunt, Mary 1987
Hunter, Adrienne 2000
Hurn, Heidi 2000

I

Irvine, Linda 1986, 87
Iverson, Mary 1989

J

Jackson, Laura 1978, 79
Jacobson, Cara 1992
Janzik, Kim 1992
Jay, Julianne 1992
Jones, Julianna 1979
Jones, Stacey 1989, 90
Jozaitis, Anne 1986

K

Kalina, Lynn 1984, 86
Kasinger, Mary 1985
Kast, Cheryl 1976, 77
Kauth, Jennifer 1986
Keesee, Tracey 1988
Kielska, Basia 1999
King, Maureen 1983
Klinefelter, Kristina 1985
Kneip, Cynthia 1985, 87
Koehler, Trish 1990
Kosovich, Wendy 1994
Kronlof, Monica 1981, 82
Krumm, Zoe 1993

L

Lake, Carol 1977, 78
Lawson, Samantha 1991
Leppink, Nancy 1981
Lueck, Dianne 1990, 92
Lueck, Susie 1990, 92
Liu, Pauline 1986, 87
Lusk, Linda 1985, 87
Lydon, Patricia 1985, 87

M

Magnuson, Marilyn 1979, 80
Maloney, Katie 1994, 96
Manipon, Sue Ann 1987, 88
Marcotte, Nichole 1992, 93
Martin, Shauna 1986
Mayer, Debora 1979
Mayer, Elizabeth 1978, 79
McBride, Julie 1986, 88
McDonald, Molly 1979
McDougall, Jane 1980, 82
McDougall, Laura 1976, 77
McElvaine, Eleanor (Mgr.) 1983, 85
86
McLauchlan, Alina 1998
McNally, Stephanie 1993
McNamara, Romany 1999, 2000
McPherson, Janet 1976, 77
Mendoza, Bernadette 1985, 86
Merriman, Shelley 1987
Michalson, Laraine 1976
Mickelson, Anna 1999, 2000
Misterek, Cindy 1987
Mitchell, Barbara 1976
Miller, Lisa 1978, 80
Miller, Martha 1981
Mohling, Karen 1981, 83
Monroe, Ramona 1986
Moore, Debbie 1981, 82
Moore, Kathleen 1981, 82
Moscrip, Amy 1992
Moss, Siri 1976
Munn, Stacy 1986
Munson, Andrea 1985

N

Nessler, Denni 1996, 98
Nevin, Sara 1983, 85
Nicoloff, Jennifer 1994
Nilles, Paige 1984
Norelius, Kristi 1981, 82
Nygren-Birkholz,
Theresa 1997, 98, 99,
2000
Nykreim, Kara 1999, 2000

O

Oates, Kimberly 2000
Oates, Shannon 2000
O'Brien, Wendy 1990, 92
O'Connell, Erin 1994, 96
Ockenden, Trudy 1986, 88
Odegaard, Kristin 1987
O'Neill, Kerry 1986, 87
O'Steen, Shyril 1980, 81
Osterhaug, Karin 1991, 93

P

Park, Ellen 1993, 95
Patterson, Trista, 1993, 94
Patton, Carolyn 1976
Pemberton, Sandra 1985
Petersen, Erin 1991, 93
Pfunder, Paige 1998, 99
Pheasant, Joann (Mgr.) 1976
Pierce, Marina 1985, 86
Piper, Amy 1994, 95
Popovice, Anna Maria 1987
Pottmeyer, Ellen 1981, 83
Pottmeyer, Susan 1984, 85
Powers, Jane 1984, 85
Pugel, Ann 1993
Purves, Alida 1997

R

Ramirez, Cindy 1995
Rattan, Leslie 2000
Rider, Jill 1985, 86
Rider, Megan 1993, 94
Rochester, Lucy 1976
Rogers, Julia 1988, 90
Roger, Nicole 1998, 99, 2000
Roling, Anne 1992, 94
Rose, Kasey 1989, 90
Rosenberg, Trisha 1999
Rousso, Kathryn 1978, 79
Rubbright, Keo 1990, 92

S

Sanford, Kristen 1986, 88
Schueler, Gail 1976
Schueler, Diane 1977, 78
Schwab, Erica 1993, 95
Schwankl, Judy 1977, 78
Scott, Ingrid 1986, 87
Seay, Meagan 1997, 98, 99,
2000
Shaver, Julie 1985, 86
Shaw, Sarah 1987, 88
Shemeta, Julie 1983
Siebold, Babette 1993, 95
Silrum, Mary 1980
Slehofer, Lori 1979, 81
Small, Marian 1976
Smart, Jo 1976
Smith, Laura 1983
Smith, Loren 1982, 83
Smith, Michelle 1996
Smith, Suzanne 1976, 77
Snow, Jonell 1997

Solem, Karen	1991, 92
Solmssen, Jennifer	1988
Spangler, Tara	1986
Spencer, Pasha	1994, 95
Steed, Teresa	1976, 77
Steele, Katie	1987, 89
Steele, Lora	1999, 2000
Steinkerchner, Denise	1986
Stewart, Brooke	1993, 94
Stewart, Gail	1984
Stingl, Kristi	1984, 86
Stoertz, Mary	1978, 79
Storey, Susan	1981
Stasiak, Carrie	2000
Strazer, Mary	1999, 2000
Sumner, Tiffani	1996, 97, 98, 99

T

Tavalero, Vanessa	1997, 98, 99, 2000
Telenska, Sabina	1997, 98, 99, 2000
Thoenig, Lucia	1993, 94
Tilmanis, Lara	1998, 99, 2000
Tuttle, Liz	1993, 95
Tylee, Kate	1997, 98, 99
Tyler, Kathleen	1979, 80

V

Van Deusen, Christie	1989
Van Pelt, Christine	1986, 88
Van Pelt, Rachael	1990, 92
Velling, Marisa	1981, 83
Vesnaver, Jenni	1999, 2000

W

Wahlstrom, Rebecca	1994
Walker, Sharon	1980
Watson, Sarah	1986, 88
Wheeler, Jennifer	1987
Whipple, Mary	1999, 2000
White, Ardath	1994, 96
White, Liz	1983, 84
Wilcox, Amanda	1993, 95
Wikstrom, Katarina	1987, 88
Williamson, Jan	1997, 98, 99
Wilson, Cynthia	1976, 79
Winters, Jenny (Mgr.)	1984, 86, 87
Winters, Susan	1981, 83

Y

Yamaura, DeAn	1986
Young, Heidi	1993, 95
Youngberg, Carrie	1994, 96

Z

Ziegler, Birgit	1984, 85
Ziobron, Cynthia	1976

Men's Cross Country

A

Albright, Richard	1969, 70, 71, 72
Alexander, Sam	1993, 94, 95
Anderson, Keith	1970, 71, 72
Anderson, Shawn	1988, 89, 90, 91
Anderson, Steve	1992
Atchison, Gary	1968

B

Baines, Simon	1993
Bannick, William Jr.	1967
Barajaz, George	1991, 92, 93
Barnett, Dave	1980, 81,82, 83
Barr, Graham	1973, 74, 75
Bazzi, David	1996, 97, 98, 99
Bell, Dan	1983, 84, 85, 86
Belz, Christian	1996, 97, 98
Bigler, Josh	1996
Bookey, Michael	1967
Bradbury, Dale	1976, 77
Brandon, Robert	1969, 71, 72
Braun, Gordon	1973, 74, 75, 76
Bronn, Gregg	1987, 89
Bullock, Hugh	1969

C

Carroll, Pat	1979, 80
Celms, John	1967
Chaffin, James	1970
Charouhas, Tom	1975, 76
Chisholm, Neil	1997
Conner, Richard	1989
Coombs, Mike	1982
Corvin, Curt	1983, 84, 85, 86
Crowell, Robert	1971

D

Davies, John	1969
Day, James	1997, 98
Dodd, Charles	1969
Donnelly, Matt	1985, 87, 88
Duke, Dustin	1999

E

Eichenberger, Paul	1977, 79
Ellison, Aaron	1984, 85, 86
Ewing, Pat	1979, 81, 82

F

Fahlman, Eric	1984
Fayant, Jason	1999
Flanagan, Kevin	1986
Flynn, Devon	1975, 76
Fovell, Peter	1976, 77
Fulton, Jeff	1967

G

Gibson, Greg	1972, 73
Glad, William	1972, 73, 74, 75
Gordon, Gavin	1982
Green, Jeffrey	1989, 90
Grote, Ryan	1993
Gustafson, Gary	1975, 76, 77, 78

H

Hallenback, Mark	1976, 77, 78, 79
Hann, Michael	1969
Hanson, Neil	1994, 95
Hardenback, Daniel	1988
Harkins, Paul	1996, 97, 98, 99
Hatzenbeler, Steve	1995
Hawkins, Lawren	1989, 91
Herbert, Alan	1972
Hildrum, Tom	1996, 97, 98, 99
Hill, Michael	1997, 98
Hilton, Daniel	1995, 96
Hjort, Alan	1988, 89
Holmes, Scott	1975
Hord, Michael	1999
Hughes, David	1991, 92, 93
Hunter, Darren	1992, 93, 94
Hutchinson, Jim	1981

I

Ihmels, Doug	1985, 86

J

Johnson, Eric	1996
Johnson, James	1969, 70
Johnson, Patrick	1988, 89, 90
Johnston, Colin	1994, 95
Jones, Greg	1983
Jordan, Tim	1970

K

Kindred, Steve	1990, 91
Kirkendall, Mike	1992
Knable, Ken	1981, 82, 83
Koch, Scott	1992, 93
Koss, William	1968, 69, 70

L

Leahy, Adam	1989, 90
Ledford, Chris	1996, 97
Lermusik, John	1979, 80, 81
Lucas, Mike	1982, 84, 85

M

MacCluer, Gavin	1995, 96
Mayer, Robert	1980
McClement, Bill	1977
McClement, Bob	1980, 81
McDowell, Robert	1985, 86, 87, 88
McKay, James, Jr.	1988, 89, 90, 91
Mesmer, Richard	1967
Metcalf, Greg	1990, 91
Minnis, Tyrone	1995
Morgan, Matt	1978
Munroe, Jeff	1993
Murray, Tim	1975, 76

N

Naesheim, Atle	1987, 88
Nelson, Kirk	1991
Newton, Brice	1994, 95, 96, 97

P

Panchen, Neil	1991, 92
Pavach, Nick	1991, 92, 94, 95
Pearson, Matthew	1996, 97
Perry, Geoffrey	1997, 98, 99
Piccillo, Mark	1976
Poole, Daniel	1968
Reid, Scott	1978
Reinke, Jim	1983, 84, 85, 86
Rickey, Paul	1997
Roe, Lawrence	1987, 89, 90
Russell, John	1999

R

Rickey, Paul	1998
Rucker, James	1998
Russell, John	1999

S

Schruth, Daniel	1998, 99
Schruth, David	1997, 98, 99
Schultz, James	1968
Scott, David	1967, 68
Shouman, Stormy	1987, 89
Smart, William	1967, 68, 69
Spangler, Kirk	1977
Stirling, Bruce	1982, 83, 84, 86
Stolp, Bill	1976, 77, 78, 79
Stonkus, Arny	1976
Surface, Steve	1973, 74, 75, 76

T

Thompson, Morgan	1999
Tolleson, Mike	1972, 73
Tungate, Paul	1968
Villani, Chris	1977

W

Webster, Rob	1981, 82
Welch, Doug	1984, 86
Williams, Simon	1987
Winger, Dan	1972, 73
Wyman, Andy	1992, 93, 94

Z

Zajac, Brad	1990, 91, 94

Women's Cross Country

A

Adams, Kathy	1977, 78, 79, 80
Aoki, Anna	1996, 97, 98, 99
Arceo, Regina	1988
Arreola, Eleanor	1984
Austin, Rachel	1993

B

Blake, Hilary	1991, 92
Bolender, Sarah	1985, 86, 87
Borgerson, Liv	1991
Bowles, Shannon	1993, 95
Bradshaw, Kate	1999
Brayton, Joelle	1992, 93, 94, 95
Buckley, Leanne	1981, 82
Buresh, Michele	1988, 89
Burns, Samantha	1995, 96
Butler, Margaret	1996, 97, 98, 99

C

Campbell, Melinda	1999
Carlson, Tara	1992, 93, 94, 95
Cassidy, Debbie	1980, 81
Coleman, Deanne	1980
Coulson, Sarah	1982
Cronin, Mary	1977

D

Dong, Mary	1987
Downey, Heidi	1989, 90
Draughon, Jennifer	1988, 89
Duryee, Diana	1984

E

English, Elizabeth	1997, 98
Eskesen, Staci	1997
Evans, Brandi	1988, 89, 92

F

Felix, Debra	1984
Flora, Amy	1995
Foianini, Ashley	1997, 98, 99
Froese, Angela	1994, 95, 96, 97
Frosch, Leslie	1974
Funk, Lara	1993

G

Gillette, Jennifer	1986, 87, 88, 89
Gregg, Sandra	1979, 80, 81, 82
Gregg, Susan	1979, 80, 81, 82

H

Hansen, Leischan	1984
Heusser, Shannon	1992, 94
Hoitink, Stacie	1989, 90, 91, 92
Howard, Anne	1989, 90
Howe, Kristen	1998

I

Ichikawa, Laura	1985, 86
Inman, Courtney	1998

J

Johnson, Emily	1992, 93, 94, 95
Johnson, Lynde	1996, 97
Jones, Alicia	1974
Joyce, Regina	1980, 81, 82

K

Kabush, Danelle	1996, 97
Keramen, Eeva	1976, 77, 78
King, Amy	1998
Knutson, Kiersten	1987
Kriz, Aimee	1991, 92, 93

L

Liebsack, Stacy	1988
Lindgren, Sara	1983, 84
Lorvick, Adrianne	1982, 83, 84, 85

M

Malm, Katherine	1991, 94, 95
Matson, Camissa	1998, 99
McVicker, Aimee	1990
Meagher, Vicki	1978, 80, 81
Minelli, Lia	1993, 94, 95, 96
Moller, Carrie	1990, 91
Morales, Carrie	1993
Moulijn, Marjan	1976, 77, 78, 79
Mullen, Emily	1999

N

Neil, Sara	1978

O

Ocken, Suzanne	1989, 90

P

Peterson, Janicka	1987, 88, 90
Petley, Karen	1980, 81, 82
Prentice, Jennifer	1984

R

Ragland, Jane	1996
Reese, Jennifer	1988, 89, 90, 91
Richard, Kristy	1991
Riley, Dana	1985
Riley, Elizabeth	1992, 93
Roetman, Rainey	1976, 77, 78, 79
Rose, Amy	1997, 98

S

Samuelson, Justelle	1994, 95
Schibig, Louise	1979
Schindler, Jen	1999
Shierk, Lia	1986
Smalley, Jennifer	1988, 89, 90
Smith, Jennifer	1998
Snyder, Julia	1984, 85
Stocker, Val	1987, 89
Swanson, Michelle	1984, 86
Syrdal, Kara	1997, 98, 99

T

Taft, Ann	1976, 77, 78, 79
Tangren, Stacy	1981, 83
Thiel, Lynn	1981
Thome, Aleah	1998

U

Urrutia, Carlene	1986, 87

V

Vanderwilde, Heidi	1985

W

Waiss, Theresa	1985
Werner, Susan	1998, 99
Williams, Heidi	1985, 86
Winney, Terry	1977, 78, 79

Y

Youngquist, Deeja 1995, 96, 97, 98

Z

Zamberlin, Mary 1984

Football

A

Abel, Bob 1919, 20
Abel, Don 1914,16
Abel, Fred 1922, 23
Able, George 1914
Agen, Dan 1983, 84, 85
Aguirre, Dick 1959, 60
Ahonen, Art 1932, 33, 34
Akbar, Hakim 1998, 99
Akina, Duane 1976, 77, 78
Akins, Al 1943
Albrecht, Ben 1970, 71, 72
Albrecht, Bill 1951, 52, 54
Albritton, Vince 1981, 82, 83
Aleaga, Ink 1994, 95, 96
Alkire, Andy 1960, 61, 62
Allen, Anthony 1979, 80, 81, 82
Allen, Cal 1969
Allen, Charles 1958, 59, 60
Allen, John 1983, 84
Allman, Mike 1987, 88
Alozie, Eric 1989
Alvarado, Tony 1980, 82, 83
Alvord, Steve 1984, 85, 86
Ames, Bill 1986 87, 88
Ames, Floyd 1906
Andersen, Hjalmer 1946, 47
Anderson, Bob 1966, 67, 68
Anderson, Herman 1911,12,13,14
Anderson, James 1973, 74, 75
Anderson, John 1999
Anderson, Johnny 1987
Anderson, Oscar 1971
Anderson, Steve 1971
Andre, Phil 1971, 72
Andrews, George 1894
Andrews, Ricky 1985, 86, 87, 88
Andrilenas, Jim 1971, 73
Antoncich, Mark 1932
Antoncich, Pete 1931, 32
Apking, Fritz 1949, 50
Apostle, Tony 1971
Armstrong, Don 1956, 57, 58
Arnason, Hal 1945
Arnold, Paul 1999
Arrivey, Pete 1953, 54
Aselin, Jeff 1994
Ask, Scott 1998
Attridge, Arthur 1896
Austin, Everett 1935, 36, 37
Austin, Gerry 1942, 43, 46, 47
Austin, Mijo, 1997, 98, 99

B

Babcock, Frank 1904, 05, 08
Bagshaw, Enoch 1903, 04, 05, 06, 07
Bailey, Bruce 1991, 92
Bailey, Cary 1981
Bailey, Mario 1989, 90, 91
Bailey, Walter 1990, 91, 92
Baker 1909
Balchunas, Tony 1942, 43
Baldassin, Mike 1974, 75, 76
Baldwin, Kenny 1983
Ballenger, Ken 1967, 68, 69
Bantz, Burwell 1905, 06, 07, 08
Barber, Rich 1984
Barmon, Jack 1942
Barnes, Bill 1964, 65, 66
Barrett Robert 1941
Barry, Damon 1991, 92
Barry, Jay 1989, 90, 91, 92
Bates, Bill 1928, 29
Battle, Eric 1994, 95
Baty, Rank 1969, 70
Bauer, Steve 1977, 78
Bayard, Ralph 1969, 70
Bayer, George 1946, 47, 48, 49
Bayle, David 1979, 80
Beall, Bruce 1985, 86, 87
Bean, Mike 1977
Beard, Colin 1998
Bearden, Garland 1984
Beaupain, Brooks 1994, 95, 96
Bechtol, Chuck 1937, 38, 39
Beck, Bill 1922, 23
Beck, Broussais 1907
Beckett, Hugh 1924, 25
Beckett, Welton 1926
Bell, Curtis 1987
Bell, Joe 1969, 70
Bellman, Verne 1922, 23, 24
Belmondo, Dave 1975
Benn, Kyle 1998, 99
Bennett, Steve 1997
Berg, Bob 1967, 68, 69
Berg, Elmer 1940, 41
Bergh, Arne 1951, 52, 53
Bergmann, Marv 1957
Berlin, Gordon 1943, 44, 46, 47
Bernhardi, Lee 1961, 62
Bertheau, Rene 1956, 57
Bethea, Cliff 1977
Beuch, William 1944
Bevandich, Louis 1945
Beymer, Jim 1965
Bianchini, Paul 1974, 75
Bibbs, Dwight 1994
Biddle, Brooks 1946 47, 48
Binkley, Jesse 1995, 96
Bird, Harry 1938, 39
Bjornson, Eric 1991, 92, 93, 94
Black, George 1951, 52, 53
Black, John 1921
Blacken, Ron 1978, 79, 80
Blake, Beull 1917,19
Blanche, Sam 1999
Blanks, Harvey 1967, 68
Bledsoe, Clarence 1930, 31
Bledsoe, Mac 1965, 66, 67
Bliss, Bernard 1911,12,13
Boggs, Ralph 1906
Bohart, Milt 1951, 52, 53
Bonamy, Douglas 1925, 26, 27
Bond, Chuck 1934, 35, 36
Bond, Chuck 1963
Bond, Randall 1935
Bonner, Glen 1972, 73
Bonwell, Tony 1971, 72
Borden, Fred 1931, 32
Borders, Phil 1958
Boulton, Silas 1932, 33
Boustead, Bob 1973, 74
Bowen, Joe 1927
Boyd, Neil 1949, 50, 51
Boyd, Skip 1972, 73, 74
Boyd, Stan 1956
Boyle, Glenn 1932, 33
Bracken, Joe, 1986
Brady, John 1970, 71, 72
Bragdon, Roger 1906
Bramwell, Steve 1963, 64, 65
Brandt Gary 1964, 65, 66
Brandt, Rich 1956, 57
Breda, Firmo 1936, 37, 38
Brennan, Bob 1981
Bresolin, Andy 1980, 81
Bridge, Todd 1992
Bridges, Corky 1953
Briggs, Gary 1977, 78, 79
Briggs, Mike 1961, 62, 63
Brigham, Jeremy 1995, 96, 97
Brimhall, Dennis 1971
Brinker, Dode 1904, 05
Briscoe, Eric 1987, 88, 89, 90
Brix, Egbert 1924, 25
Brix, Herman 1925, 26, 27
Brock, Lee 1967, 68, 69
Bronson, Gordy 1975
Brooke, Dean 1976
Brooks, Greg 1975, 76, 77
Brooks, Neil 1941, 42
Brose, Ted 1981, 82, 83
Brostek, Bern 1986, 87, 88, 89
Brougham, Dave 1945
Brougham, Milton 1934, 35
Brown, Bill 1985
Brown, Corey 1989
Brown, Dennis 1979, 80, 81, 82
Brown, Dennis 1986, 87, 88, 89
Brown, Reggie 1973, 74
Browning, Charlie 1962, 63, 64
Browning, Dave 1976, 77
Browning, Dean 1981, 82, 83
Brownlee, Brandy 1987
Broz, William 1927, 28, 29
Bruce, Gail 1945, 46, 47
Bruce, James 1913
Bruener, Mark 1991, 92, 93, 94
Brunell, Mark 1990, 91, 92
Bryan, James 1920, 22, 23
Bryant, Beno 1989, 90, 91, 93

Name	Years
Buck, Parker	1943
Bukland, Charlie	1971
Bufkin, Burl	1932, 34
Bulger, Ace	1968, 69, 70
Bullard, Barry	1958, 59, 60
Bullard, Tim	1960, 61
Burke, Tony	1933, 34
Burkhalter, Eugene	1987, 88, 89
Burleson, Alvin	1973, 74, 75
Burleson, Alvin, Jr.	1997
Burmeister, Bob	1969, 70
Burnett, Bill	1947, 48, 49
Burnham, Tim	1984, 85
Burnham, Tom	1979, 80, 81, 82
Burrell, Eddie	1996
Burrows, Rick	1896
Burton, Nigel	1996, 97, 98
Buse, August	1930, 31, 32
Bush, Blair	1975, 76, 77
Busz, Scott	1984, 85, 86
Butler, Hillary	1990, 91, 92, 93
Butler, Longie	1928
Butler, Ray	1920
Butler, Toure	1997, 98
Buzard, Bob	1928, 29
Bynum, Kai	1996

C

Name	Years
Cahill, Bill	1970, 71, 72
Cahill, Will	1910
Cain, Jim	1934, 35, 36
Cairney, Ralph	1930
Caldwell, Tony	1980, 81, 82
Calhoun, A.P.	1896,1900
Calkins, Julius	1916
Call, Wes	1999
Camarillo, Rich	1979, 80
Campbell, Chris	1994, 95, 96, 97
Campbell, W.M.	1900
Canton, Eric	1988
Carahan, Don	1962
Carlson, Wes	1945, 46
Carnutt, J.	1906
Carr, Gary	1964, 65
Carr, Luther	1956, 57, 58
Carroll, Andy	1997, 98, 99
Carroll, Charles	1926, 27, 28
Carrothers, Randy	1979
Carry, Gary	1969, 70
Carter, James	1979, 80, 81
Casarino, Dario	1980
Cass, Greg	1965, 66
Cattage, Ray	1980, 81, 82
Celoni, Dan	1973, 74, 75
Chambers, Dean	1951, 52, 53
Chambers, Richie	1991, 92, 93, 94
Chandler, Chris	1984, 85, 86, 87
Chandler, Jeff	1987, 88, 89
Chapman, John	1985
Chapman, Myers	1914
Chappell, Blaise	1983, 85
Chapple, Stan	1958, 59, 60
Charleston, William	1924, 25, 26
Chavira, Dan	1976, 77, 78, 79
Cheeks, Chris	1987
Chenevert, Cornelius	1974
Cherberg, John	1930, 31, 32
Chicoine, Ryan	1997
Chorak, Jason	1994, 95, 96, 97
Christenson, Tag	1943
Christie, Morris	1905
Claridge, Bruce	1956, 57, 58
Claridge, Pat	1958, 59, 60
Clark, Arthur	1906
Clark, Earl F.	1912,13
Clark, Gary	1961, 62
Clark, George	1907
Clark, John	1942
Clark, Newman	1919, 20, 21
Clark, Ron	1965
Clawson, David	1979, 80
Cleeland, Cameron	1994, 95, 96, 97
Cleland, Thane	1983, 84, 85, 86
Cleman, Braxton	1998, 99
Clifford, James	1988, 89, 91, 92
Clinton, Eddie	1932, 33
Clinton, Frank	1943
Clinton, James	1945
Cloidt, Joe	1948, 49, 50
Coats, Tony	1995, 96, 97, 98
Coby, Vince	1978, 79, 81
Coffey, Junior	1962, 63, 64
Coker, Cliff	1966, 67
Cole, Clarence	1905
Cole, David	1986
Cole, John	1924, 25
Cole, Kenneth	1923
Coleman, Fred	1994, 95, 96, 97
Coleman, Randy	1970, 71
Coles, Mike	1943
Collins, Brett	1988, 89, 90, 91
Collins, Greg	1970, 71, 72
Collins, Michael	1981, 82, 83
Compton, James	1987, 88, 89
Condon, Matt	1997
Conklin, Cary	1988, 89
Conley, Glen	1939, 40, 41
Conley, Ken	1973, 74
Connell, Kurth	1998, 99
Conniff, Pat	1997, 98, 99
Conrad, Pat	1982
Conwell, Ernie	1992, 93, 94, 95
Cook, Bill	1910
Cook, John	1989, 90
Cooke, Gene	1925, 26, 27
Cooney, Adam	1987, 88, 89, 90
Cope, Jim	1966, 67, 68
Corbet, G.H.J.	1901
Core, John	1955, 56, 57
Cornell, Bo	1968, 69, 70
Corson, H.W.	1900
Coryell, Don	1949
Cosgrove, J.G.	1900, 01
Coty, Paul	1980, 81, 82
Covington, Tony	1985, 86, 87, 88
Cowan, Tim	1980, 82
Cox, Bob	1954
Coyle, Michael	1997
Coyle, Wee	1908, 09,10,11
Crabbe, Jason	1991, 93
Craig, Alan	1969, 70, 71
Crawford, Mike	1957, 59
Crim, Owen	1903, 04, 05, 07
Cristie,	1923
Cromer, Marshall	1976, 77, 78
Crook, Stew	1952, 53, 54
Crow, Doug	1982, 83, 84
Cruver, Al	1936, 37
Cuesta, Tony	1976
Cunningham, Dan	1969, 70
Cunningham, Ed	1988, 89, 90, 91
Cunningham, Francois	1982
Cupic, Steve	1977
Curtis, Mike	1977, 80
Cushman, Tom	1915
Cutting, Judson	1924, 25, 26

D

Name	Years
Dahlquest, John	1927, 28
Dahlquist, Eric	1984
Dailey, Ervin	1917,19, 20
Dailey, Walter	1922
Dalan, Aaron	1995, 96, 97, 98
Daley, Bill	1982
Dallas, Marshall	1946, 47, 48
Daniels, Derrell	1997, 98, 99
Darden, Michael	1988
Dash, Wally	1945
Dasso, Gary	1959
Daste, Dominic	1996, 98, 99
Davidson, Ben	1959, 60
Davillier, Craig	1975
Davis, Mel	1949, 50
Davis, Nat	1955
Davis, Reggie	1995, 96, 97, 98
Davis, Wondame	1998, 99
Dawson, Dave	1996, 97, 98
Day, Dick	1955, 56, 57
Day, Mark	1969, 71
Dean, Fred	1974
Dean, Homer	1904
Dearborn, Phil	1944
DeCourcy, Keith	1944
Deeks, Don	1942, 43
DeFeo, Brenno	1981, 83, 84
DeGross, Mark	1987, 88, 89, 90
Derby, Dean	1954, 55, 56
DeRoin, Hurley	1932, 33
Derrow, Mike	1991
DeSaussure, Andre	1995, 98
Devers, Deke	1993, 94, 95
Devine, Richard	1911
Dibble, Robb	1994
Dicks, Norm	1961, 62
Diehl, Bill	1963
Diether, Louis	1909
Dillon, Corey	1996
Dillon, Dave	1965, 66
Dinish, Dave	1965
Dinish, Dom	1969
Dirks, Clarence	1927, 28
Dochow, Mike	1973

Name	Years
Doctor, William	1988, 89, 90, 91
Dodd, Mike	1990
Dodson, Lance	1981, 82, 83
Doheny, Brian	1971, 72, 73
Dominque, Tony	1983, 85
Dormaier, Phil	1982
Dorman, Harry	1912,13
Dorman, Ted	1940
Douglas, Bill	1962, 63, 64
Douglas, Bud	1935, 36, 37
Douglass, Don	1925, 26,27
Dow, Don	1979, 80, 81, 82
Downey, Darrell	1970, 72
Doyle, Pat	1987, 88
Driscoll, Ken	1979, 80, 81, 82
Dubois, Kinsley	1923, 24
Dubsky, Joe	1937, 38, 39
Duffy, E.J.	1900, 01
Duffy, Harold	1927
Dumas, Larry	1971
Dunlap, J.W.P.	1901
Dunn, Bob	1953, 54, 57
Dunn, Dick	1960
Dunn, Kenny	1949
Dunn, Roger	1964, 65
DuPree, Dave	1966, 67
Durham, Bert	1896
Dykes, Trent	1998

E

Name	Years
Eakins, Maxwell	1908, 09,10
Earl, Randy	1975
Earl, Robin	1973, 74, 75, 76
Earley, Bill	1950, 51, 52
Easton, Roy	1969, 70
Echols, Bob	1957, 58, 59
Eckmann, Ray	1919, 20, 21
Edwards, John	1976, 77
Edwards, Renard	1998, 99
Eernissee, Dan	1982, 83, 84
Eicher, Jim	1971
Elich, Pete	1951, 52, 53
Eliott, Walt	1937, 38
Elstrom, Todd	1998, 99
Elswick, Pete	1971, 72, 73
Emerson, P.A.	1990, 93
Emerson, Ralph	1938, 40
Emtman, Steve	1989, 90, 91
Enders, Dave	1970, 71, 72
England, Negley	1932, 33
Enslow, Dave	1957, 60
Erdman, Tom	1928
Erickson, Bob	1941, 42
Erickson, Bud	1935, 36, 37
Erickson, Walder	1923, 24
Erlandson, Tom	1985, 86, 97
Erving	1902
Esary, Tim	1987
Esser, Jerry	1953, 55
Etherington, Thomas	1924
Everett, Jim	1961
Ewaliko, Mike	1993, 94, 95
Ewing, Robert	1901

F

Name	Years
Failla, Tom	1968, 69, 70
Falk, Carl	1940, 41, 42
Farr, D'Marco	1991, 92, 93
Faulk, Ted	1916,19, 20
Fauria, Lance	1984
Fausset, Scott	1980, 81, 82
Feigner, Nick	1999
Feleay, Don	1975, 76
Fennema, Carl	1946, 47
Fenney, Rick	1983, 84, 85, 86
Ferguson, Al	1955, 56, 57
Ferguson, Bob	1970, 71, 72
Ferry, Ed	1921
Fiala, John	1993, 94, 95, 96
Field, F.	1899,1900
Fields, Jaime	1989, 90, 91, 92
Fink, Rob	1969
Finn, Ray	1931, 32
Fitzgerald, Scott	1987, 88
Fitzpatrick Dennis	1973, 74
Flaherty, Guy	1906, 07
Flanagan, John	1927, 28
Flannagan, Warren	1933, 34
Fleming, George	1958, 59, 60
Fleming, Ryan	1998, 99
Flewelling, Roger	1967
Flick, Tom	1979, 80
Folkins, Lee	1958, 59, 60
Ford, D.A	1889, 92
Foreman, Phil	1976, 77, 78, 79
Forsberg, Fred	1963, 64, 65
Forsyth, Harold	1906
Fortney, Shane	1994, 95, 96
Foster, Bob	1929
Foster, Pete	1946, 47
Fountaine, Jamal	1990, 91, 92, 93
Fraize, Matt	1997, 98, 99
Fraley, Chico	1988, 89, 90, 91
Franklin, Darryl	1984, 85, 86, 87
Frankowski, Ray	1939, 40, 41
Frazier, Gordon	1893, 94
Frazier, Jack	1945
Freeburger, Ralph	1894
Friedman, Bob	1940, 41, 42
Fudzie, Vince	1985
Fuimaono, Andy	1982, 85
Fuller, Brian	1999
Furnia, Ernie	1951

G

Name	Years
Gadke, Fred	1934, 35
Gaffney, Mike	1984, 85, 86
Gagliardi, Bret	1976, 77, 78, 80
Gaines, Robert	1975, 76, 77, 78
Gallagher, Tom	1991, 92, 93
Galligan, Glen	1921
Galoia, Willy	1975, 76, 77, 78
Galuska, Dick	1969, 70, 71
Garcia, Frank	1991, 92, 93, 94
Gardenhire, John	1980, 81
Gardner, Ken	1978, 79
Gardner, Osborne	1901
Gardner, Ray	1917
Garland, John	1969
Garnett, Scott	1980, 81, 82, 83
Garrett, Leon	1975,76
Garretson, Frank	1938, 39
Gaspard, Curtis	1990, 91
Gasson, Chades	1949
Gayton, Carver	1957, 58, 59
Geary, J.W.	1900
Geehan, John	1926, 27, 29
Gegner, Kurt	1958, 59, 60
Gehring, Rob	1974, 75, 76
Gellatley, Lester	1914
George, ODell	1998
Gillis, Phil	1950, 51, 52
Gilluly, James	1917
Gilmore, Robert	1944
Gipson, Ron	1976, 77, 78, 79
Given, Dick	1945
Glasgow, Nesby	1975, 76, 77, 78
Gleason, Bill	1938, 39, 40
Glenn, Harold	1919, 20
Glennon, Bill	1965, 66, 67
Gogan, Kevin	1984, 85, 86
Gorman, Don	1971, 72
Gosselin, Dan	1969, 71
Gossett, Dev	1948, 49
Goudeau, Marc	1988
Grabenhorst, Coburn	1937, 38
Grant, Ron	1977
Graves, Bob	1973, 74, 75
Green, Bud	1954
Green, Credell	1955, 56
Green, Mike	1973, 74, 75
Green, Phil	1992
Green, Roderick	1999
Greene, Danny	1980, 81, 83, 84
Greene, Hamilton	1921
Greenlaw, Scott	1992, 93, 94, 95
Greenlee, Tom	1964, 65, 66
Greenwood, Dick	1939, 40, 41
Greenwood, Scott	1975, 76, 77, 78
Gregor, William	1927, 28, 29
Gregory, Rusty	1974, 75
Griffith, Clay	1986
Griffiths, Burke	1913
Griffiths Tom	1909,10,11,12
Grimes, Greg	1977, 78, 79
Grimm, Huber	1905, 07, 09,10
Grimm, Warren	1908, 09,10,11
Grimm, William	1915,16,19, 22
Guinn, Gordy	1970, 71, 72
Gundlach, W.	1921
Guttormsen, George	1924, 25, 26

H

Name	Years
Habib, Brian	1986, 87
Hadley, Ron	1983, 84, 85
Hagen, Dick	1943, 44, 46, 47
Hagen, Koll	1962, 63, 64
Hagen, Leslie	1944
Hahn, Frank	1954
Haines, By	1934, 35, 36
Hainsworth, Bill	1916
Hairston, Marques	1996, 97, 98, 99

Name	Years
Hairston, Russell	1992, 93, 94
Hall, Dana	1988, 89, 90, 91
Hall, Darryl	1986, 87, 88
Hall, Wayne	1921, 22, 23
Hallock, Gene	1955, 56
Halverson, Dean	1965, 66, 67
Hamer, Ken	1980
Hammon, Ira	1970
Hammond, Ben	1956
Hanley, Myron	1922, 24, 26
Hannah, Mark	1968, 69
Hansen, Trygley	1932, 33
Hanson, J.J.	1993
Hanson, Ole	1932, 33
Hanson, Travis	1990, 91, 92
Hanzlik Steve	1969
Hardy, Warren	1913
Harlow, Herb	1946, 47
Haroldson, Bill	1932
Harper, Elbert	1920, 22
Harper, P.C.	1899
Harrais, Martin	1893, 94, 96
Harrell, Bruce	1976, 77, 78, 79
Harrell, Daren	1992
Harris, Eugene	1992
Harris, Gerald	1996, 98, 99
Harris, Jason	1996, 97, 98
Harris, Jim	1967, 68, 69
Harrison, Martin	1986, 87, 88, 89
Harrison, Walt	1940, 41, 42
Hart, John	1999
Harvey, Chet	1957
Harvey, Derek	1979, 80
Hasselbach, Harold	1989
Hatch, Larry	1946, 47, 48
Hatem, Ossim	1999
Hawkins, Dajuan	1999
Hawkins, David	1986, 87, 88
Hawkins, Pedro	1973, 74, 75
Hayes, Andre	1985
Hayes, Rick	1970, 71, 73
Haynes, Hanford	1921, 22
Haynes, Lenny	1998, 99
Hazelett, Calvin	1913
Heck, Jim	1956, 57, 58
Hein, Marvin	1945
Heinrich, Don	1949, 50, 52
Heinrich, Kyle	1976, 77, 78
Heinz, Robbie	1962, 63, 64
Hemphill, Frank	1975
Hemstad, Alf	1945, 46, 47, 48
Hendricks, Willie	1973, 74
Herring, Bob	1955, 56
Hewitt, Lynn	1961, 62
Hicks, Anthony	1996, 97
Hicks, Matt	1995
Hicks, Richard	1989, 90
Highfield, Trevor	1993, 94, 95
Hill, Bill	1938
Hill, Clinie	1896, 99
Hill, Lonzell	1983, 84, 85, 86
Hill, Ray	1921, 22, 23
Hill, S.B.	1899,1900
Hill, Stewart	1981, 82, 83
Hill, Theron	1993
Hill, William	1902, 03
Hinds, Sterling	1981, 82, 83
Hinds, Steve	1963, 64, 65
Hivner, Bob	1958, 59, 60
Hobert, Billy Joe	1991
Hobi, Edwin	1920, 21
Hoffman, Chris	1996
Hoffmann, Dave	1989, 90, 91, 92
Hoffmann, Steve	1992, 94, 95
Hollimon, Terry	1994, 95
Hollowell, Alex	1996
Holmes, Alvin	1928, 29, 30
Holmes, Bill	1938, 40, 41
Holmes, Ron	1982, 83, 84
Holzgraf, Steve	1985, 86
Holzknecht, Ted	1949, 50, 51
Hooker, JaWarren	1997, 98
Hooks, Wilbur	1999
Hopkins, Hoover	1983
Hornback, Jay	1932, 33, 34
Horton, Ray	1979, 80, 81, 82
Hosack, George	1944
Hosely, Rex	1910
Hossfeld, Walt	1952
Houlihan, Barry	1972
Houston, Herman	1969
Houston, Jim	1953, 54, 55
Howard, Colin	1930, 31, 32
Hoyt, Bill	1942
Huard, Brock	1996, 97, 98
Huard, Damon	1993, 94, 95
Hudson, Ron	1966, 67
Huebel, Jack	1939, 40
Hufford, Merle	1929, 30, 31
Huget, Jeff	1966, 67, 68
Huget, Rick	1969, 70, 71
Hughes, Dave	1949, 50
Huhta, Elmer	1926, 27, 28
Hullin, Tod	1964, 65
Hultgren, Richard	1944
Hungar, Gordon	1945, 46, 47, 48
Hunt, Ray	1912,13,14,15
Hunt, Walt	1983, 84
Hunter, Art	1987, 88, 89
Huntoon, R.W.	1899,1900, 01
Hurley, Dennis	1968, 70
Hurst, Willie	1998, 99
Hurworth, Sam	1958, 59, 60
Husby, Pete	1910,11
Hutt, Brad	1997, 98
Hyatt, Gary	1986
Hyndman, Bill	1919

I

Name	Years
Ikeda, Kevin	1982
Ilsley, David	1991, 92
Ingalls, Jerry	1971
Ingram, Robert	1920, 21, 22
Isaacson, Ted	1931, 32, 33
Issa, Jabari	1996, 97, 98, 99

J

Name	Years
Jackson, Charles	1973, 74, 75, 76
Jackson, Michael	1975, 76, 77, 78
Jackson, Ray	1959, 60
Jackson, Ron	1980, 81, 83, 84
Jackson, Vestee	1983, 84, 85
Jaeger, Jeff	1983, 84, 85, 86
Jakl, Larry	1966
James, Allen	1983, 84, 85, 86
James, Chris	1980, 81, 82
James, Gary	1967, 68
Janet, Ernie	1968, 69, 70
Janoski, Dave	1993, 94, 95, 96
Janowicz, Vince	1966, 67
Jaquot, Fred	1912,13
Jarvis, Bruce	1968, 69, 70
Jarvis, Paul	1905, 06, 08
Jarzynka, Joe	1996, 97, 98, 99
Jaton, Bruce	1946
Jeager, William	1906
Jenkins, Aaron	1985, 86, 87, 88
Jenkins, Fletcher	1979, 80, 81
Jensen, Dell	1954, 55
Jensen, Jason	1990
Jensen, Jerry	1994, 95, 96, 97
Jerome, Todd	1989
Jerue, Mark	1978, 79, 80, 81
Jessup, Paul	1927, 28, 29
Johanson, Bob	1976
John-Lewis, Kelly	1987, 88
Johnson, Ching	1916
Johnson, Clifton	1979
Johnson, Devon	1999
Johnson, Dick	1935, 36, 37
Johnson, Erling	1949, 50
Johnson, Jeff	1997, 98
Johnson, Leif	1990, 91, 92, 93
Johnson, Lynn	1994, 96
Johnson, Todd	1996, 97, 98
Johnson, Tom	1986
Johnston, Jim	1936, 37, 38
Jolley, Chris	1989
Jones, Arnold	1955, 56
Jones, Brendan	1996, 98
Jones, Calvin	1970, 71, 72
Jones, Darius	1995
Jones, Don	1937, 39
Jones, Donald	1988, 89, 90, 91
Jones, Frank	1976
Jones, Jim	1955, 56, 57
Jones, Joe	1959, 60
Jones, Louis	1991, 92, 93, 94
Jones, Marc	1989
Jones, Mark	1987, 88, 89
Jones, Matt	1990, 91, 92, 93
Jones, Rod	1984, 85, 86
Jones, Scott	1985, 86, 87, 88
Jones, Steve	1986, 87, 88
Jones, Virgil	1988, 90
Jordon, Jeff	1964, 65, 66
Jorgensen, Kermit	1959, 60, 61
Jourdan, Roberto	1972, 73, 74, 75
Judd, Charles	1948
Juergens, Chris	1998, 99
Jugum, George	1966, 67, 68
Julian, Ryan	1998

K

Name	Years
Kadletz, Ben	1996, 97, 98
Kadletz, Jon	1969
Kadletz, Ryan	1994, 95
Kahn, Dan	1987
Kaligis, Pete	1991
Kaloper, Jerry	1968
Karr, Hay	1896
Kasim, Marvin	1998
Katsenes, Jim	1970
Kaufman, Napoleon	1991, 92, 93, 94
Kean, Al	1947, 48
Keely, Rick	1969
Keiaho, George	1995, 96
Keinholtz, Leon	1921
Keller, Ward	1952
Kelley, Anthony	1999
Kelly, Joe	1982, 83, 84, 85
Kelso, Al	1971, 72
Kennamer, Buddy	1968, 69
Kennan, Washington	1971, 72, 73
Kennedy, Florren	1945
Kennedy, Lincoln	1989, 90, 91, 92
Kerley, John	1976, 77, 78
Kesi, Patrick	1992, 93, 94, 95
Kesi, Petrocelli	1996, 97
Kester, Todd	1987
Keyes, Stewart	1983
Kezer, Glen	1961, 62
Killpatrick, David	1991, 92, 93, 94
Kilpack, Mark	1987, 88
Kindred, Burdette	1937, 38
King, Richard	1944, 48
King, Tracy	1950, 51, 52
King, Whitey	1946
Kinnune, Bill	1958, 59, 60
Kirk, Douglas	1925
Kirk, Jim	1965, 66
Kirkby, Roland	1948, 49, 50
Kirkland, Dean	1988, 89, 90
Kirkpatrick, James	1982, 83, 84
Kissel, Cam	1994, 95, 96
Klinge, Dick	1938
Knoll, Jerry	1962, 63, 64
Knoll, Jon	1962, 63, 64
Knopp, Brent	1999
Knowles, Robert	1944
Knudson, Roy	1917
Kohlwes, Jeff	1987, 88
Kopay, Dave	1961, 62
Kopay, Tony	1961
Kraetz, Sam	1928, 29
Krakoski, Joe	1981, 82, 83, 84
Kralik, Joe	1990, 92, 93
Kramer, Bruce	1964, 65
Kramer, Wally	1943
Kravitz, Al	1970, 71
Kreutz, Mark	1973, 74, 75
Kreutz, Olin	1995, 96, 97
Krieg, Jim	1970, 71
Kristof, Jim	1972, 73, 74
Kronfield, Harry	1917
Kroon, Bruce	1984
Kucinskas, Stan	1951, 52, 53
Kuharski, Rob	1982, 83
Kuhn, Ed	1922, 23, 24
Kupp, Jake	1961, 62, 63
Kyllingstad, Jack	1952, 53, 54

L

Name	Years
Labrousse, Dave	1976
Lacson, Alex	1995
Lambright, Eric	1984, 85
Lambright, Jim	1963, 64
Lang, Chris	1995, 98
Lang, Le-Lo	1986, 87, 88, 89
Langehorne, Clifford	1921
Langer, Jerry	1953, 54
Lansford, Mike	1978, 79
Lantz, Clinton	1902, 03
Lappenbusch, Charles	1930
Lariza, Frank	1951, 52
Larsen, Bill	1952
Larsen, Mark	1984, 85, 86
Larsen, Tom	1999
Larson, Clarence	1894, 96, 99
Larson, Leonard	1942
Lauzon, Romeo	1925, 26, 27
Lazaravich, Dan	1933, 34, 35
Leader, Ed	1912,13
Leader, Elmer	1913,14,15
Leaphart, Robert	1981, 82, 83
Lederman, Sandy	1953, 54, 55
Lee, Ken	1967, 68, 70
Lee, Kyu	1999
Lee, Mark	1977, 78, 79
Leeland, Jeff	1977, 78
Leland, Dave	1956, 57
Lenau, Jim	1938
Lenfesty, Robert	1930, 31
Lentz, Nick	1997
Levenhagen, Robert	1944, 47, 48
Lewis, Corky	1954, 55,
Lewis, Greg	1987, 88, 89, 90
Lewis, Tony	1983, 84
Libke, Al	1963, 64, 65
Lightning, Shawn	1987
Lillis, Jack	1922, 23, 24
Lindquist, Reese	1956, 57, 58
Lindsey, Jack	1896
Lindskog, Jack	1952, 53
Lindskog, Vern	1951, 52, 53
Linnin, Chris	1978, 79
Lipe, Steve	1973, 74, 75
Lloyd, Dan	1972, 73, 74, 75
Locknane, Brent	1987
Locknane, Duane	1960, 61, 62
Logg, Charles	1917
Logg, David	1915
Logg, Elmer	1934, 35, 36
Lokovsek, Leo	1950
Long, Scot	1977
Looker, Dane	1998, 99
Loomis, Scott	1971, 72
Lorentson, Elmer	1931, 32, 33
Lorrain, Vince	1965, 66
Lovelien, Bob	1968, 69, 70
Lowe, Omare	1998, 99
Lowell, Duane	1956, 57, 58
Lustyk, Mike	1989, 90, 92
Lutes, Dave	1974, 75
Lutu, Frank	1986, 87
Lutu, Leroy	1980, 82, 83
Lyons, Lamar	1991, 92, 93, 94

M

Name	Years
Macinowski, Adam	1999
Mack, Damon	1991, 92
Mackey, Willis Ray	1979
Mackie, Brent	1978
Madarieta, Levi	1999
Madsen, Lynn	1981, 82, 83
Magee, Tom	1952, 54
Maggart, Mike	1966, 67, 68
Maguire, Ernest	1910
Mahdavi, Ben	1999
Maher, Dennis	1981, 83, 84
Malamala, Siupeli	1988, 89, 90, 91
Malloe, Ikaika	1993, 94, 95, 96
Mallory, Rick	1981, 82, 83
Malone, Art	1985, 86, 87, 88
Malvar, Caesar	1989
Mancuso, Joe	1963, 65
Mangan, Jim	1950, 51
Manke, Tom	1967, 68
Mansfield, Ray	1960, 61, 62
March, Willis	1917
Marcus, Clifton	1973, 74
Markham, Tom	1915
Markov, Ted	1933, 34, 35
Markov, Vic	1935, 36, 37
Marona, Spencer	1999
Marquiss, Guy	1975
Marsh, Bill	1929, 30, 31
Marsh, Curt	1977, 78, 79, 80
Marshall, Bill	1981
Martin, Bob	1973, 74
Martin, Don	1965, 66, 67
Martin, Doug	1976, 77, 78, 79
Martin, Elmer	1930, 31
Martin, Greg	1975
Martin, Robert	1934
Marx, William	1938, 39, 40
Mason, Andy	1990, 91, 92, 93
Mathews, Jim	1985
Mathews, Robert	1907
Matronic, Carl	1936, 37
Matter, Kurt	1970, 71, 72
Mattes, Frank	1935, 36, 37
Matthews, David	1981
Matthews, Keilan	1985, 86
Mattson, William	1907, 08, 09
Matz, Mike	1986, 87, 88, 89
Maurer, Al	1969, 70
May, Charles	1909
Mayfield, Ben	1916
Mays, Shell	1991
Mays, Stafford	1978, 79
Meader, Eilert	1928
Meamber, Tim	1981, 82, 83, 84
Means, Art	1936, 37, 38
Means, Don	1939, 40, 41

Medved, Ron	1963, 64, 65
Melusky, Henry	1944, 46, 47, 48
Meydenbaur	1893
Meyer, Ricky	1985, 86, 87
Meyers, George	1943, 46, 47
Meyers, John	1959, 60, 61
Michael, Larry	1982, 83
Michael, Mike	1948, 49, 50
Michanczyk, Ray	1954
Middleton, Bob	1969
Mikalson, Bob	1946
Miletich, Ryan	1998, 99
Millen, Hugh	1984, 85
Miller, Cedric	1912,13,14,15
Miller, Fred	1970, 71, 72
Miller, Herman	1919
Miller, Mel	1996, 97
Miller, Merle	1936, 37, 38
Millich, Don	1957, 59
Milloy, Lawyer	1993, 94, 95
Mills, Lamar	1968
Milus, Ron	1982, 83, 84, 85
Mincy, Charles	1989, 90
Minkler, Garfield	1901
Mitchell	1893
Mitchell, Charlie	1960, 61, 62
Mitchell, James	1986
Mitchell, Lamar	1990
Mitchell, Mason	1964
Mitchell, Sam	1950, 51, 52
Mittlested, Bill	1929
Mizen, John	1938, 40
Mizin, Anthony	1996, 98, 99
Mladnich, Nick	1931
Mondala, Mitchell	1934, 35, 36
Monlux, Earl	1953, 54, 55
Monroe, Bob	1960, 61, 62
Monroe, Mike	1953, 55
Moon, Warren	1975, 76, 77
Moore, Bob	1943, 44, 45
Moore, Don	1965, 66
Moore, Josh	1991, 92, 93
Moore, Shaun	1992
Mora, Jim	1981, 82, 83
Moraga, Rudy	1976, 77, 78, 79
Moran, Eric	1980, 81, 82
Moran, Malcolm	1917
Morehead, Donnie	1984
Morgan, Carl	1957
Morgan, Quentin	1999
Morrison, Steve	1995
Morrison, Victor	1916
Moses, Wayne	1973, 74, 76, 77
Mucha, Chuck	1932, 33, 34
Mucha, Rudy	1938, 39, 40
Mucklestone, Melville	1908, 09,11
Muczynski, Matt	1932, 33, 34
Mulitauaopele, Toalei	1998, 99
Murphine, Tom	1894
Murphy, Ernest	1915,16,17
Murphy, Pat	1954

Mc

MacFarlane, Doug	1950
MacKinzie, Jack	1934, 35, 36
McAdams, Dean	1938, 39, 40
McBride, Cliff	1976
McCabe, Jim	1966, 67
McCallum, John	1988, 89
McCann, Joe	1927, 28
McCarter, Jim	1955, 57
McCarthy, D.J.	1993
McClary, Doug	1951, 52, 53
McClinton, Dave	1968
McCluskey, Mike	1956, 57, 58
McCorkle, Mark	1940, 41, 42
McCormick, Walter	1944
McCullough, Ansel	1948, 50
McCumby, Don	1955, 56, 57
McCurdy, Jim	1944
McDonald, Mark	1973, 74
McDonald, Tom	1903, 04, 05
McDowell, Jay	1938, 39, 40
McElhenny, Hugh	1949, 50, 51
McElmon, Fred	1901, 02, 03, 04
McFarland, Murphy	1972, 73
McGovern, William	1944, 45, 46, 47, 48
McHale, Rick	1965, 66, 67
McIntosh, Don	1942
McIntyre, Dick	1949
McKasson, Ray	1958, 59, 60
McKay, Orlando	1989, 90, 91
McKay, Walton	1907
McKechnie, Ross	1915
McKeta, Don	1958, 59, 60
McKinnon, Mickey	1954
McLain, Jerry	1977, 78, 79, 80
McLeod, Rick	1986, 87
McMahon, Mark	1969, 70
McNair, Troy	1989
McNamee, Bob	1953, 54, 55
McPherson, Andrew	1914
McPherson, K.	1899,1900
McRae, Ed	1923, 24
McVeigh, Dick	1956, 57

N

Nakane, Tom	1992
Navarro, Joel	1986
Neal, Leon	1994, 95
Nelson, Bill	1939, 40, 41
Nelson, Bob	1945, 46
Nelson, Chuck	1980, 81, 82
Nelson, Frank	1954, 55
Nelson, John	1961
Nelson, Rock	1998, 99
Nelson, Tom	1969
Nettles, Aaron	1995
Neubauer, Lance	1979, 80
Nevelle, Jim	1991, 92, 93
Newsome, Vince	1979, 80, 81, 82
Newton, Charles	1936, 37, 38
Nicholl, Dick	1958
Nichols, Ralph	1893, 94
Niles, Wendell	1952, 53
Nisbet, Dave	1930, 31, 32
Nixon, Byng	1938, 39,40
Nnanabu, Justin	1997
Noble, Bernard	1913
Noble, Elmer	1914,15,16
Noe, Jim	1951, 52, 53
Noeltner, Rick	1976
Norton, Gene	1949, 50, 51
Norton, Jim	1962, 63, 64
Norton, John	1945
Norwood, Lyle	1964, 65
Nowogroski, Ed	1934, 35, 36
Nugent, Jack	1952, 53
Nykreim, Mike	1975

O

O'Bannon, Mike	1964
Oberg, Art	1930, 32
O'Brien, Jim	1949, 50, 51
O'Brien, John	1963
O'Brien, William	1930, 31, 32
O'Connor, Chris	1979, 80, 81, 82
Ochs, Bill	1956
Ohler, Pete	1961, 62
O'Laughlin, Sean	1997, 98
Oldes, Walter	1972, 73
O'Leary, Don	1949, 50
Oliver, Vern	1943
Olsen, Kenneth	1926, 28
Olsen, Rusty	1979, 80
Olson Bud	1949, 50
Olson, Benji	1995, 96, 97
Olson, Chuck	1947, 48, 49
Olson, Fred	1941, 42
Olson, Ron	1974, 75
Olson, Vern	1976
Olszewski, Nick	1999
Ormand, Alex	1976
Osterhout, Fred	1944, 45
Ostrom, H.C.	1893, 94
Otis, Mike	1963, 64, 65
Ottele, Dick	1944, 46, 47

P

Pahukoa, Jeff	1987, 89, 90
Pahukoa, Shane	1989, 90, 91, 92
Pallis, Chris	1980
Palmer, Bob	1930, 31
Palmer, IR	1905
Palmer, Rex	1930
Papageorgiou, George	1978
Pape, Karl	1925, 26
Parker, Bill	1966
Parker, Lester	1921
Parker, Omar	1964, 65, 66
Parker, Shirley	1906
Parks, Ralph	1981
Parmeter, Eugene	1924
Parrish, Tony	1994, 95, 96, 97
Parry, Doug	1987
Parsons, Dean	1952
Partridge, Jeff	1981, 82
Pathon, Jerome	1995, 96, 97
Patrick, Jack	1929, 30, 31
Patten, Jack	1911,12
Pattison, Mark	1982, 83, 84
Patton, Harold	1924, 25, 26

Pautzke, Clarence	1928, 29, 30
Payseno, Dick	1955, 56, 57
Peabody, Dick	1894
Pear, Dave	1972, 73, 74
Pearson, J.C.	1983, 84
Peasley, Ed	1957, 58, 59
Pedersen, Geve	1954, 55, 56
Pederson, Bob	1965, 66, 67
Pederson, Mike	1979
Pederson, Ross	1932, 33
Pelluer, Steve	1981, 82, 83
Pence, Jim	1977, 78, 79
Peoples, Tim	1982, 84, 85, 86
Perrish, Laurence	1930, 31
Perry, Loren	1949, 50
Petermann, Nelse	1973, 74, 75
Peters, Frank	1936, 37, 38
Peters, Rashad	1999
Peterson, Del	1942
Peterson, Andrew	1991, 92, 93, 94
Peterson, Bill	1950
Peterson, Verne	1933
Petrich, Doug	1987
Petrie, Roy	1922, 23, 24
Pettigrew, Jim	1973
Pharms, Jeremiah	1997, 98, 99
Phelps, Lloyd	1937, 38, 40
Phillips, Dave	1960, 61, 62
Phillips, Scott	1973, 74, 75, 76
Pierce, Aaron	1988, 89, 90, 91
Pierson, Pete	1991, 92, 93
Piety, John	1962
Pike, Roscoe	1910
Pinney, Ray	1973, 74, 75
Pitt, George	1957, 58, 59
Pittman, Bryan	1997
Plumley, Dave	1967
Pollock, Don	1934
Poole, Mark	1987, 88
Pope, Gus	1919, 20
Pope, Steve	1978, 80
Porras, Tom	1978, 79
Posey, Dan	1991
Prechek, John	1947, 48, 49
Presley, Bevan	1910,11,12,13
Preston, Ron	1969, 70
Price, Gary	1962
Prince, Geoff	1994, 95, 96
Provo, Fred	1942, 46, 47
Pullen, Dan	1903, 04, 05
Pullen, Royal	1910,11
Pulver, Elliott	1927, 28, 29
Purdue, Bob	1938

Q

Quass, Harry	1921
Quesada, Greg	1994, 95
Quinn, Lou	1973, 74, 75

R

Radke, Paul	1933, 34
Radner, Laurie	1944
Railsbuck, Llewellyn	1904
Rainwater, Dawayne	1992
Ramstedt, Julius	1930
Randle, Ivory	1988
Rawlins, Jack	1928
Rawlinson, Don	1945
Rawson, Errol	1917
Ray, Eddie	1974, 75
Reddick, Patrick	1997
Redman, Ray	1942
Redman, Rick	1962, 63, 64
Redmond, Jerry	1953
Reed, Frank	1973, 74, 75
Reed, Mike	1994, 96, 97
Reed, William	1980
Reese, H.L.	1899
Rehn, Bruce	1948, 49, 50
Reid, Jim	1933
Reilly, Mike	1979, 80
Reiner, David	1993
Rep, Ross	1905
Reser, George	1907
Reser, Reggie	1992, 93, 94, 95
Rhodes, Larry	1954
Rice, Harry	1944, 45, 46
Rice, Ray	1925
Richie, David	1993, 94, 95
Richardson, Antowaine	1976, 77, 78, 79
Richardson, Bob	1965, 66, 67
Richardson, Guy	1896
Richardson, Henry	1896
Richardson, Keith	1977, 78, 79
Richardson, Kevin	1975, 76
Richardson, Travis	1987, 88, 89, 90
Richie, David	1994, 96
Rideout, Will	1986, 87
Riggs, Thron	1940, 41, 42
Riley, Andre	1986, 87, 88, 89
Rill, David	1984, 85, 86, 87
Rios, Augie	1967, 68, 69
Roake, Steve	1953, 54, 55
Robbins, Mitch	1987
Robbins, Steve	1974, 75, 76, 77
Roberson, Dan	1969
Roberts, Jay	1984, 86, 87
Roberts, Kyle	1996, 97
Roberts, Steve	1985, 86
Robertson, Al	1983, 84
Robertson, Clarence	1952
Robertson, G.H.	1900
Robinson,	1893
Robinson, Dante	1991, 92
Robinson, Fred	1954, 55
Robinson, Jacque	1981, 82, 83, 84
Robinson, Sam	1942, 43, 46, 47
Roche, Wayne	1976, 77, 78
Rockey, Dean	1951, 52, 53
Roderick, John	1944
Rodgers, Jim	1980, 81, 83, 84
Rodgers, Tyrone	1990, 91
Rodwell, Dain	1971
Roehl, Tom	1971, 72
Rogers, Reggie	1984, 85, 86
Rogge, George	1920, 21
Rohrbach, Mike	1975, 77
Rohrscheib, Walter	1934, 35
Rongen, Kris	1991
Ronnebaum, Lane	1968, 69, 70
Rosborough, Willie	1980, 81, 82
Rose, Carl	1973
Rosenhan, Chuck	1929
Rosenzweig, Jim	1948, 49, 50
Roth, Arnold	1931
Roundun, Otis	1896
Rowland, Chris	1973, 74, 75
Rowland, Ron	1976, 77
Rudnick, Fred	1950, 51, 52
Rulis, Ed	1935
Rumberger, Trip	1977
Russell, Charley	1937
Russell, George	1893
Russo, Sam	1926
Ryan, Joe	1962, 63
Ryan, L.D.	1899,1900
Ryan, Mike	1964, 65, 66

S

Safford, Don	1962, 63
Sage, Ed	1952, 53
Sahli, Walter	1926, 27, 29
Saksa, Frank	1942, 43, 46
Sampson, Jim	1963, 64
Sandberg, Dick	1951
Sanders, Eugene	1974
Sanderson, James	1944
Sanford, Joe	1976, 78, 79
Sanford, Steve	1966
Sansregret, Norm	1945
Sapp, Bob	1994, 95, 96
Sarieddine, Sacha	1999
Sarshar, Hamid	1996
Sartoris, Jim	1964, 66
Saunders, Calvin	1978
Savage, J.R.	1949, 50
Savage, Tony	1914
Savini, Sauni	1984
Sawyer, James	1988
Scaman, Jack	1928, 29
Scheyer, Paul	1964
Scheyer, Rod	1960, 61, 62
Schlamp, Dean	1973, 74, 75
Schlepp, Eric	1995
Schloredt, Bob	1958, 59, 60
Schmidt, Donovan	1991, 92, 93, 94
Schmit, Joel	1979
Schneidermann, Harry	1928
Schoder, E.W.	1899
Schoepper, Bob	1967, 68
Schuh, Leroy	1925, 26, 27
Schulberg, Rick	1989, 90
Schulte, Steve	1970, 71, 72
Schwartz, Avery	1966, 68
Schwegler, Paul	1929, 30, 31
Scott, J.K.	1999
Scott, Tom	1971, 72
Seagrave, Louis	1913,14,15,16
Segrist, Charles	1902, 03
Seida, Judd	1998
Seiler, Clyde	1950, 51, 52
Seminavage, Opu	1995

Name	Years
Seth, Jack	1948, 49, 50
Sharp, Rick	1967, 68, 69
Shavey, Gary	1996, 97
Shaw, Bob	1925, 26, 27
Shaw, Maurice	1996, 97, 99
Shaw, Royal	1904, 05
Sheafe, James	1894, 96
Shehee, Rashaan	1994, 95, 97
Sheldrake, Tom	1937, 38
Shelley, Jason	1992
Shelton, Geoff	1999
Shelton, Leland	1927, 29, 30
Shepherd, Ron	1970, 72
Sherer, Lewis	1901, 02, 03
Sherman, Lester	1922, 23, 25
Sheron, Ed	1954, 55
Sherwood, Terry	1976, 77, 79
Shidler, Harold	1924, 25
Shiel, Walter	1912,13,14,15
Shoe, Jeff	1995
Shper, Abe	1934, 35
Sicuro, Paul	1984
Sievers, Roy	1923, 24
Sigworth, Jay	1903, 04
Siler, Bill	1961, 62
Silvers, Elliott	1998, 99
Simmons, Joe	1975
Simpson, Jess	1944
Simpson, Jim	1986
Sixkiller, Sonny	1970, 71, 72
Skaggs, Jim	1959, 60, 61
Skansi, John	1983
Skansi, Paul	1979, 80, 81, 82
Skurski, Jim	1998, 99
Slater, Brian	1985, 86, 87, 88
Sligh, Luther	1969, 71, 72
Slivinski, Steve	1936, 37, 38
Sloan, Bill	1939, 40, 41
Small, Fred	1981, 82, 83, 84
Smalling, Ralph	1932, 33
Smith, Adney	1931, 32
Smith, Bernard	1945
Smith, Bill	1931, 32, 33
Smith, Bob	1948, 49
Smith, Brett	1984, 85
Smith, Charles	1913,14
Smith, Charles	1923
Smith, Chris	1979
Smith, Dannianke	1990, 91
Smith, David	1981
Smith, Dwight	1940
Smith, Frank	1966, 67
Smith, George	1914,15,16,19
Smith, George	1986, 88
Smith, Greg	1974
Smith, Jermaine	1996, 97, 98, 99
Smith, Jim	1905
Smith, Jim	1972
Smith, Josh	1995, 96, 97, 98
Smith, Larry	1919, 20
Smith, Larry	1951, 52
Smith, Rob	1976, 77, 78
Smith, Shannon	1983
Smith, Tommie	1989
Smith, Tommie	1989, 90, 91, 92
Snider, Bill	1956, 57
Snider, William	1927, 28, 29
Snow, Bob	1940, 41
Snyder, Fred	1955
Sobhi, Mostafa	1995, 96
Sohn, Ben	1932
Soldat, Dennis	1983, 84, 85
Solid, Ken	1944
Sortun, Rick	1961, 62, 63
Sortun, Wayne	1968, 69, 70
Spague, Tom	1952, 53
Spargur, Fred	1909,10,11
Sparlin, Tom	1966, 67
Spearman, Tony	1982
Speidel, William	1902, 03
Spillers, Curtis	1926
Sprague, Dick	1950, 51, 52
Spriesterbach, Dan	1966, 67, 68
Springstead, Steve	1990, 91, 92, 93
Sprinkle, Bill	1967, 68
Sprinkle, Dick	1948, 49, 50
Squires, Roy	1928, 29, 30
Srohmeier, Paul	1973, 74, 75
Stackpool, Jack	1939, 40, 41
Stacy, Maurice	1940, 45
Stanley, Rod	1971, 73
Stapleton, Bill	1979, 80, 81, 82
Starcevich, Max	1934, 35, 36
Steel, Chuck	1961
Steele, Ernie	1939, 40, 41
Steele, Joe	1976, 77, 78, 79
Stein, Ernie	1946, 47, 48, 50
Steiner, Leslie	1944
Stephens, Dale	1964, 65
Sterling, Wayne	1939, 40, 41
Stevens, Jerramy	1999
Stevens, Kyle	1977, 78, 79, 80
Stewart, Mark	1979, 80, 81, 82
Stifter, Bill	1965
Stiger, Kim	1961, 62
Stitz, Everett	1930, 31, 32
Stombaugh, John	1926, 28, 29
Stone, Brian	1980, 81, 82
Stone, Joe	1945
Stoves, Jay	1943
Stransky, Dave	1982, 83
Strauss, Alfred	1902, 03
Stromswold, Dave	1975, 76
Stroud, Mike	1964
Strugar, George	1955, 56
Stuart, Scott	1991
Stupey, John	1961, 62, 63
Sublett, Tam	1987
Sulkosky, Paul	1932, 33, 34
Summers, Matt	1997
Susick, Pete	1940, 41, 42, 43
Sutton, Wayne	1910,11,12,13
Swartz, J.E.	1893
Swarva, G.L	1910
Sweatt, Dick	1970, 71
Sweet, Carl	1969

T

Name	Years
Tabor, Joe	1972, 73
Tadich, Dmitri	1942, 46, 47
Taggares, Pete	1971, 72, 73
Tailele, Paxton	1990, 91
Talley, Darold	1949, 50, 51
Tamble, Geoff	1994
Tarver, Roger	1980, 81, 83
Taylor, Leonard	1908, 09
Tegtmeier, Fred	1906, 07, 08, 09
Terry, Ron	1954
Tesreau, Elmer	1923, 24, 25
Tesreau, Louis	1925, 26, 27
Tharps, Terry	1999
Theisen, Art	1917,19
Theoudele, Lance	1976, 77, 78, 79
Thomas, Garth	1984, 85, 86
Thomas, Jim	1954, 55, 56
Thomas, Justin	1992, 93, 94
Thomas, Richard	1992, 93, 94, 95
Thompson, Bob	1925
Thompson, Jim	1946
Thompson, Ray	1944
Thompson, Scott	1980, 81, 82
Thompson, Steve	1965, 66, 67
Thornton, Thurle	1927, 28, 29
Tibbals, Maurice	1903, 04
Tice, Bud	1952
Tidball, Ben	1916,19
Tiedemann, Henry	1948, 49
Till, Bill	1954, 56
Tilley, Homer	1904
Tining, Norman	1921, 22
Toews, Jeff	1975, 76, 77, 78
Tormey, Pete	1977, 78, 79
Towns, Lester	1996, 97, 98, 99
Townsend, Frank	1919
Toy, David	1984, 85, 86, 87
Tracy, Jack	1941, 42, 43
Trask, Leo	1945
Travis, Greg	1986, 87, 89
Trimble, David	1983, 84, 85
Tripplett, Larry	1999
Tufono, Albert	1983, 84, 87
Tuiaea, Mac	1996, 97, 98, 99
Tuiasosopo, Marques	1998, 99
Turner, Darius	1989, 90, 91, 92
Turner, Mark	1968, 70
Turnure, Tom	1976, 77, 78, 79
Tyler, Toussaint	1977, 78, 79, 80
Tymer, Tom	1971

U

Name	Years
Ulin, Woody	1932, 33, 34

V

Name	Years
Van Divier, Randy	1978, 79
Van Hoosier, Paul	1981
Van Valkeberg, Carl	1974, 75, 76
Vaughan, Robert	1940
Verti, Tom	1967, 68, 69
Vicino, Mike	1974, 75
Vicker, Doug	1945, 47, 48, 49
Volbrecht, Ron	1968, 69, 70

Vontoure, Anthony	1999

W

Waddell, Chris	1999
Waechter, Gerald	1919
Wagner, Paul	1982
Walderhaug, Stan	1975, 76, 77
Wales, John	1994, 95, 96
Walker, Dave	1985
Walker, Ken	1998
Walker, Lacy	1983
Wallin, Steve	1971, 72
Wallrof, Paul	1957
Walsh, Andrew	1944
Walters, Chalmers	1922, 23, 24
Walters, Eugene	1940, 41, 42
Walters, Jack	1957, 58, 59
Wand, Walter	1909,10,11
Ward, Bill	1943
Ward, Chad	1997, 98, 99
Wardlow, Don	1974, 75, 76
Wardlow, Duane	1951, 52, 53
Ware, Kevin	1999
Warsinski, Jim	1951, 52, 53
Washington, Dee	1974
Washington, Otis	1967, 68
Waskom, Bob	1985
Waskom, Jim	1987, 88
Waskom, Paul	1984, 85, 86
Waskowitz, Frank	1935, 36
Waters, Donald T.	1973
Watson, Bert	1955
Watson, Dick	1942
Watts, Jerry	1971
Wea, Gerald	1966, 67
Weathersby, Vince	1985, 86, 87, 88
Weatherspoon, Hakim	1998
Wehde, Fred	1942, 47
Weindl, Jamie	1993
Weinmeister, Arnie	1942, 46, 47
Welbon, Calvin	1893, 94
Wells, Max	1902
Wenger, Barry	1968
Wentworth, Henry	1928, 29, 30
Werdel, John	1991, 92, 93
Werner, Clyde	1967, 68, 69
Wesley, Don	1972
West, Marc	1989
Westerweller, Larry	1928, 29, 30
Westlund, Roger	1975, 76, 77, 78
Weston, Doug	1979, 81, 82
Westover, Ralph	1908
Westra, John	1997, 98
Westrom, Fred	1923, 24
Wetterauer, Dick	1963, 64, 65
Weyrick, Alan	1989
Wheeler, Ron	1979, 80
Whitacre, John	1972, 73, 75
White, Bob	1957, 58, 59
White, Cedric	1993
Whitenight, David	1981, 82, 83
Whitmyer, Nat	1961, 62
Wiatrak, Joe	1931, 32, 33
Wiatrak, John	1934, 35, 36
Wiatrak, Paul	1940, 42
Wick, Sanford	1916
Wiese, Brett	1985, 86, 87, 88
Wiezbowski, Steve	1970, 71, 72
Wiggs, Sekou	1995, 96, 97
Wijchechowski, Carl	1967, 68
Wilcox, Leonard	1928, 30
Wiley, Jim	1949, 50, 51
Williams, Aaron	1979, 80, 81, 82
Williams, Curtis	1998, 99
Williams, Dave	1964, 65, 66
Williams, Demouy	1985, 86, 87
Williams, Greg	1979, 80
Williams, J.S.	1901
Williams, Jafar	1998, 99
Williams, Jerry	1964, 65, 66
Williams, Ross	1917
Willig, Bob	1985, 86, 87, 88
Willis, Dave	1986
Willis, Don	1993
Willis, Fred	1907
Willis, Gene	1968, 69, 71
Willis, Hart	1906, 07
Willis, Jamaun	1999
Wilmoth, Jeff	1984
Wilson, Aaron	1977, 78
Wilson, Abe	1923, 24
Wilson, Darren	1983
Wilson, George	1923, 24, 25
Wilson, John	1920, 21
Wilson, Kirk	1957, 58
Wilson, Pat	1925, 26, 27
Wilson, Stan	1975, 76
Windust, Fran	1931, 32, 34
Wingender, John	1942, 43
Winn, Grover	1911
Winsor, William	1905
Winters, Ralph	1963, 64, 65
Wirt, Harry	1915,16
Wise, Henry	1936, 37, 38
Witcher, Darren	1980, 82
Wolcott, Bill	1930, 31, 32
Wold, Ron	1978
Woldseth, Hans	1972, 73
Wolfe, Chad	1995
Wood, Harrison	1966, 67, 68
Wooten, Brent	1958, 59, 60
Worgan, Dave	1970, 71, 72
Worley, Al	1966, 67, 68
Worley, Larry	1970
Worthington, Rich	1937
Wren, Bob	1943
Wright, E.J.	1899,1900
Wright, William	1925, 26, 27
Wroten, Tony	1981, 82, 83, 84
Wyatt, Martin	1961, 62
Wyles, Channing	1989, 90
Wyman, Don	1933, 34

Y

Yanicks, Milt	1955
Yarr, Dan	1938, 39
Yates, Bo	1984, 85, 86, 87
Yonker, Walter	1938, 39, 40
Young, Allan	1912,13,15
Younglove, Earl	1939, 40, 41
Yourkowski, Louis	1950, 51, 52

Z

Zackery, Tony	1985, 86, 87, 88
Zajac, Elliot	1999
Zakskorn, Pat	1980, 81, 82
Zandofsky, Mike	1985, 86, 87, 88
Zatkovich, Dick	1967
Zech, Bob	1943, 44
Zeger, John	1940, 41, 46
Zeger, John	1980, 81
Zeil, Leonard	1921, 22, 23
Zemeck, Al	1938, 40
Zemeck, W.	1938
Ziebarth, Herbert	1901, 02
Zurek, Bryan	1949, 50, 51

Honorary Letter Winners

Bacon, Hank	1929
Bronson, Dick	1915
Brown, Mac	1922
Ford, Ed	1929
Green, Lloyd	1923
Haggerty, Don	1926
Hansberry, Milt	1941
Harney, Gerald	1927
Hudson, Wesley	1941
Jacobi, Lee	1935
Jones, Elton	1929
Mackie, Paul	1909
McInroe, Lloyd	1922
Mitchell, John	1927
Palmer, Burton	1923
Palmer, Rex	1929
Reeve, Stanley	1926
Schiveley, Hugh	1913
Smith, Bernard	1941
Smith, Charles	1922
Sweeney, Edward	1914
Turner, Wendall	1922
VanWoert, Ross	1929
Vaughan, Bob	1941
Watson, Ib	1929
Wiatrak, Paul	1941

Men's Golf

A

Abernathy, Bob	1937
Aden, Gordy	1964, 65, 66
Ainslie, Chuck	1962, 63, 64
Anderson, Craig	1969, 71
Anderson, Elwin	1946
Anderson, Rich	1964, 65, 66

B

Bacior, Stan	1938
Baldwin, Doug	1988, 89, 90
Banta, Neil	1937

Barnett, Michael	1983, 84, 85
Barwick, Tom	1949, 50, 51
Bashaw, Ed	1939
Bauder, Brandon	1975
Beard, James	1969
Benzin, Rich	1979, 80, 81
Benzin, Russ	1979, 80, 81
Berg, Derek	2000
Bergeson, Robb	1996, 97, 98, 99
Berry, Al	1939
Bloch, Jerry	1938
Bloom, Jeffery	1983, 84, 85, 86
Bockmann, Brett	1999
Boe, Thomas	1973, 75, 76
Boettcher, Sieg	1980
Boguch, Greg	1977
Bourne, Jim	1951, 52, 53
Bradley, William	1984, 85, 86
Brill, Earnest	1957, 58
Brottem, Johnny	1939
Brown, Chester	1960
Brown, Greg	1982, 83
Burkes, Wallace	1946
Bush, Joe	1962, 63

C

Campbell, Douglas	1970, 72
Carlson, Les	1936, 37
Carter, Paul	1982
Caruso, Pete	1991, 92
Caruso, Steve	1990
Case, Center	1935
Clark, Wayne	1985, 86, 87
Clifford, Buzz	1935
Cole, Stephen	1968
Cole, Steve	1966, 67, 68
Coleman, Gary	1956
Combs, Mike	1987, 88, 89, 90
Cone, William	1960
Congdon, Gary	1959, 60
Conrad, Bob	1994, 95, 96
Cook, Hugh	1957, 58, 59
Craig, Jack	1961, 62, 63
Cuthill, Dave	1981, 82, 83
Czarniecki, John	1935

D

Daniels, Lawrence	1973, 75
Dean, Doug	1938, 39
Draper, Ed	1947, 48, 49, 50

E

Earnest, Steve	1967, 68
Earnest, Steven	1968
Elaimy, David	1990
Elworthy, Sherman	1935
Epstein, Richard	1957, 58
Erickson, Brett	1983

F

Farris, Kelly	1962
Faulkner, Michael	1961
Field, Brian	1967
Fissel, Bob	1937
Fowlds, John	1970, 71
Frank, Draper	1950
Frei, Jack	1968
Friedman, Jay	1954

G

Gannon, Jim	1966, 67
Garner, Ben	1995
Giedt, Bruce	1957, 59
Gjolme, Harold	1941, 42, 46
Goff, Richard	1959
Glodt, Jeff	1992
Graybeal, Gordie	1979, 80, 81, 82
Greene, Joe	1946
Greene, Joe	1949
Grosz, Randal	1975
Groth, Arnie	1938, 39
Gunnerson, Elwood	1946

H

Haas, Bill	1938
Hansen, Buzz	1935
Hansen, Earl	1953, 54
Harris, Del	1960, 61
Haumann, Arthur	1957
Hazlett, Jack	1942, 46
Hemphill, Michael	1973
Henderson, Gary	1966, 67, 68
Hetsler, Justin	1996
Highsmith, Matt	1979, 80, 81, 82
Himka, Theodore	1986, 87, 88, 89
Holland, George	1948, 49
Hunt, Jeffery	1985, 86, 87
Hunter, Trevor	1992
Hynds, Jimmy	1951, 52, 53

I

Irvin, James	1971, 72, 73

J

Jacobs, Ernie	1941, 43
Jeffries, Jared	1994, 95, 96
Johanson, Paul	1951, 52, 53
Johnsen, Steven	1971
Johnson, Richard	1976, 77
Jonson, Carl	1936, 37, 38
Jonson, Ernie	1938, 39
Jonson, Michael	1969
Jonson, Mike	1968

K

Kauffman, George	1961, 62
Kelly, Troy	1999, 2000
Kemppainen, Michael	1970
Kinney, George	1950
Kline, Jeffery	1975, 76
Kral, Scott	1997, 98, 99, 2000
Kuhn, Thomas	1971, 72

L

Lamey, John	1961
Layne, Bob	1942
Leides, Keith	1984
Leitgeb, Brian	1989, 90, 91, 92
Leu, Spencer	1992, 93, 94, 95
Lewis, Lee	1939
Lodge, Joseph	1977, 78, 79, 80
Lohman, Chris	1996, 97
Longmuir, Jim	1937
Lutz, Rafer	1991, 92, 93
Lorentzen, Bob	1950, 52
Lukas, Radd	1986
Lundberg, Roger	1968
Lunder, Bjorn	1943

M

Mallory, Jim	1947, 48, 49
Manlowe, Bob	1955, 56
Martin, Aaron	2000
Martin, Brett	1996, 97
Matson, Craig	1971, 72, 73
Matson, Rob	1984
McBreen, Scott	1970, 71
McCurdy, Will	1999, 2000
McDonald, Scott	1977, 79
McDougall, Scott	1972, 73, 75
McLachlan, Kent	1952, 53, 54, 55
Meyer, Bob	1939, 42
Meyer, Paul	1980, 81, 83, 84
Miller, Justin	1996, 98, 99, 2000
Montgomery, Mike	1991, 92, 93
Morrison, Scott	1992, 93, 94, 95
Moscrip, John	1994, 95, 97, 98
Murphy, Paul	1935
Murray, Jeff	1962
Myers, Wendell	1943

N

Names, Clint	1959, 60, 61
Neville, Jack	1952
Newman, Allan	1955, 56, 57
Newsom, Brooks	1990, 93
Nicolaysen, Thor	1971
Norton, Dave	1936, 37
Nosler, Brian	1998

O

O'Shea, Norman	1942
Odell, Gary	1958

P

Perry, Len	1954, 55, 56
Philip, Bob	1939
Picht, Don	1936
Picht, Don	1937

R

Randle, John	1988, 89
Rashell, Rob	1996, 97, 98, 99
Reid, Kenneth	1969
Reuhl, Steven	1975
Rhodes, Jeff	1966
Rice, Rory	1965
Richards, Bill	1935
Richards, Bruce	1963, 64, 65
Richardson, Neil	1939

Richter, Larry 1969
Riddell, Chad 1995
Robertson, John 2000
Robbins, Conner 2000
Robinson, William 1943
Roe, Bob 1975
Rourke, Bill 1935
Rowe, Bill 1955
Runge, Louis 1975
Runte, Joseph 1975, 76
Runte, Steven 1973
Russel, Don 1951, 52, 53
Ryno, John 1977

S

Sadler, Jerry 1938
Sargent, Harrison 1956
Sater, Gary 1970, 72
Schoch, Delos 1938
Scutt, Gordy 1999, 2000
Seek, Mike 1991, 92
Shapiro, Henry 1958, 59, 60
Shore, Gary 1953
Siegel, Larry 1970
Simpson, Don 1935
Simpson, Don 1936, 37
Slackman, Darren 1994, 96, 97, 98
Slade, Erwin 1939
Smith, Cameron 1986, 87, 88
Squire, Wilbert 1941, 42
Stavney, Luther 1954
Strauhal, Charles 1943
Stroupe, Harold 1946
Sumner, Robert 1958
Swingle, Michael 1988, 89, 90

T

Taro, Bart 1941, 42
Tegeler, James 1991
Thomas, Kane 1977
Thompson, James 1971, 72
Thompson, John 1955
Thorlakson, Richard 1977
Tibke, Todd 1986, 87, 88, 89
Tindall, Bill 1963, 64, 65
Tindall, Rob 1990
Tindall, Tom 1965, 66, 67
Torrance, Jon 1943
Tudor, Joe 1938
Tullis, Ernie 1950, 53, 54
Tustin, Howard 1935

U

Utterstrom, Thomas 1971, 72

V

Vaughan, V.A. 1936, 37
Veatch, Don 1943
Vincent, O.D. 1987, 88,89

W

Welts, Fred 1942
Whaley, Scott 1988
Wickizer, Chris 1982
Willard, Ken 1943
Willhite, Don 1959, 60
Williams, Dick 1953
Williams, John 1956
Wortman, Ward 1939

Y

Yogi, Ken 1993,1994

Z

Zefkeles, Constantine 1969

Women's Golf

A

Abel, Patti 1979
Aoki, Christine 1975, 76
Au, Elisha 1998, 99, 2000

B

Bartleson, Julie 1989, 90, 91, 92
Bellotti, Paola 1996, 97, 98, 99
Britt, Elizabeth 1985, 86, 87, 88
Burkett, Angie 1993, 94, 95, 96
Burns, Heidi 1989, 90, 91

C

Colyer, Alison 1992, 93
Cooper, Mendy 1997, 98, 2000
Cordova, Andrea 1997, 98, 99, 2000

D

Drake, Stephanie 1979, 80, 81, 82

E

Eliason, Carrie 1988, 89, 90, 91

F

Foster, Janice 1976, 77, 78, 79
Friberg, Louise 2000

G

Galmanis, Kimberly 1989
Gamble, Paula 1984, 85, 86, 87
Getty, Janine 1981, 82, 83, 84
Gonder, Angie 1991
Grafos, Michelle 2000

H

Harris, Jane 1982, 83
Hildreth, Susan 1983, 84, 85, 86
Huizinga, Anne 1992, 93

K

Kamimura, Kelli 1999, 2000
Kessler, Nancy 1985, 86, 87, 88
Krieger, Tina 1984, 85, 86, 87
Kurmel, Lee 1992, 93, 94

L

Liedes, Kerry 1982, 83, 84, 85
Lippitt, Sue 1998
Litton, Janis 1976, 77
Lund, Katherine 1985, 86, 87, 88

M

Maedo, Megan 1994, 95, 96
Marquis, Patricia 1975, 76, 77
Martin, Emily 1994, 95, 96, 97
Martin, Kari 2000
Mazzuca, Dodie 1994, 95, 96, 97
McCusker, Kellee 1983
McKie, Val 1992, 93
Mulflur, Mary Lou 1977, 78, 79, 80

O

Olexio, Donna 1988, 89, 90, 91

P

Peck, Nancy 1980, 81
Pieroni, Angie 1991, 92, 93
Porambo, Lisa 1975, 76, 77

S

Sanders, Megan 2000
Sanders, Susan 1980, 81
Simkins, Sonja 1987
Spiegelberg, Caroline 1993, 94, 95, 96
Stapleton, Jennifer 1997, 98, 99

T

Thorlakson, Elisabeth 1975, 76, 77
Thompson, Greta 1979

V

Vincent, Sherri 1990, 91, 92, 93

W

Watson, Michelle 1985-88
Wellman, Janis 1975

Y

Yabe, Kim 1995, 96, 98
Yockey, Jennifer 1988, 89, 90, 91

Men's Gymnastics

B

Barnard, Doug 1960, 61
Beezhold, Wendland 1961
Bennett, Bo 1969
Bevan, Bob 1957
Bjerke, Dick 1956
Blackstock, Jim 1972, 73
Bohrmann, Gunter 1963
Boyd, Ron 1962
Brinton, Bruce 1970, 71
Buckingham, Mark 1965, 66, 67
Burson, Dale 1972, 73
Bylin, Bert 1977
Bylin, Gordie 1979, 80
Bylin, Kevin 1974, 75, 77

C

Carpenter, Bill 1971, 72, 73, 74

Clark, Jay 1973, 74, 75, 76
Clegg, John 1962
Clemmons, Dennis 1967
Cooley, Melvin 1975, 76, 77, 78
Crow, Bill 1956, 57, 59, 60
Curry, Ron 1957, 58, 59

D

Daley, John 1980
David, Jim 1963, 64, 65
Deininger, John 1962
Denny, Charlie 1957, 58, 59
Denton, Bruce 1969, 70, 71
Depue, Darrel 1966
Dieterich, Jim 1962, 63, 64
Domeier, Stu 1977, 78, 79, 80
Driscoll, Leslie 1957, 59

E

Ewald, Norm 1970, 71, 72, 73

F

Finne, Gary 1964, 65, 66
Firpo, Joe 1956
Flaathen, Eigil 1965, 66, 67
Flansaas, Mike 1964, 66, 67
Fonceca, Ricardo 1965, 66, 67
Fox, Gary 1971
Fritschen, Charlie 1977, 78, 79
Fukushima, Sho 1969, 71

G

Gaylor, Rich 1971, 72, 73, 75
Gerber, Alwyn 1978, 79
Gester, Tom 1967
Gray, Jim 1976

H

Hall, Bob 1963, 64, 65
Halverson, Rich 1980
Hansen, Kjell 1963, 64
Hanvey, Terry 1964
Hardin, Jan 1966, 67
Hauselman, Ken 1957, 59
Hayasaki, Yoshi 1970, 71
Hermansson, Bjorn 1973, 74, 75, 76
Hilton, Jim 1956
Hubbard, Jim 1962
Hughes, Joe 1971, 72, 74
Hunter, Ron 1970, 71, 72

I

Ikeda, Roy 1957, 60

J

Jackson, Dave 1973, 74, 75, 76
Jensen, Gene 1965, 66, 67
Jones, Gordon 1972, 73

K

Kamarainen, Kari 1979, 80
Kath, Gary 1976, 77, 78
Kennerud, Ken 1958, 60
Kolsrud, Lars 1970, 71
Kramer, Gerhard 1958, 59

L

Landers, Lew 1961, 62, 64
Lang, Jim 1956, 58, 59, 60
Leiman, Kerry 1970, 71, 72
Lind, Alf 1960
Lombardo, Ken 1961
Lovell, Mike 1964, 65, 66
Lovell, Steve 1965, 66, 67
Lyons, Harold 1960, 62, 63

M

Mah, Ricky 1978, 79, 80
Maseng, John 1975, 76, 77, 78
McGunnigle, Pat 1957, 59
McGunnigle, Ray 1956
Michaelson, Ernie 1956, 57
Miller, Cliff 1962
Miller, Mike 1960
Minaker, Rod 1974, 75, 76, 77
Morrow, Scott 1974
Murphy, Eugene 1956, 57

N

Nakanishi, Dave 1975, 76
Nissinen, Mauno 1969

O

O'Donnell, Tom 1972, 73, 74
Ornholt, Jan 1971
Ozora, Tomi 1969, 70, 72

P

Paulson, Peter 1972, 73, 74
Peters, Charlie 1969
Peterson, Mark 1967, 69

R

Richardson, Bruce 1961
Ruckert, Pat 1966, 67
Rule, Brent 1969

S

Sanders, Chuck 1971, 72
Shevalier, Alex 1958, 59
Skartvedt, Dave 1961, 62
Sosman, Steve 1974, 75, 76 77
Staton, George 1957
Sternberg, Brian 1963

T

Talbott, John 1973, 75
Temple, John 1958, 59
Thorne, Phil 1961
Torkelson, John 1962, 63, 64

U

Umeshita, Hide 1969, 70, 71

V

Virgillo, Mike 1961, 62

W

Wallace, Ron 1964, 66
Walrack, Perry 1978, 79, 80
Wejman, Steve 1977, 78

Y

Yates, Steve 1973
Yingling, John 1973, 74, 75

Women's Gymnastics

A

Ahten, Jan 1979, 80
Alcala, Marie 1983, 84, 85
Anderson, Kristi 1987, 88, 89, 90
Apisukh, Lanna 1998, 99, 2000
Ashbaugh, Denise 1993, 94

B

Babkes, Megan 1990
Bain, Stacie 1994, 95
Baird, Katie 1983, 84, 85, 86
Barton, Annette 1976
Boylan, Becky 1975, 76, 77
Botnen, Sandra 1989, 90
Brenneman, Nancy 1979, 80
Brown, Paige 1988
Bruce, Allison 1999, 2000
Burkett, Cindy 1984

C

Callow, Jennifer 1990, 91, 92
Campi, Michelle 1996
Casey, Marla 1983
Castillo, Eileen 1994, 95
Churchill, Lisa 1989, 90, 91, 92
Cobb, Cheryl 1980, 81, 82
Collins, Crystal 1997, 98, 99, 2000
Collins, Jill 2000
Connell, Debbie 1980, 81, 82, 83
Connolly, Stacy 1993, 94, 95, 96
Cooper, Heather 1993, 94, 95, 96
Curlee, Jennifer 1998, 99

D

DeCano, Jen-ai 1996, 97

E

Eggiman, Carrie 1978
Erdos, Amber 1996, 97, 98, 99
Erickson, Betsy 1985, 87, 88, 89

F

Field, Sidney 1999, 2000
Fine, Nancy 1976
Fitzgerald, Suzanne 1979, 80
Forrestel, Colleen 1980, 81

G

Gangwer, Wendy 1984, 85, 86, 87
Garcia, Michele 1982, 83, 84, 85
Goertzen, Heidi 1988

Goya, Wendy 1983, 84, 85, 86
Gregerich, Gail 1980, 81
Greve, Joan 1993, 94, 95, 96
Gullickson, Susan 1983

H

Hanson, Shawn 1981
Harrison, Juliana 1979
Hawkins, Kelli 1988, 89, 91, 92
Hawney, Gayle 1976, 77
Hawney, Marilyn 1976, 77, 78, 79
Hudson, Cyndie 1986, 87, 88, 89

I

Ideta, Stace 1978, 79, 80, 81

K

Kite, Liz 1977, 78
Klug, Mandi 1998, 99, 2000
Knapp, Karna 1978, 79, 80, 81
Korbein, Pat 1975, 76, 77
Kubota, Trisha 1990, 91, 93
Kudílková, Klára 1995, 96, 97, 98

L

Lajoie, Starr 1992, 93, 94, 95
Laughlin, Kim 1987
Leacock, Shelly 1982, 83, 84, 85
Logan, Kelly 1986

M

Macintosh, Catherine 1991, 92
MacLane, Sheila 1983, 84, 85, 86
Marsh, Rebecca 1991
Martin, Karin 1995
McWilliams, Becky 1981, 82, 83
Miller, Anne 1975, 76, 77
Milner, Shylo 1989, 90, 91, 92
Montalvo, Celeste 1999
Mordre, Yumi 1986, 87, 88, 89

N

Neal, Kelly 1980, 81
Newton, Dachelle 1985, 86, 87, 88
Niebling, Christine 1993, 94, 95, 96
Nygren, Nancy 1987

O

Orange, Angela 1997, 98
Osborn, Lynn 1977, 78, 79, 80

P

Pelander, Rhyan 1997, 98, 99, 2000
Pesce, Alisa 1992, 93, 94, 95
Peters, Sarah 1987, 88, 89, 90

R

Rhinesmith, Nancy 1981, 82, 83, 84
Riesenman, Lauren 1997, 98, 99, 2000
Robell, Christi 1984
Roberts, Claire 1978
Rose, Carley 1992, 93, 94, 95
Ross, Trinka 1981, 82
Rucci, Kim 1993, 94, 95, 96

S

Schedler, Jessica 1998, 99, 2000
Seabolt, Courtney 1994, 95, 96, 97
Selk, Letitia 1985, 86, 87, 88
Simpson, Sara 1986
Simpson, Tiffany 1996, 97, 98, 2000
Simonton, Tashy 1989, 90, 91
Smidt, Amy 1989
Smith, Oran 1979, 80
Stauffer, Jamie 1995, 96, 97, 98
Strother, Gretchen 1996, 97
Sun, Suzie 1981, 82, 83, 84
Sutherland, Cathy 1975, 76, 77

V

Victor, Laura 1979, 80
Voyles, Jamie 1996

W

Waaramaki, Leah 1997, 98, 99, 2000
Williams, Catherine 1993, 94
Williams, Kathleen 1980, 81
Wong, Malinda 1988, 89, 90
Wong, Stacy 1999

Y

Yasutake, Nancy 1975, 76, 77
York, Liza 1987, 88

Men's Skiing

A

Akre, Bjorn 1966
Alexander, Thomas 1959
Allsop, Jim 1968
Allsop, Jon 1963, 64, 65
Amick, Hal 1963, 64, 65
Amick, Russ 1961, 62, 63
Ammerud, Sven 1958, 59
Anderson, Graham 1954, 55
Atwell, William 1957

B

Baake, Kjell 1952, 53, 54, 55
Baldwin, Bill 1954, 55
Bekken, Einar 1968
Betzold, Doug 1964
Birkeland, Peter 1953, 56
Blom, Karl 1964, 65, 66
Borgerson, Sig 1963
Brady, Gene 1949, 50, 51, 52
Brown, Kirk Alexander 1953

C

Cadwell, Charles 1958, 60
Chetkain, Art 1952

D

Dings, Bob 1948, 49, 50
Dunaway, Bill 1948

F

Federspiel, Ralph 1956
Fischer, Clair 1950
Fisher, Allan 1949
Fite, William 1957
Franklin, James 1956

G

Garretson, Jan 1964, 66
Germundson, Gunnar 1955, 56, 57
Giese, Erik 1960, 61
Gillis, Phil 1952
Grevstad, Bennard 1955, 57
Grobey, John 1952
Guttormsen, Kristian 1965, 66, 67

H

Haase, John Albert 1953, 54, 55, 56
Hanson, Hedric 1961
Helliesen, Henry 1964
Hill, Ted 1952, 54, 55

J

Jalbert, Jay 1964, 65, 66, 67

K

Kaald, Paul 1957
Kershaw, Ed 1958, 60, 61
Kiaer, Jan 1950, 51, 52
Kohls, Richard 1968

L

Lie, Ole 1951
Liikane, Mart 1954, 55, 56
Ly, Lars 1968

M

Martin, Tom 1951
Mathis, Desmond 1957, 58, 59
McLaughlin, Ross 1954
Midelfart, Erik 1968
Mills, Benjamin Gordi 1953
Mjoen, Thor 1966, 67
Morbeck, Jack 1964
Morrison, Gordon 1951

N

Nicholson, Doug 1959
Nord, Ole Tom 1962, 63

O

Ohlckers, Harald 1968
Oldberg, Henning 1968
Oldberg, Knut 1967
Orkney, Malcolm 1965, 66, 67

P

Peterson, Per 1951
Pike, James 1958
Raaum, Gustav 1948, 49, 50
Reiswig, Richard 1958

S

Sjoberg, Nils	1966, 67
St. Louis, Bob	1948
Stevenson, Rees	1948, 49
Stiles, Henry	1961
Sunde, Gunnar	1950

T

Talbot, Bill	1948
Talbott, Wilson	1949, 50
Tallman, Gary	1951
Taulbee, Walter	1956
Thomas, Dalton	1964
Thomas, Paul	1960
Thorbjornsen, Eyvind	1954

V

Valbo, Per	1964, 65, 66

W

Wegge, Per	1961, 62, 64
Welsh, Norm	1952
Williams, Ross	1949, 50
Woodward, Ralph	1961

Y

Yggeseth, Torbjorn	1960, 61, 62

Z

Zachary, Norm	1966, 67, 68

Men's Soccer

A

Akyeampong, Seth	1968
Allen, Graham	1980
Anderson, Eric	1978
Anderton, Stephen	1969
Annis, Matt	1995, 96, 97, 98
Appia, Okyahene	1968
Ashby, William	1967, 68, 69
Aumell, Jeff	1986, 87, 88
Aune, Brent	1988, 89, 90, 91

B

Babcock, Tim	1990, 91
Baghdanian, Jahanger	1976
Bakken, Johan	1967
Barbarick, Mike	1977, 78, 79
Bede, Chris	1992
Beeson, Craig	1984, 85, 86, 87
Bell, Martin	1969
Bermudez, Ken	1985, 86, 87
Berto, David	1988, 89
Bettinger, Rees	1996, 97, 98, 99
Betts, Arthur	1973
Bialek, Tom	1985, 86, 87
Binh, Nghyen	1969
Blubaugh, Rick	1985, 86, 87
Bowers, Terrence	1973
Boyce, Jason	1994, 95, 96, 97
Boyle, James	1991
Brady, Mark	1979
Bridge, Paul	1969
Brink, Burton	1970
Brown, Cliff	1973, 74, 75, 76
Brown, Terence	1969
Browne, Mike	1978
Buck, Denny	1975, 76
Buck, Doug	1973, 74, 75, 76
Burke, Donald	1970, 71, 72
Burke, Michael	1970

C

Cairns, Mark	1987, 88, 89
Carnell, Matt	1995, 96
Carney, Michael	1970
Carroll, Kai	1997, 98, 99
Carson, Phil	1982, 83, 84, 85
Casale, Mike	1997, 98, 99
Chesler, Dave	1975, 76
Christensen, Scott	1975, 76, 77
Christianson, Tage	1972, 73, 74, 75
Christopherson, Craig	1983, 84, 85, 86
Clearman, Steve	1980, 81, 82
Cobb, Stefan	1981
Cordell, Charles	1969
Cowmey, John	1992, 93, 94, 95
Crithfield, Chad	1988, 89, 90, 91
Cullom, Robert	1975
Cvitkovic, Michael	1967

D

David, Ken	1979
DeRocco, Anthony	1980
Dickinson, James	1999
Dorn, Ken	1990, 91
Dorn, Ron	1977
Dunaway, Dave	1978
Dunlap, Mark	1977
Dunn, James	1990
Dunn, Jason	1990

E

Eckmann, Lee	1981, 82, 83, 84
Edmonston, Jon	1993, 94
Edwards, Ryan	1994, 95, 96, 97
Englebrick, Steve	1979, 80, 81, 82
Enneking, Mike	1980, 81, 82, 83

F

Farrell, Jason	1990
Felt, Dave	1978, 79, 80, 81
Fewing, Peter	1983, 84
Filion, Paul	1972
Fitchette, Ray	1976, 77, 78
Fleck, Jon	1982, 83, 84
Foisie, Greg	1998, 99
Foody, James	1975
Forgette, James	1987, 88
Forrest, Ward	1972, 73, 74, 75
Franchino, Joe	1996, 97
Fry, Brian	1983
Fuegmann, Ken	1981, 82, 83, 84

G

Gauglitz, Phil	1978
Gehling, Keith	1973
Gibson, Scott	1979, 80
Glandon, Bill	1980, 81
Godat, Kyle	1993, 94, 95, 96
Goldingay, John	1968
Goodwin, Roger	1982, 83, 84
Gradilla, Joe	1994, 95
Graves, John	1977, 78, 80, 81
Green, Daryl	1984, 85, 86, 87
Guise, Eric	1986, 87

H

Hamel, John	1985, 86, 87, 88
Hanson, Randy	1987
Hart, Wes	1998, 99
Haslam, Rick	1977
Hellyer, David	1967, 68
Henderson, Eddie	1985, 86, 88, 89
Hikida, Vern	1972
Hilmi, Milud	1968, 69, 70
Hodges, Justin	1993
Hodgson, James	1983, 84, 85, 87
Hogenhout, Mark	1997, 99
Hollingshead, Kris	1999
Hormel, Steve	1984, 85
Howell, Glenn	1988, 90
Hudock, Dusty	1991, 92, 93
Hurd, Joel	1993, 94, 95, 96
Hurme, Paul	1991, 92, 93, 94

J

Jenkins, Scott	1992, 93, 94, 95
Jerdal, Lane	1997, 98
Jeter, David	1985, 86, 87, 88
Jinneman, Skip	1977, 78, 79, 80
Johnson, Ron	1973
Jones, Michael	1968, 69

K

Kang, Hyeon	1997, 98
Kazemi, Mohammed	1967
Keenan, Ian	1978, 79, 80, 81
Keita, Manuel	1973, 74, 75, 76
Klein, John	1981, 82, 83, 84
Klein, Peter	1981, 82, 83, 84
Koch, Jeff	1987, 88
Konzen, Stewart	1975

L

Lampmann, Rob	1993
Larned, Robert	1967
Lawson, Tim	1994, 95, 96, 97
Leslie, John	1992, 93
Levensen, Albert	1972
Long, Jeff	1983, 84
Lordahl, Garrett	1985, 86
Louckes Jr., Richard	1968, 69
Lyga, Richard	1967

M

Madden, Patrick	1988, 89
Marshall, Jon	1992, 93
Martin, Andrew	1988
Martinez, Jamey	1992, 93, 94, 95

Martins, Oliver 1967, 68
Matsushita, Jon 1972
May, Bill 1994, 95, 96, 97
McCarty, Chad 1995, 96, 97
McChesney, Chuck 1982, 83
McClain, Richard 1969
McCoy, Morgan 1996, 97, 98, 99
McIntyre, Gordon 1972, 74, 75
McKeown, Brad 1977
McLane, Alexander 1969, 70
McMonigle, Mike 1980, 81
McNett, Kevin 1989
McNiel, Bryan 1992, 93, 94, 95
Mendes, Paul 1973, 74, 75, 76
Mercer, Kyle 1997
Midelfart, Finn 1967
Miller, Lyle 1969, 70
Minor, Michael 1989
Monary, Rocco 1969, 70
Moore, Carroll 1967, 68
Moore, Thomas 1970, 71
Morando, Mitch 1993
Morrill, Doug 1990, 91, 92
Morton, Randall 1969, 70
Moss, Stanley 1968
Murray, Shannon 1989, 90, 91, 92
Myrfield, Warren 1969, 70

N

Nartey, Joseph 1967, 68
Nguyen, Viet 1994, 95, 97, 98
Norton, Rolf 1989, 90
Novion, Ed 1972, 73
Novion, Rodrigo 1972

O

Oliver, Daniel 1987, 88, 89, 90
Olsen, Chad 1999
Olsen, Eirik 1985, 86, 87
Ottopal, Dale 1987
Owens, Thomas 1969, 70, 71

P

Park, Mike 1980, 81, 82, 83
Penner, Erik 1991, 92, 93, 94
Pivec, Mike 1986
Poor, Glen 1982, 83, 84
Prideaux, Brandon 1994, 95, 96, 97

Q

Quickstad, Tom 1977, 78
Quickstad, Tracy 1977, 78

R

Ramsey, Bob 1976, 77
Rasch, Theodore 1972, 73
Rauen, Jerome 1977, 78, 79
Ray, John 1970
Renkert, Jeff 1980, 81, 82
Rentschler, John 1975, 76, 77
Retchless, Paul 1977, 78, 79, 80
Ritchie, Bryn 1998, 99
Rood, Martin 1972
Russ, Jeff 1981, 82, 83, 84
Russell, Ian 1993, 94, 96, 97

S

Sagare, Jake 1999
Sarkor, Monbo 1968
Sarver, Chris 1990, 91
Sawai, Kyle 1993
Schoonmaker, Martin 1970
Schuur, Mark 1979, 80, 81, 82
Scott, John 1967
Shoemaker, Robert 1967, 68
Shugarts, Curt 1981, 82, 83
Shugarts, Greg 1985, 86, 87
Siebu, Emmanuel 1968
Siwila, Eligjah 1968
Sleeth, Billy 1998, 99
Sletten, Charles 1991, 92, 93, 94
Smith, Anthony 1973, 74, 75, 76
Smith, Jon 1987, 88, 89
Smith, Robert 1969
Somoza, Ben 1999
Stoppler, Mark 1982, 83, 85, 86
Stottlemyre, James 1970
Stout, Steve 1989, 90, 91, 92
Strom, Bernd 1986, 87, 88, 89
Strom, Dan 1978
Strom, Gerd 1991, 92, 93, 94

T

Tallman, Zachary 1999
Thomas, Mitchell 1991
Tonkin, Ed 1972, 73
Travis, Perry 1988, 89
Turnbull, Jeremy 1990, 91, 92

V

Valore, Richard 1973, 74, 75, 76
Van de Ven, Peter 1997, 98
Van Hersett, Richard 1994, 95, 96, 97
Vaughn, Dan 1973, 74, 75, 76
Vaughn, Jim 1980, 81
Virden, Jud 1978, 79, 80, 81
Virgus, Norman 1968
Volpentest, James 1988, 89, 90

W

Waibel, Craig 1994, 95, 97, 98
Walyor, Robert 1973, 74, 75, 76
Whipple, William 1968
Whitworth, Chris 1972, 73, 74, 75
Willey, Mark 1977
Willoughby, Tad 1979, 80, 81, 82
Wolff, Chris 1995, 96, 97, 98
Woodhouse, Todd 1993, 94

Y

Yi, Han 1984, 86, 87
Yourkoski, Jon 1992

Z

Zahajko Jr., Alexander 1967
Zahniser, Thomas 1970
Zohn, Joseph 1968, 69, 70

Women's Soccer

A

Adler, Melissa 1991, 92, 94
Arrant, Malia 1997, 98, 99
Ash, Erin 1998, 99

B

Bailey, Erin 1996, 97, 98
Behler, Dee 1997, 98, 99
Bennett, Tami 1997, 98, 99
Biddle, Anna 1996, 97, 98, 99
Bilanski, Tara 1992, 93, 94, 95
Brennan, Melanie 1991, 92, 93, 94
Brewer, Gina 1998, 99
Browder, Tamara 1991, 92

C

Campbell, Natalie 1996, 97, 98, 99
Cox, Sarah 1991
Conrardy, Jessica 1993
Corey, Elizabeth 1992
Coykendall, Melissa 1992
Crivello, Angie 1995, 96, 97

D

Damato, Nina 1992
Dickerson, Casey 1995, 96, 97, 98
Dowd, Amy 1991

F

Fitzpatrick, Darcy 1992, 93, 95

G

George, Heather 1994
Gleason, Terry 1993, 94, 95, 96
Goodeve, Katie 1998, 99

H

Hamamoto, Amy 1991, 92, 93, 94
Hazlegrove, Marne 1991
Hughes, Stefanie 1994

J

James, Katy 1991
Jenkins, Carolyn 1994, 95, 96, 97
Jenkins, Wendy 1991, 92
Jensen, Jeannine 1991, 92, 93
Juergens, Kathleen 1991, 94

K

Keeley, Christine 1992
Kimble, Dana 1997
Klein, Rhonda 1991, 92, 93, 94
Koepke, Krista 1993, 94, 96

L

Light, Lindsay 1996, 97
Lyons, Marisa 1996

M

McKinstry, Megan 1999
Medved, Erin 1991

Mensinger, Gretchen	1996
Merlitti, Stacy	1997, 98, 99
Morelli, Andrea	1998, 99
Murphy, Michelle	1991

O

Obara, Samantha	1992, 94
Otagaki, Erin	1999

P

Pochman, Erin	1995, 96
Putz, Caroline	1998, 99

R

Rein, Jennie	1994, 95, 96, 97
Robinson, Shelley	1991, 92

S

Saltzman, Erin	1993, 94, 95, 96
Sellers, Adrienne	1995, 96, 97
Shaw, Kristin	1997, 98
Solo, Hope	1999

T

Thompson, Emily	1992, 93, 94, 95
Thompson, Tina	1994, 95, 96
Torre, Melinda	1992, 93, 94, 95
Trandum, Sanya	1992, 93, 94, 95

W

Wagner, Theresa	1997, 98, 99
Ward, Katey	1996, 97, 99
Weeks, Leslie	1999
Wilkinson, Sarah	1993
Wilson, Jana	1996, 97, 98, 99

Softball

A

Andrews, Kim	1993, 94

B

Bennett, Angela	1997, 98
Bennett, Chellee	1993
Bork, Jessica	1999, 2000
Brown, Shelley	1994, 95, 96, 97
Burns, Stephanie	1993, 94, 95, 96

C

Church, Michelle	1993, 94, 95, 96
Clark, Jaime	2000
Cline, Jennifer	1993, 94, 95, 96

D

DePaul, Kim	1998, 99, 2000
Downs, Melissa	1997, 98, 99, 2000

E

Engen, Amber	1998

F

Francis, Leah	1995, 96, 97, 98

G

Gaw, Eve	1995, 96, 97, 98
Giordano, Jeanine	1996, 97, 98, 99, 2000
Graves, Jamie	1997, 98, 99, 2000
Gustine, Kara	1994, 95

H

Hanson, Amy	2000
Hauxhurst, Kelly	1998, 99, 2000
Helgeland, Erin	1997, 98, 99, 2000

L

Leutzinger, Rosie	1997, 98, 99, 2000
Lunzer, Amber	1997, 98

M

Marzetta, Angie	1993, 94
McJunkin, Lauren	2000
McKay, Bridget	1993, 94, 95
McLain, Megan	1994
Meyer, Heather	1995, 96
Mick, Allison	1993, 94, 95, 96

N

Newbry, Becky	1996, 97, 98, 99
Nyblod, Jami	1996, 97, 98

O

Ota, Monika	1996

P

Pickering, Sara	1994, 95, 96, 97
Pisia, Denia	1998

Q

Queypo, Beth	1993

R

Rahal, Rochelle	1994, 95, 96, 97
Redd, Jamie	1997
Rosenblad, Christie	1998, 99, 2000
Rosser, Leanne	1995, 96, 97

S

Scappini, Amy	1995
Schellenger, Dana	1996
Shaull, Karen	1993, 94
Simpson, Becky	1999, 2000
Smith, Marie	1996, 97
Spediacci, Jennifer	1997, 98, 99, 2000
Storseth, Tami	1993, 94, 95, 96
Sumsky, Jenn	1999

T

Tarr, Heather	1994, 95, 96, 97
Tawney, Traci	2000
Topping, Jenny	1999, 2000

W

Wagner, Nancy Jackson	1993, 94
Walsh, Shannon	1999, 2000
Wikstrom, Megan	1993, 94, 95
Wilcox, Bridget	1999, 2000
Williams, Mindy	1993, 94, 95, 96
Wold, Stephanie	1993

Y

Yarbrough, Michelle	1998

Men's Swimming

A

Ainslie, Michael Warren	1974, 75, 76, 77
Akina, Clem	1943
Allen, Mark	1938
Anderson, Jim	1990
Anderson, Larry Bernard	1956, 57, 59
Anderson, Steve	1963, 64, 65
Anderson, Ture	1951
Andrews, Bud	1939
Asbury, Frank	1943
Athans, George	1940, 41, 43
Aucott, Brian	1984, 85, 86
Augustine, Chris	1987, 88, 89

B

Backhaus, Robin J.	1974, 75
Bahler, David	1973, 74, 75
Bailey, Nate	2000
Baker, Gil	1936
Baker, Jonathan Harvey	1969, 70, 71, 72
Becker, Dick	1940, 41
Becker, Ricardo	1991, 92
Bell, Robert Alan	1969, 70, 71, 74
Belote, Jim	1943
Benner, Jay	1984, 86, 87
Bezanson, Jim	1990, 91, 92
Bjur, Ralph Julius	1970, 71, 73, 74
Blank, William Thomas	1973
Blean, Dave	1966
Bockman, Mack	1939, 40, 47
Bohlman, Ron	1962, 63, 64
Bonn, Mark	1986
Bonney, Roy	1966
Boone, Bob	1961
Bornfleth, Bruce	1986
Bowman, Willie	1984, 85
Braden, Jody	1988, 89, 90, 91
Branigan, Bill	1936, 37
Bray, George	1964
Brewer, Greg	1984
Brinkman, Pete	1953
Brock, Louis John	1974
Brown, Bryan	1964
Brown, John Donald	1960, 61, 62
Bruce, Ed	1936
Brundage, Walter Jr.	1957, 58
Buckley, Pete	1967, 68
Bundy, Emory Franz	1956, 57, 58
Bunje, Eric John	1977

Burleson, Gary 1967, 68, 69
Burson, Al 1967

C

Caddey, Gene 1936, 37, 39
Cady, Charles Dillon 1997, 98
Cahill, Dave 1946, 47
Call, John Gerold 1958
Campbell, Bob 1968, 70
Campbell, Daniel 1992, 94
Campbell, Dick 1946, 48, 49
Campbell,
Robert Hedgcock 1969
Capron, Alan 1990, 91, 92
Capron, David 1989
Carpe, Stanley R. 1974
Carpenter, Jim 1936, 38
Carpenter, Ted 1949
Carper, Stanley R. 1973, 75
Castner, James 2000
Cazalet, Ed 1962, 63, 64
Chisholm,
Douglas Leonard 1960, 61, 62
Clark, Christopher 1992, 95, 96
Clayton, Bob 1950, 51, 52
Cleghorn, James 1994
Close, Jason 1994, 95, 96, 97
Clowers, Jason 1990, 91, 92
Cochran, Bruce 1950
Cole, Ronald 1985, 86, 87, 88
Colella, Peter 1986, 87, 89, 90
Colella, Richard Phillip 1970, 71, 72, 73
Colella, Steven M. 1974, 75, 76
Collins, Tim 2000
Cooke, Phillip Alfred 1960, 61
Cooper, Francis 1943
Corman, Gerald Wayne 1968, 69, 70
Coulter, Joseph Murray 1960, 61, 62
Cramer, Daniel Lewis 1955, 56, 58
Creedon, Jack 1951
Cross, Eric 1991, 92, 94

D

Dalrymple,
Lawrence King 1955, 56
Danforth, Tim 1988, 89, 90
DeFrang, Gary 1989, 90, 91, 92
deHart, Greg 1994, 95, 96, 97
Deininger, John 1962, 63
DeKoster, Dean 1984, 85, 86
Deligan, Steve 1984
DeMont, Richard J. 1974, 75
Denning, Jim 1943
DeRoest, John Allen 1971, 72, 73, 74
Diaz, George Ray 1957, 58, 59
Dickson, Bernie 1936
Dietrich, Tim 1995, 96, 97, 98
Divelbess, Ken 1995, 96, 97, 98
Dolan, Stein 1990
Douglas, Michael 1985, 86, 87, 88
Douglas, Scott 1989
Drawz, Brandon 1991, 92, 93
Drips, Phil Arthur 1955, 56, 57
Dunwiddie, Richard 1984, 85, 86
Dussault, Bruce Eugene 1957
Dykes, James Alexander 1953, 55
Dykstra, Joe 1995, 96, 97, 98

E

Eagle, Rusty 1994, 95, 96, 97
Eberharter, Dick 1948, 49
Eckdahl, Bob 1940
Eder, Hyman 1948
Edwards,
Jeffrey William 1971, 72, 73, 74
Eldred, Spencer 1975
Elerding, Rocky 1998, 99
Elliott, Dick 1952
Ellis, Duffy 1984, 85
Ellis, Jeff 1986
Erikson, Gus 1936, 37
Esko, Kevin 1986, 87, 88, 89
Everard, Jason 1991

F

Fallon, Robert 1994, 95
Fankhauser, Brad 1998
Fields, David Leslie 1971, 72, 73, 74
Fisher, Donald Boyd 1955
Flaherty, Don 1954
Flightener, Barry 1994, 95, 96
Flocco, Clay 1996, 97, 98, 99
Follrich, Jay 1943, 47, 48
Fosberg, Michael 1986
Foss, Lachlan Pries 1976
Foster, Craig 1984
Fowler, Ethan 1990, 91, 92
Fowler, Evan 1990
Fox, Francis 1963
Franck, John 2000
Fuller, Gary 1988, 89, 90

G

Gage, Kenneth Davies 1956, 58
Galles, Gret 1970
Garman, Jason 1998, 99
Garrison, Tom 1962
Gaston, Dan 1998, 99
Geitz, Christian 1997, 98, 99, 2000
Gellerman,
Louis Wright 1959
Gerauld, Bill 1975
Gering, Robert Raymond 1968, 69, 70
Gillingham, James 1985, 86, 87, 88
Goetschel, Charles 1985, 86
Goldberg, Pete 1939, 40, 41
Goode, John William 1952, 53, 54, 55
Grabenhorst, Cobe 1965
Graham, Frank 1952
Gravrock, Campbell 1995, 96, 97
Greedon, John 1950
Greek, Bruce 1985, 86, 87
Griffin, Reginald Murray 1960, 61, 62
Griffith, Dale Goodrich 1958, 59, 60

H

Hagen, Daniel Phillip 1977
Hall, Dick R. 1967, 68
Hall, Larik 1986, 87, 88, 89
Hall, Richard Scott 1968, 69
Hamblin, Bob 1952, 53, 54
Hamilton, Patrick 1991
Hancheroff, Bob 1964, 65
Haney, George 1949
Hannula, Daniel Lee 1971, 72, 73, 74
Harvey, Lucian 1936, 37, 38
Haslam, Gary 1984
Hata, Lawrence 1970, 71
Haydu, Adrian 1997
Heaney, George 1947, 48
Hecht, Larry 1963, 64, 65
Heidergott, Kurt 1963, 64, 65
Henderson, Jack 1946
Hennessy, Robert 1998
Herzog, Robert 1947, 48
Heyden, Jack Robert 1967, 68, 69
Hickman, Joshua 1999, 2000
Highmiller,
James Curtis 1959, 61, 62
Hill, Bud 1947
Hilton, Ken 1938
Hodges, Merrill 1951, 52, 53
Hoeppner, Carroll 1943
Hoeppner, Fred 1939, 40
Hoff, Ernie 1946, 47, 49
Hofstetter, Rick 1975
Holden, Wally 1939, 40, 41
Holland, Jim 1948
Holt, Chris 1989, 90
Hoppe, Fred 1949, 50
Hoskins, Franz 1936, 37, 39
Hoskins, Franz 1966
Hoy, Donald James 1970, 71, 72
Hudson, Fergus 1996, 97, 98, 99
Hull, Dan 1964, 66, 67
Hurd, Paul 1941, 47
Hyatt, Ray 1940, 41, 47
Hyman, Jeff 2000

J

Jack, Richard Douglas 1956, 57, 58
Jacobs, Ronald 1970, 71, 72, 73
Jensen, Edwin K. Jr. 1960, 61, 62
Jewett, Leonard Dale 1953, 54, 55
Jochums, Dick 1961, 62, 63
Johnson, Colin 1985, 86, 87
Johnson, Pat 1936, 37, 38
Johnson, Steven Edward 1974, 75, 76
Johnston, Chril 1967
Johnston, Jerry Lee 1974, 75, 76, 77
Jubb, Eric 1952, 53, 54

K

Kauffman, Art 1965, 66, 67
Keenan, Joseph David 1967, 68, 69
Keller, Don 1966
Kimball, Kory 1991, 92, 94
Kimball, Kyle 1990, 91, 92
Kimborowicz, Mark 1986, 87, 88, 89
Kipp, Gaylon 1963, 64
Kline, Rich 1995, 96

Name	Years
Knapton, Thomas	1989, 90, 91, 92
Knipher, Kurt Frederick	1971, 72, 73, 74
Knobbs, Don	1961
Koke, Leonard	1939, 40, 41
Kruse, Kyle	1994, 95, 96
L	
Lamay, Chuck	1970
Lanam, Robert	1998, 99
Langerin, Willie	1937, 38
Larralde, Christopher	1984, 85, 86, 87
Larsen, Dennis Glenn	1971, 72, 73, 74
Larsen, Orvel Wayne	1953, 54, 55
Larson, Chuck	1967
Laughlin, Beau (Victor)	1997, 98, 99
Lautman, Scott M.	1973, 74, 75
Lawson, William	1958, 59
Lazenby, Andrew	1995, 96, 97, 98
LeClercq, Nicholas Daniel	1967, 68, 69
Lee, Pete	1947, 51
Leer, Christian	1994, 95, 96
Lewis, Bob	1952, 53, 54
Lindsay, Stephen Arthur	1958, 59, 60
Loomis, Floyd (Honor "W")	1940
Lumbard, Douglas Norman	1976
Lyons, Hal	1962
M	
MacDonald, Robert Torrance	1971, 72, 73, 74
Mackem, Greg	1988, 89, 90, 91
Magnusun, Dick	1951, 52, 53
Malmstrom, Donald Earl	1967, 68, 69
Margerum, Dick	1941, 46
Marsh, Joseph Arthur	1977
Marshall, Knox	1936
Martin, Don Robert	1960, 61
Martin, Pat	1964, 65, 66
Martinez, Adam	1997
McAdams	1939
McAllister, Chris	1992
McArthur, Bill	1947
McArthur, Thad	1948, 49, 50
McCaffray, William	1989
McCarty, Dave	1984, 85, 86, 87
McClelland, James	1989, 90, 91
McClelland, Raymond	1986, 89
McClelland, Scott	1987, 88
McClure, Horace	1936
McInnis, Mal	1948
McIntyre, Michael Edward	1973, 74, 75
McKean, Art	1963, 64, 65
McKee, Ken	1975
McMahon, Bernard	1986
McMahon, Robert Charles	1958, 59
McMahon, Steve	1984, 85
McMahon, Steven	1986
McMillan, Joseph Corey	1956, 57
McNeel, Bob	1941
McNulty, Jim	1946
Medica, Jack	1936
Meinhardt, Aldy	1965, 66, 67
Metzgar, Roy George	1960
Meyer, Jim	1965, 66
Millard, Ben	1998, 99, 2000
Miller, Andrew	1997
Miller, Balke	1991
Miller, Bob	1949, 50, 51
Miller, Jack	1964
Miller, Joe	1943
Milleson, Ted	1952
Mines, Paull	1962, 63, 64
Mitchell, Ian	1997
Mittelstaedt, Jason	1992, 94, 95
Mlakar, Christopher	1999
Moberg, Robin Carl	1975, 76, 77
Moilanen, David	1999, 2000
Mott, Stephen	1994, 95, 96, 97
Murata, Patrick	1959, 60, 61
Music, Robert W.	1971, 72, 73, 74
Music, Wayne Dale	1970, 71, 72
Mylan, Chris	1994, 95
Mynatt, Blaine	1990, 91, 92
N	
Nadal, Mark	1992, 94, 95
Nadal, Robert Jason	1994, 95, 96
Nakano, Allen Tsuyoshi	1960, 61
Nelson, Bryan	1997, 98, 99, 2000
Nelson, Ethan	1984, 85, 86
Nelson, Toy	1936
Newberg, Bob	1965
Newberg, Don	1964
Newby, Dan	1962, 63
Newlands, Harry	1936
Newman, Joshua	2000
Newton, Dick	1950, 51
Newton, Jack	1947, 48, 49, 50
Nipper, Ralph	1940
Nordyke, Brent	1994, 95, 96, 97
Northway, Douglas Dale	1974, 75
O	
O'Connor, Jay	1988, 90, 91
O'Connor, John	1989
Odman, Bill	1941
Odne, Chris	1998, 99
O'Galligan, John Anthony	1955
O'Hare, Nick	1996
Oleson, Ryan	1999, 2000
Owens, Josh	1995, 96
P	
Patterson, William Petley	1974, 75, 77
Paulson, Jeffrey David	1977
Pearson, Mark	2000
Penn, William Jared	1970, 71, 72
Perry, Tom	1937
Personette, George	1937, 38, 39
Phillips, Al	1977
Phillips, Craig Alan	1971
Phillips, Raymond Lee	1960
Phoenix, Geoffrey	1999, 2000
Portelance, Douglas Alan	1977
Portelance, Herb	1954
Portelance, Jim	1952, 53
Portelance, Ron	1976
Powell, John	1948
Power, Steven Lee	1970, 71, 72, 73
Powlison, Pete	1943, 47, 48
Price, Rob	1990, 91, 92
Prothero, Mark Wayne	1975, 76, 77
Q	
Quigley, Tom	1994, 95, 96, 97
R	
Randles, Jim	1938, 39
Ranquet, Bucky	1941
Reebs, Stephen Raymond	1975, 76
Regan, Bob	1949, 50, 51
Reichmann, Graham	1995
Reisch, Kenneth Peter	1971
Revere, Bill	1953
Revere, William Andrew	1957
Riecke, Ross	1965
Riesch, Kenneth Peter	1970, 72, 73
Roark, Tim	1965, 66, 67
Rodriguez, Mark	1964, 65
Roosa, Robert	1997, 98, 99, 2000
Root, Charles	1991, 92, 94
Ruckman, Donald Ray	1958
Rummerfield, Michael Joseph	1969
Rupert, Frank	1967, 68, 69
Russell, Brian Arthur	1976, 77
Russell, Bryant	1940, 41
Russell, James M.	1994, 95, 96
Rutherford, Carl Alvin	1967, 68, 69
S	
Salmon, Pete	1949, 51
Sangerin, Bill	1939
Santry, Daniel Douglas	1960
Sauro, Randall Craig	1974, 75, 76, 77
Sawhill, Roy	1947, 48, 49, 50
Sawhill, Wallace	1948
Schacht, Bud	1938
Schall, Myron	1951, 52, 53
Schell, Brannon	1997, 98
Schmidt, Jeff	2000
Schneider, John	1961
Schufreider, Ernie	1970
Schufreider, Jeffrey Lynn	1970, 71
Schuster, Phil	1965
Schwarz, Bud	1940
Sheehan, Leo	1940
Sheldon, Charles	1950, 51, 52
Sherwood, Gordon	1946

Sherwood, Robin 1991, 92, 94
Shigeno, Dustin 1995, 96, 97
Shilling, John Dean 1975, 76
Simmons, Dick 1952, 53
Siverston, Rick 1987, 88
Skaug, Stuart 1997, 98, 99
Slamon, Pete 1952
Slick, Daniel Ross 1968, 69
Smith, Benjamin 1992, 94, 95
Smith, Franklin Lyon 1977
Smith, George Ernest 1956, 57
Smith, Van 1950, 51
Spangler, Warren Edward 1953, 54, 55
Staples, George Gerhardt 1955, 56
Sterling, William Kelly 1975, 76, 77
Stewart, Doug 1951, 52
Stewart, George 1954
Stipek, Bill 1965, 66, 67
Stone, Jamie 1998, 99, 2000
Strah, Steve 1990, 91
Stratton, Ryan 1997, 98, 99, 2000
Sullivan, William 1992
Sussex, Steven Alan 1974, 75, 76
Swink, Don Germain, Jr. 1968, 69
Sylvester, David 1986

T

Tainter, Kit 2000
Tallman, Gerry 1987
Tallman, John 1950, 51
Tallman, Steven C. 1974, 75
Tam, Francis 1998, 99, 2000
Tauscher, Harold Thomas 1957, 58, 59
Taylor, Ronald Ernest 1954, 55, 56
Thomas, Bob 1952, 53, 54
Thomas, Chan 1938
Thome, Carl Donald 1954, 55
Thome, Edward Thomas Jr. 1956
Thompson, Robert Byrd 1958, 59, 60
Thomson, Earl 1974
Thornhill, Don 1951
Thorton, Thurle Clyde 1957, 58, 59
Torney, Jack Jr. 1952, 53
Towne, Jeffrey 1992, 94, 95
Trager, Bob 1943, 47, 48, 49
Tucker, Bob 1963
Tye, Gilbert Scott 1969, 70

U

Urquhart, Mark 1995

V

Van Pool, Ken 1995, 96, 97, 98
Van Sant, Paul 1989, 90, 91, 92
VanWart, Issac S. 1974
VanWort, Steve 1975
Veale, Mark 1984
Vela, Steve 1984
Viau, David 1997, 98, 99
Virtue, Neil 1994, 95

W

Wahl, Art 1961, 62, 63
Walker, Michael Shane 1995
Walters, James B. 1974, 75
Wang, Kuo 1994, 95
Ward, Thomas Edward Jr. 1957, 58
Wardian, Edward 1985, 86, 87, 88
Warren, Thomas Frederick 1959
Watanabe, James Mitsuo 1959, 60, 61
Watanabe, Jun 1995
Watson, Jason 1991
Webster, John 1961
Weham, Bill 1936
Weil, Stephen Robert 1968, 69, 70
Weston, John Joseph 1975, 76, 77
White, Brad 1987, 88, 89, 90
White, Jim 1947
White, Robert Lee 1977
Wilcox, Bill 1938, 39
Williams, David Alden 1971, 72, 73, 74
Willson, Ed 1949, 50
Willson, Ted 1951
Wilson, John Docherty 1967, 68, 69
Wise, Arnie 1964, 65, 66
Witzke, Paul 1966, 67
Wohle, Eric 1992, 94, 95
Wright, Kyle 1998

Y

Yake, Bill 1938, 39, 40
Yee, Justin 1990
York, Erik 1986, 87, 88, 89
Young, David Paul 1977
Young, Michael Roy 1976
Young, Roy James 1975, 77
Yurchak, Randy 1994, 95, 96

Z

Zema, Gene 1947, 48
Zielke, Matt 2000

Women's Swimming

A

Abbott, Rae 1999
Abrams, Kathleen 1976
Adamek, Lynn Rachelle 1976, 77
Allen, Kathrin 1994, 95, 96, 97
Anderson, Donna 1989, 91, 92
Arden, Irene 1976
Avicola, Amy 1994, 95, 96, 97

B

Bain, Janice 1986, 87, 88
Bart, Janella 1998, 99, 2000
Baxley, Mary 1976, 77
Beadle, Allison 1985, 86, 87
Benson, Kiki 1992
Benson, Kirsten 1989, 90, 91
Berg, Ellen 1988, 89, 90, 91
Bingman, Tekla 1998
Birkner, Joanne 1996
Birrell, Shannon Doreen 1977
Bjodstrup, Karen 1984, 85, 86, 87
Black, Jane 1984
Black, Jill 1984
Brooks, June 1976
Brown, Margaret Kay 1976, 77
Bruya, Rachel 1995, 96, 97
Brychell, Jeannette 1984, 85, 86, 87
Bugarcic, Angie-Gisele 1992, 93, 94, 95
Butts, Dana 1992
Butts, Denise 1992, 93, 94, 95
Butts-Miller, Dana 1993

C

Cameron, Jennie 1991
Cheadle, April 2000
Childs, Kelli 1996
Christensen, Shaina 1996, 97, 98, 99
Citron, Kelly 2000
Clark, Cat 1984, 85
Coddington, Megan 2000
Cole, Kelly 1994, 95, 96, 97
Cray, Jenny 2000

D

Dalton, Susie 1984, 85
DeFrancisco, Sara 1994, 95, 96, 97
Delich, Whitney 1988
Dold, Joelle 1991, 92, 93, 94
Dorman, Abby 1993
Duncanson, Lori Kay 1977
Dyer, Jessica 1997, 98, 99, 2000

E

Egan, Jeanne 1984, 85
Ellis, Jana 1985, 86
Ellis, Robin 1984, 85
Elsner, Addy 1996, 97, 98, 99

F

Fenton, Devon 1990, 91
Fish, Gretchen 1986, 87, 88, 89
Fosberg, Linda 1986, 87, 88
Fritz, Jennifer 1990
Fuller, Carrie 1994, 95, 96, 97

G

Gage, Jessica 1991, 92
Gain, Janice 1985
Geist, Christie 1989, 90, 91
Gidlof, Shelly 1984
Gillingham, Nancy 1984, 85
Goodridge, Jennifer 1991, 92, 93, 94
Gray, Heidi 1993, 94, 95, 96
Grayson, Arnissa 1990, 91, 92, 93
Griggs, Kristen 1991, 92, 93
Gurner, Sandy 1984

H

Haggland, Kristen 1991, 92
Harada, Kim 2000
Hardee, Cathie 1998
Harris, Sunny 1997, 98, 99, 2000
Hingsbergen, Evelyn 2000
Hislop, Jo A. 1976, 77
Holman, Alice 1990
Hurtgen, Cheryl 1984

J

Jackson, Kelli 1992, 93, 94
Jenkins, Mary Ellen 1993, 94, 95, 96
Johnson, Helen 1987, 88, 89, 90
Jones, Marci 1996, 97, 98, 99

K

Kain, Mary 1989, 90
Keller, Kelsey 1997, 98, 99, 2000
Kilgore, Kim 1987, 88, 89, 90
Kimura, Doris Yukiko 1976, 77
Kimura, Nikole 1998

L

Landry, Jackie Kae 1976, 77
Langin, Audrey 1992, 93, 94
Larsen, Vanessa 1985, 86, 87, 88
Latimer, Denise 1988
Lovsted, Karen Louise 1977
Lysogorski, Kim 1998, 99, 2000

M

Marsh, Carla Suzanne 1976, 77
Martinez, Claudine 1992, 93, 94, 95
Marx, Linda 1987, 88
Marx, Marilea 1986
McClelland, Lynn 1992, 93, 94
McClure, Jaina 1999
McCoid, Pamela 1976
McElvaine, Arlene R. 1977
Middleton, Catherine 1991
Miller, Dana 1994
Montreuil, Kristin 1987, 88, 89, 90
Montreuil, Laurie 1987
Mooney, Debra 1984, 85
Moore, Julie 1992, 93, 94, 95
Murray, Michelle 1991, 93, 94

N

Nagata, Kristen 1997, 98, 99, 2000
Nelson, Susan 1976
Nixon, Jenny 1990, 91, 92, 93
Novesky, Sara 1993, 94, 95, 96

O

Ocken, Julie 1997, 98
Orsag, Dena 1989, 90, 91, 92

P

Patrick, Wendy 1991, 92
Pelkey, Deborah Anne 1977
Porter, Twyla 1985, 86, 87

Q

Quan, Sara 1992, 93, 94, 95

R

Read, Lesley 1976
Reimann, Kim 1997, 98, 99
Rekate, Kim 1984, 85, 86
Riggs, Diana 1977
Roark, Brandyn 2000
Robisch, Susan 1986, 87, 88, 89
Ronning, Kristen 1990, 91, 92
Rosenbaum, Anne 1999, 2000

S

Saladin, Susette 1985, 86, 87, 88
Satow, Tisha 1995
Schlumpf, Maria 1988, 89, 90
Schneider, Irene 1998, 99, 2000
Seubert, Trish 1988, 89, 90, 91
Shaull, Nicole 1998
Shelton, Jean 1985, 86
Sherrill, Kristen 1994, 95, 96, 97
Shelton, Jean 1984
Simmons, Anne 1992, 93, 94
Smith, Ashley 1994, 95, 96
Smith, Cory 1997, 98, 99
Spanish, Kerrie 1996, 97, 98, 99
Stolz, Abigail 1976, 77
Stucka, Jennifer 2000
Sunderland, Laura 1976
Swan, Kimberly 1990, 91
Sycamore, Laura 1993, 94, 95, 96

T

Tagas, Trina 1993, 94, 95, 96
Taggert, Megan 2000
Tanabe, Dawn 1986
Taradash, Tiffany 1991
Thompson, Jessica 1997, 98, 99
Tjelle, Kristin Marie 1977

V

van der Velden, Elaine 1984, 85, 86
Velikonja, Maria 1977
Versaw, Kristen 1998

W

Watanabe, Loree 1984, 85, 86, 87
Watanabe, Machiko 1997, 98, 99, 2000
Weatherhead, Katherine 1998, 2000
Weissert, Robin 1984
Weller, Karen 1986
Wicklund, Brenda 1988, 89, 90, 91

Men's Tennis

A

Addison, Peter 1976
Adkisson, Bill 1945
Aikins, Jim 1963, 64, 65
Albano, Ray 1952, 53, 55
Allen, Marshall 1920, 21
Andrews, Richard 1974, 75
Arlati, Ornello 1993, 94, 95, 96

B

Ballard, Dean 1910
Barber, Tom 1991
Barker, Stewart 1920
Baronsky, Robert 1958
Beer, Donald 1970, 71, 72, 73
Beer, Kenneth 1972, 73, 74
Bennett, Ed 1951
Bennett, Sumner 1954
Berg, James 1970, 71, 72, 73
Berman, Evan 1985
Berman, Jeremy 1998, 99, 2000
Betts, Dick 1939
Bishop, Ralph 1934
Bismuti, Peter 1986
Blom, Karl 1964, 65, 66
Bloomberg, Brion 1962, 63
Bloomberg, Steve 1967
Bostick, Wally 1947, 49, 51
Briggs, Bob 1933, 35
Brink, Bill 1944
Brink, Jim 1947, 48, 49
Broom, David 1958, 59, 60
Brown, Henry 1927
Brown, Tim 1990, 91, 92, 93
Bubois, Dick 1925, 26
Burrows, Dick 1947
Burrows, Ken 1945, 46, 47, 48
Butterfield, Bob 1942

C

Cahoon, Kevin 1976
Calaunan, Rex 1997
Camberlain, Percy 1918
Canfield 1916
Cannon, Joseph 1972, 73, 75
Carlson, Brent 1987
Carlyon, William 1971, 72, 73
Case, Gary 1966, 67
Cate, Bill 1939
Cavanaugh, Bill 1950
Chartier, Francis 1994
Christensen, Derwyn 1950
Chvoj, Martin 1996, 97
Clarke, Fred 1931
Clarke, George 1924, 25, 26, 27
Clarke, Ted 1932, 33
Clegg, Colin 1932, 34
Clegg, Ken 1933, 35, 36, 37
Coates, Tim 1980
Coats, William 1967, 68, 69
Colen, Peter 1976
Coons, Curt 1937, 38, 39
Crapo, Bill 1936, 37, 38
Crile, Chet 1990, 91, 92, 93

D

Damascus, Jim 1948
Dapas, Tori 1994, 95
daPonte, Bud 1932

Dawson, Craig 1983, 84, 85
Dearing, Bob 1935
Dekkert, Ron 1945
DeMaine, Mark 1992, 93
Denton, Pierre 1910
Diver, John 1989
Dorsey, Steve 1982, 84
Doyle, Harry 1959, 60, 61
Dranga, Mel 1925, 26, 27
Draves, Francis 1943
Drew, Eric 1996, 97, 98, 99

E

Eden, Darrell 1941, 42, 46
Eden, Donald 1942, 46
Ehmer, Paul 1968
Eicher, Jeff 1999
Ellegood, Kyle 1978, 79

F

Finnigan, Stephen 1967, 68, 69
Fisher, Fred 1949
Fisher, Peter 1968, 69
Flye, Don 1952, 53, 57
Foster, Geordie 1981, 82
Foster, John 1985, 88
Freeman, Eric 1989, 90, 91
Freudenberger, Jon 1988
Fritsch, Matthias 1993, 94, 95

G

Gamling, Martin 1997, 98
Gant, John 1981
Gardner, Doug 1983
Gardner, Ernest 1934
Gavin, Vince 1928
Geoghegen, Ed 1940
Getchell, Jim 1954
Goff, Dave 1958, 59
Gottesman, Tim 1994, 95
Graber, Andy 1990
Grant, Bill 1988
Grant, Don 1950
Grant, Richard 1975, 76, 77, 78
Greeley, Dave 1938
Green, Mike 1963
Greenberg, Michael 1974, 75, 76, 77
Grevstad, Barney 1934, 35, 36
Grimes, John 1968
Gross, Aaron 1990, 91
Grundy, Robert 1989, 90

H

Hageman, Walt 1951
Hagen, Wayne 1983, 84
Hanlin, Matt 2000
Hansen, Bert 1908
Hanson, Bob 1953, 54
Hanson, Don 1944, 45
Harnett, Jason 1991, 92, 93, 94
Harrison, Kent 1979
Harrison, Scott 1981, 82
Hart, Brian 1993, 94
Hashiguchi, Shugo 1934
Hefter, Chris 1991
Henderson, Steven 1974, 75, 76, 77
Herrman, David 1991
Hesketh, Bob 1923, 24, 25
Higgins, Hubert 1916
Hill, Jim 1934, 35
Hodderson, Eric 1966
Holbrook, Art 1941, 42
Hoyt, George 1929, 30, 31
Hunt, Laury 1961, 62, 63
Hunt, Steven 1986, 87, 88
Hynes, John 1969, 70, 71
Hynes, Kryan 1930
Hynes, Mike 1961, 62, 63

I

Ide, Wilson 1918

J

Jacobsen, Bill 1956, 57, 60
Jacobsen, Billy 1982, 83, 85, 86
Jobs, Pete 1960, 61, 62
Johnson, David 1988, 89, 91, 92
Johnson, Fletcher 1922, 23, 24
Johnson, Steven 1966, 67, 68

K

Kaplan, Craig 1987
Kato, Kenneth 1969, 70
Kaufman 1916
Kawakami, Wayne 1978, 79
Keeney, Harold 1933
Kellock, Bruce 1970
Kendrick, Robert 1998, 99
Killingsworth, Bill 1939, 40
Kirk, Jerry 1951, 52, 53
Kirk, Jon 1994
Kitamura 1918
Knight, Dick 1968, 69, 70
Kono, Masami 1957, 58
Kopach, Michael 1978, 79, 80
Kriegal, Dick 1944
Kull, Christoph 1999

L

Lagonegro, Robert 1985
Langlie, Art 1920, 21, 22, 23
Langlie, Windy 1926, 28, 29
Lapins, Nick 1964, 65, 66
LaRoux, Archie 1939
Larson, Gary 1962
Larson, Timothy 1985
Lass, Roland 1967, 68, 69
Leaver, Dave 1963, 64, 65
Lee, Wai Ching 1977, 78, 79, 80
Lefebvre, Doug 1941
Leonhard, Kurt 1987, 89
Lieber, Carl 1945
Lim, Danny 1951, 55
Lim, Randy 1979, 80, 81, 82
Linden, Gary 1955, 56, 57
Linden, Glenn 1950, 51
Litzau, Mark 1977, 78
Livengood, Joe 1923, 25
Loquivan, Henry 1940, 41
Lotfy, Hussein 1970, 71, 72
Loveland, Kerry 1989, 90
Lowe, Jack 1946, 47, 48, 49
Lund, Knute 1989, 90, 91, 92
Lunde, Marius 1998, 99, 2000

M

Marion, Armand 1923
Mark, David 1972, 73
Marti, Inaki 1992, 93
Marti, Manuel 1991, 92, 93
Martin, Geordie 1959, 60, 61
McCormick, Don 1965
McKay, John 1978, 79
McLaren, Don 1929, 30
McLaughlan, Andrew 1978
Meacham, Dave 1981, 82
Meade, Peter 1974, 75
Mertel, Chuck 1955, 56, 57
Miller, Peter 1974
Montcrief, Ray 1909
Montgomery, Joe 1969, 70, 71
Moore, Scott 1995, 96, 97
Mordoff, Kenneth 1970, 71
Morgan, Brandt 1966, 67
Mosher, Dick 1936, 37
Mounger, Lowery 1957, 58, 59
Muira, M. 1916
Murray 1909

N

Naslund, Gordon 1945
Neubauer, Mark 1981, 82, 83, 84
Neubauer, Thomas 1988
Newkirk, Bill 1928, 29, 30
Niles, Wendell 1952
Nordstrom, Lloyd 1930, 31, 32

O

Odell, Rollin 1955, 56
Odman, Bob 1941, 42, 43
Oertli, Ron 1956
Olejar, Michael 1991
Olson, Al 1943
Olson, Walt 1944, 46
Onustock, Mark 1985, 86, 87, 88
Opperman, Jack 1945
Opperman, John 1948, 49
Ostrom, Dewey 1937, 38
Oswald, Dick 1946
Oswald, Hugo 1943

P

Page, Byron 1938, 39, 40
Parry, Jeff 1986, 87, 88, 89
Parsons, Darren 1989, 90
Parsons, Dean 1962, 63
Partain, Greg 1982
Pearson, Chris 1983, 84, 85, 86
Pearson, Scott 1980, 81, 82, 83
Peck, Don 1942, 43
Perkins, Doyle 1954, 55, 56
Perry, Bryce 1972, 73, 75
Peterson, Haller 1940, 46

Pettit, Tupper	1960
Plummer, Willis	1927, 28
Posavac, Andy	1998, 99, 2000
Preston, Hugh	1949, 50

Q

Quatrochi, Nicholas	1997, 98, 99, 2000
Quillian, Bill	1952, 53, 54, 55
Quillian, Will	1990

R

Radloff, Richard	1958, 59, 60
Rampazzo, Sasha	1995, 96, 97, 98
Rampazzo, Stefano	1993, 95, 96, 97
Rant, Dick	1984, 85, 86, 87
Ravenscroft, George	1938, 39, 40
Raymond, Chad	1997
Reid, Bill	1949
Reischling, Ted	1984, 85, 87
Remberg, Adair	1908
Rhodes, Bill	1934, 36
Rickles, Julian	1936, 37
Rieke, Mott	1931, 32, 33
Romney, Chris	1978, 79, 80
Rose, Jack	1953
Rosen, Richard	1995, 96
Rosenberg, Henry	1934, 35, 36
Rostgaard, Sverre	1931
Ruby, Dillon	2000
Ruffin, Douglas	1971, 72, 73

S

Sackett, Rod	1945
Sanders, Monroe	1918
Scharman, Michael	1972, 75
Schroeder, Ian	1987, 88, 89
Schuster, Keith	1977, 78
Scott, Harry	1922
Scott, Wallace	1924
Shanglie, Ladd	1938
Shaw, Harry	1924, 25
Short, Charlie	1984, 85, 86, 87
Skidmore, Sam	1925
Slemmons, Warren	1965
Smetheram, Herb	1954
Sporcic, Chris	1990, 92
Steiner, Herb	1943
Stephenson, Cullen	1976, 77, 78
Stewart, Jeff	1966
Strasberg, Ari	2000
Swartz, Joe	1926, 27
Sweet, John	1943

T

Taylor, Bill	1920, 21, 22
Tille, Chuck	1998, 99
Tom, Taylor	1996
Tomandl, Mark	1992, 93, 94, 95
Troeh, Arnie	1965

V

Valdez, Enrique	1977, 79, 81
Van Noy, Mark	1980
Vandenburge, Bill	1947

W

Wall, Tom	1976, 77, 78, 80
Waller, Don	1918, 20, 21
Watanabe, Frank	1942
Wendel, Hal	1980
Wendell, Robbie	1993, 94
Whiteside, Brian	1979, 81, 82
Wick, Lou	1950, 51, 52
Wilkinshaw, Walt	1937
Williams, Nick	1995, 96, 97
Wilson, Jay	1983, 84, 85, 86
Witt, Bob	1933
Witt, Clyde	1965, 66
Woodin, M.S.	1908
Woolley, Mark	1997, 98, 99, 2000
Wright, Jeff	1994

Y

Yee, Gary	1972, 73, 75

Z

Zeratsky, Dan	1980, 81, 82, 83
Zimmer, Stuart Jr.	1968, 69, 70

Women's Tennis

A

Agee, Teri	1981
Allen, Amy	2000
Allen, Elizabeth	1989, 90, 91, 92
Appel, April	1993, 94
Appel, Janie	1980, 81, 82
Appel, Jennifer	1977, 78, 79, 80
Arndt, Ann	1978, 79, 80, 81

B

Baronsky, Beth	1987, 88
Beck, Kathi	1976, 77, 78, 79
Bixler, Catherine	1986
Blitz, Lisa	1985, 86
Botts, Lara	1998, 99
Boudwin, Sherril	1980, 81, 82, 83
Buchanan, Heidi	1994, 95
Buermann, Evelyn	1982, 83, 84, 85
Burrows, Anne	1975, 76, 77, 78

C

Cadigan, Meggan	1996, 97
Cahoon, Susan	1988, 91
Calvert, Vanessa	1986
Carlyon, Caron	1975, 76
Casal, Gina	1981
Chi, Kathy	2000
Christ, Kirsten	1984, 85
Clarke, Whitney	1988, 89
Clayton, Becky	1990, 91, 92, 93
Clevenger, Kris	1989, 90
Cordry, Erin	1985, 86, 87
Corlett, Erin	1994
Costain, Katherine	1996, 97
Costi, Kari	1993, 94, 95, 96
Cummings, Sharon	1976
Cutler, Judy	1980, 81

D

Dickson, Chris	1983, 84, 85
Dorsey, Christi	1979, 80, 81, 82
Dysart, Nancy	1984

E

Eggertsen, Laura	1978
Ershig, Wendy	1986

F

Ferkins, Lesley	1988, 89
Field, Lorri	1982
Foster, Susan	1983, 84
Fountain, Melanie	1992
Fox, Rhonda	1991
Frost, Kim	1992, 93, 94, 95

G

Garside, Gretchen	1995
Goesling, Susan	1973, 74, 75, 76
Gray, Colleen	2000
Gronowick, Kathy	1981, 82, 83, 84
Guimond, Jennifer	1991

H

Hannesdottir, Hrafnhildur	1998, 99
Henderson, Gini	1981, 82
Hinkley, Lisa	1990, 91
Hoag, Tahnee	1999
Hudson, Kristin	1990
Huguenin, Katie	1995, 96, 98
Hutton, Beth	1991, 92

I

Ichikawa, Mai	1990
Irving, Lindy	1993, 94, 95, 96

J

Jacobsen, Brenda	1979, 80
Jamieson, Sharon	1976
Johnson, Laura	1976
Johnson, Sandra	1988

K

Klaic, Darija	2000
Knudson, Karla	1979
Kolb, Karly	1994, 95
Kordonskaya, Ilona	1999, 2000
Kraszewski, Kristina	1998, 99, 2000
Kristensen, Anett	1997
Kunath, Kate	1996

L

Larson, Kris	1977
Lefebvre, Michelle	1980
Leong, Shieh Yen	1993, 94
Loveland, Charlotte	1993
Luna, Kari	1995, 96, 97, 98

M

Majury, Erin	1986, 87
Maki, Janelle	1984, 85, 86, 87
Marhefka, Lynne	1976, 77, 78, 79
Matheson, Monique	1986, 87, 88, 89
Maw, Anna	1992
McCann, Laura	1983
Mead, Jennifer	1987, 88, 89, 90
Moldrem, Lisa	1978, 79, 80, 81
Mounger, Melinda	1986, 87, 88, 89

O

Olejar, Cindy	1988, 89, 90, 91

P

Payne, Delores	1975, 76, 77
Phan, Lahn	1991, 92, 93, 94
Phillips, Claudia	1978
Pollock, Andrea	1988, 89, 90, 91
Proctor, Lisa	1992, 93, 94, 95

R

Radford, Jennifer	1996, 97
Raftis, Maryann	1982, 83
Reilly, Mary	1989, 90, 91, 92
Rembold, Beth	1988, 89, 90
Ridder, Linda	1982, 83, 84, 85
Rintalla, Cindy	1977

S

Sanchez, Rachael	1997
Schaab, Lynn	1979
Schaumburg, Kim	1977, 78, 80
Schutten, Mary	1975, 76, 77, 78
Sosnowy, Kori	1995, 96, 97, 98
Stensrud, Carla	1982, 83, 84, 85
Stoloff, Erica	1995, 96, 97, 98
Strang, Lisa	1978, 79, 80, 81
Stringer, Paige	1992, 93, 94, 96
Stunova, Zuzana	1997, 98, 99, 2000
Svanfeldt, Jennifer	1997, 98, 99, 2000
Swerland, Shauna	1991, 92, 93

T

Thomas, Michelle	1991, 92, 93, 94
Tobin, Nancy	1979

V

Van Dyk, Gretchen	1978, 79, 80, 81
Vermilyea, Emily	1999
Voke, Jennifer	1994

W

Wagner, Chris	1984, 85, 86, 87
Wagner, Zeta	1997, 98, 99, 2000
Wicklund, Kari	1989, 90
Wood, Kristin	1983, 84, 85, 86
Wu, Peggy	1997, 98, 99, 2000

Z

Zier, Becki	1984, 85, 86, 87

Men's Track and Field

A

Abbey, George	1949, 50, 51
Ackermann, Carl	1948
Adams, Ben	1938
Adams, Robert	1929, 31
Aguierre, Domingo	1941
Akins, Jerrod	1992
Alan, Mark	1990, 91
Albright, Richard Gordon	1970, 72, 73, 74
Aleinikoff, Paul	1958, 59, 60
Algyer, Ray	1926
Allamano, John Eugene	1966, 67, 68
Allen, Michael	1990, 92, 93
Anabel, Scott	1996, 97, 98, 99
Anacker, Don	1957, 58, 59
Anderson	1910
Anderson, Bob	1939
Anderson, Bruce	1936
Anderson, Casey	1921
Anderson, Dean	1926, 27, 28
Anderson, Gene	1964
Anderson, Keith Leroy	1971, 72
Anderson, Oscar	1915
Anderson, Roy	1942
Anderson, Shawn	1991
Anderson, Steve	1928, 29, 30
Anderson, Sylvester	1922, 23
Anderson, Tyler	1991, 92, 93
Angell, Abe	1954, 55, 56
Angell, Anthony	1960, 61, 62
Angle, Jim	1935, 36, 37
Anshutz, Bert	1935, 36, 37
Applegate, Kenneth	1924, 25, 26, 27
Armstrong, Patrick William	1968
Arthaud, Don	1932, 33
Arthaud, Jack	1939, 40
Atkins, Herman, Jr.	1970
Atkins, Jerrod	1993
Atkinson, Dennis	1961
Atwood, Duncan Fuller	1974, 76, 77
Augerson, Casey	1920
Augustine, Webster	1924, 25, 26
Auzias-Turrene	1912
Avey, Gene	1939, 40

B

Bain, Jerry	1958, 60
Bale, Dick	1951, 52
Bale, Robert	1929, 30, 31
Ball, John	1966
Ballard, Robert	1971
Ballwey, Brian Jerome	1974
Banks, Henry	1952, 53, 54, 55
Bannick, John	1934
Bantz, Burwell	1908
Baptiste Bernard Coleridge	1967, 68
Barajaz, George	1992
Barber, Gregory	1997, 98, 2000
Barnes, Burton	1933, 34
Barr, Darrell	1940, 41
Barr, Theodore Graham	1976
Barron, Jack	1943
Bartholmey, Don	1949, 50
Baudraum, Warren	1940
Baugh, Gerald	1972
Bazzi, David	1997, 98, 99, 2000
Beall, Harry	1920, 21, 22
Bechtol, Chuck	1938, 39, 40
Beguhl, Philip Charles	1973
Belford, John	1987
Bell, Charles	1939, 40
Bell, Daniel	1985, 87
Bell, Gerry	1943
Bell, Theodore	1931, 32, 34
Belur, Jerry Jack	1972, 74, 76
Belz, Christian	1997, 98
Bender, Bert	1958, 59
Berge, Stephen Ray	1970
Bergman, Eugene	1919, 21
Bigelow, Dick	1942
Bingham, Harry	1938, 39, 40
Bingham, Jeffrey Emerson	1969
Birch, Jeff	1966, 67
Birkinshaw, Richard Grant	1971
Bjorkland, Leon	1938, 39
Bledsoe, Clarence	1930, 31, 32
Blonk (Honor "W")	1932
Blue, Eugene	1919
Blue, Nick	1998
Bohrer, Steven	1987
Bollen, Chris	1964, 65
Bollinger, Ron	1954
Bookey, Michael Thomas	1968
Bottjer, Ryan	1998, 99
Bowman, Claire	1911,13
Bowman, Hugh	1908,10,11
Bowman, John	1985
Bracken, Dan	1931, 32, 33
Bradley, Blayne	1991
Braley, Russ	1942
Brandon, Robert Alvin	1972, 73
Brandt, Michael Lee	1969
Brannon, Ernie	1957, 58, 59
Braun, Gordon	1974, 76
Braunschweiger, Bob	1958, 59
Braunstein, Tony	1991, 92, 93
Brazier, John	1955
Brewer, Philip	1947, 49
Brian, Robert	1999, 2000
Brigham, Charles	1946, 49, 50, 51
Brinkley, Jim	1941, 42, 43
Brix, Egbert	1924, 26
Brix, Herman	1926, 27, 28
Brodie, Doane	1928, 29,31
Brokaw, James Franklin	1910,11

Bronn, Greg 1987, 90
Brosseau, Joseph 1999
Brovold, Gregory Edward 1969
Brown, Dick 1949
Brown, Steve 1963, 64, 65
Bryan, Bob 1954, 55, 56
Bryan, James 1922, 23
Bryant, Beno 1990
Bryde, John Kirk 1971
Buchanan, William 1961
Buckley, John 1935, 36, 38
Burke, Jack 1947, 48, 49, 50
Burkholder, Troy 1996
Burney, Jack 1953
Burney, John 1947, 48, 49
Burston, Ray 1925, 26
Buse, August 1931
Bush, Fred 1950
Bynoe, Alex 1992, 93
Byrne, Timothy B. 1972, 74

C

Cadman, Jason 1998, 99, 2000
Cadwell, George 1932
Cairney, Ralph 1930, 32
Calder, Lester 1920
Callison, Cecil 1922, 23
Cameron, Pete 1953
Campbell, Ed 1910
Campbell, Graham 1998, 99
Campbell, Todd 1991
Carlton, Dennis 1953
Carr, Luther 1957
Carr, Michael 1973, 74
Carter, Frank 1924
Cassity, George 1955, 56
Cathcart, Ernie John 1971, 72
Cavicke, David 1946
Celms, John Valdis 1966, 67, 68
Chaffin, James Ralph 1971
Chambul, Borys 1972, 74, 76
Chang, Spencer 1990
Chapin, Ron 1990, 91, 92, 93
Charouhas, Tom Charles 1976
Charteris, James 1925, 26, 27
Childs, Boyd 1935, 36, 37
Childs, Lee Andrew, Jr. 1970
Christensen, Scott Blair 1970, 71
Chung, Aaron 1992, 93
Clark, Andy 1992, 93
Clark, Charles Stephen 1973, 74
Clark, George 1925
Clark, Lyle 1942, 46, 47
Clarke, George 1924, 26
Clarkson, Charles 1928, 29, 30
Clinton, Dick 1943
Clyde, Paul 1913,14,15,16
Coatney, David Edward 1977
Coats, William 1960
Cochran, Elvin 1913,14
Cochran, Lamont 1915
Cocking, Boyd 1926
Coddington, Travis 1997
Cole, Bruce 1940, 41, 42
Cole, Jay 1991, 92, 93
Cole, Stephen M. 1974
Coleman, Kelly 1990, 91, 92, 93
Coleman, Sam 1938, 39
Comin, Myron 1934
Condon 1911
Condon, John 1931, 32, 33
Congdon, Gordon 1935
Connell, Kurth 1996, 97, 98
Connors, Craig 1997, 98
Consecki, Scott 1930
Conwell, Ernest 1992, 93, 96
Cook, Dennis Alphonse 1977
Corbin, Merritt 1932, 33
Corvin, Curt 1985, 86
Courtney, Ira 1911,12
Courtwright, Ed 1938, 39
Coyle, Frank 1908
Craig, Lawrence Warren 1969, 71
Cram, Jack 1927, 27, 30
Cramer, John 1961, 62, 63
Crities, Newton 1912,13,15
Croasdill, Charles 1938
Cummins, Robert 1948
Custer, Ed 1933
Custer, Walt 1933
Cutts, Elmer (Honor "W") 1929

D

Dailey, Ervin 1919, 20
Dalby, Dave 1947, 48
Damberville, Andrew 1996, 97, 98, 99
Danielson, Alvin 1968, 69
Dankworth, Gary Steven 1970, 71, 72, 73
Davidson, Harry 1914
Davies, Robert 1929
Davis, Albert A. 1974, 76
Davis, John 1956, 57
Davis, Marsh 1919, 20, 21
Dawson, Bryce 1996, 97, 98
Day, James 1998, 99
Deeks, Don 1943
DeMunnik, Mike 1996
Derby, Dean 1956, 57
DeSaussure, Andre 1997
Dill, Jacob 2000
Dillaway, Steve 1965, 66, 67
Dixon, Bill 1950, 51
Dkartvedt, Darrold 1953
Dodds, Gordon 1928, 29
Dodge, Harold 1943
Dohm, Clarence 1905
Donaldson, John 1949, 50, 51
Donnelly, Matthew 1985, 86, 87
Donovan (Honor "W") 1932
Donovan, Clyde 1933
Doremus, Ralph 1933
Douglas, Donald 1920, 21, 22
Douglas, Donald 1946
Douglas, John 1959, 60, 61
Downey, Craig 2000
Driscoll, Les 1957, 58
Drury, Jim 1935, 36
DuBois, Kenneth 1923
DuBois, Kinsley 1924
Dufour, Pete 1951, 52
Dunn, Bryant 1930, 31, 32
DuPree, David Ellis 1966, 67, 68

E

Eakins 1910,11
Easton, Roger 1971
Eckman, Ray 1920
Edmiston, Ariel 1934, 35
Edmonds, Rupert 1912,13,14,15
Egbert, Vince 1938
Egtvet, Percy 1923, 24, 25
Eitelberg, Daniel 1977
Elkins, Daniel 1974
Ellison, Aaron 1985, 87
Ellison, Bernard 1990, 91
Engelstone, Eric 1985, 87
Enger, Harold 1943
England, Negley 1932, 33, 34
Erickson, Donald 1986
Erickson, Greg 1985
Erickson, Steve 1981, 82, 84, 85
Eriksen, Dick 1939
Evans, Thomas 1960, 61, 62
Evans, White 1910,11
Ewaliko, Rody J. 1974, 76

F

Faber, Fred 1942
Factory, Michael 1977
Faget, Melvin 1927, 28
Failla, Donald 1959, 60, 61
Fairleigh, Lawrence Dean 1969, 71
Fairleigh, Michael Robert 1970, 71
Fancher, John 1914
Fate, Donald Dean 1968, 69, 70
Fayant, Jason 1999, 2000
Feider, Patrick 1990
Feldman, Cary Lynn 1970, 71, 72
Fellows, Jerry Allen 1970
Fennema, Carl 1947, 48
Ferguson, Jack 1928
Ferry, Edward 1922, 23, 24
Fetter, Earl 1946, 47
Fieder, Pat 1991
Finke, Ralph 1924
Fischer 1938
Fisher, James Norman 1966, 67, 68
Fjellman, Greg 1992, 93
Flagg, Jack 1937, 38, 39
Flanagan, Patrick 1986, 87
Floberg, John 1950
Flynn, Devon Brownlee 1976, 77
Forni, Greg 2000
Fornia, Bob 1952, 53, 54
Forster, Andrew 1997
Forsyth, Elliott 1987, 91
Foster, Phil 1921
Frame, Don 1933

Franco, Pablo J. 1974, 76, 77
Frankland, Charles 1920, 21, 22
Frankland, Charles 1947
Free, A.K. 1922, 23
Frost, Eugene 1933, 34
Frostad, Knut 1961, 62
Froude, Chester 1924
Fuller, Roy 1931
Fulton, Jeff 1967

G

Gable, John 1935
Gaines, Robert 1976
Galer, Fred 1932, 33, 34
Gamach, Dan 1985
Gano, Kyle 1992, 93
Garretson, Ron 1941, 42, 43
Garrett, Brian 1967
Garrett, George 1932
Garrison, David Howard 1972, 73
Gary Jr., Robert 1986, 87
Gary, Clark 1962
Gavin, John 1933
Gayton, Carver 1959
Gayton, Gary 1952, 53, 54, 55
Genung, Eddie 1929, 31, 32
Gibson, George Gregory 1974, 76, 77
Gibson, John 1915,16,17
Giesen, Allan 1990
Giles, Don 1941
Gilliam, Darrell 1946
Gilpin, Tom 1963
Gish 1910,11
Glass, Steve 1998
Gleason, Villeroy 1915
Goiney, Bob 1972
Gonsecki, Scott 1931, 32
Goodner, Ernest 1919, 20
Goss, Lyle 1926
Gourlay, Arthur 1928
Grace 1912
Gray, Harold 1915,17,19
Gray, Larry 1954, 55
Green, Jeffrey 1990, 91
Green, Stan 1953, 54
Greene, Harold 1905
Grichunchin, Fred 1935
Griffin, Scott 1990
Guenther, Fred 1952, 53
Guerrero, Patrick 1990, 91
Guiterrez, Uriel 1996
Gustafson, Gary Leroy 1977

H

Haagen, Merrill 1941, 42, 43
Hablou, Wallace 1950
Hage, Bob 1938, 39
Hagerty, Frank 1923
Hale, Mark 1987, 90
Hall, Dana 1990, 91
Hall, Ned 1937
Hamilton, James Allen 1972, 73
Hammermaster, Gene 1955, 56
Hamre, Nelson 1991
Hanenberger, Peter Dan 1968
Hann, Michael Robert 1970
Hansen, Doug 1972
Hanson, Gary 1966, 67
Harder, Richard 1959, 60, 61
Harkins, Paul 1997, 98, 99, 2000
Harmon 1913
Harper, Steve 1992, 93
Harrell, Newson 1932
Harrell, Newton 1931
Harris, Al 1985
Harris, Albert 1970, 71
Harris, DeWitt Alvin 1986
Harrison, Donn 1948, 49, 50
Harrison, Jelani 2000
Harrison, Walt 1942, 43
Hartley, Talbot 1929, 30, 31
Haslam, Harry 1970, 71
Hatheway, Ernest 1921, 22, 24
Hattix, Carlos 1996, 97
Hatzenbeler, Steve 1996
Hawken, Harvey 1961, 62, 63
Hawkins, Harold 1934
Hay, Marion 1936, 37, 38
Hayes, John 1949
Hayes, John Frederick 1974, 76, 77
Haynes, Nat 1930
Hazelton, Scott 1987
Hazlet, Stewart 1963, 64
Heaton, Archie 1939, 41
Henning, Burt 1927
Henry, Dean 1955
Hensey, Jack 1950
Hensey, John 1947, 48, 49
Herbert, Alan James 1974
Hicks, William Lewis 1974
Hildrum, Tom 1999, 2000
Hill, Michael 2000
Hiltabidel, Charles 1946
Hilton 1912
Hilton, Daniel 1996
Hilton, Jim 1954, 55, 56
Hinkley, Wayne Henry 1974, 76
Hobbs, Richard 1960, 61
Hoelting, Kimball S. 1968, 69, 70
Hogue, Jim 1965, 66
Holmes, Scott D. 1974
Holzknecht, Ted 1951
Hooker, JaWarren 1998, 99, 2000
Horat, Albey 1992, 93
Hossman, Carl 1933
Howell, Bryan 1985
Hubbard, Harry 1939
Hubbell, John Monroe 1968, 69, 70
Hublou, Wallace 1948
Hufford, Merle 1931
Hughes, David 1991
Humber, Bruce 1935, 36, 37
Humes, Thomas 1927, 28, 29
Hunt, Woodward 1960
Hunter, David 1985
Hurd, Bob 1949
Hurley, Victor 1921, 22, 23
Husby 1912
Hutchinson, Bob 1951, 52, 53

I

Iddings, Earl J. 1997, 98, 2000
Iddings, Owen 2000
Ingraham, Reed 1928, 29
Ingraham, Woodward James 1960, 61
Iverson, Tony 1999

J

Jackson, Doug 2000
Jamerson, Jay 1987
James, Bill 1958, 59, 60
Jernigan, Noel 1955
Jessup, Paul 1928, 29, 30
Joachims, Herb 1942
Johansen, Havard 1990
Johns, Jack 1930
Johns, Paul 1940, 41
Johnsen, Ron 1993
Johnson 1911
Johnson, Benjamin Erskine 1969, 71
Johnson, Eric 1996, 97
Johnson, Erik 1987
Johnson, James Frederick 1970, 71, 72
Johnson, Jim 1950
Johnson, Kenneth 1961, 62, 63
Johnson, Pat 1990
Johnson, Rockne 1949
Johnson, Ron 1990
Johnston, Colin 1996
Johnston, Dan 1997, 98, 99
Johnston, Mike 1956
Jones, Steve 1990
Jonsson, Dwight 1998
Joslin, Scott 1990

K

Kaligis, Pete 1992, 93
Kamm, Tom 1943, 47
Kasim, Marvin 1999
Kearney, Kevin 1993
Keating, Bob 1937
Kelly, Marcus 1998
Kennon, Calvin 1985
Kent, James 1946, 47
Kerry, Bill 1952, 56, 57
Kertes, Jan C. 1968
Killien, Ken 1934, 35, 36
Killien, Phil 1963, 64, 65
Kindred, Steve 1991, 92, 93
King, Cleo 1908
King, John 1933, 34
King, Winchester 1923, 24, 25
Kintner, Bill 1937
Kipp, Dwight 1939, 40
Kirkendall, Mike 1992, 93
Kirkpatrick, Joey 1997
Kiser, Rufus 1928, 29, 30

Klein, Eric John	1967, 68
Knapp, Clarence	1915
Kneip, Neal	1985, 86
Knight	1917
Kobel, Mel	1955, 56
Koch, Scott	1991, 92, 93
Kolstad, Dayton	1958, 59, 60
Koss, Benjamin	2000
Koss, William Daniel	1969, 70, 72
Kotto, Fred	1985
Kydd, Bill	1943

L

LaBarge, Peter	1960
Labonge, Carl	1952, 53, 54, 55
LaBounty, Cliff	1957, 58, 59
Landy	1921
Lang	1911
Langer, Jerry	1952, 53, 54, 55
Larberg, Don	1947, 48, 49
Larson, Jack	1958, 59, 60
Lauber, Charles	1946, 47
LaVerdure, Darryl David	1973, 74
Lavery, Terence Kevin John	1971, 72, 73, 74
Leach, Larry	1996
Leadbetter, Bob	1954, 55, 56
Leahy, Adam	1990
Ledford, Chris	1997, 98, 99
Leffler, Mitch	1990, 91, 92, 93
Lesley, Earl	1950, 51
LeTourneau, Jack	1959
Lewis, Moses	1999
Lim, Ron	1962
Linde, Carl (Honor "W")	1930
Lindsey, Ben	1997, 98, 99, 2000
Linton, Robert	1921
Lipscombe, Jack	1935
Lockhart, Bob	1938, 39, 40
Lomax, Jon	1960, 61, 62
Long, John	1941, 42
Loudon, Dick	1951
Louie, Bob	1964
Louie, Johnny	1964
Lucci, Frank	1955, 56, 57
Luke, Fred	1966, 67, 68
Luke, Milton	1960
Lund, Harry	1934
Lund, Ron	1955
Lunsford, Walt	1935
Lynch, Jack	1964, 65
Lynn, Bob	1941

M

MacCluer, Gavin	1996, 97
MacDonald, Bill	1915,16,17,19
Macdonald, William	1943, 47
MacIntyre	1927
Mackey, James	2000
MacPherson, Mike	1996, 98
Madche, Bryan	1996, 97, 98
Mager, Gene	1941
Maginis, William	1923
Maginnis, Dave	1936, 37, 38
Mahnken, Carl	1957
Makela, George	1959, 60, 61
Manalili, Craig	1992, 93
Manhken, Carl	1956
Mantle, Vernon	1930, 31
Mapes, Gary	1957, 58
Markov, Vic	1936, 37
Marks, Kevin	1990, 92, 93
Martin, Dave	1972, 74
Martin, Paul	1940
Martin, Tim	1992, 93
Mason, Ben	1955
Mason, Earl	1921, 22, 23
Massey, Howard Robert	1969
Mathies, John	1960, 61
Matland, Conrad	1949, 50
Maxwell, Samuel	1987
McAdams, Dean	1940
McBride, Cye	1992, 93
McCallum, Charles	1927
McCallum, Don	1926, 27
McClelland, George	1913,14
McClusky, Mike	1957
McConkey, Fred	1950
McConkey, Paul	1949, 51
McCord, Murray	1964, 65
McCrory, Tom	1903, 05
McCullouch, Dave	1956, 57, 58
McDonald, Tom	1905
McDonald, William	1920
McDowell, Bruce	1990
McDowell, Robert	1986
McFee, John	1912
McFee, John	1913,14
McGaffy, Wesley	1919
McGillicuddy	1913
McGinnis, William	1924, 25
McGoldrick, Jim	1937, 39, 40
McKay	1910
McKay, Fred	1964, 65, 66
McKay, Jim	1992, 93
McKay, Orlando	1990, 91
McKimson, Dick	1956, 57
McLaren, Ian	1937
McLaughlin, Bob	1941, 46, 47
McLean, Sutherland	1942, 46
McLeod, Horace	1923
McMahon, Paul	1932, 33
McNeil, Chester	1931
McRae, Ronald	1949
Meader, Ron	1932, 33
Meier	1910
Meisnest (Honor "W")	1925
Merritt, Brent	1990, 91
Mesmer, Richard Eugene	1968, 70, 71
Metcalf, Greg	1991, 92, 93
Metlen, Dave	1921, 22
Meurer, Don	1953
Meyer, Ben	1996, 97, 98, 99, 2000
Meyer, Bill	1937
Meyer, Denny	1952, 53, 54
Meyer, Richard	1960, 61
Meyring, Don	1946
Michael, Mike	1986
Michel, Dan	1956, 57, 58
Mickelson, Erik	1998, 99
Mill, Doug	1967
Miller, James	1922
Miller, Jess	1935, 36, 37
Miller, Merle	1937
Miller, Reed	1958, 60
Miller,Henry	1926
Millett, Tom	1956
Minnis, Tyrone	1996, 97
Minnitti, Robert	1999
Molenaar, Dee	1947, 48
Mondschein, Brian Emmanuel	1976, 77
Monroe, Chase	1997
Montgomery, Bob	1963
Montgomery, Dick	1937, 38, 39
Montgomery, Robin	1934
Moody, Clifton	1996, 97, 98, 99
Moore, Lucian M.	1977
Morgan, Art	1936, 38
Morgan, Ken	1950, 51, 52
Morris, Frank	1952
Morton, Darrell	1958, 59
Moser, Bill	1957, 58, 59
Muir, Robert	1947, 48
Murphy, Tom	1938, 39, 41
Murray, Timothy Arnold	1976, 77

N

Nace, Howard	1942
Nail, Joe	1941, 42, 43
Nammermaster, Gene	1954
Nardin, Al	1926, 27
Neilson, Robert Scott	1976, 77
Neiman	1912
Neiman, Paul	1959
Nelson, Arthur	1929
Newing, Geoffrey Gerrard	1972, 73
Newton, Brice	1996, 97
Nichol, George	1930
Nickelberry, Ray	1963
Nickell, George	1928, 29
Noji, Richard	1986, 87, 90
Northcraft, Dick	1938, 40

O

O'Brien, Michael	1999
O'Brian, Daniel George	1969
O'Neil, Harley	1939
O'Neil, Paul	1930
Odegard, Cleave	1987
Oldberg, Barney	1958, 60, 61
Oldfield, Steve	1963, 64, 65
Olma, Mike	1986
Olson, Bill	1948, 49, 50

P

Palmason, Vic	1935, 36, 37

Name	Years
Panchen, Neil	1992, 93
Panton, Jim	1937, 38
Pape	1910
Parrish, Scott	1986
Parsley, Reed Dubois	1969, 70
Parsley, Tony	1991, 92, 93
Parsons, Dean	1952, 53, 54
Patten	1911,12,13
Patton, Jeff	1996
Paulsen, Shane	1990, 91, 92, 93
Pavach, Nicholas	1992, 93, 96
Pearson, Joe	1903
Pearson, Matthew	1997, 98
Pearson, Eric	1997
Pedersen, Ross	1933, 34
Peeples, Clint	1962
Peltret, Ed	1925, 26, 27
Pemberton, Al	1964, 65, 66
Penderson, Ross	1932
Pendleton, Crosby	1929, 30, 31
Perkins	1920
Perry, Geoffrey	1997, 98, 99, 2000
Perry, Loran	1950, 51, 52
Peterson, Brook	1998
Phillips, Matt	1999, 2000
Pickering, Gerry	1966, 67
Pittman, Evert	1943
Plowman, Gary	1962
Plowman, Jerry	1963, 64
Plumb, Frank	1933, 34, 35
Poole, Daniel Leo	1969
Pope, Gus	1919, 20, 21
Pratt, Reginald	1921, 22
Predmore, Jacob	1996, 97, 98, 99, 2000
Prefrement, Ernie	1933
Prior, Derek	1998, 2000
Prout, Larry	1966, 67
Pruzan, Harry	1933, 34, 35
Pulford, Larry	1956, 57, 58

Q

Name	Years
Quan, Anthony	1999
Quitslund, Gary Kitchel	1972, 73
Qvale, Kjell	1940, 41

R

Name	Years
Radford, Michael Andre	1977
Ramos, Mike	1982, 83, 84, 86
Ramsey, Finlay	1925, 26
Ramstedt, Julius	1929, 30, 31
Rector, Michael	1942
Redfern, Mel	1948
Redmond, Edward	1998
Redmund, Frank	2000
Reed, Robert	1928, 29
Reinelt, Herb	1949
Reinke, James	1986, 87
Reinking, Dick	1964, 65, 66
Remund, Frank	1999
Renz, Joshua	1998, 99, 2000
Reynolds, Robin	1996, 97, 98
Reynolds, Sewall	1946
Rhuddy, Kenneth	1930, 31, 32
Richards, Bill	1950, 51, 52
Richburg, Julio	1990
Richmond, William	1985, 86
Rickey, Paul	1998
Ridgeway	1910
Riley, Fenwick (Honor "W")	1930
Roberson, Darryl	1990
Roberts, Dave	1965, 66, 67
Robinson, Doug	1949
Robinson, Douglas	1946
Robinson, Earl	1947
Robinson, Josh	1999, 2000
Robinson, Richard	1942
Robinson, Vern	1954
Rockett, Bob	1985
Roe, (Lawrence) T.T.	1990
Roe, Bill	1965, 66, 67
Rogge, Joshua	1999
Rohrschieb, Walter	1935, 36
Rose, Tyler	1997, 98, 99
Rosencranz, Robert Michael	1976
Rosenquist, Frank	1932, 33
Ross, Fred	1928, 29, 30
Rubestello, Leo	1943
Russell, John	2000
Russell, Ray	1942, 43
Rustad, Doug	1962
Rutter, Robert L.	1974
Ryan, Field	1952, 53, 54
Ryan, Willem	1996, 97, 98, 99

S

Name	Years
Saladino, Peter	1989
Samples, Roger	1935, 36
Sanders, Leo	1998
Sarles, Trevor	1963, 64, 65
Saunders, Robert	1959, 60, 61
Sayers, Christopher Mark	1971
Scanlon, Henry	1947, 48
Schepman, Hoddy	1957
Scherer, Lewis	1903
Schloessler, Lee	1946
Schroeder, Marvin	1925, 27
Schruth, Daniel	1999, 2000
Schruth, Dave	2000
Schultz, James William Jr.	1967, 68
Schutte, Todd	1989
Schwinn, Matthew	1999
Scott, Jim	1940
Scott, Rob	1992, 93
Seferovich, Larry	1962, 63, 64
Sellers, Elbert	1929, 35
Senior, Robert Michael	1973
Senstrom, Sam	1916
Setliff, Adam	1992, 93
Seymour, James Michael	1970, 71
Shaffer, Ron	1952
Shelley, William	1927, 28, 29
Shelton, Thad	1996
Shera, Brian (Honor "W")	1925
Sheron, Ed	1955
Sherrick	1910,11
Shields, Donald Keith	1970, 71
Shinnick, Nelson	1962
Shinnick, Phil	1963, 64, 65
Shirey, Riley	1971
Short, Nathan	1985, 86, 89
Shouman, Stormy	1989, 90, 91
Sievers, Chris	1956, 57, 58
Simon, Darrell	1928
Simpson, Eric	1991, 92, 93
Simpson, Larry	1967
Simpson, Peter	1989
Sinclair, Thomas Ross	1977
Singer, Dean	1955, 56, 57
Sinhkoskey, Gary	1959
Sires, Jed	1998
Skartvedt, Darrold	1952, 54
Slade, Douglas	1923
Sloan, Bill	1940
Smart, William Burton	1968, 69, 70
Smith, Bill	1930
Smith, Bob	1941
Smith, Graham	1927, 28
Smith, Hans	1948
Smith, Jacob	1992, 93
Smith, Martin	1947
Smith, Matthew	1989, 90, 91
Smith, Rex	1905
Smith, Robert	1942
Smith, Troy	1929
Smith, Willard	1939, 41
Smyth, Gregory Rusty	1972, 73
Snyder, Loyal	1924, 25, 27
Softli, Tony	1958
Southwick, Everett	1951
Southwick, Glen	1919
Spencer, Peter Allan	1968, 69, 70
St. Clair, Justin	1998, 99, 2000
Steed, Bill	1946, 47, 48, 49
Steele, Sean	2000
Steensland, Doug	1962
Stehr, Vaughn	1986
Steinhardt, Adam	1989
Stengele, Bill	1996, 97
Stenstrom, Sam	1915
Sternberg, Brian	1963
Steward, Pete	1950, 51
Stirling, Bruce	1985, 86
Stokes, Carl	1989
Stoll	1910,11
Stolp, William C.	1977
Strathairn, Thomas	1966, 67, 68
Strickler, Howard	1961, 62
Strom, Terry	1954, 55, 56
Strub, Mike	1990, 91
Stuclell, Ed	1917
Stutfield, Fred	1936, 37, 38
Sundquist, Stanley	1950
Surface, Steven Ronald	1977

Sutherland, George	1974
Suver	1938
Swan, John	1938
Swanzey, Gene	1941, 42
Sweeney, Scott	1997, 98
Swift, Craig Timothy	1970, 71, 72
Swisher, Bob	1933, 35

T

Tabish, Dan	1985
Taylor, Art	1939
Taylor, C.	1920
Taylor, Daniel Arthur	1970, 71, 72, 73
Taylor, J.D.	1985, 86
Taylor, Jeffrey P.	1972, 73, 74
Taylor, Vincent	1985
Temple, Thomas Clyde	1966, 67, 68
Terry, Michael	1998
Teunis	1924
Thomas, Garth	1985
Thomas, Tracey	1989, 90, 91
Thomason	1912
Thompson, Don	1939
Thompson, E.B.	1903
Thompson, Morgan	2000
Thornburgh, Dale	1952
Thowsen, Jon	1972, 73
Thrall, John Michael	1961, 62, 63
Tibbals, Maurice	1903, 05
Tinner, Keith Charles	1976, 77
Tobacco, Terry	1957, 58, 59
Todd, Jim	1940, 41
Tolbert, William A.	1977
Tonning, Bjarne	1934
Torney, Jack	1925, 26, 27
Trexler, Gene	1950
Trowbridge, Bill	1937
Troy, Smith	1927, 28
Trueblood, Harold	1930
Tulin, Charles	1952
Tupper, Cecil	1924, 25
Turene	1913
Turnbull, Larry	1960, 62, 63
Turner, Edward	1996, 97
Tuson, Rodger Andrew	1947, 49

U

Ullman, Tom	1940, 41
Umsted, Louis	1950

V

Vagners, Juris	1959
Van Voris, Cecil	1923
Vanderhoof, Rod	1951, 52, 53
Vandermay, Bill	1936, 37, 38
Vavak, Roy	1965
Vegar, Joseph Stanley	1976, 77
Vernon, Frank	1908
Vierick, Girton (Honor "W")	1930
Vincent, Russell	1974, 76, 77

W

Walker, Brad	2000
Walker, Keith	1989
Walker, William Robert	1969, 71
Walmsley, Michael George	1970
Walsh, Martin Thomas	1967, 68, 69
Walter, Clement (honor"W")	1912
Walter, Ernest	1913,14,15
Walters, Anthony	2000
Walters, Gene	1942
Wardlow, Duane	1952, 53, 54
Warnock, Robert	1998
Watson, Archie	1940, 41
Webb, Ceccil	1948
Weber, Julian	1932
Weingarten, Harry	1948
Weiser, Karl	1963, 64, 65
Weiser, Philip	1961, 62, 63
Weisman, Paul	1950
Werner, Clyde LeRoy	1968
West, Wariboko	1963, 64, 65
Westlake, Doug	1966, 67, 68
Westlund, Lynn	1961
Wheaton, Dwight	1991, 92, 93
White, Coral	1903
Whiting, Keith	1929, 30, 31
Whitten, Ty	1997
Whitworth, Don	1936
Widell, Ralph F.	1974
Widenfelt, George	1951, 52, 53
Wiehl, Dick	1957
Wilde, Drummond	1925, 26
Wilde, Frank	1926
Wilkins, Jesse	1939
Wilkinson, Trevor	1947, 49
Will, John	1941
Willard, Garth	1991, 92, 93
Williams, Dave	1965, 66, 67
Williams, Harold	1921, 22, 23
Williams, John	1912,13,14
Williams, T.	1910
Williamson, Marc	1985
Willis, Bob	1964, 65, 66
Willis, Don	1992, 93
Wilson, John	1922, 23
Wilson, Todd	1989, 90, 91
Winger, Daniel Noah	1972, 73, 74
Winsor, Will	1905
Witter, Darren	1989, 90, 91
Woelful, Paul	1928
Wold, Donald	1946, 47, 48
Wood, Harrison Anthony	1967, 68, 69
Woodbridge, Dudley	1915,16
Woodward, Walter	1930, 31, 33
Wright, Garner	1911,12,13,14
Wright, Ken	1938, 39
Wuotila, Robert Thomas	1968
Wyers, Teunis	1924, 25

Y

Yantis, Richard	1941, 42
Yorke, Gregory Lorne	1970

Z

Zackery, Tony	1985
Zajac, Bard	1991, 92, 93
Zener, Robert	1922, 23
Zoccola, James	1985
Zwiebel, Gordon	1932, 33, 34

Women's Track and Field

A

Adams, Sonya	1985, 86
Aoki, Anna	1998, 99, 2000
Austin, Rachel	1994

B

Barnes, Celia	1999
Barter, Terra	1994
Bek, Margaret	1996
Bendico, Merry Jane	1998, 2000
Benjamin, Marva	1985, 86
Biere, Sondra	1996
Bledsoe, Arlene	2000
Bjone, Mari	1991
Blake, Hilary	1992, 93
Bolender, Sarah	1985, 86
Boren, Wendy	1989
Borsheim, Vickie	1985, 86
Bowles, Shannon	1994, 96
Bradshaw, Kate	2000
Brager, Natalie	1994, 96
Brayton, Joelle	1994, 96
Brown, Patricia	1977
Buresh, Michele	1989, 90
Burkhardt, Laura	1994
Burns, Karrie	1992
Burns, Samantha	1996
Butler, Margaret	1998, 99, 2000

C

Campbell, Leslie	1989, 90, 91, 92
Carlson, Carrie	1998
Carlson, Tara	1993, 94, 96
Casbere, Jessica	1991, 92, 93
Chapman, Melissa	2000
Compton, Tracey	1996
Cottingham, Tracey	1977
Couvson, Kim	1996, 98
Cressel, Marcia L.	1976, 77
Cunningham, Estenee	1989, 90

D

Dandenault, Susanne	1989, 90, 91, 92
Davis, Patrice	1996, 98, 99
Demeter, Wendy	1986
Dennis, Donna	1985, 86
Doht, Karlyn	1990, 91, 92, 93
Downey, Heidi	1989, 90
Draughon, Jennifer	1989, 90

E

Ellis, Kristen	1992
Emel, Michelle	1994, 96
English, Elizabeth	1998, 99, 2000
Erickson, Sandra	1999, 2000
Eskesen, Staci	1996, 98
Evans, Brandi	1989, 90, 91, 92

F

Fagnani, Cari	1985, 86
Faulkner, Virginia	1977
Foianini, Ashley	1998
Forster, Sonja	1989, 90, 91, 92
Franza, Megan	1998
Froese, Angela	1996, 98
Frosch, Leslie	1976, 77
Funk, Lora Jean	1992, 93, 94

G

Gamby, Kellie	1989, 90
Garrison, Mary Margaret	1977
George, September	1986, 89
Gerbatz, Brenda	1985, 86
Gheewala, Neha	1996
Gillette, Jennifer	1989, 90
Glass, Monique	1996, 98, 99
Goodlett, Helen	1976
Griffin, Tracy	1993, 94
Griffis, Keisha	1996, 98, 99

H

Haines, Margaret	1998, 2000
Hallett, Amy	1990
Hanson, Cherish	1990, 91
Hawkins, Shavon	1999, 2000
Hellett, Amy	1989
Hill, Aretha	1996, 98
Hill, Michelle	1985, 86
Ho, Evelyn	1996
Hoitink, Stacie	1990, 91, 92, 93
Howard, Anne	1990, 91
Hungar, Susan Lynn	1976, 77
Hurson, Mary	1986

I

Ichikawa, Laura	1985, 86
Inman, Courtney	1999

J

Johnson, Emily	1993, 94, 95
Johnson, Lynde	1998
Johnson, Zelda	1985
Jolivet, Diane	1985
Jones, Alicia	1976
Jones, Margie	1985
Jones, Meg	1986
Julian, Beth	1990

K

Kabush, Danelle	1996, 98
Kearsley, Jane	1976
Keller, Kendra	1985, 86
Kelley, Lara	1996, 98, 99
Kelly, Alice Louise	1976, 77
Keranen, Eeva	1976, 77
King, Amy	1999, 2000
Kriz, Aimee	1992, 93, 94
Kruse, Laura	1994
Kuyk, Kathy	1976

L

Lasater, Lorraine	1985, 86
Lewis, Pam	1992, 93, 94
Liebsack, Stacy (Brunell)	1989, 93
Lindgren, Sara	1985
Lovely, Dawn	1989, 90
Lowe, Kenya	1993

M

Makrogiannis, Eugenie	1996
Malm, Katherine	1992, 96
Mathewson, Tami	1990, 91, 92, 93
Matson, Camissa	1998, 99, 2000
McClatcher, Mikki	1994, 96
McDonald, Mary C.	1993, 94
McVicker, Aimee	1991
Milton, Shiri	1985
Minelli, Lia	1996
Moller, Carrie	1991
Moore, LeTesha	2000
Morales, Carrie	1994
Morrison, Rebecca	1998, 99
Moulign, Marjan	1977
Muhammad, Asya	1998, 99
Mullen, Emily	1999
Mullian, Tracey	1989, 90, 91

N

Newton, Nolana	1996

O

O'Connell, Catherine	1989, 90
Oelke, Sheryl	1990, 91
Ogarro, Zunilda	1999, 2000
Olsen, Sharon Lynne	1996
ONeill, Shannon	1989

P

Pacheco, Anica	1996
Parker, Monika	1992, 93
Pascoe, Shelley	1991
Patridge, Diane Jennifer	1977
Penton, Marzette	1996, 98, 99
Pentz, Chelsie	1998, 99, 2000
Perebooom, Darla Marie	1977
Petersen, Janicka	1989, 90
Peterson, Sarah	2000
Peterson, Marilee	1977
Phillips, Jackie Ann	1977
Pimley, Jill	1998
Pinkerton, DeAnn Lea	1977
Ponath, Jennifer	1985, 86
Porter, Sunny	1999
Posner, Amy	1991, 92
Prince, Mary	1989, 90
Pulley, Julie	1977

Q

Quinn, Marguerite Rute	1977

R

Reed, Jenny	1976
Reese, Jennifer	1989, 90, 91, 92
Reid, Michele	1998
Rembold, Kali	1993, 94, 96
Richard, Kristy	1992
Richardson, Francine	1998, 99
Riley, Elizabeth	1994
Robinson, Claudine	1991, 92, 93, 94
Roetman, Rainey Kay	1977
Rohweder, Roxanne	1986
Ronning, Kristen	1990, 91, 92, 93
Rose, Amy	1998, 99
Ross, Shirley	1986
Roth, Ellen Claire	1977

S

Salibian, Searan	2000
Samuelson, Justelle	1996
Sandmeyer, Toshiko	1991, 92, 93, 94
Sanford, Shelley	1986, 89
Sauter, Andrea	2000
Schorr, Terese	1990, 91, 92, 93
Schweim, Joyce	1989, 90
Shanley, Susan	1996
Shepherd, Jeanine	1977
Sheppard, Kelsey	1999, 2000
Silvis, Suzanne	1991, 92, 93, 94
Smith, Jemara	2000
Smith, Meledy	1985
Spriestersbach, Megan	2000
Stapleton, Michele	1989
Stocker, Valarie	1990
Stoertz, Mary	1976
Sutton, Kyla	1993, 94, 96
Syrdal, Kara	1998, 99, 2000

T

Taft, Ann Roberta	1977
Tasker, Angie	1989, 90
Terry, Tamanika	1993, 94
Thomas, Sesilia	1998, 99, 2000
Torkelson, Nancy	1986
Torrison, Lisa	1985
Tramposch, Jonica	2000
Trimmer, Suzanne L.	1976, 77

U

Uusitalo, Elizabeth	1986

V

Vandermeij, Melissa	1996
VanPelt, Caryl Lovsted	1977
Vermeere, Janie	1991, 93, 94

W

Walker, Shirley	1985
Warner, Kamberly	1993, 94, 96
Weil, Kari	1998, 99

Werner, Susan	2000
Whiltock, Sandy	1990
White, LaTonya	1990, 91
Whitish, Emily	1999, 2000
Whitmire, Rebecca	1989
Wilkins, Carol Lynn	1977
Williams, Barbara Catherine	1977
Williams, Heidi	1985, 86
Willis, Celia	1989, 90, 91, 92
Withey, Christina	1998, 99, 2000
Wolfe, Rebecca	1985
Woods, Patrice	1993, 94, 96

Y

Youngquist, Deeja	1996, 98, 99

Volleyball

A

Allmon, Sarah	1998, 99
Andrus, Pam	1984, 85, 86, 87
Austin, Dawn	1990, 91, 92, 93
Auzias de Turenne, Jackie	1985, 86, 87, 88

B

Baker, Julie	1994, 95, 96, 97
Bassin, Aline	1994
Baughn, Cheryl	1979
Baughn, Lisa	1979, 80, 81
Beckenhauer, Melinda	1987, 88, 89
Bell, Carolyn	1984, 85
Benjamin, Paige	1999
Benkovsky, Karen	1993
Blight, Wendy	1975
Bradner, Kandy	1978
Bransom, Angela	1993, 94, 95, 96
Braymen, Bobbi	1990, 91, 92
Brittain, Stacy	1979, 80, 83
Buse, Deborah	1975, 76
Byrtus, Andrea	1987, 88

C

Callander, Wendy	1975
Carpine, Karen	1976
Churnside, Britni	1998, 99
Clarke, Kealy	1992
Cleage, Erin	1985, 86

D

Daly, Arwen	1993
Darcey, Sue	1983, 84
Desilets, Makare	1994, 95, 96, 97
Dietz, Gretchen	1977, 78, 79
Djordjevic, Dragana	1991, 92, 94, 95
Doty, Sue	1977, 78, 79

E

Evensen, Meredith	1984, 85

F

Fitzgerald, Kelly	1982, 83
Flick, Diane	1989, 90, 91, 92

G

Garrison, Maggie	1980
Garrison, Mary	1976
Grim, Kayley	1986, 87, 88, 89
Grovey, Janelle	1999

H

Hardesty, Kara	1981, 82, 83, 84
Hartzell, LeeAnn	1984
Herrera, Tanja	1979
Heuff, Marianne	1979
Hjorth, Debbie	1991, 92, 93, 94
Houser, Shirley	1979, 80
Hurlbut, Holly	1976

J

Jacobson, Molly	1993, 94, 95, 96
Jensen, Marya	1992, 93, 94, 95

K

Kay, Nicole	1986, 87, 88, 89
Knoll, Heather	1992, 93
Koehn, Cheryl	1979, 80
Koppinger, Jolyn	1985, 86
Krayer, Lisete	1981, 83, 84
Kurrus, Julie	1981, 82, 83, 84

L

Laffling, Kristina	1996, 97, 98, 99
Lamken, Anne	1981, 82, 84, 85
Larsen, Kelley	1988, 89, 90, 91
Larson, Marcene	1979, 80, 81
Leonard, Sally	1985
Little, Lys	1975, 76
Lloyd, Gale	1980
LoDolce, Kristie	1991, 92
Lyons, Abby	1979, 80, 82

M

Maroutsos, Kiki	1998, 99
Maurer, Gretchen	1999
McCammond, Lisa	1986, 87, 88, 89
Martin, Tani	1991, 93
Mills, Susie	1979, 80
Monks, Eileen	1976, 77
Mulloy, Marci	1976

N

Netherby, Dana	1993, 94, 96, 97

P

Page, Sabrina	1999
Patton, Michelle	1994, 95, 96, 97
Poelstra, Lynn	1981, 82, 83
Polan, Julie	1994, 95, 96, 97
Potter, Claudia	1975

R

Reid, Michelle	1987, 88, 89, 90
Reinhardt, Raynani	1977, 78, 79
Richardson, Allison	1998, 99
Ringgold, Tiffany	1990, 91, 92, 93
Robertson, Ashleigh	1989, 90, 91, 92
Roche, Cheryl	1980, 81
Rodriguez, Maria	1979, 80, 81
Ross, Elizabeth	1999

S

Sappington, Lori	1985, 86
Schweizer, Kori	1994, 95, 96, 97
Seacat, Allison	1996, 97, 99
Seacat, Emily	1997, 98
Short (Coma), Angie	1996, 97, 98
Simmons, Sara	1993
Steinert, Lesli	1994, 95
Stone, Becky	1981, 82, 83, 84
Streatfeild, Jennifer	1990, 91, 92, 93
Suttich, Starry	1981, 82

T

Teagle, Mindy	1983, 84
Terry, Genevieve	1983, 84, 85, 86
Thompson, Dana	1989, 90, 91, 92
Thompson, Malena	1998, 99
Thorlakson, Carolyn	1975
Thorpe, Gail	1987, 88, 89, 90
Topham, April	1989, 90
Treseder, Brooke	1997
Tuiasosopo, Leslie	1995, 96, 97, 98
Tutt, Amy	1993, 95, 96, 97

U

Underhill, Lisa	1998, 99

V

VanEngelen, Tamara	1996
Van Peursem, Bonnie	1980, 82
Vicknair, Kymme	1994
Voss, Barbara	1975, 76

W

Welch, Cathy	1981, 82
Wetzel, Laurie	1985, 86, 87, 88
Wilson, Donna	1975
Winnie, Jeanne	1979
Woods, Jesse	1998

Men's Wrestling

A

Allan, William	1972
Allen, Bill	1973
Allen, Chuck	1936
Amunson, James	1965
Anderson	1926
Arwood, Gene	1937, 38

B

Badeaux, Dave	1973
Bahr, Rex	1975
Bardarson, Otto	1919, 20, 21
Bell, Richard	1961, 62, 63
Bergsma, Benjamin	1972
Berry, Roy	1922, 23, 24
Bickenbach, Marvin	1938, 39
Birch, Irwin	1938

Bird, Harry 1939
Block, Jack 1957
Bloom, Cliff 1929
Bolinger, Clayton 1921
Bolinger, Morris 1920
Bollman, Dean 1917, 20
Bolton 1915
Booker, Arthur 1976
Borgerson, Melvin 1932, 33, 35
Boulton, Henry 1916,17
Bramen, John 1941
Brenneman, Kelly 1976, 77
Bressler, Mike 1976, 77
Bronneman, Leroy 1935, 37
Brown, Tom 1973, 74, 76
Bush, Maurice 1961
Byrd, Carroll 1917

C

Caddey, Gene 1938, 40
Cahoon, Scott 1972
Calderon, Rich 1974, 75
Callison, Oliver 1940
Capato, Robert 1976
Carlson, Roy 1940
Carter, L. M. 1921
Cheney, Steve 1966
Clithero, Ray 1922, 24
Connor 1923
Corn, Randy 1972
Crowder, Dick 1940, 41
Crumb, Joe 1921, 22, 23
Culp, Frank 1930
Currey, James 1958
Curtis, Ad 1935

D

Dartnell, Don 1941
Davidson, Ben 1961
Davis, Paul 1922, 23, 24
de Spain, Harold 1919
Denney, John 1961, 62
Dent, Bill 1932, 33, 34
Dewey, Louis 1936
Dickson, Gordon 1911,12,13,14
Dmitrieff 1934
Dodson, Jim 1926
Downer, Michael 1972, 73
Dunham, Donald 1972, 73, 74
Dunshee, Hans 1973
Dupar, John 1977

E

Easterbrook, Arthur 1916
Englund, Mike 1924
Enos, Earl 1958
Enslow, Dave 1958, 59
Esveldt, George 1938, 39, 40

F

Fisher, Carl 1962, 63
Fisher, Jack 1920
Fitzpatrick, Mike 1973
Foreman, Byron 1918
Frankowski, Ray 1940, 41
Fudally, Paul 1957, 58, 59
Fuhrer, Frank 1961

G

Gale, Ralph 1914,15
Garrison, Mike 1977
Gibson, Blaine 1918,19, 20
Gilbert, Clark 1941
Gilbert, Murray 1940
Giske, Ragnar 1933
Graves, Dave 1973, 74
Griffin, Fred 1923, 24, 25
Grim 1911
Gronlund, William 1961

H

Haapala, Rueben 1934
Hale, Bert 1934
Hancock, Virgil 1911,14
Hardy, Warren (Mike) 1911,12,13,14
Harless, Dale 1966
Hashisaki, George 1977
Hayfield, Mark 1938, 39
Herrick, Fred 1963
Hertz, Stewart 1925
Hobi, Frank 1914
Hodge, James 1967
Hokari, Sam 1936, 37
Hollenbeck, Greg 1933, 34
Hoover, Glenn 1912
Howard, Bill 1930, 32
Howe, Ken 1921
Humphries, Chris 1977

I

Iverson, Gary 1961
Jackson, Paul 1962, 63, 64

J

Jacot, Bradley 1972, 73, 74, 75
Johnson, Hal 1919
Johnson, Michael 1961
Johnson, Ron 1962, 63, 64

K

Kacmarcik, Andy 1974
Kahler, Greg 1966
Kanazawa, Hiroshi 1939, 40
Kaseburg, Bill 1939, 41
Kaseburg, Fred 1940
Kaveny, Patrick 1972, 73, 75
Kawahara, Hitoshi 1937, 38, 39
Kegel, Richard 1958
Kempinsky, Warren 1941
Kennedy, Walter 1967
Kersey, Jerry 1973, 74
Klinge, Dick 1937, 38
Klobucher, Frank 1913
Koeneman, Tom 1936
Kondo, Mark 1972
Kondo, Michael 1972, 73
Kraetz, Sam 1930

L

La Chappelle, Oliver 1914,16
Landauer, Joee 1930
Langdon, Jack 1936
Lange, Ted 1924, 25, 26
Leak, Lloyd 1926
Learned 1926
Leavitt, Darrell 1923
Leggott, Chuck 1975
Lentz, Jerald 1958, 59
Lev, Lester 1929
Lloyd, Dan 1973
Locke, Charles 1966, 67
Lujan, Henry 1977

M

Maddock, Hal 1940
Maddock, Howard 1941
Mandles, Meyer "Bud" 1933
Mangrum, Carl 1977
Markov, Vicc 1937
Martin, Ernest 1925, 26
Masui, Leonard 1918,19
McAdams, Dick 1917
McClain, Dave 1974
McCredy, Noble 1921, 22
McGovern, Foster 1917,18
McKee, Dave 1967
McKellar, Claude 1934
McKellar, Everett 1933
McManus, Paul 1967
Means, Art 1936
Miller, Mike 1974, 75
Mitchell, Dave 1973, 74, 76
Moore, Jim 1967
Morris, Hugh 1964
Muczynski, Matt 1933
Murdock, Bill 1973

N

Newell, Bilgy 1932
North, Al 1939, 40, 41

O

O'Day, Pat 1957
Olsen, Howard 1926, 29
Onder, Yuksel 1957
Oonishi, Toshi 1974, 75, 76, 77
Owings, Larry 1970, 71, 72

P

Panowicz, Bob 1967
Papenfuse, Kaare 1974
Parberry, Sterling 1938
Parrish, Dewey 1972
Paup, Everett 1923
Phillips, P. G. 1963, 64, 65
Pleasant, Don 1972
Polatnik, Stephen 1958
Potter, Claude 1921
Prater 1911,12
Puhr, Edd 1933

Q

Renfro, Mel	1973, 74
Rice, Ray	1925
Rich, Stan	1935, 36
Robbins, Bennie	1911
Roush, Ellard	1976

S

Saato, Yozo	1939
Sartoris, George	1917, 20
Schwab, William	1959
Sellick, Harry	1918
Severyns, Andrew	1913
Shands, Al	1932
Shanley	1915
Sharpe, Harold	1932, 33, 34
Shields, Gordon	1940, 41
Shinjo, Hajime	1972, 73
Shults, Bruce	1967
Sievers, Fred	1959
Skaggs, Jim	1961
Smith, Adney	1932, 33
Smith, Chuck	1915
Smith, Doug	1967
Smith, Doug	1976, 77
Sparks, Bobby	1977
Sperber, Al	1965
Stevens, Len	1930
Strong, Chet	1939
Sullivan, Jay	1976
Summers, Tom	1939, 40
Surbeck	1961

T

Talbot, John	1915,16
Tennant, Roger	1967
Terada, George	1935, 36
Truscutt, Bill	1938
Tsuchiya, Takuzo	1939, 40, 41

U

Ulrich, Robert	1964
Upper, Barrington	1912

V

Van de Bogart, Paul	1914,15,16
Vassar	1926
Vogel, Jack	1930

W

Webster, Lloyd	1930
Webster, Mike	1929
William, Murdock	1972
Williams	1916
Willms, Gary	1964
Wooding, Dick	1962, 63, 64
Woods, James	1972, 73, 74

Y

Yamada, Art	1964, 65
Yamada, Fred	1914
Yamada, Tom	1915,16

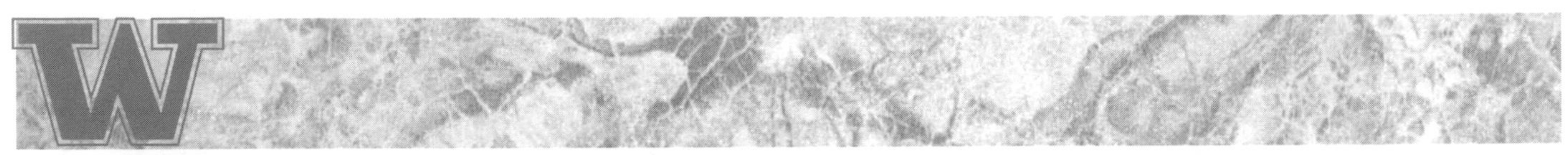

University of Washington Olympic Medalists

Below is a list of athletes who indicated on questionnaires that they attended Washington as a student. The list has been compiled from information provided by the U.S. Olympic Committee library and the Canadian Olympic Committee library.

Athlete	Sport	Event	Medal
2000 Summer Games at Sydney, Australia			
Charlie McKee	Sailing	49er	Bronze
1996 Summer Games at Atlanta			
Marc Schneider	Rowing	Lightweight four without coxswain	Bronze
1992 Summer Games at Barcelona, Spain			
Michelle Campi	Gymnastics	Team member - did not compete	Bronze
Rebecca Twigg	Cycling	3000 meter individual pursuit	Bronze
1992 Winter Games at Albertville, France			
Hilary Lindh	Skiing	Downhill	Silver
1988 Summer Games at Seoul, South Korea			
Charlie McKee	Sailing	470 class	Bronze
1984 Summer Games at Los Angeles			
Betsy Beard	Rowing	Women's eight	Gold
Carl Buchan	Sailing	Flying Dutchman	Gold
William Buchan	Sailing	Star class	Gold
Charles Clapp	Rowing	Eight	Silver
Steve Erickson	Sailing	Star class	Gold
Al Forney	Rowing	Four with coxswain	Silver
Sterling Hinds	Track and Field	4 X 400 Meter Relay (Canada)	Bronze
Blair Horn	Rowing	Eight (Canada)	Gold
Ed Ives	Rowing	Four with coxswain	Silver
Kristi Norelius	Rowing	Women's eight	Gold
Shyril O'Steen	Rowing	Women's eight	Gold
John Stillings	Rowing	Four with coxswain	Silver
Rebecca Twigg	Cycling	Road race	Silver
1976 Summer Games at Montreal, Canada			
Rick Colella	Swimming	200 Meter Breaststroke	Bronze

1972 Summer Games at Munich, Germany

Robin Backhaus	Swimming	200 Meter Butterfly	Bronze
Lynn Colella	Swimming	200 Meter Butterfly	Silver
Rick DeMont	Swimming	400 Meter Freestyle	Gold #
Doug Northway	Swimming	1500 Meter Freestyle	Bronze

1964 Summer Games at Tokyo, Japan

Ted Mittet	Rowing	Four without coxswain	Bronze

1960 Summer Games at Rome, Italy

John Sayre	Rowing	Four without coxswain	Gold

1952 Summer Games at Helsinki, Finland

Phil Leanderson	Rowing	Four with coxswain	Bronze
Carl Lovsted	Rowing	Four with coxswain	Bronze
Albert Rossi	Rowing	Four with coxswain	Bronze
Alvin Ulbrickson, Jr.	Rowing	Four with coxswain	Bronze
Richard Wahlstrom	Rowing	Four with coxswain	Bronze

1948 Summer Games at London, England

Gordon Giovanelli	Rowing	Four with coxswain	Gold
Robert Martin	Rowing	Four with coxswain	Gold
Allen Morgan	Rowing	Four with coxswain	Gold
Warren Westlund	Rowing	Four with coxswain	Gold
Robert Will	Rowing	Four with coxswain	Gold

1936 Summer Games at Berlin, Germany

Gordon Adam	Rowing	Eight	Gold
Ralph Bishop	Basketball		Gold
Charles Day	Rowing	Eight	Gold
Donald Hume	Rowing	Eight	Gold
George Hunt	Rowing	Eight	Gold
James McMillin	Rowing	Eight	Gold
Jack Medica	Swimming	400 Meter Freestyle	Gold
		1500 Meter Freestyle	Silver
		800 Meter Freestyle Relay	Silver
Robert Moch	Rowing	Eight	Gold
Roger Morris	Rowing	Eight	Gold
Joseph Rantz	Rowing	Eight	Gold
John White	Rowing	Eight	Gold

1928 Summer Games at Amsterdam, Holland

Steve Anderson	Track and Field	110 Meter High Hurdles	Silver
Herman Brix	Track and Field	Shot Put	Silver

1920 Summer Games at Antwerp, Belgium

Gus Pope	Track and Field	Discus Throw	Bronze

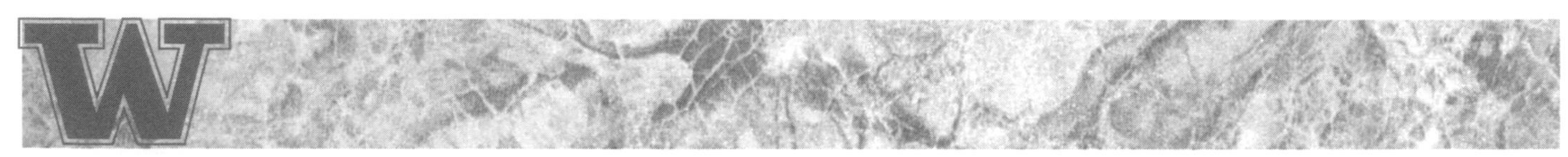

University of Washington Olympic Participants

In addition to the athletes above, many who attended the University of Washington have been members of their country's Olympic Team. Below is an alphabetical list of the athletes, the countries they represented, the years they participated, their sport and event.

Athlete	Country	Year	Sport	Event
Chris Allsopp	USA	1976	Rowing	
		1980*	Rowing	Quadruple sculls
Chuck Alm	USA	1960	Rowing	Four with coxswain
Duncan Atwood	USA	1980*, 1984	Track and Field	Javelin throw
Victoria Baker	USA	1984	Rowing	Women's alternate
Hope Barnes	USA	1980*	Rowing	Women's alternate
	USA	1984	Rowing	Women's alternate
Bruce Beall	USA	1984	Rowing	Quadruple sculls
Betsy Beard	USA	1988	Rowing	Women's eight
Christian Belz	Switzerland	2000	Track and Field	Steeplechase
Roberto Blanda	Italy	1992, 1996	Rowing	Eight
Beverly Brockway	USA	1960	Skiing	Giant slalom, slalom
Susan Broome	USA	1984	Rowing	
	USA	1988	Rowing	Women's eight
William Buchan	USA	1980*	Sailing	Star class
Norm Buvick	USA	1948	Rowing	Alternate
Dave Calder	Canada	2000	Rowing	Eight
Chris Campbell	USA	1988	Rowing	Women's eight
Suzanne Chaffee	USA	1968	Skiing	Downhill, giant slalom
Borys Chambul	Canada	1976	Track and Field	Discus throw
Rick Colella	USA	1972	Swimming	200 meter breaststroke
Ira Courtney	USA	1912	Track and Field	100, 200 meter dash, 4 X 100 meter relay
Donald Coy	USA	1936	Rowing	Alternate
William Crookes	USA	1936	Skiing	Combined
Hana Dariusova	Czech Republic	1992	Rowing	Women's eight
		1996	Rowing	Women's pair without coxswain
Rick DeMont	USA	1972	Swimming	1500 freestyle
Jennifer Devine	USA	1996	Rowing	Double sculls
Jeffrey Durgan	USA	1984	Soccer	
Rod Ewaliko	USA	1980*	Track and Field	Javelin throw
George Farmer	USA	1964	Luge	Singles
Ralph Faulkner	USA	1928	Fencing	Alternate
		1932	Fencing	Sabre
Trevor Fernandes	Tanzania	1984	Field Hockey	
Donald Fraser	USA	1932	Curling	
		1936	Skiing	Cross-country - 18Km
		1936	Skiing	Cross-country - 4 X 10Km relay
Ted Frost	USA	1960	Rowing	Pair without coxswain
Louis Gellerman	USA	1960	Rowing	Alternate

Athlete	Country	Year	Sport	Event
Ed Genung	USA	1932	Track and Field	800 meter run
			Track and Field	1600 meter relay
David Halpern	USA	1984	Canoeing	Kayak - 2500 meters
Maylon Hanold	USA	1992	Canoeing	Kayak - slalom singles
Jan Harville	USA	1980*	Rowing	Women's eight
		1984	Rowing	Women's four with coxswain
Phil Henry	USA	2000	Rowing	Alternate
Mike Hess	USA	1976	Rowing	Eight
Aretha Hill	USA	1996	Track and Field	Women's discus throw
Annette Hilliard	USA	1976	Rowing	Women's alternate
Alan Holt	USA	1972	Sailing	Star class
Ja'Warren Hooker	USA	2000	Track and Field	Alternate
Bruce Humbar	Canada	1936	Track and Field	100, 200 meter dash, 4 X 100 meter relay
Bob Hutchinson	Canada	1952	Track and Field	100, 200 meter dash, 4 X 100 meter relay
Edward Ives	USA	1988	Rowing	Pair without coxswain
Paul Jessup	USA	1932	Track and Field	Discus throw
Jannette Burr Johnson	USA	1952	Skiing	Downhill, giant slalom, slalom
Regina Joyce	Ireland	1984	Track and Field	Marathon
David Kehoe	USA	1980*	Rowing	Four with coxswain
Dale McClements Kephart	USA	1964	Gymnastics	Artistic individual all around
	USA			Team combined exercises
Nancy Lethcoe	USA	1956	Swimming	100 meter butterfly
Fred Luke	USA	1972	Track and Field	Javelin throw
Todd MacCulloch	Canada	2000	Basketball	
Katie Maloney	USA	2000	Rowing	Women's eight
Thad McArthur	USA	1952	Modern pentathlon	Individual, team
Chad McCarty	USA	2000	Soccer	
Charlie McKee	USA	1992	Sailing	Alternate
Jack Medica	USA	1932	Water Polo	Alternate
Robert Miller	USA	1956	Modern pentathlon	Alternate
Barbara Mitchell	USA	1972	Swimming	200 meter breastroke
Keith Mowen	USA	1972	Cycling	Road race
Scott Munn	USA	1992	Rowing	Eight
Scott Neilson	Canada	1980*	Track and Field	Hammer throw
Mauno Nissinen	Finland	1968, 1972	Gymnastics	All around
Kristi Norelius	USA	1980*	Rowing	Women's alternate
Mark Norelius	USA	1976	Rowing	Eight
Gus Pope	USA	1924	Track and Field	Discus throw
Bob Rogers	USA	1960	Rowing	Pair without coxswain
James Rogers	USA	1972	Team handball	
		1976	Team handball	
Chad Rudolph	USA	1972	Rowing	Four with coxswain
Charles Ruthford	USA	1972	Rowing	Four with coxswain
Laure Savasta	France	2000	Basketball (women)	
Mark Schneider	USA	2000	Rowing	Four without coxswain
Delos Schoch	USA	1936	Rowing	Alternate
Detlef Schrempf	Germany	1984	Basketball	
Joyce Tanac Schroeder	USA	1968	Gymnastics	Artistic individual all around
				Balance beam
				Floor exercise
				Side horse vault
				Uneven bars
				Team combined exercises

Athlete	Country	Year	Sport	Event
Jason Scott	USA	1996	Rowing	Four without coxswain
Adam Setliff	USA	1996, 2000	Track and Field	Discus throw
Jim Seymour	USA	1972	Track and Field	400 meter hurdles
Robert Shepherd	USA	1992	Rowing	Eight
Phil Shinnick	USA	1964	Track and Field	Long jump
Scott Shipley	USA	1992, 1996, 2000	Canoeing	Kayak - slalom singles
Al Stocker	USA	1960	Rowing	Four with coxswain
Sabina Telenska	Czech Republic	1992	Rowing	Women's eight
		1996	Rowing	Women's pair without coxswain
Nick Thometz	USA	1984	Speed Skating	Long track - 500 meters
				Long track - 1000 meters
				Long track - 1500 meters
		1988	Speed Skating	Long track - 500 meters
				Long track - 1000 meters
		1992	Speed Skating	Long track - 500 meters
				Long track - 1000 meters
Terry Tobacco	Canada	1956	Track and Field	400 meter run, 4 x 400 relay
		1960	Track and Field	400 meter run
Todd Trewin	USA	1992	Equestrian	Individual - 3 day
				Team - 3 day
Rebecca Twigg	USA	1996	Cycling	3000 meter individual pursuit
Chris Wells	USA	1980*	Rowing	Pair with coxswain
Chris Welp	Germany	1984	Basketball	
Wariboko West	Nigeria	1964	Track and Field	Long jump
George Widenfeldt	Sweden	1952	Track and Field	Decathlon
Michael Yonker	USA	1960	Rowing	Four with coxswain

* Selected for the 1980 Olympic Team and participated in the 1980 Olympic Games boycott

\# Gold medal taken away because DeMont took a prescribed asthma medication that included a banned substance. Decision on suit to regain the medal is still pending

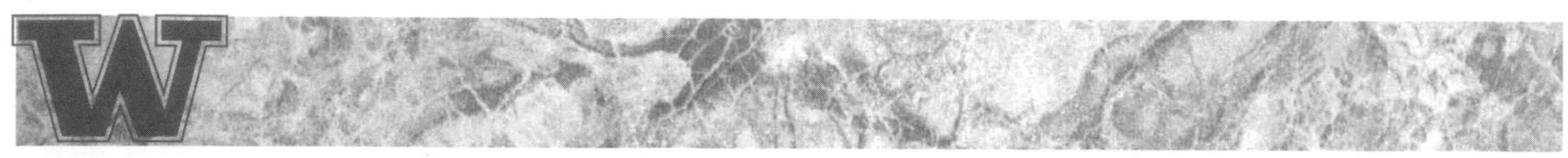

University of Washington Coaches In The Olympics

Several University of Washington coaches and one trainer have participated in the Olympic Games

Coach	Sport	Year	Participation
Hec Edmundson	Track and Field	1912	U.S. team; ran in the 400 and 800 meter events
Bob Ernst	Rowing	1976, 1980	Head U.S. women's rowing coach
		1984, 1988	Head U.S. women's rowing coach
Jan Harville	Rowing	1996	Assistant U.S. women's rowing coach
Eric Hughes	Gymnastics	1972	Manager of the U.S. gymnastics team
Frank Lee	Gymnastics	2000	Coach of Namibia, Africa team
Bob Neville	Volleyball	1968	Assistant men's Canadian volleyball coach
		1976	Head men's Canadian volleyball coach
		1984	Assistant men's U.S. volleyball coach
Chrissy Price	Soccer	2000	Athletic trainer for U.S. women's soccer team
Ken Shannon	Track and Field	1976	Javelin assistant coach
		1984	Coach of U.S. throwers and decathletes

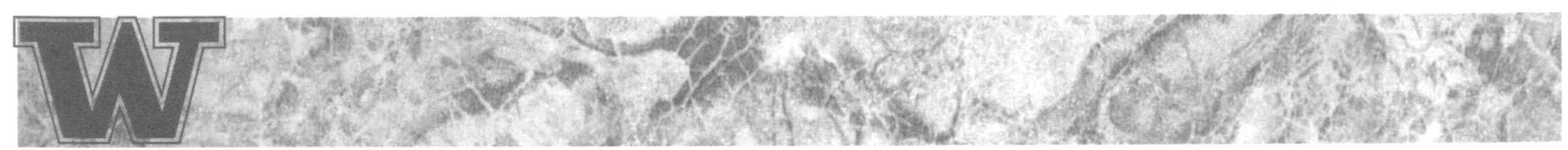

Husky Hall of Fame

Individual members of the Husky Hall of Fame are listed alphabetically, with their sport and year of induction. The list includes members inducted through 2000. Teams inducted are shown following the individual members and are grouped by sport. The Husky Hall of Fame was established in 1979.

NAME	SPORT	YEAR
Chuck Allen	Football	1994
Steve Anderson	Track and Field	1979
Irene Arden	Swimming	1985
Robin Backhaus	Swimming	1991
Enoch Bagshaw	Football	1980
Milt Bohart	Football	1989
Bruno Boin	Basketball	1992
Vicki Borsheim Beskind	Track and Field	1997
Patricia Bostrom	Tennis	1987
Jim Brink	Tennis	1989
Heman Brix	Track and Field	1980
James Bryan	Football-Basketball-Track	1981
Carl Buchan	Sailing	1998
Ralph Cairney	Basketball-Football-Track	1984
Rusty Callow	Crew	1982
Charles Carroll	Football	1979
Harvey Cassill	Athletic Director	1992
Jim Charteris	Track and Field	1986
John Cherberg	Football	1981
Joe Cipriano	Basketball	1999
Earl "Click" Clark	Football-Trainer	1990
Yvette Cole	Basketball	1996
Lynn Colella Bell	Swimming	1980
Rick Colella	Swimming	1982
Hiram Conibear	Crew	1979
Irving Cook	Basketball	1991
Melvin Cooley	Gymnastics	1994
Don Coryell	Football	2000
William "Wee" Coyle	Football-Baseball-Track	1980
Jim David	Gymnastics	1987
Karen Deden Westwater	Basketball	2000
Gilmour "Gil" Dobie	Football	1979
William "Tippy" Dye	Basketball	1996
Ray Eckman	Football-Athletic Director-Track	1982
Darrell Eden	Tennis	2000
Clarence "Hec" Edmundson	Basketball-Track and Field	1979
James Edwards	Basketball	1990
Bob Egge	Basketball	1988
Steve Emtman	Football	1999
Dick Erickson	Crew	1994
Cary Feldman	Track and Field	1990
Fred Fisher	Tennis	1989
George Fleming	Football	1980
Alan Forney	Crew	1996
Charles Frankland	Basketball-Track Athletic Director	1981
Ray Frankowski	Football-Wrestling	1986
Bob Galer	Basketball	1981
J. Wilson Gaw	Baseball	1983
Edwin Genung	Track and Field	1982
Dorsett "Tubby" Graves	Baseball	1980
Catherine "Kit" Green	Administrator	1998
Tom Greenlee	Football	1987
Frank Guisness	Basketball	2000
Bob Hall	Gymnastics	1988
Walt Harrison	Football	1999
Marv Harshman	Basketball	1985
Talbot Hartley	Track and Field	1998
Steve Hawes	Basketball	1987
Yoshi Hayasaki	Gymnastics	1983
Don Heinrich	Football	1981
Judy Hoetmer	Golf	1988
Bob Houbregs	Basketball-Baseball	1979
Merle Hufford	Football	1990
Eric Hughes	Gymnastics	1989
Bill Hutchinson	Baseball	1995
Edean Ihlanfeldt	Golf	1989
Michael Jackson	Football	2000
Alfred James	Basketball	1989
Don James	Football	1994
Paul Jessup	Track-Football	1982

NAME	SPORT	YEAR
Calvin Jones	Football	1983
Regina Joyce	Track and Field	1990
Dale McClements Kephart	Gymnastics	1999
Dick Knight	Tennis	1995
Art Langlie	Tennis-Baseball	1984
Hal Lee	Basketball-Baseball	1987
Mike Lude	Athletic Director	1998
Ray Mansfield	Football	1995
Vic Markov	Football	1980
Gordon McAllister	Smallbore rifle	1997
Jay McDowell	Football	1991
Hugh McElhenny	Football	1979
Roy McKasson	Football	1987
Don McKeta	Football	1984
Jack Medica	Swimming	1981
Charles Mitchell	Football	1992
Warren Moon	Football	1984
Yumi Mordre	Gymnastics	1995
William Morris	Basketball	1988
Rudy Mucha	Football	1990
Bill Murdock	Wrestling	1991
Karen Murray Hodgins	Basketball	1992
Scott Neilson	Track and Field	1986
Chuck Nelson	Football	1998
Ned Nelson	Baseball-Basketball	1989
Jack Nichols	Basketball	1980
Dave Nisbet	Football	1988
Mauno Nissinen	Gymnastics	1991
Rick Noji	Track and Field	1999
Jim Owens	Football	1979
Larry Owings	Wrestling	1986
Jimmy Phelan	Football	1986
George Pocock	Crew	1989

NAME	SPORT	YEAR
August "Gus" Pope	Track and Field	1983
Steve Power	Swimming	1995
Bill Quillian	Tennis	1985
Gustav Raaum	Skiing	1992
Mike Ramos	Track and Field	2000
Rick Redman	Football	1982
Peter Salmon	Swimming	1990
Bob Schloredt	Football	1981
Detlef Schrempf	Basketball	1995
Paul Schwegler	Football	1983
Wallace Scott	Tennis	1990
Phil Shinnick	Track and Field	1992
Sonny Sixkiller	Football	1985
Doug Smart	Basketball	1994
William Smith	Football	1991
Dick Sprague	Football	1995
Max Starcevich	Football	1989
Ernest Steele	Football	1999
Joe Steele	Football	1996
Brian Sternberg	Track and Field	1983
Alfred "Doc" Strauss	Football-Baseball	1981
George Strugar	Football	1988
Joyce Tanac Schroeder	Gymnastics	1998
Elmer Tesreau	Football-Baseball	1985
Jack Torney	Swimming-Tennis Track	1981
Roscoe "Torchy" Torrance	Baseball	1980
Al Ulbrickson	Crew	1979
Arnie Weinmeister	Football	1982
Jack Westlund	Golf	1987
Sammy White	Baseball-Basketball	1984
George Wilson	Football	1980
Al Worley	Football	1992

Teams

1959 Baseball team (1996)

Daryl Burke
Donald Daniels
George Grant
Peter Hanson
Floyd Harlington
Robert Hofeditz
Earl Irvine
Ken Jacobson
Bob Johnson
Carlton Olson
John Pariseau
George Pitt
Richard Reiten
Donald Rhodes
Gary Snyder
Jim Stjerne
John Swinehart
Jerry Thornton
Jack Walters
Ernie Wheeler
Robert Wyman

1953 Men's Basketball Team (1985)

H. Don Apeland
Joe Cipriano
Will Elliott
Roland Halle
Bob Houbregs
Charles Koon
Doug McClary
Mike McCutchen
Dean Parsons
Steve Roake
Don Tripp
Bill Ward

1923 Men's Eight-Oared Crew (1990)

Charles Dunn
Harry John Dutton
Rowland France
Don Grant
Max Luft
Sam Shaw
Fred Spuhn
Pat Tidmarsh
Dow Walling

1936 Men's Eight-Oared Crew (1979)

Gordon Adam
Charles Day
Donald Hume
George Hunt
Jim McMillin
Robert Moch
Roger Morris
Joe Rantz
John White

1940 Men's Eight-Oared Crew (1986)

John Bracken
Fred Colbert
Dallas "Dal" Duppenthaler
Al Erickson
Ted Garhart
Chuck Jackson
Gerald Keely, Sr.
Paul Soules
Dick Yantis

1941 Men's Eight-Oared Crew (1991)

John Bracken
Vic Fomo
Doyle Fowler
Ted Garhart
Chuck Jackson
Bill Neill
Paul Simdars
Tom Taylor
Walt Wallace

1948 Men's Four-Oared Crew with coxswain (1981)

Gordon Giovanelli
Bob Martin
Allen Morgan
Warren Westlund
Bob Will

1948-50 Men's Eight-Oared Crew (2000)

John Audett
Roger Baird
Norm Buvick
Ed Hearing
Rod Johnson
Don Landon
Floyd "Bobby" Lee
Carl Lovsted
Charlie McCarthy
Allen Morgan
Alvin Ulbrickson, Jr.
Ken Walters
Bob Will
Bill Works
Bob Young

1952 Men's Four-Oared Crew with coxswain (1998)

Fil Leanderson
Carl Lovsted
Al Rossi
Alvin Ulbrickson, Jr.
Richard Wahlstrom

1958 Men's Eight-Oared Crew (1984)

Chuck Alm
John Bisset
Dick Erickson
Louis Gellerman
Andy Hovland
Phil Kieburtz
Roger MacDonald
John Sayre
Bob Svendsen

1977 Men's Eight-Oared Crew (1999)

Jesse Franklin
Terry Fisk
Mike Hess
Ron Jackman
Mark Miller
Ross Parker
Mark Sawyer
John Stillings
Mark Umlauf

1981 Women's Eight-Oared Crew (1989)

Peg Achterman
Susan Broome
Madeline Hanson
Lisa Horn
Jane McDougall
Karen Mohling
Debbi Moore
Kristi Norelius
Shyril O'Steen

1959 Football Team (1994)

Ricardo Aguirre
Chuck Allen
Lee Bernhardi
Barry Bullard
Tim Bullard
Don Carnahan
Jim Carphin
Stan Chapple
Larry Clanton
Pat Claridge
Keith Cordes
Mike Crawford
Gary Dasso
Ben Davidson
Dick Dunn
Bob Echols
Dave Enslow
Jim Everett
George Fleming
Lee Folkins
Carver Gayton
Kurt Gegner
Serge Grant
Bob Hivner
Sam Hurworth
Ray Jackson
Joe Jones
Kermit Jorgensen
Bill Kinnune
Gary Kissell
Roy McKasson
Don McKeta
John Meyers
Don Millich
John Nelson
Ed Peasley
George Pitt
Jim Quessenberry
Bob Schloredt
Jerry Schwartz
Jim Skaggs
Barney Therrien
Jack Walters
Dan Wheatley
Bob White
John Wilson
Brent Wooten
Richie Chambers

1991 Football Team (1997)

Jeff Aselin
Bruce Bailey
Mario Bailey
Walter Bailey
Angelo Banchero
Doug Barnes
Damon Barry
Jay Barry
Eric Battle
Nathan Beedle
Eric Bjornson
Jeff Bockert
Todd Bridge
Shermonte Brooks
Mark Bruener
Mark Brunell
Beno Bryant
Brandon Bunch
Eric Butler
Hillary Butler
Geme Calman
Richard Chong
James Clifford
Brett Collins
Brian Conlan
Ernie Conwell
Shawn Cox
Jason Crabbe
Ed Cunningham
Andrew Davis
Mike Derrow
Demetrius Devers
Robb Dibble
John DiSante
William Doctor
Rodney Ellison
P.A. Emerson
Steve Emtman
Kelii Erwin
Mike Ewaliko
D'Marco Farr
Jaime Fields

Jamal Fountaine
Chico Fraley
J.J. Frank
Tom Gallagher
Frank Garcia
Curtis Gaspard
Larry Goncalves
James Goodwin
Darrell Green
Phil Green
Scott Greenlaw
Charleston Grimes
Russell Hairston
Dana Hall
Travis Hanson
Darren Harrell
Eugene Harris
Trevor Highfield
Billy Joe Hobert
Dave Hoffmann
Steve Hoffmann
Damon Huard
Eteka Huckaby
Jeff Hudson
Larry Humble
David Ilsley
Denton Johnson
Leif Johnson
Donald Jones
Louis Jones
Matt Jones
Pete Kaligis
Napoleon Kaufman
Lincoln Kennedy
Patrick Kesi
David Killpatrick
Joe Kralik
Sanjay Lal
Larry Leham
Scott Leick
Mike Lustyk
Lamar Lyons
Damon Mack
Siupeli Malamala
Matt Marino
Andy Mason
Shell Mays
D.J. McCarthy
Orlando McKay
Ardi Mekanik
Jeff Meyer
Josh Moore
Shaun Moore
Tom Nakane
Keith Navidi
Leon Neal
Eddie Nelson
Jim Nevelle
John Norman
Shane Pahukoa
Andrew Peterson
Aaron Pierce
Pete Pierson
Tyson Pollman
Eric Posenecker
Dana Posey
Terry Redmond
David Reiner
Reggie Reser
Moses Ringwood
Dante Robinson
Tyrone Rodgers
Kris Rongen
Joel Rosborough
Mark Schilder
Donovan Schmidt
Danianke Smith
Tommie Smith
Matt Spillinger
Travis Spring
Steve Springstead
Michael Steward
Scott Stuart
Paxton Tailele
Justin Thomas
Richard Thomas
Darius Turner
Peter Ullman
Richard Washington
Jaime Weindl
Jay Wells
John Werdel
Donald Willis
Greg Yasutake
Zario Ziegler
Kevin Zitkovich

1975 Mile Relay Team (1988)

Jerry Belur
Pablo Franco
Billy Hicks
Keith Tinner

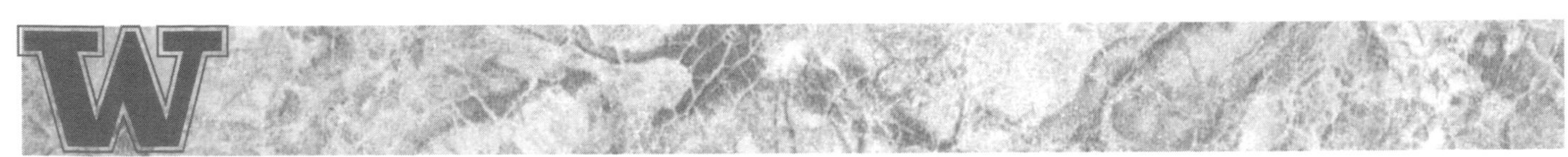

RESEARCH METHODOLOGY AND PHOTO CREDITS

We used many sources of information in the research for this book. One primary source is the University's Media Relations Department located in the Graves Building. Another primary source is the University's Manuscripts, Special Collections, and University Archives Division (UWMssSCUA) located in the University's Allen Library. A third primary source is the Microfilm and Newspaper Collections Department in the University's Suzzallo Library.

The Media Relations Department publishes annual media guides on each sport and has files on individual athletes. It also has extensive references including NCAA and PAC-10 publications.

The MssSCUA Department has data related to early university and athletic history including a complete set of the Tyee (the university yearbook), original copies of the campus newspaper (the *Pacific Wave*, the *Wave*, and the *Daily*) and many photographs of early athletes and teams.

The Microfilm Department contains microfilm on local newspapers, including the *Seattle Post-Intellingencer*, the *Seattle Times*, and the *University Daily*.

We used the following books and unpublished theses in our research.

Books

_____. *Achieving Gender Equity*. Overland Park, KS: National Collegiate Athletic Association, 1994

Blais, Madeleine. *In These Girls, Hope is a Muscle.* NY: Warner Books, Inc., 1995

Clarkston, Rich. *Notre Dame Football Today.* NY: Pindar Press, 1992

Gates, Charles M. *The First Century at the University of Washington, 1861-1961.* Seattle, WA: University of Washington Press, 1961

Gerald, Michael. *Owings! A Decade of Immortality*, 1980

Halberstam, David. *The Amateurs.* NY: William Morrow & Company, Inc., 1985

Hamlin, Rick. *A 100-Year Celebration: Tournament of Roses.* NY: McGraw Hill Publishing, 1988

Hammerbeck, ed., *Pacific Coast Conference Record Book.* CA: Publisher? 1959

Hendrickson, Joe. *Tournament of Roses: The First 100 Years, A History in Words and Pictures.* CA: The Knapp Press, 1988

Hibner, John C. *The Rose Bowl, 1902-1929: A Game-by-Game of Collegiate Football's Foremost Event, from Its Advent Through Its Golden Era.* Jefferson, NC and London: McFarland & Company, Inc., 1993

James, Don. *James*. Lincoln, Nebraska: Virgil Parker, 1991

Johnston, Norman J. *The Fountain & the Mountain*. Seattle, WA: Documentary Book Publishers and the University of Washington, 1995

Newell, Gordon. *Ready All! George Yeoman Pocock and Crew Racing.* Seattle, WA: University of Washington Press, 1987

Owen, John. *Press Pass.* Seattle, WA: The *Seattle Post-Intelligencer*, 1994

Paxton, Harry T., ed. *Sport USA:The Best From The Saturday Evening Post.* NY: Thomas Nelson & Sons, 1961

_____. *Revenues And Expenses of Divisions I and II Intercollegiate Athletics Programs.* Overland Park, KS: National Collegiate Athletic Association, 1995

Rockne, Dick. *Bow Down to Washington.* Huntsville, AL: The Strode Publishers, 1975

Rudman, Steve. *Celebrating 100 Years of Husky Football.* NY: Professional Sports Publications, 1990

Sperber, Murray. *Shake Down The Thunder.* NY: Henry Holt and Company, 1994

____. *Three Quarters of a Century At Washington.* Seattle, WA: University of Washington Alumni Association, 1941

Torrance, Roscoe C. *Torchy!* Mission Hill, SD :Dakota Homestead Publishers, 1973

Veltfort, Susan. *University of Washington National Championship, 1991.* Charlotte, NC :UMI Publications, Inc., 1992

Unpublished Theses

Hewitt, Lynn R. The History of Intercollegiate Football at the University of Washington from its Origin through 1965. An Unpublished Thesis, University of Washington, 1967

Maurer, Bruce L. A Compendium of Head Coaches of Intercollegiate Sports at the University of Washington, 1892 to 1970. An Unpublished Thesis, University of Washington, 1970

Orphan, Milton A., Jr. The Development of Intercollegiate Volleyball at the University of Washington and a Comparison of its Status to that of Other Selected Universities and Colleges in the United States. An Unpublished Thesis, University of Washington, 1966

Thornton, Thurle C. The History of Intercollegiate Swimming at the University of Washington through 1961. An Unpublished Thesis, University of Washington, 1962

Tobacco, Charles T. An Historical Study of Intercollegiate Track and Field at the University of Washington prior to 1960. An Unpublished Thesis, University of Washington, 1960

Ulbrickson, Alvin E. The History of Intercollegiate Rowing at the University of Washington through 1963. An Unpublished Thesis, University of Washington, 1963

And finally, we interviewed and received correspondence from over 100 former athletes, coaches, sports columnists, and friends of Husky sports.

PHOTO CREDITS

In the text, we cited the sources of all photos. The primary sources are the University's Media Relations Department, *Tyee* yearbooks, and the University's Manuscripts, Special Collections, and University Archives (UWMssSCUA). The negative numbers for the UWMssSCUA photos we used are:

1889 - negative UW6655
1892 - negative UW 1505
1893 - negative UW 1874
1894 - negative UW 1873
1896 - negative UW 1752
1897 - negative UW 1876, UW 6107, and UW file(Athletics -track)
1898 - negative UW 951
1900 - UW file (Athletics-football)
1903 - negative NA 608
1920 - UW file (Buildings - stadium)
1921 - UW Sports collection number 429
1927 - Hec Edmundson collection number 158
1941 - Hec Edmundson collection 158

Index

C

D

E

F

G

N

U

W

Y

Z